INTERNATIONAL HANDBOOK OF LITERACY AND TECHNOLOGY

Volume Two

INTERNATIONAL HANDBOOK OF LITERACY AND TECHNOLOGY

Volume Two

Edited by

Michael C. McKenna
University of Virginia

Linda D. Labbo
University of Georgia

Ronald D. Kieffer
Ohio Northern University

David Reinking
Clemson University

LEA
2006

LAWRENCE ERLBAUM ASSOCIATES, PUBLISHERS
Mahwah, New Jersey   London

Senior Acquisitions Editor: Naomi Silverman
Assistant Editor: Erica Kica
Cover Design: Tomai Maridou
Full-Service Compositor: MidAtlantic Books & Journals

This book was typeset in 11 pt. Palatino Roman, Bold and Italic. The heads were typeset in Palatino Roman, Bold and Italic.

Lawrence Erlbaum Associates, Inc., Publishers
10 Industrial Avenue
Mahwah, New Jersey 07430
www.erlbaum.com

CIP information for this volume can be obtained from the Library of Congress.

ISBN 0-8058-5087-2 (case)
ISBN 0-8058-5088-0 (paper)

Books published by Lawrence Erlbaum Associates are printed on acid-free paper,
and their bindings are chosen for strength and durability.

Printed in the United States of America
10 9 8 7 6 5 4 3

Contents

Section II: TECHNOLOGY APPLICATIONS WITH SPECIFIC POPULATIONS

Section III: LITERACY SOFTWARE AND THE INTERNET

Section IV: TEACHER EDUCATION AND PROFESSIONAL DEVELOPMENT

Section V: THE POTENTIAL OF TECHNOLOGY IN KEY DIMENSIONS OF LITERACY

Preface

The effects of technology on literate activity have been both sweeping and subtle, marked by an increasing variety of changes that are difficult to evaluate and project. Perhaps the only prediction that can be offered with certainty is that the impact of technology is irreversible. While specific changes may come and go, literacy and technology seem inextricably linked. This *Handbook* is dedicated to that linkage and to examining the intricacies that define it.

BACKGROUND AND OVERVIEW OF VOLUME TWO

In Volume One of this *Handbook*, we endeavored to lay essential groundwork for the study of literacy and technology. Editors and contributors alike felt obliged to define terms and offer considerable (and considerate) explanations about topics such as the nature of the Internet, differences in print and digital text, and issues surrounding hypertext and hypermedia (Reinking, 1998). The theme was transformations, thought to be especially pertinent as technology caused an epiphany in how we view the nature of literacy and what counts as literate activity. We might have been justified in assuming that readers of Volume One were conversant in these matters, but our intent was to document the full range of transformations for all literacy educators. We believe we accomplished that goal and, in so doing, created a rarity: a book about technology that is not rapidly dated, one that will retain an explanatory value.

Volume Two differs considerably in conception. Its contributors assume for the most part a higher level of expertise on the part of readers, and the projects and applications they describe are characterized by greater sophistication. The range of technology use is broader, and the challenges that have emerged are in sharper focus. The title of this volume has changed slightly to reflect our endeavor to incorporate contributions on a broad geographic basis. It is now a truly *international* handbook. Colleagues from six countries and five continents are chapter authors. Their work offers a glimpse of the communalities faced by literacy educators around the world, together with specific challenges raised by unique circumstances.

The five sections represent the principal areas in which significant developments are occurring. Section 1 addresses the role of technology in the new literacies. Issues concerning multimedia and the problems of becoming critically literate in such environments are explored. The experiences of educators in a variety of national contexts enrich this discussion. How technology is addressing the instructional needs of children at a variety of ages is the subject of section 2. The range of topics is especially broad—from phonological awareness to comprehension, and from beginning readers to struggling older children. The promise of technology for making text accessible to special populations is a recurrent theme. Contributors to section 3 examine important issues in the use of software and Internet resources. The process of software development, selection, and validation is explored from several perspectives, including those of researchers and commercial developers. Special challenges of software development in China are detailed. Emerging issues concerning information accessibility and proprietary concerns are addressed in the context of Internet use. Innovative applications of technology in teacher education are the focus of section 4. Ambitious case-based Internet projects are described in detail and preview new perspectives on how literacy educators may be prepared in years to come. Section 5 is an ambitious attempt to systematically sample the impact and potential of technology applications in various dimensions of literacy instruction. These dimensions include student engagement, emergent literacy, phonics, fluency, comprehension, vocabulary, family literacy, spelling, writing, adolescent literacy, cultural and ethnic diversity, special education, English language learners, and reading assessment. To accomplish this goal, the editors invited input from a number of researchers whose work has specialized in a particular literacy domain but has lacked a focus on technology. We asked these scholars to comment on how technology has impacted their areas and to indicate the direction future applications should take, based on available evidence.

Introduction: Trends and Trajectories of Literacy and Technology in the New Millennium

Michael C. McKenna
University of Virginia

KEY TRENDS AND TRAJECTORIES

The contributors to this volume represent a broad variety of expertise, perspective, culture, and geography. They describe a host of developments, projects, and issues that, when jigsawed together, portray a rapidly evolving and incredibly varied tableau. As a means of introducing the volume, I will attempt to distill the principal trends that appear to be underway and to offer what seem to be a few reasonable projections.

Hardware Improvements and Diversification

The evolution of hardware, driven principally by business, continues to produce computers that are faster, cheaper, smaller, more mobile, and more powerful than each previous generation. The decline in costs has made technology more accessible and has helped to address the problem of the "digital divide," at least insofar as the divide is related to relative economic advantage. The divide is now evident in countries with developing economies, such as Colombia (Alvarez, chap. 3, this volume) and China (Liu & Zhang, chap. 13, this volume). Here we see many of the same issues arising that began in the economically developed world.

The decreasing size of hardware has raised questions about what constitutes a computer. The year 2005 marked the first time that laptop sales exceeded the sales of desktop models. While few would perceive the laptop to be anything other than a computer, the progression away from conventional forms leads to murky classifications. The circuitry now commonplace in cell phones, televisions, cameras, personal digital assistants, GPS devices, gaming equipment, and scores of other applications has blurred traditional distinctions. Such devices have also juxtaposed textual and visual literacies in striking new ways, as witnessed by text messaging via camera phones and e-mailing replete with jpegs and commercial emoticons.

Software Development and Evaluation

Specific to the field of literacy instruction, new software applications have continued to develop, though not without technical challenges. Speech recognition, long touted as the key to intelligent feedback in literacy applications, has overcome many, though by no means all, obstacles. Adams (chap. 8, this volume) describes how speech recognition software is not yet sufficiently nuanced to account for dialect and idiolect variations (and for an assortment of other departures from "Standard English"). "[O]ur greatest challenge," she suggests, "has been to teach it [the software] how to distinguish genuine difficulties from (for example) accents, missing teeth, confident repairs, coughs, stuffy noses, and the incessant background voices and racket of the classroom."

A second trend has been the continuing improvements to software designed to support children as they attempt to read texts presented in digital environments. The pioneering work of Lynne Anderson-Inman and Mark Horney (1998) has occasioned further innovations in supported text. For example, Bus, de Jong, and Verhallen (chap. 9, this volume) carry on this important line of inquiry with Dutch youngsters. Dalton and Strangman (chap. 6, this volume) couch their discussion in terms of *access* to print, an idea borrowed from barrier-free architecture, designed to grant access to the physically disabled. They examine how electronic supports can offer access to a variety of struggling readers and suggest that applications intended principally for students with disabilities may ultimately assist abler readers as well.

A third trend entails the creation of increasingly sophisticated multimedia environments, housed both on the Web and in self-contained packages, such as gaming software. Lemke (chap. 1, this volume) describes how these developments mark substantive breaks from the print tradition, with consequent implications for instruction and research as media converge. The complex interplay among media that inhabit the same environment, he argues, makes it imperative that we redefine the idea of critical literacy as it applies to these emerging contexts.

Altogether new software applications have appeared as well. Formidable challenges to the digital representation of nonalphabetic languages (Liu & Zhang, chap. 13, this volume) and of scientific symbols and formulae (Fullerton, chap. 12, this volume) have been overcome. An emerging application is the use of Kintsch's method of latent semantic analysis to help students write summaries and infer main ideas (Olson & Wise, chap. 5, this volume).

Commercial software development continues apace, and the inherent tension between commerce and pedagogy remains an issue of consequence. Stafford, Miller, and Ollivierre (chap. 11, this volume) detail the steps now in place industry-wide to ensure the effectiveness of new products, steps taken by developers as in-house measures. Such studies, including those centered around print products, have long occasioned skepticism, however, because they are not conducted by disinterested parties. But practitioners—the deep-pocketed consumers of educational software—generally have had little recourse other than to accept the objectivity of commercial reports. They have had little objective guidance in choosing in the midst of what Hobbs describes as an "option overload" (chap. 2, this volume).

The potential role of the research community as arbiters in product validation has therefore been reconsidered. For example, the editors of *Reading Research Quarterly* have invited debate as to the desirability of publishing studies that independently investigate the efficacy of specific products. Olson and Wise (chap. 5, this volume) contend that success in the marketplace is no substitute for third-party empirical validation. Dalton and Strangman (chap. 6, this volume) suggest that the rapid pace of change in technology applications requires that research be likewise accelerated. But is this goal realistic given the limited resources available to engage in such research; the time required to conduct, review, and publish findings; and the almost certain divisiveness caused by the results (see McKenna, 1998)? Granted, the recent tendency of federal funding to be linked to programs grounded in scientifically-based reading research might give rise to the kind of "horse race" studies that would yield evidence of efficacy. Even so, the time and resources required would tend to constrain such an effort.

When such studies have appeared in respected forums, the consequences have been great (e.g., Paterson, Henry, O'Quin, Ceprano, & Blue, 2003; Slavin, 1990). A particular casualty may prove to be the integrated learning system (ILS). In an extensive review of available studies of these expansive diagnostic-prescriptive packages, Coiro and her colleagues (Coiro et al., 2003) identified a general tendency of an ILS to produce impressive initial gains, due to high levels of novelty-based engagement, followed by disappointing achievement when lesson formats are inevitably repeated. Coiro, Karchmer Klein, and Walpole (chap. 10, this volume) contend that establishing the effectiveness of software and Web resources is complicated by their rapid proliferation and by their tendency to embed attractive features that are designed to increase salability but that may be of questionable pedagogical value. They therefore recommend a skeptical stance and discuss the importance of selecting software with systematic care at a time when evidence is scant.

Classroom Practice and Teacher Resistance

Three of the editors have attempted to portray classroom applications of technology that reflect evidenced-based practice (McKenna, Labbo, & Reinking, 2003). At the primary level, such a classroom might be characterized by computer-guided word study, electronic storybooks with decoding scaffolds, social interaction guided by software applications, graphics packages to assist children as they illustrate their work, and software designed to reinforce concepts about print. In the upper grades, teachers might coordinate multimedia book reports, collaborative Internet projects, and keypal linkages with children in other localities.

While these classroom portraits are defensible in light of available evidence, and affordable in terms of cost allocations in most developed countries, we see few instances in which teachers have actualized these scenarios. Hardware is frequently unused, confined to lab settings, or used (often injudiciously) to occupy children in center arrangements. Despite the inroads of digital environments, literacy instructors have been slow to embrace technology and integrate it into their instruction.

This resistance to implementation may be unique to literacy education. Hobbs (chap. 2, this volume) argues that a different sort of digital divide appears to have emerged between literacy teachers, on the one hand, and science and math teachers on the other. The latter have more readily adopted technology applications, while language arts teachers tend to prefer the print tradition. Ironically, once children are immersed in technology applications in content subjects, their use of literacy is transformed irrespective of the methods and materials with which they interact in "literacy" classrooms. Hobbs speculates as to the reluctance of literacy educators to embrace the emerging view of multiple literacies. They may view technology as a threat to the print canon. They may be suspicious of the increasing informality of the written expression that characterizes e-mail (see Bromley, chap. 25, this volume). Or they may unconsciously associate technology with popular culture. My colleagues and I have expressed it this way: "It is hard for some teachers to consider, let alone accept, that emerging forms of electronic reading and writing may be as informative, pedagogically useful, and aesthetically pleasing as more familiar printed forms. To consider that electronic forms of text may in some instances even be superior is undoubtedly more difficult" (McKenna, Labbo, & Reinking, 2003, p. 325).

Turbill and Murray (chap. 7, this volume) report a different sort of resistance at the primary level. Australian primary teachers tend to view the role of technology as providing for play, not real learning. Teachers ask if there is "value added" for their investment in technology applications. To the extent that "real" learning involves teacher-directed instruction, digital environments as yet seem poorly suited to this end unless the users are independent learners. But when learning is grounded in social interaction and exploration, technology's potential may be greater. Verhoeven, Segers, Bronkhorst, and Boves (chap. 4, this volume) argue that the prevailing transmission view of pedagogy, in the Netherlands and elsewhere, works against the realization of this potential. Technology's promise, they maintain, lies in constructivist designs. In their proposed system, children collaboratively solve problems and in the process create multimedia products. "The new media," Stafford, Miller, and Ollivierre observe, "enable instruction to be targeted based on individual student needs rather than the class as a whole, thus allowing a shift from teacher-centered to more student-centered learning" (chap. 11, this volume). The question, however, may not be the technological capacity to achieve such a goal but whether it is adequately embraced by teachers whose pedagogy is transmission oriented.

Whatever the cause, an emerging factor may soon reduce teacher reluctance, at least in American settings. The standards movement may hold the potential to effect substantive changes not only in technology applications but in what counts as literacy. The *Standards for the English Language Arts*, cosponsored by the National Council of Teachers of English and International Reading Association (1996), are specific about the direction literacy education must take. They underscore more than once the importance of both "print and non-print texts," they make multiple references to "visual language," they stress that students must be able to apply "media techniques," and they indicate that students must be able to "use a variety of technological and information resources (e.g., libraries, databases, computer networks, video)." Likewise, the New Standards, co-developed by the National Center on Education and the Economy and the University of Pittsburgh (1998) have been highly influential among the states as they develop their own mandated standards and objectives. The New Standards include viewing as a pertinent domain of the language arts. If, in the coming years, such standards are reflected in state competency tests required to document adequate yearly progress, literacy educators may be pressured to broaden their instructional focus. To date the pace of change has been slow, but new developments and new pressures may at last alter the status quo.

Teacher Preparation

Turbill and Murray (chap. 7, this volume) argue that one reason teachers may be reluctant to employ technology is that those who prepare them to teach do not model its use. Such modeling might counter the tendency of teachers in preparation to follow earlier models in their future practice—namely, the models of instruction to which they were exposed as students (McKenna & Robinson, 2005). So long as these models do not implement technology, their own practice cannot be expected to implement technology. This form of intergenerational inertia may also yield to pressures brought about by the New Standards, but other developments may become factors as well. These include the use of technology (the Internet in particular) to deliver instruction to preservice and in-service teachers. Some of these applications are already commonplace, such as online course offerings, complete with downloadable documents, PowerPoints, video and audio clips, chats, message boards, and other resources, now often used in tandem.

Additional, yet still-emerging, applications are an exciting area of research and development. These applications are described in detail by the contributors to this volume. The Internet has become a repository of resources that have few precedents in earlier technologies. The common denominator of these resources is the case study, though the nature of these studies varies widely. Ferdig, Roehler, and Pearson (chap. 15, this volume) discuss how video clips of exemplary teaching, presented in the context of Reading Classroom Explorer, can be used to model instructional techniques and to ground self-appraisals. Harrison, Pead, and Sheard (chap. 16, this volume) extend the range of these clips to include non-exemplary episodes, leaving it to users to differentiate the two through critical analysis. Classroom contexts that include instructional clips, but go well beyond them, is the goal of Case Technologies to Enhance Literacy Learning (CTELL). Kinzer, Cammack, Labbo, Teale, and Sanny (chap. 14, this volume) discuss how these classroom cases were developed and how they can be used in college coursework. They comprise such a broad array of information (student data, demographics, background, etc.) that the cases are presented in a hypermedia framework, allowing users to pursue the answers to questions in a constructivist environment. A similar platform is used for the Extended Case Studies in Reading Acquisition (McKenna & Walpole, 2004), in which longitudinal data, including sequenced audio clips, are compiled for beginning readers as they progress from Kindergarten through Grade 3.

Whether the modeling of technology use that is embodied in these applications will transfer to classroom application is unclear. It seems fair to suggest that even though teachers may come to appreciate how technology can enhance their own learning, they may still remain resistant to incorporating it into their instruction of children. The key to this breakthrough, as Turbill and Murray (chap. 7, this volume) suggest, lies with teacher educators. When they see fit to model technology applications both for preservice and in-service teachers, demonstrating how such applications can enrich their teaching and help them attain their goals, then the cycle may truly be broken and classroom practice reinvented to reflect the realities of the new literacies.

Technology and Dimensions of Literacy Instruction

An important feature of Volume Two is the commentary offered by recognized literacy researchers whose primary focus has not been technology applications. These chapters abound with insights into how research has informed each dimension, with critiques of past technology applications, and with suggestions for the future. I make no attempt here to summarize these chapters. Instead I have attempted, by way of introduction, to distill common themes that link more than a single area, themes that may possess an overarching significance as we move forward. I note three in particular.

Digital divides.   The original notion of a digital divide centered on economic advantage, the purchasing power of advantaged parents to acquire technology that less-affluent families could not afford. While this divide remains (to a greater or lesser degree in particular national settings), new divides have emerged and the plural of this term is appropriate. I have mentioned two of these additional divides: the one separating countries with developing versus developed economies and another separating language arts teachers from teachers of math and science. Au (chap. 27, this volume), Edwards (chap. 20, this volume), and Bernhardt (chap. 26, this volume) all speak of cultural and linguistic divides that inadvertently limit the benefits of technology reaped by English-language learners and by families whose values have not embraced technology. Edwards decries the wrong headedness of assuming that merely providing technology to culturally diverse families will be sufficient to overcome cultural belief systems that might operate against its use. Another divide, long present among students, separates technology enthusiasts ("geeks") from students who are more popular and socially adept. This divide, Alvermann maintains (chap. 22, this volume), has all but vanished due to the ease and omnipresence of technology applications and to their protean tendency to emerge in a multitude of convenient forms. These are now in reach of nearly all and appear to offer something to everyone. In this development may lie the solution to bridging the other divides as well. As technology becomes cheaper, more convenient, and increasingly versatile, the rift that separates national economies may well be reduced, and at the same time digital literacies may inconspicuously enter the lives of diverse families, like a Trojan horse.

Student engagement.   Technology may hold the potential to increase student engagement in literacy learning, but the lessons of the past suggest that new approaches are needed to realize this potential. Gambrell (chap. 18, this volume) points out that the Internet increases the opportunities for engagement through increasing access to engaging texts and by affording nearly boundless choices to students. Technology, she contends, can support another key to engagement as well: social interaction. Alvermann (chap. 22, this volume), like Lemke (chap. 1, this volume), cautions that such interaction may take unconventional forms, especially among adolescents, as they employ digital literacies to achieve social goals. There are lessons for educators in the differences between teacher-constrained uses of the Internet and those pursued by students on their own.

Pedagogical perspectives.   Technology represents a theory-free platform from which to launch applications that embody a variety of perspectives on how children should be taught. Earlier drill-and-practice applications are now eschewed by those researchers who point to evidence that more sophisticated software must be developed to reflect what is presently known. Similar points are made with respect to phonics (Kuhn & Stahl, chap. 19, this volume), spelling (Templeton, chap. 23, this volume), emergent literacy (McGee & Richgels, chap. 28, this volume), and vocabulary (Blachowicz, Beyersdorfer, & Fisher, chap. 24, this volume). Diverse perspectives also infuse reading assessment, and it is interesting to witness how wireless and Internet technologies can support the very different approaches advocated by Walker and Goetze (chap. 30, this volume) and by Kame'enui and Wallin (chap. 29, this volume). Their goals for children are similar, but the data they value differ dramatically. Shifting perspectives also are caused by technology, as developments oblige educators to respond as they reconsider the world they are preparing students to enter. Duke, Schmar-Dobler, and Zhang (chap. 21, this volume) discuss the problem of teaching students to comprehend in hypertext and hypermedia environments. Bromley (chap. 25, this volume) mentions the need on the part of students to employ electronic aids while writing and to compose using nonverbal elements. Blachowicz, Beyersdorfer, and Fisher (chap. 24, this volume) suggest that vocabulary instruction faces new challenges as icons replace words, as technology itself generates new terms, and as words take on new properties when used in search engines.

TENSIONS IN THE EVOLUTION
OF TECHNOLOGY AND LITERACY

These trends—at once varied and dynamic, characterized at times by coherence and at times by apparent contradiction and chaos—have occasioned a host of responses on the part of literacy educators. These have ranged from consensus to controversy and from enthusiasm to resistance. These polarities suggest that it may be useful to recast the trends as *tensions* that will define important trajectories in the years ahead.

- *The tension between print and digital environments.* The emergence of new and varied hardware applications extends digital literacies to all corners of society. Print will occupy an important place for the foreseeable future, but it endures an uneasy coexistence with digital platforms.

- *The tension between users and nonusers of technology.* The multiplicity of hardware platforms has altered the image of technology. Its infusion into households via the younger generation may operate to nullify the resistance of parents. Its multiform nature makes it increasingly acceptable to socially conscious youth. These populations are now far more actively engaged in digital literacies than before.

- *The tension between explicit instruction and constructivism.* Established instructional formats are juxtaposed in the marketplace with newer applications that invite social interaction and exploration. Consumer dynamics will determine the direction of software development, and those dynamics may be influenced by research and by the success of new applications, such as speech recognition.

- *The tension between commercial developers and researchers.* Results of in-house research are frequently at odds with third-party studies of product effectiveness. The purchasing public will need to become increasingly savvy in software selection and in seeking out available evidence. Scholarly forums may increasingly yield to the pressure to publish effectiveness studies.

- *The tension between conventional and technology-based instruction.* As the nature of reading and writing are transformed, the logic of traditional instruction is increasingly challenged. The resistance of language arts teachers to placing digital literacies on a footing equal to print is an important constraint, but their resistance may wane in the face of the standards movement and of out-of-class student involvement in digital applications. The conventional position may become increasingly insular.

- *The tension between conventional and technology-based teacher preparation.* The reluctance of teacher educators in the language arts to model the use of technology now abuts the willingness to do so on the part of their colleagues in science and math education. A movement from traditional to case-based learning is a dynamic that may lead to increased implementation of technology.

FINAL THOUGHTS

The "post-typographic" world we projected in Volume One has still not been realized. Fullerton (chap. 12, this volume) points out that this very volume, though ironically treating issues of digital literacy, is nevertheless a testament to the "primacy of print.". Hobbs (chap. 2, this volume) cautions that while "the technology education world continues (as always) to hype the just-around-the-corner potential of technology to transform teaching and learning for the betterment of all," the realities lag far behind the vision. Yet it is not only the pace but the vision itself that may warrant a revised view. The chapters in this book document the progress we have made in technology applications in literacy education. They also suggest that the vision itself must change to accommodate unanticipated developments in technology driven by business applications. As these developments occur, it behooves all literacy educators—practitioners, teacher educators, and researchers alike—to embrace those changes.

The theme of Volume One of the *Handbook* was transformations, and these we now see continuing on a variety of fronts. The most prudent view is not to view these transformations as transitions from one static state to another, but to perceive them as an unending evolution. We must learn that where literacy and technology converge, our principal concern should be the journey, not the destination.

REFERENCES

Anderson-Inman, L., & Horney, M. A. (1998). Transforming text for at-risk readers. In D. Reinking, M. C. McKenna, L. D. Labbo, & R. D. Kieffer (Eds.). *Handbook of literacy and technology: Transformations in a post-typographic world* (pp. 15–44). Mahwah, NJ: Lawrence Erlbaum Associates.

Coiro, J., Leu, D. J., Jr., Kinzer, C. K., Labbo, L., Teale, W., Bergman, L., Sulzen, J., & Sheng, D. (2003, December). *A review of research on literacy and technology: Replicating and extending the NRP subcommittee report on computer technology and reading instruction.* Paper presented at the 53rd annual meeting of the National Reading Conference, Scottsdale, AZ.

McKenna, M. C. (1998). Afterword to twentieth-century literacy: Prospects at the millennium. *Peabody Journal of Education,* 73(3&4), 376–386.

McKenna, M. C., Labbo, L. D., & Reinking, D. (2003). Effective use of technology in literacy instruction. In L. M. Morrow, L. B. Gambrell, & M. Pressley (Eds.). *Best practices in literacy instruction* (2nd ed., pp. 307–331). New York: Guilford Press.

McKenna, M. C., & Robinson, R. D. (2005). *Teaching through text* (4th ed.). Boston: Allyn & Bacon.

McKenna, M. C., & Walpole, S. (2004, June). *An Internet database of longitudinal case studies in reading.* Paper presented at the meeting of the Society for the Scientific Study of Reading, Amsterdam, The Netherlands.

National Center on Education and the Economy. (1998). *New standards: Performance standards and assessments for the schools.* Washington, DC: NCEE.

National Council of Teachers of English & International Reading Association. (1996). *Standards for the English language arts.* Newark, DE: IRA/NCTE.

Paterson, W. A., Henry, J. J., O'Quin, K., Ceprano, M. A., & Blue, E. V. (2003). Investigating the effectiveness of an integrated learning system on early emergent readers. *Reading Research Quarterly, 38,* 172–207.

Reinking, D. (1998). Introduction: Synthesizing technological transformations of literacy in a post-typographic world. In D. Reinking, M. C. McKenna, L. D. Labbo, & R. D. Kieffer (Eds.). *Handbook of literacy and technology: Transformations in a post-typographic world* (pp. xi–xxx). Mahwah, NJ: Lawrence Erlbaum Associates.

Slavin, R. E. (1990). "IBM's Writing to Read: Is it right for reading?" *Phi Delta Kappan, 72,* 214–216.

INTERNATIONAL HANDBOOK OF LITERACY AND TECHNOLOGY

Volume Two

I
▾▾▾▾▾▾▾▾

THE ROLE OF TECHNOLOGY
IN THE NEW LITERACIES

Toward Critical Multimedia Literacy: Technology, Research, and Politics

Jay Lemke
University of Michigan

NEW MEDIA, NEW LITERACIES

What should critical literacy mean in the age of multimedia? The purpose of critical literacy has always been to empower us to take a critical stance toward our sources of information. In an age of print, the most significant public sources that sought to shape our social attitudes and beliefs presented themselves to us through the medium of text: school textbooks, mass circulation newspapers, government publications, advertising copy, popular novels, and so forth. Illustrations were just that: redundant, secondary content subordinate to the written text. The written word had power and prestige; it defined literacy. We taught students to carefully and critically study written text, and by and large we ignored the accompanying images.

The advent of television challenged the basic assumptions of the traditional model of critical literacy. It was clear that more people were being influenced by what they saw and heard than by what they read. The academy refused to take television seriously for its first few decades, but gradually the field of cultural studies began to emerge and critically study all popular media. The analysis of print advertising awoke to the significant ideological messages in advertising images (Williamson, 1978). Both images and commentary were seen as central to the politics of television news (Hall, Critcher, Jefferson, Clarke, & Roberts, 1978; Hartley, 1982). Feminist critique examined images in advertising media, school textbooks, and even our literacy primers.

Nevertheless, visual literacy was still nowhere to be found in the standard curriculum, and the concept of a critical visual literacy remained the province of research specialists. With the rise of the World Wide Web as a near-universal information medium, it became clear to all of us that written text was just one component of an essentially multimodal medium. My first view of a web page, using the Mosaic browser on a unix workstation, was startling not for the delivery of text, but for the inline image of (then Vice-President and Internet supporter-in-chief) Al Gore. The text introduced the World Wide Web gateway of the University of Illinois supercomputing center, but that photo of Al Gore spoke volumes about both the potential of the Web as a multimodal medium and its political significance.

Web pages and Web sites are valued today for their integration of text, images, animations, video, voice, music, and sound effects. Web site authoring is the new literacy of power. Web sites are gradually replacing printed newspapers and magazines, college catalogues and shopping catalogues, travel brochures, and corporate and government publications. Print has a certain convenience which will ensure that it remains, but the genres of print are already coming to resemble those of the Web, and each successive generation shows a stronger preference for online-information media. The most common print media and genres of everyday life, except only the popular novel so far, seem likely to be superseded by their electronic successors. The new generation of university students, even graduate students, regards a physical visit to the library, other than for quiet study, as an anachronism. If information is not available online, it is bypassed in favor of information that is.

Critical literacy needs to respond to these historic changes. We need a broader definition of literacy itself, one that includes all literate practices, regardless of medium. Books-on-tape are as much literate works as are printed books. Scripted films and television programs are no less products of literate culture in their performances than they were as texts. In printed advertisements, the message toward which we need to take a critical stance is conveyed not just by the textual copy, nor even by the copy and the images, but by the interaction of each with the other, so that the meaning of the words is different with the images than without them, and that of the image together with the words distinct from what it might have been alone. In the multimodal medium of the Web, the message is less the medium than it is the multiplication of meanings across media (Lemke, 1998a, 1998b). Critical literacy *is* critical multimedia literacy.

Media are converging. This is especially evident with commercial media. Television programs, including the network news, have associated multimedia Web sites, as do popular films, digital games, and even books. The *Harry Potter* books began as a print literacy phenomenon, but today there is a seamless web of books, films, videos, videogames, Web sites, and other media. *The Matrix* began as a theatrical-release feature film, but its fictional world is now distributed across all media. Tolkien's *Lord of the Rings* has been re-imagined as film, animation, and in a variety of videogame genres. Young readers would consider us illiterate today if we knew only the printed texts, because for them the intertextual meanings and cross-references among all these media are essential to their peer-culture understanding and "reading" of these works. *Enter the Matrix*, the videogame, advertises that *The Matrix Reloaded* film is incomplete without the events, scenes, and backstory in the game. Not only are the textual themes and content distributed over the various media in all these and many other cases, but so are the visual images and visual styles and the themes and meanings they present.

What is a text today? It is not bounded by the first and last pages of a folio book. It is distributed across multiple sites and media. It is an intertextual constellation, not just in the imagination of literary theorists, but in simple everyday fact. The principle of hypertext or hypermedia, which we associate with the Web, based on explicit links of text or images to other text and images, from web page to web page, now also applies to the social and cultural linkages among our reading of books, viewing of films and television, screening of videos, surfing the Web, playing computer games, seeing advertising billboards, and even wearing T-shirts and drinking from coffee mugs that belong to multimedia constellations. Each of these media directs us to the others, without Web-like hyperlinks; each one provides an experiential basis for making meanings differently with all the others.

We are more and more enmeshed in these multimedia constellations. More than ever we need a critical multimedia literacy to engage intelligently with their potential effects on our social attitudes and beliefs.

COPING WITH COMPLEXITY

We need conceptual frameworks to help us cope with the complexity and the novelty of these new multimedia constellations. If we are to articulate and teach a critical multimedia literacy, we need to work through a few important conceptual distinctions and have some terminology ready-to-hand.

The research field of *social semiotics* (Halliday, 1978; Hodge & Kress, 1988; Lemke, 1989; Thibault, 1991) has for some time now been trying to develop the key concepts needed for these tasks (Kress & van Leeuwen, 1996, 2001; O'Toole, 1990; van Leeuwen, 1999). In various incarnations it is also known as critical discourse studies, critical media studies, and critical cultural studies. I present here the terms and distinctions I myself find it useful to make. They are not very different from those of most people working on these problems.

The core idea of semiotics is that all human symbolic communication, or alternatively all human meaning-making, shares a number of features. In multimedia semiotics, these common features are taken as the ground which makes integration across different media possible. The fundamental conceptual unit is the signifying or meaning-making practice. It applies both to creation of meaningful media and to the interpretive work of making meaning from or with them. Such practices are culturally specific in their details, but can be described within a common framework. All meaning-making acts make three kinds of meaning simultaneously: (a) they present some state-of-affairs, (b) they take some stance toward this content and assume an orientation to social others and their potential stances to it, and (c) they integrate meanings as parts into larger wholes. In doing each of these things, they make use of cultural conventions which distinguish and often contrast the potential meaning of one act or sign with those of others that might have occurred in its place, and the meanings of each act or sign shift depending on the acts and signs that occur around it and are construed as parts of the same larger whole. The complex process by which the range of conventional meanings that any act or sign can have gets specified by context and co-text until we are satisfied that some consistent pattern has emerged is simplified by our reliance on familiar, recognizable idioms and genres.

This model of meaning-making applies to language, whether spoken or written, and also to pictorial images, abstract visual representations, music, mathematics, sound effects, cooking, dress, gesture, posture, signed languages, or actions as such. It was developed originally for the well-studied case of language, but seems to apply pretty well to all semiotic modalities. There is another core principle for multimedia semiotics: that we can never make meaning with just one semiotic modality alone. You cannot make a purely verbal-linguistic meaning in the real world. If you speak it, your voice also makes nonlinguistic meaning by its timbre and tone, identifying you as the speaker, telling something about your physical and emotional state, and much else. If you write it, your orthography presents linguistic meaning inseparably from additional visual meanings (whether in your handwriting or choice of font). If you draw an image, neither you nor anyone else (with a very few exceptions), sees that image apart from construing its meaning in part through language (naming what you see, describing it), or imagining how it would feel to draw it, sculpt it, etc. For young children, the distinction between drawing and writing has to be learned. For all of us, speech and our various body gestures form a single integrated system of communication. All communication is multimedia communication.

Or, more precisely, it is multi-modal communication. Multimodality refers to the combination or integration of various sign systems or semiotic resource systems, such as language, depiction, gesture, mathematics, music, etc. The medium, as such, is the material technology through which the signs of the system are realized or instantiated. Language is a modality or semiotic system. It can be realized in the medium of speech, or the medium of printed orthography, or the medium of Braille writing, or in manual signs. The print medium can accommodate linguistic signs and also image signs, as well as mathematical signs, abstract diagrams, musical notation, dance notation, etc. It cannot accommodate animation or full-motion video. In many cases, we have only a single name for both the modality and the medium, as for example with *video*. As a modality, it means the cultural conventions that allow us to create meanings by showing successive images in time, so that the semiotics of still images are no longer sufficient to understand what is going on. New semiotic conventions apply in the case of video (and animation). As a medium, video or film can accommodate images (as still frames), language, music, and many other modalities in addition to its own unique modality.

Because every physical medium carries abstract signs in ways that allow us to interpret features of the medium also through other systems of meaning (the grain of a voice, the style of a font, the image quality of a video), the material reality of communication is inherently multimodal. Moreover, the various modalities and sign systems have co-evolved with one another historically as parts of multimodal genres, even within a single medium. We have conventions for integrating printed words and images, video visuals and voice-over narration, music and lyrics, action images and sound effects. At the simplest level, this integration takes place by combining the contributions to the (1) presentation of a state-of-affairs, (2) orientation to content, others, and other stances, and (3) organization of parts into wholes, from each modality. This combination is really a multiplication in the sense that the result is not just an addition of these contributions, as if they were independent of each other, but also includes the effects of their mutual interaction; the contribution of each modality contextualizes and specifies or alters the meaning we make with the contribution from each of the others. The image provides a context for interpreting the words differently, the words lead us to hear the music differently, the music integrates sequences of images, and so forth.

This multiplication happens to some extent separately for the (1) presentational content, (2) orientational stance toward content and toward addressees, and (3) organizational structure. But each of these three aspects of the overall meaning also influences the other two. If the musical score links visual images into the same larger unit, then the way we read the content-meaning of those images can be different from how we would interpret them if they were separated into different units by a break or major shift in the music, so that they no longer seemed as relevant to each other, no longer as strongly interacting with each other and influencing each other's content-meaning.

This takes us, in brief, about as far as general multimedia semiotics has come in the last few decades. From these ideas, and an analysis of the typical multimodal genres of a society, we could provide a reasonable conceptual basis for a critical literacy curriculum to help students analyze meanings in a particular multimodal text or genre. But as I have tried to argue previously in this chapter, we have already moved far beyond multimodality as such. The Web is a truly multimedia medium insofar as any other medium can be embedded within a web page and linked into a Web site. As a medium, it can accommodate, in principle, and increasingly in practice, *any* modality and it can at least simulate most other media. It is also a hypertextual or hypermedia medium because elements in other media and modalities can be linked together in ways that allow the user to choose a variety of paths through the Web site in the course of time.

A trajectory across links within a Web site may already carry us across different genres and different media using different modalities. But we do not just surf within Web sites; we increasingly, perhaps normally, surf across sites, and therefore across the Web-genre conventions of different institutions—from a film-site (The Matrix, Lord of the Rings) to a commercial product site (Nike sportswear, Pepsi-Cola), to an information site (Internet Movie Database, NASA Earth

Observatory), to a portal or search site (Yahoo, Google), a news site, personal homepage, university site, etc. We are learning to make meaning along these *traversals* (Lemke, 2002a, 2002b, 2003) in ways that are trans-generic and trans-institutional. Such traversals are still relatively free of the constraints of conventional genres and represent an important potential source of radically new kinds of meanings.

All that lies still within the medium of the Web, but traversals are not limited to a particular medium. We make meanings as we move our attention, over shorter and longer periods of time, among Web surfing, television viewing, book reading, game playing, face-to-face conversations, and indeed, all the activities of daily life. As our culture increasingly enmeshes us in constellations of textual, visual, and other themes that are designed to be distributed across multiple media and activities, of the sort I have already discussed, these cross-activity and cross-medium connections tend to become coherently structured and not just randomly sequential over the course of a day. We begin to see them as relevant to each other's meanings. We begin to use the meanings from one to interpret the meanings of others. Attitudes, beliefs, and values are reinforced across media, activities, and domains of our lives. Some of these constructions are our own, but increasingly they are designed by others to influence us. In both cases, we need a genuinely critical multimedia literacy to maintain our relative autonomy in making choices about what and who to believe, identify with, emulate, admire, scorn, or hate. It is not just fiction and fantasy, or commercial products, that are promoted by multimedia constellations; it is also attitudes toward war and peace, Muslims and Jews, health-care systems, gay rights, political candidates and corporate profits.

CRITICAL MULTIMEDIA ANALYSIS

The field of critical discourse analysis is now well developed (e.g., Fairclough, 1989, 1995; van Dijk, 1998, 1997; Wodak, 2000; Wodak & Reisigl, 2000). It has its own new journal (Graham, Fairclough, Wodak, & Lemke, 2004). It grows out of functional linguistic discourse analysis (e.g., Halliday, 1985; Halliday & Hasan, 1989; Martin, 1992) and earlier initiatives in language and ideology studies and social semiotics (e.g., Fowler, Hodge, Kress, & Trew, 1979; Halliday, 1978; Hodge & Kress, 1988; Hodge & Kress, 1993; Kress & Hodge, 1979; Lemke, 1995). But it has only recently begun to address nonlinguistic media and multimedia (Kress & van Leeuwen, 2001; Lemke, 2002b; Scollon & Scollon, 2003; van Leeuwen, 1999). With these beginnings, however, we are now on the verge of developing a true discipline of critical multimedia analysis.

Here are some key questions that must be addressed as we begin to define and prepare to teach critical multimedia literacy:

- How do people from diverse backgrounds interpret images or video critically in relation to accompanying text or narration?
- How do we read text and hear spoken language differently when images or video are integrated with them in space and time?
- How do people in different cultural and subcultural communities construct informational and rhetorical messages that artfully combine language and image, and sound, music, interactive engagement, and movement in virtual space?
- What kinds of messages are less readily available for argument and critique when they are presented visually rather than verbally (e.g., lifestyle values "sold" along with product advertising)?

- What are the messages presented in popular culture media which are addressed to mass audiences, but designed to further the interests, commercial and political, of those who control these media?
- How do people from different backgrounds (by gender, age, social class, ethnic culture, etc.) interpret these media and appropriate them for their own purposes, making them part of their own cultures and communities?
- In what ways do the original messages infiltrate our lives as we appropriate these media, and in what ways do we succeed in transforming their significance for us?
- How critical are we, and how critical do we need to be?

Verbal descriptions or explanations and visual images or representations are inherently incommensurable: they always necessarily present different meanings, however similar we may think them to be according to some set of disciplinary conventions. To what extent does this inherent incommensurability tend to ensure that each will undermine the monological certainties which the other projects? There is no one-to-one correspondence of any complex image with a written description or verbal "reading" of the image. There is no real image that shows exactly and only what a verbal account says. Multimodal presentations have an inherent critical potential to the extent that we learn how to use the images to deconstruct the viewpoint of the text, and the text to subvert the naturalness of the image. Multimodal rhetorical techniques usually try to combine image and text in ways that reinforce a single attitude, but they can never entirely succeed. We need techniques of analysis that can both show how images and texts have been selectively designed to reinforce one another and show their residual potential for undermining each other. This is a key part of the job of critical multimedia analysis.

I have mainly used "text" and "image" to make my point, but clearly, full-spectrum multimedia, i.e., those which make use of not only text and images, but also sound effects, music, designed spaces, and actional affordances (interactivity), multiply both the potential for carrying implicit ideological messages and the potential for subverting their own efforts. No single consistent meaning can be projected across so many different media. The signs from each medium retain the potential for alternative interpretations which are *not* consistent with those from the other media, and combining these perverse or divergent readings opens up spaces of critique and awareness of the extent to which the designed multimedia text is deliberately trying to foreclose these alternative readings and their potential ideological implications.

MAKING MEANING IN REAL AND VIRTUAL PLACES

To understand multimedia, to learn how to be critical of its messages, and to teach others how to use it critically, we need not just a conceptual framework and a goal—we need research on how people do use them and use them in a variety of different ways. We need such research not the least because readers differ in how we interpret signs and differ systematically by culture, age, social class, gender, sexuality, etc. Researchers as a social caste are not as diverse as the readers to whom multimedia messages are, or may be, addressed. We cannot rely on our own readings and intuitions alone.

How do we do research on multimedia use? What should we be seeking to learn? I want to propose a particular kind of research agenda. It is not by any means the only one, just the one that I have been trying to develop in my own thinking about these issues.

Too often in educational research we begin from an implicit input-output model: that direct relations of cause and effect should allow us to determine what causes what by seeing which changes in some input to the situation lead to which changes in outcomes. To some extent we adopt this logic because it has been successful in other kinds of inquiry where there are relatively direct cause-and-effect relationships, or at any rate relationships that can be modeled in this very simple way. We also desire it to be so because it promises us power and control. Social science of this kind is grounded in the dream of social engineering. By and large it is a dream that in the last century has failed, not simply because most experiments in social engineering have failed, but because social science has learned that its fundamental premise is simply wrong. Social systems have such complex interdependencies among multiple relations of cause and effect that no single input, nor even any realistically specifiable constellation of inputs, reliably governs any particular output. Moreover, what matters in the case of social systems is much less the principles that they all obey and much more their unique configurations. Every effort to control some outcome ripples through the system to produce unanticipated and often uncontrollable side effects. Every possible outcome depends not just on some small combination of inputs, but on emergent properties of the system as a whole that are not analyzable into separable component effects.

How then do we do research on social systems, or aspects of them such as the ways in which diverse people make diverse meanings with complex media artifacts in the context of an ecology of economic, political, and ideological processes? We replace an input-output model with a "tracer" model. We open the black box of intermediations that lie between any input and any output and we follow, or trace in detail, the actual processes by which outcomes are arrived at. We aim for an understanding of just how the specificities of any particular social system mediate chains of cause and effect that run through them. We do this for many different individual systems. We do it for particular systems at many different scales or levels of organization, and most particularly, across many timescales, across many orders of magnitude from moments to decades.

We hold on to a well-founded faith that having done this many times over we will not have to start again totally from scratch with each new system. We will learn to be sensitive to the kinds of mediations, the kinds of interactions, the kinds of differences that are most likely to matter to our domains of interest in the system. We will have, not a general theory that applies to all social systems, but a well-informed method of identifying what matters both more and less in the next system we study. We will arrive at something a little less like knowledge and a little more like wisdom.

Where to begin? I wish to begin with the study of how people make meanings and experience feelings across real time as they interact with rich, complex multimodal artifacts and environments. I am particularly interested in the role of material tools and perceptual signs, of real or virtual artifacts that can be written on and later read from (in whatever semiotic modality), of complex meaningful spaces in which we feel that we move and act, and of all the ways in which we meaningfully cumulate moments into longer trajectories and traversals. I want to know how we make meaning across time.

We could do this as a kind of micro-ethnography, following people moment by moment through a day, as they make sense of and react affectively to people, places, and things in the spaces of our lives. Obviously this is very hard to do, technically, ethically, and ultimately, methodologically. We could easily be overwhelmed by quantity of data and by the complexity of daily life. We would also encounter a peculiarity of the spaces of modern, or postmodern, life. They are not all physically real, or more precisely, they do not all have the same relationship between their physical and semiotic affordances. I am speaking here of "virtual realities." The worlds inside the television set, behind the movie screen, at the other end of the cell-phone link, on the computer screen, in the video game all have a material basis, but as meaning-worlds they look and feel very different to us than does that material basis as such. We learn to enter virtual attentional spaces where we make meaning, act meaningfully, and experience feelings as if in a world very different from the immediate physical one. Entering a virtual attentional space is a truly amazing capacity of the human brain and body, and it takes so little to let the world we imagine affect us equally with the world we otherwise take to be real. As organisms we interact with our environments in ways that take so much for granted, that attend only to a few critical details, so that if we artificially mock up those details, we respond organically as if we were actually in the virtual world, more or less, depending on how well and how many of those critical inputs have been provided.

As a result, in the course of daily life many people make meanings and experience feelings not just in the immediate physical spaces of our ecological environment, but also in the virtual semiotic extensions of that environment, especially multimedia. There is no sharp and absolute transition from making meaning with a book or magazine to feeling emotionally, or even physically, part of a film drama or a vivid three-dimensional computer game. In modern life we have learned to cycle our attention among multiple, immediate, and virtual attentional spaces. We can drive while talking on our cell phones (a bit risky). We can do e-mail or internet chat during meetings. We can carry on conversations while watching television, or play a computer game while doing internet chat with other players, in and out of our game characters. In fact we can juggle quite a few such activities at once. How do we follow people in and out of all these virtual worlds as well as follow them around in the immediate ecological world?

Research is usually the art of simplifying a problem just enough—enough to make it possible to do it, but not so much as to make the results irrelevant to our real concerns. What if we begin research on multimedia meaning-making by following people only as they move in virtual worlds (and secondarily as they move into and out of them)? What makes virtual worlds feel real to us is that they provide many of the affordances for meaning and feeling that we are accustomed to in the non-virtual world. And that is just what we ultimately want to understand. The great advantage of virtual worlds for research is that they are readily recorded, and that traversals across different virtual worlds or among different media simulated within them are no more difficult to follow than traversals within a single virtual world.

Even if what we will see in meaning-making in and across virtual worlds will necessarily be drastically simplified compared to what happens in daily life, virtual worlds are increasingly becoming one of our dominant media for communication and for the learning and promotion of viewpoints and ideologies. What we learn about how people make sense and feel within them is useful and relevant in itself, for purposes of media design and critical media analysis, even if it is limited as a model for the complexity of these processes in the full course of daily life.

A useful place to begin such research, I believe, is with the study of highly immersive, three-dimensional computer games. They are complex, advanced multimedia that are far more successfully used by millions of students than are most present-day Web-based and stand-alone educational software media.

LEARNING FROM GAME WORLD MEDIA

Computer games (Rouse & Ogden, 2001) are the most advanced form of multi-sensory, multi-modal media with which students and the wider public have experience and which we know to be successfully designed and successfully used by a large population (Gee, 2003). They exemplify a medium in which affective elements of meaning-making are far more prominent than in present-day educational media or on the Web. Compared to other significantly affective media such as film or television, they are far more interactive and afford opportunities for exploration, choice, (virtual) artifact use, movement through places, and selective shifts among attentional spaces—all of which are characteristic of complex, extended real-world meaning-making activities such as scientific research or architectural construction. Like good educational software and unlike the Web, film, or television, computer game media also allow us to create persistent records and world-effects (such as in-game notes and persistent changes in objects and environments) which help mediate cumulative learning over longer timescales than those of moment-to-moment game play.

Perhaps most importantly for research purposes, it is possible to create real-time, synchronized video and computer log records of monitor display, keystroke and mouse or joystick input, and user speech and action. It is possible in this way to follow user activity in entering the game world, acting and moving within the primary game world and among various subsidiary screens or auxiliary attentional spaces, communicating within and parallel to the game world action (e.g., to other players, in game and/or in side-channel chat online or face-to-face), and on leaving the game world. Ideally we would also like to observe how people integrate or cumulate in-game meaning-making activity and meanings made with out-of-game life activities and identities. We would like to study real and virtual communities of people who share in multi-player games and persistent world games. We would like to understand class, gender/sexuality, cultural and subcultural differences in which games people play, how, and why; the kinds of meanings they make and feelings they experience; and what persistent learning effects result. But we need to take such an ambitious agenda one step at a time.

We are not going to be able to do sophisticated, reliable, or useful research on how to adapt features of computer games to develop advanced educational media unless we first understand the basic meaning-making practices people employ in these complex virtual environments. We need to understand:

- How linguistic and visual-graphical modes of meaning-making are integrated.
- How dynamic, cumulative meaning-making in real time differs from making meaning with static images or text.
- How the affective components of in-game experience play a role in meaning-making and in the sense of immersion or presence in the virtual world.
- How we integrate interactions with characters, artifacts, and features of places in making sense in the game world.
- How we navigate spatially in-game in relation to meanings and feelings.
- How we cycle our attention among multiple attentional spaces available in the virtual world and between the virtual and the real world.
- How we communicate with real and virtual others in-game and in parallel with game activity.
- How we characterize and understand our own in-game actions in retrospect when we are out of the game.
- How we cumulate meanings and feelings across multiple gaming sessions.

These are, I believe, the basic research priorities for the initial-phase of educational research on computer gaming. The outcomes of such research can help guide the design of new generations of educational software that can both capitalize on the game-based multimedia experience of so many students and mediate for them the transition to far more complex discipline-based multimedia practices.

In order to pursue this basic research agenda efficiently, we need to mostly defer to a second phase of research consideration of a number of equally important issues:

- How do single-player and multi-player gaming experiences differ for various game genres?
- How do we communicate, cooperate, and collaborate with other players in multi-player game play?
- How does massively multi-player online persistent-world gaming differ from gaming which lacks these features?
- How do gaming activity, meaning-making, and experienced feelings differ among users/ player/learners according to social class, gender/sexuality, and cultural/subcultural differences, both typically and atypically?
- How do people integrate in-game meanings, feelings, activity patterns, relationships, and identities with out-of-game life?
- How do we coordinate our multiple, parallel engagements with diverse attentional worlds, including game worlds, film and television worlds, work worlds, school worlds, online and software-mediated attentional spaces, etc.?

It should be clear that we cannot entirely set aside these issues even in the initial research, but while being thoughtful about them, a focus on the first set of research issues I've identified seems to me the best way to prepare ourselves to investigate these further issues in an informed and effective way. Our purpose in this research should not only be to guide the design of the next generation of advanced educational media, but also to ground a complementary critical multimedia literacy curriculum. There is nothing about which students need to be more critical than the media through which they learn, whether in school or in the rest of their lives.

THE POLITICS OF CRITICAL MULTIMEDIA LITERACY

The time is past when serious scholars can pretend to have no politics. We make value choices at every stage of our work as researchers, speakers, writers, and teachers. If we take no special thought about these choices, then we naively reinforce the value choices of others, and with them, the interests of institutions and social sectors that share responsibility for the inequities and injustices in our own society. If we feel the need for critical literacy, for a critical multimedia literacy curriculum, it is because we do not trust the messages carried in our pervasive modern media. It is not just that we may be skeptical of their facts, we are also wary of the values and assumptions they purvey. None of us, or our students, can make free and democratic choices about the kind of world we want to live in if we lack the tools of critical multimedia literacy.

For this reason, research in related fields, such as critical discourse analysis (Fairclough, 1995; van Dijk, 1998; Wodak, 2000) and critical media studies (Hall & Evans, 1999; Mirzoeff, 1998), has recognized that we cannot simply study media as artifacts and multimodal texts, not even with the addition of studies of how people read and use them. We must also inquire into their conditions of production, their institutional origins and functions, their circulation in the modern economy, and to whom their benefits accrue, directly and indirectly, economically and politically. Who creates mass media, youth media, and educational media? And who does not? What institutions and what sectors of society benefit most and in what ways from the production, sale, circulation, and consumption of multimedia? We are not asking these questions out of pure academic curiosity, and our students would not be much interested in this agenda if that were the only reason for it. We undertake this inquiry because we believe that we will uncover at least one component of the covert workings of injustice and the perpetuation of privilege and anti-democratic power in our society.

To be critical, however, is not just to be skeptical or to identify the workings of covert interests. It is also to open up alternatives, to provide the analytical basis for the creation of new kinds of meanings which can embody the hopes and dreams of people who do not choose to accept traditional literacy conventions, commercial genres, or the rational-consumer model of the future. A critical multimedia literacy curriculum will not be successful with students if it is only about analysis and critique. The dismal history of similar efforts to teach critical television viewing provides a clear warning. Critical multimedia literacy needs to be taught as creation, as authoring, as production—in the context of analysis of existing models and genres. We need to help students see how they could create multimedia different from the media that are sold to them, or offered "free." In the age of television, with rare exceptions, it was not possible to teach media production, and even when the media were produced, they were not, in the students' eyes, "real television." Today, and in the near future, it will be much more realistic for all interested students to be critically creative with multimedia; to create with greater awareness that the genres and models they imitate have histories of serving particular interests and reinforcing particular beliefs and values; to create, when they choose, *against* those traditions as well as with them.

Critical multimedia literacy is about all media. It is not an addition to studies of textual print literacy, it is a re-conceptualization of what literacy itself means now and in our students' future lives. It is as much about factual, scientific, technical, and bureaucratic literacies as it is about literate worlds of the imagination. It is as much about the rhetoric of persuading people regarding belief, values, and action as it is about presenting information or building virtual worlds. It will need to be articulated in relation to every other subject and area of the curriculum just as the current literacy curriculum does. Above all, it will need to be grounded in research: on how meanings are made across multiple media and modalities, on the role media play in the larger society, and on how to teach critical multimedia literacy not just as critique but as a resource for the creation of alternative practices, values, and lifestyles.

I am confident that the core intellectual tools exist to define and carry out successful research agendas for building a critical multimedia literacy curriculum. I think there are important social, intellectual, and political reasons for making this work a high priority. It is an effort to which many of us can and must contribute for it to succeed. What I have presented here is meant as one tentative articulation of this important enterprise. I hope that it will be joined by many others.

REFERENCES

Fairclough, N. (1989). *Language and power.* New York: Longman.

Fairclough, N. (1995). *Critical discourse analysis.* London: Longman.

Fowler, R., Hodge, R., Kress, G., & Trew, T. (1979). *Language and control.* London: Routledge & Kegan Paul.

Gee, J. P. (2003). *What video games have to teach us about learning and literacy.* New York: Palgrave/ Macmillan.

Graham, P., Fairclough, N., Wodak, R., & Lemke, J. L. (Eds.). (2004). *Critical discourse studies.* London: Routledge.

Hall, S., Critcher, C., Jefferson, T., Clarke, J., & Roberts, B. (1978). *Policing the crisis.* London: Macmillan.

Hall, S., & Evans, J. (Eds.). (1999). *Visual culture: The reader.* London: Sage.

Halliday, M. A. K. (1978). *Language as social semiotic.* London: Edward Arnold.

Halliday, M. A. K. (1985). *An introduction to functional grammar.* London: Edward Arnold.

Halliday, M. A. K., & Hasan, R. (1989). *Language, context, and text*. London: Oxford University Press.

Hartley, J. (1982). *Understanding news*. London: Methuen.

Hodge, R., & Kress, G. (1988). *Social semiotics*. Ithaca: Cornell University Press.

Hodge, R., & Kress, G. (1993). *Language as ideology* (2 ed.). London/New York: Routledge.

Kress, G., & Hodge, R. (1979). *Language as ideology* (1 ed.). London/New York: Routledge.

Kress, G., & van Leeuwen, T. (1996). *Reading images: The grammar of visual design*. London: Routledge.

Kress, G., & van Leeuwen, T. (2001). *Multimodal discourse*. London: Arnold.

Lemke, J. L. (1989). Social semiotics: A new model for literacy education. In: D. Bloome (Ed.), *Classrooms and literacy* (pp. 289–309). Norwood, NJ: Ablex Publishing.

Lemke, J. L. (1995). *Textual politics: Discourse and social dynamics*. London: Taylor & Francis.

Lemke, J. L. (1998a). Metamedia literacy: Transforming meanings and media. In: D. Reinking, L. Labbo, M. McKenna, & R. Kiefer (Eds.), *Handbook of literacy and technology: Transformations in a post-typographic world* (pp. 283–301). Hillsdale, NJ: Lawrence Erlbaum Associates.

Lemke, J. L. (1998b). Multiplying meaning: Visual and verbal semiotics in scientific text. In J. R. Martin & R. Veel (Eds.), *Reading Science* (pp. 87–113). London: Routledge.

Lemke, J. L. (2002a). Discursive technologies and the social organization of meaning. *Folia Linguistica, 35*(1–2), 79–96.

Lemke, J. L. (2002b). Travels in Hypermodality. *Visual Communication, 1*(3), 299–325.

Lemke, J. L. (2003). The role of texts in the technologies of social organization. In R. Wodak & G. Weiss (Eds.), *Theory and interdisciplinarity in critical discourse analysis* (pp. 130–149). London: Macmillan/Palgrave.

Martin, J. R. (1992). *English text*. Philadelphia: John Benjamins.

Mirzoeff, N. (Ed.). (1998). *The visual culture reader*. New York: Routledge.

O'Toole, L. M. (1990). A systemic-functional semiotics of art. *Semiotica, 82*, 185–209.

Rouse, R., III, & Ogden, S. (2001). *Game design: Theory and practice*. Plano, TX: Wordware Publishing.

Scollon, R., & Scollon, S. W. (2003). *Discourses in place: Language in the material world*. London: Routledge.

Thibault, P. (1991). *Social semiotics as praxis*. Minneapolis: University of Minnesota Press.

van Dijk, T. (1998). *Ideology*. London: Sage.

van Dijk, T. (Ed.). (1997). *Discourse studies*. London: Sage.

van Leeuwen, T. (1999). *Speech, music, sound*. New York: St. Martin's Press.

Williamson, J. (1978). *Decoding advertisements: Ideology and meaning in advertising*. London: Marion Boyars.

Wodak, R. (2000). *Methods of text and discourse analysis*. London: Sage.

Wodak, R., & Reisigl, M. (2000). *Discourse and discrimination: Rhetorics of racism and antisemitism*. London: Routledge.

Multiple Visions of Multimedia Literacy: Emerging Areas of Synthesis

Renee Hobbs
Temple University

Screen activity is a central fact of life for American children and teens, with children ages 8 to 18 spending an average of eight hours per day using media, including television, videogames, the Internet, newspapers, magazines, films, radio, recorded music, and books (Kaiser Family Foundation, 2001). Even American babies and toddlers spend two or more hours per day using media (Kaiser Family Foundation, 2003a). In contemporary society, with rapid changes taking place in the way that information is created and distributed, children and young people need to be able to find, select, comprehend, and evaluate information and entertainment messages. While educators rightly emphasize the development of language competencies, it is also valuable for students to learn to use symbol systems, including images, sound and music, as a means of self-expression and communication, as these are now an integral part of contemporary life. While educational technologists have privileged interactive computing, online synchronous and asynchronous communication as focal issues (Fouts, 2000; Oppenheimer, 2003), consumption of popular culture and mass media messages is still the central leisure activity for Americans, Europeans, and an increasingly large number of people around the world. Mass media messages provide most people with their primary source of information about the world (Kubey & Csikszentmihalyi, 1990) and the use of media messages—particularly popular music, film and television—continues to be a primary component of adolescent social interaction (Lenhart, Rainie & Lewis, 2001) and socialization (Calvert, 1998). Adolescents' interest in mass media and popular culture may drive much of their electronic reading and writing (using Web sites and interactive online communication experiences), particularly for youth from high-poverty communities (Bussiere & Gluszynski, 2004; Chandler-Olcott & Mahar, 2003; Monroe, 2004). As a result, literacy educators are recognizing the need to respond to the changing array of media technologies and resources used in the world outside the classroom in order to make education more responsive to the needs of learners in the 21st century.

As a result, more and more scholars and educators are using terms such as *visual literacy, media literacy, critical literacy, information literacy* and *technology literacy* to expand the concept of literacy so that visual, electronic, and digital forms of expression and communication are included as objects of study and analysis. Academic scholars in the fields of literary theory, cultural studies, history, psychology, library and information science, medicine and public health, linguistics, rhetoric, communication and media studies have become increasingly interested in how people comprehend, interpret, critically analyze and compose texts of various kinds. Literacy educators no longer "own" the concept of literacy. Questions about the processes of literacy are being interrogated by many different scholars using a variety of theoretical and disciplinary lenses. Each year, a growing number of K–12 educators are using technologies to bring students access to online newspapers, magazine articles, audio programs, narrative films and television documentaries, blogs, and other multimedia resources to help students build critical thinking, communication, creativity and collaborative problem-solving skills (Hobbs, 2004). They are involving students in creating their own messages using visual, electronic and digital media tools. Stakeholders also include business leaders, youth development specialists, federal and state education officials, parents, community activists and artists who have voiced their ideas about issues related to the uses of media and technology in literacy education. Like the parable of the blind man and the elephant, each stakeholder group approaches the topic of *multiliteracy* from different perspectives, and as a result, there are numerous, differentially nuanced visions of what these skills encompass (Hobbs, 1998a; Tyner, 1998).

This paper reviews the disciplinary traditions and key concepts of some of the new literacies and examines the consensus (and disjunctures) that are beginning to emerge among diverse stakeholders and scholars as some key ideas are beginning to circulate in a range of disciplines. A model that synthesizes this literature is created in order to support the work of scholars interested in investigating how teachers translate the "big ideas" of multiliteracies into classroom practice and to support the development of measures to assess students' learning. This paper then reviews the small, but growing, body of evidence about the uses of film, video, newspapers, and computers as tools for literacy learning and identifies research opportunities for future interdisciplinary scholarship focused on understanding how multimedia and popular culture texts can be used as tools to support literacy development among K–12 learners.

DISCIPLINARY FRAMEWORKS SHAPE PRIORITIES
FOR THE NEW LITERACIES

Throughout the 20th century, calls to expand the concept of literacy have arisen from a number of scholars from different disciplinary and intellectual backgrounds, including media studies, technology education, literary studies, library and information sciences, education, cultural studies, and the visual arts. By and large, the discourse between these scholarly fields has been limited, and only a few scholars have served as intermediaries and translators, framing ideas across multiple fields (Flood, Heath & Lapp, 1997; Kellner, 1995). Increased access to scholarship online has probably been a contributing factor in the growth of border crossing and cross-disciplinary or inter-disciplinary work in literacy education.

Visual Literacy. Based on nearly 100 years of work by cognitive psychologists, artists, literary scholars, graphic designers, art historians, and philosophers on the psychology of vision, aesthetics, and spatial intelligence (see reviews in Gregory, 1970), academics and K–12 classroom teachers in both arts and humanities fields have long incorporated visual materials into the classroom in order to demonstrate how factors like selection, framing, composition, sequence, and aesthetic dimensions of images influence viewers' interpretations and emotional responses. While critics identify longstanding questions about the coherence and viability of assertions about the value of visual literacy made by practitioners and scholars (Avgirinou & Ericson, 1997), visual literacy education aims to demonstrate how genres, codes, conventions and formats shape perceptual and interpretive processes. Scholars with interests in visual literacy have examined how images are comprehended and interpreted, how language and images interact in the meaning-making process (Worth & Gross, 1981), how exposure to visual images affects general cognitive and intellectual development (Messaris, 1994), and how semiotic and aesthetic dimensions of images can be examined and appreciated (Eco, 1979; Natharius, 2004). In comparing the differences in emphasis among various multiliteracies, it is clear that visual literacy privileges the "reading" process of "viewing and interpreting" images more than the "composing" process of creating and constructing images (Tyner, 1998).

Learning about the visual conventions of images gives viewers a foundation for heightened conscious appreciation of artistry and the ability to recognize the manipulative uses and ideological implications of visual images (Messaris, 1994). A fundamental dimension of teaching visual literacy is the emphasis on distinguishing between pictures and reality, as naïve viewers imagine that images produced by photographic media are simple mechanical records of actuality with high levels of correspondence and fidelity (Griffin & Schwartz, 1997). The problem of "representation" has been articulated by film scholars throughout the 20th century (see Nichols, 1992 for review). Texts are only representations of reality, but scholars have been intrigued by the ways in which people process visual texts as if they were veridical experience (Messaris, 1994). While in elementary and secondary educational practice a focus on the aesthetics of images has its locus in visual arts education, there is a tradition of exploring visual literacy in language arts, particularly in film (or film and literature) courses often offered as electives in U.S. and some European high schools. Concepts including realism, truthfulness, accuracy, bias, objectivity, and stereotyping have shaped classroom activity not only in English language arts, but also in social studies, science, and even health education (Aufderheide, 1993).

Information Literacy. Information literacy has been defined as a set of abilities requiring individuals to recognize when information is needed and have the ability to locate, evaluate, and use it (American Library Association, 2000). At the heart of it, information literacy emphasizes the need for careful selection, retrieval and choice-making in response to the abundant information available in the workplace, at school, and in all aspects of personal decision-making, especially in the areas of citizenship and health. Deriving from the influential *A Nation at Risk* report in 1983, a coalition of 65 national organizations founded the National Forum on Information Literacy which was highly influential in outlining the role of the library and information resources in the development of K–12 and higher education (Plotnick, 1999).

Information literacy education emphasizes the critical thinking, meta-cognitive, and procedural knowledge used to locate information in specific domains, fields, and contexts. A prime emphasis is placed on recognizing message quality, authenticity and credibility. Personal and contextual factors activate or suppress people's evaluative stance towards information, and scholars have examined the conditions under which people are likely to critically assess information or accept information at face value (see Fitzgerald, 1999 for review).

Critics have claimed that information literacy does not emphasize the ways in which meaning is constructed through interpretation (Lankshear, Snyder & Green, 2000). Among some K–12 practitioners, information literacy may be defined more narrowly as mere skills, as in the process of locating information using library classification systems and Boolean search strategies, using checklist-type criteria to evaluate Web-based source materials, and avoiding plagiarism through correct citation of source materials (Dibble, 2004). Critics perceive that information literacy appears to emphasize the simple acquisition of "facts" to be sought and used to make a case for an argument, without the recognition that information and knowledge are the products of cultural practices that exist within the context of economic and political relations (Kapitzke, 2003; Vandergrift, 1987). But since the process of finding, using and handling information is always context-specific, it is never only just a routine application of a particular set of operations. In line with this perspective, some scholars see information literacy as more broadly and more closely akin to processes involved in reading. Dissatisfied with the focus on information and eager to connect the critical thinking tradition of information literacy with newer forms of online communication, Gilster (1998) has coined the term *digital literacy* as the ability to understand, evaluate, and integrate information in multiple formats. Even more broadly, Lloyd (2003, 90) has rejected information as a set of skills, describing it instead as a meta-competency, where individuals are able to "recognize the nature of their need for information, actively navigating cognitive and environmental barriers, and accommodating and assimilating information as they create new knowledge."

Media Literacy. Media literacy education in the United States has been deeply influenced by the work of British, Canadian and Australian educators and scholars who have developed a significant body of writing about instructional practices that engage children and young people in critically analyzing mass media messages and popular culture (see Alvarado & Boyd-Barrett, 1991 for review). This approach is theoretically aligned with communication scholarship in audience reception studies, which emerged from mid–20th century research in the fields of literary studies, cultural studies, and media effects. Scholars have used concepts including uses and gratifications, spectatorship, resistant and oppositional reading of media texts, conceptualizations of active and passive audiences, fan culture and interpretive communities, and screen theory (see Brooker & Jermyn, 2003 for an identification of central texts and scholars). Positioned in the 1970s as a response to television's supposed deleterious impact on childhood socialization, and originally labeled "critical viewing skills" (Brown, 1991), educators and scholars have broadened the focus to emphasize an expanded conceptualization of literacy as the ability to access, analyze, evaluate, and communicate messages in a wide variety of forms (Aufderheide, 1993). As used here, the term *critical* refers to the recognition that visual and electronic messages are constructed texts that present particular, distinctive points of view as a result of the economic, political and social contexts in which they circulate. In this view, critical readers and viewers are aware of the "constructedness" of media messages and explore who produces texts, their motives and purposes for communication and expression, and the role of media institutions, economics, and ideology in the construction and dissemination of cultural messages (Brunner & Tally, 1998; Buckingham & Sefton-Green, 1994). A "generic" focus is evident among media literacy educators, as media literacy educators emphasize specific ways of reading messages in the genres of print and television news media, advertising, non-fiction television, and narrative film. Issues including advertising and materialism, media violence, the First Amendment and freedom of expression, and the representation of gender and race in the media are also featured in curriculum for secondary students. This reflects the enduring traditions of media literacy which have been associated with questions whether to conceptualize the audience as innocent victim, active text reader, hedonistic pleasure-seeker, or political dupe (McLuhan, 1964).

Media literacy education is often defined by its emphasis on pedagogy: it stresses a more active, student-centered, participatory style that emphasizes inquiry and learning by doing (Buckingham, 2003; Kist, 2000). Rather than emphasize teachers as providers of knowledge, media literacy pedagogy stresses 1) the process of inquiry, with critical questions guiding the process of message analysis and 2) situated action learning, based on the work of Freire and Macedo (1987), which emphasizes the cycle of awareness, analysis, reflection, action and experience in a community context that is responsive to the needs of individuals, particularly as they relate to social inequalities and political injustices. Media literacy educators emphasize the centrality of "composition" using media tools and technologies and advocate for moving media production away from its historically vocational track in secondary education to align it more closely within English education. Media literacy practices involve students in actively creating messages using publishing software, digital cameras, video, and other media. Recently, the National Council of Teachers of English (NCTE) approved a resolution stating that they will 1) encourage preservice, in-service, and staff development programs that will focus on new literacies, multimedia composition, and a broadened concept of literacy 2) encourage research and develop models of district, school, and classroom policies that would promote multimedia composition, and 3) encourage integrating multimedia composition in English language arts curriculum and teacher education, and in refining related standards at local, state, and national levels (NCTE, 2003). As yet, however, there is little evidence to know the extent to which increasing access to low-cost, home video, editing software, and Web publication tools have affected instructional practices in secondary English education. But more than 40 states in the U.S. have included media literacy outcomes in their state education frameworks (Kubey & Baker, 2001), which reflects the gradual perceptual changes among educational leaders concerning the value of these skills for life in a media-rich and technology-saturated society.

Critical Literacy. Arising from traditions established by work in semiotics and cultural studies, literacy scholars have begun to define reading as not just extracting meaning from text, but the process of constructing meaning through interaction and involvement. "Meaning," in this view, is understood in the context of social, historic and power relations, not just the product of the author's intentions (Kellner, 1995; Cervetti, Pardales, & Damico, 2001). For these scholars and practitioners, "texts" are any form of symbolic expression used in the communication of meaning (Barthes, 1972). As used by critical literacy scholars, the term *critical* refers to the recognition of oppression and exploitation as embedded in texts and textual activity; critical literacy is a component of the struggle for a better society, with an explicit ideological focus on issues of inequity as related to race, gender, class, and sexual orientation (Kellner, 1995). Critical literacy education emphasizes that identity and power relations are always part of the process of composing and interpreting texts, and that these processes occur in a socio-culturally and historically-bound framework.

Connected to Freire and Macedo's (1987) exploration of reading within a sociocultural context, critical literacy scholars and educators examine and understand how various texts, including pictures, icons, and electronic messages (as forms of symbolic expression) are used to influence, persuade, and control people. Critical literacy emphasizes that literacy cannot be understood as just "cracking the code" or "analyzing the author's intentions" but must be understood as an embodiment of social and political relationships. This perspective foregrounds sociocultural factors within a framework of power relations, incorporating within literacy practices an understanding of the identity of the participants, how the activity is defined or executed, the timing of the activity, where it occurs, and why participants are motivated to perform the activity (Rand Reading Study Group, 2004). At the same time, these scholars emphasize the importance of not just reading texts critically, but understanding how people can control their experience of the world through constructing messages as part of transforming society (Gee, 1996). A central component of critical literacy pedagogy is its focus on examining multiple perspectives and points of view, often through juxtaposing diverse materials, including photos, videos and artifacts of popular culture (Luke, 1997; McLaughlin & DeVogel, 2004) and exploring themes related to power, identity, pleasure, and transgression (Alvermann, Moon & Hagood, 1999).

A MODEL FOR SYNTHESIZING EMERGING
CONSENSUS IN MULTILITERACIES

Led by the rapidly changing communications media in contemporary society, scholars and practitioners are working as fast as possible to re-conceptualize literacy in ways that reflect emerging perspectives on the communicative competencies required for life in the 21st century. As Tyner

(2004, 373) notes, each of the new literacies described above is "provisional, speculative and distinguished by the subtle ideological and professional differences of its various constituents." At the present time, it is unclear whether various terms for new literacies will continue to multiply as a result of increased attention from diverse interest groups, or whether they will slowly decline as consensus gradually emerges among scholars, educators, and policy makers. But an array of similar terms for distinctive concepts and ideas has real-world implications for educational practice, as Cervetti, Pardales and Damico (2001) pointed out in explaining how the distinctions between *critical reading* and *critical literacy* were confusing to practitioners and policy makers. There is a risk that misunderstandings of the multiple formulations of these new literacies could twist and warp how these concepts are understood by the public and by policy makers.

Fortunately, the emerging consensus among these different perspectives is obvious and considerable: all of the proponents reflect an appreciation that visual, electronic, and digital media are reshaping the knowledge, skills and competencies required for full participation in contemporary society, and all view these abilities as fundamentally tied to the intellectual and social practices known as literacy (New London Group, 1996). Multiliteracies proponents recognize that the acquisition and development of these competencies will require changes to the K–12 learning environment, including significant changes in teacher preservice and in-service education, design of learning experiences, access to tools, resources and materials, and techniques of classroom management (Buckingham, 2003; Film Education Working Group, 1999). And one can find scholars and practitioners in each of these new literacies who frame these concepts within a social, political, and economic context, a stance which recognizes literacy as a form of social power which enables fuller control over the circulation of messages and meanings in society (Giroux & Simon, 1989; Luke, 1997).

What tenets or principles do the practitioners and scholars advocating new literacies share? A typology developed by the Film Education Working Group (1999) identified broad categories of inquiry focusing on authors, audiences, messages, language, values, and representation. Table 2.1 presents a synthesis of the key conceptual tenets or working principles that are emphasized in the work of media literacy, visual literacy, critical literacy, and information literacy scholars and practitioners from the United Kingdom, Canada, and the United States, whose work has been briefly described above. Tenets from all four multiliteracies are collapsed into three broad categories: AA (authors and audiences), MM (messages and meanings), and RR (representations and reality). These three categories cut across print, visual, electronic and digital forms and genres and represent a simplified way to express the key dimensions of multiliteracies education in a framework that may be resonant and useful to K–12 classroom practitioners.

This model may also support research on staff development and the development of new methods and tools for assessing student learning. In my work with practitioners of information literacy, media literacy, visual literacy and critical literacy in elementary and secondary schools, I have found teachers' perceptions of their own goals and aims to be critically implicated in the shape of the curricular choices they make in the classroom (Hobbs, 1998b; 1994). Among teachers, there is a wide range of motivations and beliefs concerning multiliteracies that leads to a proliferation of instructional methods and approaches to classroom practice. As a result, it is difficult to recognize "best practices" in new literacies. By synthesizing the key ideas of multiliteracies into three broad categories, it may be easier to describe instructors' objectives and goals with more precision and identify the types of overt and covert instructional aims and priorities now extant among practitioners in K–12 settings. For example, use of this model may enable researchers to observe and document differences between teachers' stated aims and their instructional practices, a phenomenon described as ubiquitous by Hart and Suss (2002) in their cross-national case studies of teachers of adolescents. Future research might explore how these three broad conceptual

TABLE 2.1
A Model for Integrating the Conceptual Tenets of Multimedia Literacies

Themes	Tenets	Sources
AA		
AUTHORS AND AUDIENCES	AA1. Consumers of texts make selections and choices of texts to meet various needs and gratify different desires.	M, I
	AA2. Consumers of texts are defined, targeted, and conceptualized by producers of texts.	M, C, V, I
	AA3. Texts are consciously created by authors and involve the coordination of different types of labor.	M, C, V, I
	AA4. Texts are often produced and distributed for power, gain and profit; economic and political factors shape the content and format of texts.	M, C, V, I
MM		
MESSAGES AND MEANINGS	MM1. Texts use a variety of combinations of symbol systems (language, image, sound, music) and delivery systems (print, visual, electronic) and employ genres, codes, and conventions that can be identified and classified.	M, C, V, I
	MM2. Individuals and social groups select, use, interpret, and respond to texts by using their unique life experiences, prior knowledge, and social positions.	M, C, V
	MM3. People's interpretation of texts influence aspects of decision-making, attitude formation, world view, and behavior.	M, C, V, I
RR		
REPRESENTATIONS AND REALITY	RR1. Texts reflect the ideologies and world views of their authors, and as a result, they selectively omit information and have distinctive points of view.	M, C, V, I
	RR2. Texts use techniques that affect people's perceptions of social reality.	M, C, V, I
	RR3. Texts can be examined in relationship to people's different understandings about social reality within various political, social, and economic contexts.	M, C, V

Support for this tenet found in Visual literacy (V), Media literacy (M), Information literacy (I), and Critical literacy (C).

tenets may help characterize the changes in students' growth that may result from learning opportunities with print, visual, electronic, and digital media in (and out of) the classroom.

What do the new literacies have in common? How are they different? These new literacies have as a central focus the development of students' engagement with texts and their concern for the meaning-making process, the constructed process of authorship, and questions about how texts represent social realities. They differ in their relative emphasis on the reader, the text, and the socio-historical and political contexts in which interpretations take place. For example, media literacy emphasizes an understanding of the processes involved in "constructing texts" and conceptualizes the audience as a construction designed within a particular economic framework. Information literacy emphasizes the process of "selection and choice" of texts as a component of the meaning-making process. By contrast, critical literacy emphasizes the constructed nature of "meaning," recognizing that meaning-making occurs as individuals interact with texts and make sense of other readers' interpretations in relation to their own social positions and lived experiences of the world. Visual literacy emphasizes the "aesthetic and rhetorical" functions of images, examining how people make connections between the visual texts they encounter and their own experience of reality, examining media texts for their plausibility and correspondence with other media representations.

The disjunctures among these new literacies reflect important differences in emphasis, pedagogy, and ideology. While media literacy, critical literacy and technology literacy emphasize the connection between reading and writing, this is less emphasized in visual literacy and information literacy, which are both primarily centered on the process of accessing, reading, and using texts. There is a disjuncture between multiliteracies regarding the appropriate message genres deserving attention, from those include or emphasize popular culture (media literacy, visual literacy, cultural literacy) and those which focus primarily on informational messages (information literacy). This disjuncture reflects well-entrenched arguments in English language arts education, as Robert Scholes (1998) articulates when he proposes replacing the canon of literary texts with a canon of methods of critical analysis (including theory, history, production, and consumption) that enable a reader to read all kinds of texts in all kinds of media, including entertainment and popular culture, while opposite arguments are made by E. D. Hirsch (1987), who calls for a focus on core literary and historical texts so that students can acquire the world knowledge they need to be culturally literate.

Another disjuncture concerns fundamental conceptualizations of teaching and learning, as some practitioners and scholars in all the new literacies described in this chapter emphasize participation and peer-interaction, inquiry-based learning, and constructivist learning principles, while others tend to view learning as a form of skills and content delivery from experts who guide instruction. The teacher-centered transmission model of instruction is common to most classrooms in the United States, and this model tends to emphasize textbooks as the *de facto* curriculum, whereas in participatory classrooms, a wider range of textual materials (including visual, multimedia and popular culture texts) is used (Wade & Moje, 2000). As yet, there is little consensus among K–12 practitioners about how visual texts, digital media, and technology tools are best infused into learning environments. Even though this debate will continue to create divisions among scholars and practitioners, it is likely that a hybrid of teacher-centered and participatory approaches will be used in most K–12 settings by selectively structuring learning experiences to match students' needs (Tyner, 2004).

Examining Multimedia Literacy Practices in Schools

Much research in the past 20 years has examined the impact of television on the development of children's reading skills (Neuman, 1991), but relatively little is known about the ways that visual media (including film and television programs) or mass media (like newspapers, magazines, radio or audio resources) may be useful in the context of literacy instruction in primary or secondary education. By contrast, there is a substantial literature that examines how computers, online, and digital information technologies are used (or not used) in schools (Fouts, 2000; Norris, Sullivan, Poirot & Soloway, 2003). Historians of education should investigate the factors that led to shift towards conceptualizing educational technology as focused exclusively on computers, thus marginalizing film and video forms as technologies.

Although neither "fish nor fowl" in its status as non-print media, film and video use is ubiquitous among secondary educators, with at least 90% of teachers using video, film or documentaries, and 1 in 4 teachers using video once a week or more often (PBS, 2004). No one is startled to learn that English teachers use films like *To Kill a Mockingbird* and *Hamlet*, but a survey of English teachers in Minnesota found that a wide variety of genres and types of films are in use (from Hollywood classics to low-budget independent films). More than 200 unique titles were described among the 161 teachers who participated in the study (Larsson, 2001). Researchers know much less about why and how teachers use video in the classroom as a learning tool, but based on field observations, it appears that the content transmission model is dominant, along with a pervasive attitude that video is a form of entertainment and useful primarily for non-academic students, and only rarely used to support literacy learning or the development of critical thinking skills (Hobbs, in press; Hobbs, 1994). Future research should explore how teachers' current uses of film and video in the classroom may be more meaningfully connected to students' literacy development in elementary- and secondary-education contexts, as well as in home-school and family literacy initiatives.

Another under-researched mass media form that is highly relevant to the work of literacy educators is newspapers and magazines. Newspaper use has been a common feature of instruction in many schools since the 1960s, with more than 950 U.S. daily newspapers sponsoring year-round programs providing newspapers to 106,000 schools at reduced rates. Used by 381,000 teachers as a text for learning in the classroom, newspaper-in-education programs reach almost 14.5 million students each year (NAA Foundation, 2004). A study of home literacy practices has shown that newspapers are a valuable resource for family communication, particularly with boys (Sullivan, 2004). One wonders why there is such a dearth of scholarly research on how newspapers (and their new online variants) are used in schools. The newspaper industry has produced some evidence that newspaper use in the classroom influences newspaper reading in later life. Researchers interviewed a large representative sample of 18 to 34 year olds, finding that 64% of those who had had a class where newspapers were part of the curriculum were regular readers of newspapers; by contrast, only 38% of those who didn't have exposure to newspapers in the classroom were regular newspaper readers (Saba, 2004). Further research should investigate how comparing and contrasting online newspapers and televison news media might support literacy development.

Emerging Evidence from Research on Multimedia Literacies

How have the new literacies been shown to affect student learning? Most examinations of multimedia literacy look at very small numbers of students, usually a single classroom (Alvermann, Moon, & Hagood, 2001; Anderson, 1983). Studies have explored whether students learned the facts, vocabulary, and information provided as part of the instruction (Baron, 1985; Kelly, Gunter & Kelly, 1985) or whether a video broadcast about media literacy affects cognitive or critical analysis skills (Vooijs & Van der Voort, 1993). In addition, case studies from a number of countries have documented teachers' instructional strategies in implementing media literacy in classrooms (Hart & Suss, 2004; Hart, 1998; Hurrell, 2001; Kist, 2000), and a further body of research has examined media literacy as an intervention tool for prevention and public health (see Kaiser Family Foundation, 2003b for review).

There is emerging evidence that media literacy instruction affects the development of reading comprehension and writing. In a quasi-experimental study, eleventh grade students who participated in a year-long English language arts/media literacy curriculum were compared to students from a demographically matched group who received no instruction in critically analyzing media messages. Critical message analysis skills were measured by examining students' ability to identify the purpose, point of view, and construction techniques used in print newsmagazines, TV news segments, print advertising, and radio news segments. Statistically significant differences were found in students' reading comprehension, writing skills, critical reading, critical listening, critical viewing, and knowledge of media production, media history, media economics, and understanding of media terminology (Hobbs & Frost, 2003).

Information literacy skills have been measured among students in middle school and high school. A large-scale study of New Zealand students showed students have only limited understanding of the information literacy skills involved in using library-related resources, specifically libraries, parts of a book, and reference sources (Brown, 2001). Instructional models intended to foster the acquisition of research, problem-solving, and metacognitive skills were found to be effective with a class of eighth-grade students who were asked to research and write about events surrounding the African-American Civil Rights Movement (Wolf, 2003). Students were provided support in the activities required to solve information-based problems through six processes: task definition, information seeking strategies, location and access, use of information, synthesis, and evaluation. Such models, maps, and organizers should continue to be tested among many groups of learners to determine the full range of their value for increasing metacognitive awareness of the processes involved in using information for problem solving.

While numerous teacher staff development programs are available to preservice and in-service teachers to learn to integrate multiliteracies into instruction, few have been evaluated. Begoray and Morin (2002) investigated a teacher summer institute that brought English teachers from Manitoba Canada together to explore music, visual arts, media, and drama, finding that even after one year, teachers believed they increased their use of technology, art, music, drama, and media in their classrooms. Begoray (2002) videotaped and interviewed teachers in a Canadian city who were learning to use visual literacy concepts over a period of two years. Teachers implemented lessons involving the use of cameras and photography, made active use of videotaping to document students' learning progress, and involved students in mental visualization as a means to promote reading comprehension. Further research should continue to explore why and how teachers decide to implement new literacies instruction, the role of staff development in supporting teachers' growth and change, and outcomes including student motivation, literal and inferential comprehension, listening skills, and collaboration.

CONCLUSION

There is no shortage of theories about the promise of media, technology, and popular culture in education. However, as Bazalgette, Bevort and Savino (1992, 3) point out, "the realities of teaching and learning are harder to define and share." In reviewing accounts of practice of media education in more than a dozen countries, they emphasize that what is institutionally appropriate in one setting may not be so in another. The conceptual model which presents tenets of the four new literacies represents an effort to synthesize some key themes in a rich and varied literature now emerging from many academic disciplines and fields. Such synthesis may support the development of new research which examines teachers' and students' engagement with popular culture and mass media texts in the context of learning in English language arts. The current range and diversity of philosophies and approaches to new literacies, like Solomon's beard, may be a prime source of strength for the future of the field. But the diverse perspectives and areas of emphasis may also lead to academic sniping, divisiveness, and sheer exhaustion. Models that support cross-disciplinary dialogue and continued border crossing, now routinely appreciated as an essential component of postmodern scholarship, should move forward the development of this emerging field of inquiry.

The growing band of literacy educators now interested in popular culture, mass media, and online and digital technologies must be responsive to what Masterman (1985, 24) has identified as a central objective for media education: the ability to apply knowledge and skills learned in the classroom to the world of everyday life. In reflecting on the appropriate learning outcomes for teaching information literacy, media literacy, visual literacy, and critical literacy, teachers must design learning experiences that help students, as quickly as possible, to stand on their own two feet and apply critical thinking skills to the media and technology experiences they have at home. Future research must more systematically begin to explore the student learning outcomes that result from instruction that emphasizes information literacy, visual literacy, media literacy, and critical literacy and to find better ways to help teachers assess when and how such learning occurs.

In contrast to the idealistic visions of education scholars and academics, the institutional nature of schooling demands that teachers adapt and modify their work to fit with the normative values of school culture. As a result, teachers often encounter situations and experiences in using media, technology, and popular culture in the classroom that are not described in the scholarly academic literature, whose voices "demand that the repertoire of acceptable cultural objects be expanded" (Aronowitz & Giroux, 1993, 182). The dynamism and complexity of contemporary life in a media-saturated and information-rich culture remind us that the use of media, technology, and popular culture in the classroom is not for the faint of heart. Such work vitally depends on the initiative and perseverance of individual teachers, who are inspired and motivated by a wide range of different understandings about the role of the mass media, technology, and popular culture in society. These individuals need to have courage, imagination, and creativity to enable students to develop the competencies they need to be citizens of an information age.

REFERENCES

Alvarado, M., & Boyd-Barrett, O. (1991). *Media education: An introduction.* London: British Film Institute.

Alvermann, D., Moon, J., & Hagood, M. (1999). *Popular culture in the classroom: Teaching and researching critical media literacy.* Newark, DE: International Reading Association.

American Library Association (2000). Information literacy competency standards for higher education. Accessed September 1, 2004 online at http://www.ala.org/ala/acrl/acrlstandards/informationliteracy competency.htm.

Anderson, J. A. (1983). The theoretical lineage of critical viewing curricula. *Journal of Communication, 30*(3), 64–70.

Aronowitz, S. & Giroux, H. (1993). *Education still under siege.* Westport, CT: Bergin & Garvey.

Aufderheide. P. (1993). *Media literacy: A report of the national leadership conference on media literacy.* Queenstown, MD: Aspen Institute.

Avgirinou, M., & Ericson, J. (1997). A review of the concept of visual literacy. *British Journal of Educational Technology 28*(4), 280–291.

Baron, L. (1985). Television literacy curriculum in action. *Journal of Education Television, 11*(1), 49–55.

Barthes, R. (1972). *Mythologies.* New York: Hill and Wang.

Bazalgette, C., Bevort, E., & Savino, J. (1992). *New directions: Media education worldwide.* London: British Film Institute.

Begoray, D. (2002). Visual literacy across the middle school curriculum: A Canadian perspective. Paper presented at the American Educational Research Association, New Orleans, LA, April 1. ERIC ED467283.

Begoray, D. L., & Morin, F. (2002, November). Multiple literacies in language arts: Sustainable teacher change through a summer institute. *Reading Online, 6*(4). Available: http://www.readingonline.org/articles/art_index.asp?HREF=begoray/index.html

Brooker, W., & Jermyn, D. (2003). *The audience studies reader.* New York: Routledge.

Brown, J. A. (1991). *Television "critical viewing skills" education: Major media literacy.* Hillsdale, N.J.: L. Erlbaum Associates.

Brown, G. (2001). Locating categories and sources of information: How skilled are New Zealand children? *School Library Media Research, 4.* Accessed November 2, 2004 at http://www.ala.org/ala/aasl/aaslpubsandjournals/slmrb/slmrcontents/volume42001/brown.htm

Brunner, C., & Tally, W. (1998). *The new media literacy handbook.* New York: Anchor.

Buckingham, D. (2003). *Media education.* London: Polity Press.

Buckingham, D., & Sefton-Green, J. (1994). *Cultural studies goes to school: Reading and teaching popular media.* London: Taylor & Francis.

Bussiere, P., & Gluszynski, T. (2004, May). The impact of computer use on reading achievement of 15-year olds. SP-599-05-04E. Learning Policy Directorate, Human Resources and Skills Development, Government of Canada. Accessed November 28, 2004 online at http://www11.hrsdc.gc.ca/en/cs/sp/lp/publications/2004–002625/page01.shtml

Calvert, S. (1998). *Children's journeys through the information age.* New York: McGraw-Hill.

Cervetti, G., Pardales, M., & Damico, J. (2001, April). A tale of differences: Comparing the traditions, perspectives and educational goals of critical reading and critical literacy. *Reading Online 4*(9). Available: http://readingonline.org/articles/art_index.asp?HREF=/articles/cervetti/index.html

Chandler-Olcott, K., & Mahar, D. (2003). Tech-savviness meets multiliteracies: Exploring adolescent girls' technology mediated literacy practices. *Reading Research Quarterly, 38*(3), 356–386.

Dibble, M. (2004). Directory of online resources for information literacy: The information literacy process. University of South Florida, Tampa Library. Accessed online September 1, 2004 at http://www.lib.usf.edu/ref/doril/

Eco, U. (1979). *A theory of semiotics.* Bloomington: Indiana University Press, Midland Book Edition.

Film Education Working Group (1999). *Making movies matter.* London: British Film Institute.

Fitzgerald, M. (1999). Evaluating information: An information literacy challenge. *School Library Media Research 2.* Accessed online December 1, 2004 at http://oldweb.ala.org/aasl/SLMR/vol2/evaluating.html

Flood, J., Heath, S. B., & Lapp, D. (1997). *Handbook of research on teaching literacy through the communicative and visual arts.* International Reading Association. New York: Macmillan.

Fouts, J. (2000). Research on computers and education: Past, present and future. A report prepared for the Bill and Melinda Gates Foundation. Seattle Pacific University, Seattle, WA. Accessed online November 28, 2004 at http://www.esd189.org/tlp/images/TotalReport3.pdf

Freire, P. & Macedo, D. (1987). *Literacy: Reading the word and the world.* South Hadley, MA: Bergin & Garvey Publishers.

Gee, J. P. (1996). *Social linguistics and literacies: Ideology in discourses* (2nd ed.). London: Taylor & Francis.

Gilster, P., (1998). *Digital literacy.* New York: Wiley.

Giroux, H., & Simon, R. (1989). *Popular culture, schooling and everyday life.* New York: Bergin & Garvey.

Gregory, R. (1970). *The intelligent eye.* New York: McGraw-Hill.

Griffin, M., & Schwartz, D. (1997). Visual communication skills and media literacy. In J. Flood, S. B. Heath & D. Lapp (Eds.). *Handbook of research on teaching literacy through the communicative and visual arts.* International Reading Association. New York: Macmillan.

Hart, A. (1998). *Teaching the media: International perspectives.* Mahwah, N.J.: Erlbaum.

Hart, A., & Suss, J. (2002). Media Education in 12 European Countries. Research report from the Euromedia Project. E-collection of the Swiss Federation Institute of Technology. Zurich. Accessed December 3, 2004 at: http://e-collection.ethbib.ethz.ch/ecol-pool/bericht/bericht_246.pdf

Hirsch, E. D. (1987). *Cultural literacy.* Boston: Houghton Mifflin.

Hobbs, R. (in press). Non-optimal uses of media in the classroom. *Learning Media and Technology.*

Hobbs, R. (2004). A review of school-based initiatives in media literacy. *American Behavioral Scientist 48*(1), 48–59.

Hobbs, R., & Frost, R. (2003). The acquisition of media-literacy skills. *Reading Research Quarterly 38*(3), 330–355.

Hobbs, R., (1998a). The seven great debates in media literacy education, *Journal of Communication 4*(2), 9–29.

Hobbs, R. (1998b). Media literacy in Massachusetts. In A. Hart (Ed.) *Teaching the media: International perspectives.* Mahwah, NJ: Lawrence Erlbaum Associates, (pp. 127–144).

Hobbs, R. (1994). Pedagogical issues in U.S. media education. In S. Deetz (Ed.), *Communication Yearbook 17.* Newbury Park: Sage Publications (pp. 453–466).

Hurrell, G. (2001). Intertextuality, media convergence and multiliteracies: Using *The Matrix* to bridge popular and classroom cultures. *Journal of Adolescent and Adult Literacy, 44*(5): 481–483.

Kaiser Family Foundation (2003a). Zero to six: Children and electronic media. Accessed November 1, 2004 at http://www.kff.org/entmedia/entmedia102803pkg.cfm

Kaiser Family Foundation (2003b). Key facts: Media literacy. Accessed November 1, 2004 at http://kff.org/entmedia/Media-Literacy.cfm

Kaiser Family Foundation (2001). *Kids and media @ the new millennium.* Accessed online October 27, 2003 at: http://www.kff.org/content/1999/1535/

Kapitzke, C. (2003). Information literacy: A positivist epistemology and a politics of outformation. *Educational Theory, 53*(1), 37–53.

Kelley, P., Gunter, B., & Kelley, C. (1985). Teaching television in the classroom: Results of a preliminary study. *Journal of Educational Television, 11*(1), 57–63.

Kellner, D. (1995). *Media culture: Cultural studies, identity and politics between the modern and postmodern.* New York, Routledge.

Kist, W. (2000). Finding "new literacy" in action: An interdisciplinary high school Western civilization class. *Journal of Adolescent and Adult Literacy, 45*(5), 368–377.

Kubey, R., & Baker, F. (1999). Has media literacy found a curricular foothold? *Education Week, 19*(9).

Kubey, R., & Czikszentmihalyi, M. (1990). *Television and the quality of life: How viewing shapes everyday experience.* Hillside, NJ: Lawrence Erlbaum Associates.

Lankshear, C., Snyder, I., & Green, B. (2000). *Teachers and technoliteracy: Managing literacy, technology and learning in schools.* St. Leonards, New South Wales: Allen and Unwin.

Larsson, D. (2001). Use of film in Minnesota high schools. Unpublished manuscript, Minnesota State University. Accessed online November 1, 2004 at: http://www.english.mnsu.edu/larsson/SCS/MNSurvey.html

Lenhart, A., Rainie, L., & Lewis, O. (2001, June 20). *Teenage life online.* A report of the Pew Internet and American Life Project. Accessed November 28, 2004 at http://pewinternet.org/reports/oc.asp?Report=36

Lloyd, A. (2003). Information literacy: The meta-competency of the knowledge economy? An exploratory paper. *Journal of Librarianship and Information Science, 35*(2), 87–92.

Luke, C. (1997). Media literacy and cultural studies. In S. Muspratt, A. Luke, & P. Freebody (Eds.), *Constructing critical literacies: Teaching and learning textual practice.* Cresskill, NJ: Hampton, (pp. 19–49).

Masterman, L. (1990). *Teaching the media.* London: Routledge.

McLaughlin, M., & DeVogel, G. (2004). Critical literacy as comprehension: expanding reader response. *Journal of Adolescent and Adult Literacy, 48*(1), 52–62.

McLuhan, M. (1964). *Understanding media: The extensions of man.* New York: McGraw-Hill.

Messaris, P. (1994). *Visual "literacy": Image, mind, and reality.* Boulder CO: Westview.

Monroe, B. (2004). *Crossing the digital divide: Race, writing, and technology in the classroom.* New York: Teachers College Press.

NAA Foundation. (2004). *Measuring up! The scope, quality and focus of newspaper in education programs in the United States.* Vienna VA: Newspaper Association of America Foundation.

Natharius, D. (2004). The more we know, the more we see: The role of visuality in media literacy. *American Behavioral Scientist, 48*(2), 238–247.

National Council of Teachers of English. (2003). On Composing with Non-Print Media. Resolution passed December 2003. Accessed November 1, 2004 at: http://www.ncte.org/about/over/nty/resol/115073.htm

Neuman, S. (1991). *Literacy in the television age: The myth of the TV effect.* Norwood, NJ: Ablex.

New London Group. (1996). A pedagogy of multiliteracies: Designing social futures. *Harvard Educational Review, 661*, 60–92.

Norris, C., Sullivan, T., Poirot, J. & Soloway, E. (2003). No access, no use, no impact: Snapshot surveys of educational technology in K–12. *Journal of Research on Technology in Education, 36*(1), 15–28.

Nichols, B. (1991). *Representing reality: Issues and concepts in documentary.* Bloomington: Indiana University Press.

Oppenheimer, P. (2003). *The flickering mind.* New York: Random House.

Plotnick, E. (1999). Information literacy. ERIC Clearinghouse on Information and Technology, Syracuse University. ED–427777. Access online September 1, 2004 at http://www.ericfacility.net/ericdigests/ed427777.html

Public Broadcasting Service (2004, August 25). PBS programming tops the list of teacher favorites for second consecutive year. Accessed November 29, 2004 at http://www.pbs.org/aboutpbs/news/20040825_teacherfavorite.html

Rand Reading Study Group. (2004). Reading for Understanding: Toward a R&D Program in Reading Comprehension. Accessed September 24, 2004 at http://www.rand.org/multi/achievementforall/reading/readreport.html

Saba, J. (2004, September 26). NAAF study bolsters newspapers-in-school notion. *Editor and Publisher.* Accessed November 29, 2004 at http://www.editorandpublisher.com/eandp/search/article_display.jsp?schema=&vnu_content_id=1000642391

Scholes, R. (1998). The rise and fall of English. New Haven, CT: Yale University Press.

Sullivan, M. (2004). Why Johnny won't read. *School Library Journal, 50*(8), 36–40.

Tyner, K. (2004). Beyond boxes and wires: Literacy in transition. *Television and New Media, 4*(4), 371–388.

Tyner, K. (1998). *Literacy in the digital age.* Mahwah, NJ: Lawrence Erlbaum Associates.

Vandergrift, K. (1987). Critical thinking misfired: Implications of student responses to *The Shooting Gallery. School Library Media Quarterly, 15*(2), 86–91.

Vooijs, M., & Van der Voort, T. (1993). Teaching children to evaluate television violence critically: The impact of a Dutch school's television project. *Journal of Educational Television, 19*(3), 139–152.

Wade, S., & Moje, E. (2000). The role of text in classroom learning. In M. Kamil, P. Mosenthal, P. Pearson & R. Barr (Eds.) *Handbook of reading research* (Volume 3, pp. 609–627). Mahwah, NJ: Lawrence Erlbaum Associates.

Wolf, S. (2003). The Big Six information skills as a metacognitive scaffold: A case study. *School Library Media Research, 6.* Accessed November 1, 2004 at http://www.ala.org/ala/aasl/aaslpubsandjournals/slmrb/slmrcontents/volume62003/bigsixinformation.htm

Worth, S., & Gross, L (1981). *Studying visual communication.* Philadelphia: University of Pennsylvania Press.

3

Developing Digital Literacies: Educational Initiatives and Research in Colombia

Octavio Henao Alvarez
University of Antioquia
Medellín, Colombia

As in other countries, in Colombia printed texts no longer comprise the only materials for reading and writing. Information access, knowledge acquisition and building, and indeed participation in culture, are mediated by a variety of audiovisual and electronic devices centered around the computer. Consequently, Colombian teachers, like their counterparts around the world, face the challenge of transforming the concept of literacy by taking into account reading and writing through various digital media and genres including web pages, e-mail, chat room discussions, and hypermedia documents. Likewise, educational researchers in Colombia are trying to understand more fully the dimensions of reading and writing in digital environments.

In this chapter, I provide a glimpse into the efforts of Colombian society to grapple with the educational challenges of developing programs that contend with the new digital literacies. Specifically, I provide a brief overview of the socio-cultural context of education in Colombia and how digital technologies are integrated into that context, including several educational initiatives sponsored by various agencies. Subsequently, I describe some ongoing programs of literacy research that emanate from Colombian universities and that are aimed at understanding reading comprehension when students read hypermedia texts as opposed to printed texts.

COLOMBIAN EDUCATION AND DIGITAL LITERACIES IN SOCIO-CULTURAL CONTEXT

Sixty percent of the Colombian population, which is currently more than 40,000,000, live in poverty (www.dnp.gov.co). In Colombia's large cities, it is not unusual to see children sleeping under the bridges and walking down the streets searching for food in the trash cans. The free snack food offered by public schools to children and youngsters may be the only food they receive each day.

Recent figures indicate an approximate 16% unemployment rate nationwide. Eighty percent of the work force (approximately 4,000,000 people) earn a minimal monthly salary equivalent to approximately 116.7 US dollars. At this level of income, buying a standard computer for personal use would require saving an entire month's salary for most of a year. These figures illustrate the high cost of technologies in Colombia (see www.dnp.gov.co; www.dane.gov.co).

Regarding the current status of literacy and education in Colombia, 27% of adults 24 years or older, and 10% of the total population, do not know how to read or write. Sixty-two percent of Colombian families own fewer than 20 books, including school texts. Recent reports show that 80% of basic education students do not achieve the expected learning standards in mathematics and language (www.camlibro.com.co). Due to the lack of economic resources, only 17% of Colombian youngsters have access to higher education (El Tiempo, 2003).

However, despite this widespread poverty, Colombia, like many other countries, cannot afford to ignore the possibilities that the new digital technologies offer. For indeed, new digital technologies will not only determine future forms of literacy, but will afford opportunities to increase the economic development of the country and its citizens. Although Colombia is poorer than many nations where technology is more affordable and more fully integrated into daily life, new information and communication technologies (ICTs) are reconfiguring the landscape of education and the work place. Students increasingly need a higher level of skills in using these technological resources to be able to perform in school and at work. Businessmen, in Colombia as in many other countries, prefer to hire employees skilled in using digital technologies, and who are able to search quickly and efficiently for information, to assess the quality of this information, and to use it to solve problems.

With the support of the national, regional and local governments, many programs have been developed in cities and municipalities which are aimed at incorporating new technologies into educational processes, thus expanding opportunities for developing new literacies. Three projects are illustrative: a national project called "*Computadores para educar*" (Computers to Educate), and two projects that are currently under way in two large cities entitled "*La Red Integrada de Participation Educativa*" (Integrated Network of Educational Participation), in Bogotá, and "*Computadores e Internet Gratis para la Educación*" (Free Internet and Computers for Education), in Medellín.

The purpose of the national "Computers to Educate" program is to collect computers that are no longer used by companies and organizations in Colombia and other countries, to update them, and to deliver them freely to public schools for use in educational activities throughout Colombia. These computers are delivered completely operative to various educational institutions and are equipped with a network card and some basic software. At least one computer with multimedia capabilities and a modem is donated to each school. In order to facilitate the integration and use of these computers in academic programs, some teacher training and support for the development of appropriate curricula are offered. Thus far, this program has delivered 23,000 computers to 2,591 schools located in 700 municipalities of the country, especially in rural areas, benefiting approximately 868,000 students and 32,000 teachers (www.computadoresparaeducar.gov.co).

In Bogotá, the purpose of the "Integrated Network of Educational Participation" is to offer new computer technology to teachers and to the community, which is aimed at improving the quality of education and creating a more active participation of citizens in the betterment of their city. Some components of this program are the following: computer hardware; communication infrastructure and educational software; training for the educational community; an information system to support operative academic processes; and an educational Web site. At the time this chapter was written, 662 educational centers, 16 small libraries and three large libraries had been equipped and connected. In addition, 4,776 teachers and 2,498 administrative staff had begun computer training, not to mention the fact that 316 educational institutions are using virtual learning environments (www.redp.edu.co).

In Medellín, a program entitled "Free computers and Internet for Education" has been under way since 2002. This program has provided all public educational institutions of the city with computer labs, each with 21 computers and an Internet connection via modems. Thus far,

492 labs and approximately 10,000 computers have been installed. These computers will not only benefit approximately 400,000 students, but also the entire community, which will eventually have access to these labs. With the support of a research group from the University of Antioquia that works in the area of reading-writing and new technologies, a process to raise consciousness and training has begun for the teachers and students in the use of these resources. This project has transformed Medellín into the Colombian city with the school system best equipped in terms of ICTs (www.funfacionepm.org.co).

In addition to these programs, in order to improve the quality of the educational system from the basic to the higher levels and to enable it to better meet the future demands of the country in different fields, the National Ministry of Education has recently initiated a program to incorporate ICTs in education. That effort has three objectives: establishing equipment and infrastructure; developing curricular content; and defining processes and standards to use ICTs in basic and middle education. One of the strategies available for this program is an agreement between the Ministry of Education and Microsoft called "*Alianza por Colombia*" (Alliance for Colombia), the objectives of which are: training teachers in the use ICTs as didactic support; the development of ICT-based projects that help to improve education; and the development of computer-based learning materials for public distribution. The teaching training process will be oriented towards incorporating ICTs into the classroom, developing academic contents for various purposes, and establishing academic centers in order to train teachers to use ICTs in Education.

Thus, Colombia, despite it relatively poor citizenry when compared to the rest of the developed world, has clearly recognized the importance of developing new digital literacies. Further, the country and educational system have taken steps to initiate programs aimed at promoting the development of new digital literacies. Although the scope of these efforts is not as broad, and the hardware and software is not as current as in more economically developed countries, the commitment is strong and much progress is being made. In addition, Colombian researchers are engaged in on-going programs of research aimed at better understanding reading comprehension in multimedia environments, both to inform efforts in Colombia and to contribute to the knowledge base of the field more broadly. In the next section, after outlining relevant theory, I describe some representative research projects.

COLOMBIAN RESEARCH ON COMPREHENDING DIGITAL TEXTS

Like many other developing countries, Colombia cannot support or model the adoption of new digital technologies in its schools by relying entirely on the experiences and the results of studies carried out in other areas or contexts which present distinctly different social, economic, and cultural conditions. The fact that in Colombia a relatively small percentage of students attending public schools have a computer at home, and public education institutions have on average a ratio of only 1 computer for 85 students (www.ccit.org.co), limits the feasibility of applying experiences and findings about the use of ICTs in education that have proved successful in developed countries. Questions such as "What do these ICTs contribute to the quality of teaching reading and writing?" and "How to use these technologies to improve the reading skills of students?" are especially relevant in a country where the great majority of the population have limited access to these resources.

In an effort to make a contribution to the design of strategies that capacitate Colombian teachers and students in the efficient use of these ICTs, my assistants and I have conducted five experiments aimed at studying the comprehension of digital texts. The objectives of these experiments were: to contribute to an appropriate incorporation of new technologies into the school curriculum, especially in the area of reading and writing; to research and compare the functioning of some factors associated with reading comprehension, such as the use of a dictionary, contextual analysis, semantic associations, recognition of main ideas, summary, and recall, when students read digital and print texts; and to contribute to an understanding of teaching of reading and writing using digital materials. However, currently the scope of these studies is relatively small and our findings thus far have not been published in peer-reviewed outlets. Thus, these studies are presented only as illustrative of the type of research we have conducted thus far and the kind of questions we are interested in exploring, not as a source of definitive findings or conclusions. The length of a book chapter does not permit me to provide much relevant detail about the experiments that we have conducted, nor to identify and acknowledge the limitations of the investigations and analyses. Therefore, readers of this chapter are urged not to cite these studies in literature reviews without these important caveats.

All of these experiments involved 40 children who were 11 or 12 years old and enrolled in the sixth grade at a middle-class private school located in Medellín, Colombia. Thus, this sample of participants is not necessarily representative of all Colombian school children at this age or level of schooling. In several of these experiments, we were interested in comparing the comprehension of digital texts among proficient and less proficient readers. Therefore, the 40 students in our experiments were selected from a group of 70 students based on reading comprehension scores on a standardized test (Henao Alvarez, 2001). Twenty children with the highest scores and 20 children with the lowest scores were selected. To complement this selection criterion, the Spanish teacher was requested to match the list of students with the highest and lowest scores in the reading comprehension test, according to her own criteria and evaluations. In her opinion, the 40 students selected on the basis of the test results accurately reflected her independent assessment of the students' reading comprehension. All 40 children were familiar with the Windows Operating System and had previously engaged in reading and writing digitally in relation to various applications on the computer.

The experiments were carried out during two-and-a-half weeks in the children's school for the part of the experiments that required reading printed texts and at a nearby university computer room where the children were bussed to read the digital texts. My assistants and I, not the classroom teacher, led all experimental activities.

These experiments address the following questions: When reading digital and printed texts, are there differences in readers' utilization of the dictionary, contextual analysis, the content and quality of semantic maps, the quality of summaries produced, and the recall of main ideas?

Experiment 1: Use of dictionary and contextual analysis. The purpose of this experiment was to compare the frequency of using the dictionary and the capacity of contextual analysis of two groups of competent readers as they read a hypermedia and a printed text. Our work in this experiment is guided by previous research suggesting that word meaning in a text is a decisive factor for its comprehension and that inadequate vocabulary knowledge is related to lower comprehension (Johnson and Pearson, 1978; Nagy and Herman, 1987). To evaluate a reader's familiarity with the words contained in a text or speech is a relatively reliable way of predicting their ability to understand the text or speech. Further, a good reading program should include effective strategies to develop vocabulary, helping students to know the meaning of many words, and to use them appropriately in reading, writing, and oral expression (Johnson and Pearson, 1978; Nagy and Herman, 1987). Further, as some authors maintain, reading is an effective instrument to learn the meaning of words (Nagy and Anderson, 1984; Nagy and Herman, 1987). Digital texts can offer readers a wide variety of readily available information during reading, including resources that provide rich possibilities for conveying definitions of concepts and terms, providing dynamic means for actively constructing knowledge representations (Bagui, 1998; Stemler, 1997).

In the first experiment, 20 competent readers participated. They were randomly divided into two groups. The first group read a digital text, "*Algunos datos de Fernando Botero*" (*Some data about Fernando Botero*), accompanied by digital resources in the form of videos, pictures, and audio. A second group read a printed version of the same text, but without the digital supporting resources. Both groups were told to carefully read the corresponding text, at least twice. Reading time was not controlled, neither were there restrictions on the use of audiovisual resources among the group reading the digital version

In the digital version, a dictionary with appropriate definitions appears by activating an icon on the screen. The meanings of selected words could be accessed alphabetically or by typing in a word from the text. In the digital version, the computer registers the reader's navigation, indicating what links are activated, what nodes are visited, and how long the reader remains at a particular node. Thus, it is possible to establish accurately what word meanings a reader investigated and how many times a word was investigated. The readers of the printed version were given a booklet with the same words contained in the dictionary of the digital version, and they were asked to mark every word they searched.

Contextual analysis was evaluated with a Cloze Test designed by the researcher, using a text composed of different segments drawn from the experimental text and in which every fifth word was deleted for a total of 25 deletions. There were no deletions in the first and final sentence of the text.

Results indicated that the participants reading the digital version of the text investigated statistically more word meanings in the dictionary than the readers of the printed text. These results coincide with those from a study carried out many years ago in the U.S. (Reinking and Rickman, 1990). However, it is worth noting that in that experiment the average number of words investigated was relatively low in both groups when compared to the number of words not known by the children before the reading experience (approximately 60%). In the case of the digital texts, the access to the dictionary may have not been attractive enough for the users, because the search was not made by clicking directly on the unknown word, but by opening the dictionary through an icon. More research is needed to investigate how user interfaces might affect the number of words investigated and whether such factors have effects that vary by reading ability.

In relation to contextual analysis, the readers of the digital text outperformed readers of the printed text; however, the difference was not statistically significant. When readers try to decipher a word by means of contextual analysis, they transcend the smaller lexical unit represented by words, focusing their attention on the structure of a sentence or paragraph. If readers are able to take advantage of the context, they can perhaps use diverse means to help themselves acquire the meaning of an unknown word and thus understand the text more globally.

Experiment 2. Construction of semantic maps. The purpose of the second experiment was to determine if there were differences among semantic maps produced from key words identified in printed or digital versions of the text. In this study, a semantic map was defined as a representation of the different meanings of a word by creating a visual representation of relations among words of a text. In other words, it was a graphic representation of the diverse categories of meanings associated with a word. Semantic maps are often used as a teaching strategy based on the aptitude that students have for relating new words to their own experiences or previous knowledge, and for organizing them into categories (Heimlich and Pittelman, 1986). Semantic maps have been used as a didactic strategy for vocabulary building, because theoretically they help students to structure new learning by relating it to their previous knowledge. Likewise, they may contribute to developing more active readers, motivating them to evoke what they know about a specific topic, and to use this information in their reading. This activation of previous knowledge has long been considered essential for reading comprehension. For example, when a specific conceptual schema is activated, the whole structure of the memory for this concept is also activated, thus facilitating the comprehension process (Johnson and Pearson, 1978; Johnson, Toms-Bronowski, and Pittelman, 1982; Heimlich and Pittelman, 1986).

The subjects of Experiment 2 were the same 20 children who participated in Experiment 1, but the students who read the printed text in the first experiment read the digital text in Experiment 2, and vice versa. The concept of a semantic map and the procedures for its construction were explained to both groups. During a 50-minute session prior to the experiment, the researcher used an overhead projector to explain semantic mapping of a word using an example of the concept "dog," which in the example entailed approximately 20 nodes with their respective links, illustrating the following relations: class, attributes, and examples.

Ten students read a digital version of "*Flora y Fauna del Pacífico Colombiano*" (Flora and Fauna of the Colombian Pacific Region). The other 10 students read a printed version of the same text. Both groups were instructed to read the text attentively, at least twice. The reading time was not controlled. There were no restrictions on the exploration and use of the audio-visual resources such as videos, photographs, and audio. Immediately after they finished reading, they were given three blank sheets and requested to construct three semantic maps illustrating the following topic words: *birds, deer, and dolphin*. It was suggested that they include in the map as many words or associated concepts as they could, illustrating in the links the three types of relations presented in the instruction phase.

The resulting semantic maps for each word were scored as follows: three points if the three types of relations were included; one point was assigned for each word/node included in the map whose relations was appropriately described. The total score was the sum of the scores obtained across the three maps. The results reveal that semantic maps developed by readers of the digital texts were of higher quality as indicated by their statistically higher scores.

A possible explanation of these results would be in the structural similarity between the presentation of the digital text and a semantic map. Both represent a group of nodes interconnected through multiple links. It is possible that when readers read digital texts that emphasize the interrelations among concepts, they can perceive more clearly the relations and connections among the diverse concepts being discussed.

Experiment 3. Identifying important ideas. The purpose of the third study was to investigate whether competent readers would vary in their ability to identify the main ideas of textual content presented either digitally or in print. Finding main ideas has been argued to be an important dimension of reading comprehension because there is evidence that identifying the main ideas of texts explains a statistically significant proportion of the variance in measures of reading comprehension among elementary school students, even when differences in general intelligence and decoding ability were controlled (Baumann, 1985).

Participants in this third experiment were the same 20 children who participated in Experiments 1 and 2, with the treatment conditions (digital vs. printed texts) again reversed. Again, both groups participated in an instructive session about the concept of main idea as separate from the details in a text. Then, for the sake of practice, they each received a sheet with three texts and were asked to identify the main ideas. Participants provide their individual responses orally with an explanation of their respective selections.

The students assigned to the digital text read "*Geografía del Pacífico Colombiano*" (Geography of the Colombian Pacific Region). The other group read a printed version of the same text. Both groups were again told to read attentively the respective text at least twice, with no restrictions on time. When finished, the students received a sheet with blank spaces to write

10 important ideas of the text they had read. When they finished that task, they were presented with a sheet listing 49 ideas drawn from the experimental text, organized according to their order of appearance in the text. Each of the 49 ideas was preceded by a blank space allowing the student to indicate on a scale from 1 to 5 the importance of each idea. None of the ideas were drawn from the supplementary material available to readers of the digital version of the text.

To increase the validity and reliability of the measures, a group of six expert readers (three professors and three doctoral students), using a scale from 1 to 5, evaluated the importance of each one of the 49 unitary ideas of the text "Geography of the Colombian Pacific Region." Before rating the ideas, the experts read the text attentively, first in hypermedia version, and then in its printed form. Later, the *median* of the six scores given by the experts to each unitary idea was calculated, and then used as the standard for scoring participants' responses. The ideas with a median value between 3.5 and 5.0 were considered to be important ideas; those with a median value below 3.5 were considered to be details. The result was a total of 27 important ideas and 22 details.

The following procedure was adopted for scoring participants' responses: when the assessment given by a student to an idea coincided with that of the experts, or differed, two points were assigned; when the difference between a participant's scoring and that of the experts was 1 or 1.5, one point was assigned; when this difference was greater than 1.5, no points were assigned. The maximum score possible using this procedure was 98.

Results indicated that readers of the digital version statistically outperformed those reading the printed version on both measures of main ideas. There are several possible explanations for these results from a theoretical standpoint. For example, authors often leave certain rhetorical signs in their texts, by which they suggest what contents or segments have more relevance. A competent reader can use these signs or marks to find the most important information. The digital version of the text used in this experiment included a set of words highlighted in yellow that work as hypertext links, which changed to orange when a reader followed a link. By clicking on these links, some windows are opened up with specific textual and graphical information about the topic. Nonetheless, to make both formats comparable, all the information offered in these links was also presented in the printed version, including graphics and pictures.

However, most of the important ideas from the text "Geography of the Colombian Pacific Region" are related to topics that were provided in the highlighted links. It seems reasonable to suppose that the increased visibility of these words helped readers to identify more easily the important information. In the printed version, we did not highlight these words, which we might have done, and, if we had, it may have affected results.

Experiment 4. Capability to summarize. The purpose of this study was to compare and analyze the quality of summaries produced by participants after reading a digital or printed text. In this experiment, we also compared the performance of competent and less competent readers. A summary synthesizes the content of a text, indicating what is the essential information presented by a text (Perelman de Solarz, 1994). The production of a good summary implies text comprehension. It demands from the reader an analysis and selection of the most essential information, which implies the successful exercise of fundamental comprehension processes. According to Kintsch and van Dijk (1978), in order to derive, synthesize and organize the global meaning of a text, a reader employs several general rules that produce a macro-level understanding of a text. Thus, investigating whether digital texts affect competent and less-competent readers' ability to generate summaries seems to be an appropriate way to assess potential comprehension differences when compared to reading printed texts.

In this experiment, there were a total of 40 students, the same 20 children that were part of Experiments 1, 2 and 3, and the 20 children that obtained the lowest scores in the test "Evaluación de Habilidades para la Comprensión Lectora (Reading Comprehension Skill Assessment) (Henao Alvarez, 2001). For the group of competent readers, the assignment to digital or printed text was again reversed. The 20 students classified as less-competent readers were randomly assigned to one of the two groups.

Participants were instructed on the concept of summary. By using an overhead projector and photocopies, three texts were presented individually to introduce and practice summarizing. Students had an opportunity to share their summaries orally, while others in the group could comment about them. The performance of these exercises convinced the researcher that participants had a clear understanding of how to summarize.

Both in the sub-group of competent readers and in the sub-group of less-competent readers, the 10 students read "*Usos del Agua*" ("Water Uses") as a digital text and 10 as a printed texts. Participants in the digital group were told to carefully read the text at least twice, completely reading the main body of the text and subsequently activating each of the link words. The reading time was not controlled, and there were no restrictions on the exploration and use of the audio-visual resources such as videos and audio. When the students indicated that they had read through all the text at least twice, they were given a blank sheet and were asked to write a summary of the text. They could review the text, if they considered it necessary. Likewise, they were recommended to write in the clearest possible way and to use complete sentences. The time for performing this task was not limited. Following the same instructions, group B of competent and low-skilled readers read a printed version of the texts and were asked to complete the same task with the same directions.

Following the procedures of the previous experiment, the same group of six expert readers evaluated the importance of the 64 idea units that comprised the text "Water Uses," generating 40 important ideas and 24 details. A researcher and another professor of reading and writing scored the summaries independently, using the idea units generated by the group of expert readers. Results indicated that the competent and less-competent readers reading the digital version of the text included statistically more of the important ideas in their summaries of the hypermedia than in the summary of the printed text.

These results might be explained by considering that generating a summary demands a process of selection, analysis, and synthesis of the most relevant information. The possible interpretation of the results in Experiment 3 regarding the identification of important ideas may have the same relevance in interpreting the results of the present experiment. The digital text used in the present experiment also presents a series of words that function as links, highlighted in yellow, and by activating them, they display other topical textual units on screen. In this case also, so that the reading in both formats was comparable, the printed text included the same textual and graphical information as the hypermedia. If most of the important ideas of the text "*Water Uses*" are related to these highlighted words, indicating links and their respective contents, it is natural to suppose that the highlighting of these links helped readers reading the digital text recognize more easily the important ideas, and thus led to participants including them in their summaries.

Experiment 5. Ability to recall information. The purpose of this study was to replicate Experiment 4 using recall of main ideas as the dependent measure, because researchers have considered the recall of textual information as evidence of comprehension. The subjects of this experiment were the same 40 students who participated in Experiment 4. The assignment to groups A and B was inverted for both competent and less-competent readers.

The 20 students of group A, skilled and low-skilled, read the hypermedia "*La Imprenta*" (The Press). Conditions were the same as in the previous experiments. When participants were finished reading, they were given a blank page with instructions to write everything they remembered from the text, using complete sentences and trying to write as clearly as possible. To lessen the effects of short-term memory, each participant was asked to provide orally the name and description of the last TV program they had watched.

In accordance with Experiments 3 and 4, the same group of six expert readers evaluated the importance of the ideas units that comprised the text, thus generating a scoring template consisting of 18 important ideas and 10 details. Recalls were scored independently carried by a researcher and another professor of the reading and writing, based on the scoring template. Results revealed that both competent and less-competent readers who read the digital version of the text outperformed those reading the printed text at statistically significant levels.

In agreement with the assumptions of several authors such as Goldman (1996), Mayer and Sims (1994), and Stemler (1997), a possible explanation of these results lies in the interactivity that a hypermedia allows. The reader's choice of selecting, relating, and organizing the different contents of the text might positively affect recall of information. The rich audio-visual support in the digital text used in this experiment may be another factor that influenced amount of recall. Regarding this type of text, it has been indicated that the design quality of on-screen components can contribute to greater attention from the user, a more effective activation of previous knowledge, and a deeper processing of information (Stemler, 1997; Bagui, 1998).

The digital text that participants in this experiment read generated a data base indicating which links readers follow and how long they remain at the nodes accessed. Thus, it is possible to accurately establish how long the reader watches a video, looks at a picture or listens to an audio recording. Examining this information indicated that less-competent readers invested more time examining the audio-visual resources of the text than did competent readers. This finding could explain why the performance of the less-competent readers was better when they read the digital texts.

The results of this experiment on recall contrast with the findings of other previous studies. For example, Aust, Kelley, and Roby (1993) did not find statistically significant differences in recall of information when comparing information presented in a printed or a digital text. Likewise, Gordon, Gustavel, Moore, and Hankey (1988) found that participants in their study recalled more information in articles written in a conventional linear format when compared to articles written as hypertexts. In addition, Jakobson and Spiro (1993) found that students who studied using computerized drill-and-practice materials recalled more than those who studied hypermedia materials.

General discussion. The results of these experiments reveal that readers' comprehension of the digital texts designed for this research consistently surpassed readers of conventionally printed information. This conclusion held for less competent, as well as competent readers, at least in the experiments where this distinction was investigated. Thus, under the conditions of these experiments, the digital textual formats used might contribute to the improvement of reading comprehension among Colombian students, at least those in private schools.

Paivio's (1991) theory of dual coding offers one theoretical interpretation for the results observed in these experiments. According to dual coding, learning improves when the information is processed through two channels instead of one channel (visual and linguistic). This double processing generates several cognitive trajectories that a learner can use later to retrieve information from memory. Because the digital texts used in these experiments presented information codified in several symbolic modes (audio, graphical illustrations, pictures, and videos), this theory may explain the results obtained.

Other researchers have argued that digital texts make available to the reader the means and dynamic tools to actively construct knowledge representations (Bagui, 1998; Stemler, 1997). The wealth and variety of information that these textual formats offer configure new spaces and possibilities so students may achieve a more nuanced comprehension. Therefore, if these new textual formats foster the development of abilities required for comprehension and learning, the importance of their use in school as reading and study materials becomes evident.

CONCLUSION

In Colombia, a country actively involved in the process of economic globalization, the new digital technologies are reconfiguring the notion of literacy. The initiatives pursued by the various localities and education agencies in Colombia illustrate the importance of new digital literacies and how seriously they are being attended to in preparing Colombia's citizenry for the future. Such efforts must be supported by research that ideally provides guidance to the development of ICT technologies and their integration into Colombia's educational system and the sociocultural context it serves, but that also contributes to the literature seeking to clarify the role of digital texts in fostering reading comprehension. It is hoped that the experiments described in this chapter illustrate the potential in both of these domains.

REFERENCES

Armbruster, B. B., Anderson, T. H., & Ostertag, J. (1987). Does text structure/summarization instruction facilitate learning from expository text? *Reading Research Quarterly, 22*(3), 331–346.

Armbruster, B. B., Anderson, T. H., & Ostertag, J. (1989). Teaching text structure to improve reading and writing. *The Reading Teacher*, Noviembre, 130–137.

Aust, R., Kelley, M. & Roby, W. (1993). The use of hyper-reference and conventional dictionaries. *Educational Technology Research and Development, 41*(4), 63–73.

Ayersman, D. J. (1996). Reviewing the research on hypermedia-based learning. *Journal of Research on Computing in Education, 28*(4), 500–525

Bagui, S. (1998) Reasons for increased learning using multimedia. *Journal of Educational Multimedia and Hypermedia, 7*(1), 3–18.

Baumann, J. F. (1985). La eficacia de un modelo de instrucción directa en la enseñanza de la comprensión de ideas principales. *Infancia y Aprendizaje*, 31–32, 89–105.

Bolter, J. D. (2001). *Writing space. Computers, hypertext, and the remediation of print.* Mahwah, NJ: Lawrence Erlbaum Associates.

Cliff Liao, Y. (1998). Effects of hypermedia versus traditional instruction on student's achievement: A meta-analysis. *Journal of Research on Computing in Education, 30*(4), 341–359.

Coiro, J. (2003). Reading comprehension on the Internet: Expanding our understanding of reading comprehension to encompass new literacies. *The Reading Teacher, 56*, 458–464.

Dillon, A., & Gabbard, R. (1998). Hypermedia as an educational technology: A review of the quantitative research literature on learner comprehension, control, and style. *Review of Educational Research, 68*(3), 322–349.

El Tiempo (2003). Edición del Domingo 19 de Octubre, sección 3, p. 5.

Gipe, J. P. (1980). Use of a relevant context help kids learn new word meaning. *The Reading Teacher, 33*, 398–402.

Goetz, E. T., & Ambruster, B. B. (1980). Psychological correlates of text structure. In R. J. Spiro, B. C. Bruce, and W. F. Brewer (Eds.) Theoretical issues in reading comprehension. Hillsdale, NJ: Lawrence Erlbaum Associates.

Goldman, S. R. (1996). *Reading, writing, and learning in hypermedia Environments.* In H. van Oostendorp and S. de Mul (Eds.) Cognitive Aspects of Electronic Text Processing. Norwood, NJ: Ablex Publishing Corporation.

Gordon, S., Gustavel, J., Moore, J., & Hankey, J. (1988). The effects of hypertext on reader knowledge representation. *Proceedings of the Human Factor Society 32nd Annual Meeting*, 296–300.

Heimlich, J. E., & Pittelman, S. D. (1986). Semantic mapping. Classroom applications. Newark, Del: International Reading Association.

Henao Alvarez, O. (2001). Competencia lectora de los alumnos de educación básica primaria: una evaluación en escuelas públicas de Medellín. *Revista Interamericana de Bibliotecología, 24*(1), 45–67.

Jakobson, M., & Spiro, R. (1993). Hypertext learning environments, cognitive flexibility, and the transfer of complex knowledge: An empirical investigation. (*Technical Report #573*). Champaign: Center for the Study of Reading, University of Illinois.

Johnson, D. D. (2000). Just the right word: Vocabulary and writing. In R. Indrisano and J. R. Squire (Eds.), *Perspectives on writing. Research, theory, and practice* (pp. 162–186). Newark, DE: International Reading Assocation.

Johnson, D. D., & Pearson, P. D. (1978). *Teaching reading vocabulary*. New York: Holt, Rinehart & Winston.

Johnson, D. D., Toms-Bronowsky, S., & Pittelman, S. D. (1982). *An investigation of the trends in vocabulary research and the effects of prior knowledge on instructional strategies for vocabulary acquisition*. Wisconsin Center for Education Research. Theoretical Paper No. 95.

Kamhi-Stein, L. D. (1997). Las estrategias de resumen de alumnos universitarios de "alto riesgo". *Lectura y Vida*, Año 18, No. 4, 17–24.

Kamil, M. L., & Lane, D. M. (1998). Researching the relation between technology and literacy: An agenda for the 21st Century. In D. Reinking, M. C. McKenna, L. D. Labbo, & R. D. Kieffer (Eds.), *Handbook of literacy and technology. Transformations in a post-typographic world* (pp. 323–341). Mahwah, NJ: Lawrence Erlbaum Associates.

Kaufman, A. M., & Perelman, F. (1999). El resumen en el ámbito escolar. *Lectura y Vida, 20*(4), 6–18.

Kintsch, W., & van Dijk, T. A. (1978). Toward a model of discourse comprehension and production. *Psychological Review, 85,* 363–394.

Landow, G. P. (1997). HYPERTEXT 2.0 *The convergence of contemporary critical theory and technology*. Baltimore, Maryland: The Johns Hopkins University Press.

Lemke, J. L. (1998). Metamedia literacy: Transforming meanings and media. In D. Reinking, M. C. McKenna, L. D. Labbo, & R. D. Kieffer (Eds.), *Handbook of literacy and technology. Transformations in a post-typographic world* (pp. 283–301). Mahwah, NJ: Lawrence Erlbaum Associates.

Leu, D. J., Kinzer, C. K., Coiro, J. L., & Cammack, D. W. (2004). Toward a theory of new literacies emerging from the Internet and other information and communication technologies. In R. B. Ruddell & N. J. Unrau (Eds.), *Theoretical models and processes of reading* (5th ed., pp. 1570–1613). Newark, DE: International Reading Association.

Leu, D. J., & Reinking, D. (1996). Bringing insights from reading research on electronic learning environments. In H. van Oostendorp and S. de Mul (Eds.) *Cognitive aspects of electronic text processing*. Norwood, NJ: Ablex Publishing Corporation.

Marzano, R. J., & Marzano, J. S. (1988). *A cluster approach to elementary vocabulary instruction*. Newark, DE: International Reading Association.

Mayer, R. E., & Sims, V. K. (1994). For whom is a picture worth a thousand words? Extensions of a dual-coding theory of multimedia learning. *Journal of Educational Psychology, 86,* 389–401.

McKenna, M. C., Reinking, D., Labbo, L. D., & Kieffer, R. D. (1999). The electronic transformation of literacy and its implications for the struggling reader. *Reading & Writing Quarterly, 15*(2), 111–126.

McKnight, C. (1996). What makes a good hypertext? In H. van Oostendorp and S. de Mul (Eds.) *Cognitive aspects of electronic text processing* (pp. 213–238). Norwood, NJ: Ablex Publishing Corporation,

Nagy, W., & Anderson, R. (1984). How many words are there in printed school English? *Reading Research Quarterly, 19,* 304–330.

Nagy, W., & Herman, P. (1987). Breadth and depth of vocabulary knowledge: Implications for acquisition and instruction. In M. G. McKeown and M. E. Curtis (Eds.), *The nature of vocabulary acquisition*. Hillsdale, N. J: Lawrence Erlbaum Associates.

Nagy, W., & Herman, P. (1987). Limitations of vocabulary instruction. Champaign, Illinois: University of Illinois, Center for the Study of Reading.

Nagy, W. E., Herman, P. A., & Anderson, R. C. (1985). Learning words from context. *Reading Research Quarterly, 20,* 233–253.

Paivio, A. (1991). Dual coding theory: Retrospect and current status. *Canadian Journal of Psychology, 45,* 255–287.

Pearson, P. D., & Johnson, D. D. (1978). *Teaching reading comprehension*. New York: Holt, Rinehart and Winston.

Perelman de Solarz, F. (1994). La construcción del resumen. *Lectura y Vida, 15*(1), 5–20.

Reinking, D. (1998). Introduction: Synthesizing technological transformations of literacy in a post-typographic world. In: D. Reinking, M. C. McKenna, L. D. Labbo, & R. D. Kieffer (Eds.), *Handbook of literacy and technology. transformations in a post-typographic world* (pp. xi–xxx). Mahwah, NJ: Lawrence Erlbaum.

Reinking, D., & Rickman, S. S. (1990). The effects of computer-mediated texts on the vocabulary learning and comprehension of intermediate-grade readers. *Journal of Reading Behavior, 22*, 395–411.

Salomon, G., Perkins, D. N., & Globerson, T. (1992). Compartiendo el conocimiento: la ampliación de la inteligencia humana con las tecnologías inteligentes. *Comunicación, Lenguaje y Educación, 13*, 6–22.

Spires, H. A., & Estes, T. H. (2002). Reading in Web-based learning environments. In C. C. Block & M. Pressley (Eds.), *Comprehension instruction: Research-based best practices*. New York: The Guilford Press.

Stemler, L. K. (1997). Educational characteristics of multimedia: A literature review. *Journal of Educational Multimedia and Hypermedia, 6*(3–4), 339–359.

Winograd, P. N. (1985). Dificultades de estrategia en el resumen de textos. *Infancia y Aprendizaje*, 31–32, 67–87.

Winograd, P. N., & Bridge, C. A. (1986). The comprehension of important information in written prose. In J. F. Bauman (Ed.) *Teaching main idea comprehension*. Newark, DE: International Reading Association.

4

Toward Interactive Literacy Education in the Netherlands

Ludo Verhoeven, Eliane Segers, John Bronkhorst, and Lou Boves
Radbond University, The Netherlands

Beginning in the late 1990s, in the Netherlands, an attempt has been made to transform literacy education for primary school pupils. In a nationwide initiative, the practice of learning and education is evolving from traditional knowledge transmission approaches to constructivist approaches of knowledge construction. This evolution is supported and strengthened by recent insights in cognitive science, which suggest that knowledge must be considered as an active and social process, rather than as a static, context-free concept (see Bransford, Brown & Cocking, 2000). Constructivist theories of learning hold that students use their prior knowledge to construct new knowledge that is relevant to their individual experiences and situations. This view differs fundamentally from the instructivist view that learning occurs by absorbing information presented by teachers.

With regard to that new perspective, there is a widespread belief that Information Communications Technologies (ICT) offers many possibilities to facilitate knowledge construction. At the start of the 21st century, an awareness of new forms of literacy has emerged. In the literature, such terminology as *informational literacy* (Leu & Kinzer, 2000) and *Web literacy* (Sutherland-Smith, 2002) have been introduced to refer to a wide range of abilities directly related to ICT, of which the ability to find needed information in the enormous amount of available material on the Internet is considered to be very important. Because ICT is increasingly being integrated into the school curriculum, the convergence of literacy instruction and networked technologies seems inevitable, as well as the integration of reading and writing instruction and learning in subject areas. This change creates complex learning situations, in which it is important to provide enough instruction to keep children focused on the task (McEneaney, 2000). In this context, the role of ICT is fundamentally different from the drills implemented in conventional computer-aided instruction systems. ICT, if properly applied, should be able to support the cognitive processes involved in knowledge construction.

The long-term objective of the Dutch initiative is to implement interactive literacy education which stimulates meaningful, social and strategic learning processes, encourages children to learn independently, and can be adapted to the various learning needs of children (cf. Verhoeven & Aarnoutse, 1999). Therefore, an attempt is made to develop and validate operational models of the cognitive processes underlying constructive learning and a theory of the ways in which ICT technologies can support those cognitive processes to make constructive learning more efficient, effective and appealing for the students. Moreover, a learning environment will be developed that supports individual and collaborative knowledge construction. This environment will then be used to study constructive learning in the domain of reading and writing in the content areas. The learning environment will enable pupils to interact with a large repository of electronic, multimedia documents that can be searched and consulted to find new information that helps to construct individual knowledge about the subject under study. At the same time, students must be able to communicate between themselves and a teacher, both through a learning environment enhanced with ICT and directly through personal interaction. All parts of the environment will be designed to help students increase their literacy skills, in addition to their knowledge of the subject under study.

In the present chapter, we will uncover how technology may facilitate the processes that are involved in literacy learning in an ICT environment that combines literacy and subject learning with access to the world via the Internet. Starting from an evaluation of current practices of literacy education, we will discuss what is needed from the point of view of research aimed toward guiding the development of ICT environments that support interactive literacy education. In addition, a learning environment on the Internet will be presented that integrates meaningful reading, writing and learning in subject areas. Furthermore, the results of some pilot studies will be described, that were conducted to get a glimpse of the way children could work and learn using the Internet as a tool to gather knowledge about a subject and merge this into a piece of work that can be presented to others. In the final section, we will provide some general conclusions about the feasibility of an Internet-based environment for children learning to write in the subject areas.

CURRENT PRACTICES OF LITERACY INSTRUCTION

The literacy teaching methods currently used in many elementary schools in the Netherlands and elsewehere are characterized by a number of problems. First of all, literacy eduction is not really aimed at the transaction of meaning, but rather at the teaching of skills. The compartmentalization of literacy subjects forms a case in point. Literacy education has been divided into disjointed areas of instruction such as oral proficiency, reading, writing, vocabulary, and linguistic awareness. Often, these areas are broken down into even smaller instructional units. However, there is clear evidence that development in one of these domains also leads to development in the other domains (cf. Allington & Cunningham, 1996). In teaching methods, this phenomenon may actually be used to pursue the integration of knowledge and skills: a text that has been read, may be discussed in class, and then students may be asked to write essays on the same topic, which subsequently can be read and discussed by other students. Furthermore, in traditional literacy education, the emphasis is on the development of skills, without taking into account the students' learning motivations. Through teacher-based texts and subject matter, children are taught to maintain practice and expand their repertoire of skills. They are given tasks that help them to develop their capacity to complete assignments and perform tasks independently. The assumption is that the students will remain motivated: intrinsically, on the basis of their task-oriented self-motivation, and extrinsically, on the basis of the teachers' recognition of that self-motivation. However, intrinsic motivation in literacy education is often lacking on the part of students and also among teachers who don't take motivation into account (cf. McKenna, 2001). In order to promote the intrinsic motivation of children, teachers should focus on the children's experiences and interests as much as possible by offering interesting subject matter (see Guthrie, Schafer, Wang, & Afflerbach, 1995; Verhoeven & Snow, 2001).

A second current issue in literacy teaching is the lack of space for social interaction. Co-operation among students actually helps to reinforce cognitive strategies (cf. Slavin, 1990). In social networks, children gradually learn to explicitate (explicate?) their own sources of knowledge and problem-solving strategies and to test them against those of others (Bloome & Egan-Robertson,

1993). Through social processes, children learn to demarcate meanings within a certain domain, which is not only important for the development of their language, but also in many ways for the development of their thinking (cf. Rogoff, 1990). Literacy learning is often considered to be a passive process. At school, children are often given materials that require receptive processing, for example, the use of collections of texts, workbooks, and work sheets that are based on only one educational route to literacy or only one answer to knowledge-related questions. This approach reinforces the passive orientation of students. However, acquiring literacy skills requires active participation on the part of the students. Research has shown that students achieve better results when they are more actively involved in the literacy acquisition process (cf. Bruner, 1986; Gallimore & Tharp, 1990).

Third, the quality of the materials used in current literacy teaching leaves much to be desired (Allington & Cunningham, 1996). This shortcoming applies to instructional materials as well as to the stock of school library books. Moreover, present-day education does not focus enough on environmental opportunities for using literacy and on reading literature. In addition, the potential of information technology as a tool in language teaching is not yet fully recognized, even though research has shown that modern communication media (computers, CD-ROMs, DVDs) can be very useful in engaging students in acquiring literacy (Cameron, 1989; Reinking, McKenna, Labbo, & Kieffer, 1998).

Finally, the lack of continuity in education is a universal problem in developed societies (see Verhoeven, 1994). Educators often do not know how to avoid the abrupt changes in literacy teaching that occur in elementary education at crucial stages (between the preschool socialization phase, junior level, intermediate level, and senior level). There is an urgent need for continuous learning routes that, for various subject areas, concretize the best possible structure for language and literacy teaching in education. It should also be noted that many teachers find it difficult to teach students who are linguistically and/or culturally diverse (cf. Au, 1993). For many school teachers and educators in societies throughout the world, the education of ethnic minority children poses a real problem (cf. Durgunoglu & Verhoeven, 1998). Minority children often have difficulties acquiring a vocabulary, distinguishing sounds, and understanding and constructing larger text units such as sentences and texts. The limited vocabulary of these children is perceived as the most serious problem (see Droop & Verhoeven, 2003).

TOWARDS INTERACTIVE LITERACY EDUCATION

In order to overcome the phallacies of traditional education, literacy teaching needs to become much more interactive and better geared to the educational needs of the child (see Cazden, 1988; Slavin, 1995; Newman, 1998; Verhoeven, 1996). Interactive literacy teaching presupposes that children acquire literacy skills in an environment that stimulates meaningful social and strategic learning processes (cf. Verhoeven & Aarnoutse, 1999). With respect to meaningful learning it is important that children get the opportunity to determine their own learning pathway on the basis of their own interests in a rich and realistic context (cf. Au, Scheu, Kawakami, & Herman, 1990). By providing attractive subject matter, the teacher may reinforce the children's interests. By creating a powerful learning environment, she may teach children how to attribute their own meanings to the subject matter. With respect to social learning, much importance is attached to the social interaction between teacher and students, and between the students themselves. Communication with their peers enables children to reinforce their cognitive strategies (see Stahl, 1995; Johnson & Johnson, 1999). In social networks, children gradually learn to explicate their own sources of knowledge and problem-solving strategies and to test them against those of others. Moreover, through social interaction, children become increasingly better at demarcating meanings within a certain theme, and also learn to take into account divergent views and misconceptions, and to make a distinction between subjective and objective knowledge. Finally, with respect to strategic learning, it is essential that students become aware of their own rules of behavior in learning (cf. Pressley, 1998). It is essential that instruction is not only geared to knowledge and understanding, but also to the integration of the newly acquired knowledge into the children's own knowledge system. Strategic learning increases the children's ability to transfer their knowledge and skills from one situation to another (see Palincsar & Brown, 1984; Slavin, 1990).

One way to ground learning in meaningful contexts is to use ICT-supported learning environments providing rich and cohesive informational formats that enable students to identify and define problems, to specify reasons for problem solution, to generate strategies for solving identified problems and to observe results of attempted solutions (Bransford, Sherwood, Hasselbring, Kinzer & Williams, 1990; Schwarz, Brophy, Lin & Bransford, 1999; Leu & Kinzer, 2000). In such environments, teachers expect students to use their knowledge to solve realistic problems rather than to simply memorize information in order to pass a written test. Students are provided with multiple opportunities to interact during the solution of real-life problems and they form learning communities to collaborate in the classroom. In these learning communities, students are active participants who interact and analyze divergent views and alternative approaches to solving problems that are discovered during the learning process. They critically examine and evaluate ways to approach problem situations or to discuss issues that have been raised in the classroom. They are encouraged to ask hard questions, evaluate data, analyze information, describe issues, challenge assumptions, reflect on their background knowledge, and discuss new information and research to generate links between new information and their existing knowledge. These activities are designed to enable students to draw conclusions and to transfer knowledge to new situational problems (Bransford, et al., 2000).

Instead of simply assigning fact-based instruction, children need to have the opportunity to start their lessons with challenging problems in order to learn information that is relevant to them. Instructional innovations such as problem-based or project-based learning have successfully been designed for students in advanced education (e.g., Barrows, 1985; Williams, 1992), and more recently in primary education (e.g., CTGV, 1993, 1996, 1998; Vye, et al., 1998). The learning results in such environments turn out to be most effective when students form learning communities in which individual accountability is connected to group collaboration in order to achieve predefined objectives and when there is access to expertise and opportunity for tutoring according to students' needs (for an overview, see Bransford, et al., 2000). Moreover, frequent opportunities for formative assessment and systematic feedback on ongoing learning processes appear to effectively promote student progress (e.g., Barron, et al., 1998).

It can be concluded that ICT can be extremely helpful in flexibly promoting children's literacy learning and knowledge construction. However, only a very few attempts have been made to develop software for use in open learning environments to create guided generative learning environments that use rich macro contexts as anchors for learning. As a case in point, the Cognition and Technology Group at Vanderbilt has forwarded STAR. Legacy, a software shell that organizes student activity into typical phases of inquiry to make their learning processes visible to themselves and to the teacher (see Schwartz, et al., 1999). Learning cycles are defined in terms of five distinct components: challenge, initial thoughts, perspectives and resources, assessment, and final conclusions. This type of software offers a good example of how to organize and facilitate learning in challenge-based environments. Yu (2001) examined the effect of computer-assisted co-operative learning situations on pupils' cognitive, affective, and social outcomes. He found that co-operation without competition engendered better attitudes towards the subject matter and promoted more interpersonal relationships. However, the software does not incorporate any tools for communication, collaboration, or feedback.

The design of an open literacy learning environment should therefore build on a socio-cultural or neo-Vygotskian tradition of research informed by the insight that literacy is a cognitive tool used in classrooms to support the construction of shared knowledge. A series of studies investigating talk and computers in classrooms can be seen as helpful in this respect (Edwards & Mercer, 1987; Mercer 1995; Mercer, 2000; Bereiter, et al., 1997). The methods of discourse analysis, combining computer-based text analysis with a qualitative analysis of orientations, ground rules, speech-acts, and surface language, has also been applied with some success to analyze types of teacher-student dialogue and relate these, using computer-based text analysis, to outcome measures (see, for example, Wegerif, Mercer & Dawes, 1999). This work develops a well-established line of socio-cultural research on the ways in which teachers use language to stimulate, support, and guide learning (Mercer 1995; Wells, 1999; Mercer, 2000).

With respect to collaboration, electronic conferencing can be seen as a promising tool. In several studies, electronic conferencing is promoted as a new form of communication sharing features of both written and spoken modes of communication (Barron, et al.,1998; Yates, 1996; Herring, 1996). Electronic conferencing has distinctive strengths as a support for conversations about teaching and learning. Some have claimed, for example, that electronic conferencing provides a particularly valuable support for teaching and learning writing (Columb & Simutis, 1996; Galin & Latchow, 1998; Bonk & King, 1998). It is also common in the literature to claim that electronic conferencing can be an effective support for collaborative learning. A few attempts have been made to develop software for student collaboration in open learning environments. For example, the Computer-Supported Interactive Learning Environments (CSILE) software (Scardamalia & Bereiter, 1984, 1994; Scardamelia, Bereiter, Swallow, & Woodruff, 1989; Scardamelia, et al., 1992) is a system designed to support students in purposeful, intentional, and collaborative learning, in a local network. Students can select alternative communication modes (text, video, audio, animation) to generate nodes containing ideas or information that are related to the topic under study. Nodes are available for others to comment on, leading to dialogues and an accumulation of knowledge. CSILE emphasizes on building a classroom culture supportive of active knowledge construction that can extend individual intentional learning to the group level. The body of CSILE research has shown the educational potential of technology for support of communication collaborative learning. However, more research is necessary in two directions. First, it should be noticed that electronic conferencing is different from regular communication classrooms (see Salomon, Perkins & Globerson, 1992; Sherry & Meyers, 1996; Wegerif, 1996). Electronic conferencing is speech-like in that it supports learning through conversations. It is, however, sufficiently different to mean that insights derived from research on types of teaching and learning conversations undertaken in face-to-face classrooms do not automatically apply. Research is needed to disentangle the pedagogical possibilities of electronic conferencing. Second, it will be important to determine how educational software can help students to initiate ideas, to make such ideas explicit, to elaborate on these using multiple resources, and to transform ideas into coherent text. Therefore, we need fine-grained studies to uncover how students' thinking and reflective processes can be optimized in electronic conferencing.

With regard to feedback, the question is how the process of literacy learning can be fostered. A distinction can be made between the process of knowledge construction and the process of spoken and written language processing. So far, few attempts have been made to develop intelligent tutoring systems containing explicit representations of the knowledge to be taught and the way this knowledge has to be transferred to the students. In such systems, the knowledge the student has acquired at any phase of the learning process is captured in a database. The development of such systems thus far has represented formal knowledge bases, as in mathematics (see e.g., Anderson, Boyle, Corbett & Lewis, 1990). Studies on intelligent tutoring for young students in the domain of knowledge construction are generally lacking. Feedback on language processing research is also quite limited. There are a number of specific language measurements that are feasible for providing online feedback with a sufficient level of reliability: spelling, lexicon, grammar, and (to some extent) style. Several studies have been conducted on feedback on speech, oral reading, and spelling (see e.g., Sharp, et al., 1995; Mostow, 2001). It was shown that devices such as speech recognition and speech synthesis can be effective tools in supporting children's literacy processes. However, studies in this respect are highly limited to contexts of direct instruction for children with special needs. No attempts have been made so far to integrate feedback systems in more open learning environments.

CREATING A LITERACY LEARNING ENVIRONMENT ON THE INTERNET

Design

For a computer-based instructional program to create an educational environment consistent with a constructivist approach, there are a few basic requirements. Figure 4.1 presents the outline of a technology-enhanced learning environment which is being developed in order to promote interactive literacy education in the Netherlands.

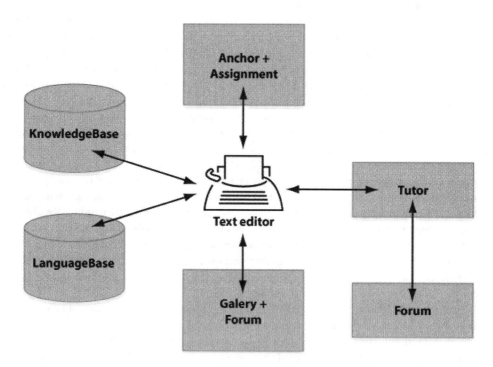

FIGURE 4.1.   The proposed learning environment.

By means of anchors and subsequent assignments, the learning task is made meaningful for the child. Prototypically, the assignment involves the construction of a digital paper including text, audio, and video materials able to play any taped materials, such as sound, pictures, and films. Central to this system is an *editor* that the pupil can use as a basic word processor in addition to audio and video processing. The editor is the control center for which language technology can help create a number of roles beyond that of a typewriter. Children work out their assignment by searching the Web and by using WebQuests (http://webquest.sdsu.edu/webquest.html). Other assistance is also available in the form of a knowledge base and a language base. The knowledge base helps children to organize their knowledge in the direction of the assignment being given. Therefore, automated layered tools can be implemented in the system in the form of a digital encyclopedia or an assignment-specific knowledge base. The language base provides the opportunity to search for word meanings in a digital dictionary and to receive feedback as regards the spelling and the grammar of the text being produced by the child. As is the case with the knowledge base, the ingredients of the language base can also be implemented as automatic layered tools. The gallery and forum allow children to present their materials and discuss them with others. In such a forum, children have the opportunity to experience that what is clear for the writer is not always that clear for the reader. Motivation to communicate is a strong vehicle in all levels of literacy learning. This calls for a community with which to communicate. The Internet provides an ideal podium for such a community. The result of this approach is that it gives the children a tangible aim: a publication for all their friends to see and read. Even parents, neighbours, and grandparents, can have a look. Finally, the tutor—the classroom teacher or a teacher student—may help the child to find their way in the environment and/or to fulfill the requirements which follow the assignment. In the case of student teachers there is the option of communication in a forum of other student teachers. The environment also enables the teacher to monitor the pupil's progress. All the component tools have the task of monitoring the pupil's progress. The learning environment has global means of measuring progress, such as keeping track of which lessons are finished and which documents are produced. In addition, language proficiency can be assessed in the fields of spelling, lexicon, grammar, and (to some extent) rhetorical style.

Automated feedback may play an important role in providing children with feedback on their output. Feedback on children's knowledge construction and language use can be given on-line, immediately after the assignment is finished, or later on, for instance in specific writing lessons. In the present environment, the monitoring of knowledge construction will be managed by identifying the relevant problem-solving methods to be applied and by organizing the knowledge resources so that it is easy to access for maintenance. Automated layered tools that handle multiple problem-solving methods will be developed to assist the learner in the knowledge acquisition process. Such layered tools will help the learner to select the relevant problem-solving method, to use this method to query for domain terms and knowledge, and to conduct completeness and consistency analyses.

With respect to language use, the present environment foresees in feedback on spelling and grammar. An attempt is made to go beyond existing spelling checkers by means of a monitor in which three types of spelling errors are distinguished: typing errors (typos), orthographical errors and morphological errors. Typing errors are slips of the keyboard, typically made when typing too quickly. Orthographical errors generally occur when the writer isn't certain how the word is spelled, and writes down how he or she thinks the word sounds. Morphological errors concern errors resulting from not or incorrectly applying grammatical rules for word formation. The spelling monitor basically handles the problem of spelling error detection and correction as follows. Given a word, the existence of that word in the vocabulary of the language at hand is checked. If the word is absent from that vocabulary, the word is highlighted in the text, and suggestions are given of word forms that are "near" to the original form. Since there are different spelling error types, the distance between the original word and the suggestions is calculated using three dimensions. The first dimension concerns typing. Words are considered "near" if they are a result of swapping two letters, omitting a letter, or hitting neighboring keys. The second dimension refers to orthographical "nearness," which is determined by the phonological proximity. The letter combinations *ay* (as in *may*) and *ai* (as in *main*) are phonologically very close. The third and final dimension relates to morphology. Morphologically, words that have the same stem, will be considered "nearer." The incorrectly spelled *fishi* will have the morphologically related *fish*, *fished* and *fishes* and *fishy* as suggestions, for instance.

In the same way that we can make use of a spelling monitor, we can trace the syntactic proficiency of a pupil with the aid of a grammar monitor. With such a monitor, it is possible to provide more information on the context and the type of grammatical error. When checking the grammatical correctness of a sentence, the following steps can be taken. First, a sentence is divided into tokens. In addition, each token is looked up in a lexicon and it is tagged with corresponding grammatical categories. Then, a parser is used to determine the grammatical category that is applicable in the context of the input sentence. Grammar rules are applied to determine whether the user has made any grammatical or style errors. Finally, information about the error is provided, possibly with a suggestion for improvement.

The modular approach of the grammar monitor allows for easy adaptation of the grammar checker for various levels of learning. This difference in levels will mainly be achieved by adding user-specific grammatical rules and adjusting the wording of the messages. For rhetoric style information, rules can be added to identify a number of typical stylistic errors children often make, such as long chains of sentences starting with *and then*, or the lack of iterative sentences.

Preliminary Findings

The ideas of the proposed learning environment have been tested in several pilot studies. In this section, we will go through the different parts of the learning environment and share our observations.

Anchor and assignment. A video on the subject can serve as an anchor conforming to the ideas of Bransford et al. (1990). For teachers, it turns out to be a challenge to discuss the videos in a meaningful way in the classroom and have children come up with their own learning questions. It is also of great importance to have other materials than just the computer environment in the class. The integration of different subjects, as discussed in the introduction of this chapter, is also an issue, for example, in reading and discussing texts together, discussing in small groups, writing assignments, and so on.

The assignment of, for instance, making a piece of work on Australia using a kind of start page on the Internet, turned out to cause some problems for the children. In a pilot study (Segers & Verhoeven, 2003), we found when looking through the history of the Internet Explorer that many children have wrong search strategies. Most children only used the start-page they were given and did not try to find other pages. The children who did would type a complete question in the Google search window, instead of a search term. The "free" assignment of writing a piece of work on such a broad topic caused another problem. The teacher instructed the children not just to write about kangaroos, for example, but to insert several topics. This led in a number of cases to pieces of work with several unrelated topics and little coherence.

In other studies, we explored the use of WebQuest as an assignment. A WebQuest consists of an introduction, a task, information sources, description of the process, guidance on how to organize the information, and a conclusion (Dodge, 2002), and has the potential of giving children more guidance in surfing the Web. However, when using WebQuests one should be aware of the following: First of all, children can have problems with finding out the exact nature of the assignment. The assignment is often to create something for the "real world," like writing a newspaper article or, in the case of one of our studies, a travel brochure. However, many children do not know what a travel brochure is, because that is something they do not see often. More information, or perhaps an example, should be given, so that the assignment becomes clear for the children. We also found that a WebQuest can be too much guidance for some children. Children should also have the freedom to explore their own questions in a self-guided search on the Internet. This freedom can easily be added into a WebQuest. Another critical point is that in a WebQuest children have to answer questions by inspecting several Internet resources. Many children in our study were overwhelmed with the amount of information in which they had to search. Children often started reading on the top of a page and could not skim the text in order to find the answer. One should therefore be careful not to put too many open resources in one WebQuest.

The Knowledge Base. This should contain at least a children's dictionary. Although children in interviews report that they do not find the texts on the Internet difficult, an example of a child in our first pilot study shows differently—one girl wrote a paper about Pearl Harbor, believing this was situated in Australia. She had not understood that the text on the Internet was about how the attack on Pearl Harbor drew Australia into World War II. The teacher should stimulate the children to use this dictionary, but it would also be good to have some Internet texts read and discussed together in the classroom or in small groups.

The Language Base. Online spelling and grammar feedback as given by Microsoft Word causes problems for the children. Although their spelling does improve, many errors are not seen because they form other "real" words. Also, children can spell a word so phonetically that the spelling checker does not have a clue. A special spelling checker for children, based on their type of errors, needs to be designed to overcome this problem.

The Tutor. The tutor turned out to be a very important part of the learning environment. Children need feedback during their research, before and during their writing process, and during rewriting. The tutor can teach children not to copy and paste texts but to use their own words, and can look after writing style, content, and presentation. The tutor can also play a role by being present in the Forum and by giving feedback examples and reflections on pieces of work.

The Galery+Forum. Children love this part of the environment. However, they have much trouble in giving feedback on each others' texts. Instead, most attention is paid to saying hellos and goodbyes and to approving or disapproving of a text. The reason why one does not like a text or what could be changed is hardly ever mentioned. Children can also often not resist using the forum as a kind of chatbox and so discuss all kinds of subjects irrelevant to the presented material. The teacher is the one to guide children in this process.

It can be concluded that an Internet-based learning environment for children in the upper grades of primary school is quite feasible. However, one should not forget that children need guidance from the teacher while working in an open learning environment and dealing with the amount of information that is available. The classroom environment needs to be in line with the learning environment, and the role of the teacher seems more important than ever.

PERSPECTIVE

To conclude, research and development has so far focused on just small parts of an ICT-supported constructivist learning environment for children. No attempt has been made to integrate evidence from cognitive science, language technology, and education in order to develop, validate, and implement a fully-integrated technology-enhanced constructivist literacy learning environment. It is clear that the implementation of technology-enhanced interactive learning environments will put new demands on the development of new courseware. By setting standards for high-quality interactive learning environments and by developing and testing such environments in the field, an attempt should be made to offer guidelines for the construction of new software, knowledge, and course material that enable educators to optimally foster the literacy development of children (see Bransford, Brown & Cocking, 2000; Leu & Kinzer, 2000).

In an ICT-supported interactive learning environment, knowledge construction should be seen as a process that is essentially social in nature. The literacy learning process in an ICT-supported constructivist environment can be accelerated by guiding the students in this process in such a way that they ultimately will be able to guide themselves (see Labbo, 1996; Leu & Kinzer, 1999). The teacher may stimulate self-monitoring by helping the students to organize and structure information (planning), by teaching them how to ask themselves questions or correct themselves (evaluation), or by helping them to focus their attention, maintain their motivation, and minimize their fear of failure (social emotion). As children learn to control their own learning processes, they become increasingly less dependent on their environment for their development. In future work, it is important to pay much attention to the role and function of the technological and educational components in the organization in which learners and teachers will work. The role of the social context may be investigated at several levels, starting at the micro level (where teachers interact with individual students and students interact in dyads or small groups, via the meso level of the class), to the macro level of the school, or even a set of schools that collaborate in one or more projects.

Although pedagogical theory provides convincing arguments for the superior performance of constructivist learning, the implementation of innovative constructivist learning environments in schools for primary and secondary education has not been without problems. To a large extent, these problems can be linked to the fact that the present generation of teachers is not adequately educated to organize open learning in classroom situations. The experience gained in the present project, and especially the ICT support developed in the project, will ask for new teacher competencies. This will put high demands on the education of future generations of teachers and professors. As Reinking, Labbo, and McKenna (2000) stated, there is an urgent need to prepare teachers today to cope with the changes in literacy education brought forward by digital forms of communication. Case-based studies of exemplary practice can be seen as a promising tool to promote the professional development of teachers in this respect (see Kinzer & Teale, this volume).

REFERENCES

Allington, R. L., & Cunningham, P. M. (1996). *Classrooms that work*. New York: Harper Collins.
Anderson, J. R., Boyle, C. F., Corbett, A. T., & Lewis, M. W. (1990). Cognitive modelling and intelligent tutoring. *Artificial Intelligence 12*, 7–49.
Au, K. H. (1993). *Literacy instruction in multicultural settings*. New York: Harcourt Brace.
Au, K. H., Scheu, J. A., Kawakami, A. J., & Herman, P. A. (1990). Assessment and accountability in a whole language curriculum. *The Reading Teacher, 43*, 574–577.

Barron, B. J., Schwartz, D. L., Vye, N. J., Moore, A., Petrosino, A., Zech, L., & Bransford, J. D. (1998). Doing with understanding: Lessons from research on problem- and project-based learning. *Journal of the Learning Sciences 7*, 271–311.

Barrows, H. S. (1985). *How to design a problem-based curriculum for the preclinical years.* New York: Springer Verlag.

Bereiter, C., Scardamelia, C., Cassells, C., & Hewitt, J. (1997). Postmodernism, knowledge building, and elementary science. *The Elementary School Journal 97*, 4, 329–340.

Bloome, D., & Egan-Robertson, A. (1993). The social construction of intertextuality in classroom reading and writing lessons. *Reading Research Quarterly, 28*, 4, 304–333.

Bonk, C. J., & King, K. S. (Eds.) (1998). *Electronic collaborators: Learner-centered technologies for literacy, apprenticeship, and discourse.* Hillsdale, NJ: Lawrence Erlbaum Associates.

Bransford, J., Sherwood, R., Hasselbring, T., Kinzer, C., & Williams, S. (1990). Anchored instruction: why we need it and how technology can help. In: D. Nix & R. Spiro (Eds.), *Cognition, education and multimedia: Exploring ideas in high technology* (pp. 114–141). Hillsdale, NJ: Lawrence Erlbaum.

Bransford, J. D., Brown, A. L., & Cocking, R. R. (2000). *How people learn. Brain, mind experience and school.* Washington: Academic Press.

Bruner, J. (1986). *Actual minds, possible worlds.* Cambridge, MA: Harvard University Press.

Cameron, K. (1989). *Computer-assisted language learning.* Norwood, NJ: Ablex.

Cazden, C. (1988). *Classroom discourse: The language of teaching and learning.* Portsmouth, NH: Heinemann.

Cognition and Technology Group at Vanderbilt (1993). Anchored instruction and situated cognition revisited. *Educational Technology, 33*(3), 52–70.

Cognition and Technology Group at Vanderbilt (1996). Looking at technology in context: A framework for understanding technology and education research. In: D. C. Berliner & R. C. Calfee, (Eds). *The handbook of educational psychology* (pp. 807–840). New York: Macmillan.

Cognition and Technology Group at Vanderbilt (1998). Designing environments to reveal, support, and expand our children's potentials. In S. A. Soraci and W. McIlvane, (Eds.) *Perspectives on Fundamental Processes in Intellectual Functioning (Vol. 1)* (pp. 313–350). Greenwich, CT: Ablex.

Columb, G., & Simutis, J. (1996). Visible conversation and academic inquiry: CMC in a culturally diverse classroom. In L. Herring (Ed.), *Computer-mediated communication: Linguistic, social and cross-cultural perspectives* (pp. 203–222). Philadelphia: John Benjamins.

Dodge, B. *Some thoughts about WebQuests.* Retrieved February 4th, 2002, from the World Wide Web: edweb.sdsu.edu/courses/edtec596/about_webquests.html

Droop, M., & Verhoeven, L. (2003). Language proficiency and reading ability in first- and second-language learners. *Reading Research Quarterly 38*, 78–103.

Durgunoglu, A. Y., & Verhoeven, L. (1998). *Literacy in a multilingual context.* Mahwah, NJ: Erlbaum.

Edwards, D., & Mercer, N. (1987). *Common knowledge: The development of understanding in the classroom.* London: Methuen/Routledge.

Galin, J. R., & Latchow, J. (Eds.) (1998). *The dialogic classroom: Teachers integrating computer technology, pedagogy, and research.* Urbana, IL: National Council of Teachers of English.

Gallimore, R., & Tharp, R. (1990). Teaching mind in society: Teaching, schooling and literate discourse. In L. C. Moll (ed.), *Vygotsky and education.* Cambridge: Cambridge University Press.

Guthrie, J., Schafer, W., Wang, Y., & Afflerbach, P. (1995). Relationships of instruction to amount of reading: An exploration of social, cognitive and instructional connections. *Reading Research Quarterly, 30*, 8–25.

Herring, S. (1996). *Computer-mediated communication: Linguistic, social and cross-cultural perspectives.* Philadelphia: John Benjamins.

Johnson, D. W., & Johnson, R. T. (1999). *Learning together and alone: Cooperative, competitive, and individualistic learning* (5th ed.). Boston: Allyn and Bacon.

Kinzer, C., Gabella, M., & Rieth, H. J. (1994). An argument for using multimedia and anchored instruction to facilitate mildly disabled students' learning of literacy and social studies. *Technology and Disability, 3*, 117–128.

Labbo, L. D. (1996). A semiotic analysis of young children's symbol making in a classroom computer center. *Reading Research Quarterly, 31*, 356–385.

Leu, D. J., & Kinzer, C. K. (1999). *Effective literacy instruction, K–8*. Upper Saddle River, NJ: Prentice Hall.

Leu, D. J., & Kinzer, C. K. (2000). The convergence of literacy instruction with networked technologies for information and communication. *Reading Research Quarterly, 35*, 108–127.

McEneaney. (2000). *Learning on the Web: A Content Literacy Perspective*. Retrieved May 23rd, 2003, from the World Wide Web: http://www.readingonline.org/articles/mceneany/

McKenna, M. (2001). Development of reading attitudes. In L. Verhoeven & C. Snow (Eds.), *Literacy and motivation* (pp. 135–158). Mahwah, NJ: Lawrence Erlbaum Associates.

Mercer, N. (1995). The quality of talk in children's joint activity at the computer. *Journal of Computer Assisted Learning, 10*, 24–32.

Mercer, N. (2000). *Words and minds: How we use language to think together*. London: Routledge.

Mostow, J. (2001). Evaluating tutors that listen: An overview of the project LISTEN. In K. Forbus & P. Feltovich (Eds.), *Smart machines in education* (pp. 169–234). Menlo Park, CA: MIT Press.

Newman, R. S. (1998). Students' help seeking during problem solving: Influences of personal and contextual achievement goals. *Journal of Educational Psychology, 90*(4), 644–658.

Palincsar, A. S., & Brown, A. L. (1984). Reciprocal teaching of comprehension-fostering and comprehension-monitoring activities. *Cognition and Instruction, 2*, 117–175.

Pressley, M. (1998). *Reading instruction that works: The case of balanced teaching*. New York: Guilford Press.

Reinking, D., Labbo, L. D., & McKenna, M. C. (2000). From assimilation to accommodation: A developmental framework for integrating digital technologies into literacy research and instruction. *Journal of Research in Reading, 23*(2), 110–122.

Reinking, D., McKenna, M. C., Labbo, L. D., & Kieffer, R. D. (1998). *Literacy and technology*. Mahwah, NJ: Lawrence Erlbaum Associates.

Rogoff, B. (1990). *Apprenticeship in thinking*. New York: Oxford University Press.

Salomon, G., Perkins, D. N., & Globerson, T. (1992). Partners in cognition: Extending human intelligence with intelligent technologies. *Educational Researcher, 20*(3), 2–9.

Scardamalia, M., & Bereiter, C. (1984). Teachability of reflective processes in written composition. *Cognitive Science, 8*, 173–190.

Scardamalia, M., Bereiter, C., Brett, C., Burtis, P. J., Calhoun, C., & Lea, N. S. (1992). Educational applications of a networked communal database. *Interactive Learning Environments, 2*, 45–71.

Scardamalia, M., Bereiter, R. S., Swallow, M. J., & Woodruff (1989). Computer-supported intentional learning environment. *Journal of Educational Computing Research, 5*, 51–68.

Scardamelia, M., & Bereiter, C. (1994). Computer support for knowledge-building communities. *Journal of the Learning Sciences, 3*, 265–283.

Schwartz, D. L., Brophy, S., Lin, X., & Bransford, J. D. (1999). *Educational technology, research and development*. Washington: Association for Educational Communications and Technology.

Segers, E., & Verhoeven, L. (2003). Writing in the subject areas: a new learning environment on the internet. In A. M. Vilas, J. A. M. Gonzalez, & J. M. Gonzalez (Eds.), *Advances in Technology-Based Education: Toward a Knowledge-Based Society, Volume II* (pp. 1141–1146). Badajoz: Junta de Extremadura.

Sharp, D. L., Bransford, J. D., Goldman, S. R., Risko, V. J., Kinzer, C. K., & Vye, N. J. (1995). Dynamic visual support for story comprehension and mental modeling by young, at-risk children. *Educational Technology Research and Development, 43*, 25–42.

Sherry, L., & Myers, K. M. (1996). Developmental research on collaborative design. In *Proceedings of 43rd Annual Conference of the Society for Technical Communication* (pp. 199–204). Charlottesville, VA: Society for Technical Communication.

Slavin, R. E. (1990). *Cooperative learning: Theory, research and practice*. Englewood-Cliffs, NJ: Prentice Hall.

Slavin, R. E. (1995). *Cooperative learning: Theory, research and practice* (2nd ed.). Boston, MA: Allyn and Bacon.

Stahl, R. J. (1995). *Cooperative learning in language arts*. Menlo Park, CA: Addison-Wesley.

Sutherland-Smith, W. (2002). Weaving the literacy web: Changes in reading from page to screen. *The Reading Teacher, 55,* 662–669.

Verhoeven, L. (1994). *Functional literacy: Theoretical issues and practical implications.* Amsterdam/Philadelphia: John Benjamins.

Verhoeven, L. (1996). Language in education. In F. Coulmas (Ed.), *Handbook of sociolinguistics* (pp. 389–404). London: Basil Blackwell.

Verhoeven, L., & Aarnoutse, C. (1999). Verbetering van het onderwijs Nederlands: een plan van aanpak. (A plan for improvement of education in Dutch.) *Spiegel, 14,* 53–70.

Verhoeven, L., & Snow, C. (Eds.) (2001). *Literacy and motivation.* Mahwah, NJ: Lawrence Erlbaum.

Vye, N. J., Schwartz, D. L., Bransford, J. D., Zech, L., & CTGV (1998). SMART interventions that support monitoring, reflection and revision. In D. Hacker, J. Dunlosky & A. Graesser (Eds.), *Metacognition in educational theory and practice* (pp. 305–346). Mahwah, NJ: Lawrence Erlbaum Associates.

Vygotzky, L. S. (1964). *Thought and language.* Cambridge: University Press.

Wegerif (1996). Collaborative learning and directive software. *Journal of Computer Assisted Learning, 12,* 22–32.

Wegerif, R., Mercer, N., & Dawes, L. (1999). From social interaction to individual reasoning. *Learning and Instruction, 32*(6), 493–516.

Wells, G. (1999). *Dialogic inquiry: Towards a sociocultural practice and theory of education.* Cambridge: Cambridge University Press.

Williams, S. E. (1992). Putting case-based instruction into context: Examples from legal and medical education. *Journal of the Learning Sciences, 2,* 367–427.

Yates, S. (1996). Oral and written aspect of computer conferencing. In S. Herring (Ed.), *Computer-mediated communication: Linguistic, social and cross-cultural perspectives* (pp. 29–46). Philadelphia: John Benjamins.

Yu, F. Y. (2001). Competition within computer-assisted cooperative learning environments: cognitive, affective and social outcomes. *Journal of Educational Computing Research, 24,* 99–117.

II
▼▼▼▼▼▼▼▼

TECHNOLOGY APPLICATIONS WITH SPECIFIC POPULATIONS

5

▼▼▼▼▼▼▼

Computer-Based Remediation for Reading and Related Phonological Disabilities

Richard K. Olson and Barbara Wise
University of Colorado, Boulder

I. THE NATURE OF GENETIC AND ENVIRONMENTAL CONSTRAINTS ON READING DEVELOPMENT

It may seem odd to begin a presentation on computer-based interventions for reading disability by discussing research on genetic factors. However, the evidence for strong genetic influence in many cases of reading disability has been one of the main motivations for our work on computer-based methods for remediation. A brief review of the genetic evidence will help clarify why such extraordinary environmental support may be needed for many children with reading disabilities.

Before turning to the genetic evidence, it must be emphasized that there are substantial differences in literacy levels both between and within countries that are obviously related to cultural and subcultural differences in education and reading practice that have no relation to genetic factors. For example, in a study conducted by the Organization for Economic Co-operation and Development (OECD), France and the U.S. are close to the literacy mean for industrialized countries (www.pisa.oecd.org). Finland has the highest level of literacy in this survey. Finland, which has high requirements for reading teachers, has a language with a simple phonological structure (five vowel sounds and no consonant clusters) and a transparent orthography. The Finns' high literacy level may also be related to their very high level of newspaper subscription and reading practice, including subtitled movies. In contrast, the average literacy level in Brazil is far below the mean for the OECD countries, and this is clearly related to a lack of instruction for many poor children in Brazil.

Literacy differences within countries are substantially greater than between countries, and much of these within-country individual differences may also be related to subcultural and individual differences in quality of education, socio-economic status, and reading habits. For example, in the U.S., there are many urban areas of extreme environmental deprivation related to reading, including very poor reading education, limited access to print in the schools and homes, and difficulties due to reading instruction in a child's second language (Olson, 2004). It is clear that environmental factors are the main reasons for poor reading in such deprived contexts.

When environmental conditions are generally supportive for reading development in higher income U.S. communities with good schools and access to print, average reading scores are much higher than in poorer communities. Nevertheless, the normal distribution of reading skills in these favorable environments still includes many children with mild to severe difficulties in learning to read, in spite of apparently good reading instruction. The unexplained failure of these children has led us to study the potential role of genetic factors in reading disability.

In our behavior-genetic research with twins and our intervention research with computers in the schools, we have used the term *reading disability* rather than *dyslexia* because of the latter term's assumptions about etiology. According to Lyon, Shaywitz, & Shaywitz (2003, p. 2),

> Dyslexia is a specific learning disability that is neurobiological in origin. It is characterized by difficulties with accurate and/or fluent word recognition and by poor spelling and decoding abilities. These difficulties typically result from a deficit in the phonological component of language that is often unexpected in relation to other cognitive abilities and the provision of effective classroom instruction. Secondary consequences may include problems in reading comprehension and reduced reading experience that can impede growth of vocabulary and background knowledge.

Our research does not assume a neurobiological origin or that effective classroom and home-based instruction is always present among the children with reading disabilities that we study. We are equally interested in environmental influences and genetic influences on reading disability for children in Colorado schools that are near or above the national norms for academic achievement.

The Colorado Learning Disabilities Research Center (CLDRC) began a behavior-genetic twin study of reading disability in 1982 by comparing the similarities of identical and fraternal twins (DeFries et al., 1997). The basic logic of twin studies is that identical twins share all their segregating genes (genes that make us different), while fraternal twins share half their segregating genes on average. Both types of twin pairs share their home and school environments, so greater similarity for reading disability in identical pairs compared to fraternal pairs provides evidence for genetic influence.

The CLDRC twins between 8 and 18 years of age were identified from school records in Colorado. With parental permission, their files were examined for any evidence of reading problems. If any such evidence was found for one or both twins in a pair, they were both invited to our laboratory at the University of Colorado for extensive standardized and experimental testing of reading and potentially related skills. We also tested a comparison group of twins without evidence of reading disability in either member of the pair. To date, we have tested over 3000 twin pairs and their siblings. About 2/3 of the pairs have at least one member with a school history of difficulty in learning to read.

A basic premise of our twin study of reading disability is that reading is a complex process involving several basic cognitive skills. Therefore, in addition to basic standardized measures of word reading, spelling, and reading comprehension, we have also assessed several component skills in word reading, including phonological decoding, measured by oral and silent nonword reading. In oral language, three of our measures assess phoneme awareness, defined as the ability to isolate and manipulate phonemes in spoken words and nonwords. We and others have found that phonological decoding and phoneme awareness tend to be worse than expected in children with reading disabilities, compared to their reading level (Rack, Snowling, & Olson, 1992), and therefore are a potential cause of reading disability, as well as a target for remediation in our computer-based remediation studies described in the next section.

At various times during the twin study, we have also included measures of basic sensory processing of visual and speech-related auditory stimuli to see if deficits in these skills might contribute to failure in the development of phoneme awareness, phonological decoding, and reading. We will return to these measures in section III where we discuss computer programs for training basic sensory processes in children with reading disabilities, and their influence on reading development.

The behavior-genetic results for deficits in word reading, phonological decoding, and phoneme awareness are of direct relevance for our remediation studies described in the next section. Briefly, group deficits in word reading have a strong average genetic influence for disabled readers in our twin sample, currently estimated at 54% (this implies 46% for environmental influences), while genetic influences on related group deficits in phonological decoding (oral nonword reading) and phoneme awareness (phoneme deletion) were estimated at 71% and 72% respectively (Gayan & Olson, 2001). Moreover, the genetic influences on deficits in these three reading and language skills were due largely to the same genes, as estimated from their high genetic correlations.

The common causal view of the correlation between reading, phonological decoding, and phoneme awareness is that deficits in phoneme awareness constrain the development of phonological decoding in reading, which constrains growth in fluent word reading, and ultimately reading comprehension (e.g., Share & Stanovich, 1995). In this view, remediation directed primarily toward phoneme awareness and phonological decoding skills should be uniquely beneficial for subsequent growth in word reading and comprehension. Our evidence for strong genetic influences on phonological deficits suggests that extraordinary environmental intervention (including intensive computer programs, of course) may help overcome these genetic constraints.

Other genetic evidence suggests a different or at least complementary approach to computer-based remediation of reading disabilities. Our studies of preschool twins have demonstrated genetically compromised learning rates for pre-reading skills that influence subsequent reading growth (Byrne et al., 2002); non-genetic studies have shown that young poor readers have seriously compromised learning rates for new words, though they eventually learn those words with more extended practice (e.g., Reitsma, 1983). Unfortunately, genetically compromised learning rates in reading development are typically coupled with genetically influenced deficits in reading practice, in spite of the need for greater than normal practice for most children with reading disabilities to reach, or more closely approach, normal reading levels (Olson, 2004).

Even without explicit intervention for the deficits in phoneme awareness and phonological decoding that are presumed to play a causal role in reading disability, an intervention that substantially increased accurate reading practice on the computer should serve to promote more rapid growth in reading for many children with reading disabilities. Thus, the potentially distinct needs for more accurate reading practice and/or improved phonological skills through explicit training guided our focus on two different computer-based remediation programs titled "Accurate-Reading-in Context" and "Phonological-Analysis" (Wise, Ring, & Olson, 2000). These computer programs did require rather extensive staffing beyond the regular classroom teacher. We staffed the programs with one trained assistant for every three or four students. This is considerably less than some one-on-one intervention studies with a human tutor (c.f., Torgesen et al., 2001) and similar to the small-group size of many resource rooms, but it is much more than the regular classroom teacher can provide in a class of 25–30 students. If benefits for reading from either or both programs were roughly equivalent to those from individual tutoring, the cost advantage for computer-based remediation should be obvious. In addition, from a scientific point of view, the programs provided a well-controlled experimental platform for comparing different methods of remediation that were delivered with equal intensity and enthusiasm by the computer. This may be very difficult to achieve when training in different conditions is administered by a researcher who believes in the superiority of one condition over others. See Rosenthal (2003) for a general discussion of researchers' unintentional communication of expectations and their influence on subjects' behavior. Also, teachers' primary responsibility is to students, so they may modify a program to meet children's needs. While this is exactly what a good teacher should do, it makes it harder to assure "treatment fidelity" in classroom studies. Thus, while classroom studies are essential to evaluate transfer and scalability of research ideas, computer studies add a unique component of studying variations in methods with reduced bias and with assured treatment fidelity at least during computer time.

II. RESULTS FROM OUR COMPUTER-BASED REMEDIAL PROGRAMS TO SUPPORT ACCURATE READING PRACTICE, PHONOLOGICAL DECODING, AND PHONEME AWARENESS

Before turning to the Wise et al. (2000) study that will be the primary focus of this section, we will say a few things about some of our computer-training studies that preceded and motivated this large study. When talking computers with high-quality synthetic speech (DECtalk) became available in the mid 1980s, we thought that they could support poor readers in their reading of more advanced grade-level appropriate text by encouraging them to target difficult words for orthographic and speech support. Prior to our formal training studies in the schools, we confirmed in pilot studies that synthetic computer speech was equal to natural speech for supporting the recognition and learning of targeted words in stories (Olson, Foltz, & Wise, 1986a). We also determined that feedback for difficult words in the stories was far more effective in promoting learning of those words compared to reading the stories without feedback (Olson, Foltz, & Wise, 1986b). This second result may seem obvious now, but we had to counter the claims of some advocates for the "Whole Language" approach to reading instruction, who argued that guessing difficult words from first-letter sounds and context was more natural and would lead to better growth in reading. "Whole Language" was the dominant approach to reading instruction in the Boulder schools during the 1980s. To gain acceptance of our research studies in those schools, we had to convince the teachers and administrators that our computer programs might provide greater benefits than reading and guessing difficult words. (Some teachers remained concerned that their students might start talking like the computer, but this only happened as a joke.)

Our initial formal training studies in the schools were designed to provide greater practice in accurate reading than children with reading disabilities would typically experience in their reading classrooms. Therefore, we displaced a half hour per day of regular classroom reading instruction and substituted individual reading of stories on the computer in quiet school locations outside the classroom. We compared the experimental groups' performance to a randomly assigned control group that was given the same pre- and post-tests, but remained in their regular reading classroom. To address the previously discussed phonological deficits in children with reading disabilities, we also assessed the added benefits from helping children attend to the onset-phoneme, rime, and syllable–sound relations in their targeted words, as described below. Our strong hypothesis was that explicitly drawing attention to these relations would provide greater benefits for growth in phonological decoding and reading than would simply providing whole-word feedback for targeted words.

Thus, in our first small training study (Wise et al., 1989), we asked poor readers in the third through sixth grades to read stories on the computer that were selected to be at an instructional level that was 1–5 difficult words per 100, not so difficult that their reading would be disrupted by very frequent targeting of difficult words, but not so easy that they would learn few new words. The computer-trained poor readers (lower 10% of readers in their classes) were randomly assigned to one of three different levels of orthographic and speech segmentation for the targeted words. Targeted words were broken into onset-rime units, syllables, or left as whole words. "Exception" words were not segmented, for example words like *said*, with no orthographic "neighbors" with similar pronunciations. In the two segmented conditions, the segments were sequentially highlighted as they were pronounced by the computer. We hypothesized that the segmented conditions would lead to greater growth in phonological decoding skills and perhaps in word reading skills as well.

In this, and all our future studies, we were surprised at how much training and teacher support some children needed to know when to "target" difficult words. Our trainers worked explicitly to help children improve from targeting sometimes as few as 1 in 20 word errors to reach levels where they targeted most of the words they needed to. We compared how many words the children targeted on their independent reading days, to the number of words they targeted when reading aloud with the computer with the trainer sitting beside them. Trainers worked intensively with the students to help them notice when they were struggling with a word, and trainers rewarded students with stickers which could be traded for incentives, for improving their targeting ratios. An improved ratio indicated that they were asking for help on most of the words they would have missed. The fact that training awareness of errors was so intense as to support accurate reading for most children is a challenge for scalability. Programs will need to detect errors, or to train students to detect errors, without such intensive human support in order for speech-supported reading programs to be both effective and scalable to classrooms without the 1:4 teacher-student ratio that we had.

The results of this first study showed greater growth in reading for all computer-trained conditions compared to the regular reading classroom control group, and the onset-rime segmentation condition yielded significantly greater growth in phonological decoding (but not for standardized measures of word reading) than the whole-word or syllable feedback conditions. Encouraged by these preliminary results, we trained a substantially larger sample for a longer time with these same three onset-rime, syllable, and whole-word orthographic and speech feedback conditions. Much to our surprise, although computer-based remediation in the larger study resulted in more rapid growth in phonological decoding and word recognition than in the classroom control group, there were no significant differences in gains for the three segmentation conditions on any of our reading or phonological decoding measures (Olson & Wise, 1992). We also noted that across all conditions, better pretest phoneme awareness was related to greater reading gains. These results motivated the inclusion of explicit training in phoneme awareness for one of the two main conditions of the Wise et al. (2000) study.

Training time in the Olson and Wise (1992) study was limited to about 10 hours in half-hour sessions, and there was no explicit training to improve poor readers' deficits in phoneme awareness or phonological decoding beyond what we hoped would come from the segmented feedback for targeted words. Therefore, we subsequently initiated a much longer study that included 50–60 half-hour sessions for 2nd–5th graders over a semester, and compared two training conditions. (An untreated control group was omitted because earlier studies had shown clear advantages over classroom controls after limited computer remediation, and we wanted to maximize power to test for differential treatment main effects and interactions.)

The two training conditions included one that was called "Accurate-Reading-in-Context" (ARC), wherein children spent 22 computer hours reading stories with speech feedback, and 7 small-group hours practicing the Palincsar & Brown (1984) comprehension strategies while reading together. The second training condition, called "Phonological Analysis" (PA), included 7 small-group hours using the articulatory training methods developed by Lindamood and Lindamood (1975). About half of the PA group's 22 individualized hours on the computers included exercises designed to support phoneme awareness and phonological decoding, and half was spent reading stories on the computer with segmented speech feedback for targeted words. Both experimental groups answered multiple-choice comprehension questions every 5–9 pages and reviewed targeted words at the end of each session (Wise, Ring, & Olson, 2000). In these studies, as in the earlier studies, many students required extensive training and much support (and stickers!) from teachers to learn to ask for help on the difficult words.

Pretests, midtests, and posttests were given before, during, and at the end of training. Follow-up tests were given one and two years after the end of training for a subset of the generally younger subjects who remained in their elementary schools and thus available for testing. The PA group showed significantly greater gains in phoneme awareness, phonological decoding, and untimed word reading at the end of training. Their advantage in phoneme awareness and phonological decoding was significant one and two years after the end of training, but their initial advantage in untimed word reading had disappeared. The ARC condition showed significantly greater growth in time-limited word reading at the end of training, but this advantage over the PA condition also disappeared in the one- and two-year follow-up tests.

The main effects of treatment at the end of training were qualified by interesting interactions with grade level or reading level. In general, the PA condition yielded better results for untimed word reading and spelling for children with reading disabilities in grades 2 and 3, while the ARC condition yielded greater gains in all measures of word reading and spelling for children with reading disabilities in grades 4 and 5. The interactions with grade level were statistically significant for an untimed measure of word recognition and for WRAT spelling. Thus, at the end of training, word reading and spelling benefits were greater in the PA condition for the youngest and weakest poor readers, while the benefits were greater for the older and stronger readers in the ARC condition. In these post-hoc analyses, we cannot determine whether it is reading level or age driving these effects.

The good news from the study is that there were substantially larger gains in standard word-reading scores for *both* training conditions, compared to similar reading-classroom controls in a separate study (Wise, Ring, & Olson, 1999). Moreover, our gains per hour of computer-based instruction supported by and supplemented with 1:4 instruction with well-trained research associates were comparable to those in other intensive remediation studies that used one-on-one tutoring with expert instructors (Torgesen, 2002)! We were also pleased that the PA group had clearly better phoneme awareness and phonological decoding at the end of training and at follow up. However, we were very disappointed that the PA group's advantage in these skills did not transfer to consistently greater growth in word reading, spelling, and reading comprehension in follow-up tests, or for the older poor readers even at the end of training. It is possible that the differential gains in phonological awareness and decoding at the end of 29 hours of training, though large in effect size, statistical significance, and close to normal levels, were still not sufficiently strong to transfer to lasting differences in reading accuracy one year later. However, similar null results from a one-on-one tutoring study with longer training (88 hours) have led Torgesen et al. (2001) to conclude that we still don't know how to connect remedied phonological skills in 3rd–6th grade poor readers to greater growth in fluent reading.

Wise et al. (2000) speculated that greater long-term benefits for reading from phonological training might be achieved by doing three things: by increasing the training time beyond 29 hours as most experts suggest, by explicitly training and rewarding transfer of skills to independent reading, and by moving beyond accuracy and improving the speed and automaticity of lexical (whole word) and sublexical (phonemes and syllables) phonological processing. On the other hand, additional training in lexical fluency and automaticity alone might be just as, or even more effective, particularly in older poor readers. Further study is needed to compare more intensive computer-based approaches that include the suggested three improvements for the remediation of reading disabilities across the grades.

Before turning to the auditory training studies in the next section, we will comment on our attempts to identify the important elements of the PA condition in the Wise et al. (2000) study that led to superior growth in phoneme awareness and phonological decoding. We believed that our training of articulatory awareness, including some aspects of methods developed by Lindamood and Lindamood (1975), was an essential component of that training for at least the children with the most severe deficits. Several studies had shown that poor readers seem to have less awareness of the articulatory movements associated with different speech sounds, and it seemed to us that training this awareness should support better growth in phoneme awareness and phonological decoding, than phonological training without this support.

To test our hypothesis that articulatory awareness training was an important component of our PA training condition, Wise, Ring, and Olson (1999) conducted a large study with second through fifth grade poor readers, comparing the PA training condition used in Wise et al. (2000) with two variations of that condition. The variation of PA training most relevant to our hypothesis replaced the time devoted to articulatory awareness training, with practice in organizing block patterns to represent changes in spoken phoneme sequences, manipulating graphemes to correspond to phoneme changes in nonwords and words spoken by the computer, spelling words spoken by the computer with feedback for their responses (Wise & Olson, 1992), and practicing the reading of nonwords. The group with training in articulatory awareness also practiced with these programs, but for less time due to their work with small-group articulatory awareness activities and a computer program for articulatory awareness provided by the Lindamood Bell Company. As in Wise et al. (2000), both groups read stories on the computer for part of their training time. Total training time of about 40 hours in half-hour sessions was the same in both conditions.

Much to our surprise, at the end of training and in one-year follow-up tests, there were no significant differences for gains in phoneme awareness, phonological decoding, or reading from the articulatory and non-articulatory training conditions described above (Wise et al., 1999). Results of a previous smaller study by Wise, Ring, Sessions, and Olson (1997) suggesting that there might be differences for the poorest readers were not confirmed. Thus, we soundly rejected our favored hypothesis that training in articulatory awareness was an essential component of the Wise et al. (2000) PA training condition that had led to its impressive gains in phoneme awareness and phonological decoding. On the other hand, we were very encouraged that both conditions in Wise et al. (1999) yielded substantial gains in phoneme awareness (Effect Size = .92–1.73), phonological decoding (Effect Size = 1.46), and standard scores in word reading (Effect Size = .73–.98), compared to gains for a regular reading-classroom control group.

One recent study without computers examined treatment benefits for articulatory (mouth) vs. auditory (ear) phonological awareness training vs. an untrained control group. One of the authors of the study trained non-readers who knew their alphabet but could not read words (Castiglioni-Spalten & Ehri, 2003). Children received 3–6 sessions of training using mouth pictures to specify different sounds or undifferentiated "ear" blocks just to count sounds in words. The children were tested one day and one week after training, by testers who were unaware which training condition the children were in. The two trained groups did not differ significantly from each other on any measures of phonological awareness, spelling, or reading at post tests, one day, or one week after training. Both the "mouth" and the "ear" trained groups scored higher than the control group on most measures. On a "cued reading" measure, only the mouth group outscored the controls significantly, but it still did not differ significantly from the ear group. The fact that only one group differed significantly from a control does not statistically support that the two trained groups differ from each other. Thus, to date, no study clearly supports an advantage for articulatory over non-articulatory phonological-awareness training.

In summary, Wise et al. (1999) showed that our computer-based remediation programs were very effective for promoting disabled readers' growth in phoneme awareness, phonological decoding, and word reading, but the inclusion or exclusion of training in articulatory awareness had no differential effect on gains in these skills. Wise et al. (2000) further demonstrated that similar long-term gains in reading were attained from accurate reading practice on the computer, with or without explicit training in phoneme awareness and phonological decoding. We suggested that the addition of training time, more training and rewarding of independent transfer activities, and including more intensive automaticity training in phoneme awareness and phonological decoding might yield greater long-term benefits for reading growth compared to the ARC condition, but this hypothesis remains to be tested. Still, we are encouraged that simply practicing accurate reading on the computer, reviewing targeted words, and answering occasional comprehension questions had such powerful effects on reading growth in disabled readers. In the concluding section of this chapter, we will discuss current commercial computer programs that can be used to support this type of accurate reading practice.

Failure to find greater long-term benefits for reading growth from training older disabled readers' phoneme awareness and phonological decoding might suggest that trained improvement on our phonological measures failed to impact some deeper constraint on normal growth in these skills and in reading (Olson, 2002; Scarborough, 2001). We alluded earlier to hypotheses of possibly greater benefits from making phonological skills either more automatic so they would promote more rapid growth in fluent reading or to making them better-grounded with more active thinking and self-checking, so they would transfer better to independent reading. A different view is that there are more basic deficits in disabled readers' auditory-temporal processes and related deficits in speech perception that constrain normal growth in phoneme awareness, phonological decoding and reading (Tallal, 2003). Perhaps training in these more basic and possibly causal deficits would lead to greater growth in reading. In the next section we briefly review the evidence for this idea, and we critique several studies claiming to show unique benefits for reading from computer-based training in speech perception.

III. RESULTS FROM COMPUTER-BASED PROGRAMS FOR TRAINING BASIC AUDITORY PROCESSING SKILLS

We first explored possible deficits in auditory-temporal processes and categorical speech perception in disabled readers when we were developing a test battery in 1981 for our subsequent behavior-genetic studies with twins. Tallal (1980) had recently presented evidence that poor readers' phonological decoding difficulties were strongly linked to their deficits in perceiving the temporal order of rapidly presented tone sequences, but that their reading ability was not related to the perception of slowly presented sequences. Then, Godfrey, Syrdal-Lasky, Milay, and Knox (1981) published the first study showing deficits in poor readers' categorical perception of speech. These results resonated with our interest in assessing more basic reading-related processes that might reflect genetic influence, so we worked with the investigators of both studies to see if we could replicate their findings and include the measures in our twin test battery.

However, our attempts at replication did not support the inclusion of these measures in our battery. The Tallal (1980) temporal-order judgment task was only modestly correlated with phonological decoding and reading skill in our sample, and we found that the correlation was largely due to some outliers who did very poorly on *both* the slowly and rapidly presented tone sequences. A similar result has recently been published by Share, Jorm, Maclean, and Matthews (2002). The Godfrey et al. (1981) task showed a statistically significant but modest difference between good and poor readers' apparent categorical perception of phonemes, and this difference was also driven by a few outliers who were very inconsistent in their categorical judgments, even when the stimuli were well on either side of the formant-transition boundary that yielded nearly 100% correct performance in normal readers. (This pattern is evident in at least one more recent study by Joanisse, Manis, Keating, and Seidenberg (2000) that showed plots of individual subjects' data.) Thus, it seemed to us that only a minority of disabled readers had deficits in the Tallal and Godfrey et al. tasks, and at least some of these deficits were related to subjects' difficulties in attending to the task, rather than more fundamental deficits in temporal-order perception or speech perception. Other more recent studies have also suggested that much of the poor-reader group deficit in auditory and visual sensory processing tasks is limited to outliers and/or problems in maintaining attention in difficult psychophysical tasks (Bretherton & Holmes, 2003; Hulslander et al., 2004; Marshall, Snowling, & Bailey, 2001; Olson & Datta, 2002; Ramus, et al., 2003; Rosen, 2003; Stuart, McAnally, & Castles, 2001; Wood, 2003). Unfortunately, we were too busy developing the twin test battery, and did not take the time to publish the results of our early replication attempts.

Although the current status of auditory-temporal and speech-processing deficits in children with reading disabilities is controversial, any evidence that computer-based training in auditory-temporal tasks and speech processing can help remediate reading disability should be considered on its own merits. In fact, such evidence has recently been published for a widely used computer-based program titled FastForWord Language™ (Temple et al., 2003). This study has been cited by Tallal (2003, p. 210), as showing that FastForWord Language™ "… training raised the dyslexic readers' [reading] scores into the normal range."

In our view, the Temple et al. (2003) study was not appropriately designed to interpret the results as support for the value of FastForWord Language™ in the remediation of reading disability or dyslexia. The most fundamental problem was that it did not have an appropriate untreated or alternately treated reading-disabled control group. The reading-disabled group improved significantly in several reading scores from the beginning to the end of the eight-week FastForWord Language™ training program, but there are several possible reasons for these gains that are not directly related to the specific effects of the training. The first is that when extreme groups are selected in the population based on test performance, they often show better performance on a second testing. This can be due to "regression to the mean" from simple error variance on the first test. It can also be due to increased familiarity with the test and the testers, an effect that we have seen in our own research. At a minimum, a randomly assigned untreated control group with reading disability is needed that has the same experiences outside the training program. It is not clear what the experimental group's outside experience was in the Temple et al. (2003) study. There is no information on how or where the subjects were recruited, and the secondary reference cited to provide this information did not clarify this. In addition, there was no discussion of the reading instruction or practice outside of FastForWord Language™ that might also have accounted for subjects' gains in reading.

The untrained control group that was used in the Temple et al. (2003) study was a group of readers that scored well above the national norms on reading measures at pretest. Consistent with possible regression to the mean artifacts, the above-normal readers actually showed a statistically significant decline from pre- to post-test on one of the reading measures (passage comprehension). In any case, this above-normal untreated control group did nothing to control for the possible confounds mentioned above related to training effects on reading.

Ideally, a treated control group would be used that did not contain the element of training deemed essential for the method's benefits. In the case of FastForWord Language™, the element of training that was purported to be essential for improving the language skills of children with specific language impairment was the modified speech training (initially stretching certain formant transitions in stimuli) (Tallal et al., 1996). Habib et al. (2002) addressed this question in a well-controlled study that Tallal (2003) cited as support for the FastForWord Language™ program. Habib et al. Study 1 compared auditory training with modified speech training with the same listening activities but with natural speech support in computer exercises requiring subjects to find the "odd one" of four spoken syllables (e.g., pin win sit bin) that did not share a common consonant sound with the others, in a pre-specified position. Children improved in this task more quickly with modified than with natural speech during training, and the modified speech group scored higher in post-training tests on the same task. That result might be viewed as support for FastForWord Language™, but the rest of the Habib et al. results could not generally be viewed as support for gains in language or reading. Except for performance in the trained "odd one" task, children's performance increased more in eight out of the remaining 12 reading and language measures in the condition with natural speech than in the condition with the modified speech, though these differences were not significant in this small sample of six children in each group. One measure, complex nonword spelling, did improve more for the group with modified speech support ($p = .043$), but this result depended in part on an unexplained decline from pre- to post-test in the natural speech condition.

Tallal et al. (1996) had previously reported greater gains from their modified speech condition across a wide range of language tasks. However, the Habib et al. Study 1 found no support for such broad benefits in language or reading specifically from the modified speech training. Habib et al. (2002) did show significant pre- to post-test gains in both groups on most of their 12 reading and language measures, and they suggested that modified speech in the auditory training programs was responsible for this improvement. However, for reasons discussed above regarding the Temple et al. (2003) study, an untrained or differently trained control group is needed to confirm this hypothesis, and the authors acknowledged this.

In Studies 2 and 3, Habib et al. (2002) shifted their auditory training in the laboratory to the offices of speech therapists and the homes of disabled readers, using exercises recorded on a CD. In Study 2, training over a period of 6 weeks, 15 minutes per day, yielded significant gains in phonological and oral language composite scores for some subgroups. Nonword spelling and regular-word reading showed small but significant gains in only one of three subgroups. In Study 3, more extensive results for reading and spelling gains were reported. Nonword reading showed modest but significant improvement, but nonword spelling, regular-word reading, and exception-word reading did not. Again, an untreated control group is needed to conclude that any significant gains were due to speech training. In general, there did not seem to be much change in reading from pre- to post-test in Studies 2 and 3, and there was no Bonferoni correction for the multiple tests of significance.

Two other recently published studies of speech perception training have also failed to find significant effects on reading. Gonzalez, Espinel, and Rosquete (2002) administered training in phoneme awareness and letter sounds with or without additional training in speech perception. The authors claimed that their results supported better reading for the group that also had training in speech perception, but it was clear from a close examination of their data that this was because the speech perception group was at a higher reading level at pretest. The non-speech training group actually had slightly greater gains in reading. In a second study, Hayes, Warrier, Nicol, Zecker, and Kraus (2003) trained children diagnosed with a learning disability and/or with ADHD with a popular commercial auditory training program called Earobics (Cognitive Concepts, 1998). The study found improved auditory processing abilities that were also reflected in some brain EP changes after training when children listened to phonemes, but there were no significant changes in reading and spelling skills. Similarly, a recent report by Segers and Verhoeven (2004) on studies of training with modified speech in the Netherlands concluded that there was little or no benefit from such training for reading in older children with dyslexia, or in younger children at risk for reading disabilities. Finally, a recent study by Bishop, Adams, Lehtonen, and Rosen (2005) found no additional benefit from the use of modified speech in a computer-based spelling intervention program for children with poor reading and language skills.

Of course, Tallal and colleagues might argue that the other studies reviewed here, including the Habib et al. (2002) study she cited as support for FastForWord Language™, were not using exactly the same methods as FastForWord Language™. Fortunately, there are three recently published independent studies that did use FastForWord Language™. The first study by Hook, Macaruso, and Jones (2001) used a value-added control-group design. The children with reading disabilities in the study were all receiving multisensory language and reading instruction during the two-year study period. One group (FWL) was also trained at the beginning of the study with FastForWord Language™, a second group (OG) initially received Orton Gillingham training, and a third group (LC) was a longitudinal control group that received the regular multisensory language and reading instruction also given to the other two groups. The results were clear: At the end of the FWL and OG training sessions, both groups gained in phoneme awareness compared to the LC group, but only the OG group gained significantly in nonword and word reading. The FWL group did show significantly greater gains in speaking and syntax in measures that were similar to the training exercises, but this advantage was not maintained in a two-year follow-up test.

A second study by Pokorni, Worthington, and Jamison (2004) randomly assigned 60 poor readers to 60 hours of computer-based instruction in FastForWord Language™, the LIPS program from Lindamood and Lindamood (1998), or the Earobics program previously mentioned in our review of the study by Hayes et al. (2003). Six weeks following the intervention, there were no significant gains from pretest in reading standard-scores for any of the treatment conditions, although there were significant gains in phoneme awareness associated with the Earobics and LIPS programs. Unfortunately, those gains did not transfer to reading.

Finally, a third study by Rouse and Krueger (2004) may provide the most powerful test of the independent contribution of FastForWord Language™ (FFWL) to the development of reading skills. They compared gains in language and reading measures for as many as 485 children who were below the 20th percentile on state standardized reading assessments. The children were randomly assigned to the FFWL treatment group or an untreated control group. In spite of the large sample size, there were no significant ($p < .05$) differences in gains for the two groups on the state standardized reading tests, on reading assessments used in the Success for All program, or on a computerized language and reading assessment marketed by the Scientific Learning Corporation. The 95% confidence interval for effect size on the state standardized test was $-.08$ to .16, very slightly and non significantly favoring FFWL. This indicates that any benefit from FFWL on reading is likely to be very small. Rouse and Krueger cited a similar unpublished study by Borman and Rachuba (2001) with 415 children in the Baltimore public schools, where the 95% confidence interval for differences in gains between FFWL and an untreated control group was $-.08$ to .13. As in the Rouse and Krueger study, this tiny effect did not approach statistical significance.

Scientific Learning Corporation has conducted several of its own unpublished field studies of FastForWord Language™ benefits for reading. Brief technical reports of some of these studies can be accessed on the company's Web site. It is beyond the scope of this chapter to critique these studies. The reports that were available as of June, 2003 were independently reviewed by Wahl, Robinson, and Torgesen (2003). They concluded at the end of their review that the results from FastForWord Language™ were "... mixed or indeterminate (no control groups) for reading outcomes such as phonemic decoding, word recognition, or reading comprehension." (p. 7). Several more recent technical reports from Scientific Learning Corporation have included untreated control groups with greater gains on some reading measures reported for groups trained with the FastForWord programs (Steven Miller, personal communication, 1/6/2005). Again, it is beyond the scope of this chapter to critique these unpublished studies, but even if there are some apparent benefits of FastForWord programs for reading compared to untreated control groups, there is a further concern. As Wahl et al. noted, "What is not clear from the research at this point is whether the FastForWord Language product has unique instructional advantages when compared to conventional methods of direct instruction in phonemic awareness or reading." (p. 7). In our view, the best way to address this problem is to include a treated control group that includes intense direct instruction in reading with equal time on task, but with or without the FastForWord Language™ program. This value-added design, similar to the one used in the study of FastForWord Language™ by Hook et al. (2001) and by us in our study of articulatory awareness training (Wise et al., 1999), also provides a good control for effects related to experimenter and subject expectations that may arise from special treatment, regardless of the specific content of that treatment (Rosenthall, 2003).

In summary, the three peer-reviewed, published, independent, and controlled experimental assessments of FastForWord Language™ effects on reading that we are aware of (Hook et al., 2001; Pokorni et al., 2004; Rouse & Krueger, 2004), along with one large independent but unpublished study (Borman & Rachuba, 2001), failed to demonstrate significant additional gains in reading at the end of training. Moreover, in the study by Hook et al., FastForWord Language™ trained children were also no better in reading than the LC control group in a two-year follow-up test. Unfortunately, Rouse and Krueger (2004) interpreted their null results from FastForWord Language™ training as generally negative evidence on the benefits of computer programs for reading development. They suggested that since FastForWord Language™ was represented widely as the "… leading edge of scientifically based computer technology in the schools.… if students reap no benefit…, then it is unlikely that the average use of computers in the schools generates any sizeable gains either." (p. 325). However, the published studies we have reviewed in this section, including those on FastForWord Language™, did not explicitly train reading, and that may be the reason they failed to improve reading development. In the previous section, we reviewed our own research that revealed significant benefits from computer-based instruction that focused directly on reading. In the next section we consider other programs that have directly focused on reading skills. We should note in concluding this section that Scientific Learning Corporation has added some new programs that do focus on basic reading skills. To our knowledge, the benefits of these new reading programs have not been independently evaluated.

IV. OTHER COMPUTER PROGRAMS FOR BEGINNING AND REMEDIAL READING INSTRUCTION

Several commercial programs that actually teach reading seem to have had some market success. As far as we know, there have been no independently published studies of their benefits for children with reading disabilities. We have used some of the Lexia (www.lexialearning.com) early reading programs in parts of our research. Although the benefits of the Lexia programs were not evaluated in isolation from other components of our training studies, the younger children with reading disabilities seemed to respond well to the exercises that explicitly teach basic grapheme-phoneme correspondences. Researchers in the Netherlands have developed and evaluated several similar computer-based remediation programs that seem to be efficient and effective training tools for children and adults with dyslexia (Tijms, Hoeks, Hoogeboom, & Smolenaars, 2003).

Currently there is a large U.S. Department of Education funded ($10,000,000) study being conducted by Mathematica Policy Research of Princeton on the use of educational technology in the classroom for reading and math. Of interest in this chapter are commercial programs selected for beginning reading instruction in the first grade, and for reading comprehension in the fourth grade. Companies participating in the first grade comparisons with random assignment to programs include the Academy of Reading (AutoSkill International, Inc.), Destination Reading (Riverdeep, Inc.), The Waterford Early Reading Program™ (Waterford Institute), Headsprout™

(Headsprout, Inc.), Plato FOCUS™ (PLATO Learning, Inc.), and Read, Write, and Type™ (Talking Fingers, Inc.). Programs focused on reading comprehension in the fourth grade incude Academy of Reading®, Read 180 (Scholastic, Inc.), KnowledgeBox® (Pearson Digital Learning), and Leaptrack™ (Leapfrog Schoolhouse). A search through the project Web site (http://www .ed.gov/news/pressreleases/2004/02/02132004.html) for the study did not find much detail about its design, but it appears that whole classrooms are the target population. In our view, most children do fine in their beginning reading classrooms without computers, and the real benefits are for children who need extra support and extra time on task in reading and writing. Nevertheless, it will be interesting to see the results of this independent study.

One commercial program of particular interest to us is marketed by Kurzweil Educational Systems Inc. (KESI), for which both authors of this chapter have served as consultants. The program supports color scanning of printed material, character recognition, and high-quality text-to-speech translation for scanned materials that are presented on the computer screen. The program enables children and adults with reading disabilities to read materials of their choosing, including Web content, with speech support. Other useful functionality includes dictionary support, writing with speech translation, and support for second language learning. Of course the functionality that most interests us is speech support requested specifically for difficult words while children are reading text for meaning. KESI has traditionally marketed their program as a prosthetic for children and adults whose poor reading impairs their comprehension, for whom the text is typically spoken by the computer continuously while it is highlighted on the screen. We think that for learning to read, it would be best to have children actively read and request help when they need it, as the KESI system can also support. We hope to see a test of this hypothesis. We would also like to see independent tests of overall benefits from the KESI system and other commercial programs for children with reading disabilities, in well-controlled experimental designs.

V. NEW DIRECTIONS FOR COMPUTER-BASED SUPPORT OF EARLY READING DEVELOPMENT

In this last section, we briefly describe two new technologies that may enhance the capability of computer reading software. These include Latent Semantic Analysis (LSA, Landauer & Dumais, 1997) and computer speech recognition (Pellom & Hacioglu, 2003). Some current research is underway with both of these capabilities as part of the Colorado Literacy Project (COLit, 2004), and some other research (Mostow et al., 2003) and a marketed product (Soliloquy) are using speech recognition in reading software.

The Colorado Literacy Tutor (COLit) is a collaborative project at the University of Colorado, with principal investigators R. Cole and W. Kintsch. Part of that project includes Summary Street, a program developed at the Institute for Cognitive Science (ICS) to train higher-level comprehension and summarization using Latent Semantic Analysis (LSA). The other part of the program, developed at the Center for Spoken Language Research (CSLR), involves an integrated program of foundational exercises and interactive books with an animated, talking Tutor.

The Summary Street program analyzes summaries of text automatically and provides feedback to the student about the completeness and the conciseness of information presented for each main section of the text. In an earlier study, small groups of middle-school children who used Summary Street during language arts time spent more time writing summaries and wrote more complete and concise summaries than did small groups of students who practiced writing summaries without Summary Street (Kintsch, Steinhart, Stahl, Matthews, & Lamb, 2000). The

Summary Street portion of the Colorado Literacy Project is studying LSA for summarization with a set of 27 books at fourth-, fifth-, and sixth-grade levels (SSWeb, 2004). While efficacy for differences in reading comprehension has not yet been established, we believe the ability to support summarization with software holds promise for improving writing and comprehension with computer support, and future research will clarify how effective it is and how it can best be implemented in programs.

The early reading program at CSLR, Foundations to Literacy, involves foundational exercises and interactive books with an animated "Virtual Tutor" that gives instructions, pronounces words, and gives hints and expansive feedback, with accurate speech movements and recorded, clear speech. These programs have been in development for almost three years, and space does not allow us to describe them fully here. They are described in another chapter, which also reports the results from the first pilot in Spring, 2003 (Wise, Cole, Van Vuuren, Schwartz, Snyder, Pellom, Ngampatipatpong, Tuantranont, in press). A promising functionality in these programs involves providing real time feedback for oral reading. The program highlights the paragraph that the student reads aloud, and a cursor moves to the beginning of each word very soon after the child reads it. The cursor is controlled by SONIC, a continuous speech recognition system for this capability (Pellom, 2001; Pellom & Hacioglu, 2003). SONIC, developed at CSLR, is now achieving recognition accuracy for children's words spoken while reading books on computers at around 90%, and further improvement is expected (Hagen et al., 2003; Pellom, 2004). This capability is exciting because it may improve students' engagement and their ability to recognize and correct errors during computer reading. The hypothesis is that the speech tracking and the animated, hinting Tutor should replace the need for the 1:4 human helper needed in the ROSS programs and in most effective small group instruction.

Another program of research (Mostow et al., 2003) uses different speech recognition technology to track reading errors on short text segments. Children improve in reading when they use the program, but the unique contribution of speech recognition to their improvement has not yet been demonstrated, since reading practice may improve reading by itself. Soliloquy Learning (http://soliloquylearning.com/) has produced a commercial program that uses speech recognition in book reading (see Adams, this volume). The company has formed partnerships with several prominent publishers and their program has been approved for funding in several states. Currently, there are no published reports of its efficacy for children with reading disabilities. We do believe that speech recognition technology shows great promise for providing corrective feedback while reading, especially as speech-recognition error rates come down, and as difficulties with ambient noise in classrooms are resolved. We eagerly await further developments in these areas.

SUMMARY AND CONCLUSIONS

We began with a discussion of the need for computer support in learning to read from the perspective of evidence for genetic and environmental constraints on some children's learning rates for reading. This evidence suggested the need for extraordinary environmental intervention. We then reviewed our research with talking computers that did show significant benefits for reading in experimental comparisons with regular classroom controls, though the benefits of two different methods interacted with reading level and age. We then shifted to discussion of computer-based programs, particularly FastForWord™, that claim to remediate underlying speech processing deficits, and thereby reading disabilities. An analysis of peer-reviewed and published research by independent investigators did not support these claims. We then briefly reviewed other commercial programs that focused directly on reading and writing skills, noting their apparent success in the market place and the need for independent studies of their efficacy for children and adults with reading disabilities. Finally, we concluded with an outline of some exciting new approaches with computer technology that also need to be validated in carefully controlled studies. We are encouraged about the potential benefits of computer technology for children with reading disabilities, but independent research must tell what works, how it works, and for whom.

ACKNOWLEDGMENTS

We acknowledge the support of NIH grants HD11683 and HD22223 for our studies on the use of talking computers in the schools to help children with reading disabilities.

REFERENCES

Bishop, D. V. M., Adams, C. V., Lehtonen, A., & Rosen, S. (2005). Computerised training of spelling skills in children with language impairments: A comparison of modified and unmodified speech input. *Journal of Research in Reading, 28*(2), 144–157.

Borman, G. D., & Rachuba, L. T. (2001). Evaluation of the Scientific Learning Corporation's Fast ForWord computer-based training program in the Baltimore city public schools. *A Report Prepared for the Abell Foundation,* August.

Bretherton, L., & Holmes, V. (2003). The relationship between auditory temporal processing, phonemic awareness, and reading disability. *Journal of Experimental Child Psychology, 84*, 218–243.

Byrne, B., Delaland, C., Fielding-Barnsley, R., Quain, P., Samuelsson, S., Hoien, T., Corley, R., DeFries, J. C., Wadsworth, S., Willcutt, E., & Olson, R. K. (2002). Longitudinal twin study of early reading development in three countries: Preliminary results. *Annals of Dyslexia, 52*, 49–74.

Castiglioni-Spalten, M., & Ehri, L. (2003). Phonemic Awareness Instruction: Contribution of articulatory segmentation to novice beginners reading and spelling. *Scientific Studies of Reading, 7*, 25–52.

COLit. (2004). Colorado Literacy Tutor project. [Online]. http://www.colit.org

CSLR. (2004). Reading Web site. [Online].http://cslr.colorado.edu/beginweb/reading/reading.html

Cognitive Concepts, Inc. (1998). *Earobics auditory development and phonics program step 2.* Evanston, Ill: Author.

DeFries, J. C., Filipek, P. A., Fulker, D. W., Olson, R. K., Pennington, B. F., Smith, S. D., & Wise, B. (1997). Colorado Learning Disabilities Research Center. *Learning Disabilities, 8*, 7–19.

Gayan, J., & Olson, R. K. (2001). Genetic and environmental influences on orthographic and phonological skills in children with reading disabilities. *Developmental Neuropsychology, 20*, 487–511.

Godfrey, J. J., Syrdal-Lasky, A. K., Millay, K. K., & Knox, C. M. (1981). Performance of dyslexic children on speech perception tests. *Journal of Experimental Child Psychology, 32*, 401–424.

Gonzalez, M., Espinel, A., & Rosquete, R. (2002). Remedial interventions for children with reading disabilities: Speech perception—An effective component in phonological training? *Journal of Learning Disabilities, 35*, 334–342.

Habib, M., Rey, V., Daffaure, V., Camps, R., Espesser, R., & Demonet, J. F. (2002). Phonological training in dyslexics using temporally modified speech: A three-step pilot investigation. *International Journal of Language & Communication Disorders, 37*, 289–308.

Hagen, A., Pellom, B., & Cole, R. (Dec, 2003). "Children's Speech Recognition with Application to Interactive Books and Tutors," in IEEE Automatic Speech Recognition and Understanding Workshop, St. Thomas, USA.

Hayes, E. A., Warrier, C. M., Nicol, T. G., Zecker, S. G., & Kraus, N. (2003). Neural plasticity following auditory training in children with learning problems. *Clinical Neurophysiology, 114*, 673–684.

Hook, P. E., Macaruso, P., & Jones, S. (2001). Efficacy of FastForWord training on facilitiating acquisition of reading skills by children with reading difficulties—A longitudinal study. *Annals of Dyslexia, 51*, 75–96.

Hulslander, J., Talcott, J., Witton, C., DeFries, J., Pennington, B., Wadsworth, S., Willcutt, E., & Olson, R. K. (2004). Sensory Processing, Reading, IQ, and Attention. *Journal of Experimental Child Psychology, 88*, 274–295.

Joanisse, M. F., Manis, F. R., Keating, P., & Seidenberg, M. S. (2000). Language deficits in dyslexic children: Speech perception, phonology, and morphology. *Journal of Experimental Child Psychology, 77*, 30–60.

Kintsch, E., Steinhart, D., Stahl, G., Matthews, C., & Lamb, R. (2000). "Developing summarization skills through the use of LSA-based feedback," *Interactive Learning Environments, 8*, 87–109.

Landauer, T., & Dumais, S. (1997). A solution to Plato's problem: The Latent Semantic Analysis theory of acquisition, induction and representation of knowledge, *Psychological Review, 104*, 211–240.

Lindamood, C., & Lindamood, P. (1975). *Auditory Discrimination in Depth.* Science Research associates Division, MacMillan/McGraw Hill: Columbus: OH.

Lindamood, C. H., & Lindamood, P. C. (1998). *Lindamood Phoneme Sequences Program (LIPS).* Austin, TX: PRO-ED.

Lyon, G. R., Shaywitz, S. E., & Shaywitz, B. A. (2003). A definition of dyslexia. *Annals of Dyslexia, 53*, 1–14.

Marshall, C. M., Snowling, M. J., & Bailey, P. J. (2001). Rapid auditory processing and phonological ability in normal readers with dyslexia. *Journal of Speech, Language, and Hearing Research, 44*, 925–940.

Mostow, J., Aist, G., Burkhead, P., Corbett, A., Cuneo, A., Eitelman, S., Huang, C., Junker, B., Sklar, M. B., & Tobin, B. (2003). Evaluation of an automated Reading Tutor that listens: Comparison to human tutoring and classroom instruction. *Journal of Educational Computing Research, 29*, 61–117.

Olson, R. K. (2002). Phoneme awareness and reading, from the old to the new millenium. In E. Hjelmquist and C. von Euler (Eds.), *Dyslexia and literacy: A tribute to Ingvar Lundberg* (pp. 100–116). London: Whurr Publishers.

Olson, R. (2004). SSSR, environment, and genes. *Scientific Studies of Reading. 8*(2), 111–124.

Olson, R., & Datta, H. (2002). Visual-temporal processing in reading-disabled and normal twins. *Reading and Writing, 15*, 127–149.

Olson, R. K., Foltz, G., and Wise, B. (1986a). Reading instruction and remediation using voice synthesis in computer interaction. *Proceedings of the Human Factors Society, 2*, 1336–1339.

Olson, R. K., Foltz, G., & Wise, B. (1986b). Reading instruction and remediation with the aid of computer speech. *Behavior Research Methods, Instruments, and Computers, 18*, 93–99.

Olson, R. K., & Wise, B. W. (1992). Reading on the computer with orthographic and speech feedback: An overview of the Colorado Remedial Reading Project. *Reading and Writing: An Interdisciplinary Journal, 4*, 107–144.

Organization for Economic Cooperation and Development (OECD). Program for International Student Assessment (PISA), retrieved October 21, 2004, from www.pisa.oecd.org

Palincsar, A. S., & Brown, A. L. (1984). Reciprocal teaching of comprehension-fostering and comprehension-monitoring activity. *Cognition and Instruction, 2*, 117–175.

Pellom, B. (2001). "SONIC: The University of Colorado Continuous Speech Recognizer," University of Colorado, tech report #TR-CSLR-2001-01, Boulder, Colorado, March.

Pellom, B., Hacioglu, K. (2003). "Recent Improvements in the CU SONIC ASR System for Noisy Speech: The SPINE Task," in Proceedings of IEEE International Conference on Acoustics, Speech, and Signal Processing (ICASSP), Hong Kong. April, 2003.

Pokorni, J. I., Worthington, C. K., & Jamison, P. J. (2004). Phonological awareness intervention: Comparison of Fast ForWord, Earobics, and LiPS. *The Journal of Educational Research, 97*, 147–157.

Rack, J. P., Snowling, M. J., & Olson, R. K. (1992). The nonword reading deficit in developmental dyslexia: a review. *Reading Research Quarterly, 27*, 28–53.

Ramus, F., Rosen, S., Dakin, S. C., Day, B. L., Castellote, J. M., White, S., & Frith, U. (2003). Theories of developmental dyslexia: Insights from a multiple case study of dyslexic adults. *Brain, 126*, 841–865.

Reitsma, P. (1983). Word-specific knowledge in beginning reading. *Journal of Research in Reading, 6,* 41–56.

Rosen, S. (2003). Auditory processing in dyslexia and specific language impairment: Is there a deficit? What is its nature? Does it explain anything? *Journal of Phonetics, 31,* 509–527.

Rosenthal, R. (2003). Covert communication in laboratories, classrooms, and the truly real world. *Current Directions in Psychological Science, 12,* 151–154.

Rouse, C. E., & Krueger, A. B. (2004). Putting computerized instruction to the test: A randomized evaluation of a "scientifically based" reading program. *Economics of Education Review, 23,* 323–338.

Scarborough, H. S. (2001). Connecting early language and literacy to later reading (Dis) Abilities: Evidence, theory, and practice. In S. Neuman and D. Dickinson (Eds.), *Handbook for Early Literacy Research* (pp. 97–110). NY: Guilford Press.

Segers, E., & Verhoeven, L. (2004). Computer-supported phonological awareness intervention for kindergarten children with specific language impairment. *Language, Speech, and Hearing Services in Schools, 35,* 229–239.

Share, D. L., & Stanovich, K. (1995). Cognitive processes in early reading development. *Issues in Education: Contributions from Educational Psychology, 1,* 1–35.

Share, D. L., Jorm, A. F., Maclean, R., & Matthews, R. (2002). Temporal processing and reading disability. *Reading and Writing, 15,* 151–178.

Stuart, G., McAnally, K., & Castles, A. (2001). Can contrast sensitivity functions in dyslexia be explained by inattention rather than a magnocellular deficit? *Vision Research, 41,* 3205–3211.

Summary Street. (2004). Information about Summary Street and its use in COLit. [Online]. http://lsa .colorado.edu/summarystreet/ and http://www.knowledge-technologies.com/cu.html

Tallal, P. (1980). Auditory temporal perception, phonics and reading disabilities in children. *Brain & Language, 9,* 182–198.

Tallal, P. (2003). Language learning disabilities: Integrating research approaches. *Current Directions in Psychological Science, 12* (6), 206–211.

Tallal, P., Miller, S., Bedi, G., Byma, G., Wang, X., Nagarajan, S., Schreiner, C., Jenkins, W., & Merzenich, M. (1996). Language comprehension in language-learning impaired children improved with acoustically modified speech. *Science, 271,* 81–84.

Temple, E., Deutsch, G., Poldrack, R., Miller, S., Tallal, P., Merzenich, M., & Gabrieli, J. (2003). Neural deficits in children with dyslexia ameliorated by behavioral remediation: Evidence from functional MRI. *Proceedings of the National Academy of Sciences, 100,* 2860–2865.

Tijms, J., Hoeks, J., Hoogeboom, M., & Smolenaars, A. (2003). Long-term effects of a psycholinguistic treatment for dyslexia. *Journal of Research in Reading, 26*(2), 121–140.

Torgesen, J. (2002). The prevention of reading difficulties. *Journal of School Psychology, 40,* 7–26.

Torgesen, J., Alexander, A., Wagner, R., Voeller, K., Conway, T., & Rose, E. (2001). Intensive remedial instruction for children with severe reading disabilities: Immediate and long-term outcomes from two instructional approaches. *Journal of Learning Disabilities, 34,* 33–58.

Wahl, M., Robinson, C., & Torgesen, J. (2003). Florida Center for Reading Research: Fast ForWord Language. On line report accessed 1/5/2005 at http://www.fcrr.org/FCRRReports/PDF/Fast_ForWord_ Language_Report.pdf

Wise, B., Olson, R., Anstett, M., Andrews, L., Terjak, M., Schneider, V., & Kostuch, J. (1989). Implementing a long-term computerized remedial reading program with synthetic speech feedback: Hardware, software, and real-world issues. *Behavior Research Methods, Instruments, and Computers, 21,* 173–180.

Wise, B., Ring, J., & Olson, R. K. (1999). Training phonological awareness with and without attention to articulation. *Journal of Experimental Child Psychology, 72,* 271–304.

Wise, B., Ring, J., & Olson, R. K. (2000). Individual differences in gains from computer-assisted remedial reading with more emphasis on phonological analysis or accurate reading in context. *Journal of Experimental Child Psychology, 77,* 197–235.

Wise, B., Ring, J., Sessions, L., & Olson, R. K. (1997). Phonological awareness with and without articulation: A preliminary study. *Learning Disability Quarterly, 20,* 211–225.

Wise, B., Cole, R., Van Vuuren, S., Schwartz, S., Snyder, L., Ngampatipatpong, N., Tuantranont, J., & Pellom, B. (In Press). Learning to Read with a Virtual Tutor: Foundational exercises and interactive books. In Kinzer, C., & Verhoeven, L. (Eds). *Interactive Literacy Education.* Lawrence Erlbaum.

Wood, C. (2003, June). A longitudinal study of spoken word recognition, temporal information processing awareness and literacy. Paper presented at the meeting of the Society for the Scientific Study of Reading, Boulder, CO.

Improving Struggling Readers' Comprehension Through Scaffolded Hypertexts and Other Computer-Based Literacy Programs

Bridget Dalton and Nicole Strangman
CAST, Inc.

Literacy demands are higher than at any time in our history as information and communication technologies drive our global economy and forge new means of knowledge production, application, and communication. And yet, in the United States alone there are 8.7 million students in Grades 4–12 who have little chance of developing the academic skills essential to success in a highly literate society because they are unable to read and understand their textbooks (Kamil, 2003). The results of the NAEP 2003 report underscore the urgency of the problem: 37% of students in Grade 4 and 26% of students in Grade 8 could not read at a basic level (National Center for Education Statistics, 2003). Often described as struggling readers, this group is comprised primarily of students with special needs, students who are English Language Learners, and students who are poor. For students who struggle to read, print is a traditional technology that often serves as a barrier, rather than a gateway, to learning. The damaging consequences of poor reading are pervasive and far-reaching; students shut out of grade-level curriculum read less and learn less than their typically achieving peers, resulting in the Matthew Effect, where the rich get richer and the poor get poorer (Stanovich, 1986).

Perhaps because the need is so urgent, and the promise of technology apparent, there has been a continued line of research focusing on students with reading problems (for recent reviews, see MacArthur, Ferretti, Okolo, & Cavalier, 2001; Strangman & Dalton, 2005; for a review integrating general and special-education research, see Coiro, Leu, Kinzer, Labbo, Teale, Bergman, Sulzan & Zheng, 2003). Technology and computer-mediated text have the potential to support struggling readers in two important ways: as a compensatory tool, providing access to text; and as a learning tool, helping students learn how to read with understanding. The 1997 Individual with Disabilities Education Act (IDEA) mandates that all students with disabilities have both access to the general education curriculum and make meaningful progress in that curriculum. While possible, these goals are difficult to accomplish with a print-based curriculum when many students lack the requisite literacy skills.

In contrast, the characteristics of digital text—nonlinearity, integrated media (audio, graphics, video, animations, and text), and interactivity—make it possible to transform text in multiple ways in accordance with learner needs and preferences. For example, students with decoding or fluency problems may bypass these difficulties and access materials at their grade and/or interest level via text-to-speech (TTS) or digital voice that reads aloud a word, sentence or passage. Students who lack vocabulary or background knowledge might benefit from a hyperlinked multimedia glossary or supplemental information, such as background information, an historical time line, or an explanatory animation (Anderson-Inman & Horney, 1998; Reinking, 1988), while others might learn to read strategically as they interact with texts containing embedded strategy instruction and computer avatars that function as coaches. Students who avoid reading might read more in a digital reading environment that communicates through multimedia and provides options for interacting with the text in multiple ways. In each of these cases, whether the goal is to provide access to text, or to serve an instructional role, transformation of the text in ways that potentially support and extend the capacity of the reader has redefined the traditional notion of readability (McKenna, 1998; Reinking, 1988; Rose & Dalton, 2002).

The role of computers and digital text in supporting struggling readers' comprehension is the focus of this chapter. The Rand Reading Study Group Report (Snow, 2002) defines reading comprehension as the process of simultaneously extracting and constructing meaning. In a print-based model of reading comprehension, text, reader, and activity interact as the reader, operating within a larger sociocultural context, extracts and constructs meaning. This chapter will examine how digital reading environments are redefining the relationship between the reading comprehension dimensions of text, reader, and activity in ways that potentially extend and build the capacity of the reader to engage productively with a wider range of texts at varying difficulty levels. First, we address the role of TTS and digital speech feedback as an indirect means of improving comprehension. Second, we consider research on hypertext enhanced with learning supports and other computer-based approaches to improving comprehension. Finally, we end with a presentation of key issues to address in the research and development of new digital reading technologies in today's diverse classrooms.

IMPROVING COMPREHENSION THROUGH DECODING AND FLUENCY SUPPORT

For struggling readers, weak decoding skills and lack of fluency are major impediments to comprehension (Ehri, 1994). Reading becomes an effortful process of extraction, reducing capacity for attention to meaning, which is the purpose of reading. Digital text has the capacity to bypass decoding and fluency problems via TTS functionality and digitized speech. Although implementations vary, readers typically click on a word or passage and have it read aloud, with or without synchronized highlighting (see Figure 6.1). When users click *Read* on the toolbar, the text is spoken using synthetic speech. As each word is read aloud, it is highlighted in contrasting colors. By clicking on a single word in the text, users can access syllable-level speech feedback with simultaneous highlighting

The rationale behind studies investigating the value of speech feedback for struggling readers' comprehension (Aist & Mostow, 1997; Elbro, Rasmussen, & Spelling, 1996; Lundberg & Olofsson, 1993) is that providing students more fluent access to the text will free up capacity for constructing meaning, thereby improving comprehension. At its most basic, it seems reasonable to think that TTS will serve a compensatory function, enabling struggling readers to understand a particular text that might otherwise be inaccessible. Providing access to text at students' grade and interest level would be an important outcome, ensuring access to the general education curriculum, which is the goal of recent educational reform in special education (IDEA, 1997). Another

FIGURE 6.1.   Screenshot displaying Kurzweil 3000, an example of a product offering TTS feedback and synchronized highlighting.

important outcome would be increasing students' engagement with text and, with it, their volume of reading. In addition, TTS and digital speech feedback may serve an instructional function, indirectly improving comprehension by developing word recognition skills that would facilitate more fluent reading and understanding of print texts.

The question "What is the effect of TTS on students' comprehension?" seems rather straightforward, but the research results are not. Variations in research design and technology applications make it difficult to interpret results, although there is some evidence to suggest that the instructional effect of speech feedback varies as a function of the readers' age and initial literacy levels

Corroborative research in the United States, Denmark, & Sweden has shown that reading with speech feedback positively affects comprehension (Elbro et al., 1996; Elkind, Cohen, & Murray, 1993; Lundberg & Olofsson, 1993; Mostow et al., 2003), although only two of these studies found that improvement transferred to the comprehension of text without speech feedback (Elbro et al., 1996; Mostow et al., 2003). A strong, compensatory effect was demonstrated in Elkind and colleagues' (1993) study of middle school students with dyslexia who read digital literature with TTS support for a semester using a preliminary version of Bookwise (Xerox Imaging Systems). The authors report that students were able to engage productively with the literature and that 70% of the students improved comprehension on a TTS-supported version of the Gray Oral Reading Test by approximately one grade level, with 40% achieving gains of two-to-five grade levels. However, this improvement did not transfer to performance when tested without TTS support. Elkind et al. also found that not all students benefited from TTS; 14% decreased performance when tested in this medium, perhaps due to kinesthetic motor weaknesses (Elkind et al., 1993).

The latter finding highlights the importance of looking beyond group results to examine effects on individual learners, since there are likely to be important differences in learner attributes that will influence outcomes. For example, Lundberg and Olofsson (1993) found that Scandinavian students with reading disabilities in Grades 4–6 improved comprehension when reading text with TTS support, while students in Grades 2–3 did not. The teachers in the study suggested that the older students benefited more from the use of TTS because they were reading more challenging texts with a higher percentage of complex, multisyllabic words, and thus the

TTS was more beneficial in closing the gap between their decoding level and the reading level of the text. Another explanation may be that the younger students were not as strategic in using speech feedback. In a series of studies, Mckenna and Watkins (1994, cited in McKenna, 1998) found that kindergarten and first-grade children reading talking books often underaccessed or overaccessed speech pronunciations and decoding help.

The use of speech feedback may be structured in a way that encourages a more active experience, and this may strengthen the positive impact on reading comprehension. For example, Elbro et al. (1996) found a remedial effect of TTS for Danish students with reading and language disabilities who read with TTS support for 20 minutes a day for 40 days. Students' experience with TTS was enhanced in this study. Rather than clicking on a word and having it read aloud, students were presented the word broken into visual and auditory segments (either by syllable or letter names). Then, they had to attempt their own pronunciation before clicking on the word and hearing the word pronounced. This is a far more active experience for the reader than simply listening to a word or passage and may well have been a factor in the positive transfer results. When tested with a standardized reading achievement test, students outperformed a control group who had received traditional reading remediation.

However, not all learners may benefit from efforts to improve the value and use of speech feedback. For example, McKenna and Watkins (1994, cited in McKenna, 1998) embedded instructional feedback within the TTS feedback offered in talking books. When students clicked on a word for pronunciation help, they received phonics analogies feedback. McKenna and Watkins found that many of the K–1 students in their study were so distracted by the phonics analogies feedback that they could not follow the story. McKenna and Watkins continued to explore variations of types of speech feedback support with and without accompanying instructional feedback in primary classrooms with learners representing a wide range of beginning reading skills (McKenna & Watkins, 1995; 1996, cited in McKenna, 1998). These studies did not report effects on comprehension, but they are worth mentioning because they point to the importance of examining the relationship between learner attributes and digital text features. McKenna and Watkins concluded that students needed alphabetic knowledge and a minimal level of sight vocabulary to realize improvements in incidental word recognition. Further, they found that relying on students' independent accessing of word pronunciation support was problematic since students tended to access words they already knew and to not access words they did not know. They also observed that contextualizing phonics analogy support in the reading of authentic text did not result in learning transfer.

Studies by Mostow and Aist and their colleagues at Carnegie Mellon's Project Listen (http://www–2.cs.cmu.edu/~listen/) further underscore the relevance of learner characteristics to the impact of decoding and fluency interventions on reading comprehension. Over several years they have designed and tested an interactive Reading Tutor for struggling readers that uses speech recognition to listen to students' oral reading of connected text and offer instructional feedback. Students may also use the Reading Tutor to write or dictate their own texts (Mostow, Aist, Burkhead, Corbett, Cuneo, Eitelman, Huang, Junker, Sklar, & Tobin, 2003). While students may access help on their own, the Reading Tutor also initiates a variety of support based on its evaluation of students' reading accuracy. For example, the Reading Tutor might read a word or sentence aloud or provide audio and graphical support to sound out, syllabify, rhyme, or spell words. In an early descriptive study of six low achieving third grade students using the Reading Tutor under the supervision of an aide, Aist and Mostow (1997) found that students made two years of progress in 8 months on an informal reading inventory administered before and after treatment. Subsequently, Aist and Mostow added features so that students could use the software independently and tested it in a year-long experimental study. The study compared the effects of daily

20 minute sessions of the Reading Tutor, tutoring with a certified teacher, and regular classroom instruction on 131 struggling readers in 12 Grade 2 and 3 urban classrooms (Mostow et al, 2003). Results of the Woodcock Reading Mastery Test indicate that the human-tutored group outperformed the Reading Tutor group in word attack only, with students making comparable gains in word identification, word comprehension, and passage comprehension. In Grade 3, students in both the human- and computer-tutored groups made significantly greater gains than the control group in word comprehension, with a trend for improved passage comprehension. It is important to note that Grade 3 students in the control group did not make progress relative to the norm group on any subtest, while both the human- and computer-tutored groups grew at a significantly faster rate than the norm group on word comprehension and passage comprehension. This progress relative to the norm group was weaker for second graders, providing additional evidence that there are likely to be important interaction effects for learner characteristics.

Other research on speech recognition has produced positive results. Raskind and Higgins (Higgins & Raskind, 2000; Raskind & Higgins, 1999) found that students with learning disabilities (ages 9–18) who performed writing exercises with the use of discrete—but not continuous—speech recognition, improved reading comprehension, as well as targeted phonemic awareness and decoding skills.

Another indirect approach to improving reading comprehension is training in word recognition. There have been some studies of computer software programs designed to increase automatic word recognition for students with reading disabilities that resulted in transfer to improved comprehension at the sentence (Holt-Ochsner, 1992) and passage level (Lundberg, 1995). Lundberg and Olofsson (1993) used their word recognition instructional software with a 15-year-old boy with severe reading disabilities who was deemed illiterate. After a year using the software, the boy was able to read the newspaper and short stories, a significant and potentially life-altering achievement for this individual. A study in the Netherlands investigated the impact of a pseudoword naming program on sentence comprehension, but the presence of a ceiling effect undermined any meaningful conclusions in this regard (van den Bosch, van Bon, & Schreuder, 1995).

In contrast to these studies that report beneficial outcomes of fluency and decoding support on reading comprehension, a number of researchers have found that decoding support in the form of TTS has no effect on comprehension (Farmer, Klein, & Bryson, 1992; Leong, 1995; Wise & Olson, 1995; Wise, Ring, & Olson, 1999, 2000). These studies varied in important ways such as student population, type of TTS used, duration of the intervention, comparison condition, and experimental measures; there does not appear to be a common pattern that might explain the lack of results.

In summary, the research does not yield a single answer to the question "Does TTS/voice audio and fluency support improve struggling readers' comprehension?" There are promising findings regarding the effectiveness of speech recognition and word recognition training programs, but these kinds of interventions are under-researched. The TTS literature offers many positive findings in different international settings, but it also offers strong suggestions that the effectiveness of TTS interventions may depend on a number of variables. These may include the age and initial literacy skills of the learner and the gap between the learner's independent or instructional reading level and the level of the text. For middle grade and secondary students who are reading substantially below grade level, TTS offers access to age appropriate text. In comparison to primary grade students, they are more likely to experience a gap between what they want and need to read and what they are able to read on their own, and thus may use TTS support to greater advantage. It is also likely that older students are more strategic than their younger peers in accessing supports appropriately. At the same time, if the text is too challenging, containing unfamiliar vocabulary and concepts, complex syntax, or requiring background knowledge that students do not have, simply having access to the text via TTS will not suffice. Just as many of us may decode the words in an advanced physics text with limited comprehension, a student with reading disabilities may be able to "hear" the words via TTS and not have the requisite vocabulary or background knowledge to make sense of the text. Further, while older students may be more strategic than younger students, struggling readers may still lack sufficient metacognitive skills to make good decisions about when to access TTS support.

The duration of treatment also seems to be an important factor in the effectiveness of TTS use. Two of the studies reporting positive impact on students' comprehension took place over several months. That raises the possibility that the increase in volume of reading made possible by TTS accounts, at least in part, for the positive effect on comprehension.

It is not necessary to design a digital environment as one size fits all. TTS can be a meaningful part of a more flexible, individually supportive approach. It is possible, and we would argue, desirable, to build in supports to accommodate the needs of the full range of learners encountered in today's diverse classrooms. IDEA mandates that all students have access to the general education curriculum. This means that students with decoding problems should be reading the same texts as their typically achieving peers. They can no longer be relegated to reading high-interest/low readability books (which often belie the term high interest) or as is often the case, reading worksheets rather than authentic text. TTS makes it possible for many struggling readers to read grade-level material. This is not to suggest that students only read grade-level material in a digitally supported context. At the same time they are reading age-appropriate material with TTS support, they would benefit from direct instruction to improve decoding and fluency with material at their instructional and independent levels.

IMPROVING COMPREHENSION THROUGH ENHANCED HYPERTEXTS AND OTHER COMPUTER-BASED INTERVENTIONS

Readers struggle for many reasons other than weak decoding and fluency. Unfamiliar vocabulary and concepts, complex syntax, lack of background knowledge, and unfamiliar text structures may all interfere with comprehension (Gaskins, 2003; Lipson & Wixson, 1997). Struggling readers also tend to be less strategic in their approach to text, lacking a flexible repertoire of strategies that can be deployed to accomplish a variety of reading purposes (Graham & Harris, 1996). Monitoring understanding and knowing when and how to seek resolution to textual confusion is a challenge (Swanson & Alexander, 1997). Not surprisingly, many struggling readers do not view themselves as in charge of their learning and may avoid reading whenever possible.

There is a promising body of research investigating the potential of digital text to function as a scaffolded learning environment, providing supports to students with diverse learning needs. Digital learning environments, by virtue of the flexibility of the medium, have the potential to scaffold instruction in a rich variety of ways. For example, images and animated graphics can be incorporated into digital texts to supplement textual definitions, supporting vocabulary understanding and reading comprehension (Anderson-Inman, Horney, Chen, & Lewin, 1994; Boone & Higgins, 1993). Texts can be electronically altered to offer strategic scaffolds such as note-taking tools, self-monitoring questions, and graphic-organizer overviews (Anderson-Inman & Horney, 1998). These features provide focused support that enables students to focus on one essential aspect of a task at a time and work in their zone of proximal development (Vygotsky, 1978). And all these features can be accessed or not, depending on the student's needs and interests, providing a way to gradually remove support as it is no longer needed. They offer supportive rather than directive scaffolding, offering support tailored to specific learner needs (Dennen, 2004). Several valuable frameworks have been developed for describing and organizing digital learning scaffolds.

Anderson-Inman and Horney (1998) describe a useful taxonomy of eight types of supports, five of which focus on content representation (translational, illustrative, secondary, summarizing, general purpose) and three of which support students in manipulating content and/or expressing their understanding (instructional, collaborative, notational and structural).

Others have proposed a cognitive apprenticeship framework to describe scaffolded reading environments that guide students in actively constructing meaning from authentic texts and support them in developing important metacognitive skills (Cognition and Technology Group & Vanderbilt Learning Technology Center, 1993; Collins, Brown, & Newman, 1989). Several design features characterize a cognitive apprenticeship model: reading processes are made explicit for the learner via modeling and demonstration, skills are developed in the context of reading connected text with multiple opportunities for feedback and practice, support is scaffolded, fading as competence increases, and learners engage in self-reflection and exercise increasing control over their learning as they become more proficient. There is the expectation that students will internalize needed skills and dispositions, and will be able to transfer them to the reading of other texts, both print and digital.

A cognitive apprenticeship model is also associated with Universal Design for Learning (UDL) (Meyer & Rose, 1998; Rose & Meyer, 2002). The concept of universal design originated in the field of architecture, where it is now accepted practice to design physical structures and spaces so that all users, including those with disabilities, have full access. Curb cuts and captioned TV are two examples of universally designed applications that were initially created for individuals with disabilities and that now benefit the mainstream population. Universal Design for Learning applies this concept to the design of text and other instructional materials and practices, making a similar case that all learners benefit when curricula are designed from their inception with the broadest range of learners in mind.

The UDL framework draws upon the work of Lev Vygotsky (1978) and recent advances in the neurosciences regarding how the brain processes information. Developments in brain research suggest that the three essential elements of learning identified by Vygotsky (recognition of the information to be learned, application of strategies to process that information, and engagement with the learning task) are overseen by three sets of learning networks in the brain: recognition networks, strategic networks, and affective networks (Rose & Meyer, 2002). Individual differences in these networks lead to considerable person-to-person differences in how students access, use, and engage with learning materials. There is also considerable within-person variation, depending on the interplay of learner, task, and activity variables, represented by Vygotsky's (1978) notion of the zone of proximal development. Three principles provide a foundation for Universal Design for Learning: (1) To support students' diverse recognition networks, provide multiple means of representation; (2) to support students' diverse strategic networks, provide multiple means of expression within a cognitive apprenticeship environment; and (3) to support students' diverse affective networks, provide multiple means of engagement (Rose & Meyer, 2002).

Hypertext Research

The research on hypertext (sometimes referred to as computer-mediated text, hypermedia, integrated media and hypertext) comprehension in K–12 settings has focused primarily on enhancing an existing piece of literature or textbook with hyperlinked resources and supports. In contrast, very little is known about students' comprehension of hypertexts that are designed as non-linear multimedia reading experiences, such as informational web pages and hypertext stories with multiple decision points that allow the reader to construct one of several possible story paths and outcomes.

Boone and Higgins (1993) carried out a series of hypertext investigations with students with learning disabilities and other struggling readers. Their initial research focused on K–3 students' use of a hypertext version of basal reader stories as a supplement to the students' core literacy curriculum. The hypertexts were developed over three years: Year 1 hypertexts included links to a multimedia glossary and decoding supports; Year 2 hypertexts added anaphoric reference support; and Year 3 added comprehension strategy support, such as summarizing or rereading the text. Questions were embedded within the text, with incorrect responses generating instructional feedback (e.g., highlighting the relevant information from the passage). The results varied across grade level and year of study, with low achieving students in the experimental group significantly outperforming students in the control group on a standardized reading achievement test in Grades K, 2, and 3 in Year 1; in Grades 1, 2, and 3 in Year 2; and in Grade K in Year 3. The lack of results in Year 3 is difficult to interpret and suggests the complexity of designing multifaceted support systems for diverse learners.

In a year-long study of urban fourth and fifth graders, including many of whom were struggling readers, Moore-Hart (1995) found that students using Multicultural Links, a hypermedia program with a variety of content resources about different cultures (including Japanese, Chinese, French, African, and British) and a word-processing program, gained higher scores on the California Achievement Test than did students using the Multicultural program without the computer supports, or students in a control group. However, the report does not indicate whether these differences were statistically significant.

Reinking and Schreiner (1985) and Reinking (1988) investigated fourth and fifth grade good and poor readers' comprehension of hypertexts with four types of comprehension support: vocabulary definitions, passage paraphrases at a lower readability level, additional background information, and a main idea statement. In one of the few studies to manipulate user versus computer control of help access, they found that good and poor readers learned more when they were required to use all of the enhancements (Reinking & Schreiner, 1985). However, a follow-up study found that user control was not a factor, with good and poor readers obtaining similar comprehension benefits from the two versions of the enhanced hypertexts (Reinking, 1988). In light of these mixed findings, the notion of student control over accessing resources is an important area to continue to study.

There is additional disagreement in the hypertext research literature. In contrast to the beneficial impact of supported hypertexts demonstrated in the above studies, two other studies of students in Grades 4–6 did not find any treatment effects for enhanced hypertexts (Leong, 1995; Swanson & Trahan, 1992). Leong (1995) found that average and below average Canadian readers' passage comprehension did not vary as a function of four different types of support: TTS, TTS with vocabulary explanations, TTS with vocabulary explanations and reading awareness prompts, and TTS with lower readability passages. In another study, students with learning disabilities and their typically achieving peers also failed to benefit from a re-reading enhancement feature (Swanson & Trahan, 1992).

For struggling adolescent readers, who may be reading several years below grade level, access to grade and age appropriate text is particularly problematic. Two important studies have targeted research at this population of readers. Results here are also somewhat mixed. MacArthur and Haynes (1995) developed two hypertext versions of a tenth grade biology chapter, a basic version that presented the digital equivalent of the printed textbook with an online notebook for students to take notes as they studied, and an enhanced version that added TTS, an online glossary, links between questions and text, main idea highlighting, and explanations summarizing key ideas. Students with learning disabilities and low achieving students using the enhanced hypertext demonstrated significantly greater comprehension than their peers reading the basic hypertext, suggesting that students were able to use supports productively, although it is not possible to determine which supports were most useful.

Higgins, Boone, and Lovitt (1996) also targeted high-school content literacy, developing history textbook chapter hypertext study guides for struggling readers that included links to explanatory information, provided simpler substitutions for selected vocabulary and phrases, and embedded comprehension questions. Each screen presented comprehension questions with corrective feedback, and students could not progress to a new screen until they had answered correctly. Comparison of students in hypertext versus hypertext-plus-lecture versus lecture-only conditions indicated that students with learning disabilities tended to obtain higher test retention scores in the hypertext-plus-lecture condition than in the hypertext condition and did least well in the lecture-only condition. Remedial students similarly did least well in the lecture-only condition, while obtaining comparable scores in both the hypertext and hypertext-plus-lecture conditions. However, none of these results were significant, perhaps due to the small sample size.

Much of the existing hypertext research with struggling readers has focused on supporting students' access to the text and learning of specific content, with some attention to cognitive and metacognitive processing. Further, most applications have provided a range of supports that are either presented to all readers, regardless of need, and/or are student selected, allowing the user to determine the level of support needed. The Universal Design for Learning Group at CAST has taken a different approach, developing a scaffolded hypertext reading environment for struggling readers, entitled Thinking Reader, that provides several levels of support (Dalton et al., 2002).

Drawing on principles of UDL (Rose & Meyer, 2002; Rose & Dalton, 2002) and research-based strategy instruction (Palincsar and Brown, 1984), the Thinking Reader is designed to improve students' reading comprehension and engagement. Figure 6.2 illustrates the various supports available in a Thinking Reader version currently under study. Supports include TTS, a multimedia glossary, background knowledge links, and embedded strategy instruction. As students read the text, they are periodically prompted to "stop and think" and apply one of the reading strategies they have learned, such as predicting, clarifying, questioning, summarizing, and visualizing, to connect in a personal way to the text, and to self-reflect on their progress as a reader.

Strategy coaches in the form of computer avatars (an animated virtual 3D character) offer strategy hints, model responses, and think alouds. Students type, or in some cases, audio-record, their responses, which are captured in a work log that can be accessed at any point by the student and teacher and which serves as a concrete artifact of their thinking and progress for self-reflection and evaluation purposes. Students' strategic learning of the strategies is scaffolded by varying the amount and type of help provided by the coach and the modality and structure of the student response format. For example, coaches provide text-specific models at level 1 and generic hints at level 4. Similarly, since summaries are the most challenging for students to learn, they move from a closed format (identifying the best summary) to a constructed format (constructing a summary based on key points presented in a list) to an open format (writing a summary independently). In contrast, predictions are open-ended at all levels, since even the weakest students are able to generate predictions that they can evaluate and revise as they read further in the text. And finally, the mode of response is varied to accommodate students who might benefit from the option to audio-record their response, rather than write it (Dalton & Herbert, 2003).

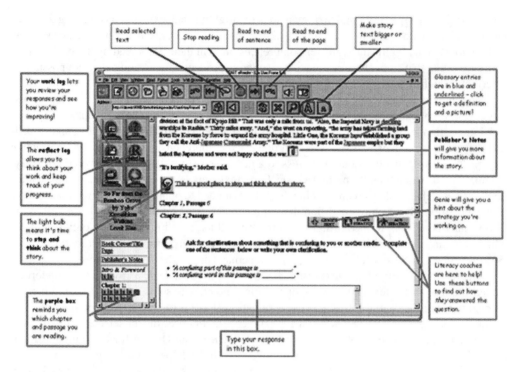

FIGURE 6.2.   Student guide sheet with screen shot of the 2002–3 version of CAST's Thinking Reader, a universally-designed digital reading environment.

Research on Version 1 of the Thinking Reader with 102 middle school students reading at the 25th percentile and below compared two instructional treatments—reciprocal teaching with Thinking Reader versions of three highly appealing novels versus reciprocal teaching with print versions of the same novels (Dalton et al., 2002). Controlling for initial reading levels and gender, students in the Thinking Reader group made significantly greater gains in reading achievement on the Gates-MacGinitie Reading Achievement Test than did students in the strategy instruction group. Although it is not possible to determine what specific aspect(s) of the Thinking Reader approach contributed to students' greater success, these findings suggest that addition of digitized flexible, leveled supports and an engaging multimedia environment to the reciprocal teaching methodology can improve students' ability to develop comprehension skills. To learn more about the impact of such digital reading environments on specific populations, Dalton and colleagues are continuing to refine and expand the Thinking Reader in studies of children in primary, intermediate and middle school grades, with students who are English Language Learners, students with reading disabilities, and students with severe cognitive disabilities, and with informational and narrative text.

The Internet is another important avenue to providing students with flexible approaches to content. In a series of descriptive studies, Anderson-Inman and Horney designed hypertexts and electronic study tools for struggling readers, including students with learning disabilities, students who are deaf or hard of hearing, and children of migrant workers. For their federally funded initiative Project Intersect, they are creating a set of online digital books, offering a wide variety of resources to support reading comprehension, including background information, glossary entries, and ideas for reading strategies (Anderson-Inman, Horney, & Blair, 1991–2001). Figure 6.3

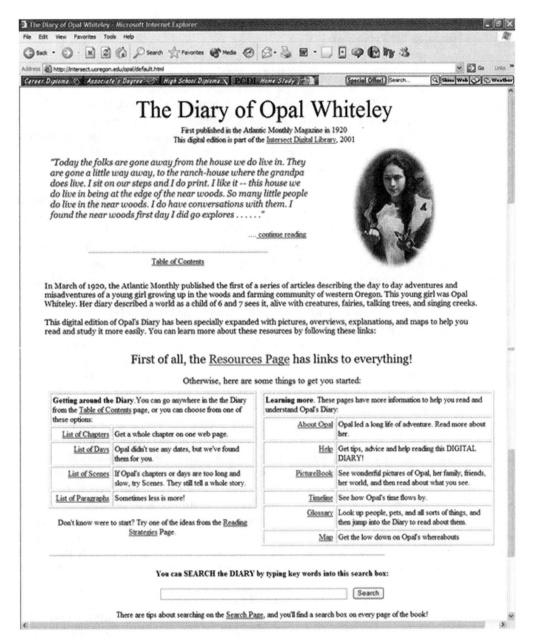

FIGURE 6.3.   Screen shot of The Diary of Opal Whiteley web site (Anderson-Inman and Horney, Project Intersect).

shows a screenshot from their online version of the Diary of Opal Whiteley, a young girl living in western Oregon at the turn of the 20th century. It is an excellent illustration of how a Web-based hypertext can provide multiple avenues into content, providing background knowledge and extending connections between Opal's world and that of the larger society. There are as yet no published data with which to directly gauge these texts' effectiveness for improving reading comprehension, but texts such as these are worthy of study.

Developing Reading Comprehension with Computer
Software Instructional Programs

Another fruitful approach to improving reading comprehension is through the development of comprehensive technology-based programs that address various components of reading. One illustrative model is RAVE-O (Retrieval, Automaticity, Vocabulary, Elaboration, and Orthography), a beginning reader intervention program developed by Maryanne Wolf and colleagues (Wolf and Katzir-Cohen, 2001; Wolf, Miller, & Donnelly, 2000). RAVE-O is designed to develop fluency in the reading outcomes of word identification, word attack, and comprehension, while also building automaticity in the underlying reading processes of visual recognition, auditory recognition, semantic development, and lexical retrieval. It includes both on and offline instructional activities, and addresses metacognitive and motivational issues. The results of a series of experimental studies have been impressive, with RAVE-O significantly improving the reading comprehension of beginning readers with reading disabilities (Wolf, 2001).

Positive comprehension results have also been found with two other comprehensive reading programs. Lynch, Fawcett, and Nicolson (2000) developed RITA, a computer-based literacy system that includes computerized, curriculum-based activities in phonics, fluency, vocabulary, spelling, and comprehension and tested it with eight struggling readers in the UK. The researchers derived a set of RITA activities for each of the eight readers based on their IEP goals (including basic phonics, sound differentiation, word attack, spelling, and comprehension). In this way, computer time focused on students' individual needs. Students significantly improved comprehension and demonstrated meaningful progress toward IEP goals. Another study of a computer-supported comprehensive literacy program for first grade students demonstrated greater comprehension for the computer users versus a control group, but the effect was only significant for males (Erdner, Guy, & Bush, 1998).

Hypertext is here to stay. Its design and form will continue to evolve as information communication technologies advance, and it is likely to look and function quite differently 10 years from now. Kress (2003), Lemke (1998), and others suggest oral and visual communication forms will become increasingly important in integrated media environments, with written verbal text losing its currently privileged status. Our challenge will be to advance research commensurately so that all students, and especially those currently viewed as struggling readers, are able to successfully read, view, and learn in diverse digital literacy environments. While the research results on hypertext enhancements to date are somewhat variable, there is a growing body of support for improving struggling readers' comprehension by embedding supports that are tied to the various sources of comprehension difficulty, and particularly for struggling readers at the intermediate grade levels and above.

However, we know very little about which supports work best for which students, and in relation to different types of texts and reading tasks. This should be a major area of investigation. There is some research to suggest that the very students who would benefit most from supports are least likely to access them appropriately (Anderson-Inman, Horney, Chen, & Lewin, 1994; Horney & Anderson-Inman, 1999; McKenna, 1998; van Daal & Reitsma, 1993). The degree of control over a hypertext environment is an equally important target for research, as available research is divided on the issue.

Studies that focus on hypertexts that teach students how to learn and to become more strategic in their use of the various supports available to them are also needed. The need is further heightened when you consider that digital texts are in a state of constant evolution, requiring the learner to adapt accordingly. Leu & Kinzer (2000) make a compelling argument that success in the rapidly evolving new digital literacies environments will go to those learners who are highly strategic and metacognitive, traits that are areas of weakness for many struggling readers, and especially those with learning disabilities. And very little work has focused on how digital text can support students' responses in these environments, especially in relation to response modalities and levels of structure. With just a few exceptions, students have been limited to answering multiple choice comprehension questions embedded in the hypertext or writing in an electronic notepad. The opportunity to respond to text by other means, such as audio-recording, constructing and manipulating graphics, or interacting with video are prime areas for investigation.

The goal, as stated previously, is not to design one optimal hypertext learning environment, but rather to design learning environments that can be customized for the full range of individual learners. There is a danger in making instructional design decisions that do not address the needs of learners traditionally considered *outliers*, since it is often those students who push us to new solutions (Rose & Meyer, 2002). Reporting overall results based on group means can mask important effects on individual students. The flexibility of digital environments potentially frees us from making decisions based on what works on average, enabling us to base them instead on what works for a particular student in a particular reading context.

IMPROVING COMPREHENSION THROUGH SUPPORTS FOR ENGAGEMENT AND MOTIVATION

Engagement is clearly an important literacy outcome for reading in digital environments. While little research has directly focused on this as an outcome, there are many descriptive accounts in the United States and Sweden of struggling readers' increased engagement while reading on the computer (Dalton & Coyne, 2002; Dalton et al., 2002; Heimann et al., 1995; Lewin, 1997; 2000; Lundberg & Olofsson, 1993; Montali & Lewandowski, 1996; Xin et al., 1996). In addition to the novelty effect, potential sources of students' positive affective response to digital texts include the integration of multiple media, varied levels of decoding and comprehension supports that provide an optimal mix of challenge and support, and student opportunities for control and choice. However, some studies argue against these possibilities (Elkind et al., 1993; Moore-Hart, 1995). Further, students' engagement may be at a surface level and not reflect an in-depth connection to the content or task (Horney & Anderson-Inman, 1994). On a positive note, in one of the few studies to directly examine the role of engagement in improving comprehension, Reinking and Watkins (2000) found that some of the struggling readers in their study became more engaged in reading as a result of creating multimedia book reviews to share in a class database and also made gains in reading comprehension.

Despite the lack of empirical research, it seems clear from descriptive accounts that struggling readers enjoy reading on the computer. This is not surprising, given that the alternative for these students is reading print texts that are either far above their reading level, or below their grade and interest level. Much work is needed to be done in this area, especially given the decreasing levels of engagement evidenced by struggling readers as they advance through the grades. It will be important to learn more about the features, and combinations of features, that prove motivating for different learners, and to identify those which not only heighten engagement, but also result in improved comprehension outcomes. The text and activity will be mediating variables to consider, since it is less likely that students will view digital reading environments positively if they perceive the text to be boring or the task as simply another school assignment.

CONCLUSIONS

New technologies offer great opportunity and great challenge. While the research is somewhat equivocal, international research studies create an overall picture for struggling readers that is quite optimistic. These studies demonstrate the positive effects of TTS, hypertexts enhanced with access and learning supports, as well as other more comprehensive computer programs. However, there are numerous areas that need further investigation, in particular the issue of learner control in digital environments, the role of sociocultural factors, and the relationship between various individual learner characteristics and the impact of digital comprehension supports.

Technology-based literacy is deictic in nature (Leu, 2002), rendering our usual approach to developing a research base infeasible. It is no longer feasible, or desirable, to carry out multiple replications of a particular intervention, given the rapid development of the underlying technology base. We will need to move forward more quickly than we are used to. Technology can be not only the focus for research but also a research tool. We have not taken advantage of the capability of technology to track and analyze students' use of support systems and to relate patterns of use with learning outcomes, student factors, text factors, activity factors, and sociocultural factors. Nor have we taken advantage of the options for developing a shared database of results that would allow us to mine results across studies to answer questions about the effects of various design features. This would require greater specification regarding learner, text, activity, and technology characteristics.

And finally, there is virtually no research that has examined the effect of providing struggling readers more comprehensive access to technology-based literacy support. What would it mean if struggling readers had their entire curriculum available in a universally-designed digital format? How would the usual educational projectory of a struggling reader change if from the very beginning of their schooling they were allowed to learn in a digital literacy environment that adapted dynamically to their needs and interests? States are now requiring that educational publishers provide accessible versions of their curricula for students with disabilities, with great interest in the potential to embed in these curricula learning and assessment supports, as well as supports for professional development. While these requirements are currently targeted to students with disabilities who meet specific eligibility criteria, it is reasonable to assume that once these kinds of materials are available in schools, teachers will want to apply them to the broader range of students that they teach.

This larger shift in the educational publishing landscape is currently underway with the creation of the National Instructional Materials Accessibilty Standard (NIMAS) (http://www.cast.org/ncac/NationalFileFormat3138.cfm). Under the auspices of the U.S. Department of Education, Rose and the Universal Design for Learning Group at CAST led a panel of 40 education experts, disability advocates, technical experts, textbook publishers, and the School Division of the American Association of Publishers to establish a new standard for the provision of digital textbooks (Rose, personal communication, 2003). This strongly suggests that educational textbook publishers will be working to bring accessible digital offerings to market and providing content in a manner that will need to be made usable by all learners. To inform this new movement in educational publishing of digital textbooks, Web sites, and other educational materials a strong program of research and development in technology and struggling readers will be required.

Finally, the recent NAEP results (NCES, 2003) present an incomplete picture of students' literacy achievement, for they do not tell us how students are reading and understanding the new texts they encounter on the Internet (Leu & Kinzer, 2000). More than 75% of 12- to 17-year-olds use the Internet to accomplish such varied purposes as e-mailing and instant-messaging friends, downloading music, and conducting educational research (Pew Internet & American Life

Project, 2003). Further, Internet-savvy teens who rely on the Web to accomplish school work complain that their teachers either are not aware of, or do not use to full advantage, the teaching and learning resources available on the Web. For the most part, students are turned loose on the Internet with very little instruction and support in how to successfully learn and navigate in that complex literacy environment. While there is very little research on struggling readers' comprehension on the Internet, it is likely that difficulties with traditional print literacies will carry over, and perhaps be compounded by the additional demands of searching, evaluating, and integrating information across multiple sources and in multiple media formats (Eagleton, Guinee, & Langlais, 2003; Leu, 2000). At the same time, the Internet offers affordances that may allow struggling readers to engage more productively in learning, especially if they are provided supports to access content and actively construct meaning. Research is needed to ensure that we do not create even more struggling readers, or worse yet, new categories of readers who fail to thrive in the digital literacy place of their future.

REFERENCES

Aist, G. S., & Mostow, J. (1997). *Adapting human tutorial interventions for a reading tutor that listens: Using continuous speech recognition in interactive educational multimedia.* Paper presented at the CALL'97 Conference on Multimedia, Exeter, England.

Anderson, L. M., Horney, M., & Blair, J. (1999–2001). *Project intersect and the intersect digital library.* Retrieved April 8, 2005, from http://intersect.uoregon.edu/default.html

Anderson-Inman, L., & Horney, M. A. (1998). Transforming text for at-risk readers. In D. Reinking & M. C. McKenna (Eds.), *Handbook of literacy and technology: Transformations in a post-typographic world.* (pp. 15–43). Mahwah, NJ: Lawrence Erlbaum Associates.

Anderson-Inman, L., Horney, M. A., Chen, D., & Lewin, L. (1994). Hypertext literacy: Observations from the electrotext project. *Language Arts, 71*(4), 37–45.

Boone, R., & Higgins, K. (1993). Hypermedia basal readers: Three years of school-based research. *Journal of Special Education Technology, 12*(2), 86–106.

Cognition and Technology Group & Vanderbilt Learning Technology Center. (1993). Examining the cognitive challenges and pedagogical opportunities of integrated media systems: Toward a research agenda. *Journal of Special Education Technology, 12*(2), 118–124.

Coiro, J., Leu, D. J., Kinzer, C. K., Labbo, L., Teale, W., Bergman, L., Sulzen, J., & Zheng, D. (2003). *A review of research on literacy and technology: Replicating and extending the NRP subcommittee report on computer technology and reading instruction.* Paper presented at the 53rd Annual Meeting of the National Reading Conference, Arizona.

Collins, A., Brown, J. S., & Newman, S. E. (1989). Cognitive apprenticeship: Teaching the craft of reading, writing, and mathematics. In L. B. Resnick (Ed.), *Knowing, learning and instruction: Essays in honor of Robert Glaser* (pp. 453–494). Hillsdale, NJ: Lawrence Erlbaum Associates.

Dalton, B., & Coyne, P. (2002). Universally designed digital picture books to support beginning reading in children with cognitive disabilities, *52nd Annual Meeting of the National Reading Conference.* San Antonio, Texas.

Dalton, B., & Herbert, M. (2003, December). *Scaffolding students' response to digital literature with embedded strategy supports: The role of audio-recording vs. Written response options.* Paper presented at the 53rd Annual Meeting of the National Reading Conference, Arizona.

Dennen, V. P. (2004). Cognitive apprenticeship in educational practice: Research on scaffolding, modeling, mentoring, and coaching as instructional strategies. In *Handbook of research on educational communications and technology* (2nd ed., pp. 813–828). Mahwah, NJ: Lawrence Erlbaum Associates.

Eagleton, M. B., Guinee, K., & Langlais, K. (2003). Teaching Internet literacy strategies: The hero inquiry project. *Voices from the Middle, 10*(3), 28–35.

Ehri, L. C. (1994). Development of the ability to read words: Update. In R. B. Ruddell & M. R. Ruddell (Eds.), *Theoretical models and processes of reading (4th ed.)*. (pp. 323–358): International Reading Association.

Elbro, C., Rasmussen, I., & Spelling, B. (1996). Teaching reading to disabled readers with language disorders: A controlled evaluation of synthetic speech feedback. *Scandinavian Journal of Psychology, 37*, 140–155.

Elkind, J., Cohen, K., & Murray, C. (1993). Using computer-based readers to improve reading comprehension of students with dyslexia. *Annals of Dyslexia, 43*, 238–259.

Erdner, R. A., Guy, R. F., & Bush, A. (1998). The impact of a year of computer assisted instruction on the development of first grade learning skills. *Journal of Educational Computing Research, 18*(4), 369–386.

Farmer, M. E., Klein, R., & Bryson, S. E. (1992). Computer-assisted reading: Effects of whole-word feedback on fluency and comprehension in readers with severe disabilities. *Remedial and Special Education, 13*(2), 50–60.

Gaskins, I. (2003). Taking charge of reader, text, activity and context variables. In A. P. Sweet & C. E. Snow (Eds.), *Rethinking reading comprehension* (pp. 141–165). New York: Guilford Press.

Graham, S., & Harris, K. R. (1996). Addressing problems in attention, memory, and executive functioning: An example from self-regulated strategy development. In G. R. Lyon & N. A. Krasnegor (Eds.), *Attention, memory, and executive function* (pp. 349–365): Paul H. Brookes Publishing Co.

Heimann, M., Nelson, K. E., Tjus, T., & Gillberg, C. (1995). Increasing reading and communication skills in children with autism through an interactive multimedia computer program. *Journal of Autism and Development Disorders, 25*(5), 459–481.

Higgins, K., Boone, R., & Lovitt, T. (1996). Hypertext support for remedial students and students with learning disabilities. *Journal of Learning Disabilities, 29*(4), 402–412.

Higgins, E. L., & Raskind, M. H. (2000). Speaking to read: The effects of continuous vs. Discrete speech recognition systems on the reading and spelling of children with learning disabilities. *Journal of Special Education Technology, 15*(1), 19–30.

Holt-Ochsner. (1992). Automaticity training for dyslexics: An experimental study. *Annals of Dyslexia, 42*, 222–241.

Horney, M. A., & Anderson-Inman, L. (1994). The electrotext project: Hypertext reading patterns of middle school students. *Journal of Educational Multimedia and Hypermedia, 3*(1), 71–91.

Horney, M. A., & Anderson-Inman, L. (1999). Supported text in electronic reading environments. *Reading & Writing Quarterly, 15*(2), 127–168.

Individual with disabilities education act. (1997).

Kamil, M. L. (2003). Adolescents and literacy: Reading for the 21st century. Washington, D.C.: Alliance for Excellent Education.

Kress, G. (2003). *Literacy in the new media age*. London: Routledge.

Lemke, J. L. (1998). Metamedia literacy: Transforming meanings and media. In D. Reinking, M. C. McKenna, L. D. Labbo & R. D. Kieffer (Eds.), *Handbook of literacy and technology: Transformations in a post-typographic world*. (pp. 283–301). Mahwah, NJ: Lawrence Erlbaum Associates.

Leong, C. K. (1995). Effects of on-line reading and simultaneous dectalk auding in helping below-average and poor readers comprehend and summarize text. *Learning Disability Quarterly, 18*, 101–116.

Leu Jr., D. J. (2002). Internet workshop: Making time for literacy. *Reading Teacher* (Vol. 55, p. 466): International Reading Association.

Leu, D. J., & Kinzer, C. K. (2000). The convergence of literacy instruction with networked technologies for information and communication. *Reading Research Quarterly, 35*(1), 108.

Lewin, C. (1997). "Test driving" cars: Addressing the issues in the evaluation of computer-assisted reading software. *Journal of Computing in Childhood Education, 8*(2/3), 111–132.

Lewin, C. (2000). Exploring the effects of talking book software in UK primary classrooms. *Journal of Research in Reading, 23*(2), 149–157.

Lipson, M. Y., & Wixson, K. K. (1997). *Assessment & instruction of reading and writing disability: An interactive approach*. (Second ed.). New York: Longman.

Lundberg, I. (1995). The computer as a tool of remediation in the education of students with reading disabilities—a theory-based approach. *1995, 18*, 89–99.

Lundberg, I., & Olofsson, A. (1993). Can computer speech support reading comprehension? *Computers in Human Behavior, 9*, 283–293.

Lynch, L., Fawcett, A. J., & Nicolson, R. I. (2000). Computer-assisted reading intervention in a secondary school: An evaluation study. *British Journal of Educational Technology, 31*(4), 333–348.

MacArthur, C. A., Ferretti, R. P., Okolo, C. M., & Cavalier, A. R. (2001). Technology applications for students with literacy problems: A critical review. *The Elementary School Journal, 101*(3), 273–301.

MacArthur, C. A., & Haynes, J. B. (1995). Student assistant for learning from text (salt): A hypermedia reading aid. *Journal of Learning Disabilities, 28*(3), 50–59.

McKenna, M. C. (1998). Electronic texts and the transformation of beginning reading. In D. Reinking, M. C. McKenna, L. D. Labbo, & R. D. Kieffer (Eds.), *Handbook of literacy and technology: Transformations in a post-typographic world* (pp. 45–59). Mahwah, NJ: Lawrence Erlbaum Associates.

Meyer, A., & Rose, D. H. (1998). *Learning to read in the computer age* (Vol. 3). Cambridge, MA: Brookline Books.

Montali, J., & Lewandowski, L. (1996). Bimodal reading: Benefits of a talking computer for average and less skilled readers. *Journal of Learning Disabilities, 29*(3), 271–279.

Moore-Hart, M. A. (1995). The effects of multicultural links on reading and writing performance and cultural awareness of fourth and fifth graders. *Computers in Human Behavior, 11*(3–4), 391–410.

Mostow, J., Aist, G., Burkhead, P., Corbett, A., Cuneo, A., Eitelman, S., Huang, S., Junker, B., Sklar, M. B., & Tobin, B. (2003). Evaluation of an automated reading tutor that listens: Comparison to human tutoring and classroom instruction. *Journal of Educational Computing Research, 29*(1), 61–117.

National Center for Education Statistics. (2003). *Digest of education statistics, 2003*. Retrieved March 31, 2005, from http://nces.ed.gov//programs/digest/d03/

Palincsar, A. S., & Brown, A. L. (1984). Reciprocal teaching of comprehension-fostering and comprehension-monitoring activities. *Cognition & Instruction, 1*(2), 117.

Pew Internet & American Life Project. (2003). *America's online pursuits: The changing picture of who's online and what they do*. Washington, D.C.: Madden, M.

Raskind, M. H., & Higgins, E. L. (1999). Speaking to read: The effects of speech recognition technology on the reading and spelling performance of children with learning disabilities. *Annals of Dyslexia, 49*, 251–281.

Reinking, D. (1988). Computer-mediated text and comprehension differences: The role of reading time, reader preference, and estimation of learning. *Reading Research Quarterly, 23*(4), 484–498.

Reinking, D., & Schreiner, R. (1985). The effects of computer-mediated text on measures of reading comprehension and reading behavior. *Reading Research Quarterly, 20*(5), 536–552.

Reinking, D., & Watkins, J. (2000). A formative experiment investigating the use of multimedia book reviews to increase elementary students' independent reading. *Reading Research Quarterly, 35*(3), 389–419.

Rose, D. H., & Dalton, B. (2002). Using technology to individualize reading instruction. In C. C. Block, L. B. Gambrell, & M. Pressley (Eds.), *Improving comprehension instruction: Rethinking research, theory, and classroom practice* (pp. 257–274). San Francisco, CA: Jossey Bass Publishers.

Rose, D. H., & Meyer, A. (2002). *Teaching every student in the digital age: Universal design for learning*. Alexandria, VA: Association for Supervision and Curriculum Development (ASCD).

Snow, C. (2002). Reading for understanding: Toward a research and development program in reading comprehension. Pittsburgh, PA: Office of Educational Research and Improvement.

Stanovich, K. E. (1986). Matthew effects in reading: Some consequences of individual differences in the acquisition of literacy. *Reading Research Quarterly, 21*, 360–406.

Strangman, N., & Dalton, B. (2005). Technology for struggling readers: A review of the research. In D. Edyburn, K. Higgins, & R. Boone (Eds.), *The handbook of special education technology research and practice* (pp. 545–569). Whitefish Bay, WI: Knowledge by Design.

Swanson, H. L., & Alexander, J. E. (1997). Cognitive processes as predictors of word recognition and reading comprehension in learning-disabled and skilled readers: Revisiting the specificity hypothesis. *Journal of Educational Psychology, 89*(1), 128–158.

Swanson, H. L., & Trahan, M. F. (1992). Learning disabled readers' comprehension of computer mediated text: The influence of working memory, metacognition, and attribution. *Learning Disabilities Research & Practice, 7,* 74–86.

van Daal, V. H. P., & Reitsma, P. (1993). The use of speech feedback by normal and disabled readers in computer-based reading practice. *Reading and Writing: An Interdisciplinary Journal, 5,* 243–259.

van den Bosch, K., van Bon, W. H. J., & Schreuder, R. (1995). Poor readers' decoding skills: Effects of training with limited exposure duration. *Reading Research Quarterly, 30*(1), 110–125.

Vygotsky, L. S. (1978). *Mind in society: The development of higher psychological processes.* Cambridge, MA: Harvard University Press.

Wise, B. W., & Olson, R. K. (1995). Computer-based phonological awareness and reading instruction. *Annals of Dyslexia, 45,* 99–122.

Wise, B. W., Ring, J., & Olson, R. K. (1999). Training phonological awareness with and without explicit attention to articulation. *Journal of Experimental Child Psychology, 72,* 271–304.

Wise, B. W., Ring, J., & Olson, R. K. (2000). Individual differences in gains from computer-assisted remedial reading. *Journal of Experimental Child Psychology, 77,* 197–235.

Wolf, M., & Katzir-Cohen, T. (2001). Reading fluency and its intervention. *Scientific Studies of Reading, 5*(3), 211–239.

Wolf, M., Miller, L., & Donnelly, K. (2000). Retrieval, automaticity, vocabulary elaboration, orthography (RAVE-O): A comprehensive, fluency-based reading intervention program. *Journal of Learning Disabilities, 33*(4), 375.

Xin, J. F., Glaser, C. W., & Rieth, H. (1996). Multimedia reading using anchored instruction and video technology in vocabulary lessons. *Teaching Exceptional Children,* 45–49.

Early Literacy and New Technologies in Australian Schools: Policy, Research, and Practice

Jan Turbill and Joy Murray

Each of us has been working in the area of technology and education in one way or another for the past 15 years. Murray has been responsible for the development and delivery of state-wide professional development (PD) in technology in the classroom across the K–12 perspective. The PD program known as Technology in Learning and Teaching (TILT) has trained 25,000 teachers with the major focus being on skill-training and incorporating Information Communication Technologies (ICT) into the classroom (Murray, 1996, 1997, 1998, 1999, 2000; Murray & Phillips, 2000; Lenzen & Murray, 2001). Turbill has been interested in two ends of the educational spectrum—integrating technology into the literacy curriculum at the Kindergarten level and creating effective online learning environments at the higher education level (Turbill, 2001a, 2001b, 2003).

While we both believe that our respective work has been exciting and relatively successful, we both constantly feel frustrated at what we actually see happening in classrooms with respect to the integration of information technology into the K–6 curriculum. This is most evident in the early years of schooling within the literacy curriculum.

It is our belief that currently most teachers of early literacy view technology as something that their students can "play" with during "free time" or as a "reward" after the real "work" has been completed. Even though many teachers of the young children we work with and observe in classrooms are now quite skilled themselves in using technology for their personal and professional purposes, there seems to be reluctance, for whatever reasons, in them being able to integrate the technology into their instructional practices. Thus, while there is much written about embedding information technology (IT) and, more recently, the second generation information communication technologies (ICT) into the classroom literacy curriculum, we propose that teachers of early childhood continue to operate within the paradigm that literacy is a set of skills to be mastered and technology is a tool to be used to master those skills.

We are not alone in our beliefs. In their federally funded review of teacher professional development in the area of ICT across the K–12 perspective, Downes et al. (2001) conclude that despite an "enormous investment in ICT-related continuing professional development" there seems to be little evidence of change that goes "beyond the act of embedding ICT into existing curriculum to the act of transforming curriculum frameworks (both pedagogies and content)" (p. 58).

Furthermore, they suggest that professional development should be reframed "within a package of curriculum reform, pedagogical reform and a redefinition of the teaching profession as one of knowledge generation" (p. 77). Downes et al. (2001) quote the 1996 OECD study *Changing the Subject* which says that to achieve the benefits of technological innovations,

> . . . teachers will have to change almost every aspect of their professional equipment. They will have to reconsider themselves entirely, not only the structures of their material and their classroom techniques, but even their fundamental beliefs and attitudes concerning learning (p. 63).

In this chapter, we want to explore why such little change seems to have occurred in Australia and offer some suggestions as to how teachers of early literacy may begin to change almost every aspect of their professional equipment.

More specifically we intend to address the following questions:

- What are current views of what constitutes literacy in a technology environment?
- What are the realities of policy and pedagogy in teaching literacy in the early years in a technology environment?
- What seem to be the barriers to change for the teaching of early literacy in a technology environment?
- What are some possible solutions for beginning to change the paradigm of early childhood teachers?

CURRENT VIEWS OF WHAT CONSTITUTES LITERACY IN A TECHNOLOGY ENVIRONMENT

Contemporary views define literacy as social practice (Gee, 1990; Harris, Turbill, Fitzsimmons, & McKenzie, 2001; Makin & Jones Diaz, 2002; Muspratt, Luke, & Freebody, 1999; Zammit & Downes, 2002, to name a few). Thus, literacy incorporates those practices which we use to communicate and function in our everyday lives, including digital literacies that we use with the computer, Internet, e-mail, CD ROMs, DVD, digital cameras and so on. Makin and Jones Diaz (2002) suggest that "literacy is a tool with which our values, attitudes, aspirations, opinions, dreams, goals and ideas about the world are constructed, represented and reconstructed" (p. 8).

Zammit and Downes (2002) take an even broader view when they argue that "literacy can no longer be seen as just a set of cognitive abilities or skills based on an identifiable technology, for example, alphabetic script on paper. It needs to be recognised as a social activity embedded within larger practices and changing technologies" (p. 24).

Such a broadening of what constitutes literacy and literacy practices clearly has implications for literacy pedagogy. In 1990, Freebody and Luke proposed a framework that emphasized that to be literate in contemporary society readers and writers need to take on four roles:

1. code breaker/code maker (how do I crack this code?)
2. text participant (what does this mean?)
3. text user (what do I do with this text?)
4. text analyst (how is this text positioning me?)

Each of these roles requires the reader/writer to use a range of skills and practices. Luke and Freebody (1999) argued that they developed this framework so that it would serve to shift the focus from what is *the* best method to what is the range of practices children need to learn to be effective literate members of their community. Harris et al. (2001) demonstrate that such a framework can be used to guide the classroom literacy curriculum so that teachers provide a balanced literacy program that is situated in social contexts.

Zammit and Downes (2002) agree that a more contemporary view of literacy must include a far more diverse and complex set of texts and technologies, and therefore they argue that to be literate in today's society means being multiliterate (Cope & Kalantzis, 2000). Many researchers agree that reading and writing in the electronic, digital environments in which our students are living and learning are very different from reading and writing paper-based texts only. And learning to be literate using such texts involves more than simply adapting the paper-based skills to the new environments. It requires the learning of additional and new skills (Labbo & Reinking, 1999; Lankshear & Snyder, 2000; Leu & Kinzer, 2000). Zammit & Downes (2002) suggest that these essential skills include, "locating, comprehending, using, critiquing and creating texts within personal, social, educational, historical, cultural and workplace contexts" (p. 25). Such learning, it is argued, must begin with the emergent and beginning readers and writers (Labbo, 1999; Labbo, 2000; Labbo, Sprague, Montero, & Font, 2000, Labbo & Kuhn, 2000, Turbill, 2001a).

Literacy, ICT, and the First Years of Schooling

It is clear from our review of the literature that a contemporary view of literacy must now incorporate new technologies or ICT. So what does this mean for the first years of schooling? Luke (1999) suggests that children's early literacy and play experiences are shaped increasingly by the electronic media. Furthermore, he argues that children "process these multi-modal information sources simultaneously in the process of moving through multimedia text. What this suggests is many more parallel cognitive demands rather than the serial linear processing required of print" (p. 97).

However, the limited research into early childhood literacy and technology practices in Australia indicates that home literacies shaped by new technologies are often mistrusted in the formal setting of the school. For example. in reporting on research commissioned by the New South Wales (NSW) Department of Education and Training (DET) and NSW Department of Community Services (McNaught et al., 2000; Makin et al., 1999) into popular culture and early literacy learning, including many families from non-English speaking backgrounds, Arthur et al. (2001) go so far as to suggest that pre-school experiences involving the literacies of technology and popular culture are likely to be not only ignored, but also devalued, in early schooling. They quote one early childhood educator commenting that:

> Mum makes a big deal and 'oh, he can write his name', but it turns out to be on the computer. When he comes in to do it here he has no idea. He might write an M (quoted in Arthur, 2001, p. 299).

In her reporting of three major research projects, Downes (2002) confirms this attitude to preschoolers and suggests that this view also dominates children's early school experiences. She notes that "Many of these kindergarten children enter school with informal competencies and predispositions for learning that have developed from the use of computer technologies in their homes" (p. 184). Downes' (2002) work (also supported by the Australian National Schools Network KidSmart, 2002 evaluation) confirms the notion that "young children enjoyed socializing around the computer. They liked talking about what they were doing on the computer with their family and friends" (p. 187). Moreover she suggests that there is evidence to support earlier findings that early introduction to computers is useful in counterbalancing gender imbalance in both the usage and access within the family.

Downes (2002) reported that children in the early childhood years enjoy using educational games, drawing programs, talking books, and the Internet, tending to discuss these in terms of play. She quotes children's comments such as, "I play typing games" or "I can play painting," as examples of how the children incorporate computers into their dramatic play and imitate "adults' computer behaviors" from familiar settings (p. 192). It seems that through such acculturation young children are not only being shaped by their interactions with computers, but they are also reshaping the computer to their own ends within their own contexts. For example, young children seem quite content to "pretend-write" by tapping any letter on the keyboard in order to imitate adult behavior. Such play, or pretend-write, is well documented in young children writing in the paper-based mode (Bissez, 1980; Cambourne & Turbill, 1987).

The three research reports analyzed by Downes (2002) provide strong support for the idea that children who have regular opportunities to use the computer at home for games and other uses are more likely to be predisposed to exploratory learning and learning by doing in school. Specifically, Downes (2002) suggests that "children as young as three can use computer technology to be creative and represent their ideas in symbols, words, sounds and images" (p. 194). Similarly, Moulton-Graham and Oxenbould (1997) suggest that the way children "are being defined as 'literate' and the way they are defining themselves as 'literate', differ" (p. 81). All of which suggests that many children come to school with different orientations to learning and different sets of orientations to traditional texts, literacies, and technologies. Such differences challenge the current curriculum in terms of both content and pedagogy. Most children interviewed in the studies felt that their control over computer activities at school was severely limited. It seems children were not allowed to fiddle or try to fix things. Their computer experiences were either heavily teacher-directed, in order to achieve syllabus outcomes in key learning areas, or were at the other extreme of incidental, occasional game playing during free time or lunch" (Downes, 2002, p. 194). Downes' review clearly demonstrates the limited role that technology seems to be playing in the classrooms of young children.

This issue is further highlighted by Fleer's (2000) review of the research in early childhood education that hardly mentions the existence of computer and information technology. Fleer, however, does suggest that there is general agreement that investing dollars in early childhood education has the potential for "a cost saving ratio of one to six" (p. 1). However, it is evident from Fleer's work that such investment does not include new technologies. Luke and Luke (2001) go so far as to argue that the current enthusiasm for investment in early intervention programs is "dedicated to the restoration and preservation of print-based early childhood" (p. 91). They see it as a bureaucratic response to the "new forms of identity, technological competence and practice, and new life pathways" that children are forging for themselves outside of organized education and control. Luke and Luke (2001) interpret what they call the "crisis over print literacy" as "a generational crisis over our lack of critical and technical engagement with new technologies and new economies and their complex influences on childhood, adolescence and youth" (p. 114). Similarly, Lloyd (2002) sees the "generational crisis" reflected in popular media that reinvents childhood and new technologies at different times as either "utopian" or "apocalyptic."

For whatever reason—teacher insecurity, low school regard for popular culture, bureaucratic control of an agenda that looks to conserve a "when-I-learned-to-read" past—it seems there is a battening down of the hatches when it comes to schools and teachers acknowledging that the world is changing in fundamental ways. Something is preventing teachers from applying their usual wisdom of starting where children are at, at least where use of new technologies is concerned.

The rhetoric seems to make good sense. However, teachers in NSW as in all states in Australia, operate within centralized educational state systems. This means that teachers must work within the realities of their respective government policies, including a mandated literacy curriculum. While such curriculum may have been negotiated with teachers and supported with suitable resources, the practicalities of school life operating in such large systems often mean that teachers' beliefs and practices remain with what is known and safe. In addition, teachers often operate in old school buildings with never enough PowerPoints in a classroom and not enough space to accommodate more than one or two computers.[1]

THE REALITIES OF POLICY AND PEDAGOGY IN TEACHING LITERACY IN THE EARLY YEARS IN A TECHNOLOGY ENVIRONMENT

In 1997, the NSW government launched the NSW Literacy Strategy. While referred to as a "literacy strategy," there was a strong refocus on the teaching of reading, particularly in the first three years of school. The first year of this strategy saw the release of a document, *Teaching Reading: A K–6 Framework (1997),* with professional development and other materials to support teachers. Reading Recovery (Clay, 1979) was also a major component of this strategy. The "Framework," as it became known, offered the following definition from Marie Clay in response to the posed question: What is reading?

> I define reading as a message-getting, problem-solving activity which increases in power and flexibility the more it is practised. My definition states that within the directional constraints of the printer's code, language and visual perception responses are purposefully directed by the reader in some integrated way to the problem of extracting meaning from cues in a text, in sequence, so that the reader brings a maximum of understanding to the author's message (Clay, M (1991) Becoming Literate The Construction of Inner Control. p. 6).

The document went on to point out that:

> Reading is an essential part of literacy. Any discussion of reading must take place in the context of what it means to be literate in today's society. The following definition of literacy underpins these materials.
>
> *Literacy is the ability to read and use written information and to write appropriately, in a range of contexts. It is used to develop knowledge and understanding, to achieve personal growth and to function effectively in our society. Literacy also includes the recognition of numbers and basic mathematical signs and symbols within text.*
>
> *Literacy involves the integration of speaking, listening and critical thinking with reading and writing. Effective literacy is intrinsically purposeful, flexible and dynamic and continues to develop throughout an individual's lifetime.*
>
> *All Australians need to have effective literacy in English, not only for their personal benefit and welfare but also for Australia to reach its social and economic goals.* (Australia's Language: The Australian Language and Literacy Policy, Department of Employment, Education and Training (1991) p. 6).

---

[1]Murray visited a Year 1 classroom recently where the computers were so close together that the mouse had to be operated by moving it around on the top of the computer.

This definition of literacy is broader than merely focusing on reading and writing, however it does not explicitly mention technology or digital literacies. Contrast for example the Queensland Literacy Strategy for Public Schools released in 2000. In *Literate Futures: The Teacher Summary Version* (2000), literacy is defined:

> Literacy is the flexible and sustainable mastery of a repertoire of practices with the texts of traditional and new communication technologies via spoken language, print, and multimedia (p. 3).

The South Australian (SA) view of literacy expressed in the SA Curriculum Standards and Accountability Framework released in 2001 by the SA Department of Education, Training and Employment states:

> Learners develop and use operational skills in literacy to understand, analyse, critically respond to and produce spoken, written, visual and multimedia communications in different social and cultural contexts (p. 16).

However, regardless of such policies in most states in Australia, the teaching methods proposed by Marie Clay, and first introduced through Reading Recovery, have become the major practices for the teaching of reading and writing at the emergent and beginning reading levels. These methods include using Running Records to assess student reading, matching children with an appropriate reading level book, and a strong focus on the systematic and explicit teaching of phonics. Such methods tend to view literacy as a set of skills and to restrict the definition of literacy to "the reading and writing of paper-based texts" (Makin & Jones Diaz, 2002, p. 9). Therefore while the researchers and reviews and some state curriculums argue for a change in what constitutes literacy and literacy practices in a technology environment, the reality for most teachers in Australia who teach the beginning years of school is still a strong focus on teaching traditional skills that are restricted to paper-based views of literacy learning.

SUPPORT FOR THE TEACHING OF EARLY LITERACY
IN A TECHNOLOGY ENVIRONMENT

Given the rhetoric espoused in the literature discussed above, one would expect to find a variety of supports for the teaching of early literacy in a technology environment. These supports might be in the form of useful Web sites that could be used by teachers of the early years as demonstrations of how they can incorporate ICT into their literacy programs, or sites that are interactive and relevant for young children to use, or classroom research that highlights classroom practices that link literacy and ICT.

And so we searched. In preparation for writing this chapter, we searched: the Federal Government's Department of Education, Training and Youth Affairs Web site; major Australian teacher professional development and support Web sites, including those of several state governments; and various online databases of journals, research reports, and articles. We were looking for: major policy documents that might specifically frame the work of early childhood teachers (which we found and discussed earlier in this chapter); major research reports that might guide their practice (e.g., Fleer, 2000; Lankshear et al., 1997; Downes et al., 2001, also referred to earlier); and accessible classroom supports for day-to-day teaching in the form of journal articles and sites. It is this latter group that we now turn our attention to having attempted to identify the key issues from the many reviews and reports that have been carried out over the past 10 years or so.

We spent a great deal of time exploring online teacher support sites because we believed that useful interactive sites would provide teachers with ideas and demonstrations of what they might be able to incorporate into their classrooms. We specifically explored Australian sites. What we discovered was a woeful collection of resources from the major Australian providers of online teacher support. These various sites offered as a resource for early childhood educators echo Lankshear and Knobel's (2002) reviews which revealed "drill and skill activities masquerading as amusing stories, busy work in the form of online 'painting' activities, or printable blackline images that can be hand-coloured offline, one-to-one correspondence activities in the form of 'match these shapes' and activities written for parents to employ at home with their child" (p. 184). Like Lankshear and Knobel, we found that most sites are variations on text-based, alphabetic literacies. We agree also that many sites tend to dumb-down learners (and teachers) and decrease value from learning opportunities. Rarely did any of the sites engage with new literacies at all. Rather, most sites we found were simply repositories for teachers to run off busy work or drill-and-practice work sheets. Such sites not only reinforce a paper-based set of literacy skills, they support a direct instruction view of learning.

It was certainly disappointing to find that most of the examples of online technology use in early childhood education in Australia, with a few non-government and commercial exceptions, are out of a "Direct Instruction" pedagogy. In addition, apparently teachers are not concerned about such a lack of useful support sites into this area (Fleer, 2000). However, we believe that if teachers are to achieve the benefits of technological innovations indicated earlier in this chapter, then they will have to be prepared to make huge changes in pedagogy and curriculum content. How they are to do this is a mystery when the very technology supports provided for them present a restricted and restrictive image of its use that in turn tend to reinforce governments' investments in early childhood print-based literacy intervention programs. We agree with Lankshear and Snyder (2000) when they say that limitations in classroom work are not a reflection on the personal shortcomings of teachers, but "go to the heart of important issues that include: the conditions under which teachers learn to be teachers; policy directions and directives; resourcing decisions; and administrative and political agendas" (p. xix).

The teacher in-service and preservice communities (Downes et al., 2001) tend to reflect the changing views of what constitutes literacy and the role that new technologies can play in literacy practices, however, as Lankshear et al. (1997) and Lankshear and Snyder (2000) suggest, resulting fundamental changes in pedagogy and curriculum content are rarely found. If there are changes, they tend to be that new technologies are often added on to old book-based content and used within traditional teaching frameworks. It is not surprising therefore, that Jones (2002) reports that "pre-service students rarely see their supervising teachers making use of ICT to assist and improve teaching and learning" (p. 5). Therefore, teacher-training programs seem to be making little impact, and so the status quo continues.

All of which seems to indicate that it is easier said than done! Easier to theorize on the transformative potential of new technologies than to transform classroom practice over night; easier to talk about innovative uses of technology than to find them in practice and easier to spend scarce teacher time on traditional issues than seek out some new and time-consuming technologies.

Our analysis of all that we have read and viewed clearly demonstrates that there are many comprehensive reports and reviews that could guide policy and curriculum development in linking literacy and technology in the early years in Australia. These certainly indicate where we should be heading and why. There are also many small excellent research projects that demonstrate how ICT technologies can be incorporated into the literacy curriculum. From these it is clear that possibilities exist.

Yet there is a conundrum. While we have offered some possible explanations as to why so little seems to have changed in the teaching of literacy and technology in the early years, we wonder, as does Downes et al. (2001), why all teachers of children in the early years are not enthusiastically moving into embracing "curriculum reform, pedagogical reform and a redefinition of the teaching profession as one of knowledge generation" (p. 77).

One other possible answer to this dilemma is that there appears to be little research that is readily available to teachers that resonates with their particular experiences. Such research needs to begin at the ground level of teachers and children in the busy daily and often chaotic lives of schools. In the next part of this chapter, we describe research that documents the slow and often frustrating process that a group of Kindergarten and Grade 1 teachers experienced as they attempted to incorporate ICT into their literacy curriculums.

A CASE STUDY OF THE PROCESS OF CHANGE IN ONE SCHOOL (OR "WHERE THE RUBBER MEETS THE ROAD")

For some four years, Turbill has been visiting one large urban multicultural school on a weekly basis. As a "critical friend" to the school and its staff, she has played a significant role in helping Kindergarten and Grade 1 teachers implement the use of the computers into their literacy practices. It has been a long and slow process. However, there has been change, slow incremental change, and each phase of that change needed to occur in order to support and enhance the next. The now well-known cliché "change is a process not an event" was very evident in this school. This process of change can be best described in a series of phases.

Phase 1: Mapping the Territory

The first year (1999) was spent working with several Kindergarten and Grade 1 classrooms. The focus of the research at this point was to ascertain what emergent literacy users could do with computers, what skills they had, and what skills they needed to learn in order to use them. During the year, all 12 Kindergarten and Grade 1 teachers were interviewed formally, and many informal conversations took place as well about technology and its use in their classrooms. Classroom observations of the traditional literacy teaching were also recorded, often with the support of video. From these initial data, four main themes emerged. These were labeled under the broad heading "lessons learned." Briefly, these were (for more detail refer to Turbill 2001a):

Computer-related lessons

Computer-related lessons included the need for the computers to work, to have access to printers, the Internet, digital cameras, and so on. Teachers found it very frustrating when the computers did not work, for whatever reason. They also stated that while two computers in each room were better than one, it was like having "two pencils to be shared by all children."

Software-related lessons

Suitable software and time to explore such software was a major issue. Teachers knew little about the software that was available, and those who had seen software "that looked interesting" in catalogues had little or no idea of what might be involved in their use. Time to explore the potential use of software was cited as a major issue.

Curriculum-related lessons

Teachers questioned whether they needed the additional technology to teach literacy anyway. They felt they had been successfully teaching children to read and write using traditional technologies and paper and pencils, and many questioned the added value of using technology. What was clear was that the teachers held a traditional view of literacy that included only paper-based print and these views needed to be challenged.

Teacher-related lessons

Teachers, themselves, felt apprehensive about how to use the computers, and those who did use them for their personal and administrative purposes could not see the potential other than "play" within their existing framework of what constituted literacy and how it was best taught. They also found it difficult to organize the use of the computers when there were 26+ children, two computers, and one teacher.

The information gleaned from this phase was then used to attempt to change teachers' pedagogy and their traditional views of literacy so that they began to view ICT as an integral component of their literacy curriculum. It was the beginning of a long, slow, often frustrating, and chaotic process.

Phase 2: Setting Up the Volunteer Program

The first step in supporting teachers was to provide some classroom support for them. There was no additional money, so the principal and Turbill decided to implement a volunteer program (taking its impetus from the fact that it was the Year of the Volunteer). A cadre of volunteers (mostly "mums") were invited to come daily and observe and support the children as they "played" at the computers during the literacy block. Turbill's role during this phase was to act as a liaison with the volunteers, provide workshops to show them what to do, and to monitor the program. This program worked well, although required constant maintenance to make sure at least one volunteer was active in each classroom during their literacy time and to provide the ongoing workshops needed to support the volunteers (Turbill, 2001b).

The volunteers used a basic framework developed by Turbill called "Concepts of Screen" (after Clay 1991), in order to assess Kindergarten and Grade 1 children's basic skill levels in using the computer (use of the mouse, matching cursor and mouse, understanding the function of icons, and so on) as well as developing a language for talking about the computer use (mouse, icon, click, double click, drag, and more). This knowledge was then used by teachers to group the children into pairs so that at least one child in the pair had some of the basic concepts of screen (See Turbill, 2001b for details). It did not take long for the less-skilled children to learn the concepts of screen from their partners.

Thus, children began to "play" with the computers. They played the "talking books," and used "drill-game" type CDROMS software. However, this was hardly incorporating ICT, and teachers indicated concern that the students were only "playing." The literacy lessons proceeded as in the past, focusing on print and paper-based technology. It was clear that the teachers needed to see a purpose for using the computers that would enhance their existing literacy curriculum. They also needed to have confidence in the fact that the computers, printers, and Internet would work effectively when they did want children to use them. (This was and still is a constant problem, indicating a need at the government level to supply schools with in-school, ongoing technical support. Teachers cannot be asked to become technicians, too!)

Phase 3: Digital Language Experience Approach (DLEA)

Some two years later, Turbill first heard about Digital Language Experience Approach (DLEA) at the International Reading Conference in 2002. DLEA is clearly described by Labbo, Eakle, & Montero (2002 posted May). Their research indicated that "as promising as recent research and instructional ideas have been, we realized that much remains to be learned about effective ways to integrate LEA with digital photography and creativity software in the early years classroom." It was hoped that introducing DLEA to the teachers in this school could be the starting point of incorporating ICT into the curriculum. Language Experience Approach (LEA) was a traditional teaching method already widely used by the Kindergarten, Grade 1, and ESL teachers in the school, so it was hoped that the addition of a digital format would be readily accepted by the teachers.

It was decided to make several adaptations to the procedures, as outlined by Labbo et al. (2002). These included:

- The teachers in this research had access to Microsoft's PowerPoint software and many had used it in their own work or university studies, thus it was felt that this software would suit our purposes better than the creativity software used by Labbo and her colleagues.
- The children would take the lead and select the photos they wanted to take with the digital camera (after Espinetti, 2002).
- The children in Grade 1 would be encouraged to compose and write their own stories, rather than have the teacher or volunteer scribe the story as in Kindergarten.

Before providing teachers with the necessary professional development to be able to use DLEA, it was deemed necessary to trial the whole process so there were both a model to demonstrate to teachers and an understanding of the process. Therefore, it was decided that Turbill should trial DLEA with two Grade 1 children.

Phase 4: Exploring the Potential of DLEA

A mix of action research (Kemmis & McTaggart, 1988) and case study (Merriam, 1998) methodologies were used for this phase of the project. Burns (1990) indicates, "action research is the application of fact-finding to practical problem-solving in a social situation with a view to improving the quality of action within it, involving the collaboration and cooperation of researchers, practitioners and laymen" (p. 346).

Two 6-year children, Penny and Justin, were chosen to trial DLEA. Both were in Grade 1 and deemed to be average readers and writers for their age by their class teacher. Penny was the only English-speaking child in the class. Justin came from a Chinese-speaking background and, in fact, returned to China for several months with his parents during this project.

The children were told they were going to make a digital book. They would take the photos, decide on the order of the photos, write the captions, and then they would present their digital books to the rest of the class. The purpose given to the two children for their digital books was: to prepare a digital book that could be used to introduce the newly enrolled children to the key people and places in the school. These books would be used to help the new children get to know their way around more quickly (see Turbill 2003 for details).

The end of this project saw the development of two digital books that the children had made that they could find on the computer and read to the class. The class teacher was thrilled and could see many opportunities for creating more digital books. It was now time to introduce the practice to all the Kindergarten and Grade 1 teachers.

I am Penny in 1M. That means Year 1.

FIGURE 7.1.   A slide from Penny's digital book.

Phase 5: Sharing with All the Teachers

The next phase was to share what was found in the action research project with all the teachers for Kindergarten and Grade 1. A series of short, 1-hour sessions were set up with two teachers at a time to work with Turbill. The teacher-pair were to become support buddies back in their class-rooms. Using a PowerPoint presentation, we reviewed what we had already done and was in place in the school (e.g., volunteer program, Concepts of Screen checklist). The digital books that were developed by the Grade 1 children with Turbill were used to demonstrate the creation of a DLEA book and to identify the literacy and ICT skills being used. Teachers were quick to indi-cate additional learning outcomes and adaptations that could be used. For example, one teacher suggested creating a "photo bank" on the school's intranet so children could access them in order to create new DLEA digital books. This, it was suggested, would alleviate the need to access the school's scarce digital cameras. Another teacher suggested creating "cloze" activities using the digital books, and another suggested highlighting certain phonic blends or high fre-quency words.

Each teacher was then given the opportunity to use the digital camera, take some photos and develop her own digital book. During the 1-hour workshop, teachers quickly saw the benefits of DLEA in their literacy programs, especially for their ESL children. They expected the ESL children would benefit by the repetition of English structures such as "I am Fadi. I can run fast." Another teacher suggested developing a DLEA digital book with the children that highlighted the use of English prepositions. For example, "Where is the orange? The orange is **on** the table" (with a relevant photo to support the text. "Where is the orange now? The orange is **under** the table." (with matching text) and so on. In the weeks that followed, several teachers began to experiment with DLEA. One Grade 1 class created a DLEA presentation of their field trip. Each child had taken at least one photograph and when returning to school had been responsible for uploading their respective photograph into a PowerPoint slide. With the students working in pairs, the teacher had shown the first pair how to upload the photo into PowerPoint and write the caption; this pair then demonstrated the process to the next pair, and so on. In this way, every child had a chance to learn how to upload the photograph into a slide and to write his/her caption. The whole process took a week with the support of a parent volunteer and, the final product was proudly shown and read to anyone who came into the classroom. It was eventually posted on the school's intranet for all Grade 1 children to read.

RESULTS AND RECOMMENDATIONS

This action research project with its adaptations supports both the findings of Labbo et al. (2002) and Espinetti (2002). Like Labbo et al., it was found that DLEA incorporates all the best aspects of the Language Experience Approach, with the added advantages of teaching children and their teachers to also use digital literacies. Indeed, it seemed to be an approach that suited the needs of both the teachers and their children in this particular school. DLEA began with what teachers knew and trusted, namely LEA, and allowed them to learn new ICT skills within this context.

What was evident in this phase of the project was that because the children chose their own images to photograph from a known context (i.e., their school) all the children in the class could recognize them and talk about them. For children from ESL backgrounds, the more opportunities to talk about shared experiences such as these made great sense to the teachers. Children would happily revisit their digital books and therefore English structures and vocabulary. The teachers also talked about the possibilities of developing digital books in English and the children's first language. This they suggested could be another role for the parent volunteers who were literate in their first language. These bilingual digital books could be printed off of the computers so the children could take them home to practice with their parents.

Furthermore, the digital books could be shared easily amongst all Kindergarten and Grade 1 classrooms by putting them onto the school's intranet. Because the photographs are common images, children could talk about them, add to them, or even write their own captions and create a personalized slide show. Children love to see the photos of themselves and their friends on the computer, and teachers predicted that the children would want to read the digital books over and over again. Thus, children and teachers are beginning to use ICT for authentic purposes and not just as something to do when the children finished their "real" work.

Finding authentic purposes for young children's writing has always been a difficult challenge for teachers. DLEA seems to respond well to such a challenge. The children had a real purpose and audience for their digital books and they worked hard to make sure that their books were "right" for their audience. They were prepared to edit and proofread their books so that they were clear to that audience. Their sense of audience and willingness to edit and proofread is indeed unusual for this age group. Yet, the children were not only willing, but insistent. Teachers could see that digital books easily became published versions and thus could become additional reading resources via the schools intranet. Several teachers also pointed out that soon the children would be able to access these from home, and thus this would include parents in the process.

The small case study reported here has helped explore the potential of DLEA not only as a new teaching method but also as a bridge for teachers to begin to think of literacy as more than paper-based skills. Furthermore, it has served to open the doors for incorporating ICT into the literacy curriculum and begin the process of change that the theorists propose is needed. It seems that if young learners are to be able to operate effectively in that "different space" in the school setting as easily as many of them do outside the school, we must give support to teachers at the ground level in a such a way that they can take ownership of the change process for themselves. Once they do, they will continue to move onwards. However, what is also imperative is that resources—hardware, software and Internet sites—must reflect the theoretical frameworks described above.

IMPLICATIONS FOR FURTHER RESEARCH

The project reported above occurred over a period of five years. Changes have happened, and are still happening, but at a frustratingly slow pace. Yet, there is change, and it has occurred not only because of the reports, reviews, and theorizing that has been reported earlier in this chapter. It has occurred mainly because the research began at the grassroots level. The research methodology has been "action research" or what is often called "teacher research." In other words. teachers have taken a strong role in the research, and thus the research not only reflects their needs, but also responds to these needs. Such research brings about not only changes in practices, but also in beliefs (Turbill, 2001a). Further research needs to be situated in classrooms with researchers working with teachers in their classrooms in order to document and help initiate changes in practice and beliefs. Most importantly this research needs to be long term.

Finally, it is our belief that the major challenge ahead is helping teachers of children in the early years to understand that ICT is indeed a critical component of a literacy curriculum. The theorizing explored in this chapter leads us to accept almost without question that ICT is already strongly embedded within today's society and the culture of early childhood outside the school. It is clearly not the case inside the classrooms. Much needs to be done if classrooms are to reflect the same use of ICT as society in general. Moreover, for some children ICT is very much part of their home. However, for others it is not. Thus the issues of equity are exacerbated and the "great divide" increases.

If we are to make any headway in these challenges, there needs to be innovative thinking and research into how ICT can become part of every early childhood classroom. This means changing the existing paradigm that literacy is a set of skills to be mastered and technology is a tool for early childhood teachers, school leaders, bureaucrats, and politicians alike. A challenge faces us all!

REFERENCES

Arthur, L., Beecher, B., & Jones Diaz, C. (2001). Early literacy: Congruence and incongruence between home and early childhood settings. In M. Kalantzis (Ed.), *Languages of learning: Changing communication and changing literacy teaching.* Melbourne: Common Ground.

Australian National Schools Network. (2002). KidSmart Evaluation. Australian National Schools Network, amended and approved August, 2002.

Bissex, G. (1980). *Gnys at wrk: A child learns to read and write.* Cambridge, Mass: Harvard University Press.

Burns, R. (1990). *Introduction to research methods.* Melbourne: Longman Cheshire.

Cambourne, B., & Turbill, J. (1987). *Coping with chaos*, Primary English Teaching Association, Portsmouth NH: Heinemann Educational Publishers.

Clay, M. (1991). *Becoming Literate: The construction of inner control.* Auckland: Heinemann Educational Books.

Cope. B., & Kalantzis, M. (Eds.) (2000). *Multiliteracies: Literacy learning and the design of social futures.* Melbourne: Macmillan.

Department of Employment, Education and Training (1991). *Australia's Language: The Australian language and literacy policy.* Department of Employment, Education and Training, Canberra: AGPS.

Downes, T., Fluck, A., Gibbons, P., Leonard, R., Matthews, C., Oliver, R., Vickers, M., & Williams, M. (2001). *Making better connections.* Canberra: Department of Education, Science and Training, Commonwealth of Australia.

Downes, T. (2002). Children's and families's use of computers in Australian homes. *Contemporary Issues in Early Childhood, 3*(2), 182–196.

Espinetti, G. (2002). *Images that capture stories of our worlds: A new literacy for preschoolers.* Paper presented at International Reading Association Conference, San Francisco.

Fleer, M. (2000). *An early childhood research agenda: Voices from the field.* Canberra: Department of Education, Training and Youth Affairs.

Freebody, P., & Luke, A. (1990). Literacies programs: Debates and demands in cultural context. *Prospect: Australian Journal of TESOL, 5*(7), 7–16.

Gee, J. (1990). *Social linguistics and literacies, ideologies in discourse.* London: Taylor and Francis.

Harris, P., Turbill, J., Fitzsimmons, P., & McKenzie, B. (2001). *Reading in the primary school years.* Sydney: Social Science Press.

Jones, A. (2002). *Integrating ICT in the early years: Literacy, maths and multimedia.* ACEC Proceedings: refereed papers section Australian Computers in Education Conference, Hobart, July 2002. Retrieved from the Web [9/9/03] http://www.tasite.tas.edu.au/acec2002

Jones Diaz, C., Arthur, L., Beecher, B., & McNaught M. (2000). Multiple literacies in early childhood: What do families and communities think about their children's early literacy learning? *Australian Journal of Language and Literacy, 23*(3), 230.

Kemmis, S., & McTaggart, R. (1988). *The action research planner (3rd ed).* Vic: Deakin University Press.

Knobel, M., & Lankshear, C. (1995). Literacies, texts and difference in the electronic age. In *Celebrating Difference Confronting Literacies.* Conference Papers Australian Reading Association Conference, Sydney, July 12–15.

Labbo, L. & Reinking, D. (1999). Negotiating the multiple realities of technology in literacy research and instruction. *Reading Research Quarterly, 34*(4), 478–492.

Labbo, L. (1999). A semiotic analysis of young children's symbol making in a classroom computer center. *Reading Research Quarterly, 31*(4), 356–385.

Labbo, L. (2000). 12 things young children can do with a talking book in a classroom computer center. *The Reading Teacher, 53*(7), 542–546.

Labbo, L., & Kuhn, M. (2000). Weaving chains of affect and cognition: A young child's understanding of CD-ROM talking books. *Journal of Reading, 32*(2), 187–210.

Labbo, L. D., Eakle, A. J., & Montero, M. K. (2002, May). Digital Language Experience Approach: Using digital photographs and software as a Language Experience Approach innovation. *Reading Online.* 5(8). Available:http://www.readingonline.org/electronic/elec_index.asp?HREF=labbo2/index.html

Labbo, L., Sprague, L., Montero, M. K., & Font, G. (2000). Connecting a Computer Center to Themes, Literature and Kindergarteners' Literacy Needs. *Reading Online,* http://readingonline.org/electronic/labbo/index.html

Lankshear, C., Bigum, C., Durrant, C., Green, B., Honan, E., Morgan, W., Murray, J., Wild, M., & Snyder, I. (1997). *Digital rhetorics: Literacies and technologies in education—Current practices and future directions. Volume Three Issues and Innovations.* Department of Employment, Education, Training and Youth Affairs. Canberra: Commonwealth of Australia.

Lankshear, C., & Knobel, M. (2003). New technologies in early childhood literacy research: A review of research. *Journal of Early Childhood Literacy, 3*(1), 59–82.

Lankshear, C., & Snyder, I., with Green, B. (2000). *Teachers and techno-literacy: Managing literacy, technology and learning in schools*. St Leonards: Allen and Unwin.

Lenzen, M., & Murray, J. (2001). The role of equity and lifestyles in education about climate change: Experiences from a large-scale teacher development program. *Canadian Journal of Environmental Education,* Vol. 6.

Leu, D., & Kinzer, C. (2000). The convergence of literacy instruction with networked technologies for information and communication, *Reading Research Quarterly, 35*(1), 108–127.

Lloyd, M. (2002). Reinvention of childhood in a networked world. In McDougall, A., Murnane, J. & Chambers, D. (Eds.) (2002). Vol. 8—*Computers in Education: Australian Topics*. Papers presented at the 7th World Conference on Computers in Education, Copenhagen, Denmark, July/August, 2001. http://crpit.com/vol8.html accessed 31/10/03.

Luke, C. (1999). What next? Toddler Netizens, Playstation Thumb, Techno-literacies. *Contemporary Issues in Early Childhood, 1*(1).

Luke, A., & Luke C. (2001) Adolescence lost/childhood regained: On early intervention and the emergence of the techno-subject, *Journal of Early Childhood Literacy, 1*(1), 91–120.

Luke, A., & Freebody, P. (1999) A map of possible practices: Further notes on the four resources model, *Practically Primary, 4*(2), 5–8

McNaught, M., Clugston, L., Arthur, L., Beecher, B., Jones Diaz, C., Ashton, J., Hayden, J., & Makin, L. (2000). *The early literacy and social justice project: Final report*. Sydney: NSW Department of Education and Training and NSW Department of Community Services.

Makin, L., Hayden, J., Holland, A., Arthur, L., Beecher, B., Jones Diaz, C., & McNaught, M. (1999). *Mapping literacy practices in early childhood services*. Sydney: NSW Department of Education and Training and NSW Department of Community Services.

Makin, L., & Jones Diaz, C. (Eds.) (2002). *Literacies in early childhood: Changing views and challenging practices*. Sydney: Maclennan and Petty.

Merriam, S. (1988). *Case study research in education: A qualitative approach*. San Francisco, California: Jossey-Bass Publishers.

Moulton-Graham, K., & Oxenbould, M. (1997). Windows and doors: Computers in early literacy programs: The early years: Embracing the challenges. *1997 Early Years of Schooling Conference Proceedings* (Melbourne, Australia, July 20–21, 1997). Victoria Education Dept. (Australia). #16.

Murray, J. (1996). *Technology in learning and teaching*. Paper presented at the Learning Environment Technology Australia (LETA) Conference, Adelaide.

Murray, J. (1997). *New technology, new literacy: What is it? Who's doing it? Where is it going?* Paper presented to the Australian College of Education NSW Chapter, 22 Oct. (published on ACE Web site).

Murray, J. (1998). *Computer technology and teacher development: A systems perspective on pedagogical change*. Creative Systems Practice. Australia New Zealand Systems (ANZSYS) conference, Sydney, 7–10 October.

Murray, J. (1999). *Computer Technology and Teacher Development: A program to support pedagogical change*. Communication and networking in education: Learning in a networked society. International Federation of Information Processing (IFIP) conference Hameenlinna, Finland, 13–18 June.

Murray, J. (2000). Computer technology and teacher development: A program to support pedagogical change. In Watson, D., & Downes, T. (Eds.) *Communications and networking in education: Learning in a networked society*. Boston: Kluwer Academic.

Murray, J., and Phillips, G. (2000). *Technology in Learning and Teaching (TILT) and TILT PLUS: NSW school technology training*. Retrieved June 12, 2004 from http://www.flexiblelearning.net.au/nw2000/talkback/p128.htm

Muspratt S., Luke, A., & Freebody, P. (Eds.) (1997). *Constructing critical literacies: Teaching and learning textual practice*. Sydney: Allen and Unwin.

NSW Department of Education. (1997). *Teaching Reading: A K–6 Framework*. Sydney: NSW Department of Education.

South Australia Department of Education, Training and Employment. (2001). *South Australian Curriculum Standards Framework* (SACSA). Adelaide: Department of Education, Training and Employment.

The State of Queensland (Department of Education) 2000, Literate Futures: Report of the literacy Review for Queeensland Schools, The Teacher Summary Version, Retrieved June 10, 2004 from http://education .qld.gov.au/

Turbill, J. (2001a). A researcher goes to school: The integration of technology into the early literacy curriculum. *Journal of Early Literacy, 1*(3), 255–279.

Turbill, J. (2001b, July/August). Getting kindergarteners started with technology: The story of one school. *Reading Online, 5*(1). http://www.readingonline.org/international/inter_index.asp?HREF=turbill2/ index.html

Turbill, J. (2003). March, Exploring the potential of the digital language experience approach in Australian classrooms, *Reading Online, 6*, (7), Available: http://www.readingonline.org/international/inter_ index.asp?HREF=turbill7

Zammit, K., & Downes, T. (2002). New learning environments and the multiliterate individual: A framework for educators, *Australian Journal of Language and Literacy, 25*(2), 24–36.

8

The Promise of Automatic Speech Recognition for Fostering Literacy Growth in Children and Adults

Marilyn Jager Adams
Soliloquy Learning and Brown University

**THE PROMISE OF AUTOMATIC SPEECH
RECOGNITION FOR FOSTERING LITERACY
GROWTH IN CHILDREN AND ADULTS**

Few challenges are more important in the classroom than that of ensuring that every student invests adequate time and attention in reading. At the same time, unfortunately, few challenges are more difficult for the classroom teacher to pull off.

In the hopes of engaging children in the reading they need, all manner of classroom tactics have been invented: Round Robin reading, choral reading, DEAR (drop everything and read), SSR (sustained silent reading), personal reading logs, and partner reading. Yet none of these tactics is fail-safe, particularly for those children who need the time on text most. Reading together, their turns are too long for comfort and too short for good practice. Reading alone, their attention wanders; they get distracted; some even fake reading or hide out, covertly engaging in other activities. Soon enough, the reading period is over for the day—but, alas, they have not read, or not enough.

Basically, kids are kids and, for many, learning to read is hard. It requires concentration, perseverance, and is rewarding only to the extent that it is successful. Young readers need text that is appropriate to their own individual level in words, language, information, humor, and ideas. But even the best book can fail to keep a child's attention so long as reading itself is effortful. Until children can read comfortably on their own, they need someone or something to keep them engaged—someone to help them across the difficulties, to support their on-going understanding, and to allow them to sense and enjoy their own progress and accomplishment.

This chapter is about the promise of speech recognition technology for helping to meet this need. In the effort to explain why I so strongly believe in its potential, I begin by discussing the nature and the magnitude of the problem for both children and adults. This discussion is divided into two sections: The first is built on archival research, and the second on observation. At the end of the paper, I describe a software system that my colleagues and I have been developing and some preliminary indications of its usefulness in classrooms.

The Need for One-on-One Reading Support

Across many decades and tutoring methods, research has amply demonstrated that virtually all children are able to make normal or accelerated progress in reading given early and adequate one-on-one support (Elbaum, Vaughn, Hughes, & Moody, 2000; Monroe, 1932; Pinnell, Lyons, DeFord, Bryk, & Seltzer; 1994; Slavin, Karweit, & Wasik, 1994; Slavin, Karweit, & Madden, 1989; Vellutino et al., 1996; Wasik & Slavin, 1993). Of special value is the practice of engaging children, one-on-one, in reading aloud to a helpful listener. Moreover, the benefits of such read-aloud sessions are substantial at least through Grade 4 or 5 for virtually all students and well beyond for students who are struggling (Chard, Vaughn, & Tyler, 2002; National Reading Panel, 2000).

As documented by the National Reading Panel (2000), such read-aloud sessions promote not just fluency, but also word recognition, comprehension, and full-scale reading scores. Though some (e.g., Garan, 2002) have expressed dismay that the National Reading Panel would endorse oral over silent reading, that's not the point. The goal of teaching children to read is precisely to instill in them the confidence and competence to read silently and independently on their own. The message of the National Reading Panel is that listening to and helping children as they read aloud is an exceptionally valuable practice toward improving students' reading—toward increasing the productivity with which they can read all by themselves.

Why Oral Reading?   Several different hypotheses can be offered for the special power of oral reading for promoting reading growth. An obvious one is that when a child is reading aloud, it is far easier to be sure that she or he is staying on task. Second, because listeners can hear difficulties as they happen, they can offer help exactly when it matters most, that is, exactly when the child is attending to the difficulty and exactly where its resolution best supports and is supported by the meaning of the text. Similarly, because listeners know exactly where the child is in the text, they can choose optimal moments to probe understanding, to elicit predictions, or to invite reflection or discussion. In this vein, it is worth noting that many of the most effective practices for developing vocabulary and comprehension strategies also rest on read-aloud dynamics (see National Research Panel, 2000).

To be sure, neither of these explanations has to do with modality per se. Yet there is also a third hypothesis, which should not be dismissed. Within psychology, there is an age-old and well-respected theory that anything people learn to do with automaticity is necessarily anchored in motor learning (see Freeman & Nuñez, 2000). Indeed, herein is the origin of the word *information*, as Aristotle proposed that the *forms* in the mind are built through actions of the body. To read with fluency, it is precisely automaticity that is required—with the spellings, the meanings, and the flow of the words. Only then can active, thoughtful attention be focused on the meaning and message of the text.

Over the decades, experimental psychology has richly documented the integral dependence of perceptual development on motor experience and practice. Though much of this work has centered on people's knowledge of time and space, motor activity seems equally core to speech and text apprehension.

As a basic example, the building blocks of spoken language are the phonemes. The distinctive features of phonemes are a function of their place and manner of articulation (e.g., labial, dental, alveolar, . . . ; voiced, unvoiced, plosive, . . .). Yet, across speakers and linguistic contexts, these features are not acoustically definable. Instead, people "hear" these distinctive features motorically, by mentally co-producing the speech to which they are listening (Liberman & Mattingly, 1985). At the level of everyday examples, perhaps this is why the ability to understand a once-difficult accent is so often accompanied by the ability to imitate it. Almost certainly it is why engaging children in active production and contrast of the phonemes is so important a component of good phonemic awareness programs.

With respect to text, Huey (1908) wrote:

> The fact of inner speech forming a part of silent reading has not been disputed, so far as I am aware, by any one who has experimentally investigated the process of reading. . . . Although there is an occasional reader in whom the inner speech is not noticeable, and although it is a foreshortened and incomplete speech in most of us, yet it is perfectly certain that the inner hearing or pronunciation, or both, of what is read, is a constituent part of reading by far the most of people, as they ordinarily and actually read. (pp. 117–118).

Indeed, electromyographic recordings of the vocal musculature of readers have long shown that silent reading is commonly attended by subvocalizing, and more so as text difficulty is increased. Such motor activity has sometimes been dismissed as a nonfunctional or even dysfunctional vestige of early reading instruction. Yet this does not seem correct, for efforts to reduce or interfere with subvocalization activity serve equally to reduce reading comprehension (Hardyck & Petrinovich, 1970). More recently, brain-imaging studies confirm the involvement of motor and articulatory centers in the normal reading circuit and their disturbance or damping among disabled readers (see Sandack & Poldrack, 2004).

How Much Guided Oral Reading Do Children Need?   Such argument notwithstanding, research affirms that in the general education classroom, one-on-one reading sessions are generally both rare and brief (Moody, Vaughn, & Schumm, 1997). Through an observational study, McIntosh et al. (1993) found that, except for purposes of clarifying information, checking for understanding, or answering specific questions, classroom teachers rarely ask individuals to read to them and, when they do, the readings generally last less than one minute. Even in special education classrooms, one-on-one reading tends to be limited, as students are found to spend far more time doing worksheets and waiting around (Vaughn, Moody, & Schumm, 1998; Vaughn, Levy, Coleman, & Bos, 2002). Further, by all indications, the amount of classroom time spent reading is only less in poorer schools and with poorer readers (Allington, 1983, 1989; Birman et al., 1987).

Thus, the National Reading Panel's (2000) urging that classroom teachers find ways to increase the time they engage their students in guided oral reading on a regular basis is well taken. With respect to how much time to devote to this activity, however, the Panel's report is less helpful, offering only that more research (or better reporting) is needed. Similarly, though the datasets of several recent meta-analyses of the intervention literature seem to indicate that read-aloud sessions are the most valuable component of reading tutorials (Brooks, Flanagan, Henkhuzens, & Hutchison, 1998; Elbaum et al., 2000; Swanson, 1999; Vaughn et al., 2002), none pulls out time itself as an independent variable.

My suspicion is that, provided it is well spent, precious little additional time on text would make a huge difference in students' reading growth. The scientific basis for this opinion is my own, personal, deep-seated conviction that, given the basics, children learn almost anything remarkably quickly—if only one can get them to pay attention.

In any case, if we can't get a hard estimate of the additional time that might be warranted, we can at least speculate. For first graders, let us consider a study by Pinnell, Lyons, DeFord, Bryk, and Seltzer (1994). The purpose of this study was to compare the efficacy of the full Reading Recovery Model, complete with fully trained tutors, against four alternatives. The first alternative model was designed in all ways after the Reading Recovery model, except that the teachers had only two weeks rather than a full year of prior training. For the second alternative model, certified Reading Recovery teachers were asked to implement the full Reading Recovery Program, but with small groups rather than one-on-one. The third alternative again involved one-on-one tutoring, but was built around direct instruction of distinct skill strands. For the fourth alternative, called the "control group," the treatment was the Chapter 1 (small-group) pullout program already in place in each study school. All of the interventions were implemented with first-grade students from similar student populations and over the same time period.

In brief, the results of this study across a variety of outcome measures were strongest for the one-on-one Reading Recovery tutoring, and that is how they were interpreted. Even so, an alternative (and not mutually exclusive) explanation lay in the amount of reading done by the children in the course of their tutoring. In the two one-on-one Reading Recovery formats, which were by far the most effective treatments, the children read an average of about five books per session. In contrast, the children in the small-group implementation of Reading Recovery averaged only 2.38 books per session. For the two least successful treatments, the Direct Skills (one-on-one) tutoring and the Chapter 1 groups, the average number of books per session were 0.22 and 1.33, respectively. If we extrapolate across 50 sessions, the total number of books read by children ranged from 250 for those in the one-on-one Reading Recovery tutoring, to 120 for those receiving Reading Recovery in small groups, to as few as 11 for the children in the Direct Skills Intervention. Extrapolating from the Pinnell et al. study, it would appear that even struggling beginners need only 10 minutes a day of active reading time in order to catch up and keep up with grade-level expectations across the first grade.

What about older children? Again, hard data is wanting, but consider the statistics in Table 8.1. The numbers in the panel at left represent the amount of time that middle-class fifth graders read outside of class as reported by Anderson, Wilson, and Fielding (1988). As can be seen, the amount of reading in which these children engaged decreased by at least one-third with every 10 percentile points. The numbers in the panel at right show how much the children's total, yearly reading would increase in percentage and in number of words if they were somehow

TABLE 8.1
The Effect of Increasing Fifth-Graders Reading by 10 Minutes Per Day.
Baseline Numbers from Anderson, Wilson, & Fielding (1988).

Percentile	Current Reading		Plus 10 Minutes per Day	
	Minutes per Day	Words per Year	Percent Increase	Words per Year
98	65.0	4,358,000	15%	5,029,000
90	21.1	1,414,000	47%	2,085,000
80	13.2	885,000	76%	1,555,000
70	9.6	643,000	104%	1,313,000
60	6.5	435,000	154%	1,105,000
50	4.6	308,000	217%	978,000
40	3.2	214,000	313%	884,000
30	1.3	87,000	769%	757,000
20	0.7	47,000	1429%	717,000
10	0.1	6,700	10000%	677,000
0	0	0	∞	670,000

induced to read just 10 minutes more per day. If, somehow, this could be managed, the tenth percentile reader would end up reading as much as the seventieth percentile child does now. Similarly the amount of time the average child spends reading would be tripled—and so, too, would their exposure to the language, vocabulary, information, ideas, and modes of thought that texts present.

The classroom challenge. Ten minutes per day doesn't sound like much, but consider the logistics. Suppose you were a teacher who was totally committed to reading one-on-one with each of your students every day. To meet this goal, let's say you decided to devote one full hour of every school day to one-on-one reading sessions. Assuming about 25 students in your classroom, the time you could spend reading with each would be only about 2 minutes per day—assuming, of course, no disruptions, zero transition time, that you did absolutely nothing else for the duration, and that the other 24 students were unfailingly behaving and spending their time well. To read with each child for 10 minutes, you would need to maintain these conditions for four or five hours. For purposes of classroom management, of course, you could spread these sessions across the school week, but the result would be that you were, on average, reading with each child for only 2 minutes per day, an amount we've already shown to be barely manageable, in any case.

In recent years, much emphasis has been placed on improving the effectiveness of early reading instruction, and especially alphabetic basics, with the promising result that children from historically low-achieving schools are leaving first grade with reading scores that are at or above national norms. Many had hoped that such early success would snowball, compounding itself across the school years. To the contrary, however, where follow-up data exist, they indicate that even among students from highly regarded and well-controlled programs (e.g., Foorman et al., 1998; Hiebert, 1994; Slavin et al., 1996), reading progress tends to slow across the elementary school years, such that by the middle grades, many students are once again behind despite their strong start.

The data from the fourth-grade National Assessment of Educational Progress (NAEP) tell a similar tale. Since 1992, reading achievement has increased consistently and significantly among more advantaged children (National Center for Education Statistics, 2001). In contrast, scores of the lowest performing children have declined ever so slightly, but significantly. Alas, the gap has only widened. Staring at the NAEP results, cycle after cycle, I have often wondered just how much of the achievement difference between our have and have-not schools reflects the likelihood with which parents succeed in causing their children to read aloud with them at home. If so, it redoubles the social urgency of finding ways to increase the availability of supported reading at school. After all, public schooling was invented exactly and only to ensure all children full educational opportunity, regardless of what their homes could offer.

The adult literacy obligation. Time after time, we are reminded how strongly children's literacy achievement is influenced by the educational levels and literacy practices of their parents. Yet, the situation is at least as dire for the adult literacy population. According to the 2003 National Assessment of Adult Literacy (National Center for Education Statistics, 2006), more than 40% of adult Americans cannot manage more than the simplest literacy tasks. In all, that equals nearly 100,000,000 adults, including more than 80% of those who never finished high school (NCES, 2006).

A particularly troubling fact is that, of eligible adults, only about 8% ever enroll in basic skills instruction (Mikulecky, 2001). In Canada, which has an adult literacy situation that is very similar to that of the U.S. in terms of both the percentage of adults in need of help and the nature of the services available, a study was recently undertaken to determine why participation is so low (Long & Middleton, 2001). Of a national cross-section of 866 adults who had never finished high school, 60% said they had considered enrolling in an adult education program. Less hopefully, only 20% thought they were likely do so within the next five years. Of those who actually did contact an adult literacy center, less than half actually enrolled and 30% of those dropped out within a few months. Of those who enrolled but dropped out, the most frequent reason given was that the program was not helpful to them in level, content, pace, or instruction.

What type of instruction do adult literacy students need? In an assessment of 676 students enrolled in Adult Basic Education (ABE) classes in the U.S., Strucker and Davidson (in press) identified three broad categories of ABE readers. At the high end, making up about 20% of the ABE population, GED Readers were found to possess adequate high-school level reading skills. At the other extreme, Beginning Readers, who represent about 10–12% of the population, were found to lack basic skills and to demonstrate word recognition and comprehension at or below a level considered equivalent to second grade.

In the middle, making up nearly 70% of the ABE population, are the *Intermediate Readers*. Although basic word recognition abilities are essentially in place among these students, their reading fluency and vocabularies remain markedly weak (Davidson & Strucker; 2002; Greenberg, Ehri, & Perin, 1997; Sabatini, 2002). As measured by Davidson and Strucker (2002), expressive vocabulary of adult Intermediates averaged GE 6.6 while receptive vocabulary (PPVT-III) fell below the 9th percentile (Davidson & Strucker, 2002). As a group, the adult Intermediates also demonstrate poor reading fluency (Davidson & Strucker; 2002; Greenberg, Ehri, & Perin, 1997; Sabatini, 2002; Strucker and Davidson, in press), averaging about 100 words correct per minute in oral reading (Davidson & Strucker, 2002.)

It goes without saying that adult learners have no time to waste. It is imperative that instructional reading materials be selected in deference to their reading levels and informational needs. Further, as with our school children, adult literacy students have great need for someone to sit with them as they read—to help them appreciate their progress and to assist them with the vocabulary, language, and background knowledge required by their texts. But who is there to do this? In 2003, ProLiteracy (the recent merger of Laubach Literacy and Literacy Volunteers of America, Inc.) launched an aggressive national campaign to recruit 100,000 new volunteer literacy tutors <http://www.proliteracy.org>. With 100,000,000 adults in need, that would be 1,000 students per tutor—*if* they succeed.

According to Sum, Kirsch, and Taggart (2002), "Workers in the U.S. with literacy skills in the highest levels (Levels 4/5) are 10 times as likely to receive training from their employer as workers with the most limited (Level 1) skills. U.S. spending on higher education is far above average, but spending on adult basic education and job training for the low skilled is below average" (p. 31). "Unfortunately," they add, "inequality is deeply rooted in the education system and in the workplace in the United States. Those entering any level of the educational system with below-average skills are far less likely to advance to the next level, receive far fewer hours of applied learning time, and hence gain far fewer skills" (p. 31).

An inability to read stands as an enormous barrier to one's potential knowledge and social participation. What is in balance for adults is not merely the information in instructions, newspapers, memos, and manuals but, further, the major archives of human invention, philosophy, literature, study, and experience. Literacy affords access to jobs, people, events, places, times, language, perspectives, thoughts, and modes of thought that extend broadly and deeply beyond what any person could ever encounter in her or his day to day existence. And, both directly and indirectly, it also limits what one can do for or hope for one's children.

For adults and children, both, our country must find more powerful ways of making literacy achievable.

The Need for One-on-One Reading: Up Close and Personal

For children. After I finished writing *Beginning to Read* (Adams, 1990), I was often invited to work with teachers and schools around the country, especially in low-income districts. In those classrooms, I saw the reality of the challenges about which I had studied. I watched the painful futility of teaching reading to children who did not know their ABCs. I watched the bright eyes and efficiency of teaching and learning where phonemic awareness was taught playfully and well. From the back of the class, I watched finger-point reading and choral reading, always impressed by how many children were not even on the same page. And I watched lots and lots of independent reading. For a few children in every classroom, learning to read seems remarkably easy, almost magically so. For most, it is genuinely difficult. I watched the beaming pride of accomplishment when children chose books and read them successfully. I also watched children's heartrending disappointment when they found themselves defeated. Not infrequently I watched as children encountered words beyond their vocabulary in the books they were reading.

I vividly remember one eager young reader who asked me to sit with him. He read his first book splendidly. His second, William Steig's *Doctor De Soto* (1990), was one of his own choice, and he opened it with glee. This, clearly, was a guy book, and funny, too. Unfortunately, it is also a book that is much more difficult than its layout suggests. Within a page or two, he encountered a word he did not know. He tried valiantly to sound it out. But his efforts were in vain, for neither was the word in his listening vocabulary. Disappointed, he moved on, only to encounter another, and another, and another such totally elusive word. The joy was gone and so, quite decisively, my little reader shifted his strategy. For the remainder of the book, he simply skipped every single word that was not instantly familiar, including many that I was sure he really knew. I have since watched many low vocabulary children adopt this same strategy. If this is an understandably pragmatic strategy for getting through the text at hand, it is tragically self-limiting over the long haul. In its use, not only do children forfeit the opportunity to learn about words that are not already in their vocabularies but, equally, the opportunity to learn to read many that are.

For adults. Around the same period of time, there appeared an article on adult literacy in the *Boston Globe*, in which it was reported that Massachusetts' waitlist for enrollment was more than 8,000 long (the statewide waitlist has since grown from 15,000 to 22,500 <http://www.sabes.org>). I asked my friend and long-time adult literacy instructor, John Strucker, to take me to an adult literacy class. The center occupied two rooms upstairs from an old-fashioned soda fountain and grill—a "spa," as they are called in New England. The anteroom/office was stacked high with dusty old books and yellowing paper copy. If there was something worthwhile to read in that stash, who knows who could find it.

The class I attended was scheduled from 10:00 to 11:00 A.M. During that hour, the 15 students reviewed their homework, did some round-robin reading from a vintage 1950s controlled-vocabulary book, had a spelling test and a spelling lesson, and went over the homework for the next class. Then the class was over. I asked two students how long they had been enrolled at the center. One said four years. The other said seven. I couldn't help but wonder: If they depended entirely on these classes for learning to read, how many more years would it take until they were done? What these students desperately needed was a tutor—someone who could guide them to the confidence and competence they needed to read on their own.

Propitious Accidents

Writing *Beginning to Read* (Adams, 1990) had given me the opportunity for all this classroom work and, ironically, it had also given me the time. The politics of the book were too much for BBN Technologies (formerly Bolt, Beranek and Newman), where I had worked since graduate school. Shortly after finishing the book, I was reduced to part time and, soon thereafter, laid off all together. Actually, it was even worse; both the psychology and the education departments were riffed entirely. Whether in protest or sympathy, the Speech Department offered me some free space in their area. They discouraged me from bringing my too-many books, but I had an office, a phone, and lots of wonderful new colleagues, albeit with an expertise about which I knew next to nothing. Sometimes fate drops us in odd situations. The only thing to do is to ask why that might be and to go for it. And so, from that jobless exile, I embarked on what has now been a 15-year project to build a speech-recognition-based reading tutor.

BBN had the best speech recognition team in the world, but this was not an easy task. Our first challenge was to port the recognizer from a workstation to a desktop machine. Management was firm that it could not be done, and we spent countless hours petitioning and meeting about its feasibility. Finally, one of my colleagues had a brilliant idea. He proposed to management that they fund one person for 6 weeks to generate an informed estimate of whether the port was possible and, if so, how much labor it would require. Management conceded, and within 3 weeks the port was done.

We brought in children to read, and we hired some teachers to transcribe and annotate their recordings. Of interest, it turns out that people, including teachers, are remarkably unreliable at marking the presence or locations of pauses in children's reading records. On the other side, a common complaint about speech recognizers is that they are not sufficiently accurate for a task such as this. To the contrary, my biggest problem with the recognizer was its exacting accuracy. Repeatedly, it would call errors where I heard none. Sure enough, when I looked at its phonetic transcriptions, it was always right (unless the microphone was out of place). For example, the text word was *hill*; I heard *hill*, but the speech recognizer quite accurately heard /h ē ō/ and marked the word wrong. Technically, the speech recognizer was correct but, pragmatically, this would not do. During normal hours, the big machines belonged to the paid employees, so I burned barrels of midnight oil, shut in the vault with the VAX, trying to figure out the physical signatures of reading difficulty (as distinct from difficulties of articulation or delivery). Happily, there was somebody down the hall who would keep me company through the wee hours, practicing his clarinet.

In 1995, we were given the opportunity to try our technology out in the DODEA (Department of Defense Education Agency) schools through the White House Technology Initiative. In quest of electronic storyware for the kids to read, we chose to partner with the Waterford Institute. Unfortunately for us, Waterford's storyware was supported by an operating system that they had built themselves; with pre-Y2K computers, we were in DLL hell. And there were other problems. The only speech-quality headsets available at the time were too big for the kids and would flop out of position with every movement. Worse still, the total system—stories, graphics, and recognizer—required color monitors, sound cards, and 16MB of memory. None of the schools had machines this fancy. Finally, President Clinton issued a class-size reduction order to the DODEA schools. The funds vanished, and the project folded.

Soon thereafter, the telephone company bought BBN. This seemed to mean the bitter end of our hobby-shop habits. But then, out of the blue, I got a phone call from California. A veritable angel named Joe Costello had heard what we were trying to do and wanted to build a company for exactly that goal. That company would be Soliloquy Learning.

For Soliloquy Learning's first effort at creating its own reading software, we used the Microsoft speech recognizer. The advantages of using the Microsoft recognizer were significant: It was inherently compatible with all Windows machines, and it was free. In terms of disadvantages, the first was that it would not work on Apple computers, though at the time, that didn't seem to bother anybody much besides me. The greater disadvantage was that, for our purposes, it did not work very well. Although the hacking skills of my colleagues were impressive, the Microsoft code was too securely encapsulated. We could not gain clean access to the parameters with which we needed most to work.

Carus Publishing generously helped us out with content, and, somehow, by the spring of 2002 we ("we" were principally seven engineers, a refrigerator, and me, all squeezed into a tiny office in Medford, MA) managed to tape together a little application, the Soliloquy *Reading Assistant* V.1. In fact, it was rather crude and kludgy (see www.answers.com), but the kids seemed pleased. Our funder was pleased, too, giving us the go-ahead to build our own recognizer, starting with Carnegie-Mellon's Sphinx2 Toolkit. What we created, the *Reading Assistant* V.2, worked on both PCs and Apples, but it was still a bit lacking in grace. We, therefore, devoted the following year to making it better, doing our best to optimize its responsiveness as appropriate to the reading situation and as distinct from the sorts of open-ended speech applications for which the Sphinx technology was principally designed. We released the *Reading Assistant* V.3 in the spring of 2005.

The *Reading Assistant*

The technological maturity of automated speech recognition is attested by its sudden burst into the industrial sector, most visibly, perhaps, in telephone and call-routing applications. In contrast, use of automatic speech recognition for assisting student's reading has yet to gain significant following. This is despite the fact that a number of groups have attempted to build such systems. The best known of these may be IBM's ***Watch! Me Read*** project, which stretches back to the 1980s (Nix, Fairweather, & Adams,1998; Williams, 2002). A broad review of the history, promise, and special technical considerations of building speech-recognition-based reading tutors can be found in Mostow and Aist (2001). Jack Mostow himself has surely been the single busiest and most creative contributor to the scientific questions and technical issues involved in this challenge (see Mostow's website, <http://www.cs.cmu.edu/~listen/>).

When automatic speech recognition and reading are used in the same sentence, many people instantly respond, "Phonics!" Certainly, we could have done phonics, and maybe someday we will. For now, however, we feel the greater educational need is for novice and intermediate readers than for beginners, and for fluency, vocabulary, and comprehension than for word attack skills. As such, the *Reading Assistant* never interrupts for phonics work (though, again, there are foreseeable applications where doing so would be appropriate). Instead, when a child mangles or struggles with a word, the machine produces it, asking the child to repeat it and continue reading. Problem words are then listed in the performance reports and marked in the text itself for review. Thus, the emphasis during reading sessions is squarely on providing the ongoing assistance to enable students to continue reading with comprehension, as well as the audience and feedback, both online and cumulatively, to motivate them to do so. As one child confided in me, "I really like it because it gives you something to *do* when you're reading."

As of today, we have developed two different kinds of applications for the *Reading Assistant*. Both are targeted at novice and intermediate readers—readers who essentially know how to decode but lack the automaticity, vocabulary, and comprehension control to read with adequate confidence, speed, and productivity on their own. In one, the technology version of Hiebert's

QuickReads (2003), the focus is on reading and rereading short passages for fluency development per se. In the other, the materials are extended texts, from trade books and Scott Foresman's leveled readers, and the emphasis is more generally on guided oral reading. In either case, the applications are designed with two purposes in mind: (1) to offer students the oral reading opportunities and guidance they need to learn through reading, and (2) to provide teachers with the assistance and information they need to monitor and guide their students' growth.

Presenting texts and supporting graphics to the student on the computer monitor, the *Reading Assistant* is designed to offer supported opportunity for orally reading and rereading level-appropriate text (see Figure 8.1). Whether in the course of their own reading or during preview or review of a text, students can ask the computer for the pronunciation of any word. Alternatively, if a student requests that a word be explained, the computer presents the word's contextually appropriate meaning, a sentence to illustrate its usage, and, wherever possible, a graphic as well. Some of our applications also include Spanish glossary support for English language learners (see Figure 8.2).

Students can also request that the text, or any segment of it, be read aloud to them. The narrators are professional voice models whose readings are expressive and carefully enunciated. So as to make it easier for the student to read along during such modeling, the text is highlighted in time to the narrator's voice, and the pause between sentences has been computationally set

FIGURE 8.1.   A screenshot of the *Reading Assistant* in Read and Record mode with intervention highlighting on the word *ocean*. The text is from *Dory Story* by Jerry Pallotta, illustrated by David Biedrzycki, published by Charlesbridge, Watertown, MA ©2000.

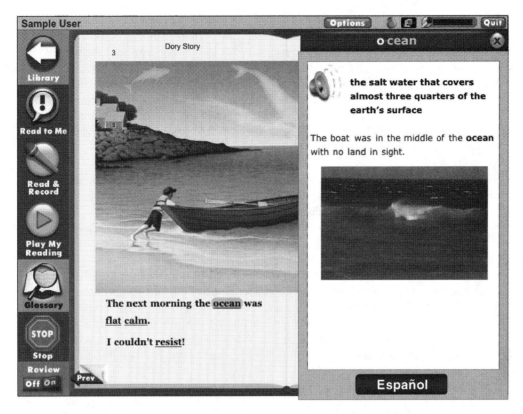

FIGURE 8.2. A screenshot of the *Reading Assistant* with the Glossary open to the entry for *ocean*. The text is from *Dory Story* by Jerry Pallotta, illustrated by David Biedrzycki, published by Charlesbridge, Watertown, MA ©2000.

to ensure enough time for the student to understand and keep up. In addition, each text is followed by a set of comprehension activities. Although these activities vary from publisher to publisher, all are structured to prepare students to read the text with more focus and purpose the next time through.

The key attribute of the *Reading Assistant* lies in the support it provides for students themselves to read. Specifically, by virtue of its speech-recognition layer, the software listens to the student as she or he reads aloud. Monitoring for signs of difficulty, it autonomously provides assistance when the student stumbles or gets stuck. In the background, meanwhile, it builds ongoing records of what the student has read and reread, of her or his fluency on each reading, and of the specific words and segments of text with which the student had difficulty. Tied to each text is a Progress page, which summarizes progress and performance and displays problem words and the student's Personal Glossary (i.e., text words whose meanings the child has looked up). In addition to Progress Reports for the students, the software includes a Review Mode in which miscues are color-coded in the text so that students can selectively focus on difficulties, playing, practicing, repairing, and replaying their readings to their own satisfaction.

The *Reading Assistant* provides the teacher with more detailed reports of students' performance, including accuracy, fluency, amount read, problem words, comprehension, and usage statistics. These reports are available cumulatively and for each separate reading and title and, indeed, in the network version, collapsible almost any which way one wants (classrooms, titles, groups, marking period, . . .). The software also maintains digital recordings of the student's reading so that teachers can build performance portfolios for monitoring growth or sharing with parents. Because these recordings are tied to the text and the performance reports, teachers can listen to them selectively, using the color-coding shown in Review Mode to identify and access segments of special concern or lesson-relevance. The network version also gives teachers the option of assigning specific titles to individuals or the class. Our hope is that these features will help teachers knowingly choose books and challenges on which to focus during the precious one-on-one time they can schedule with each student.

Vignettes.   After putting on her headset and logging in, Pat Miehead spends a minute doing the microphone-check activities. This two-minute activity allows the machine to adjust the input volume and be sure that the microphone is positioned acceptably. Pat then turns to the list of reading selections that her teacher has chosen for her. Pat clicks on a title called *Dory Story*. The cover page pops up, and Pat listens as the machine provides a brief overview of the story. She then clicks on the cover image to open the book.

Pat has never read this story before, so she begins by turning through the pages, stopping on each folio to examine the pictures and to browse the text. She looks for words of which she is uncertain and clicks on each to hear its pronunciation. If she is unsure of the meaning of a word, she clicks on the Glossary button to read (and hear) its syllabified pronunciation and its contextually appropriate definition and usage. If she wants to hear the text, or any part of it, read by an expressive, professional reader, she clicks the "Read to Me" button and then clicks on the text to tell the machine where to begin.

When she has finished browsing, Pat returns to the first page of the book. She clicks the Read & Record button, and all but the first sentence on the page are grayed slightly. As she reads the story aloud, the machine follows along, monitoring and evaluating her progress in the background. When she reads/ŏ sseen/for *ocean*, it paints the word yellow, a signal that she needs to return to that word and try it again. Pat does try, but without success. The machine does not let her struggle for more than a few seconds. Then it distinctly says, "ocean," whereupon Pat repeats the word and continues reading. When she reaches the end of each sentence, the machine automatically shifts the visual emphasis to the next. When she gets to the end of each page, it waits, knowing she may want to dwell on the text or pictures for a bit before moving on. When she turns the page, it is ready to listen. After Pat finishes the story, she completes the comprehension activities which, for this text, are multiple-choice questions.

She then opens her Progress Report to see her PowerPoints. The PowerPoints goal for a selection is a function of its length and difficulty. To reach the PowerPoints goal, the student must read the entire selection with adequate fluency and answer at least 80% of the comprehension questions correctly. Pat sees from the graph that she has almost, but not quite reached the PowerPoints goal for this story. The accompanying tables show her that, although she has read the whole story and answered all of the comprehension question correctly, her reading rate (in correct words per minute) was a bit low. The words on which she stumbled are listed in the Progress Report, but Pat prefers to go back to the story text to study them.

Pat returns to the beginning of the story and switches the display to Review Mode. All of the words she read splendidly are now displayed in green fonts. Those she mangled or with which she needed help are printed in red. Those that were iffy are printed in yellow. Clicking on the Play My Reading button, Pat asks the machine to play back her own reading. Again, it highlights the sentences as it goes. When it gets to sentences containing red or yellow words, she listens carefully. Then she stops the playback and clicks on the problem words, listening carefully to their correct pronunciation and reading them again. Occasionally, she goes to the Glossary for help with a word's meaning, usage, or syllable-by-syllable pronunciation. After reviewing her work, she reads the whole story again. The PowerPoint graph for her second reading shows that, this time, she has mastered the story. She is very pleased with herself.

Pat Miehead is an easy student. She is spending her time well, making good use of the software, learning a lot, and enjoying her progress. But on any given day, not all the students in a class are as easy as Pat Miehead.

There is also, for example, Neva Guittouette. Neva opens lots of stories, but she tends to close them quickly, too. When she is inside a story, she enjoys flipping through the pages, clicking on the words, listening to the narrator, and looking at the pictures. But she is not inclined to read much of them. Fortunately, the Teacher's Progress Reports show exactly how much Neva has read of what in each session as well as how she otherwise spent her time. Seeing this, Neva's teacher may want to sit down with her and show her how to use the software well. She may also want to shorten the list of titles she makes available to Neva in the next few sessions. Some versions of the software are programmed to require that students finish reading a selection before moving to the next.

Carefully reviewing the Teacher Progress Reports, Pat and Neva's teacher is happy to see that most of the children are progressing nicely, as shown by the titles they've read, their comprehension scores, and their fluency. But she also notices that Jung Scientist's fluency and progress looks surprisingly poor. She drills down to Jung's last reading to listen to what is going on. Looking at Jung's reading in Review Mode shows large sections of the text that are almost entirely red, indicating great difficulty. The teacher plays Jung's reading to find out what the problem is. She hears whistling, burping, funny voices, funny words—no wonder his fluency was so poor. The teacher invites Jung to her desk so that he can listen to his reading with her. The problem does not recur.

Sitting next to Jung are the Challenger twins. The twins are in constant motion at their stations. They stand up, sit down, rock, and bounce. When they read, they have a penchant for fiddling with the microphone boom and especially for rolling the windsock back and forth in their fingers. When they are not reading, they like to swing the microphone boom up over their heads— but they frequently neglect to swing it back to their mouths when it is time to read again. The Challenger twins also have a number of issues that compel them to leave their seats. In so doing, they have both developed a preference for unplugging the headset over taking it off; unfortunately, they often forget to plug it back in when they return. The problem is that if the machine does not get a good signal, it cannot tell when the twins are reading correctly. Because there is a bit of the Challenger twins in so many children, V.3 includes a continuous microphone check. When the *Reading Assistant* finds that the microphone signal is lost or otherwise unacceptable, a dialog box pops up with troubleshooting instructions.

Diagnostic sensitivity. In engineering the *Reading Assistant*, our greatest challenge has been to teach it how to distinguish genuine difficulties from (for example) accents, missing teeth, confident repairs, coughs, stuffy noses, and the incessant background voices and racket of the classroom. To find out how well it is doing, we established a "ground truth," by asking two experienced reading teachers to listen, rewinding and re-listening as often as they wished, to the children's readings and to agree with each other for each content word whether they would have intervened or tagged it for review, or whether, flawlessly delivered or not, they judged the word to be secure to the student. Table 8.2 compares the computer's judgments to those of the teachers.

The numbers in Table 8.2 are based on the oral reading of 349 passages representing 153 children in Grades 2–6. The children attended a public elementary (Grades 2–5) or middle school

TABLE 8.2
A Comparison of the *Reading Assistant*'s Error Judgments with Those of Two Reading Teachers

	Diagnostic Sensitivity of the Reading Assistant		
	% FN	*% FP*	*Text Words*
Grade 2	2.19	2.30	1040
Grade 3	2.60	1.96	5078
Grade 4	1.50	2.03	1040
Grade 5	1.60	0.89	624
Grade 6 (all)	1.60	1.39	11177
Grade 6 (ELL)	1.66	1.1	2289

(Grade 6) in districts of median income and educational achievement in the Boston Metropolitan area. English is the second language for about 15% of the Grade 2–5 students and 38% of those in Grade 6. In addition, many of the others had pretty good Boston accents. False Positives are instances where the teachers felt a word warranted intervention or review, but the machine did not. False Negatives are instances where the teachers judged a word to have been read with acceptable comfort, but the machine flagged it for intervention or review. Totaling the False Positives and the False Negatives, the machine agreed with the teachers on upwards of 95% of the words. By comparison, though only given ample opportunity to rewind and re-listen, the teachers ultimately agreed with each other on nearly 98% of the words. We are still working, but we are getting close.

Classroom efficacy.   The most important question, of course, is whether the *Reading Assistant* does indeed promote students' reading growth. To begin to ask this question, we undertook a study using the *Reading Assistant* V.2 with mainstream Grade 2–5 classrooms in the famously representative town of Framingham, MA (for more detail, see Adams & Sullivan-Hall, in preparation). In conducting the study, we worked with a pair of schools: in one school, classrooms in Grades 2 and 3 received the *Reading Assistant* software, while those in Grades 4 and 5 participated as controls; in the other school, the Grades 4 and 5 classrooms received the software, while those in Grades 2 and 3 participated as controls. We used school achievement test profiles and demographics to choose schools that were matched as nearly as possible, although a last-minute school-closing within the district altered the planned balance in the distribution of classrooms. All children who obtained parental permission participated, which included 97.2% of the eligible treatment population and 91.6% of the eligible controls. In addition, 4.7% and 3.3% of the children in treatment and control conditions, respectively, moved away during the course of the year. The number of participating students and teachers is summarized in Table 8.3.

Importantly, the question we were asking through this study was whether having students read for a few more minutes per week with the help of the *Reading Assistant* would boost their reading growth? We were *not* asking whether the *Reading Assistant* might supplant classroom reading instruction. Sessions with the *Reading Assistant* were therefore held during the students' scheduled computer time. Software use began the first week in December and continued for 17 weeks through March. Through February, the students worked with Hiebert's (2003) *Quick-Reads Technology Version*; in March, tradebook titles from Charlesbridge Publishing's *Insights* collection were made available. Each participating class scheduled the computer lab for two

TABLE 8.3
Number of Teachers and Children Participating in the *Reading Assistant* Field Test

	Grade				
Condition	2	3	4	5	Total
Reading Assistant					
Teachers	3	3	2	3	11
Students	59	63	43	63	228
Control					
Teachers	3	3	2	2	10
Students	48	57	42	35	182
Total					
Teachers	6	6	4	5	21
Students	107	120	85	98	410

30-minute sessions as often as twice a week, and usage of the software was observed through periodic visits to the schools and measured by means of the student usage records maintained by the software.

Using Edformation's Standard Oral Reading Fluency Assessment Passages (<http://www.edformation.com>), with standard paper and pencil procedures, the children's fluency was pre-tested in November and the post-tested in June. To analyze the children's fluency gains, we used a Group (2) × Grade (4) × Pre-/Post-Post-Test fluency (2) repeated measures analysis of variance, where Treatment and Grade were between-subjects while the comparison of Pre-/Post-test fluency in correct words per minute was within-subjects. The main effect of Group was not significant ($F(1, 402) = 0.189, p = 0.66$), indicating that the overall reading levels of the software and control classrooms were quite comparable. Regardless of Group, fluency increased with Grade-Level ($F(1,402) = 48.76, p < .001$) and between the Pre- and Post-Test (from fall to spring) ($F(1, 402) = 1,085.9, p < .001$). In addition, the size of the Pre-/Post-Test gain interacted with grades ($F(3,402) = 5.13, p < .002$). Most importantly, as shown in Figure 8.3, fluency gains were significantly greater for those children who had worked with the *Reading Assistant* than for those who had not ($F(1,402) = 12.11, p < .001$).

In Figure 8.3, the fluency gains for the children in our study are also compared to normative expectations as based on the average of two large, national samples (Hasbrouck & Tindal, 1992, and Edformation <www.edformation.com>; before averaging, fall to spring gains from each norm were adjusted for the total number of weeks between the dates of the pre-test and post-test, i.e., 22 weeks for the children in Grades 2 and 3, and 24 weeks for those in Grades 4 and 5). As can be seen, the gains of the children who worked with the *Reading Assistant* were consistently greater than predicted from the norms, where the relative advantage was 20%, 63%, 71% and 19% for children in Grades 2, 3, 4, and 5, respectively.

Given that the maximum possible number of sessions with the *Reading Assistant* was 34, these would seem healthy gains. But, of course, due to snow days and other realities of school time, none of the classes used the computer lab for all of its scheduled sessions. Nor, obviously, could the children have read for the full 30 minutes of any session. Exactly how much did they read? The answer, collated from the *Reading Assistant's* User Logs, is shown in Table 8.4, totaling a little more than 2 hours for the younger children and a little more than three hours for the older children. The actual number of sessions for which students used the software ranged from

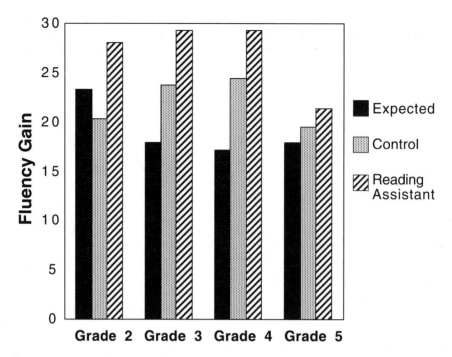

FIGURE 8.3.   Fluency gains in correct words per minute for children who read with the *Reading Assistant* twice a week from December through April as compared to experimental controls and gains as predicted by fluency norms.

about 15 for the younger children to about 24 for the older children, with actual reading time, as measured through the software, averaging only about 8 minutes per session. The remaining time per session was spent not just in miscellaneous and transition activities, but also a number of instructionally and cognitively relevant activities, including teacher-led text and task discussions, selecting and browsing the selections, comprehension activities, review of progress and problems, and thinking. Indeed, for much of the remaining time per session, the children had their books open and looked, for all practical purposes, like they were in fact reading.

TABLE 8.4
Reading Assistant Usage for Each Grade, Including Mean Number of Sessions,
Mean Reading Time Per Session, and Mean Total Reading Time Across Sessions

| | *Reading Assistant Usage* | | |
| | | *Reading Time (minutes)* | |
	Number of Sessions	*Per Session*	*Total*
Grade 2	14.8	8.8	131
Grade 3	20.3	7.5	152
Grade 4	24.3	7.9	192
Grade 5	23.4	8.4	197

That the children averaged only about 8 minutes of actual reading per half-hour session seems a bit surprising at first. But then, we must ask: How much reading do they, themselves, actually do when we sit and read one-on-one with them for a half hour? When we conduct choral reading sessions? When we set aside a half hour for them to read on their own?

Closing

To the question of how much reading must children do to make a difference, these data again indicate an answer of "surprisingly little." Yet there are so many more questions that are begged: How much reading need children do before reaching the point of diminishing returns? How might such sessions be optimally distributed in time? How do the effects weather with time? Do they shrink? Might they grow? What, more specifically, is the nature of the learning or improvement that accrues with reading practice? The problems that beset young readers vary individually, developmentally, and as a function of the text at hand. Can the computer be programmed to detect the specific and distinct needs of different students? What other kinds of feedback and interactions would effectively promote reading, learning, and literacy growth?

Indeed, the questions provoked by this sort of technology are almost innumerable. But so, too, is the technology's potential for helping us answer them. Speech recognition-based readingware affords precise tracking of when, what, how much, and how well students have read, as well as of the words and textual segments with which they had difficulty, whether they received help and, if so, exactly what kinds. Some have conveyed to me a concern that I "vanished" from the reading scene. I didn't vanish. I just felt I had to try to do this. Speech-recognition-based readingware offers an unprecedented platform for melding research and practice and, hopefully, for making real contributions to the vital challenge of closing the literacy gap. Indeed, looking to the future, one way to imagine the potential of the *Reading Assistant* is as a book with ears, voice, evaluative precision, and an instantaneously accessible library of texts and references. This, we believe, is a book of enormous possibility, not just for supporting reading growth, but for making all kinds of literature and literacy both physically and cognitively accessible to students of all ages.

We are currently working in partnership with John Strucker and Mary Beth Curtis to develop and test modules designed especially for adult literacy students. As we learn more and more about what makes texts difficult and how to detect different kinds of uncertainty in readers, our goal is to develop the software's capacity for richly interactive text-based tutoring, and especially for supporting reading, thinking, and learning in the content areas.

ACKNOWLEDGMENTS

The author wishes to thank The Carlisle Foundation for their generous support of the Framingham Reading Project, the teachers and students of the Framingham Public Schools for their participation in this study, Patti Sullivan-Hall for her collaboration and assistance in all, and the engineers at Soliloquy Learning for their extraordinary brilliance and hard work.

REFERENCES

Adams, M. J. (1990). *Beginning to read: Thinking and learning about print.* Cambridge, MA: The MIT Press.
Adams, M. J., & Sullivan-Hall, P. (in preparation). Speech recognition-based software for developing reading fluency.

Allington, R. L. (1983). The reading instruction provided readers of different reading abilities. *Elementary School Journal, 83*, 95–107.

Allington, R. L. (1989). Coherence or chaos? Qualitiative dimensions of the literacy instruction provided low-achievement children. In A. Gartner and D. Lipsky (Eds.). *Beyond separate education.* New York: Brookes.

Anderson, R. C., Wilson, P. T., and Fielding, L. G. (1988). Growth in reading and how children spend their time outside school. *Reading Research Quarterly, 23*, 285–303.

Brooks, G., Flanagan, N., Henkhuzens, Z., Hutchison, D. (1998). *What works for slow readers? The effectiveness of early intervention schemes.* Slough, UK: National Foundation for Educational Research.

Birman, B. F., Orland, M. E., Jung, R. K., Anson, R. J., Garcia, G. N., Moore, M. T., Funkhouser, J. E., Morrison, D. R., Turnbull, B. J., & Reiser, E. R. (1987). *The current operation of the Chapter 1 program: Final report from the National Assessment of Chapter 1.* Washington, D.C.: Government Printing Office.

Chall, J. S. (1983). *Stages of reading development.* New York: McGraw-Hill.

Chard, D. J., Vaughn, S., & Tyler, B. J. (2002). A synthesis of research on effective interventions for building reading fluency with elementary students with learning disabilities. *Journal of Learning Disabilities, 35*, 386–406.

Cipielewski, J., & Stanovich, K. E. (1992). Predicting growth in reading ability from children's exposure to print. *Journal of Experimental Child Psychology, 54*, 74–89.

Cunningham, A. E., & Stanovich, K. E. (1990). Assessing print exposure and orthographic processing skill in children: A Quick measure of reading experience. *Journal of Educational Psychology, 82*, 733–740.

Cunningham, A. E., & Stanovich, K. E. (1991). Tracking the unique effects of print exposure in children: Associations with vocabulary, general knowledge, and spelling. *Journal of Educational Psychology, 83*, 264–274.

Cunningham, A. E., & Stanovich, K. E. (1998). What reading does for the mind. *American Educator, 22*(1–2), 8–15.

Davidson, R., & Strucker, J. (2002). Patterns of word recognition errors among Adult Basic Education native and nonnative speakers of English. *Scientific Studies of Reading, 6,* 299–316.

Edformation. Standard Oral Reading Fluency Assessment Passages. <http://www.edformation.com>

Elbaum, B., Vaughn, S., Hughes, M. T., & Moody, S. W. (2000). How effective are one-to-one tutoring programs in reading for elementary students at risk for reading failure? A meta-analysis of the intervention research. *Journal of Educational Psychology, 92*, 605–619.

Finn, J. D. (2001). School noncompletion and literacy. In C. F. Kaestle, A. Campbell, J. E. Finn, S. T. Johnson, & L. J. Mikulecky (Eds.). *Adult literacy and education in America (NCES 2001–534),* pp. 41–72. Washington, DC: National Center for Education Statistics.

Foorman, B. R., Francis, D. J., Fletcher, J. M., Schatschneider, C., & Mehta, P. (1998). The role of instruction in learning to read: Preventing reading failure in at-risk children. *Journal of Educational Psychology, 90*, 37–55.

Freeman, W. J., & Nuñez, R. (2000). Restoring to cognition the forgotten primacy of action, intention, and emotion. In R. Núñez & W. J. Freeman (Eds.). *Reclaiming cognition: The primacy of action, intention and emotion,* pp. ix–xix. Exeter, UK: Imprint Academic.

Garan, E. M. (2002). *Resisting Reading Mandates: How to Triumph with the Truth.* Portsmouth, NH: Heinemann.

Greenberg, D., Ehri, L. C., & Perin, D. (1997). Are word reading processes the same or different in adult literacy students and third-fifth graders matched for reading level? *Journal of Educational Psychology, 89*, 262–275.

Hardyck, C. D., & Petrinovich, I. F. (1970). Subvocal speech and comprehension level as a function of the difficulty level of reading material. *Journal of Verbal Learning and Verbal Behavior, 9*, 647–652.

Hasbrouck, J. E., & Tindal, G. (1992, Spring). Curriculum-based oral reading fluency norms for students in grades 2 through 5. *Teaching Exceptional Children,* pp. 41–44.

Hiebert, E. (1994). Reading recovery in the United States: What difference does it make to an age cohort? *Educational Researcher, 23*(9), 15–24.

Hiebert, E. R. (2003). *QuickReads: A research-based fluency program (Technology Edition)*. Parsippany, NJ: Pearson Learning.

Huey, E. B. (1908/1968). *The psychology and pedagogy of reading*. Cambridge, Mass.: MIT Press.

Juel, C. (1994). *Learning to read and write in one elementary school*. New York: Springer-Verlag.

Kirsch, I., Jungeblut, A., Jenkins, L., & Kolstad, A. (1993). *Adult illiteracy in America: A first look at the National Adult Literacy Survey*. Washington, DC: National Center for Education Statistics.

Liberman, A. M., & Mattingly, I. G. (1985). The motor theory of speech perception revised. *Cognition, 2*(1), 1–36.

Long, E., & Taylor, L. (2002). *Nonparticipation in literacy and upgrading programs: A national study*. Ontario, CA: ABC CANADA Literacy Foundation.

Long, E., & Middleton, S. (2001). *Patterns of participation in Canadian literacy and upgrading programs: Results of a national follow-up study*. Ontario, CA: ABC CANADA Literacy Foundation.

Mcintosh, R., Vaughn, S., Schumm, J., Haager, D., & Lee, O. (1993). Observations of students with learning disabilities in general education classroom. *Exceptional Children, 60*, 249–261.

Mikulecky, L. J. (2001). Education for the workplace. In C. F. Kaestle, A. Campbell, J. E. Finn, S. T. Johnson, & L. J. Mikulecky (Eds.). *Adult literacy and education in America (NCES 2001–534)*, pp. 109–142. Washington, DC: National Center for Education Statistics.

Monroe, M. (1932). *Children who cannot read*. Chicago: University of Chicago Press.

Moody, S. W., Vaughn, S., & Schumm, J. S. (1997). Instructional grouping for reading: teachers' views. *Remedial and Special Education, 18*, 347–356.

Mostow, J., & Aist, G. (2001). Evaluating tutors that listen: An overview of Projet LISTEN. In K. Forbus & P. Feltovich (Eds.). *Smart machines in education:* Cambridge, MA: The MIT Press.

National Center for Education Statistics. (2006). *A First Look at the Literacy of America's Adults in the 21st Century (NCES 2006-470)*. Washington, DC: National Center for Education Statistics, U.S. Department of Education.

National Center for Education Statistics. (2001). The nation's report card: Fourth-grade reading highlights (NCES 2001–513). Washington, DC: U.S. Department of Education, Office of Educational Research and Improvement.

National Reading Panel. (2000). *Teaching children to read: An evidence-based assessment of the scientific research literature on reading and its implications for reading instruction*. Rockville, MD: National Institutes of Health.

Nix, D., Fairweather, P., & Adams, W. (1998). *Speech recognition, children and reading. Human factors in computing systems*. New York: Association for Computing Machinery.

Pinnell, G. S., Lyons, C. A., DeFord, D. E. Bryk, A. S., & Seltzer, M. (1994). Comparing instructional models for the literacy education of high-risk first graders. *Reading Research Quarterly, 29*, 8–39.

Núñez, R., & Freeman, W. J. (Eds.). (2000). *Reclaiming cognition: The primacy of action, intention and emotion*. Exeter, UK: Imprint Academic.

Rosen, D. J. (2002). Adult Literacy Advocacy: In for the Long Haul. Keynote Presentation. New York Association for Continuing/Community Education, Kerhonkson, NY.

Sabatini, J. P. (2002). Efficiency in word recognition of adults: Ability group comparisons. *Scientific Studies of Reading, 6*, 267–298.

Sandak, R., & Poldrack, R. A. (Eds.) (2004). The cognitive neuroscience of reading. Scientific Studies of Reading, 8 (whole no. 3), 199–304.

Slavin, R. E., Karweit, N. L., & Wasik, B. A. (1994). *Preventing Early School Failure: Research, Policy, and Practice*. Boston: Allyn & Bacon.

Slavin, R. E., Karweit, N. L., & Madden, N. A. (1989). *Effective programs for students at risk*. Boston: Allyn & Bacon.

Slavin, R. E., Madden, N. A., Dolan, L. J., Wasik, B. A., Ross, S., Smith, L., & Dianda, M. (1996). Success for All: A summary of research. *Journal of Education for Students Placed At Risk, 1*, 41–76.

Stanovich, K. E. (1993). Does reading make you smarter? Literacy and the development of verbal intelligence. In H. Reese (Ed.). *Advances in child development and behavior, 24*, 133–180. San Diego: Academic Press.

Steig, W. (1990). *Doctor de Soto*. New York: Farrar, Straus and Giroux.

Stotsky, S. (1984). Research on reading/writing relationships: A synthesis and suggested directions. In J. Jensen (Ed.). *Composition and comprehending*, pp. 627–742. Urbana, IL: ERIC Clearinghouse on Reading and Communication Skills and National Conference on Research in English.

Strucker, J., & Davidson, R. (in press.). *NCSALL Report: The Adult Reading Components Study*. Boston: World Education/NCSALL.

Sum, A., Kirsch, I., & Taggart, R. (2002). *The twin challenges of mediocrity and inequality: Literacy in the U.S. from an international perspective*. Princeton, NJ: Educational Testing Service.

Swanson, H. L. (1999). Reading research for students with LD: A meta-analysis of intervention outcomes. *Journal of Learning Disabilities, 32*, 504–532.

Vaughn, S., Levy, S., Coleman, M., & Bos, C. S. (2002). Reading instruction for students with LD and EBD: A synthesis of observation studies. *Journal of Special Education, 36*, 2–15.

Vaughn, S., Moody, S., & Schumm, J. S. (1998). Broken promises: Reading instruction in the resource room. *Exceptional Children, 64*, 211–226.

Vellutino, F., Scanlon, D. M., Sipay, E., Small, S., Pratt, A., Chen, R., & Denckla, M. (1996). Cognitive profiles of difficult-to-remediate and readily remediated poor readers: Early intervention as a vehicle for distinguishing between cognitive and experiential deficits as basic causes of specific reading disability. *Journal of Educational Psychology, 88*, 601–838.

Wasik, B. A., & Slavin, R. E. (1993). Preventing early reading failure with one-to-one tutoring: A review of five programs. *Reading Research Quarterly, 28*, 178–200.

Williams, S. M. (2002). Speech recognition technology and the assessment of beginning readers. In *Technology and assessment: Thinking ahead*, pp. 40–49. Washington, DC: National Academy Press.

CURRICULUM MATERIALS

Hiebert, E. R. (2003). *QuickReads: A research-based fluency program (Technology Edition)*. Parsippany, NJ: Pearson Learning.

Insights: Reading Fluency Software. (2000). Watertown, MA: Charlesbridge Publishing.

9

▼▼▼▼▼▼▼

CD-ROM Talking Books:
A Way to Enhance Early Literacy?

Adriana G. Bus, Maria T. de Jong, and Marian Verhallen
Leiden University

We introduce young children to the world of reading by means of fictional literature. Research suggests that children's concepts about stories develop as a result of their adult led encounters with books (Sulzby, 1985). For instance, research by Sulzby (1985) indicates that as children's adult-led encounters with storybooks increase, they begin to represent story structure and linguistically sophisticated story language in their retellings. When reading a book with adults, emergent readers do not focus exclusively on illustrations, as they are likely to do when looking at a book independently. Through paying more attention to the written text, they are likely to have occasions to notice sound symbol correspondences and become aware of orthographic patterns. Additionally, over time young children begin to memorize features of the text from repeated shared readings of the same book. It is clear that when adult caregivers read and discuss books with children, they enter into a cognitive apprenticeship that scaffolds or supports youngsters' literacy learning. Recent advances in multimedia, CD-ROM technologies offer new possibilities for introducing children to the world of reading through the computer. For example, in the Netherlands and other parts of the world, adults can read books to children or young children can independently experience electronic versions of those same books on a computer screen. According to a recent survey (Mullis, Martin, Gonzalez, & Kennedy, 2001), 9% of Dutch families have access to educational reading software at home. Access to this software could result in unique literacy learning experiences through joint activities between parents and their young children or through children's independent explorations of interactive, multimedia stories on CD-ROM.

CD-ROM storybooks have the potential to effect a literal interaction between the reader and the story, because digital storybooks are by nature dynamic entities that are adaptable to the needs and wishes of individual readers. At the very least, CD-ROM books include an oral reading of the story (Reinking, Labbo, & McKenna, 1997), a multimedia feature that allows nonreaders to have access to the text without adult intervention. However, CD-ROM books also frequently include additional features, narration, digital graphics, animations, movie clips, highlighted text, music, and sound effects, which may be supportive of young children's literacy development. Multimedia features of CD-ROM stories, such as interactive animations, blur the distinction among various types of popular, entertaining media (e.g., computer games, movies, and cartoons) that children seem to effortlessly comprehend. Although it is likely that CD-ROM books do not replicate entirely the adult-child interactions that occur when reading print-based books, electronic text may function as a unique scaffold that supports children's comprehension, language development, and concepts about print (cf. Chomsky, 1990; Labbo & Kuhn, 2000; McKenna, 1998).

Due to the potential impact of CD-ROM storybooks on early literacy development, researchers have begun to conduct research on how encounters with picture storybooks, which are similar in illustrations and story content but have an electronic format, figure into young children's emergent reading development (de Jong & Bus, 2002, 2003, 2004; Greenlee-Moore & Smith, 1996; James, 1999; Labbo & Kuhn, 2000; Labbo, Reinking & McKenna, 1995; Lewin, 1997, 1998, 2000; Matthew, 1996; McKenna, 1998; Miller, Blackstock, & Miller, 1994; Reinking, 1988, 1994, 1997; Reinking & Bridwell-Bowles, 1991; Ricci & Beal, 2002; Segers, Takke, & Verhoeven, 2004; Smith, 2001; Turbill, 2001). Thus, as we enter a new technological era where computers are readily accessible to young children, questions arise as to the potential of this type of software on early literacy development (Labbo, 1996). Do CD-ROM storybooks support young children's print based, emerging literacy development? Do electronic literacy experiences stimulate unique learning experiences and effects? We wonder to what extent the unique multimedia features of CD-ROM stories create a cognitive apprenticeship that enables young children to read stories in ways that supports their literacy development.

THE COMPUTER AS AN ELECTRONIC SCAFFOLD

Researchers who are interested in learning how young children construct story meaning have been most interested in how adults facilitate comprehension (e.g., Bus & van IJzendoorn, 1988; Whitehurst et al., 1988). Because books have been viewed as static objects that consist of fixed words on pages, and because young children cannot decipher those words independently, it is only logical that research has focused on how adults' comments scaffold children's comprehension. Thus, the role of pictures and printed text has clearly been de-emphasized in the literature about storybook reading in previous decades (cf. Reinking, 1994). More recently, over the past decade, researchers have suggested that computer programs have the potential to serve as "electronic scaffolds" that support children's story-related literacy development (Labbo & Kuhn, 2000; McKenna, 1998; McKenna, Reinking, & Bradley, 2001; McKenna & Watkins 1994, 1995, 1996). CD-ROM stories foster children's comprehension and focuses their attention on relevant aspects of the plot because digital storybooks are by nature dynamic entities easily capable of being adapted to the needs and wishes to individual readers. Animations that augment text may help youngsters understand a character's state of mind, point of view, or motives. For instance, in a research study, Smith's (2001) son James (2 to 3 years old during the study), who attended to computer animations that supplemented the text, frequently chose to interact with the story by speaking directly to the screen, not to his mother. For instance, reading the CD-ROM version of Aesop's fable *The Tortoise and The Hare*, he clicked eight times on Hare, thus revealing a hypertext ("Hey I was supposed to win.") and he answered talking directly to Hare on the computer screen ("Well, he already winned.") and not to his mother. According to Smith (2001), who compared various ways in which young children encounter books, this type of meaning making is evident only with CD-ROM storybooks, where the characters seem to talk directly to James and he responds to them, rather than to his mother.

It is clear that the CD-ROM talking books offer interactive features that may serve as "electronic scaffolds." Additionally, CD-ROM talking books (also referred to as electronic storybooks) incorporate more symbolic elements on screen than printed books do on the page. For example, CD-ROM stories may include live-action video, sound effects, animations, narration, and music that are responsive to moves by young readers. However, different types of interactive features such as automatic text narration, text read aloud on demand, pronunciation of unfamiliar words, animations that stray from the storyline, and decoding phonics analogies prompts, such as "if m-a-t- is mat then r-a-t- is [pause] rat," have had various degrees of success with children in different stages of reading development (McKenna, 1998). Questions remain as to which features of software programs offer effective alternatives for adult support in ways that help children maneuver independently and purposefully through the maze of letters, words, sentences, illustrations, unfamiliar vocabulary, and concepts that are inaccessible for nonreaders on the printed page.

Findings from recent studies suggest that various factors play important roles in whether CD-ROM, multimedia talking books serve as competent scaffolds for children of various literacy ability levels. For instance, Segers et al. (2004) sought to find out if computer programs were as successful in promoting children's book-related vocabulary development as were teachers. They found that teachers outperformed the computer program. However, results may be due to the quality, content, and limited interactive features of the program used in the study. The CD-ROM storybook in the Segers et al. (2004) study was limited to an occasional, small animation, followed by a question posed by the computer after each story segment. Other features may have been more supportive of vocabulary growth. A potentially productive approach to studying this issue is to test whether separate features of talking books such as video, sound effects, animations, interactivity of text, and responsiveness of the screen to student demands, have the potential to enhance specific literacy learning activities. Furthermore, to test whether CD-ROM stories promote literacy and literary learning, classroom intervention studies are necessary (Roskos, Christie, & Vukelich, 2004). As Reinking and Watkins (2000) noted, creative researchers need to devise new approaches and frameworks for addressing the complex factors affecting instruction and learning with computers in classrooms.

DIGITAL GUIDANCE TO FOCUS CHILDREN'S ATTENTION ON PRINT

Research focused on adult/child book sharing suggests that when children focus their attention on print as adults read aloud, they are more successful in internalizing features of written words (Mason, Peterman, & Kerr, 1989; Murray, Stahl, & Ivey, 1996; Smolkin, Conlon, & Yaden, 1988). It is also clear that children's orthographic knowledge of print when reading books is reinforced in two types of conditions: first, when the text has special characteristics such as bold letters, single letters, text in balloons, or when text is used as part of the illustrations (Smolkin, Yaden, Brown, & Hofius, 1992); and second, when a child or an adult points to the text, focusing children's attention on print (Ehri & Sweet, 1991). Thus, it is likely that CD-ROM multimedia storybooks may enhance young children's orthographic knowledge through digital guidance that may focus children's attention on print (e.g., words or phrases are highlighted while text is read aloud) (de Jong & Bus, 2003). For example, we (de Jong & Bus, 2003) noted that in 84.4% of CD-ROM books with text that we analyzed, the written and spoken words were emphasized through various digital effects that ranged from letter color changes to blocks of highlighting around words or phrases. Additionally, some of the CD-ROM talking books we analyzed also offer the option of reading separate words or phrases of text aloud at a time.

In our own work (de Jong & Bus, 2002), we have studied if multiple readings of the CD-ROM talking book *P. B. Bear's Birthday Party*, which includes digital highlighting of the text while it is pronounced and interactivity both fostering young children's ability to read words. Findings indicate that some junior and senior kindergarten children (4 to 6-year-olds) who explored the CD-ROM book six times were able to read nouns from the focal text in a decontextualized list. We speculated that children made gains in word reading because the program provided opportunities for children to make connections between iconic, written, and spoken forms of story words. Contrary to the notion that book experiences only support story comprehension and vocabulary development (cf. Sénéchal, LeFevre, Thomas, & Daley, 1998), our findings indicate that kindergarten children who have attained basic levels of literacy development (e.g., some letter recognition, invented spelling abilities, limited word recognition) strongly improved in reading words from the story text as a result of multimedia storybook reading. On the other hand, children who according to a pretest demonstrated low levels of alphabetic knowledge, did not internalize features of written words. Thus, it is likely that children deny aspects of books too remote from what their present knowledge includes and that they do not internalize features of written words in a multimedia storybook learning environment until they have begun to consider letters to be important sources of information (Ehri & Sweet, 1991).

HOW CONSIDERATE ARE TALKING BOOKS?

Labbo & Kuhn (2000) suggest that a productive way to evaluate the potential effectiveness and quality of CD-ROM storybooks to support children's story-related literacy development is to determine if the digital text is considerate. Based on Armbruster's (1984) notion of considerate text in books printed on paper, this construct postulates that coherence of text, clarity of writing, and congruity across structural story element are key factors in fostering children's language development and story comprehension. In other words, the way stories are told in CD-ROM storybooks may be considerate, assisting young readers in following and remembering the story, or inconsiderate, not assisting readers in following and remembering the story. Labbo and Kuhn (2000), regard a CD-ROM multimedia story feature to be inconsiderate if it is not related to the main aspects of the story (e.g., characters, location, time, problem, goal, events, resolution, or theme). From this perspective, engaging but largely peripheral animations may distract children from figuring out story events, making logical predictions, determining cause-and-effect connections, or drawing relevant conclusions. Indeed, some children may shift from a story-related to a game-playing stance—a shift in cognitive perspective which may interfere with their comprehension of the story (cf. Bolter, 1998; Greenfield et al., 1996).

In our own work, we have found that about 90% of the multimedia effects present in 55 Dutch CD-ROM books that we analyzed are inconsiderate with the story, a result that was replicated by Korat and Shamir (2004) for an Israeli collection of CD-ROM books. These visual and sound effects, discovered by moving the cursor over the illustrations, are appealing and humorous, but mostly unrelated to the story, a factor that may negatively impact story comprehension (cf. Bolter, 1998; Greenfield et al., 1996; Labbo & Reinking, 1999; Leu, 2000). For example, in the CD-ROM story *Big Party for Tiger*, with the click of a mouse a tea towel morphs into a dove, an animation that is incongruent with the main storyline, which involves a complex telephone conversation between Aunt Goose and Bear.

Labbo and Kuhn (2000) report that Roberto, a kindergarten case-study child who displayed a basic concept of story structure, often lapsed into passive viewing of a CD-ROM story because each screen page of the story had numerous multimedia special effects which were inconsiderate with the story. For example, when interacting with and viewing a series of incongruent special effects in the CD-ROM story *Arthur's Teacher Trouble*, Roberto tended to passively watch the screen. He seemed to enjoy the multimedia effects, but this affective motivation did not lead to understanding the story. On the other hand, when interacting with *Stella Luna*, a CD-ROM story with more integrally related multimedia effects, Roberto consistently engaged in complex and explicitly stated chains of story events. Because 90–95% of *Stella Luna's* multimedia effects were related to the central story, Roberto's story experience was enhanced. He made comments that indicated how he was constructing story meaning. For instance, looking at a supplemental animation clip that showed Stella Luna's mother looking for her in spite of a hostile owl's pursuit, Roberto planned how to access additional story information on screen (e.g., "Let's look and see here . . ."); he connected new information to previous events (e.g., "It's mother. She was looking for her baby before."); and he responded to humorous events (e.g., he giggles when a baby bird pokes Stella Luna with his beak and she acts startled).

Other research supports Labbo and Kuhn's (2000) findings, noting that young children were not successful in navigating through an entire story without being distracted by pictorial details and sound effects hidden in screen illustrations (e.g., James, 1999; Turbill, 2001). Our P. B. Bear experiment (de Jong & Bus, 2002) suggests that the iconic modes of electronic books (e.g., mouse access to illustrations, animations, games) attract 4 and 5-year-olds at the expense of reading a full page of story text. Indeed, after six 15-minute sessions, only a minority of the children we studied had read the entire story more than once, even though they had sufficient opportunities to read the story six times. For example, children explored *P. B. Bear's Birthday Party* in bits and pieces, activating animations, accessing text fragments, and ignoring connected text. As a result, the children in the experimental condition did not know the story content better than those in a control condition. However, the absence of negative effects of animation in other studies may suggest that older or more advanced children are capable of separating inconsiderate features from the essentials of the story (cf. Underwood & Underwood, 1998).

In Ricci and Beal's (2002) randomized experiment among a group of 66 first-grade students, visual and sound effects did not negatively affect comprehension. The interactive storybook format offered many more potential distractors away from the main story line than other forms of media (e.g., teacher read alouds). On each page screen, a child could click on any object to see an animation and sound effect that was not central to the story. For example, when a duckling hatches on screen, the child can subsequently click on a pond reed in the background and see a parade of costumed ants march across the foreground, accompanied by music. Children in the study were able to recall many details from stories presented in a CD-ROM format, even though they explored dozens or, in some cases hundreds, of animations that were completely irrelevant to the storyline. In other words, interaction with unrelated story animations did not affect first graders' memories for story facts, their ability to make inferences, or their performance on a picture-sequencing task. Instead of interfering with the story, the animations produced some positive effects as evidenced by increased enjoyment children reported on a rating scale. Thus, it is conceivable that animations unrelated to the story may enhance older or more advanced children's engagement and motivation to explore stories and thus their understanding of stories (Cordova & Lepper, 1996).

To pursue this line of questioning, we (de Jong & Bus, 2004) recently studied 4 to 5-year-old Dutch kindergarten children who were still in the initial stages of story comprehension but retelling a story their responses were more than just responding by labeling pictures or commenting at pictures. All 18 children listened to picture storybooks read by adults and also explored a CD-ROM storybook that included numerous animations, for more than 90% inconsiderate with the story (de Jong & Bus, 2003). Most children seemed engaged with the content of the electronic, CD-ROM books. Indeed, each of the children activated more than 20 animations unrelated to the story in each session. Nonetheless, over time, children heard approximately 90% of the screens 3.5 times. Despite their encounters with distracting, inconsiderate animations, they continued to focus on the story. This comparison of CD-ROM storybook encounters with traditional print book reading adds nuance to the argument that inconsiderate animations distract children from listening to the story text (de Jong & Bus, 2004). Indeed, children's understanding of the printed book was as good as their understanding of the electronic version of the book. These results, however, do not rule out the possibility that access to numerous incongruent or inconsiderate inserts in each screen could foster passive viewing and lead children to suspend efforts to make sense out of the story when they are younger and less knowledgeable. Unlike the CD-ROM storybooks used by Labbo and Kuhn (2000), there were fewer (different) animations available in the CD-ROM storybooks used in our study (19 or more animations per screen used by Labbo & Kuhn as opposed to five per screen in our study). Additional work is needed to learn more about the effects of considerate animations as scaffolds to children's story comprehension.

TELEVISED PRESENTATIONS OFFERED
SIMULTANEOUSLY WITH NARRATION

Many CD-ROM storybooks offer a multimedia presentation of the story that allows children to simultaneously view animations while hearing the story read aloud. For example, in the CD-ROM version of *The Ugly Duckling* (1993), the focal book of a study conducted by Ricci & Beale (2002), one screen shows the text and an illustration of mother duck sitting on her eggs. As the text is narrated, the illustration becomes animated in ways that dramatize the story content: the eggs hatch, ducklings emerge, and mother looks surprised and distressed at the appearance of the ugly duckling. Thus, the presentation mode is similar to that of a televised cartoon—a mode in which children hear a narrator describe animated actions, music, sound effects, and accompanying character dialogue.

In 50% of the Dutch CD-ROM storybooks we analyzed (de Jong & Bus, 2003), stories included music and cinematic effects that added a film-like depth to the story, thus potentially supporting children's ability to make inferences about story events. For example, the dynamic visuals in the CD-ROM, *Well Again*, make visible how a garden-hose telephone works and how it is possible that one of the characters, Gossipmonger, is able to overhear a call from Bear to Aunt Goose. The dynamic visuals of the English CD-ROM title, *The Cat in the Hat*, show how the cat takes the children by surprise by rushing into the children's house. In 34.5% of the Dutch CD-ROM storybooks we analyzed (de Jong & Bus, 2003), complete scenes were dramatized in concert with the story. For example, in the CD-ROM *Little Flatfoot*, one can see how the main character, Nicky, flies in animated scenes; however, other story events are represented by static pictures. Even though these features are considerate with the story (Labbo & Kuhn, 2000), they may cause cognitive overload.

A small body of literature provides detailed analyses of young children's comprehension of stories across audio and audiovisual media. Researchers (e.g., Gibbons, Anderson, Smith, Field, & Fisher, 1986) strictly controlled for complexity and difficulty of information. They found no strong evidence for the visual superiority hypothesis, a theoretical frame that assumes that children are better equipped to process visual rather than verbal information. As Neuman and Koskinen (1992) note, the crowdedness of televised presentations that require children to process simultaneously through multiple modalities quickly might interfere with comprehension and encourage children to "look and not to listen." Children may have a tendency to remember more dialogue and make more inferences about stories when there are no visual actions to attract their attention (Neuman & Koskinen, 1992). Gibbons et al. (1986) note that highly salient visual information available through televised presentations does not interfere with children's processing of auditory information, thus reducing or shifting their attention away from narration toward visually depicted information. We hypothesize that in so far as studies report results in line with the visual superiority hypothesis, they may have inadvertently confounded effects of media with the type of information actually presented. Audio information including utterances may be more complex and difficult for young children to comprehend than video information that depicts actions.

On the other hand, video fragments, short animations that depict story events or a character's actions and that are considerate with story narration, may help viewers build mental representations of stories. A case in point is provided in Field and Anderson's (1985) research, in which visual orientation and recall of auditory content were positively correlated, particularly in a sample of 5-year-olds. They compared children's recall of three types of information, visual (animated stories mostly communicated visually with very little information provided via auditory channels), mainly auditory (puppet skits composed primarily of dialogue and little or no puppet movement on a fixed background), and audiovisual (same information could be learned by listening or viewing with a soundtrack signaling what was to happen visually). In general, recall for younger children was significantly better for the audiovisual condition. Other work in this area suggests that visual information supports children's understanding of factual information and their ability to make inferences. Gibbons et al. (1986) presented 30-second audiovisual stories to 4-year-old children. Audiovisual content consisted of animated dolls performing setting-appropriate actions in a dollhouse, school, hospital and street scene. Actions, accompanied by standard cinematic techniques (e.g., zooms, pans, cutaway shots), were accompanied by character utterances. The other half of the group of children heard stories in audio form that included character utterances accompanied by actions described by a narrator. Narrated action statements were carefully matched to utterances in length (number of words) and complexity (number of propositions per statement). The researchers found that the 4-year-olds remembered dialogue better in the audio-visual condition than in the audio condition alone. Audiovisual input led to better memory for actions and produced more elaborations. Thus, the presentation mode had a positive effect on so-called constrained relevant inferences, those inferences defined as logically or pragmatically derived from information in the text. For instance, the fact that Joe drives a bus in the story is derived from the statement, "Joe started up the bus with a key." Calvert, Huston, Watkins and Wright (1982) observe that cinematic effects (e.g., zoom shots, music, and sound effects such as a loud crash) announce events and may help focus children's attention on central story content. Additionally, dynamic images may support a more complete model of a story, resulting in a child's improved ability to make inferences. In line with Neuman's (1997) theory of *synergy* we therefore hypothesize that additional filmic representations, music and sounds may add new dimensions to children's story understanding. Simultaneous presentation of information in various modes may foster what good readers seem to do best—namely, transforming information in a text to mental models that include visual-spatial information about story scenes (Sharp et al., 1995).

Paivio's (1986) dual-coding hypothesis may also provide a theoretical perspective for viewing positive effects of dynamic visuals and sound effects on comprehension processes. Dual-coding perspectives assume that textual information is more memorable when it is encoded visually and linguistically. Thus, Paivio posits that the words-with-visualizations condition encourages the building of referential connections between elements in verbal and visual representations, thus helping to create a more complete story model. Therefore, it is not the images themselves that are beneficial for later recall, but the association links they create that are important (Dubois & Vial, 2000). In other words, it is assumed that referential connections between verbal and visual input promote creation of coherent mental images of the story that is unrealizable in isolation (Mayer & Anderson, 1992).

DYNAMIC IMAGES AS A FRAMEWORK FOR
UNDERSTANDING A STORY

When taking a dual encoding hypothesis perspective, it is logical to assume that kindergarten children will understand complex stories better with dynamic visualizations available in a CD-ROM storybook than with static visualizations available in picture storybooks. One may expect that multimedia features support children's ability to make inferences and promote their understanding of more complex facets of stories. Sharp et al. (1995), testing this notion in a within-subject experiment, found that stories accompanied by dynamic video images supported young children's recall and retelling of stories. However, questions remain as to the exact role dynamic video plays in mental model building. It is clear to us that dynamic visuals have an advantage over static pictures because zoom and close-up shots can focus a child's attention on important details that might not be noticed when inspecting a static picture. A more complete visual representation of the story may promote text understanding, thus supporting more of story aspects that often are only implied or conveyed aurally, such as main characters' internal responses and motives for actions.

To further explore these issues, we (Verhallen, Bus, & de Jong, in press) conducted a follow-up study on whether young at-risk children, who were given multiple multimedia exposures of a similar story, would recall more story elements than those students who received the same repeated exposures to an onscreen version of the picture storybook alone (cf. Neuman, 1989). This study is noteworthy because it explores if CD-ROM stories can support the literacy development of 5-year-old children who are considered to be at-risk for academic achievement because they were low scoring on a language test and as a consequence of inexperience with story language. Thus, two versions of the same book, *Winnie the Witch*, were presented on the computer; however, one version included static images and the other included multimedia additions (e.g., cinematic techniques such as zooms, pans, cuts, film sound effects). The static version resembled the book version, only the oral reading of text read aloud was added. With the click of an icon, the text is read aloud. In the dynamic version, multimedia effects were coordinated with text. For example, when the text explains that Winnie is waving her wand, the animation depicts Winnie waving her magic wand and her cat Wilbur changing from black to green. On the other hand, the illustration in the static image condition is far less informative. The screen displays Winnie with her wand held high and the cat the color of green. In the static version, the transition from black to green is not visualized. Even though *Winnie the Witch* is a simple story, it contains all of the elements of a complete story grammar: setting (a black cat in a black house), a problem (Winnie can't see the black cat against the black house furnishings), initiating event (Winnie falls over the cat), internal response (Winnie decides something must be done), attempt (Winnie changes Wilbur into a green cat), direct consequence (Winnie can see Wilbur, even in places he is not allowed to go), reaction (Wilbur is put outside, on the green grass). As such, the story lends itself to retellings that may include a complete story grammar. Findings suggest that after four readings, dynamic visuals provided more support for kindergarten children's story understanding than did their independent encounters with static image, picture storybooks. In the dynamic condition, children's retellings included more complex layers of the story (e.g., mentioning reasons for actions and direct consequences). Importantly, at-risk students who scored low on language tests profited more from listening to multimedia versions of the story than they did from static image versions.

These results underscore the advantages of animated illustrations and sound effects in fostering story comprehension and in supporting children's ability to make inferences about story events. These advantages appear to be related to the capacity of the multimedia version of the story to enhance and enrich representations of texts that are necessary to understanding deeper layers of the story (cf. Gyselick, Ehrlich, Cornoldi, de Beni, & Dubois, 2000). Multimedia storybooks enable kindergarten children to build more complete models of stories. Stories in other media presentations are not just a variation on picture storybooks that may enrich children's understanding of story, but with such additions, children seem to reach more complex levels of story understanding.

Additionally, young children who are at-risk for school failure frequently lack the necessary background knowledge and metacognitive strategies to create images for scenes, events, and objects that are incompletely described by text. Children with non-mainstream heritage languages may also lack a sufficient vocabulary to comprehend stories encountered in school settings. The work by Verhallen et al. (in press), which focused on 5-year-olds from Moroccan-Arabic, Moroccan-Berber or Turkish speaking families living in the Netherlands, demonstrates that these children have difficulties in understanding stories read aloud by adults. For example, when non-Dutch speaking 5-year-old children hear a simple picture book like *The Very Hungry Caterpillar*, they encounter difficult words (e.g., *cocoon, scramble, outside, nibble*) and complex sentence structures (e.g., "and that big caterpillar built a little house for himself, named cocoon."). Less verbal children may have to expend more working-memory resources on basic language comprehension processes, leaving too few resources available for creating rich, comprehension-supporting imagery (Pressley, Cariglia-Bull, Deane, & Schneider, 1987). Thus can be explained why the immigrant children in the Verhallen et al. study profited more from CD-ROM, multimedia storybook reading.

In our work (Verhallen et al., in press), we have also found advantages of the multimedia CD-ROM storybook condition for linguistic content. When filmatic images, cinematic techniques, and sounds were added to a picture storybook on the computer screen, immigrant children learned more new words and sentence structures than they did with static pictures alone. A gain of six or seven words (12–14% of words we suspected children would not know) is substantial in comparison to the number of words children on average learned with static pictures (three or four new words). Learning effects also occurred in a relatively short period as children spent a total of 24 minutes watching the *Winnie the Witch* CD-ROM. We suggest that when immigrant children hear the story in combination with animations, they derive meaning of a number of unknown words and sentences. As a result, this new knowledge supports story comprehension. An interactive cycle occurs—when children understand more of the story, they will understand more of the text. When language is better understood, this will stimulate their understanding of the story, and so forth. Thus, we propose that children who experience second language acquisition difficulties profit from computer enhanced, multimedia additions to picture storybooks.

It is clear that we need further studies to test this hypothesis. Future work may employ sophisticated eye-movement equipment to pinpoint what children are attending to on screen, when the information is presented as static illustrations, animated illustrations, animated illustrations supported by sound, etc.

CONCLUSIONS AND FUTURE DIRECTIONS

Previous research has highlighted the importance of adult-child interactions for scaffolding young children's emerging literacy development (Bus, van IJzendoorn, & Pellegrini, 1995; Scarborough & Dobrich, 1994). The recent infusion of computers into homes and early childhood classrooms in various countries around the world makes it possible for us to gain insights into young children's opportunities for story comprehension and literacy development while interacting with new story telling media (e.g., DVD, CD-ROM storybooks, televised stories, or interactive stories online). The studies reported in this chapter draw attention to the potential of multimedia versions of stories to provide alternative venues, less dependent on adult scaffolding, for supporting young children's literacy development.

Currently, research suggests that children who are very early in emergent literacy development, without any knowledge of the alphabet or the alphabetic principle, do not seem to make progress in word recognition as a result of interacting with CD-ROM versions of stories (e.g., clicking on a word to lead to its pronunciation). Thus far, only children who have some basic insights into the workings of literacy seem to show evidence of computer story-related development in reading words. On the other hand, it is possible that children who are less advanced in emergent literacy may be able to develop meaning-making skills through repeated encounters with CD-ROM stories. More studies are needed to determine which particular features of electronic books might be most helpful (de Jong & Bus, 2002, 2004).

According to results of our content analysis of over 50 CD-ROM books in the Netherlands from 1995–2002, most CD-ROM stories offer interactive resources that are inconsiderate (Labbo & Kuhn, 2000) with traditional notions of meaning making processes and comprehension. Therefore, we agree with Labbo and Kuhn (2000) that inconsiderate programs may coax children into habits of thinking or dispositions toward meaning making that are nonproductive when viewed from the perspective of print-based reading skills. Even when these additions are engaging and inviting, alternative genres and multimedia content may be preferred. Children may be allowed to playfully explore the screen environment of a story for the first readings, but then be limited to hearing the story and seeing considerate animations upon subsequent rereadings.

Other forms of interactivity that may support children's emerging literacy development are rarely included in CD-ROM storybooks. For example, programs may stop after a story segment and pose a question that invites children to reflect upon the story. Traditional question and answering may be replaced by a purpose activity, such as making an electronic version of the book that retells a video version of the story (e.g., Labbo, 2000, 2004).

It is clear that even 2 and 3-year-olds spend time with media of various types; however, it is less clear what cognitive processes these children engage in as they interact with multimedia (Lewin, 2003). Are children passively viewing screens that divert their attention away from active meaning making? Educators and researchers must play an important role in exploring the effective design of interactive media in the future to ensure that the interactions enhance, amplify, and extend children's learning. Through continued efforts that build upon a growing body of research evidence, it is becoming clearer which types of resources ensure appropriate support for the maximum number of readers and how those electronic resources can be presented effectively. Suitable CD-ROM talking books are only sparely available. In addition, much of the suitable materials (see de Jong & Bus, 2003 and Korat & Shamir, 2004 for a summary) have been withdrawn from the market and are no longer available to parents or educators. Publishers of educational materials would do the field a good service by publishing new series. Award-winning picture storybooks of well known authors should be complemented with dynamic, cinematic effects and sounds.

Data from recent studies suggest that multimedia technologies may provide valuable tools for accelerating literacy development in young children. The most surprising finding is that children's ability to comprehend complex elements of stories is facilitated by dynamic video information and sound effects. Such experiences appear to enrich children's understanding of stories, thus extending their engagement in literacy practices. Furthermore, the audiovisual capabilities of electronic storybooks suggest new possibilities for enhancing early literacy experiences for some groups at-risk for school failure. Using multimedia technologies can readily be justified as a valued and important pedagogical goal. There is early, yet clear evidence that kindergarten children from immigrant families profit from interacting with CD-ROM multimedia stories. Indeed, groups that lag behind in language and literacy seem able to create basic mental models from stories encountered via multimedia, CD-ROM books (Lewater, 2003). Additional questions need to be pursued if we are to learn how to best utilize computer technologies, such as CD-ROM talking books and television to facilitate young children's literacy development. What role should teachers and parents play in matching children with particular types of CD-ROM stories? What new literacies are young children learning when they engage with books on screen? Will intensifying immigrant children's CD-ROM storybook reading experiences in classrooms compensate for the lack of caregiver-shared book reading that is common in some immigrant homes? We invite the educational and research community to join us in answering these and other intriguing questions so we may be better prepared as a field to best utilize computer resources, such as CD-ROM talking books.

REFERENCES

Armbruster, B. B. (1984). The problem of "inconsiderate text." In G. Duffy, L. Roehler, & J. Mason (Eds.). *Comprehension instruction: Perspectives and suggestions* (pp. 202–217), New York: Longman.

Bolter, J. D. (1998). Hypertext and the question of visual literacy. In D. Reinking, M. C. McKenna, & L. D. Labbo, & R. D. Kieffer (Eds.). *Handbook of literacy and technology: Transformations in a post-typographic world* (pp. 3–13). Mahwah, NJ: Lawrence Erlbaum Associates.

Bus, A. G., & van IJzendoorn, M. H. (1988). Mother-child interactions, attachment, and emergent literacy: A cross-sectional study. *Child Development, 59*, 1262–1272.

Bus, A. G., van IJzendoorn, M. H., & Pellegrini, A. D. (1995). Joint book reading makes for success in learning to read: A meta-analysis on intergenerational transmission of literacy. *Review of Educational Research, 65*, 1–21.

Calvert, S. L., Huston, A. C., Watkins, B. A., & Wright, J. C. (1982). The relation between selective attention to television forms and children's comprehension of content. *Child Development, 53*, 601–610.

Chomsky, C. (1990). Books on videodisc: Computers, video, and reading aloud to children. In D. Nix & S. Rand (Eds.). *Cognition, education, and multimedia* (pp. 31–47). Mahwah, NJ: Lawrence Erlbaum Associates.

Cordova, D. I., & Lepper, M. R. (1996). Intrinstic motivation and the process of learning: Beneficial effects of contextualization, personalization, and choice. *Journal of Educational Psychology, 88*, 715–730.

De Jong, M. T., & Bus, A. G. (2002). Quality of book-reading matters for emergent readers: An experiment with the same book in a regular or electronic format. *Journal of Educational Psychology, 94*, 145–155.

De Jong, M. T., & Bus, A. G. (2003). How well suited are electronic books to supporting literacy? *Journal of Early Childhood Literacy, 3*, 147–164.

De Jong, M. T., & Bus, A. G. (2004). The efficacy of electronic books in fostering kindergarten children's emergent story understanding. *Reading Research Quarterly, 39*, 378–393.

Dubois, M., & Vial, I. (2000). Multimedia design: The effects of relating multimodal information. *Journal of Computer Assisted Learning, 16*, 157–165.

Ehri, L. C., & Sweet, J. (1991). Fingerpoint-reading of memorized text: What enables beginners to process the print? *Reading Research Quarterly, 26*, 442–462.

Field, D. E., & Anderson, D. R. (1985). Instruction and modality effects on children's television attention and comprehension. *Journal of Educational Psychology, 77*, 91–100.

Gibbons, J., Anderson, D. R., Smith, R., Field, D. E., & Fisher, C. (1986). Young children's recall and reconstruction of audio and audiovisual narratives. *Child Development, 47*, 1014–1023.

Greenfield, P. M., Camaioni, L., Ercolani, P., Weiss, L., Lauber, B. A., & Perucchini, P. (1996). Cognitive socialization by computer games in two cultures: Inductive discovery or mastery of an iconic code?

In I. E. Sigel (Series Ed.), P. M. Greenfield, & R. R. Cocking (Vol. Eds.). *Advances in applied developmental psychology: Vol. 11. Interacting with video* (pp. 147–167). Norwood, NJ: Ablex.

Greenlee-Moore, M. E., & Smith, L. L. (1996). Interactive computer software: The effects on young children's reading achievement. *Reading Psychology: An International Quarterly, 17*, 43–64.

Gyselinck, V., Ehrlich, M. F., Cornoldi, C., de Beni, R., & Dubois, V. (2000). Visuospatial working memory in learning from multimedia systems. *Journal of Computer Assisted Learning, 16*, 166–176.

James, R. (1999). Navigating CD-ROMS: An exploration of children's reading interactive narratives. *Children's Literature in Education, 30*, 47–63.

Korat, O., & Shamir, A. (2004). Do Hebrew electronic books differ from Dutch electronic books? A replication of a Dutch content analysis. *Journal of Computer Assisted Learning, 20*, 257–268.

Labbo, L. D. (2000). 12 things young children can do with a talking book in a classroom computer center. *The Reading Teacher, 53*, 542–546.

Labbo, L. D. (1996). A semiotic analysis of young children's symbol making in classroom computer center. *Reading Research Quarterly, 31*, 356–385.

Labbo, L. D. (2004, February). *Screenland revisited: Young children's use of computer screen symbols as social, cultural and cognitive tools.* Paper presented for The Netherlands Organization for Scientific Research, Leiden, Holland.

Labbo, L. D., & Kuhn, M. R. (2000). Weaving chains of affect and cognition: A young child's understanding of CD-ROM talking books. *Journal of Literacy Research, 32*, 187–210.

Labbo, L. D., & Reinking, D. (1999). Negotiating the Multiple Realities of Technology in Literacy Research and Instruction. Invited for theory and research into practice section of *Reading Research Quarterly, 34*, 478–492.

Labbo, L. D., Reinking D., & McKenna, M. (1995). Incorporating the computer into kindergarten: A case study. *Perspectives on literacy research and practice: 44th Yearbook of the National Reading Conference.* In A. Hinchman, D. Leu, & C. K. Kinzer (Eds.). Chicago, IL: National Reading Conference, Inc., (pp. 459–465).

Leu, D. J. (2000). Literacy and technology: Deictic consequences for literacy education in an information age. In M. L. Kamil, P. B. Mosenthal, P. D. Pearson, and R. Barr (Eds.). *Handbook of Reading Research* (Vol. 3, pp. 743–770). Mahwah, NJ: Lawrence Erlbaum Associates.

Lewater, D. (2003). Cognitive strategies for learning from static and dynamic visuals. *Learning and Instruction, 13*, 177–189.

Lewin, C. (1997). Evaluating talking books: Ascertaining the effectiveness of multiple feedback modes and tutoring techniques. In C. K. Kinzer, K. A. Hinchman, & D. J. Leu (Eds.). *Inquiries into literacy theory and practice.* Forty-sixth yearbook of the National Reading Conference, Chicago, IL: National Reading Conference.

Lewin, C. (1998). Talking book design: What do practitioners want? *Computers and Education: An International Journal, 30*, 87–94.

Lewin, C. (2000). *Talking book software and beginning to read: Exploring the effects of talking books software in UK primary classrooms.* Unpublished manuscript. The Open University, Walton Hall, Milton Keynes.

Lewin, T. (2003). A growing number of video viewers watch from the crib. *The New York Times*, October 29.

Mason, J., Peterman, C., & Kerr, B. (1989). Reading to kindergarten children. In D. Strickland & L. Morrow (Eds.). *Emerging literacy: Young children learn to read and write* (pp. 52–62). Newark, DE: International Reading Association.

Matthew, K. I. (1996). The impact of CD-ROM storybooks on children's reading comprehension and reading attitude. *Journal of Educational Multimedia and Hypermedia, 5*, 379–394.

Mayer, R. E., & Anderson, R. B. (1992). The instructive animation: Helping students build connections between words and pictures in multimedia learning. *Journal of Educational Psychology, 84*, 444–452.

McKenna, M. C. (1998). Electronic texts and the transformation of beginning reading. In D. Reinking, M. C. McKenna, L. D. Labbo, & R. D. Kieffer (Eds.). *Handbook of literacy and technology: Transformations in a post-typographic world* (pp. 45–59). Mahwah, NJ: Lawrence Erlbaum Associates.

McKenna, M. C., Reinking, D., & Bradley, B. A. (2001, November). *The effects of electronic trade books on the decoding growth of beginning readers.* Paper presented at NATO Advanced Study Institute on literacy acquisition, assessment, and intervention: The role of phonology, orthography, and morphology, Il Cioco, Italy.

McKenna, M. C., & Watkins, J. H. (1994, December). *Computer-mediated books for beginning readers.* Paper presented at the meeting of the National Reading Conference, San Diego.

McKenna, M. C., & Watkins, J. H. (1995, November). *Effects of computer-mediated books on the development of beginning readers.* Paper presented at the meeting of the National Reading Conference, New Orleans.

McKenna, M. C., & Watkins, J. H. (1996, December). *The effects of computer-mediated trade books on sight word acquisition and the development of phonics ability.* Paper presented at the meeting of the National Reading Conference, Charleston, SC.

Miller, L., Blackstock, J., & Miller, R. (1994). An exploratory study into the use of CD-ROM storybooks. *Computers in Education, 22,* 187–204

Murray, B. A., Stahl, S. A., & Ivey, M. G. (1996). Developing phonemic awareness through alphabet books. *Reading and Writing, 8,* 307–322.

Mullis, I. V. S., Martin, L. E., Gonzalez, E. J., & Kennedy, A. W. (2001). *PIRLS2001 International Report. IEA's Study of Reading Literacy Achievement in Primary Schools in 35 countries.* Chestnut Hill, MA: Boston College.

Neuman, S. B. (1989). The impact of different media on children's story comprehension. *Reading Research and Instruction, 28,* 38–47.

Neuman, S. B. (1997). Television as a learning environment: A theory of synergy. In J. Flood, S. Brice Heath & D. Lapp (Eds.), *Handbook of research on teaching literacy through the communicative and visual arts* (pp. 15–30). New York: Simon & Schuster.

Newman, S. B., & Koskinen, P. (1992). Captioned television as comprehensible input: Effects of incidental word learning from context for language minority students. *Reading Research Quarterly, 27,* 94–106.

Paivio, A. (1986). *Mental representations: A dual coding approach.* Oxford: Oxford University Press.

Pressley, M., Cariglia-Bull, T., Deane, S., & Schneider, W. (1987). Short-term memory, verbal competence, and age as predictors of imagery instructional effectiveness. *Journal of Experimental Child Psychology, 43,* 194–211.

Reinking, D. (1988). Computer-mediated text and comprehension differences: The role of reading time, reader preference, and estimation of learning. *Reading Research Quarterly, 23,* 484–498.

Reinking D. (1994). Electronic literacy. *Perspectives in Reading Research, 4,* 1–7.

Reinking, D. (1997). Me and my hypertext ☺ A multiple digression analysis of technology and literacy (sic). *The Reading Teacher, 50,* 626–43.

Reinking, D., & Bridwell-Bowles, L. (1991). Computers in reading and writing. In B. Barr, M. L. Kamil, P. Mosenthal, & P. D. Pearson (Eds.). *Handbook of Reading Research: Vol. 2* (pp. 310–340). New York: Longman.

Reinking, D., Labbo, L. D., & McKenna, M. (1997). Navigating the changing landscape of literacy: Current theory and research in computer-based reading and writing. In J. Flood, S. B. Heath, & D. Lapp (Eds.). *Research on Teaching Literacy Through the Communicative and Visual Arts* (pp. 77–92). New York: Simon & Schuster Macmillan.

Reinking, D., & Watkins, J. (2000). A formative experiment investigating the use of multimedia book reviews to increase elementary students' independent reading. *Reading Research Quarterly, 35,* 384–419.

Ricci, C. M., & Beal, C. R. (2002). The effective of interactive media on children's story memory. *Journal of Educational Psychology, 94,* 138–144.

Roskos, K. A., Christie, J. F., & Vukelich, C. (2004, April). Young children learning new words in a theme-based reading curriculum. In R. A. Roskos (chair), *Helping Young Children At Risk: Early Literacy Interventions with Promise.* Annual Meeting of the American Educational Research Association, San Diego, CA.

Scarborough, H. S., & Dobrich, W. (1994). On the efficacy of reading to pre-schoolers. *Developmental Review, 14,* 245–302.

Segers, E., Takke, L., & Verhoeven, L. (2004). Teacher-mediated versus computer-mediated storybook reading to children in native and multicultural kindergarten classrooms. *School effectiveness and school improvement, 15*, 215–226.

Sénéchal, M., LeFevre, J. A., Thomas E. M., & Daley, K. E. (1998). Differential effects of home literacy experiences on the development of oral and written language. *Reading Research Quarterly, 33*, 96–116.

Sharp, D. L. M., Bransford, J. D., Goldman, S. R., Risko, V. J., Kinzer C. K., & Vye, N. J. (1995). Dynamic visual support for story comprehension and mental model building by young at-risk children. *Educational Technology Research and Development, 43*, 25–41.

Smith, C. R. (2001). Click and turn the page: An exploration of multiple storybook literacy. *Reading Research Quarterly, 36*, 152–183.

Smolkin, L. B., Conlon, A., & Yaden, D. B. (1988). Print salient illustrations in children's picture books: The emergence of written language awareness. *Thirty-seventh Yearbook of the National Reading Conference*, 59–67.

Smolkin, L. B., Yaden, D. B., Brown, L., & Hofius, B. (1992). The effects of genre, visual design choices, and discourse structure on preschoolers' responses to picture books during parent-child read-alouds. *Yearbook of the National Reading Conference, 41*, 291–301.

Sulzby, E. (1985). Children's emergent reading of favorite storybooks: A developmental study. *Reading Research Quarterly, 20*, 458–481.

Turbill, J. (2001). A researcher goes to school: Using technology in the kindergarten literacy curriculum. *Journal of Early Childhood Literacy, 1*, 255–279.

Underwood, G., & Underwood, J. D. M. (1998). Children's interactions and learning outcomes with interactive talking books. *Computers and Education: An International Journal, 30*, 95–102.

Verhallen, M. J. A. J., Bus, A. G., & de Jong, M. T. (in press). The promise of multimedia stories for kindergarten children at-risk. *Journal of Educational Psychology*.

Whitehurst, G. J., Falco, F. L., Lonigan, C. J., Fischel, J. E., DeBaryshe, B. D., Valdez Menchaca, M. C., & Caulfield, M. (1988). Accelerating language development through picture book reading. *Developmental Psychology, 24*, 552–559.

CD-ROMS/DVDS/BOOKS

Arthur's Teacher Trouble [CD-ROM]. (1994) Brown.

Big Party for Tiger (Groot Feest voor Tijger) [CD-ROM]. (1998). Baarn, The Netherlands; Het Spectrum Electronic Publishing.

Little Flatfoot [Platvoetje] [CD-ROM]. (2000). Weesp, The Netherlands: Keec.

P. B. Bear's Birthday Party [CD-ROM]. (1994). London: Dorling Kindersley, Multimedia. Stellaluna [CD-ROM]. (1996) Canon.

The Cat in the Hat [CD-ROM]. (1997). Novato, CA: Borderbund.

The Tortoise and the Hare [CD-ROM]. (1994). Novato, CA: Borderbund.

The Ugly Duckling (Version 1) [CD-ROM]. (1993). San Francisco, Morgan Interactive.

The Very hungry caterpillar (by E. Carle) (1969). London: Puffin.

Well Again [Ik Maak je Weer Beter, zei Beer] [CD-ROM]. (1998). Baarn, The Netherlands, Het Spectrum Electronic Publishing.

Winnie the Witch [Heksenspul met Hennie de Heks en de Kat Helmer] [CD-ROM]. (1996). Nieuwegein, The Netherlands, Bombilla/VNU Interactive Media.

III

LITERACY SOFTWARE AND THE INTERNET

10
▼▼▼▼▼▼▼

Critically Evaluating Educational Technologies for Literacy Learning: Current Trends and New Paradigms

Julie Coiro
University of Connecticut

Rachel A. Karchmer Klein and Sharon Walpole
University of Delaware

Educational software and Internet resources are increasingly being recognized for their potential to foster literacy learning in and out of the classroom. Recent studies have shown the benefits of using technology to develop skills such as phonological awareness (Wise & Olson, 1995), word recognition (Davidson, Elcock, & Noyes, 1996), comprehension (Matthew, 1997), spelling (Higgins & Raskind, 2000), writing (Rowley, Carson, & Miller, 1998), and motivation to read (Nicolson, Fawcett, & Nicolson, 2000), each of which represents an important facet of a comprehensive literacy curriculum. Furthermore, software and/or Internet technologies can improve literacy learning for typical students (Allen & Thompson, 1995) and at-risk learners (Howell, Erickson, Stanger, & Wheaton, 2000) as well as for students with learning disabilities (MacArthur & Haynes, 1995) or mixed handicaps (Heimann, Nelson, Tjus, & Gillberg, 1995). Studies also illustrate the positive effects of technology in out-of-school literacy contexts (Hull & Schultz, 2001). These benefits and the evolving role of technology have the potential to greatly influence the ways in which educators think about effective literacy instruction.

Recently, however, the beneficial aspects of technology in education have been overshadowed by four confounding issues that challenge those responsible for evaluating which particular educational technologies to use with students. First, the sheer number of software programs and Internet websites available to evaluate is overwhelming for educators already short on time and resources. The number of software programs has grown exponentially in the last decade (Buckleitner, 1999)—as of January 1, 2003, there were 171,638,297 Web hosts worldwide (Zakon, 2003). As a result, identifying quality materials from this array of electronic resources can be a particularly time consuming and arduous task.

The nature of many digital media products poses a second set of challenges for educators. Much of the children's educational market is dominated by shallow drill and practice programs with slick technical features and fancy packaging (Shade, 1996), and many websites designed for children incorporate product advertisements merged with content (Aufderheide, 2001). Now, more than ever before, educators must look "beyond the catch phrases, bargains, flashing animations and online sales pitches to ensure that it [the information] addresses the range of diverse literacy needs that challenge educators in the classroom" (Geissenger, 1997, p. 3). Furthermore, new multiliteracy perspectives (e.g., Cope & Kalantzis, 2000) support the careful consideration of the effects that using a particular electronic resource will have on the social and cultural literacy practices that occur in the classroom. The lack of quality control applied to these technologies (e.g., Ciolek, 1996; Luke, 2000) requires educators to not only assume higher levels of screening responsibility, but also to better prepare students to make good decisions about the information they find on their own.

A third challenge to effective technology evaluation is that new technologies often require new ways of thinking about reading, writing, and communicating (e.g., Lankshear & Knobel, 2003; Leu, Kinzer, Coiro, & Cammack, 2004). Applications of technology such as non-linear hypertext, multimedia software, interactive simulations, and real-time chat rooms present new literacy experiences for students. Nicholls and Ridley (1997) have observed a tendency for literacy educators to consider these technologies in the same way as print-based instructional materials for students, yet, they argue, today's digital instructional materials require qualitatively different evaluation practices. Specific guidelines for evaluating emerging technologies in the context of authentic literacy practices need to be established and validated by curriculum coordinators and classroom teachers if we are to make progress in this area.

Finally, teachers attempting to learn more about effective technology evaluation practices are hindered by the challenge to keep up with the current demands for school-wide curriculum integration and accountability. Most states have imposed standards making computer learning an essential part of the curriculum (ISTE, 2000), while federal guidelines encourage schools to incorporate scientifically research-based literacy practices and materials into daily instruction (No Child Left Behind, 2001). Strategies for integrating technology into the literacy curriculum have been outlined, for example, by literacy organizations such as the International Reading Association (1984; 2001) and by technology organizations such as the Southern Regional Education Board's EvaluTech (1997) and Florida's Panhandle Area Educational Consortium (2004). However, with regard to evaluating the technology materials themselves, there are few acceptable models with theoretically grounded guidelines (Bader, 2000; Buckleitner, 1999). The issue of evaluating instructional technologies and their impact on literacy learning demands a complex process (Bader, 2000), yet research suggests that preservice and in-service teachers are given little instruction, support, or time in learning how to evaluate technology resources (Education Market Research, 1999).

It is within the context of the challenges outlined above that we frame this chapter and reconsider effective evaluation practices. Technologies for learning have considerable potential when selected carefully to fulfill a logical purpose. Yet, as we move into the future, great difficulty lies with trying to arrive at a flexible set of evaluation criteria that characterize the potential for literacy learning with different technologies, for different purposes and for different audiences. In fact, as we move forward with evaluation of technology, it will be important to develop procedures that allow us to begin with the learner and his or her purpose rather than the technology and its potential.

At the outset, we want to stress that it is not our intention in this chapter to cite specific research-based reviews of particular software or websites for literacy instruction. Instead, we seek to provide a critical pathway through the literature as it more generally pertains to the following three questions:

- What can we learn from existing research and recommendations about effective and ineffective practices for evaluating and selecting technology resources for literacy learning?

- Do recommended evaluation practices align with emerging theories and perspectives of literacy and learning with software, Internet, and other information and communication technologies?
- What new approaches to technology evaluation should be considered in light of the dynamic and changing notions of literacy and learning within digital environments?

With these questions in mind, we began by informally reviewing the literature since 1980 on evaluation of software (Coiro), print-based resources (Walpole) and Internet technologies (Karchmer-Klein). Each of us identified emerging themes related to current and past evaluation practices of technology for literacy learning within each medium. Then, we examined the similarities and differences across mediums to arrive at a set of common themes that characterize the literature in this area.

In structuring the chapter, we begin with a brief review of the perspectives that guided the nature of our review of technology evaluation practices. Because we chose to pursue a more critical discussion of the literature in this area, we felt it was important to define our particular stance early on. We follow with a discussion of seven themes in evaluation practices that we argue fall short of the multidimensional considerations required for effective evaluation of current technologies. We then match these arguments with a parallel set of seven promising practices that we believe more carefully consider current and emerging theories of literacy and technology. Finally, we conclude this chapter with a series of recommendations for an updated model of technology evaluation that reflects current perspectives of literacy and learning, new technological capabilities, and new learning outcomes for students.

THEORETICAL ISSUES

Interpreting the effectiveness of technology for learning (and of practices for evaluating technology) is greatly influenced by the lens with which one sees the world (Labbo & Reinking, 1999). It is important to understand from the beginning, then, that we have adopted an approach to evaluation that embraces multiple perspectives of literacy, learning, and technology integration in an effort to avoid what Dole (2000) describes as "a series of pendulum-swinging fads" (p. 65) that continue to plague education and more specifically, literacy instruction (see more in Venezky, 1987). Because technologies change so rapidly and new technologies emerge faster than we can keep up (Leu, 2000), our thinking about evaluation needs to be flexible, open to new perspectives and considerate of more traditional ones. What works for one learner may be different than what works for another, and educational technologies for literacy learning are no exception.

Several dynamic perspectives of learning with technology informed our critique of evaluation practices in this chapter. One perspective emphasizes the relationship between the learner and the computer. For example, drawing upon the work of Jonassen, Peck and Wilson (1999), technology in learning should serve at least five functions including: (1) a knowledge construction tool; (2) an information vehicle; (3) an intellectual partner; (4) a context; and (5) a social medium that supports learning. Similarly, Clements (1985) recommends computer experience in which the learner plays an active role in controlling the direction of both experiential and drill environments placed in the context of authentic higher-level experiences. He also directs educators to consider children's preferences and developmental levels, while looking for materials that offer a wide variety of applications that are integrated into the curriculum for the means of achieving educational goals.

A second perspective demands that we broaden our conception of literacy instruction beyond practice in singular skill areas *and* expand our evaluation practices to consider opportunities to engage in multiple literacies of the Internet. We should consider how multiple sign systems (e.g., Kress & Van Leeuwen, 2001), multiple settings of literacy practice (e.g., Chandler-Olcott & Mahar, 2003), and new forms of Internet literacies (e.g., Lankshear & Knobel, 2003; Leu et al., 2004) impact our choices of technologies with the potential to most effectively enhance these new literacies.

Our critique of evaluation practices is also influenced by the belief that opportunities for learning with technology should integrate instructional practices that are comprehensive, authentic, and individualized. Green's (1988) socio-cultural conception of literacy as having "three interlocking dimensions of learning and practice—the operational, the cultural, and the critical" (Lankshear & Knobel, 2003, p. 10) effectively accounts for dimensions of language, meaning, and context simultaneously and inspires new ideas about how technology evaluation practices can achieve this as well. Furthermore, constructivist notions of the literacy learner as one who uses technology tools to construct, reflect, and transform meaning into something more suitable for personal purposes (Cope & Kalantzis, 2000; Jonassen, 1996) inform our thinking as well.

Finally, and perhaps most importantly, our position is informed by the work of others who insist that the teacher plays a critical role in the successful use of computers (e.g., Balajthy, 2000; Karchmer, 2001). We consider technologies in schools as facilitating a critical interaction among multiple learners, teachers, and goals. Thus, it is imperative that valid technology evaluation practices consider the diverse purposes and perspectives that teachers bring to any computer-based learning situation when evaluating its utility in the literacy curriculum. With each of these perspectives in mind, we turn to our critical review of current and past evaluation practices of technology for literacy learning.

EVALUATING TECHNOLOGIES FOR LITERACY LEARNING: LIMITED EVALUATION PRACTICES

The first theme we noted in our review is that many early evaluation practices of both print and electronic materials relied on evaluations made by outside reviewers having little contact with the individuals who would actually be using the materials. Before computers emerged on the scene, and even now, textbooks have been reviewed every 5–8 years by representative groups composed mainly of classroom teachers, who examined the wares of publishers at the state level (in 22 states), or the district level (in 28 states), and then again at the school level. At each of those levels, the publishers provided the materials for review for free (as they stood to benefit from future large sales) and often sent sales representatives to make presentations. The general trend has been for the state or district to produce a short list of acceptable programs and then for the district or school to repeat the review process with materials on that list. Interestingly, these evaluators often relied on popular media (e.g., television, radio, newspaper) rather than on traditional research (Reutzel, Sudweeks, & Hollingsworth, 1994). These are insufficient sources for informing such high-stakes decisions as materials evaluation.

As educational computer software appeared on the market in the early 1980s, most educators resorted to outside compilations of reviews to inform their decisions about effective programs (Buckleitner, 1999). "Teachers often selected software from catalogs, choosing almost any software that remotely touched on the subjects they were teaching" (Komoski, 1995, para. 1). With the advent of the Internet, searchable databases grew in popularity. The first and largest evaluation database, published by Educational Products Information Exchange, or EPIE, is still accessible today (learn more at http://www.epie.org/epie_tess.htm) as are other collections of reviews by outside organizations such as SuperKids Educational Software Review (http://www.superkids .com/), KidsDomain (http://www.kidsdomain.com/reviews/), and The Learning Village (http:// www.learningvillage.com/). However, many of these contain commercialized technical reviews of software features (Buckleitner, 1999) as opposed to more specific evaluations of how these features may be used by children in real classrooms for literacy learning.

The second recognizable theme in early evaluation practices involves the process of categorizing instructional resources by technology type as a means of understanding how computer-assisted programs can support instruction. Evaluators typically reviewed a piece of courseware by identifying the category to which it belonged and then compared a list of available technical features to those deemed important within that category (Duchastel, 1987). We suppose this practice grew out of a need to develop operational definitions of the newly emerging technological learning opportunities of the time, while also finding manageable commonalities between the growing numbers of software programs in the 1980s. Taylor (1980), for example, grouped computer resources according to three functions: tutor, tool, or tutee; others (e.g., Spenser, 1986; Robyler, 1997) grouped them according to their design structure: drill and practice, tutorial, instructional game, or simulation. In both cases, emphasis was placed on what a particular program could do and the types of technical features it offered.

Early guidelines for evaluating Internet resources, although developed almost 20 years later, proposed similar categorization schemes that emphasize Web site functions over individual learner or curriculum considerations. Some framed the evaluation process of websites on functional dimensions such as information dissemination; education and training; commerce and advertising; or entertainment and communication (e.g., Trochin, 1996). Payton (1998), meanwhile, evaluated websites based solely on the categories of design, content, technical elements, and credibility. This emphasis on the functions and categories of technology tools is certainly an important consideration in the evaluation process, and in fact, these categories can help structure the type of support each tool requires. However, technology function should not be the only focus as it often draws attention away from the different ways that students might interact with the technology and how these materials might actually mesh with classroom literacy instruction.

Another shortcoming of early evaluation practices that emerged in our review is that most evaluations of textbooks, software, and even Internet websites were limited to filling out a short checklist or rating sheet. Typically, this checklist included a set of predetermined criteria that the evaluator deemed to be present or absent during the review process. Generally, however, this checklist approach encouraged a simplistic and monolithic approach to evaluation and did not reflect the true nature of a material's use for instruction or the individual influences of teachers (Balajthy, 2000) and students (e.g., Sturm, Rankin, Beukelman, & Schutz-Muehling, 1997). With regards to software and Web site checklists, most included short and simple yes/no questions about technical features (e.g., Scott & Barker, 1987), and only a few revealed an underlying assumption that technology evaluation is multi-dimensional and complex (e.g., Ellsworth & Hedley, 1993; Wepner, 1989). Although traditional checklist-type approaches can be helpful in weeding out materials in the initial phases of evaluation, they do not sufficiently capture the multiple dimensions of effective evaluation in light of what we know about literacy learning today.

A fourth concern we have with early evaluation practices is that they tended to focus attention primarily on physical attributes and technical features and less on actual student learning potential and application in the literacy classroom (McDougall & Squires, 1995). This is clearly evident in Scott and Barker's (1987) guidelines for selecting and evaluating reading software. Although these authors discuss the importance of making certain "that the courseware is founded on sound pedagogical assumptions ... [and that it] ... matches with the skills and objectives in the reading curriculum" (p. 884), the sample checklist they provide includes 12 yes/no items about technical issues such as access to the correct hardware and peripherals to run the software, quality of the documentation, cost efficiency issues, preview policies, and backup disk management, and only two items dealing with instructional issues such as matching objectives to the general curriculum or to a specific literacy lesson.

Web site evaluation practices also tend to emphasize design features over quality of content. Most sets of guidelines incorporated what The Children's Partnership (2003), a nonprofit children's advocacy organization, calls *baseline requirements*. These include things such as organization name, contact information, professional design, ease of navigation, updated content, and use of advertisements. A recent study by The Stanford University Persuasive Technology Lab (2002) surveyed 1,410 Web users asking what they felt were the components of a valid Web site. Participants reported that sites including a physical address, employees' names, and photographs were the most credible. On the other hand, sites with typographical errors, advertisements, and broken links were the least credible. We found very few Web site evaluation practices that move beyond a consideration of technical features to examine student literacy learning potential in these new environments.

The overemphasis on the technical features of literacy materials continues even today in some circles. Robyler (2003), for example, includes criteria like categorical design features, user flexibility, and technical soundness as "essential" to the technology evaluation process, whereas considerations like educational significance, ease of integration, and adaptability are deemed "optional" (p. 110), implying that they are less important in the overall decision-making process. As a result, many technology evaluation practices lack attention to the potential match (or mismatch) of the curriculum materials to the context in which they will be used, and they ignore the knowledge and skills of the teachers and children who will be using the materials. In effect, they employ a cursory survey of whether the proposed technology will be operational in the target setting rather than whether it will be effective for teaching and learning. Such a compatibility survey is perhaps necessary, but certainly not sufficient.

A fifth trend we observed is that early evaluation methodologies primarily consisted of one-dimensional treatment and control group comparisons of traditional tasks completed on and off the computer screen (e.g., Keene & Davey, 1987; Gambrell, Bradley, & McLaughlin, 1987) or comparisons of main effects of computer instruction with those resulting from traditional teacher instruction (e.g., Nicolson, Fawcett, & Nicolson, 2000). These studies emphasized the effectiveness of drill-and-practice treatments as a substitute for human instruction. In addition, these studies rarely considered the impact of the teacher's role, how new technologies were implemented into the curriculum, and other variables that we now know impact the effectiveness of technology use in the classroom (Cope & Kalantzis, 2000; Labbo & Reinking, 1999; Paterson et al., 2003).

Next, we found that early research focused on the effects of technology on distinct skill-based literacies while little attention was paid to more holistic or multiple conceptions of literacy. Karchmer, Mallette, and Leu (2002) report most of the published research that measures the effectiveness of technologies on literacy learning emphasizes the effects of singular dimensions of literacy such as phonological awareness, word recognition, expressive writing, or fluency. While studies of this type may be important to guide selection of resources to meet very specific curriculum needs, it is important to broaden our conception to include how technology can support multiple literacy skills in a range of electronic environments.

A seventh theme we observed in most early evaluation processes is that almost all thoughtful evaluations of a particular material took place *prior* to its selection and its actual use in the classroom. Evaluation tended, therefore, to focus on a material's potential for learning rather than on actual student learning. Rarely is time spent directly examining a material's impact on literacy learning outcomes or gathering teachers' perceptions of a material's utility once it is integrated into classroom instruction. Similarly, within these limited evaluation formats, there is little consideration of children's own conversations about a particular software program or Internet resource as they interact with these materials for their own literacy learning purposes (Wilson, 1998). Case and Truscott (1999) stress the importance of previewing software while students interact with the program to get a more comprehensive picture of a certain resource's strengths and weaknesses.

Fortunately, however, the seven themes outlined above provide only one side of a larger story for those seeking to more effectively evaluate the potential for technology in today's classrooms. In our review, we discovered a small, yet growing, body of work slowly emerging since the mid–1980s that reflects an intellectual shift from earlier thinking about what characterizes effective evaluation of technology materials for literacy learning. These evaluation practices are more closely aligned with theories of technology integration in the 1990s and beyond. In this next section, we present a series of promising practices that we feel may extend the limited ones discussed previously (see Table 10.1).

EVALUATING TECHNOLOGY MATERIALS: PROMISING PRACTICES

The first promising practice we found in the literature on evaluating educational technologies is the move toward a more systematic consideration of interactions before, during, and after use in

TABLE 10.1
Trends in the Literature on Evaluation Practices of Technology for Literacy-Learning

Limited Evaluation Practices	*Promising Evaluation Practices*
Rely on evaluations developed by outside reviewers removed from the specific context and untrained in literacy instruction	Involve local students and teachers in the development of evaluation criteria and subsequent selection and review of technology materials
Classify materials by technology design that aligns with technology-based outcomes	Classify materials by authentic literacy practices that aligns with research-based comprehensive literacy learning outcomes
Utilize yes/no checklists in a simplistic and often commercialized review process	Utilize multidimensional leveled rubrics and open-ended formats that consider the dynamic nature of evaluation
Focus on similar technical and physical aspects inherent within the text, software program, or website	Focus on diverse human aspects of the learner and the teacher
Emphasize quantitative, simplistic comparisons that replace the teacher and/or traditional instruction	Emphasize quantitative and qualitative aspects of social interactions between students, teachers and the instructional materials
Focus only on distinct singular skill-based literacies	Consider the impact of new literacies as multi-modal and multicultural experiences that require a more global critical stance
Involve a static evaluation of potential before technology is used with minimal follow-up in evaluating student literacy outcomes as a result of using these technologies	Involve dynamic evaluation of interactions before, during, and after technology is used and directly measure its impact on student literacy outcomes

a process that directly relates back to student literacy outcomes. Current research applauds evaluation practices that do not end when the material is selected, but rather those that continue to evaluate the quality and utility of a certain resource both during and after instruction. Draper (1996) recommends a method of *illuminative evaluation* during instruction, when students can be observed within their daily classroom literacy practices with technology to get a clearer picture of how they think and feel about the experience and what they consider to be important issues. Evaluation practices can also involve gathering post-use feedback (Komoski, 1995) from students and teachers that compares the material's stated learning objectives with actual student performance or gathering evidence of student processes and products as a result of engaging with literacy learning technologies (Wepner, Valmont, & Thurlow, 2000). Such practices more effectively situate new technologies selection within the real-life classroom contexts of teaching and learning—the places where they matter most.

Another encouraging practice we observed in our review is a combined effort to first, classify technology materials by authentic literacy practices (e.g., reading, writing, and thinking practices) instead of by technology type, and second, to connect these practices with theory-informed frameworks and local learning outcomes within a comprehensive literacy curriculum instead of just using technology for its motivational value or as a break from real instruction. Several researchers direct our attention to using computers for meaningful and authentic reading and writing purposes (Case & Truscott, 1999; Hickey, 1995; Simic, 1999) for which learners are viewed as active, social designers of new literacy forms (Cope & Kalantzis, 2000). Although we were unable to locate specific evaluations that addressed all of the literacy-learning issues in one cohesive format, we found evidence that thinking is moving forward in this area.

For instance, instead of directing educators to identify which technology function a certain material addresses (e.g., skill reinforcement, tutorial, or simulation), more recent evaluation systems point us to literacy-related categorization schemes. Important aspects of software for teaching phonics, word recognition, comprehension, and reading appreciation are highlighted in recent evaluation guidelines (e.g., Walpole & McKenna, 2004, Meyer & Rose, 1998), whereas others propose that we assess the potential of technology as it relates more holistically to major categories of real-world reading and writing connections (e.g., Wepner, 1989).

Internet classification systems have similarly evolved to reflect authentic literacy practices. Judi Harris (1998) highlights the educational value of certain Web-based activities by categorizing them into three structures that address social literacy practices including interpersonal exchanges, information collection and analysis, and problem solving, while the popular Blue Web'n portal Web site (http://www.kn.pacbell.com/wired/bluewebn/contentarea.cfm?cid=5) sorts Web resources by potential literacy outcomes in reading, speaking, writing, and literature. Literacy-based evaluation categories such as these assist educators in seeing the potential connections between literacy learning and technology use.

We also found literature to support the notion that once material has been observed to encourage authentic literacy practices, further consideration needs to be paid to how well these practices correspond to school-based student learning objectives (e.g., Balajthy, 2000; Wepner et al., 2000). Yet, researchers are quick to remind educators not to fall into the trap of "a technology solution looking for a problem" (Norton & Sprague, 2001, p. 27). Rather, when evaluating the utility of technology materials, we should first carefully rethink how instruction is designed and, second, examine how technology may most significantly impact these instructional and social literacy practices.

A third practice emphasized in recent literature about technology evaluation shows a progression from the simple yes/no checklist toward more open-ended formats such as rubric-based observations (McVee & Dickson, 2002), tables with scores to indicate leveled degrees of usefulness (Hall & Martin, 1999), and space for anecdotal preferences, individualized options, and application ideas (Sturm et al., 1997). Furthermore, evaluations should prompt teachers to identify their own approach to learning (e.g., skills-based vs. strategic application, objectivist vs. constructivist) and then evaluate the compatibility of this approach with a certain literacy learning technology (McVee & Dickson, 2002; Leu & Kinzer, 2003).

Efforts to develop evaluation systems for print-based literacy materials have similarly responded to the need for more in-depth evaluation practices that extend beyond one-dimensional checklists. Simmons and Kame'enui's *Consumer's Guide to Evaluating a Core Reading Program* (2003), for example, expanded their older checklist analysis of critical reading elements addressed by a potential instructional material by providing space for more open-ended reflection of these criteria. This forces a more thorough analysis than the earlier version and directs evaluators both inside and across the lessons. However, the checklist format still encourages reviewers to "find" evidence in the print that discreet bits of content are included; the program as a whole is not really considered for its holistic match to models of literacy teaching and learning. Thus, in our review, many evaluation formats seem to encourage this type of open-ended reflection, but few researchers appropriately define the crucial considerations that should be guiding the direction of these reflections.

A fourth consideration that shows promise for effective evaluation practice is movement toward a greater focus on a wide range of diverse human dimensions that students and educators bring to the computer-learning situation. Sturm et al. (1997) and Bader (2000) asserted that a careful focus on a student's particular learning needs at each step in the evaluative process is crucial for supporting literacy development with technology. Specifically, evaluation practices should consider the mode of instructional delivery (Hickey, 1995), student reading level (Leu & Kinzer, 2003), the format of instructions and learning feedback (Bader, 2000), and individual learner characteristics, including self-confidence, humor, and learning style (Burmark & Thornburg, 1996).

Several published guidelines for evaluating Internet websites encourage educators to consider the accessibility of a site's particular audience. The American Library Association, for example, recommends sites be compliant with the Americans with Disabilities Act as much as possible and provides a link to the World Wide Web Consortium site (W3C), an organization that promotes the accessibility of websites to people with disabilities. The W3C site also includes evaluation guidelines and a set of criteria used to create *Bobby*, a free software tool (http://bobby .watchfire.com/bobby/html/en/index.jsp) that evaluates the accessibility of a Web site.

As the Internet increases accessibility to the global community (The New London Group, 2000), many believe it is important to create culturally aware and representative websites (Gorski, 1999). Gorski developed evaluation questions to specifically pinpoint diverse perspectives framed in such questions as: Does the site encourage participation among users through intercultural, interactive or collaborative opportunities? Does this site provide voice to other perspectives through links or other connections? Likewise, The Children's Partnership (2003) criteria include a section on *Cultural Focus of Content* asking readers to consider if the site is maintained by members of the population reflected in its content and whether the site is specifically directed towards a certain cultural/ethnic group.

Recent literature from the last decade also calls for technology evaluators to pay greater attention to the ways that individual teachers can impact the overall effectiveness of technology. Judge (2001) noted that "after selecting software, the success of its use with students weighs heavily on the teacher's ability to set the environment appropriately" (p. 26). Others report that a teacher's purpose for using technology and his/her beliefs about literacy and learning has the potential to influence student achievement (Balajthy, 2000), selection of software (Bain, McNaught, & Mills, 1997), and the use of the Internet and other new technologies for learning and instruction (Becker,

1999). The results obtained from a newly developed Technology and Reading Inventory (Christenson & Knezak, 2001) affirm the idea that teaching style, reading instruction preference, and technology beliefs can differentially impact the effectiveness of technology used to develop reading, writing, and thinking skills. Clearly, integrating technology into literacy instruction is a complex task, necessitating thoughtful, insightful, and knowledgeable teachers.

A fifth theme that characterizes more promising practices in technology evaluation focuses attention not only on the quantitative effects of technology on literacy learning, but also on the qualitative aspects of social interactions between students, teachers, and the instructional materials. Because technology creates the potential for new types of relationships among teacher, student, content, and context (Frick, 1991), evaluators should carefully consider the ways in which young learners interact with the computer and with each other as active and social agents of change (Shade, 1996). Bruce and Peyton (1999), for example, explore this notion of situated evaluation in their assessment of computerized writing tools. Their study provides a helpful model for how to examine the relationships among classroom context, computer-based innovations, and particular literacy practices while evaluating certain technologies.

Socio-cultural perspectives to technology evaluation also consider the interactions between the multiple perspectives of students, teachers, and designers (McDougall & Squires, 1995). In their paper, they introduce their "perspectives interaction paradigm" and argue that this new evaluation system presents a more valid and holistic review of a technology's impact on learning. Turkle (as cited by Kelly, 1998) argues a similar point when she writes, "Too much of the time we think the computer is supposed to do it all, and we don't really appreciate how important the people are . . . it's the computer plus the human environment around the computer that matters" (p. 55).

There is also a trend for evaluation practices of print-based materials to use more situated and integrated procedures. Stein, Stuen, Carnine, and Long (2001) direct evaluators to consider depth of exposure to content, explicit strategies, opportunities for teachers to scaffold instruction, and strategic integration of skills and concepts across lessons. Walpole and McKenna (2004) ask evaluators to consider the school-wide implications of the materials, including teacher training, daily teacher preparation, and issues of differentiated instruction. Simmons, Kuykehdall, King, Cornachione, and Kame'enui (2000) embed materials evaluation within a school-wide improvement model, beginning with careful description of the school setting in which the materials would be used and the specific academic needs of the children who would use the materials. Likewise, we see considerations of the context as essential to evaluation procedures.

A sixth promising practice we found in our review prompts evaluators to focus attention on the range of new and multiple literacies converging within information and communication technologies and the need to adopt a healthy dose of informed skepticism (Lankshear & Snyder, 2000) while critically considering its impact on social interactions and literacy learning (Cope & Kalantzis, 2000). Evaluators must be able to critically examine educational technology resources in search of those that support, conceptualize and extend technology resources, and not simply those resources that add glitz and glamour in an electronic learning environment. Phillips (1996) reminds us that, during the evaluation process, we need to be more aware of critical issues such as "who created the title, what their point of view might be, and to what type of audience the program was written" (p. 16). Similarly, McVee and Dickson (2002) encourage educators to build on their practices of critically thinking about the role that children's books have in shaping learning to consider how particular software programs impact learning and social interaction as well. Technology evaluators should apply these critical evaluation literacies when following Judge's (2001) recommendation to rely on preexisting databases of technology reviews.

When developing procedures for evaluating informational websites for literacy learning, Coiro (2003) argues that the need to critically evaluate electronic text becomes greater for several reasons. For example, the fact that there is little consistency in the multimedia formatting of information on the Internet suggests that we need to select resources that support learners in locating important ideas in the text instead of those that distract students with unrelated animations and blinking advertisements. Second, whereas the reader is, for the most part, guaranteed that a traditionally printed text has been subject to a review process, there is no same guarantee with electronic text posted on the Web. Thus, when selecting Web site materials for classroom use, educators need to consider whether or not their students are able to assume editing responsibilities such as investigating author qualifications, paying attention to Web site sponsors, and verifying information with multiple resources.

Another area of concern is the upsurge of deception through visual imagery presented on the Internet. "Images were never tinkered with as they are today where, with computer technology, such alterations are not only easy, but also undetectable" (Center for Media Literacy, 2002). Informational websites may include images with faces that are changed, bodies that are reshaped, or objects that are inserted or resized, often with the intention of creating a good laugh. Real photos are sometimes paired with fictitious reports or doctored to match deceiving captions (see, for example, the collection compiled by library-media specialist Kathy Schrock at the end of her list beneath the heading "Sites to Use for Demonstrating Critical Evaluation" at http://school.discovery.com/schrockguide/eval.html). Evaluators should be attuned to strategies for detecting digital images that have been constructed to trick, persuade, or misinform students who read information on the Internet and should choose Internet resources with images that can be checked for validity. Finally, because information on Internet websites is often intertwined with hidden social, economic, and political agendas (Cope & Kalantzis, 2000; Kinzer & Leander, 2003), educators need to critically evaluate the proportion of information within a Web site that is driven by these hidden agendas with that information which is driven by a sincere interest in the education of our children. For instance, advertisements, interactive games, search functions, informational passages, related links, and consumer surveys at popular children's websites like American Girl (http://www.americangirl.com) and Scholastic (http://www.scholastic.com) are often woven into the same web page, causing confusion about the author's underlying intentions. Each of the dimensions of Web-based informational resources described in this section should be considered as part of the technology evaluation process.

A final promising trend we found in recent evaluation methodologies is that evaluators are making greater attempts to involve students and educators in the development of evaluation criteria and in the subsequent selection and review of educational technologies for literacy learning. Researchers have found that educators who construct evaluation criteria and then apply these criteria to evaluation practices are less fearful of the process and much more likely to use technology effectively in their classrooms (Hall & Martin, 1999; McVee & Dickson, 2002). McDougall and Squires (1995) also note the advantages of this generative approach to evaluation, whereby educators who were involved in this process were able to better "determine selection criteria, explain issues and structure thinking about the use of software" (p. 100).

Others posit that children can also provide new insights into a certain resource's strengths and weaknesses (e.g., Komoski, 1995; Wilson, 1998). Wepner (1989) found this to be true as well, when she observed student reactions to technology features that may be distasteful to teachers (e.g., robot speech), but nonetheless motivating to students. Some researchers even go so far to suggest that as a general rule, if there is no way to preview software with your students, you should avoid that software (Case & Truscott, 1999). Certainly, these are important considerations in our efforts to develop valid and reliable methods of evaluating technology resources for literacy learning.

RECOMMENDATIONS

In our analysis thus far, we've traveled down two divergent paths in the literature on evaluating technologies for literacy learning: one that we believe is limited in its utility and the other that we argue more accurately addresses the dynamic and multidimensional potential of integrating technology and literacy learning. Based on the lessons that each body of knowledge teaches us, we end by proposing the following recommendations to the process of critically evaluating educational technologies for literacy learning:

- The technology evaluation process should begin with individual student needs and a specific school, classroom, and curricular context. Technology resources should link learning objectives to authentic reading, writing, and thinking situations.
- The technology evaluation process should target meaningful knowledge construction using multiple media formats.
- The technology evaluation process should consider technology-based social interactions.
- The technology evaluation process should be informed by (rather than constrained by) reviews and evaluations conducted by individuals outside the local teaching and learning situation.
- The technology evaluation process should follow a before, during, and after format— identifying potentially useful technologies before using them with students, tracking their usefulness with students during literacy work, and examining the real effects that the technologies have on student learning after using the technology.
- The technology evaluation process should encourage expanded, mixed methods research methodologies that can be shared within the literacy community.
- The technology evaluation process must include the role of the teacher in implementing the technology.

SUMMARY AND CONCLUSIONS

It is clear that one practical technology evaluation format does not exist. In fact, we would argue that one format would limit the flexibility needed to evaluate technology use from the multiple and complex dimensions we describe in this chapter. However, findings from recent independent effectiveness studies (e.g., Mallette, Henk, & Melnick, 2004; Paterson et al., 2003, Slavin, 1990) coupled with the current evaluation models available (e.g., Bitter & Pierson, 2002, McVee & Dickson, 2002) may inform the development of our future evaluation practices. For instance, Mallette et al. (2004) examined the influence of a reading-incentive software program on the affective literacy orientations of intermediate grade students. Understanding that often not all students respond to a certain technology in the same way, the researchers used several two- and three-factor experimental designs to investigate the differential effects of the software. Their assumptions led to important findings including the notion that "when paired with levels of gender and ability, this program differentially influenced reader self-perceptions" (p. 82). Differential considerations such as these that go beyond the one-sided issue of whether or not a certain software program is effective are crucial for both researchers and classroom teachers involved in the evaluation process.

In another example, Paterson et al. (2003) examined the effects of an integrated learning system on literacy learning, behavior, and attitudinal changes towards literacy learning, and eventual transfer to classroom literacy learning. The researchers selected a mixed methods approach, since "experimental designs may miss results of the use of technology that go beyond what is traditionally measured" (p. 176), and they used rigorously triangulated qualitative data to further inform them of any "pertinent classroom factors that might influence the programs' success or failure in supporting early reading learning" (p. 183). These methodological choices allowed for broad reflection on the impact of the technology situated in the complex environment of the classroom and provided crucial insights into how different variables beyond the program itself impact its potential utility for literacy learning. Though a study of this breadth may not be realistic from a classroom teacher's perspective, on a smaller scale, the methods of Paterson and her colleagues provide a thoughtful model of what classroom factors are important to consider beyond the technology as playing a role in the overall impact of a certain software program.

Much is also to be learned from the evaluation models currently available. Each reflects some of the positive trends outlined in this chapter and may be quite helpful in helping teachers make critical decisions about appropriate technology implementation in their classrooms. These models include:

- a comprehensive list of guidelines for review of educational software and educational websites by Bitter & Pierson (2002);
- an open-ended rubric evaluation for software activities that could easily be extended to Internet resources (McVee & Dickson, 2002);
- a list of questions for evaluating reading and writing instructional software that links back to one's own theoretical orientation (Leu & Kinzer, 2003);
- a list of criteria for software selection that considers curricular, pedagogical, and individual learner dimensions (Burmark & Thornburg, 1996); and, finally,
- a generative and situated approach that considers a holistic awareness across the perspectives of classroom culture, teaching style, and student needs (McDougall & Squires, 1995).

When we consider the practical application of evaluation processes informed by the resources above, we realize that we have placed a tall order. We invite teachers to join us by specifying their teaching and learning purposes before selecting technologies. We ask that teachers first consider the factors within their classrooms and the technologies themselves which either support or prevent those purposes from being realized and then, reflect on the effects of specific technologies on their literacy teaching and learning. Similarly, we invite researchers to develop and conduct studies that employ dynamic methodologies and multiple lenses to examine the effects of literacy learning with technology. As we plunge ahead into a future where literacy learning undoubtedly involves software and Internet technologies, these recommendations may be useful for framing new paradigms in technology evaluation.

REFERENCES

Allen, G., & Thompson, A. (1995). Analysis of the effect of networking on computer-assisted collaborative writing in a fifth grade classroom. *Journal of Educational Computing Research, 12*, 65–75.

Aufderheide, P. (2001). *Activities available on children's websites: A survey.* Retrieved March 16, 2003 from http://www1.soc.american.edu/faculty/aufderheide/Research/kids-url%20survey.htm

Bader, M. J. (2000). Choosing CALL software: Beginning the evaluation process. *TESOL Journal, 9*, 18–22.

Bain, J., McNaught, C., & Mills, C. (1996). *Relationship between academics' educational beliefs and conceptions and their design and use of computer software in higher education.* Paper presented at

"Researching Education in New Times," Australian Association for Research in Education Annual Conference, Brisbane, Australia. Retrieved November 11, 2003 from http://www.aare.edu.au/97pap/bainj134.htm

Balajthy, E. (2000). The effects of teacher purpose on achievement gains. *Reading & Writing Quarterly, 16*, 289–294.

Becker, H. (1999). *Internet use by teachers*. Retrieved November 1, 2003 from http://www.crito.uci.edu/TLC/FINDINGS/internet-use/startpage.htm

Bitter, G., & Pierson, M. (2002). *Using technology in the classroom* (5th ed.). Boston, MA: Allyn & Bacon.

Bruce, B. C., & Peyton, J. K. (1999). Literacy development in network-based classrooms: Innovation and realizations. *International Journal of Educational Technology, 1*. Retrieved October 14, 2003 from http://www.ao.uiuc.edu/ijet/v1n2/bruce/index.html

Buckleitner, W. (1999). *The state of children's software evaluation: Yesterday, today, and in the 21st century*. Retrieved September 15, 2003 from http://www.childrenssoftware.com/evaluation.html

Burmark, L., & Thornburg, D. (1996). *Criteria for software selection*. Retrieved November 2, 2003 from http://www.tcpd.org/Burmark/Handouts/SoftwareSelection.pdf

Case, C., & Truscott, D. M. (1999). The lure of bells and whistles: Choosing the best software to support reading instruction. *Reading & Writing Quarterly, 15*, 361–369.

Chandler-Olcott, K., & Mahar, D. (2003). "Tech-savviness" meets multiliteracies: Exploring adolescent girls' technology-mediated literacy practices. *Reading Research Quarterly, 38*(3), 356–385.

Christenson, R., & Knezak, G. (2001). *Developing the teacher attitudes toward reading and technology questionnaire*. Retrieved November 2, 2003 from http://www.iittl.unt.edu/KIDS2001/html/ch12.htm

Ciolek, T. M. (1996). The six quests for the electronic grail: Current approaches to information quality in WWW resources. Retrieved October 10, 2003 from http://www.ciolek.com/PAPERS/six-quests1996.html

Clements, D. (1985). *Computers in early and primary education*. Englewood Cliffs, NJ: Prentice-Hall.

Coiro, J. (2003). Rethinking comprehension strategies to better prepare students for critically evaluating content on the Internet. *The NERA Journal, 39*, 29–34.

Cope, B., & Kalantzis, M. (Eds.). (2000). *Multiliteracies: Literacy learning and the design of social futures*. London: Routledge.

Davidson, J., Elcock, J., & Noyes, P. (1996). A preliminary study of the effect of computer-assisted practice on reading attainment. *Journal of Research in Reading, 19*, 102–110.

Dole, J. A. (2000). Explicit and implicit instruction in comprehension. In B. Taylor, M. F. Graves, P. VanDenBroek, & P. W. VanDenBroek. *Reading for meaning: Fostering comprehension in the middle grades*. New York, NY: Teacher College.

Draper, S. (1996). *Observing, measuring and evaluating courseware: A conceptual introduction*. Retrieved November 10, 2003 from http://www.icbl.hw.ac.uk/ltdi/implementing-it/measure.htm

Duchastel, P. C. (1987). Structures and methodologies for the evaluation of educational software. *Studies in Educational Evaluation, 13*, 111–117.

Education Market Research. (1999). *National Survey of Teachers' Use of Digital Content*. Retrieved November 1, 2003 from http://www.edweek.org/sreports/tc99/articles/survey.htm#teach

Ellsworth, N. J., & Hedley, C. N. (1993). What's new in software? Selecting software for student use. *Reading & Writing Quarterly: Overcoming Learning Difficulties, 9*, 207–211.

EvaluTech. (1997). *EvaluTech Review Criteria*. Retrieved June 3, 2004 from http://www.evalutech.sreb.org/criteria/index.asp

Florida's Panhandle Area Educational Consortium. (2004). *Evaluating Educational Software*. Retrieved June 1, 2004 from http://www.paec.org/training/SoftwareEvaluation/

Frick, T. W. (1991). *Restructuring education through technology*. Bloomington, IN: Phi Delta Kappa Educational Foundation. Retrieved December 10, 2003 from http://education.indiana.edu/%7Efrick/fastback/fastback326.html

Gambrell, L. B., Bradley, V. N., & McLaughlin, E. M. (1987). Young children's comprehension and recall of computer screen displayed text. *Journal of Research in Reading, 10*, 156–163.

Geissenger, H. (1997). *Educational software: Criteria for evaluation.* Paper presented at the 14th annual meeting of the Australian Society for Computers in Learning in Tertiary Education in Perth, Western Australia.

Gorski, P. (1999). *Toward a multicultural approach for evaluating educational websites.* Retrieved November 5, 2003 from http://www.edchange.org/multicultural/net/comps/eval.html

Green, B. (1988). Subject-specific literacy and school learning: A focus on writing. *Australian Journal of Education, 32,* 156–179.

Hall, V. G., & Martin, L. E. (1999). Making decisions about software for classroom use. *Reading Research and Instruction, 38,* 187–196.

Harris, J. (1998). *Virtual architecture: Designing and directing curriculum-based telecollaboration.* Eugene, OR: International Society for Technology in Education. [Online Version]. Retrieved October 15, 2003 from http://virtual-architecture.wm.edu/index.html

Heimann, M., Nelson, K. E., Tjus, T., & Gillberg, C. (1995). Increasing reading and communication skills in children with autism through an interactive multimedia computer program. *Journal of Autism and Developmental Disorders, 25,* 469–480.

Hickey, M. G. (1995). More than drill and practice: Selecting software for learners who are gifted. *Teaching Exceptional Children, 27,* 48–50.

Higgins, E. L., & Raskind, M. H. (2000). Speaking to read: The effects of continuous vs. discrete speech recognition systems on the reading and spelling of children with learning disabilities. *Journal of Special Education Technology, 15,* 19–30.

Howell, R. D., Erickson, K., Stanger, C., & Wheaton, J. E. (2000). Evaluation of a computer-based program on the reading performance of first grade students with potential for reading failure. *Journal of Special Education Technology, 15,* 5–14.

Hull, G., & Schultz, K. (2001). Literacy and learning out of school: A review of theory and research. *Review of Educational Research, 71,* 575–611.

ISTE (2000). *National Educational Technology Standards for Students: Connecting curriculum and technology.* International Society for Technology in Education.

International Reading Association. (1984). Guidelines for educators on using computers in the schools. *Reading Research Quarterly, 20,* 120–122.

International Reading Association. (2001). *Integrating literacy and technology in the curriculum: A position statement.* Retrieved September 3, 2003 from http://www.reading.org/positions/technology.html

Jonassen, D. H. (1996). *Computers in the classroom: Mindtools for critical thinking.* Columbus, OH: Merrill/Prentice-Hall.

Jonassen, D. H., Peck. K. L., & Wilson, B. G. (1999). *Learning with technology: A constructivist perspective.* Upper Saddle River, NJ: Merrill/Prentice Hall.

Judge, S. L. (2001). Integrating computer technology within early childhood classrooms. *Young Exceptional Children, 5,* 20–26.

Karchmer, R. A. (2001). The journey ahead: Thirteen teachers report how the Internet influences literacy and literacy instruction in their K–12 classrooms. *Reading Research Quarterly, 36,* 442–466.

Karchmer, R. A., Mallette, M. H., & Leu, D. J., Jr. (2000). Early literacy in a digital age: Moving from a singular book literacy to the multiple literacies of networked information and communication technologies. In D. M. Barone & L. M. Morrow. (Eds.). *Literacy and young children: Research based practices.* New York, NY: Guilford Press.

Keene, S., & Davey, B. (1987). Effects of computer-presented text on LD adolescents' reading behaviors. *Learning Disability Quarterly, 10,* 283–290.

Kelly, K. (1998). *New rules for the new economy: 10 radical strategies for a connected World.* New York: Viking.

Kinzer, C. K., & Leander, K. (2003). Technology and the language arts: Implications of an expanded definition of literacy. In J. Flood, D. Lapp, J. R. Squire, & J. M. Jensen (Eds.), *Handbook of research and teaching the English language arts* (pp. 546–576). Mahwah, NJ: Lawrence Erlbaum Associates.

Komoski, P. K. (1995). *Seven steps to responsible software selection.* ERIC Digest: Clearinghouse on Information & Technology. Retrieved September 20, 2003 from http://www.netc.org/software/eric_software.html

Kress, G., & van Leeuwen, T. (2001). *Multimodal Discourse: The Modes and Media of Contemporary Communication.* London: Arnold.

Labbo, L. D., & Reinking, D. (1999). Negotiating the multiple realities of technology in literacy research and instruction. *Reading Research Quarterly, 34,* 473–492.

Lankshear, C., & Knobel, M. (2003). *New literacies: Changing knowledge and classroom learning.* Buckingham: Open University Press.

Lankshear, C., & Snyder, I. (2000). *Teachers and techno literacy: Managing literacy, technology and learning in schools.* Crows Nest, AU: Allen & Unwin.

Leu, D. J., Jr. (2000). Literacy and technology: Deictic consequences for literacy education in an information age. In M. L. Kamil, P. Mosenthal, P. D. Pearson, and R. Barr (Eds.) *Handbook of Reading Research, Volume III* (pp. 743–770). Mahwah, NJ: Lawrence Erlbaum Associates.

Leu, D. J., Jr., & Kinzer, C. K. (2003). *Effective literacy instruction: Implementing best practices, 5th Edition.* Upper Saddle River, NJ: Merrill Prentice Hall.

Leu, D. J., Jr., Kinzer, C. K., Coiro, J., & Cammack, D. (2004). Toward a theory of new literacies emerging from the Internet and other ICT. In R. Ruddell and Norman Unrau (Eds.) *Theoretical models and processes of reading (5th ed.)* (pp. 1570–1613). Newark, DE: International Reading Association.

Luke, C. (2000). Cyber-schooling and technological change. In B. Cope & M. Kalantzis (Eds.). *Multiliteracies: Literacy learning and the design of social futures* (pp. 69–91). London: Routledge.

MacArthur, C. A., & Haynes, J. B. (1995). Student Assistant for Learning from Text (SALT): A hypermedia reading aid. *Journal of Learning Disabilities, 28,* 150–159.

McDougall, A., & Squires, D. (1995). An empirical study of a new paradigm for choosing educational software. *Computers & Education, 25,* 93–103.

McVee, M. B., & Dickson, B. A. (2002). Creating a rubric to examine literacy software for the primary grades. *The Reading Teacher, 55,* 635–639.

Mallette, M. H., Henk, W. A., & Melnick, S. A. (2004). The influence of Accelerated Reader on the affective literacy orientations of intermediate grade students. *Journal of Literacy Research, 36,* 73–84.

Matthew, K. (1997). A comparison of the influence of interactive CD-ROM storybooks and traditional print storybooks on reading comprehension. *Journal of Research on Computing in Education, 29,* 263–275.

Meyer, A., & Rose, D. (1998). *Learning to read in the computer age.* Cambridge, MA: Brookline Books.

New London Group. (2000). A pedagogy of multiliteracies designing social futures. In B. Cope & M. Kalantzis. (Eds.). *Multiliteracies: Literacy learning and the design of social futures* (pp. 9–38). London: Routledge.

Nicholls, P., & Ridley, J. (1997). Evaluating multimedia library materials: Clues from hand-printed books and art history. *Computers in Libraries, 17,* 28–31.

Nicolson, R., Fawcett, A., & Nicolson, M. (2000). Evaluation of a computer-based reading intervention in infant and junior schools. *Journal of Research in Reading, 23,* 194–209.

No Child Left Behind Act (2001), PL 107–110, 115 Stat. 1425, 20 U.S.C. §§ 6301 *et seq.*

Norton, P., & Sprague, D. (2001). *Technology for teaching.* Needham Heights, MA: Allyn & Bacon.

Payton, T. (1998). *Web evaluation for intermediate grades.* Retrieved October 30, 2003 from http://www.siec.k12.in.us/~west/edu/rubric2.htm

Paterson, W. A., Henry, J. J., O'Quin, K., Ceprano, M. A., & Blue, E. V. (2003). Investigating the effectiveness of an integrated learning system on early emergent readers. *Reading Research Quarterly, 38,* 172–207.

Phillips, M. (1996). Beyond the best CDs list. *Electronic Learning, 15,* 16.

Reutzel, D. R., Sudweeks, R., & Hollingsworth, P. M. (1994). Issues in reading instruction: The views and information sources of state-level textbook adoption committee members. *Reading Research and Instruction, 34,* 149–171.

Robyler, M. D. (1997). *Integrating educational technology into teaching.* Upper Saddle River, NJ: Merrill Prentice Hall.

Robyler, M. D. (2003). *Integrating educational technology into teaching* (3rd ed.). Upper Saddle River, NJ: Merrill Prentice Hall.

Rowley, K., Carlson, P., & Miller, T. (1998). A cognitive technology to teach composition skills: Four studies with the R-WISE writing tutor. *Journal of Educational Computing Research, 18,* 259–296.

Scott, D., & Barker, J. (1987). Guidelines for selecting and evaluating reading software: Improving the decision making process. *The Reading Teacher, 40,* 884–887.

Shade, D. D. (1996). Software evaluation. *Young Children, 51,* 17–21.

Simic, M. R. (1999). *Guidelines for computer-assisted reading instruction.* Retrieved August 10, 2003 from http://www.kidsource.com/kidsource/content2/Guidelines.computers.html

Simmons, D. C., Kuykehdall, K., King, K., Cornachione, C., & Kame'enui, E. J. (2000). Implementation of a school wide reading improvement model: "No one ever told us it would be this hard!" *Learning Disabilities Research & Practice, 15,* 92–100.

Simmons, D. C., & Kame'enui, E. J. (2003). *Consumer's guide to evaluating a core reading program.* Retrieved on November 1, 2003 from http://reading.uoregon.edu/appendices/con_guide_3.1.03.pdf

Slavin, R. E. (1990). "IBM's Writing to Read: Is it right for reading?" *Phi Delta Kappan 72,* 214–216.

Spenser, M. (1986). *Choosing software for children.* ERIC Clearinghouse on Elementary and Early Childhood Education, ED267914, Urbana IL. Retrieved September 20, 2003 from http://www.ericfacility.net/databases/ERIC_Digests/ed267914.html

Stanford University Persuasive Technology Lab. (2001). How do people evaluate a website's credibility?: Results from a large study. *Consumer WebWatch.* Retrieved September 18, 2003 from http://www.consumerwebwatch.org/news/report3_credibilityresearch/stanfordPTL_abstract.htm

Stein, M., Stuen, C., Carnine, D., & Long, R. M. (2001). Textbook evaluation and adoption practices. *Reading and Writing Quarterly, 17,* 5–23.

Sturm, J. M., Rankin, J. L, Beukelman, D. R., & Schutz-Muehling, L. (1997). How to select appropriate software for computer-assisted writing. *Intervention in School and Clinic, 32,* 148–161.

Taylor, R. (1980). *The computer in the school: Tutor, tool, tutee.* New York, NY: Teachers College Press.

The Children's Partnership (2003). *The search for high-quality online content for low-income and underserved communities: Evaluating and producing what's needed.* Retrieved November 10, 2003 from http://www.contentbank.org/research/QualityContent.pdf

Trochin, W. M. (1996). *Evaluating websites.* Retrieved October 1, 2003 from http://trochim.human.cornell.edu/webeval/webintro/webintro.htm.

Venezky, R. L. (1987). Steps toward a modern history of American reading instruction. *Review of Research in Education, 13,* 129–167.

Walpole, S., & McKenna, M. C. (2004). *The literacy coach's handbook: A guide to research-based reform.* New York, NY: Guilford.

Wepner, S. B. (1989). Stepping forward with reading software. *Reading, Writing, and Learning Disabilities, 5,* 61–81.

Wepner, S. B., Valmont, W. J., & Thurlow, R. (2000). *Linking literacy and technology, Grades K–8.* Newark, DE: International Reading Association.

Wilson, L. J. (1998). Children as software reviewers. *Childhood Education, 74,* 250–252.

Wise, B. W., & Olson, R. K. (1995). Computer-based phonological awareness and reading instruction. *Annals of Dyslexia, 45,* 99–122.

Zakon, R. H. (2003). *Hobbes' Internet Timeline v.6.1.* Retrieved November 4, 2003 from http://www.zakon.org/robert/internet/timeline/

A Science-Based Development and Implementation Model for Online and CD-ROM Curriculum Programs

Bernice Stafford, Libbie Miller, and Muriel Ollivierre,
PLATO Learning, Inc.

This chapter focuses on multimedia technology as a learning form, explores the themes that influence multimedia designs, and examines their relationship to classroom instruction. We begin by noting the characteristics of hypermedia and its potential for learning, and highlighting current trends in education policy and practice that frame its use. We discuss the evolution of technology-based instructional design and concurrently evolving theories about learning. Drawing on our years of experience at an innovative education technology company, we use our company's unique development model to discuss the factors and philosophies that must guide the design and use of technology materials in schools. Throughout this paper we present our developmental model as an exemplar of a broadly replicable process, though we acknowledge at the outset that it is one in which we have had an economic interest.

We describe in detail the use of an individual piece of software by a classroom teacher, using this example to illustrate how design, development, and implementation principles manifest themselves in the real world. Finally, we look to the future of instructional technology and its important role in education, highlighting several key issues to consider as the field moves forward.

HYPERMEDIA AND ITS POTENTIAL FOR LEARNING

As technology rapidly moves through the fourth wave of technological advancement, text, video, animation, sound, and 3D interactivity are continuously converging. These rich hypermedia worlds are challenging the $360 billion K–12 sector to redefine the forms and functions of learning in and outside the classroom. The information needs and challenges of an increasingly competitive global marketplace force creation of new technological forms and functions that are defined within existent social and cultural contexts. As such, high-performance workers—those equipped with conceptual knowledge as well as the adaptive ability to formulate and apply new learning and skills—are required to quickly access and gather information in dynamic environments and collaboratively work to solve problems and produce, and communicate solutions. These changes are rapidly becoming the norm in the marketplace, and are defining the accountability-driven, standards-based classroom model presented in national and global policy agendas.

Increasingly, we construct meaning from highly interactive microworlds, simulations and games that are more encompassing, but less permanent than text-based forms of literacy. In these new environments, meaning is not solely shaped by traditional forms in which print symbolizes language, conveys meaning and holds information (Adams, 1990; Clay, 1991), but rather by fluid, non-linear streams of information drawn from text, image, sound, graphics, and animated characters linked together in an extensive hypermedia web of meaning. Hypermedia can be thought of as digitized, interactive networks of multimedia sound, video, and animation elements associated to related pieces of information by hypertext links that allow the user access to information across mutually related themes. Multimedia is understood to mean computer synthesized graphics, voice, animation, and video that may include limited amounts of hypertext (www.hyperdictionary.com); this term is closely related to CD-ROM because of the large amounts of information delivered in this software format.

In reference to multimedia, the terms *information*, *data* and *knowledge* are often used interchangeably to describe the streams of electronic outputs. Blum's framework is useful here in communicating the key relationships between these terms. He defines "data as discrete entities that are described objectively without interpretation; information as data that are interpreted, organized and structured; and knowledge as information that has been synthesized so that interrelationships are identified and formalized" (Blum, 1986). In this work, the terms *information* and *knowledge* are used interchangeably to refer to actions and processes that transform information and enliven knowledge.

In classrooms, the rapidly changing forms and functions of technology demand new instructional approaches; teachers access the new resources and create new networks to share effective resources and strategies. These act as transformative drivers altering the constructions of knowledge, literacy, and literacy instruction (Leu & Kinzer, 2000). In this instability, knowledge and information become fluid, embedding interactive learning activities into the daily work of schools. Within this fluidity, multimedia technology transforms literacy and meaning. The management of the instructional process, its resources, and strategies are functional components of learning. Donald Leu argues, "in a world of rapidly changing technologies and new envisionments for their use, literacy appears to be increasingly deictic; its meaning regularly redefined, not by time or space, but by new technologies and the continuously changing envisionments they initiate for information and communication" (Leu, 2000).

CLASSROOMS IN THE POLICY CONTEXT

K–12 instructional material developers ignore current social and political trends at their peril. Since 2000, the political environment in Washington, DC, has brought about the most significant changes in education publishing since passage of the Elementary and Secondary Education Act (ESEA) in 1965 nearly 40 years earlier. The reauthorization of ESEA as the No Child Left Behind Act of 2001, with its focus on state accountability systems, is designed around curriculum standards and assessments to measure learner attainment of standards. The current Administration and the U.S. Department of Education argue that the new law provides greater flexibility in return for increased accountability, yet many state and local education officials struggle to mesh their local accountability plans with requirements under the new law. As high-stakes accountability drives standards, instruction, and assessment, educators are being forced to look for ways to increase learner productivity. One such way is to make it possible for learning to extend beyond the walls of the schoolhouse and into the community and home (Steinberg, 1996). This suggests that our approach to teaching and learning will have to change.

In this new policy environment, instructional technology programs must "work in concert with other factors such as effective leadership, instructional priorities, and day-to-day demands of classroom practice" (Culp, Honey, & Mandinach, 2003, p. 22). In addition to commonly considered applications of technology for instruction, new multimedia resources can begin to bridge the gap between what education reform aims to accomplish and the inadequate set of tools currently available. Indeed, technology can assist with professional development, data analysis and information-sharing in ways previously impossible. In "A Retrospective on Twenty Years of Education Policy," a report commissioned by the U.S. Department of Education, researchers argue that there is a need for products to help educators use assessment data more effectively and to support their professional development needs and the overall productivity of the education enterprise.

CHANGING PERSPECTIVES IN TECHNOLOGY-BASED INSTRUCTIONAL DEVELOPMENT AND DESIGN

A prominent research group at Utah State University has defined instructional design as a set of principles and a technology for implementing those principles in the development of instructional experiences and environments (Merrill, Drake, Lacy, & Pratt, n.d.). According to these experts, "the field of instructional design involves . . . two important activities: the discovery of the natural principles in instructional strategies; and the use of these scientific principles to invent instructional design procedures and tools." As the process employed by experts to determine the best teaching methods for learners in a specific context for the purpose of obtaining a specific goal, this implies an inextricable link between instruction and assessment. Shepard (2000, p. 4) argues that to obtain the increased productivity from teaching and learning demanded by today's policy environment, instruction, and assessment must necessarily become interrelated tasks.

The U.S. military has for decades been a leader in the use of technology-based instructional design, and continues to lead the way in making advances in the field as it trains all-volunteer armed forces. During World War II, when faced with the task of mounting a standing army of untrained personnel, the military worked in partnership with academics, research and development centers, and the private sector to meet their training requirements. Today, each branch of the military continues to aggressively seek out and work with leading academicians and those who have demonstrated success in applying proven research to the practice of maintaining a force structure at the ready.

In the 1940s, Gagne and Briggs brought their knowledge and practice of psychometrics and behavioral techniques to this new developing field, designing both instruction and tests to identify and train citizen soldiers (Prestera, n.d.), and it is this approach today that largely dominates thinking in the field. For the first time, technology incorporated text, video, graphics, and sound into an integrated delivery platform. This made it possible for instructional designers to experiment with precise, but less rigid, presentations of knowledge by creating products that gave equal consideration to learner behavior and to the lessons being taught. This new medium, called *multimedia*—a term believed to have first been coined circa 1965 by Ted Nelson—enabled designers to create instructional materials linked to crossover references. These "hyperlinks" made it possible for learners to easily move between and among the material. Eric Hansen in 2000 defined *multimedia* as a presentation that synchronizes both auditory and visual information, such as a movie with sound, animations, and audio (Hansen, 2000).

Early computer-assisted instructional systems, developed by such companies as Computer Curriculum Corporation (CCC) and PLATO Learning, contained more text than graphics and video and very little sound and adopted this new medium for their courseware. They continued to use mainframe or mini-computer as hosts and dumb terminals as student stations. In the mid-1980s, the San Diego-based Education Systems Corporation (ESC, later known as Jostens Learning and now as Compass Learning), developed the first computer-assisted instructional system to take advantage of state-of-the-art technology by incorporating video, color, sound, and graphics into their software. Additionally, the company pioneered delivery of courseware content on microcomputers that used Microsoft's MS-DOS operating system. It was during this period that the field of instructional design began to explore a more constructivist approach to courseware development. For the most part, these software systems continued in the tradition of behaviorally-based branching and drill-and-practice techniques to teach segmented content and/or skills (Valdez, McNabb, Foertsch, Anderson, Hawkes, & Raack, 2000, p. 5). Valdez and associates concluded: "the educational practices at this time were heavily dominated by behavioral learning principles ... [and] computer software reflected these principles" (p. 5).

At the same time, these comprehensive courseware systems, known as computer-assisted instruction (CAI) or computer-managed instruction (CMI), began to be called *integrated learning systems* or (ILS). John Kernan, then head of ESC, is believed to have coined the term *ILS*, which to this day remains the popular name for managed curriculum software systems linked by local area networks. Throughout the 1980s and into the 1990s, the ILS dominated the educational software market. In the late 1990s, growth of the ILS market slowed (Educational Marketer, 1994, p. 8) as more constructivist, comprehensive software innovations and the Internet were introduced to the education marketplace and the nation's classrooms.

EDUCATION SOFTWARE AND THE EVOLUTION OF LEARNING THEORY

While technology was evolving into multimedia, advances in the study of learning theory were taking hold in education. Learning is a complex, multifaceted interpretation of the world. Three disparate, but interdependent theoretical approaches to learning—*behaviorism*, *cognitivism* and *constructivism*—have, for the past 50 years, widely influenced thinking about how to create instructional interactions that help learners acquire knowledge and meaning about themselves and the world. Behaviorist and cognitive approaches are "guided by an objective view of the nature of knowledge and what it means to know something" (Saettler, 1990; Mergel, 1998). Both models separate knowledge into component units of planned instructional sequences and assessments. Behaviorists view learners as passive recipients, and constructivists see learners as active participants in the learning process, acting on, rather than simply responding to, their external environment (Clay, 1998).

The cognitive scientist, however, analyzes information, organizes it into connected chunks that link meaningfully with remembered networks of information or schema, and then builds on internal mental processes designing tools and instructional processes that move concepts from the simple to the complex (Saettler, 1990; Mergel, 1998). Graphic organizers, metaphors, semantic models, and computers all help the learner link concepts, analyze, and process information in non-linear ways; this parallels hypermedia systems, which link related segments of information.

In a constructivist context, new knowledge is gained through engaging problem-solving experiences from which the learner makes sense of, derives meaning from, and interprets the world. "Conceptual growth comes from the negotiation of meaning, the sharing of multiple perspectives and the changing of our internal representations through social interaction and collaborative learning" (Merrill, 1991; as cited in Mergel, 1998). The shared progression of cognitivism and constructivism are evident when one realizes:

> Information processing models have spawned the computer model of the mind as an information processor. Constructivism has added that this information processor must be seen as not just shuffling data, but wielding it flexibly during learning—making hypotheses, testing tentative interpretations, and so on. (Perkins, 1991, as cited in Mergel, 1998)

Jonassen points out that the design of instruction anchored in constructivist environments should be concerned with creating mental models that facilitate the construction and invention of authentic contexts for learning; of problem solving situated in the real world with all its complexities; and the learner's internal negotiation of knowledge that promotes reflection of one's own thinking and understanding processes (Jonassen, 1994; Mergel, 1998). Other required elements in this design include actions of the teacher-facilitator, mentoring, and collaboration with others, and appropriate tools for modeling, building, and production.

There are those who would argue that instructional theories and models, teaching models, and instructional development models are closest to the phenomenon of learning—closer than most other fields that study this phenomenon (including cognitive psychology, educational psychology, educational theory and policy, curriculum and instruction, and others) (Barob, Squire, & Dueber, 2000). Furthermore, they argue, that it is the responsibility of the instructional designer to integrate the appropriate learning theory and instructional design model. As the Internet has become ubiquitous, constructivism takes on a different meaning for learners who view materials in parallel, and not sequentially, and simultaneously obtain information from multiple-linked pages (Prensky, 2001, p. 44). The Web allows learners to examine graphics first and then read text to further their understanding of the material. This is a profound difference from previous generations of learners, who read text first and then used graphics to amplify their understanding of it (Hostetter, 2002, p. 4).

"SERIOUS PLAY" AND THE LEARNING POWER OF GAMES

As one of the oldest forms of play known to man, the use of games has been well documented in the research. "The more children play, the more likely they are to read early, to write well, and to have advanced language skills" (Mann, 1996). Other researchers have documented that free play increases problem-solving ability and effectively guides children from simple to more complex solutions (e.g., Sylva, Bruner, & Genova, 1976). Susan Myhre (1993) sees play as valuable in children's attainment of language and literacy skills "[b]ecause dramatic play has no right or wrong answers" (p. 7). It is the self-directed and self-initiated factors of play that are important to learning and autonomy.

"Serious play," the term coined by Dale Mann of Teachers College at Columbia University, is a deliberate strategy akin to that espoused by Edward DeBono, who argues: "In a game, you have to make decisions at every moment. You have to work out your moves. You have to guess what the opponent might do. There is an *objective* (emphasis added) ..." (1995, p. 1). Players—and, in this context, learners—make tactical or moment-to-moment decisions. They plot out an overall strategy they believe will lead to winning the game and must think on their feet as they receive quick feedback from each of the moves they make—successful or unsuccessful.

While engrossed in game play—board games or electronic games—learners observe their thinking in action, and observers have noted that when children play a game they tend to take on a more mature persona and perform feats that, were they not exhibited during play, most adults would label as too difficult for a child of that age to attempt. Yet when these more difficult tasks are pursued by children in the form of a game, adult attitudes change as do their expectations for young learners. Standards-based education reform at its core relies on the power of expectation, and any activity that both motivates learners and re-evaluates expectations of them cannot be overlooked.

Games at their simplest provide a structured context for play. Wilson (1997) argues that it is a false dichotomy to suggest that an objective design can have no place in a constructive environment. Context matters, he says, "You can't tell by looking only at the strategy: you have to look at the entire situation and make a judgment" (1997, p. 4). A classroom practitioner, Obe Hostetter, who has observed the power of the educational video game on his students says, "... they teach deductive reasoning, memory strategies, and eye-hand coordination ... and, can be used effectively in the classroom ... as a part of constructivist learning in education" (2002, p. 2.) Or, put another way, according to Wilson (1997, p. 3), "an instructional strategy that imposes structure may actually help learners make constructions needed for learning."

As a strategy incorporated within a constructivist instructional design model, serious play promotes memory in children and becomes a foundation for children to construct even more sophisticated memory strategies. In our work, we designed learning games to support the development, enrichment, and reinforcement of language, literacy, and mathematical skills operationalized as a "cognitive approach to instructional technology [that] emphasized looking at how [students] know rather than how [students responded] (behaviorism), and [how students analyzed, planned] and strategized their own thinking, remembering, understanding, and communicating" (Valdez, McNabb, Foertsch, Anderson, Hawkes, & Raack, 2000, p. 6). The next sections of this chapter describe this work.

Our own research, and that of other respected commercial providers of game and simulation software, show that students tend to be even more interested and motivated and persist longer at the task of acquiring relevant knowledge, skills, and information (Birch, 2002; Cognitive Concepts, 2000; Metiri Group, 2001). Students also develop cognitive strategies that help them organize, understand, and remember the content learned (McEwan, 1997, pp. 52–55). Evidence suggests that the short-term outcome of a student use of cognitive strategies is deeper understanding of the current assignment, and the longer-term outcome is internalization and consistent adaptive use of [the strategy] when encountering demanding text (Pressley, Woloshyn, Burkell, Cariglia-Bull, Lysynchuk, McGoldrick, Schneider, Snyder, & Symons, 1995).

BUILDING PRODUCTS THAT WORK: INSTRUCTION
AND THE PRODUCT DESIGN PROCESS

As we have seen, the design of instructional technology is directly linked to the learning theory it attempts to exploit. In this section, we draw on our experience developing, implementing, and evaluating multimedia technology in order to explain how the design process itself can affect instruction and learning. Our company, formerly Lightspan, Inc. and now part of PLATO Learning, Inc. developed and implemented a system of comprehensive reading, language arts, and mathematics software for use both in the classroom and in students' homes at more than 5,000 elementary and middle schools, and an integrated system of support for classroom teachers, consisting of manuals, quick start cards, and online and CD-ROM professional development support. While our work was in the constructivist mode, it was not open-ended. We created closed, "intentional" learning environments in the form of curriculum games launched from a story where learning objectives and activities were scaffolded as tasks within the game.

The company's product development methodology can be described as a form of rapid pro-totyping that we have named "hybrid rapid prototyping" because the development, implementation and field-testing processes take place almost simultaneously. As the first commercial educational software company to develop and market a technology-based, full-screen, full-motion video, comprehensive curriculum program—a costly product development endeavor—it was essential that we limit costly errors and mistakes and get to market quickly. This meant we would be working in a development environment that required frequent feedback from all client levels, from expert advisory boards and user panels of teachers to students and parents. Acknowledging the shifting policy environment, we continuously consulted emerging policy initiatives at the state and federal levels to inform the development process.

Being a new company, without a hardware platform legacy meant we could work with state-of-the-art technology and development processes at the time and we took advantage of that freedom. When ready to expand the product line a few years later, the marketing and development teams put in place the level of discipline required to ensure that the resources for new development would be available. Every other development phase was undertaken as iterative, rather than sequential, in order to bring the product to market in a timely manner. Although it took several years to complete the product and get 100 CDs in the hands of our customer base, by Spring 1994 we released for final field-testing one K–2 reading/language arts CD and mathematics CD. Initially the field test took place in schools in the local area and ultimately we were able to expand this program beyond the three local schools to 16 schools. At the mid-point of this phase of field testing, we began distributing our first production run and the beginning of the 1994–95 school year, with regularly scheduled releases continuing at timed intervals into the 1995–96 school year and beyond.

From the beginning, we dual-tracked the process; one track was product development, and the second track was product implementation and professional development. While the core product team worked on technology-based development, the core implementation team worked to construct paper-based curriculum support materials. Over time, these paper-based materials were augmented by CD-ROM and Web-based professional-development support.

In 1996, a nationally known research-and-development organization was hired to conduct a formal evaluation of those materials and the curriculum-based learning games. It is important to note that this evaluation was another concurrent activity overseen, not by the implementation or professional-development departments, but by a separate department. It took place alongside continued product development, continued curriculum support materials development, and the design of what would eventually become the rollout professional-development plan. At this stage of the process, the summative evaluation served as a "traffic cop" for both the development team and the implementation team. This was a messy process, but it worked remarkably well. It allowed the teams to receive input on key aspects of the product; this feedback loop was invaluable for the team designing professional development (Gianola, Ratkiewicz, Siach-Bar, & Grogan, 2000).

See Table 11.1 for typical commercial product development processes, which can span any-where from six to 28 months and involve a cross-disciplinary team of as many as 100 people (Foshay, 2003, pp. 1–2). Phases I through IV were simultaneous, and development was iterative with changes in the product necessitating changes in curriculum support materials and, if necessary, changes in the design of planned professional development.

This multifaceted design process is carefully followed in developing curriculum programs. The design team first develops the scope and sequence strands identifying the concepts or skills to be taught. Once these are identified, sub-objectives are developed along with suggested activities. At the same time, content specialists—educators working with a Curriculum Advisory Board—correlate the objectives with the standards developed by professional organizations

TABLE 11.1
The Achieve Now™ Product Development Process

Phase I	**Pre-concept and Concept** **Business Plan Requirements drive product planning process** Pre-concept and concept stages define target audience and game goals; explore development of concept, story, characters, environment and interactive screens. • Develop and design curriculum with internal experts and advisory boards. (Alpha test story and software components).
Phase II	**Design Development** • Develop concept document for scripts and characters and from these design storyboards and integrated product specifications (1) Senior Design Staff completes CD template concept and design (exploration of characters, environments, interactivity, look and feel) (2) Content writers, program managers, curriculum specialists and editors write content, dialogue and continuously review content (develop story/script, story/boarding staging, flow boards, interactivity). Alpha Testing character. **Curriculum Support** • Proceed with initial curriculum, script, character, and music development and review continuously with internal team • Develop and review plan for curriculum support materials; conduct alpha testing at local sites • Develop and review criterion-referenced assessment specifications; conduct alpha testing at local sites • Conduct integrated alpha testing of product at local sites • Develop and review initial professional development plan • Develop and review plan for summative evaluation • Interactive Game Plan (IGP) group writes, reviews game format, revises story script, and obtains character, script, storyboard, flow board and prototyping approvals • Conduct pre-alpha testing of software components using storyboards, pencil tests, etc. with select client groups and advisory boards • Develop specifications for the software and subsystems; conduct alpha testing at national sites
Phase III	Production Interactive/Audio/Animation. Animation layouts, record dialogue. Background and graphics animation. Animation pencil test. Retakes. Sound Effects and Animation Composite Delivery
Phase IV	Programming/QA Process Conduct beta and technical testing; complete final product revisions prior to product release. Iterative development and review process in Phase II should negate additional revisions
Phase V	Evaluation Implement annual summative evaluation plan in the form of School-Based Action Research and Meta-analysis; product continues to be monitored and reviewed by both internal and external teams

such as the NCTM, IRA, NCTE, or with the goals of major referenced state frameworks or basal texts. The product development team, including designers, writers, producers, and software engineers, then came together to produce the CD structure and the challenging interactivity of the games. Prototypes were then taken to schools and tested with students and teachers, with necessary revisions made before the product was introduced to the implementation sites. Teachers and students throughout the design process provide opinions on the characters and music. They also receive hard-copy versions of the activities in order to check difficulty levels.

Throughout the early stages of the process, assessments of the impact of the materials focused on three areas of research: participant surveys documenting perceptions and reports of improved learning, implementation, and behavioral studies including observations of students' use of the products in schools and homes, and summative studies connecting achievement data with product implementations. A comprehensive study was conducted by RMC Research Corporation, which specializes in research, evaluation, training, and technical assistance for educational and human service agencies. The RMC Implementation Study surveyed the 16 test sites, and at four of them carried out interviews and observations and examined documents to "explore implementation procedures and gauge the effectiveness of the strategies used to introduce the materials into the schools" (Adler, Dwyer, Godin, Graham, & Keirstead, 1996). Spending two days at each site, researchers collected data from parents and teachers using survey and focus group techniques. They also interviewed administrators and home/school coordinators and observed classes. This study ultimately shaped the wider school adoption and implementation process.

Their research findings stressed the need for the assessment and evaluation of the products' impact on student learning outcomes and connections to the school curriculum. Leadership responsibilities, implementation guidelines, teacher and parent training, and support systems were identified as key requisites for successful implementations. As a result, the RMC study proposed a three-year Comprehensive National Evaluation Plan to link the Achieve Now Program to student outcomes. The plan called for Year-One research to concentrate on school implementation and schooling outcomes. Starting in Year-Two when teachers would use the program to launch a lesson which would then be sent home with students to complete as home work, the analysis focused on the impact of home use on student achievement. Year-Three when the program was used by teachers to launch the lesson to be taught, enable student practice opportunities in a classroom learning center, and be used at home, the evaluation measured the impact of the program on student achievement from use at school and home. The evaluation design proposed pre- and post-measurements, experimental/control group comparisons, multi-site implementations, and stratified random sampling on a national basis. The study also clearly informed the professional development process, content, and outcomes for classroom and home.

The professional development design and evaluation process was equally rigorous. From the start, the professional development model focused on classroom interactions that reshaped learning for students and teachers. The integration of multimedia, interactive technology as classroom curricula, redefined traditional roles of teacher and students. Students equipped with clear goals concentrated on standards-based curriculum challenges, experienced success, and gained immediate feedback and a sense of control and self-esteem. Teachers and students were now sharing knowledge; no longer were teachers only passing their knowledge on to students, but students were helping teachers and parents master the games and learn the curriculum in new, relevant ways.

Teachers found the new learning context offered students more opportunities to learn and apply knowledge of the real world to the worlds of the characters. Interactivity prompted possibilities and more questions and encouraged collaborative learning, problem solving, and critical and creative thinking. The games created optimal learning environments that increased the potential for parents, teachers, and students to help each other develop and grow. Parents and other learners revisiting their elementary school curriculum in this new and different way mastered concepts they had never understood, or had memorized but long forgotten. Teachers also found the amount of information that students could be taught expanded, and game play allowed them to introduce a theme or concept and then guide student engagement in specific games. They assessed performance within the games, with performance-based projects and applications in the classroom as well as with traditional tests.

Lightspan Achieve Now™, renamed PLATO Achieve Now, the product line developed using the aforementioned processes, was designed to easily integrate into a school's K–8 reading/language arts and mathematics instructional programs. It includes interactive software, curriculum support materials, and on-site and online professional development. Curriculum support materials and professional development serve as resources to help teachers integrate the software into the classroom. They include teacher's guides, lesson plans, activity sheets, student formative and summative assessments, and family involvement activities. The professional development model is ongoing, and process-driven; it consists of both face-to-face and electronic interactions designed to be integrated into a capacity-building professional development design unique to a particular school.

Five recommended implementation model options were developed to demonstrate how the set of products can support the classroom teacher as he or she implements research-based instructional practices. The classroom model was designed to support explicit teacher-led instruction in skills and strategies and to support the introduction of independent practice. A learning center model was designed for teachers using the curriculum in regular classroom instruction during the nine-month school year to assist with the integration of skills with comprehension strategies. The third option was a family homework model, or home deployment, where students would take an assigned curriculum CD and PS one™ game console home and work the CD games with assistance from a parent/guardian or older sibling. In this model, teachers used the curriculum CDs in their classrooms to introduce instructional concepts and in student learning centers for guided and independent learning opportunities, with home deployment the added component. The tutorial model focused on professional development consultants working with schools to design a preliminary individual student tutorial plan for each enrolled student, using existing data or data from the administration of Achieve Now assessments. A tutorial intervention was designed to provide intensive, data-driven support for under-performing students. The final option was a summer school model, which was designed for the purpose of providing extra support in short duration intensive program to halt or prevent failure and/or to support the acceleration of learning.

A LOOK AT INSTRUCTIONAL DESIGN THROUGH
THE LENS OF CLASSROOM IMPLEMENTATION

Rapid prototyping quickly pushes changes in technology, but as new knowledge and data rapidly become available they alter how students learn and teachers teach. Challenged to combine interactive technologies with effective instruction, teachers supported by our consultants determined how best to align and integrate this flexible programming with their changing instructional needs. An example of this can be seen in a program we developed: "Calamity®: The Natural World, Ocean Occupants 'On the Trail of Baby Sea Turtles.'" We worked with a teacher to integrate this CD into her lesson plan and use it to support a unit designed to teach the following stated objective: "understands explicit and implicit ideas and information in third grade or higher texts (e.g., knowing main idea or essential message, connecting important ideas with corresponding details, making inferences about information, distinguishing between significant and minor details, knowing chronological order of events)." The CD was used by the teacher in the classroom as a way to introduce the topic, and students also completed some activities at home.

Prior to introducing the CD in the classroom, the teacher developed a reading list compiled from the recommended resource list included in the teacher support materials, each child was required to make one or two selections from this reading list. Believing children would be more actively engaged with materials they selected, the teacher did not assign specific books for them to read. To start the CD lesson, the teacher led the class in both a group reading and a discussion of a passage about baby loggerhead sea turtles not having been seen for at least one year after they hatched. During the discussion, some children wondered what the turtles had been doing during their long absence. Among the more introspective answers, since some of the students had parents who had recently deployed on a military assignment abroad, was that the parents must have been very sad not to have seen the baby turtles in such a long time and how happy the parents would be to once more be reunited with the baby loggerhead sea turtles.

Another classroom activity paired students with partners to reread and discuss the article, looking for information from the text to define their thoughts and ideas. This activity gave them ample opportunities to reexamine the text and identify details to support their opinions and test them on each other. This served the purpose of helping students better understand the materials, explain and elaborate, and defend a position to others. By assigning learners this activity, the classroom teacher "evaluate and integrate their knowledge in new ways" (Capper, 1996, p. 22). Yet another activity was assigned to be completed in small groups consisting of three pairs of partners. The teacher instructed the groups to draw the device used by the researchers in the story to follow the baby sea turtles. They were told they could make as many illustrations of other items—both real and fanciful—as they chose, but the assigned drawing was a requirement because they would need to use it to accompany the paragraph they had been assigned to write. With this activity, the teacher assigned learning activities that students would use to help them reflect and refine their thoughts and resolve inconsistencies.

Not only did this teacher demonstrate an understanding of both the short- and long-term value of using cognitive strategies to support instruction, she also included authentic reading and writing tasks to extend use of the technology, and she also embedded assessment activities throughout the instructional process to check for understanding as students moved from one learning activity to another. Learning assignments were structured to assist students in developing foundational skills as well as making judgments and interpretations about the information presented in the story: to draw inferences and analyze information.

Research tells us that students become good readers when given enough time to practice and build their skill. When this teacher gave the assignment to read the text to themselves and to each other, she was devoting classroom time to reading practice with a purpose that could be immediately assessed. And by starting this lesson not just with the CD materials but also with a list of appropriate, high-interest reading materials from which students would be required to make a selection, this teacher ensured that they would extend their reading practice during the regular classroom period. She counted on the audio-supported text assisting those students encounter words and phrases unknown to them. And, since she had carefully assigned a strong reading partner to each pair, there was added peer assistance. In turn, each student listened to each other as they read: another valuable learning activity built into classroom instruction. Furthermore, when students worked in small groups there were at least three strong readers in each group, thereby weaker readers. Learning in social settings is motivating to students; it helps them articulate what they are learning as well as learn from each other (Capper, 1996, p. 20). The careful scaffolding this teacher provided, including the reading and writing assignment, was designed to support every step of the teaching and learning process in the classroom.

In addition to the classroom activities that evolved out of reading the passage, the teacher assigned both electronic game-playing and print-reading activities for students to complete at home with their families. This meant that when necessary friends, or adults in the household would be able to provide needed support. As students read the nonfiction articles and successfully completed the games, they developed confidence in their ability to apply reading strategies and earn game points that would lead them to a desired game objective—to unearth the directions to a time machine. After a school year of such focused and directed teaching and learning activities, this teacher had ample evidence that demosntrated her students were in lieu of a test preparation regimen.

PLANNING FOR SUCCESSFUL
IMPLEMENTATION IN SCHOOLS

Technology can of course be used in a multitude of ways to improve education, from the enrichment of student learning opportunities to the development of a data-based decision making community but a strategic plan and clear goals are critical for any successful implementation. Careful planning at all levels ensures that, prior to any implementation attempt, the following essential factors are addressed: 1) Support of district leadership; 2) Involvement of community and educational stakeholders; 3) Clear curriculum-based technology objectives; 4) Staff development; 5) Technology maintenance and support services; and 6) Identification of funding resources (Cradler, 1996; Pennsylvania Department of Education, 2001; Rodriguez & Knuth, 2000). Districts where technology has transformed teaching and instruction tend to have administrative leadership committed to a systematic, learner-centered plan that focuses on increasing student performance by using technology to enhance learning for all students (Cunningham, 2003).

Salpeter (2003) discusses how successful educational communities have responded to current pressures by transforming their professional development into more effective, ongoing processes that focus on real needs and real uses of technology. Educational software is only as good as the manner in which it is used for learning. It should be the mission of all education technology companies to serve as partners with schools to improve knowledge and skills among teachers and administrators to create systems that improve achievement for all students. Professional development provided by vendors should prepare school leadership to design improvement efforts, implement action plans, evaluate results, and systematically re-engage in the process to continuously improve the school's standards-based instructional program (Cancelli, 2003). In addition, instructors must receive training in the multiple strategies for integrating technology into the curriculum as well as information regarding the various types of education technology available.

Typically, instructional software falls into three general categories: supplementary, which adds little or no new content and parallels teaching already done in other modes; complementary, which adds new content to the curriculum, often in ways for which there is no non-computer alternative; and primary, which acts as the main source of initial teaching, as a replacement for non-electronic modes of instruction (Foshay, 2003). Based on the general goals for program improvement, a specific instructional model software to be used. Examples of four generic instructional models and their corresponding software types are: review/reinforcement (supplementary); enrichment/exploration (complementary); problem-centered (complementary); and skill development (primary).

For education software to be viewed as effective, it must be utilized as part of an ongoing process for improvement rather than a separate, isolated activity. Products require a strong curriculum basis to support what is being taught in the classroom, as well as a high level of flexibility to enable cohesion with the variety of materials teachers may already be using. Research in early childhood education indicates that education technology, if used in developmentally appropriate ways, can serve as a useful learning tool to supplement traditional teaching methods (Clements, 1994; Shade & Watson, 1990). The introduction of technology into the educational arena has provided educators with a set of instructional tools that contain a variety of benefits for students. These include an interactive approach appealing to all learners; opportunities for the development of higher-level reasoning and problem-solving skills; and a format that encourages communication and collaboration, as well as the development of a solid foundation for life-long learning (Feldman, 2002; Hutinger, Bell, Beard, Bond, Johanson, & Terry, 1998; NAEYC, 1996; Sanyal, 2001; Schacter, 1999).

In its "Report to the President on the use of technology to strengthen K–12 education in the United States," the Panel on Educational Technology (1997) outlined six strategic recommendations for technology to make an impact in schools: 1) Focus on learning with technology, not about technology; 2) Emphasize content and pedagogy, and not just hardware; 3) Give special attention to professional development; 4) Engage in realistic budgeting; 5) Ensure equitable, universal access; and 6) Initiate a major program of experimental research. These recommendations were directed towards the K–12 education community, but have also had an immense impact on the developmental direction of education software companies.

THE FUTURE OF TECHNOLOGY IN EDUCATION

Over the past 20 years, innovations in technology have greatly impacted and changed our lives; yet educational processes used to educate our students show only minimal effects. Children, who have been surrounded and influenced by digital technology in all aspects of their lives, are expected to excel while attending schools that have maintained the same organizational structure and instructional delivery model over the past 40 years (Hay, 2000; McCain & Jukes, 2001). Education as a whole must evolve, embracing technology and change adequately prepare students for the high-tech world in which we now live.

To teach effectively, educators must engage the minds of their students through whatever means available. Education needs to exploit all possible avenues, non-traditional as well as traditional, to involve students in the learning process. Computer games have become a part of children's culture over the past 10 to 15 years (Fromme, 2003) and have been found to be the most frequently used interactive media for children and youths (Beentjes et al., 2001). In spite of these and other similar data, there is still resistance for using this type of technology as a tool when instructing students (Malkin, 1999). Technology will not replace teachers, but it will challenge and modify their instructional strategies and methodologies. The new media enables instruction to be targeted based on individual student needs rather than the class as a whole, thus allowing a shift from teacher-centered to more student-centered learning (McCain & Jukes, 2001; Tapscott, 1999). Teachers will still play a significant role in ensuring effective learning by structuring and framing the activity of the learner when technology is utilized in the classroom. Indeed, the Computer Games in Education Project showed that a combination of game software, teacher input and collaboration from peers was necessary to provide powerful learning experiences (BECTA, 2001).

A greater focus on research of all types, from school-based action research to large-scale and experimental, is necessary to determine the value that technology can bring to education, and to identify the best practices needed for the effective implementation of these new tools. We must keep in mind, however, the fact that technology is constantly evolving and to remain viable and useful, education must keep pace.

REFERENCES

Adams, M. (1990). *Beginning to read.* Cambridge, MA: MIT Press.

Adler, R., Dwyer, C., Godin, K., Graham, W., & Keirstead, C. *Lightspan test site evaluation.* (Available from PLATO Learning, Inc., 10801 Nesbitt Avenue South, Bloomington, MN 55437.)

Barab, S. A., Squire, K. D., & Dueber, W. (2000). A co-evolutionary model for supporting the emergence of authenticity. *Educational Technology Research and Development, 48*(2), 37–62.

Beentjes, J. W. J., Koolstra, C. M., Marseille, N., & van der Voort, T. H. A. (2001). Children's use of different media: For how long and why? In S. Livingstone & M. Bovill (Eds.), *Children and their changing media environment* (pp. 85–111). Los Angeles, CA: Erlbaum. (Lawrence Erlbaum Associates?)

Birch, J. H. (2002). *The effects of the Delaware challenge grant program on the standardized reading and mathematics test scores of second and third grade students in the Caesar Rodney School District.* Unpublished doctoral dissertation, Wilmington College, Delaware.

Blum, B. L. (Ed.). (1986). *Clinical information systems.* New York, NY: Springer.

British Educational Communications and Technology Agency. (2001). *Computer games in education project.* Retrieved April 2, 2004, from http://www.becta.uk/research/research.cfm?section=1&id=2826

Cancelli, A. A. (2003). *The Lightspan Achieve Now meta-analysis: 2001–2002 school year.* (Available from PLATO Learning, Inc., 10801 Nesbitt Avenue South, Bloomington, MN 55437.)

Capper, J. (1996). *Testing to learn.* Newark, DE: International Reading Association.

Cazden, C. (1974). Play with language and metalinguistic awareness: One dimension of language experience. *The Urban Review, 7,* 28–39.

Clay, M. (1991). *Becoming literate: The construction of inner control.* Portsmouth, NJ: Heineman Education.

Clay, M. M. (1998). *By different paths to common outcomes.* York, ME: Stenhouse Publishers.

Clements, D. H. (1994). The uniqueness of the computer as a learning tool: Insights from research and practice. In J. L. Wright & D. D. Shade (Eds.), *Young children: Active learners in a technological age* (pp. 31–50). Washington, DC: National Association for the Education of Young Children.

Cognitive Concepts. (2000). *Earobics Chicago public schools pilot: Research report.* Evanston, IL: Author.

Cradler, J. (1996). *Implementing technology in education: Recent findings from research and evaluation studies: Policy brief.* Retrieved January 8, 2004, from http://www.wested.org/techpolicy/recapproach.html

Culp, K. M., Honey, M., & Mandinach, E. (2003). *A retrospective on twenty years of education technology policy* (p. 22). Washington, DC: U.S. Department of Education, Office of Educational Technology.

Cunningham, J. (2003). Between technology and teacher effectiveness: Professional development. *Technology & Learning.* Retrieved January 5, 2004, from http://www.techlearning.com/story/Article.jhtml?articleID=1051

DeBono, E. (1995). *Mind power* (pp. 1). New York: DK Publishing, Inc.

Feldman, D. (2002). *Technology and early literacy: A recipe for success.* Retrieved April 26, 2004, from http://www.mcps.k12.md.us/curriculum/littlekids/resources/recipe.pdf

Foshay, R. (2003). *Instructional models: Four ways to integrate PLATO into the curriculum.* Bloomington, MN: PLATO Learning, Inc.

Fromme, J. (2003*).* Computer games as a part of children's culture. *The International Journal of Computer Game Research* (3)1. Retrieved April 5, 2004, from http://www.gamestudies.org/0301/fromme/

Gianola, S. P., Ratkiewicz, K. J., Siach-Bar, Y., & Grogan, K. E. (2000). *Evaluation results of the Delaware challenge grant project.* University of Delaware: Delaware Education R & D Center.

Hansen, E. (2000, June 20). *History and meaning of the term 'multimedia.'* Message posted to http://lists.w3.org/Archives/Public/w3c-wai-au/2000AprJun/0503.html

Hay, L. E. (2000, April). Educating the net generation [Electronic version]. *School Administrator.* Retrieved April 2, 2004, from http://www.aasa.org/publications/sa/200_04/hay.htm

Hutinger, P., Bell, C., Beard, M., Bond, J., Johanson, J., & Terry, C. (1998). The early childhood emergent literacy technology research study: Final report. Washington, DC: Office of Special Education and Rehabilitative Services. (ERIC Document Reproduction Service No. ED418545)

Hostetter, O. (2002). *The necessity of incorporating video games as part of constructivist learning* (pp. 2–4) Retrieved April 26, 2004, from www.learningthroughsports.com/img.asp?id=1573

Jonassen, D. (1994). Thinking technology toward a constructivist design model. *Educational Technology, 34*(4), 34–37.

Leu, D. J. (2000). Literacy and technology: Deictic consequences for literacy education in an information age. In M. L. Kamil, P. Mosenthal, P. D. Pearson, & R. Barr (Eds.), *Handbook of reading research* (Vol. III). Mahwah, NJ: Lawrence Erlbaum Associates.

Leu, D. J., & Kinzer, C. K. (1998). *Effective literacy instruction* (4th ed.). Englewood Cliffs, NJ: Merrill.

Lightspan, Inc. (2002). *2001–2002 Lightspan Achieve Now self evaluation results.* San Diego, CA: Author.

Malkin, M. (1999, December). *Reading, writing, PlayStation?* Retrieved April 7, 2004, from http://www.jewishworldreview.com/michelle/malkin122799.asp

Mann, D. (1996, Spring). Serious play. *Teachers College Record, 97*(3), 446–469.

Mann, D., & Shakeshaft, C. (1997). *The Lightspan Partnership, Inc. and the home-school connection: A synthesis of available evidence and a national evaluation plan.* (Available from PLATO Learning, Inc., 10801 Nesbitt Avenue South, Bloomington, MN 55437.)

McCain, T. D. E., & Jukes, I. (2001). *Windows in the future: Education in the age of technology.* Thousand Oaks, CA: Corwin Press, Inc.

McEwan, E. K. (1997). *The principal's guide to raising reading achievement.* Thousand Oaks, CA: Corwin Press, Inc.

Mergel, G. (1998). *Instructional design and learning theory.* Retrieved June 4, 2004, from www.usask.ca/education/coursework/802papers/mergel/brenda.htm

Merrill, M. D., Drake, L., Lacy, M. J., & Pratt, J. (n.d.). Reclaiming the discipline of instructional design. Retrieved April 9, 2004, from http://it.coe.uga.edu/itforum/extra2/extra2.html

Metiri Group. (2001). *The adventures of Jasper Woodbury.* Retrieved June 9, 2004, from http://www.metiri.com/Kentucky2001/Jasper.htm

Myhre, S. M. (1993). Enhancing your dramatic-play area through the use of prop boxes. *The Journal of the National Association for the Education of Young Children, 48*(5), 6–18.

National Association for the Education of Young Children. (1996). *Position statement on technology and young children: Ages 3 through 8.* Washington, DC: NAEYC.

Panel on Educational Technology. (1997). *Report to the president on the use of technology to strengthen K–12 education in the United States.* Washington, DC: President's Committee of Advisors on Science and Technology, Executive Office of the President of the United States.

Pellegrini, A. D. (1980). The relationships between kindergartners' play and reading, writing and language achievement. *Psychology in the Schools, 17,* 530–535.

Prensky, M. (2000). *Digital game-based learning.* New York: McGraw-Hill.

Pennsylvania Department of Education. (2001). *Technology plan table of contents: Critical success factors for technology planning.* Retrieved January 8, 2004, from http://www.etechplanner.org/overview/2a.asp

Pressley, M., Woloshyn, V., Burkell, J., Cariglia-Bull, T., Lysynchuk, L., McGoldrick, J. A., Schneider, B., Snyder, G. L., & Symons, S. (1995). *Cognitive strategy instruction that really improves children's academic performance.* Cambridge, MA: Brookline Books.

Prestera, G. (n.d.). *History of ISD.* Retrieved April 26, 2004, from http://www.personal.psu.edu/users/g/e/gep111/html/M4/LI%20-%20ISD/M4LIP7.htm

Rodriguez, G., & Knuth, R. (2000). *Critical issue: Providing professional development for effective technology use.* Retrieved January 8, 2004, from http://www.ncrel.org/sdrs/areas/issues/methods/technlgy/te1000.htm

Rogers, C. S., & Sawyer, J. K. (Eds.). (1988). *Play in the lives of children.* Washington, DC: National Association for the Education of Young Children.

Saettler, P. (1990). *The history of American educational technology.* Englewood, CO: Libraries Unlimited, Inc.

Sales of technology to schools to reach $1.9 billion by 1998. (1994, August 15). *Educational Marketer*, p. 8.

Salpeter, J. (2003). Professional development: 21st century models. *Technology &* Learning. Retrieved January 5, 2004, from http://www.techlearning.com/story/showArticle.jhtml?articleID=13000492.

Sanyal, B. (2001, August). *New functions of higher education and ICT to achieve education for all.* Paper presented at the meeting of the University and Technology-for-Literacy/Basic Education Partnership in Developing Countries, Paris, France. Retrieved January 8, 2004, from www.literacy.org/products/ili/pdf/UTLPsanyal.pdf

Schacter, J. (1999). *The impact of education technology on student achievement: What the most current research has to say.* Retrieved January 8, 2004, from http://www.mff.org/publications/publications.taf?page=161

Shade, D. D., & Watson, J. A. (1990). Computers in early education: Issues put to rest, theoretical links to sound practice, and the potential contribution of microworlds. *Journal of Educational Computing Research, 6*(4) 375–392.

Shepard, L. A. (2000, October). The role of assessment in a learning culture. *Educational Researcher* (29) 7.

Steinberg, L. (1996). *Beyond the classroom.* New York: Simon and Schuster.

Sylva, K., Bruner, J. S., & Genova, P. (1976). The role of play in the problem-solving of children 3–5 years old. In J. S. Bruner, A. Jolly, & K. Sylva (Eds.), *Play—its role in development and evolution* (pp. 244–257). New York: Basic Books.

Tapscott, D. (1999, February). Integrating technology into the curriculum: Educating the net generation. *Education Leadership (56)* 5.

Valdez, G., McNabb, M., Foertsch, M., Anderson, M., Hawkes, M., & Raack, L. (1999). *Computer-based technology and learning: Evolving uses and expectations* (pp. 5–6). Oak Brook, IL: North Central Regional Educational Laboratory.

Wilson, B. (1997). The postmodern paradigm. In C. R. Dills, & A. Romiszowksi (Eds.), *Instructional development paradigms.* Englewood Cliffs, NJ: Educational Technology Publications.

Wilson, B. G. (1995). Situated instructional design: Blurring the distinctions between theory and practice, design and implementation, curriculum and instruction. In M. Simonson (Ed.). *Proceedings of selected research and development presentations.* Washington, DC: Association for Educational Communications and Technology.

Can Information Get What It Wants? Barriers to Open Access in Literacy Education

Anne Fullerton
International Reading Association

A professor considers the morning's tasks: finish a literature review for an article he's preparing for submission, identify some readings for his graduate seminar and arrange copies for his students, and send off a paper for a volume of conference proceedings. He's working from home, and he's never really paid attention when his students have explained the proxy server arrangement to access his institution's library holdings of e-journal subscriptions, database subscriptions, and e-books. And he's certain he doesn't remember his password.

But he doesn't need to be concerned about proxy servers, passwords, or subscriptions. He simply goes to a single Web site, freely and openly available to all but designed for scholars, teachers, and researchers in his field, and performs a few simple searches. An hour or two later, he has downloaded and printed a dozen articles, conference papers, and book chapters relevant to his own article, including a couple of studies about to be published in a new European journal he's heard about but never seen; identified two further papers for his graduate students to read and e-mailed them the URL for access; and made his own conference paper available to his academic community. Oh, and he's also noticed some interesting work being done by someone who's new to the field and has sent off an e-mail to her to explore the possibility of a collaboration.

For at least a decade, Internet technologies have existed to facilitate this sort of availability of the scholarly record and to encourage broad and active dialogue within academic communities. Indeed, open access is the natural promise of the Internet age, the realization of Internet pioneers' and programmers' claim that "information wants to be free." At present, however, this application of available technologies has been embraced in relatively isolated disciplines. The utopian vision described above, for example, has been reality for more than a decade in hard sciences such as high-energy or astrophysics; it now shows some possibility of evolving in a more limited fashion in medicine and biology. But can or should this vision become a broader reality in academia, particularly in the social sciences and humanities? Does scholarly information from all subject areas really want to be free? If it does (or if those working in particular areas wish that it did), can it get what it wants? And what does this all mean for the academic enterprise?

PHYSICS UTOPIA: ARXIV.ORG

The Web site that allowed the professor just described to be so very efficient and so connected to his community from the solitude of his home office is arXiv.org, an "e-print service in the fields of physics, mathematics, non-linear science, computer science, and quantitative biology" (arXiv.org, 2003). Since 1991, the site has been a gateway for access to scientific literature and data of a variety of types: manuscripts submitted simultaneously to the archive and to a journal for peer review; preprints of accepted articles awaiting publication; reprints of published papers (or links to them); and "gray" literature including unrefereed articles and reports, conference papers, and miscellaneous other publications. Its approximately 350,000 documents (as of January 2006) are fully searchable by author, title, abstract keyword, subdiscipline, and year of submission. Both searching and retrieving of articles can be done by anyone with Web or e-mail access, without restriction or barrier of any kind, and at no cost. The tremendous worldwide appeal of this resource to readers is clear from access numbers that indicate 2 million visits per week (more than 60% from outside the United States; see arxiv.org/todays_stats) and more than 20 million article downloads per year (Ginsparg, 2003; "Online physics archive . . . ," 2001).

There are, however, certain restrictions placed on those who wish to submit articles. Authors must register, and registration depends on affiliation with a recognized institution or research organization; those who have no such affiliation must be sponsored by someone who does. New authors must be "endorsed" by a known author in the field who has already made his or her own publications available. Authors are also cautioned not to submit incomplete manuscripts or abstracts without full text, since "such submissions are unhelpful to readers and of very limited archival value" (arXiv.org, 2003). Articles must be submitted as particular document types—no word-processed documents need apply. Authors must select the subarchive to which they are submitting their material, and they are requested to include a brief note, indicating the nature of each article—whether unrefereed manuscript or document accepted for publication in a journal, book, or some other resource.

This may begin to suggest to readers familiar with publishing production functions just how arXiv.org can offer what it offers for free. Authors are advised that "the best choice" for file preparation and format is TeX/LaTeX, a typesetting system particularly useful for displaying mathematical equations and formulae (see Knuth, 1984), and further that "because putting papers on the archives entails certain responsibilities, authors must make their own submissions. Third-party submissions (by secretaries for example) are often the ones that cause the most problems, presumably due to lack of self-interest and related factors" (arXiv.org, 2003). That is, arXiv.org takes no responsibility for the production processes most frequently undertaken by publishers, which are instead firmly placed on the shoulders of authors; nor does it provide any peer-review or editorial services, which remain the responsibility of the publishers to whom those authors might also choose to submit their work. The site makes no mention of copyright, and one assumes that responsibility for compliance rests with the authors rather than the site administrators or hosts (as is possible under Title II of the U.S. *Digital Millennium Copyright Act*; see U.S. Copyright Office, 1998).

In fact, arXiv.org is an almost entirely automated system. It exists firmly in the academic community, in a space beside the world of traditional professional, scholarly, or academic publishing. As such, it provides access to content not bound by a particular publisher or publishers and made available solely at the discretion of its registered authors. It is based at Cornell University, where most of those involved in maintaining it have other responsibilities; Paul Ginsparg, for example, who created and continues to participate in overseeing the archive, is a professor cross-appointed to the physics and computer and information sciences departments. When an article is submitted, automated functions behind the scenes scan the document for completeness and adherence to format specifications. As long as the submitter is recognized as a registered and endorsed author, and as long as the document passes automated muster, it is posted and available for searching and retrieval; publication within 24 hours of submission is the norm. Because of the level of automation, the whole thing costs only approximately US$300,000 a year to maintain ("Online physics archive . . . ," 2001), with funding from Cornell and the National Science Foundation. This is an astonishingly low figure when compared to the $30 per year the scholarly publishing community estimates that it costs publishers to maintain an article online (Dryburgh, 2003); at that rate, arXiv.org should now require a minimum annual budget of $10,000.

In this sense, arXiv.org is an example of an electronic "self-archiving" tool that allows publication (in the broadest sense of "making public") of scholarly work at all stages of development (see, e.g., Guédon, 2003; Harnad, 1994)—from manuscript to peer-reviewed paper to published postprint to, potentially, periodic updates of the formally published record. Self-archiving is also found in the institutional repositories at many universities, which allow faculty and staff to upload, organize, and maintain their work online. ArXiv.org, however, crosses publication, institution, and even national boundaries, making available a huge amount and variety of material from disparate sources and scholars worldwide. This makes it a particularly valuable resource— more so than an institutional repository or an open-access online journal, which, by definition, include material from only one source. (This is not to suggest that open-access journals are not useful, just that they are not as useful as open-access archives, both because of their limited scope and because they are not uniformly indexed or cross-linked to other available online resources. For a list of open-access journals in education, see the Directory of Open Access Journals at http://www.doaj.org/ljbs?cpid=127.) Consider, for example, how useful it could be to have the contents of this book and the first *Handbook of Literacy and Technology*, the *Handbook of Reading Research* (all three volumes), *Theoretical Models and Processes of Reading* (all five editions), National Reading Conference yearbooks, and articles from *Reading Research Quarterly*, the *Journal of Research in Reading*, the *Australian Journal of Language and Literacy*, *Reading and Writing*, *Cognitive Psychology*, the *Journal of Educational Psychology*, and any number of other sources gathered together and fully searchable and cross-linked at one Web address. For physicists, arXiv.org permits one-stop shopping of this kind, regardless of ultimate publication vehicle and publisher, and is equally available to scientists worldwide.

Although arXiv.org is perhaps the best known, it is only one of a growing number of open-access initiatives in scholarly communication. In February 2005, for example, the U.S. National Institutes of Health (NIH) began to implement its "public access policy" and to "strongly encourage" scholars to deposit reports and articles based on NIH-funded research into the open-access PubMed Central database within 12 months of their publication ("NIH calls on scientists . . . ," 2005; "Policy on enhancing public access . . . ," 2005; see also www.nih.gov/about/publicaccess/index.htm). Other related approaches include those promoted through the Public Library of Science (PLoS; www.plos.org), BioMed Central (www.biomedcentral.com/) the Open Archives Initiative (www.openarchives.org), the Scholarly Publishing and Academic Resources Coalition (SPARC; www.arl.org/sparc/), the Cognitive Sciences Eprint Archive (cogprints.ecs.soton.ac.uk/), and the Budapest Open Access Initiative (www.soros.org/openaccess/). At present, most of these initiatives are based in the sciences and medicine, and many focus on open-access journals rather than archives that might contain material from a variety of sources. But, according to self-archiving proponent Stevan Harnad (1999a), "the fact that the rest of us are being so slow to follow [the arXiv.org] example . . . risks becoming the cosmic joke."

So, can some form of open access happen on a similar large scale in disciplines in the social sciences or humanities—or, more specifically, in literacy education? Well, no. Or, at least, not right now, and not without a significant shift in thinking and practice among all those involved in the academic enterprise: university and college administrators, junior and senior faculty, graduate students, granting agencies, professional and scholarly societies, publishers, and readers alike.

THEORETICAL PHYSICISTS ARE NOT LIKE YOU AND ME

When arXiv.org was created in 1991, Paul Ginsparg was based at the Los Alamos National Laboratory in New Mexico. It is no coincidence that this new Internet service would begin at such an institution, several years before most publishers were contemplating online publication of scholarly journals and only two years after Tim Berners-Lee (1989), himself based at the particle physics laboratory CERN, proposed the protocols that would allow the World Wide Web to evolve. Scientists at Los Alamos and other physics research institutes had used networked online tools since about 1970, when the Internet's precursor, the Arpanet, was expanding with funding from the U.S. Department of Defense specifically to support their work (see, e.g., Abbate, 2000; Bardini, 2000). And both the Arpanet and Berners-Lee's World Wide Web were specifically conceived for the storage and retrieval of information housed in a variety of documents to meet the needs of scientists, who often work in large collaborative groups and often wait a year or more for accepted papers to appear in print.

So, the particular community within which Ginsparg worked was both highly technically literate and already accustomed to sharing information (pre and post publication) through digital means. Further, many traditional publishers within physics disciplines had by 1991 begun to require authors to apply their technical skills in production of their own manuscripts, with many moving to strict online-only submission and peer review as early as the mid–1990s. The University of Chicago Press, for example, has been encouraging authors of submissions to *The Astrophysical Journal* (which it publishes on behalf of the American Astronomical Society) to typeset their own papers using Teχ/LaTeχ for close to a decade. Many authors eagerly do so in order to ensure correct rendering of mathematical symbols and equations. Use of online versions of traditionally paper-based journals has been commonplace for years among physicists, and numerous science publishers have declared that online versions should be considered the journals of record for the purposes of citation. The creation of arXiv.org merely centralized and made more convenient the online sharing of documents that was already a well established part of the culture of the physics community.

By way of contrast, the largest professional society publisher in literacy education, the International Reading Association (IRA), continued to accept manuscripts submitted only on paper until late 2004, and to provide reviewers with paper copies on request. Digital copies are almost always submitted as word-processed documents, not the more sophisticated formats common in the sciences. Full text of all IRA's leading print journals was not available online directly from the association in a systematic, structured way until 2004, and print versions are very definitely still regarded as the publications of record in the field.

Traffic to online publications in literacy education, such as those now offered by IRA and numerous other associations and publishers, clearly indicates, however, that the community wants to read and use Internet-based resources. And the volume of traffic to open-access literacy resources confirms the obvious: Making content freely accessible is very appealing to readers. Though not at the levels seen at arXiv.org, the resources that IRA makes available without subscription, password restriction, or cost are viewed collectively hundreds of thousands of times each month.

Even so, there are numerous barriers that make it unlikely that a utopian arXiv.org model will evolve for education researchers. Some of these are financial, but many relate to fundamental dif-

ferences in the culture of scholarly publishing in science, technical, and medical (STM) disciplines as compared to disciplines in the arts, humanities, and social sciences, differences that
will make it difficult and slow for those in education to realize the potential of technology in their
own academic work.

PERISHING BY (ONLINE) PUBLISHING

In spring 2001, a small group of leading science and medical researchers and scholars (including
former NIH director Harold Varmus, who had presented the idea for the now-evolving PubMed
Central in 1999) caused a stir in the world of higher education and scholarly publishing by calling for colleagues to join them in pledging to "publish in, edit or review for, and personally sub-
scribe to only those scholarly and scientific journals that have agreed to grant unrestricted free distribution rights to any and all original research reports that they have published, through . . . online
public resources, within 6 months of their initial publication date" ("Open letter," n.d.; Roberts
et al., 2001). A year later, this boycott of almost all scholarly journals was declared "a bust"
(Young, 2002), although the initiative to build a "Public Library of Science" (www.plos.org) continued, with the group's leaders changing their focus to the launch of the open-access journals
PLoS Biology and *PLoS Medicine*.

Calls for more open, easier sharing of scholarly information and communication have come
from every department and school in the academy, and have greatly increased with increased
access to and use of Internet technologies. (Recently, too, such calls have come from government
and the public, who quite reasonably assert that they should have open access to results of
research conducted with tax-funded grants from government agencies. It was largely pressure
from patients and patients' families, for instance, that prompted development of a formal NIH
public access plan.) Indeed, the demise of traditional, subscription-based print journals has been
foretold for more than a decade (see, e.g., Rogers & Hurt, 1989), and publishing sector journals
and conferences now routinely contain messages of doom and gloom for the industry. This comes
on the heels of a 20- to 30-year period of great growth and prosperity for publishers, during which
numbers of print journals published and average page counts per issue increased steadily (see,
e.g., Bergstrom & Bergstrom, 2002; Bolman, 2003). Not coincidentally, the population of academic authors seeking publication venues that "count" for tenure and promotion also grew significantly in the same period (Association of American Universities Committee on Graduate
Education, 1998).

The fact of the matter is that the publish or perish system of dissemination of scholarly work
seems more ingrained today in the social science and humanities disciplines than ever before, so
that very few, if any, authors, reviewers, editors, or readers can afford (figuratively) to boycott
journals or take risks in submitting outside the traditional publications of record. In the case of
many non-STM disciplines, where acceptance of online publications has been slow, this means
the leading, traditional, paper-based journals in each field. But neither can scholarly publishers,
commercial or nonprofit, afford (literally) to make those traditional journals freely available
online if doing so risks subscription revenue when no alternative sources of income readily present themselves.

And here we hit hard against the economic reality of scholarly publishing. The academic
communities that have been most vocal in calling for open access to information and published
work are in the sciences and medicine, where commercial publishers stepped in when university
presses and society publishers were unable to meet the publishing needs of a growing author base.
Commercial publishers are, of course, in business to make as large a profit as possible. As the cost

of journals published by for-profit entities climbed, many libraries began to experience a "serials crisis" and were forced to cut back on subscriptions (and so the subscription costs climbed further). The serious budget shortfall in many academic libraries has resulted in a steady decline in availability of the literature in many institutions, beginning more than two decades ago (see, e.g., Cummings, Witte, Bowen, Lazarus, & Ekman, 1992). Subsequently, there have been growing calls for open access, along the lines of those heard from the organizers of the Public Library of Science.

It is important to note that journals in education research for the most part did not precipitate the serials crisis, the responsibility for which is usually ascribed to commercial STM publishers. Many of the major English-language education journals are published by learned societies or professional associations (or by commercial publishers on behalf of such societies). Unlike commercial publishers, these nonprofit entities generally have as their mission furthering research and practice in particular fields; hence, subscription rates to the journals they produce remain fairly low. Nevertheless, libraries faced with difficult budget decisions may well eliminate subscriptions to journals with narrowly focused content, since they are in less demand among students and faculty than are some higher-priced, broader-interest publications. But whether for financial reasons or simply because of convenience, the appeal of open access is strong for those working in education. It is also the case that in literacy education particularly, a sense of furthering the public good goes hand in hand with calls for making more information freely accessible. There is very great appeal in making the literature available to a broader range of interested parties outside the academy—to parents of struggling learners, say, or to volunteer tutors in adult literacy programs—and to universities in countries with developing economies where even low-cost journal subscriptions are out of reach.

But even for nonprofit society publishers interested primarily in dissemination of information, financial realities associated with open access make it difficult to pursue: Revenues from journal subscriptions are often the basis on which many other association or society activities are financed. Though it may be clear that open access would benefit a society's members and further the mission of promoting knowledge in the discipline, societies that support a variety of programs are themselves "not among the prime beneficiaries of open access" (Velterop, 2003, p. 169).

It is often assumed that online publishing is, essentially, free. (The sometimes-heard extension of this is that once everything is available online and the role of publishers in organizing printing, binding, and mailing of journals is removed, publishers themselves become dispensable. Although the role of publishers is clearly changing, this particular argument is advanced only by the most naive authors and ardent Internet enthusiasts, who believe not only that information yearns to be free, but that it is all created equal. Regardless of the form of publication, publishers continue to play an important role in managing peer review, substantive and copyediting, design, production, dissemination, marketing, and so on. See Morris, 2003, for a summary of value-added functions conducted by publishers in both online and traditional publishing.) It is certainly true that costs associated with printing and distribution of traditional paper journals are a significant portion of overall publication expense. However, even with these costs removed, journal publishing as it exists today is a surprisingly expensive undertaking—costs for managing peer review, for example, are estimated at $400 per article submitted (whether accepted or rejected) (Rowland, 2002). The Wellcome Trust (2004, pp. 10–14) estimates that the total cost of publication of a single article in a good- to high-quality research journal averages $2,750, regardless of whether it appears in print, online, or both.

A society publisher or university press, then, would need to find some means of recovering costs associated with publication if an open-access model were pursued. Most reject significant reliance on grant funding (too precarious) or advertising income (tends to compromise professional tone). The usual route is to levy "page charges" that cover or subsidize publishing expenses and are paid either by authors themselves or by their institutions. This author-pays model was adopted by the Public Library of Science for its open-access journals, and it is commonplace for both paper and online journals in many STM disciplines. (One interesting alternative, proposed at the journal of the Florida Entomological Society, allows the author to choose: traditional publisher-pays model for articles that appear in the traditional subscription-based journal, print and online, or author-pays model if the author decides that he or she would like the content to be freely and immediately available online.) But these are disciplines in which research grants are frequently exceedingly large. In education, it is difficult to imagine authors routinely having the resources to contribute several hundred or more dollars toward publication of their work—and, obviously, those who could not would be disenfranchised, unless some means of subsidization were established.

WHAT IF WE FORGET ABOUT THE HORSE?

At least in scholarly publishing, it is clear that we are not yet living in the "post-typographic world" described in this volume's predecessor (Reinking, McKenna, Labbo, & Kieffer, 1998). Although new technologies are very much in play in the academic community, they are being used in most disciplines purely to power dissemination of information produced—and sold— according to an old model. With few exceptions, online publications consist of replications of traditional typographic texts (usually PDF files of journal articles) intended for searching and accessing online by paying subscribers who then download and print. In this sense, a new technology is being harnessed to perpetuate the status quo, and it is possible that opportunities for innovation that might benefit the academic enterprise are being overlooked.

It's claimed that car engines wound up in the front because that's where the horse used to be. Cars get us where we need to go, but maybe they would have done so more efficiently, more cheaply, or more cleanly if the new technology of the combustion engine hadn't been fit into the old framework of the horse and buggy. If research and publication in literacy education is to capitalize on the possibilities of Internet technologies—if it is going to do something other than replace the printing-and-mailing horse with the online-dissemination engine—it is perhaps time to rethink not only the method of delivery but the entire enterprise of published scholarship. It is clear that the financial implication for publishers is a significant obstacle to use of the Internet to provide more scholarly information more freely, as are the academy's tradition-bound requirements for publishing in leading, and largely print-based, journals of record. But other aspects of today's approach to academic publishing—including the entrenched peer-review system, the perceived primacy of print, the uncertain role of publishers, and copyright—erect as significant, or more significant, obstacles.

Alternatives to peer review.   As noted previously, peer review adds considerable expense to the publication process. At arXiv.org and at university-based online repositories and initiatives such as the Massachusetts Institute of Technology's DSpace (where gray literature including conference papers, research reports, preprints, and images created by MIT faculty is housed; see libraries.mit.edu/dspace-mit/), a considerable percentage of the information available is not peer reviewed, at least not in a traditional sense. For literacy researchers and scholars, the U.S. Department of Education's "new ERIC" (Education Resources Information Center) database, freely accessible to all at www.eric.ed.gov, promises to include full text of significant numbers of reports, conference proceedings, and other content not previously subjected to traditional peer review, contributed by U.S. publishers, other agencies and groups, and authors directly. Not only can this reduce the costs associated with creation and maintenance of such open archives, but it capitalizes on technology to organize and make broadly available information that previously had been highly limited in circulation.

Here again, however, differences in culture and climate among academic disciplines come into play in considering whether a rethinking of peer review could allow the education community to exploit technology more fully. Interestingly, ERIC, perhaps the most promising large-scale initiative in access to education research, has simply replaced traditional peer reviewers with contractors paid to vet, at least on a broad level, both author- and publisher-submitted content. A more innovative challenge to peer review restricts the author base to, say, physicists employed by recognized research institutions or to faculty at a major research university. In this way, systems such as arXiv.org or DSpace engage in what Ginsparg (2003) calls "career review"—that is, an assumption is made that the contents of these archives are for the most part of refereeable quality (defined by Ginsparg as "not obviously incorrect, not obviously uninteresting") simply by virtue of who the authors are. Ginsparg suggests that such career review could be conceived as the first tier in a two-tier peer-review system, in which only content that demonstrates superiority or extreme utility (according to criteria such as frequency of citation, number of accesses in the open archive, amount of comment or correspondence attached by readers to an archived paper, etc.) would move on to a second tier of formal review and publication that mirrors the traditional peer-review approach.

This automation of certain peer-review functions would reduce costs by assuming some of the book-keeping (logging manuscripts in an editorial office) and initial assessments of suitability often undertaken by journal editors or editorial staff. Determination of suitability for detailed assessment then falls to the community, an appealing suggestion for those who advocate an open publishing model based on a sort of self-policing or "let the scholars decide" approach. For physicists, this works well, but almost entirely because the author community, reviewer base, and readership for material at arXiv.org overlap so thoroughly. Readers of arXiv.org content are almost exclusively *expert* readers who work in small academic communities—the very people who might be called on to review the papers posted when or if they are submitted to traditional journals, and who are likely to cite the posted content in their own work. Indeed, arXiv makes most of its content invisible to casual Web browsers—inexpert readers—by blocking large sections of its holdings from Web search engines such as Google. This is in sharp contrast to recent initiatives in the library and scholarly publishing communities, which have sought to have Google and other search engines provide better indexing of more formal online publications, including those that are subscription based (Young, 2004). Traditional publishers would obviously much prefer that services such as Google Scholar point to online versions of articles housed at publisher or journal Web sites, rather than at open-access repositories; arXiv.org is only too happy to contribute to ensuring this is the case.

Many physicists are quite happy to accept this automated approach to peer review. Its results are actually not that different from the end-product of traditional peer review and publication in physics subdisciplines, where acceptance rates can be as high as 90% (see, e.g., Abt, 1988). (It should be noted, however, that arXiv does have detractors, physicists who feel its jumbling of reviewed and unreviewed content from a wide variety of sources of differing quality tends to undermine scholarship and leads potentially to sloppy research.) In disciplines such as education, where the author and reviewer base could be conservatively estimated at 10 to 20% of the reader base (for, say, *The Reading Teacher* or even *Reading Research Quarterly*), the community obviously does not consist exclusively of the expert readers seen in some other disciplines. The seal of approval offered by traditional peer review in a community accustomed to rejection rates of 70 to 90% is therefore viewed by readers as an essential indication of the value of the published work. Clearly, readers of an arXiv.org-type resource in literacy education would need to read and evaluate that content quite differently than they now do the articles in an issue of the *Journal of Educational Psychology*.

A more broadly plausible approach to rethinking peer review is suggested by Harnad (1999b), who advocates "peer commentary" in addition to peer review. He also favors the tiered approach, with the use of technology to filter out submissions that could be described as obviously uninteresting or obviously incorrect. The remaining material is then made available through an open-access archive. (Assume, for the sake of argument, that costs of creating and maintaining the archive could be held at a reasonably low level, so that funding support for it could conceivably be obtained from a scholarly society, research institution, modest author or institutional subsidies, or relatively stable grants.) Harnad suggests that peer commentary then be solicited and attached to the open-archive material, which would allow inexpert readers to be made aware of possible flaws in the content. He points out that this would also use technology to make more publishable material available more quickly. One assumes, for example, that at least some of the 80 to 90% of manuscripts rejected from *Reading Research Quarterly*, for example, are actually publishable, but that limitations of space and time make difficult decisions necessary.

For scholars, this approach is appealing in that it would encourage open, collegial dialogue that would remain accessible (and would acknowledge the ill-concealed fact that anonymous peer review is not always terribly anonymous in communities with small and overlapping author-reviewer bases). Harnad proposes that peer commentary would not replace peer review but supplement it, with only the most interesting articles moving on to traditional publication. The result would be increased and more rapid availability of information of refereeable quality and a decrease in the amount of content included in traditional subscription-based peer-reviewed journals, with a resulting reduction in both subscription fees and costs incurred by publishers for those journals.

Although there is much to like in Harnad's proposal, its implementation would quickly fail unless the academic community were willing to consider something other than traditional peer review as the gold standard for publication—a change that seems unlikely as long as tenure and promotion continues to rely on the current publication model, and as long as journal publishers have no financial incentive to propose alternative approaches. It is interesting to note that peer review as it exists today is a relatively recent creation, dating only from about the late 1940s (see, e.g., Williamson, 2003). That it has become so ingrained in academic culture and scholarly publishing so quickly, and that shaking it loose seems such a radical proposal, is quite remarkable.

Challenging the primacy of print.   If open access is to become more prevalent across disciplines, print content needs to cease being considered without question as more worthy than online. That print is thought by almost all scholars in education research to be more worthwhile, more authoritative, than online publication is clearly the case. It is perhaps particularly true in literacy education, a discipline obviously deeply invested in words on paper. By virtue of its focus, this book, for example, would seem ripe for online publication, but the editors solicited papers for publication in a traditional bound volume, to be disseminated through a commercial publisher with no plans for an online version (open access or otherwise).

Interestingly, online publication is no longer undervalued in STM publishing, where online journals are now frequently considered the publications of record. Studies undertaken by Thomson ISI (Pringle, 2004), keepers of the influential "impact factor" that assigns relative value to journals in particular fields, indicate that online journals, whether open access or subscription based, are as influential as print journals in many disciplines. Here, again, is an area where those working in arts and humanities disciplines are approaching online access in very different ways from their colleagues in the science faculties, to the detriment of their ability to capitalize on technology to improve their own access to information.

Cooperation of publishers.   If we're to forget about the horse, then authors, reviewers, and readers will need to change their thinking about academic publishing—but so, too, will publishers need to rethink their roles. Both the product and process remain largely unchanged when publishers put journal and book content through the established cycle of peer review, revision, editing, and typesetting, and then simply substitute creating and uploading of PDF files for traditional printing and distribution. Those that have the resources attempt to make connections across the literature by providing citation links (in which hyperlinks in reference lists point to online versions of cited sources, to which a reader may or may not have a subscription that will allow access) and occasional online-only supplementary material, but the end product is really very similar to the print version.

In order to create a disciplinary archive that would include peer-reviewed content, publishers would need to cooperate to make their peer-reviewed material equally and freely available. This is obviously not likely to happen among commercial publishers, or among any publishers at all, as long as the traditional book publication or subscription-based print journal model is the standard. But in attempting to use technology to further knowledge and scholarship, there is a role for which society and association publishers seem particularly suited. Since their mission is to disseminate information about their subject, rather than purely to make shareholders happy by increasing publishing revenue, some might be willing to take on managing such an archive as long as reasonable financial compensation could be obtained from some source (author or institutional subsidies, membership dues, stable grant funding, or, less appealing, advertising). Societies would, however, need to be willing to change their roles—to begin seeing themselves as disseminators of information generally, rather than exclusively of the information produced in their own publications.

The arXiv.org model is again of interest here. As noted previously, the site makes no mention of copyright. However, in many physics journals (as in other disciplines), it remains usual for authors to assign their copyright to the publisher but retain the right either by agreement or convention to reuse their work in any way they see fit. Undoubtedly, when they drew up the language on their copyright assignment agreements, the journal publishers did not anticipate that the work would be freely available and downloaded millions of times from an online archive. So far, though, the publishers have not changed the language of the assignment documents or objected to scientists posting and retrieving of material from the archive. It seems that revenue for the journals has not been significantly threatened, since institutions continue to seek out the print publication for their own archival and research purposes.

Physics, then, has arrived at the best of both worlds. Whether this would hold true in other disciplines, where more money is at stake in different ways, is unclear. The success of PubMed Central, for example, may well depend on the extent to which commercial medical publishers are willing to allow deposit of works to which they have been given copyright by authors, or the extent to which authors may begin to demand the right to withhold copyright assignment. (In education publishing, a small impact of PubMed Central may be felt since NIH includes the National Institute for Child Health and Human Development, the source of some education research grants. Of more concern to education publishers is the speculation—at present based on no supporting evidence—that the U.S. Department of Education may follow in NIH's footsteps, urging deposit of full-text journal articles to the new ERIC database.) The Association of American Publishers, obviously much concerned about the implications of PubMed Central, lobbied hard and successfully to deny NIH the right to *require* such deposit—hence the rather toothless "strong encouragement" issued by the agency. In the United Kingdom, home of the open-access initiative BioMed Central, the government has been even less willing to impose open-access requirements on authors and publishers (Science and Technology Committee, United Kingdom Parliament, 2004; Suber, 2004b).

Regardless of how conservatively one might choose to apply copyright, however, it does seem reasonable to suggest that both authors and society publishers should consider whether they want to approach copyright issues in the most draconian way allowed by current legislation, particularly in light of a shared desire to make information available to a wide audience. That a research paper in literacy education should be held outside the public domain for the same period as a Walt Disney movie—that is, for a minimum of 75 years—seems ludicrous.

WE HAVE THE TECHNOLOGY . . .

. . . but finding a way to use it effectively will require innovation and cooperation among all stakeholders in the academic enterprise. The answer is not for individual authors or academic departments to make material available in isolation, nor is it for the academic community to defer to conventional publishing models and for publishers to isolate themselves by resisting innovation in the face of a society greatly changed by Internet technologies.

In 2004, Elsevier, one of the leading commercial publishers in the sciences, announced with considerable fanfare that it would allow "postprint archiving"—that is, authors can post final, published versions of their Elsevier journal articles online, at their own or their institution's Web sites. Celebrations of this decision in academic and library circles included hints of cynicism, with many wondering why Elsevier—often held to be among the publishers most guilty for the serials crisis—would take such a step. (Suber, 2004a, suggests that it will give Elsevier an edge in the increasing competition for submissions from top authors.) After many years working in education publishing, and several years of focus on online publication issues, I know which frequent contributors to the professional literature are likely to have personal Web sites, and which of those are likely to contain links to full-text files of their articles, chapters, and conference papers. This makes me among a very few who is ever likely to find or look at this material. Without indexing, broad-based linking, a permanent and stable URL, and incorporation of identifying "metadata" in the files—that is, without features and services that are generally outside the realm of authors' expertise and resources to provide—these articles are essentially invisible to scholars browsing the Internet or to Web search engines or directories. Google Scholar, for example, is much more likely to find an article posted to Elsevier's own mammoth, highly structured, deeply interlinked, and well-organized ScienceDirect (http://www.sciencedirect.com/) than the same article posted to an author's amateur Web site on a university server. Perhaps Elsevier simply felt that allowing postprint archiving would be a good public relations gesture with little risk of negative financial impact.

Interestingly, Elsevier's change in policy affected postprints; the firm had long allowed posting of preprints, as long as they differed from the final, published work. Many education researchers do post preprints on their own or university Web sites—that is, manuscripts submitted or accepted for publication, but not revised because of peer review or editorial suggestions to their final form. Many of these preprints differ, sometimes significantly, from the final published works, and they almost always lack bibliographic notations to identify them once they are downloaded and thereby removed from the context of the author's site. Posting articles in this way may be a convenience for the author, but it does almost nothing to provide information to the academic community or the broader public. It can also serve to undermine scholarship, when multiple versions of a work are available for citation and quotation in addition to the published version of record.

On the other hand, the interests of scholarship and the desire for broad dissemination of information are not served by publishers who attempt to lock up content in ways that make it inaccessible to many in the field. Here publishers, and particularly nonprofit society publishers, have an obligation to explore ways of using technology to make content accessible as broadly as possible. This means finding ways to ensure that subscription costs can remain within the reach of most academic institutions or interested individuals, including those in countries with developing economies.

This also means finding a willingness among all interested parties to consider greater cooperation and collaboration in exploring new publishing models, whether by establishing page charges for authors who seek the large readerships afforded by open-access journals (see, e.g., Prosser, 2003, for an example of this approach); reconceptualizing peer review; shifting certain responsibilities from publisher to author, from library to publisher, or from author to computer; working to enhance the prestige of online publication; or campaigning for copyright legislation that recognizes the difference between scholarly and popular work. There are many opportunities to create a new collaborative partnership among those involved in the creation and dissemination of scholarly work, opportunities that could make important resources available not only to the professor working from his home office, but also to a public increasingly interested in access to information. New technology is in place; now what's needed is new thinking to match it.

REFERENCES

Abbate, J. (2000). *Inventing the Internet*. Cambridge, MA: MIT Press.

Abt, H. A. (1988). What happens to rejected astronomical papers? *Publications of the Astronomical Society of the Pacific, 100*, 506–508.

arXiv.org. (1991–2003). Ithaca, NY: Cornell University. Retrieved October 2003, from http://arxiv.org

Association of American Universities Committee on Graduate Education. (1998, October). *Report and recommendations*. Washington, DC: Author. Retrieved October 2003, from http://www.aau.edu/reports/GradEdRpt.html

Bardini, T. (2000). *Bootstrapping: Douglas Engelbart, coevolution, and the origins of personal computing*. Stanford, CA: Stanford University Press.

Bergstrom, C., & Bergstrom, T. (2002). *The economics of scholarly journal publishing*. Seattle, WA: University of Washington.

Berners-Lee, T. (1989). *Information management: A proposal*. Geneva, Switzerland: CERN.

Bolman, P. (2003, Summer). Chairman's corner. *Professional/Scholarly Publishing Bulletin, 4*(2), 1, 5.

Cummings, A. M., Witte, M. L., Bowen, W. G., Lazarus, L. O., & Ekman, R. H. (1992). *University libraries and scholarly communication: A study prepared for the Andrew W. Mellon Foundation*. Washington, DC: Association of Research Libraries.

Dryburgh, A. (2003). A new framework for digital publishing decisions. *Learned Publishing, 16*(2), 95–101.

Ginsparg, P. (2003, March 13). *Can peer review be better focused?* Ithaca, NY: arXiv.org. Retrieved October 2003, from http://arxiv.org/blurb/pg02pr.html

Guédon, J.-C. (2003). Open access archives: From scientific plutocracy to the republic of science. *IFLA Journal, 29*(2), 129–140.

Harnad, S. (1994). Overture: The subversive proposal. In A. S. Okerson & J. J. O'Donnell (Eds.), *Scholarly journals at the crossroads: A subversive proposal for electronic publishing*. Washington, DC:

Association of Research Libraries. Retrieved October 2003, from http://www.arl.org/scomm/subversive/sub01.html

Harnad, S. (1999a). Free at last: The future of peer-reviewed journals. *D-Lib Magazine, 5*(12). Retrieved October 2003, from http://cogprints.ecs.soton.ac.uk/archive/00001685/00/12harnad.html

Harnad, S. (1999b). The invisible hand of peer review. *Exploit Interactive, 5*. Retrieved October 2003, from http://www.exploit-lib.org/issue5/peer-review/

Knuth, D. (1984). *The Teχbook*. Boston, MA: Addison-Wesley.

Morris, S. (2003). Open publishing. *Learned Publishing, 16*(3), 171–176.

NIH calls on scientists to speed public release of research publications [press release]. (2005, February 3). Bethesda, MD: National Institutes of Health, U.S. Department of Health and Human Services. Retrieved April 2005, from http://www.nih.gov/news/pr/feb2005/od–03.htm

Online physics archive that is transforming global science communication, "arXiv.org," is moving from Los Alamos to Cornell University [press release]. (2001, July 16). Ithaca, NY: Cornell University. Retrieved October 2003, from http://www.news.cornell.edu/releases/July01/ginsparg.archive.ws.html

Open letter. (n.d.). San Francisco, CA: Public Library of Science. Retrieved October 2003, from http://www.plos.org/support/openletter.shtml

Policy on enhancing public access to archived publications resulting from NIH-funded research. (2005, February 9). *Federal Register, 70*(26), 6891–6900. Retrieved April 2005, from http://www.nih.gov/about/publicaccess/Enhanced_Public_Access.pdf

Pringle, J. (2004, May 7). Do open access journals have impact? In *Web Focus: Access to the literature*. New York: Nature Publishing Group. Retrieved May 2004, from http://www.nature.com/nature/focus/accessdebate/19.html

Prosser, D. C. (2003). From here to there: A proposed mechanism for transforming journals from closed to open access. *Learned Publishing, 16*(3), 163–166.

Reinking, D., McKenna, M. C., Labbo, L. D., & Kieffer, R. D. (1998). *Handbook of literacy and technology: Transformations in a post-typographic world*. Mahwah, NJ: Lawrence Erlbaum Associates.

Roberts, R. J., Varmus, H. E., Ashburner, M., Brown, R., Eisen, M. B., Khosla, C., Kirschner, M., Nusse, R., Scott, M., & Wold, B. (2001, March). Building a "GenBank" of the published literature. *Science, 291*(5512), 2318–2319.

Rogers, S., & Hurt, C. (1989). How scholarly communication should work in the 21st century. *Chronicle of Higher Education*, Oct. 18, p. A56.

Rowland, F. (2002). The peer-review process. *Learned Publishing, 15*, 247–258.

Science and Technology Committee, United Kingdom Parliament. (2004, November 8). *Science and technology—Fourteenth report*. London: Her Majesty's Stationery Office. Retrieved March 2005, from http://www.publications.parliament.uk/pa/cm200304/cmselect/cmsctech/1200/120002.htm

Suber, P. (2004a, June 2). Elsevier permits postprint archiving. SPARC *Open Access Newsletter, 74*. Retrieved March 2005, from http://www.earlham.edu/~peters/fos/newsletter/06–02–04.htm

Suber, P. (2004b, December 2). The UK government responds to the Gibson committee report. SPARC *Open Access Newsletter, 80*. Retrieved March 2005, from http://www.earlham.edu/~peters/fos/newsletter/12–02–04.htm#uk

U.S. Copyright Office. (1998). The Digital Millennium Copyright Act of 1998: U.S. Copyright Office summary. Washington, DC: Author. Retrieved October 2003, from http://www.copyright.gov/legislation/dmca.pdf

Velterop, J. (2003, July). Should scholarly societies embrace open access (or is it the kiss of death)? *Learned Publishing, 16*(3), 167–169.

Young, R. (2002). Boycott over lack of online access to journals is a bust. *Chronicle of Higher Education*, May 31, p. 34.

Wellcome Trust, The. (2004, April). *Costs and business models in scientific research publishing*. Histon, Cambridgeshire, UK: Author.

Williamson, A. (2003). What will happen to peer review? *Learned Publishing, 16*(1), 15–20.

Young, J. (2004, May 21). Libraries aim to widen Google's eyes. *The Chronicle of Higher Education*, 1.

13

▼▼▼▼▼▼▼

ICT and Chinese Literacy Education: Recent Developments in China

Yongbing Liu and Dongbo Zhang
National Institute of Education, Singapore

The advent of information and communications technologies (ICT) and electronic texts characterized by the popularization of computers and the Internet since the 1980s has had profound effects on both literacy practices and literacy education in the Western countries (e.g., Bourgerie, 2003; McKenna, Reinking, Labbo, & Kieffer, 1999; Reinking, McKenna, Labbo, & Kieffer, 1998). In the post-industrial societies saturated with the multimodal texts—onscreen reading and writing, online navigation, e-mailing, and computer game playing—people have been developing new literacy skills and knowledge in and for a world significantly changed from what it was a generation ago (Carrington, 2004). In turn, these changes have impacted how literacy is defined and how literacy can be effectively learned in both formal and informal contexts. Reinking (1995) and others (e.g., McKenna et al., 1999; Topping & McKenna, 1999) argue convincingly that with the electronic transformation of literacy, literacy can no longer be traditionally defined in terms of basic skills in reading and writing; electronic literacy effectively supplements print literacy and renders it multidimensional. Thus, literacy is now viewed as plural. The term *literacies* or *multiliteracy* is commomly used in the current international literature to "refer to the ability to accumulate and demonstrate the practices necessary to interact effectively in the social, cultural and technological contexts of our lives" (Carrington, 2004, p. 224). To accommodate the social and technological changes and to train students' "new ability," schools are trying to capitalize on ICT by equipping themselves with advanced computers and access to the Internet, and integrating various multimedia programs into their literacy education (e.g., see Reinking et al., 1998; Tao & Reinking, 2000; Warschauer, 2001 for reviews).

Reseachers in the West have long noted the impact of ICT on modes and means of communication (e.g., Kress, Van Leeuwen, 1996; Lemke, 1998; New London Group, 1996; Reinking, 1995), and on the ways in which literacy education is undertaken (e.g., Blok, Oostdam, Otter, & Overmaat, 2002; Reinking, 1998 for reviews). There is a substantial international literature on the relationship between literacies and ICT, instructional strategies involving electronic texts, and ICT-related pedagogic innovations, just to name a few (e.g., Kinney & Watson, 1992; Reinking et al., 1998; Schlechter, 1990; Tao & Boulware, 2002). However, little is known in the international literacy research community about the development of ICT and its application in Chinese literacy education in China. Although some studies on computer use in language education were reviewed (e.g., Bourgerie, 2003; Zhang, 1998), these studies were mainly conducted outside of China, targeting the learners of Chinese as a foreign or second language. A literature search reveals that so far there is no review of studies on ICT and Chinese literacy in the current international literature.

Therefore, in this chapter we provide an overview of recent developments of ICT and some applications in Chinese literacy education in China. First of all, we provide a brief account of the availability of computers and diffusion of the Internet in China, since these are the prerequisites for discussing the ICT impact on literacy education. Second, we discuss some major methods for inputting characters into the computer. This is important because the skill of inputting characters into the computer constitutes beginning electronic literacy and it is essential for further Chinese literacy development. Third, we review some studies on the use of ICT in Chinese literacy instruction. We conclude the chapter by pointing out some limitations of and the prospects for the use of ICT in Chinese literacy education in China.

AVAILABILITY OF COMPUTERS AND DIFFUSION
OF THE INTERNET IN CHINA

As noted earlier, in the Western countries ICT enjoyed booming growth in the 1980s, its impact was keenly felt in 1990s, and research on the relationship between ICT and literacy education is quite substantial. However, the development of ICT is only a recent phenomenon in China. This is due largely to the overall lower economic status (lack of purchasing power) of the large Chinese population. It is also due to the technical factors, especially the specific features of the Chinese language which make it more difficult, compared to Western languages such as English, to process written language via the computer. In a certain sense, the latter is a bottleneck for the deployment of ICT in China, a problem to which we return later.

China began to reform its economic system and opened its doors to the world in the beginning of the 1980s. After roughly two decades of reform, China has seen rapid economic development. Due to the rapid growth of the economy and the increase of personal income, a large consumer market has been in formation. The hot area of mass consumption had shifted in the late 1990s to personal computers, communication devices, air conditioners, body building machines, and tourism (Yan, 2000). This focus has laid down a logistical foundation for the rapid ICT development in China since the late 1990s. As a matter of fact, over the past few years, ICT development has been phenomenal in China. Almost a decade ago, computers were little more than exhibits or laboratory equipment in Chinese universities and research centers. Today, however, they have infiltrated almost every part of society and they are widely used in workplaces, schools, and homes. Statistics show that by the end of 2001, the number of personal computers per 1,000 Chinese was 19.0, while the number in 1995 was only 2.3 (World Bank, 2003). In some big cities, the use of computers has been greatly popularized. In Shanghai, for example, it is estimated that in 2003 60% of residential households had at least one computer (Wenhui Daily, 2004). With many of these computers having access to the Internet, people in China can now easily communicate with the outside world. In 1997, when the China Internet Network Information Center (CNNIC, 1997) released its first semi-annual report on the development of the Internet in China, there were only 29,900 computer hosts and 62,000 Internet users. But by the end of the year 2004, the number of Internet users had increased to more than 41 million and the number of computer hosts had reached about 94 million, which are, respectively, more than 139 and 151 times of the numbers of computer hosts and Internet users in 1997. In some big cities, such as Beijing and Shanghai, Internet users have accounted for more than a quarter of the urban population (CNNIC, 2005).

The development of ICT has also begun in the field of education as the government attaches great importance to the construction of educational ICT infrastructure. The educational authorities at both national and local levels have set up specific benchmarks for the deployment of ICT in the modernization of Chinese education (e.g., Liu, Lin, & Gu, 2004; Wang, 2001). In 1994, the government began to construct the nonprofit China Education and Research Network (CERNET). As the first nationwide education and research computer network in China, CERNET has one backbone center and ten regional centers distributed among 10 universities and 30 provincial centers throughout China. By the end of 2000, more than 900 education and research institutions, 1.2 million computers, and 8 million users have connected to the CERNET (CERNET, 2001). Computers have also begun to be installed and the campus network connected to the Internet in China's primary and secondary schools. According to the data released by the Ministry of Education (2003), nationwide primary and secondary schools had been equipped with 5.84 million computers by the end of 2002. The ratio of students to computers had increased to 1:35 in comparison to 1:121 as of 1999 (Ministry of Education, 2003). By the end of 2002, the number of campus networks in primary and secondary schools with Internet access had exceeded 26,000 nationwide, which is twice as many as the number of campus networks with Internet access in the year 2001 (Ministry of Education, 2003). This is supported by the increase of avalibility of computers. In the year 2003, the number of computers had reached over 6.6 million. In other words, there was an average of one computer for 32 students, and 34,749 schools have established their campus network (China National Commission for UNESCO, 2004). To further help more schools gain access to the Internet and to promote the integration of ICT into the school curriculum, in November 2000, the Ministry of Education decided to start the *Xiaoxiaotong* Project (Every-Campus-Connected-to-the-Internet) and proposed that more than 90% of all the public primary and secondary schools would have access to the Internet before 2010; for schools which have no access to the Internet at the moment, computers will be installed and multimedia programs provided for assisting classroom instruction (Ministry of Education, 2000a).

The development of ICT in education has begun to have great impact on school curricula at the turn of this century. In the early 1980s, computer literacy was only an elective subject in the curriculum of a few top schools in some parts of China. By the end of 1999, about 60,000 primary and secondary schools had offered compulsory digital literacy courses to about 30 million students (Nan, 2001). To further promote digital literacy in schools, in 2000 the Ministry of Education (2000b) issued the "Guide for ICT Curriculum in Primary and Secondary Schools" (Trial; hereafter, the Guide). In this Guide, the ICT course for primary and secondary schools aims to train students to be digitally literate, with basic knowledge and skills in information technology. Students are also expected to use ICT for their lifelong learning and cooperative learning. This Guide divides the curriculum into seven modules, including software and hardware; operations systems; word processing and electronic text editing; Internet and its application; multimedia product design; database; and programming methods. It also requires that ICT be used to facilitate the teaching and learning of other school subjects. The Ministry of Education (2000c) proposed in the "Special Anouncement on Universalizing ICT Education in Primary and Secondary Schools," issued in late 2000, that ICT courses should be offered in over 90% of the primary and secondary schools in China in the next 5 to 10 years.

In 2001, the Ministry of Education (2001) reformed the Chinese language syllabus and issued the "Chinese Language Arts Curriculum Standards for Compulsory Education" currently in use (from Grades 1–9; hereafter, the Curriculum Standards). Different from the earlier syllabi, this Curriculum Standards document defines the objectives of Chinese language arts education in the context of four learning phases: Grades 1–2, Grades 3–4, Grades 5–6 and Grades 7–9; it is the first national language syllabus in which the use of ICT for developing literacy skills is emphasized, and ICT skill is defined as one of the objectives of the subject curriculum. For example, in defining the objectives of character learning for the Grades 3–4 phase, it is recommended that students would be enabled to use a keyboard to input characters into the computer; and for the development of reading skills, students in Grades 5–6 and Grades 7–9 should try exploratory reading approaches by using the Internet to locate and get neccesary information and materials. The syllabus also encourages teachers to use ICT such as the Internet and CD-ROMs to facilitate their teaching of the Chinese language.

As shown above, the development of ICT in China has come a long way in a very short time. However, despite the rapid spread of ICT, research into its impact on the culture and society in general, and on Chinese literacy education in particular, is fragmental. Unlike research in the Western countries, past research conducted in China has almost exclusively focused on infrastructure development and policy issues (see Du, 1999; Liu, et al., 2004; Wang, 2001 for reviews). It has largely been driven by the government and education authorities. Nonetheless, there are two promising lines of current research that, we believe, have already contributed, or will contribute, to the further development of ICT and its impact on Chinese literacy education. These are input methods and their application in Chinese literacy instruction. Since the Chinese characters are a requisite gatekeeper to Chinese literacy, and since how to process them in digital environments is fundamental to gain access to ICT, we next turn to input methods of Chinese characters before discussing experiments involving Chinese literacy instruction by using ICT.

CHINESE CHARACTER ENCODING AND INPUT METHODS

As we know, the application of ICT, such as information retrieval, e-mail, and word processing, requires the basic computer literacy skills of inputting relevant information in a specific written-language form into the computer. Since characters (the basic units of the Chinese written language) are large in quantity and complicated in structure, how to input them efficiently into the computer is one of the most challenging issues in the deployment of ICT, in general, and literacy education, in particular. Consequently, the acquisition of electronic literacy is typically assumed to start with learning the method of inputting characters. This is why the Chinese language curriculum and ICT curriculum for primary and secondary schools place great emphasis on the learning of characters and character inputting.

To input information pertaining to written language into the computer, the most common way is to type the letters through the keyboard. For alphabetic languages, like English, this is relatively easy because such languages have a limited set of letters, which can be directly input into the computer by using the standard small keyboard. The process, however, is rather difficult for Chinese, which is different from the alphabetic languages, for there are many more characters than there are keys on a standard computer keyboard. For example, *Hanyu Da Zidian* (*A Comprehensive Dictionary of Chinese Language*; 1990), contains more than 56,000 characters. To assign all these characters to different keys on a keyboard seems unrealistic and perhaps impossible. A choice, maybe the only choice, is to first resolve characters into a limited number of components. Then, by typing the keys to which the components are assigned, one can input Chinese characters into the computer. The research has been greatly advanced recently into how to engineer computers and develop software.

Until now, three broad types of sophisticated character-encoding methods have been developed and widely used not only in China but throughout the world by Chinese-speaking individuals. However, each of them has its advantages and disadvantages, depending on its efficiency in character input and their pedagogical significance. In what follows, we discuss briefly the major features of each approach separately.

1. Graphic Method, Encoding Based on the Structure of Chinese Characters

Although there are thousands of Chinese characters, the components of these characters are not as numerous as commonly assumed. The components are estimated to total 560 (National Committee for Language Affairs, 1997). Moreover, there are regularities in the character and word formation. The structure of characters can be roughly divided into three levels: character, radical, and stroke (Feng, 1989). For example, for the character "湖" the highest level is the character itself. The second structural level is the three radicals (氵 representing the genetic meaning, 古 and 月 representing the pronunciation in general), which can be further divided into several basic strokes to make the third structural level. The higher the level, the fewer symbols. At the highest level, only one symbol is needed to represent the character—that is, the character itself—thus, thousands of symbols are needed to represent all Chinese characters. However, at the third (the lowest) level, only a few dozen strokes are needed, and all these strokes can be classified into a few basic stroke symbols such as ⌐, 丨, 丿, 丶, and ⌐. The graphic method of encoding is based on this structural feature of Chinese characters. Encoded with a limited number of different units, which are called roots, characters can finally be input with certain key combinations of the computer with a standard keyboard. Because it is based on the structure of Chinese characters (the roots) rather than pronunciation, it is possible and easy to input all characters, as long as the rules for assigning the roots to the keyboard or the relations between the roots and the keyboard are well remembered, be they frequently used characters that can be correctly pronounced by the user or infrequently used words that cannot be correctly pronounced due to the influence of dialect (Feng, 1989). In typing with the graphic input method, there is almost no need to choose from a candidate list because virtually all characters have unique key combinations. The efficiency of character inputting therefore increases. As the graphic method is designed on the analysis of the structure of characters, it is argued that such a method, when used by students in typing characters, can help them to be more aware of the features of character structure, which is beneficial to conventional Chinese literacy development in print contexts (Lu et al., 2002).

However, the graphic input method has inherent problems in terms of "think-typing" (Xu, 1999, p. 130). To use the method, one has to memorize different roots and know how the components of characters are mapped onto the keys. As a result, when inputting characters into the computer, the user has to constantly recall the rules, which unavoidably distracts him/her from thinking. As there are many rules to memorize (it takes time to learn them and they are easy to forget), the user has to continue practicing on a regular basis in order to maintain easy control of the system (Dew, 1996). Otherwise, the typing will be slow if the rules have to be constantly recalled during typing. Therefore, this input method is typically assumed to be suitable for professional typists rather than for common use, especially by children (Xu, 1999).

Another problem is that this input method cannot contribute to early Chinese literacy development, because its effective use is preconditioned by the fact that the user should be literate. In other words, although users, with the rules memorized, can key in any character, they may not know how to recognize the character or understand what the character means. To learn and use this method, users have to have sufficient knowledge of the structure of characters to input them into the computer. For those characters whose structures are not known to the user, the input is impossible even though these characters may frequently occur in the user's oral vocabulary. In addition, some scholars argue that the rules of character structures designed for the input method are quite different from the rules for pedagogic purpose. Therefore, the early learning of them is apt to make students confused about the structure of the characters, which will in turn be detrimental to students' early literacy development (Dai, 1999; Xu, 1999).

2. Phonetic Method, Encoding Based on the Pronunciation of Chinese Characters

This method of Chinese character encoding is based on *Hanyu Pinyin Fang'an* (Scheme of the Chinese Phonetic Scripts), which was adopted as an official system parallel to the existing Chinese character script (used for thousands of years in China) by the Chinese government in 1958 (for reviews, refer to DeFrancis, 1984; Wang, 2003). This scheme, which consists of 22 initials (similar to the English consonants) and 36 finals (similar to the English vowels), uses the 26 standard Roman letters with only one extra/ü/. The system of phonetic symbols has proved easy to learn (the Chinese language is a monosyllabic language). Within a few weeks, people can learn how to use it to help pronounce characters. Therefore, it has been widely employed in education as an annotated means to facilitate early Chinese literacy development (for recent development, see Liu, 2005). Due to its use in Chinese literacy education for years since 1958, almost all the literate mainland Chinese know how to use the phonetic system. That is why the phonetic input method is most celebrated in the application of ICT in China. Knowing the *pinyin* (the Roman letters corresponding to the pronunciation of a character), one only needs to type the letters of *pinyin* and the input program will convert them into characters automatically. This popular encoding method has recently developed into two major types: *Shuangpin* (Double *pinyin*) and *Quanpin* (Full *pinyin*).

Although *Shuangpin* and *Quanpin* are both developed from a *pinyin*-based encoding method, they are different in terms of the number of letters to be keyed in. As *Shuangpin* assigns the 22 initials and 36 finals to the different 26 letter-keys on the standard computer keyboard, it is not necessary to input all the letters—unlike *Quanpin*, which requires keying in all the letters of the *pinyin* with regard to the character in question to get it on the screen. Instead, only by typing the first letter standing for the initial and the first letter for the final, the character concerned can be input into the computer via *Shuangpin*. In other words, to input a character into the computer by using *Shuangpin*, usually only two letters need to be typed and therefore the efficiency of input increases (Zhang, 1992). On the contrary, *Quanpin*, as its name implies, requires that the user type all the letters of *pinyin* in order to enable the program to convert them into a particular character on the screen. Obviously, it is slower to use *Quanpin* in terms of input efficiency than to use *Shuangpin*. However, *Quanpin* is actually much easier to use than *Shuangpin* because *Shuanpin* involves certain rules for the user to memorize. To meet the different user preferences, the two methods are now usually combined in the software readily available to be used in Internet applications, and thereby users can easily shift between the two systems.

As the phonetic input method in general is based on the pronunciation of characters and the *Hanyu Pinyin Fang'an*, it is more compatible with the English input method, thus making it easier for Chinese-English bilinguals to shuttle between Chinese and English both in terms of word processing and Internet nevigation. More importantly, the phonetic method is assumed to be helpful for users to standardize their pronunciation. Therefore, wide use of it will further promote the popularization of the standard Chinese or Mandarin (Wang, 1995), because one has to know how to pronounce the character correctly in order to use the input method efficiently. Another feature of this input method is that there is no need for the user to memorize any extra rules as long as he/she knows how to pronounce the character. Chinese researchers have successfully seized this advantage to facilitate Chinese literacy instruction of children, a subject to which we return in next section.

Even though the phonetic input method is the most widely used in Chinese word processing and Internet navigation, it has been critiqued in two main aspects. One is that the speed of information input is slow, much slower than in English, for example. The Chinese language is basically tonic and very rich in homophones and thousands of Chinese characters are annotated by the *Hanyu Pinyin Fang'an* with a limited set of phonetic symbols (Feng, 1989). When the phonetic method is used for input purposes, the user has to choose from a list of the candidates that have the same pronunciation (many are different in tone). If the candidate list is not very long and there are only several homophones to be chosen from, the problem is not particularly serious, but when some characters such as those annotated with the *pinyin* of "ji" or "yi" (estimated to represent more than 100 characters), the selection takes time and inputting efficiency is greatly reduced. Even though the phonetic input computer program arranges the characters more or less in order of general frequency of occurrence so as to enable the user to choose a needed character at or near the beginning of the list, the continuous paging down to select the right character from a list of candidates would still break the normal thinking process, rendering "think-typing" practice impossible (Xu, 1999). However, this problem has been partly solved with the recent development of "intelligent" word or full-sentence input technology. Supported by a large corpus of language data, new input software is being developed and tested in China. It enables the user to type full sentences in *pinyin* without much need to go through all homophones listed to get the specific character wanted (Su, 2003). This new input software is revolutionary, but its true sophistication and practical results are unknown at present.

The other critique is that the phonetic input method is biased against dialect Chinese speakers. As noted earlier, the prerequisite for using the phonetic method is that computer users have to be able to speak Chinese with correct pronounciation; otherwise character inputting would be very slow and problematic (Zhang, 1992). This is a problem in China, where many dialects are spoken. Although standard Chinese has been promoted since the first Republic government in the 1920s, many Chinese speak it with local accents due to dialect influences. A recent national survey conducted by the National Committee for Language Affairs (2004) shows that only 53% of Chinese can communicate in standard Chinese. Despite the claim that the phonetic input method can help computer users standardize their speech (Wang, 1995), it meets strong resistance from dialect speaker communities where the graphic input method is the preferred practice (Lu & Su, 2004). To accommodate the different preferences and to promote PC sales, high-tech firms are competing to develop new software in which favorable features of the graphic and phonetic inputs are combined. At this writing, such a product is already in the consumer market. We next examine this hybrid approach.

3. Graphic-Phonetic (Phonetic-graphic) Method, Encoding Based on Both Structure and Pronunciation of Chinese Characters

Whether the input method is called *phonetic-graphic* or *graphic-phonetic* depends on the ratio of features of character structure to pronunciation. Generally speaking, the graphic-phonetic method combines certain features of the graphic encoding and the phonetic methods mentioned earlier. The basic principle is that a character is encoded with the initials of the syllables of the roots from which a character is formulated. For example, the structure of the character 树 /shu/ is composed of three roots: "木 /mu/", "又 /you/" and "寸 /cun/", all of which are characters themselves (called simple characters in a grammatical sense). Based on the *pinyin* of these three roots, 树 is encoded as "myc", the initials of the syllables of the three roots. Therefore, by typing the three letters "m", "y" and "c", the character 树 will be input into the computer. Another example is the character "冀 /ji/". Although one may not know how to pronounce the word, he/she may be aware that the character can be broken down into three roots: 北 /bei/, 田 /tian/ and 共 /gong/. Again, by typing the initials of the syllables "btg", the character will be input into the computer.

Although this approach is claimed to be the best since it combines the advantages of both phonetic and graphic methods, the graphic-phonetic encoding method still involves complicated rules for the user to memorize. In practice, users have to think about how to divide the character into components before they can input what they want into the computer. Therefore, the "think-typing" ideal, routine in English, is still very much impossible (Sheng, 2004).

In this section, we have provided a sketch of three basic input methods used in ICT in China. Among them, the phonetic approach is most sophisticated and used most widely in the ICT context in China. Although these methods cannot be compared with English input in terms of efficiency, they nevertheless facilitate the spread of ICT in China. With continuing research, these input methods will become more sophisticated and easier to use. With updated technologies, increasing purchasing power, and a large population, China will very soon have more computers and Internet users than any other country except the USA, as predicted in 1999 (Warschauer, 2001). However, as noted earlier, Chinese academics have almost exclusively focused their research on ICT infrastructure development and policy issues (Du, 1999; Liu, et al. 2004; Wang, 2001 for reviews) rather than on the impact of ICT on Chinese culture and society. Research is virtually nonexistent into how ICT influences Chinese identities and power relations, into modes and means of communication in Chinese, into how electronic Chinese reading and writing are approached, and so on. Nonetheless, research on the relationship between ICT and early Chinese literacy instruction has yielded some promising results. In the next section we highlight some of these studies.

ICT AND EARLY CHINESE LITERACY EDUCATION: SOME STUDIES IN CHINA

China has a long literate tradition and it was perhaps the first to unify its technology of writing in history (Coulmas, 1989). Although the technology of writing has been an integral part of the Chinese civilization for millennia, the learning of this technology (in the form of Chinese characters) is considered to be the most challenging problem faced by the Chinese people. The complexity and "opaque sound-shape" of characters are largely assumed to be responsible for this difficulty (e.g., Lu, 1987). Since there are no explicit and reliable grapheme-phoneme correspondence rules, many assume that the learning of characters is basically a matter of memorization, especially for the mastery of the first few hundred simple characters. Coulmas (1989), for example, maintained that "until [relatively] recently, mastery of the Chinese script was the prerogative of a very small elite, with this mastery . . . invariably acquired in conjunction with learning Mandarin" (p. 106).

Given this context, it is understandable why Chinese literacy researchers have made much more effort to use ICT, especially computers and input methods, to reform Chinese literacy instruction rather than in any other areas of ICT impact. The motive driving most research on applications of computers and input methods in Chinese literacy instruction is the desire to improve the learning of character recognition and writing, which are typically viewed as a requisite gatekeeper to Chinese literacy. The early phase of acquiring Chinese literacy is the most difficult period in the learning process (see Liu, 2005, for a review). In what follows, we discuss briefly some main principles, processes and results of some input methods studies in early Chinese literacy instruction.

1. Input Methods and Early Chinese Literacy Instruction

There are some reports in the current literature (in Chinese) on using the *Shuangpin* input method (noted earlier) to facilitate early Chinese literacy development. The experiment was first conducted in an elite primary school in Shanghai, China (Zhou, 1999) and its results were very promising. Different from the conventional way of teaching Chinese characters, which requires the learning of all syllables of *pinyin* in the two months before characters are taught with the aid of *pinyin*, in this experiment, children were taught *pinyin*, characters and the phonetic input method silmultaneously from their first day of formal schooling. The major premise of the experiment was "to use *Dian Nao* (electronic brain, a popular Chinese term for the computer) and to develop *Ren Nao* (human brain)." Therefore, this experiment in Chinese character instruction was named *Shuang Nao* (Two brains) Character Teaching Method (Zhou, 1999). The experiment was first tried in 1991 with the input method integrated into character instruction. It was thereafter continuously improved, with multimedia technology integrated since 1997 for subsequent experiments conducted in similar types of primary schools. The results of the 1997 experiment show that students taught with the new method can, in the first 10 weeks, learn to recognize on average about 900 characters and to command *pinyin*. This is a remarkable achievement, since with the conventional approach of teaching *pinyin* first, during the first 8 weeks, students can only command *pinyin* without having been taught any characters. The experiment was replicated in the year 1999 and showed that the average number of characters that students can recognize reaches about 1,400 (Zhou, 1999), far more than the 330 characters required by the official syllabus and learned by students with the conventional approach in the same period of time. This method has also been proved to be effective in developing early writing skills. Normally, most Chinese children cannot write anything when they first start their formal schooling. With the help of the computer and using the *Shuangpin* input method, they can type what they want to say into the computer and write compositions within a year. Some students who were already trained to recognize about 1,000 characters before their formal schooling could write stories on the computer after a few weeks' instruction in the *Shuangnao* experiment (Zhou, 1999).

As noted earlier, the main feature of the *Shuang Nao* experiment is that learning *pinyin*, recognizing characters, and developing computer literacy are combined, with one reinforcing the other. For example, through learning the *Shuangpin* encoding method, students' knowledge of *pinyin* for corresponding characters is enhanced, and this in turn contributes to the efficiency of character input into the computer. In addition, when typing characters into the computer, students' recognition of the characters is reinforced. After two months' training in using the *Shuangpin* input method, it was found that primary students could on average input more than 20 characters into the computer in one minute (Zhou, 1999).

Another notable study involved the use of *Renzhi Ma* (Cognitive Code), a graphic-phonetic input method to enhance literacy learning. It is called *Renzhi Ma* simply because it is assumed (He et al., 1996) that learning of it could not only maximize input efficiency but also contribute to the cognition of the written Chinese language (referring mainly to character formation or structure). This was part of a large project using ICT to reform Chinese language education in primary and secondary schools (He et al., 1996). The project began in 1994 and the first phase concerned the development of students' early Chinese literacy. Adopting *Renzhi Ma* recommended by the National Center for Research on Computer Education to supplement the use of the *pinyin* input method in primary and secondary schools (Wang, 1996), the project intends to integrate into one the four aspects of "recognizing characters, finding characters in dictionary, character encoding and character computer input" (*Si Jiehe*) (He et al., 1996). Like the *Shuang Nao* experiment, the project is another effort to integrate literacy learning with the development of basic computer literacy involving inputting Chinese characters. When the project was first initiated at the end of 1994, it involved 13 primary schools in seven cities, but at the end of 1995, the experiment was expanded to more than 170 primary schools in 16 provinces; by the year 2002, about 600 schools in 22 provinces and regions were involved in the experiment (Yu et al., 2002).

The main feature of this experiment is to teach the students the cognitive codes, which are used in encoding characters in the *Renzhi Ma* character input system at the same time they are learning the *Hanyu Pinyin*. The pedagogic process of this experiment is divided into six inter-related steps: (1) looking at the character and analyzing the structure; (2) listening to the teacher's explanation of the structure and the pronunciation of the character; (3) speaking out the *pinyin*, stroke order, and the cognitive codes of the character; (4) writing the cognitive codes of the character and the character; (5) encoding the character and typing it into the computer; and (6) making words, phrases, and sentences with the character, and inputting the words, phrases, and sentences into the computer to better understand the meaning of the character and to train typing while thinking (He et al., 1997).

It was found that students were greatly motivated in Chinese character learning and the learning of computer skills (Xie, 1998), and their knowledge of characters in terms of character strokes order, spatial structure, and pronunciation of characters was greatly promoted and reinforced (He et al., 1996). At the same time, the students learned, too, how to encode Chinese characters and input them into the computer (He et al., 1996; Xie, 1998). In 1996, a test was organized to assess the effects of the experiment, which involved 94 Primary 2 and Primary 3 students from the 26 schools participating in the experiment during the years 1994 and 1995 (Xie, 1997). The test showed that the 66 Primary 2 students on average input 25.86 characters per minute with 91.05% accuracy and the 28 Primary 3 students on average input 27.67 characters per minute with 92.73% accuracy. The effectiveness of the experiment in developing both literacy and computer skills is also reflected in the result of the test of students' ability to think-type (without looking at the keyboard) words, sentences, and composition. It was shown that both Primary 2 and Primary 3 participants were good at think-typing their composition into the computer, gauged in terms of the length of their composition and the few typing mistakes made. The result also indicated that Primary 3 students who had been trained to use the *Renzhi Ma* character input system for two years performed much better than their Primary 2 counterparts, who only had one year experience of using the method (Xie, 1997).

2. The Multimedia Program and Early Chinese Literacy Instruction

Different from the experiments mentioned earlier, which are mainly based on the character input method for literacy teaching, a character instruction experiment was conducted to determine the effects of a multimedia package on students' oral vocabulary knowledge (Chen & Huang, 2001). Research has shown that children have mastered about 3,500 words in their spoken Chinese when they reach the age of six (Li, 1995; Shi, 1990). This knowledge of oral Chinese is the foundation for early literacy development, specifically in acquiring the form and meaning of Chinese characters (Pan, 1981), but the use of this knowledge is usually restrained because the opaque orthographic-phonological relation in Chinese makes it difficult for children to link together the shape, sound, and meaning of characters. Although children have already acquired an extensive oral vocabulary before their early formal literacy education, the use of this knowledge in early literacy learning is very much restricted by the curriculum (Dai, 1999). Chen & Huang (2001) believed that with the help of multimedia presentations characterized by combining sounds, pictures, and animations, the relation between the orthography, pronunciation, and meaning of characters could be made easier for children to understand, and that therefore character learning would be greatly facilitated. They proposed that with such a method, it is possible for children to acquire a large number of the most frequently used characters in a much shorter period of time than through the conventional way of teaching. A multimedia package was designed and developed. In this package, 5,000 thousand words are provided that are believed to have been already in children's typical repertoire of oral vocabulary. Apart from animated presentations of pictures showing the shape and the meaning of characters, the multimedia package also provides various other modules for students to better understand the relationship between pronunciation, shape, meaning, and the use of characters, including exemplary text reading, *pinyin* of the characters, and various other interactive exercises for students to strengthen the understanding of the use of the characters. The package consists of three pairs of discs, with each pair based on one volume of electronic character learning textbooks compiled for the experiment. In all, there are three volumes of electronic textbooks (each for one school term) and all of them are to be finished in one-and-a-half years. The selected texts are of three main genres: simple poems, children's rhymes, and short stories. These texts were mainly selected from conventional textbooks and some of them were composed for the experiment. Altogether, there are 119 texts, which are organized into units in each electronic textbook for each school term.

The teacher and students focus on reading texts and on studying characters in texts on screen. The characters used in texts are mainly selected from children's oral vocabulary. The main features can be summarized as follows:

- Students first listen to exemplary oral reading of a text on the screen, while looking at pictures or watching animated demonstrations which show both form and meaning of characters, words, and text.

- Students use the multimedia program independently for individual learning. If they want to learn or read a particular character or text, they can simply click on the new character or text in question to get their pronunciations, forms, and meanings with certain picture presentations. For example, a picture of a mountain is provided on the screen to show its original shape of the pictoric character 山 (mountain). If it is a text describing a particular scene, it is accompanied with a picture of the scene. As all the characters, words, and texts can be animated and repeated, students can view and listen to a particular character, word, or text repeatedly if they like or need to.

- Students explore more characters, words, and texts relevant to the text concerned in terms of similar topics that are provided for extensive electronic reading.

- Students do some exercises to reinforce their learning of the characters or text in question. Some examples of the exercises are: to find characters or words that can be used to describe a particular object or place in a provided picture on the screen; to find a corresponding character by listening to its pronunciation; to use new characters to create words; to fill in sentences with characters or words; and to combine words/phrases into sentences. These exercises are believed to help students better understand the use of characters or words at the sentence level.

- The software and the electronic textbook also provide four groups of characters for the students to compare and contrast to better understand the structural differences. The computer also demonstrates strokes and stroke order of characters; students can practice writing them with the guidance provided by the computer to understand what components a character contains and how it is formed.

- The teacher checks, monitors, and guides the student learning process.

The experiment was conducted with a class of 38 students in 1999, and the results showed that the multimedia program-based teaching method was effective both in terms of helping students acquire a large number of characters within a short period of time and in accelerating the development of early reading and writing. In mid–2000, when the class was about to finish the second school term, a test was administered to the 38 participants. The test was divided into two parts: one devoted to learning the characters and the other to oral reading and writing skills. In the first part of the test, the participants were asked to recognize the 1,660 characters covered by the experiment curriculum and to write down the 120 randomly selected characters from dictation. It was found that on average 97.2% of the characters were correctly recognized and 87.7% of the 120 characters were correctly written. The participants were also required to use some randomly selected characters to create word combinations and sentences orally. For the 100 characters selected for creating word combinations, 95% of the combinations were found to be correct; for the 10 characters for making sentences, 97.8% of the sentences were found to be properly composed. The second part of the test asked the participants to orally read some texts chosen from the conventional Chinese textbook for Grade 5 and 6 students, and it was found that on average they could recognize 169 characters per minute. The participants' performance on the writing test was also found to be satisfactory, because they could use the computer to write a composition on a specified topic, containing on average 213 characters.

These experimental studies have yielded significant findings. By using certain features of ICT as intervention tools, these studies have proved that it is possible to speed up the development of children's early literacy in one way or another. At the same time, they have facilitated children's electronic literacy at a very early age. We agree with the researchers' claim that appropriate use of computer technologies can optimize Chinese literacy instruction. However, we assume that these studies are inadequate in more than one aspect. For example, pre- and post-tests are important criteria to judge the effects of experimental studies, but the experiments discussed here reported only the post-test means, and did not provide any information of whether pre-tests were conducted. In all cases, the researchers did not report whether a control group was used and whether retention rates were assessed in their experiments. Therefore, we cannot assume that the positive results can be attributed to the instructional approach. Nonetheless, they are encouraging preliminary investigations that might be used to frame more rigorous studies.

CONCLUSIONS: LIMITATIONS AND PROSPECTS

In this chapter, we have provided an overview of recent ICT developments, some input methods, and some experiments involving ICT use in Chinese literacy education. As shown, the computer availability and Internet access in China have increased dramatically in the past few years. The ICT infrastructure has been largely put in place, and the Chinese character input methods have become more sophisticated. More and more Chinese people are now reading and writing electronic texts, e-mailing, and Internet surfing. A decade ago, the Chinese people were watching the same few TV programs and listening to a few radio stations. Now, many Chinese people have gained access to a much greater variety of media/channels, despite the safeguards of the government (Du, 1999), not just for receiving information but also for producing and publishing it. For better or for worse, these changes will definitely have a great impact on Chinese culture and society in general and education in particular.

However, at the same time, this will also intensify the existing social stratification of Chinese society. Although the expansion of computer use and the Internet is very rapid and the availability and accessibility will continue to grow in the years to come, ICT use is still very much limited to the "newly rich" and the urban population. Much of China's large population is still on the wrong side of the digital divide. The data of CNNIC (2005), for example, show that about 94 million Internet users by the end of 2004 only account for 7.2% of the 1.3 billion people in China. The disparities are still very great between the East and the West, the coastal and the inland, the urban and the rural. In 2001, in Shanghai, for example, about 16.7 students had one computer, but the ratio of students to computer in Yunnan, a province in southwest China, was only 186:1 (Zhong, 2003). In some remote areas, owning a computer is still a dream.

Of the population with access to the computer and the Internet, the social stratification can also be magnified. With many media/channel choices available, educational differences have become more important in determining who can take advantage of these choices. In other words, those who have ICT skills and multiliteracies will make the best choice possible for their personal gain, either in economic or sociocultural terms. Thus education will play an important role in the incoming ICT-dominant age in China. Then the question is, "is the Chinese educational system well prepared for it?" Unfortunately the answer is "not yet." While recognizing the importance of education policy and socioeconomic factors, we assume that teachers' knowledge of and attitude toward the use of ICT are likewise important if the advantages of ICT are to be harnessed. Although teachers are encouraged to use ICT in classroom instruction and professional development in the official syllabus, the current situation is not that optimistic. A recent survey conducted on the integration of ICT in the school curriculum in Beijing showed that more than 80% of the 4,255 participating teachers never used computers in their classroom instruction, and only a very small portion of them could use the Internet to search for information and to send e-mails. Primary school teachers used computers or the Internet for about 24 minutes in school during a week, and 85% of the time in question was used for preparing of lesson plans. Only about 4% of the time was used for classroom instruction (Beijing Education Research Institute, 2001). Consequently, many teachers still appear to view computers primarily as teacher utilities rather than instructional tools.

As noted earlier, the research on ICT and literacy instruction are fragmental. Most published articles we consulted in the process of preparing this overview are about personal views on how ICT should be integrated into the school curriculum and the possible effects of the computer in Chinese literacy education. For those few data-driven studies, almost all of them focus on early literacy development in Chinese characters as shown in this chapter, with little attention given to the impact of ICT on modes and means of communication, ways of electronic Chinese reading and writing, and so on.

These problems among many others, of course, cannot be solved in a short period of time. They require continuing efforts of governments, ICT technologists, educational researchers, teachers, and students to search for solutions. But one thing is certain: China has already been connected to cyberspace, many people are beginning to communicate and learn in new and different ways, and the seas of education are no longer calm. We believe that Chinese educational researchers and practitioners will, in due time, come to grips with the changes, and make the best use of the advantages of ICT in what Reinking (1995) termed a "post-typographic world."

REFERENCES

Beijing Education Research Institute. (2001). *Beijing zhongxiaoxue xinxi jishu yu xueke jiaoxue zhenghe baogao (Report on the integration of ICT in primary and secondary school curriculum in Beijing).* Retrieved February 2, 2005, from http://www.edu.cn/20030221/3077877_1.shtml.

Blok, H., Oostdam, R., Otter, M. E., & Overmaat, M. (2002). Computer-assisted instruction in support of beginning reading instruction: A review. *Review of Educational Research, 72,* 101–130.

Bourgerie, D. S. (2003). Computer aided language learning for Chinese: A survey and annotated bibliography. *Journal of the Chinese Language Teachers Association, 38*(2), 17–47.

Carrington, V. (2004). Texts and literacies of the Shi Jinrui. *British Journal of Sociology of Education, 25,* 215–228.

CERNET. (2001). CERNET profile. Retrieved January 10, 2005, from http://www.edu.cn/20010101/22189.shtml

Chen, Q., & Huang, D. (2001). Xiaoxuesheng shizi xin qidian: Duomeiti shuyu shizi (The new start of character learning for primary students: A multimedia, oral vocabulary-based method for Chinese character learning). *Zhongguo dianhua Jiaoyu, 24*(2), 32–35.

China National Commission for UNESCO. (2004). *Educational Development in China 2004.* Retrieved January 10, 2005, from www.ibe.unesco.org/International/ICE47/English/Natreps/reports/china_ocr.pdf

CNNIC. (2005). *The 15th statistical survey report on the Internet development in China.* Beijing: China Internet Network Information Center.

CNNIC. (1997). *The first statistical survey report on the Internet development in China.* Beijing: China Internet Network Information Center.

Coulmas, F. (1989). *Writing systems of the world.* Oxford: Blackwells.

Dai, R. Q. (1999). *Hanzi jiao yu xue (Chinese character teaching and learning).* Jinan: Shandong Jiaoyu Chubanshe.

DeFrancis, J. (1984). *The Chinese language: Facts and fantasy.* Honolulu: University of Hawaii Press.

Dew, J. E. (1996). Advances in computerization of Chinese. *Journal of the Chinese Language Teachers Association, 31*(3), 15–31.

Du, X. (1999). Internet adoption and usage in China. *The 27th Annual Telecommunications Policy and Research Conference.* Retrieved January 15, 2005, from http://www.tprc.org/ABSTRACTS99/DUPAP.PDF

Feng, Z. W. (1992). *Zhongwen xinxi chuli yu hanyu yanjiu (Chinese information processing and Chinese language studies).* Beijing: Shangwu Yinshuguan.

Feng, Z. W. (1989). *Xiandai Hanzi yu jisuanji (Characters in Modern Chinese and computer science).* Beijing: Bejinjing Daxue Chubanshe.

Hanyu Da Zidian (A Comprehensive Dictionary of Chinese Characters) (Vol 1–8). (1990). Chengdu: Sichuan Cishu Chubanshe/Wuhan: Hubei Cishu Chubanshe.

He, K. K., Li, K. D., Xie, Y. R., & Wang, B. Z. (1997). Xiaoxue yuwen "sijiehe" jiaoxue gaige shiyan de lilun jichu yu shiyan moshi (Theoretical framework and models for *sijiehe* Chinese language pedagogic reform in primary schools). *Dianhua jiaoyu yanjiu, 18*(1), 28–38.

He, K. K., Li, K. D., Xie, Y. R., & Wang, B. Z. (1996). Xiaoxue yuwen "sijiehe" jiaoxue gaige shiyan yanjiu (A study of *sijiehe* Chinese language pedagogic reform in primary schools). *Dianhua jiaoyu yanjiu, 17*(1), 12–21.

Kinney, S. T., & Watson, R. T. (1992). The Effect of Medium and Task on Dyadic Communication. *Proceedings of the International Conference on Information Systems,* 107–117.

Kress, G., & Van Leeuwen, T. (1996). *Reading images: The grammar of visual design.* London: Routledge.

Lemke, J. L. (1998). Metamedia literacy: Transforming meanings and media. In D. Reinking, M. C. McKenna, L. D. Labbo, & R. D. Kieffer (Eds.), *Handbook of literacy and technology: Transformation in a post-typographic world* (pp. 283–302). Mahwah, NJ: Lawrence Erlbaum Associates.

Li, Y. M. (1995). *Ertong yuyan fazhan (Child language development).* Wuhan: Huazhong Shifan Daxue Chubanshe.

Liu, C., Lin, H. F., & Gu, W. (2004). Bring Internet into campus: Experience from Mainland China and Taiwan. *AEIMC Midwinter Conference.* Retrieved January 4, 2005, from http://iip.ist.psu.edu/publication/students/aejmc2004.pdf

Liu, Y. B. (2005). A pedagogy for digraphia: An analysis of the impact of *Pinyin* on literacy teaching in China and implications for curricular and pedagogical innovations in a wider community. *Language and Education, 19*(5), 400–414.

Lu, K. X., Yu, N. H., & Zuo, S. T. (2002). *Xiandai xiaoxue shizi xiezi jiaoxue (Reading and writing Chinese characters in contemporary primary schools).* Beijing: Yuwen Chubanshe.

Lu, J. M., & Su, P. C. (Eds.). (2004). *Yuwen xiandaihua yu Hanyu Pinyin Fang'an (Modernization of Chinese language and scheme of Chinese phonetic scripts).* Beijing: Yuwen Chubanshe.

Lu, S. X. (1987). *Lu Shuxiang lun yuwen jiaoxue (Lu Shuxiang's essays on language education).* Jinan: Shandong Jiaoyu Chubanshe.

McKenna, M. C., Reinking, D., Labbo, L. D., & Kieffer, R. D. (1999). The electronic transformation of literacy and its implications for the structure for the struggling reader. *Reading & Writing Quarterly, 15*, 111–126.

Ministry of Education. (2003). *Woguo yiwu jiaoyu qude xin jinzhan qingkuang (The new development of compulsory education in China)*. Retrieved January 15, 2005, from http://www.edu.cn/20030312/3079536.shtml

Ministry of Education. (2001). *Yiwu jiaoyu yuwen kechengs biaozhun (Chinese language arts curriculum standards for compulsory education)*. Beijing: Beijing Shifan Daxue Chubanshe.

Ministry of Education. (2000a). *Jiaoyubu guanyu zai zhongxiaoxue shishi "Xiaoxaoatong" gongcheng de tongzhi (Special Announcement on the project of every campus connected to the Internet)*. Retrieved January 15, 2004, from http://www.moe.edu.cn/zhuanti/jyxxh/xxtong/02.htm

Ministry of Education. (2000b). *Zhongxiaoxue xinxi jishu kecheng zhidao gangyao (shixing) (Guide for ICT curriculum in primary and secondary schools)*. Retrieved January 15, 2005, from http://www.edu.cn/20020327/3023657.shtml

Ministry of Education. (2000c). *Guanyu zai zhongxiaoxue puji xinxi jishu de tongzhi (Special announcement on universalizing ICT education in primary and secondary schools)*. Retrieved January 15, 2005, from http://www.edu.cn/20020327/3023658.shtml

Nan, G. N. (2001). *Xinxi jishu jiaoyu yu chuangxin rencai peiyang (ICT education and the training of creative people)*. Retrieved January 10, 2005, from www.etc.edu.cn/articledigest10/xin-xi.htm

National Committee for Language Affairs. (2004). Retrieved February 2, 2005, from http://www.people.com.cn/GB/paper464/13727/1227328.html

National Committee for Language Affairs. (1988). Xiandai hanyu changyong zibiao (A list of frequently used characters in modern Chinese). In *Yuyan wenzi guifan shouce (Handbook of language standardization)*. Beijing: Yuwen chubanshe.

New London Group. (1996). A pedagogy for multiliteracies: Designing social futures. *Harvard Educational Review, 66*, 60–92.

Pan, S. (1981). *Jiaoyu xinlixue (Educational psychology)*. Bejing: Renmin Jiaoyu Chubanshe.

Reinking, D. (1998). Synthesizing technological transformations of literacy in a post-typographic world. In D. Reinking, M. C. McKenna, L. D., Labbo, & R. D. Kieffer (Eds.), *Handbook of literacy and technology: Transformation in a post-typographic world* (pp. xi–xxx). Mahwah, NJ: Lawrence Erlbaum Associates.

Reinking, D. (1995). Reading and writing with computers: Literacy research in a post-typographic world. In A. Kathleen, D. J. Leu, & C. K. Kinzer (Eds.), *Perspectives on literacy research and practice* (pp. 17–33). Chicago: National Reading Conference.

Reinking, D., McKenna, M. C., Labbo, L. D., & R. D. Kieffer (Eds.) (1998). *Handbook of literacy and technology: Transformation in a post-typographic world*. Mahwah, NJ: Lawrence Erlbaum Associates.

Sheng, Y. L. (2004). Cong Hanzi bianma dao Hanyu bianma (From Chinese character encoding to Chinese language encoding). In J. M. Lu, & P. C. Su (Eds.), *Yuwen xiandaihua yu Hanyu Pinyin Fang'an (Modernization of Chinese language and scheme of Chinese phonetic scripts)* (pp. 293–300). Beijing: Yuwen Chubanshe.

Shi, H. Z. (1990). 3–6 sui ertong yuyan fazhan yu jiaoyu (The language development and education of 3–6-year-old children). In Z. X. Zhu (Ed.), *Zhongguo ertong qingshaonian xinli fazhan yu jiaoyu (Psychological development and education of children and youth in China)* (pp. 94–127). Beijing: Zhongguo Zhuoyue Chubanshe.

Schlechter, T. M. (1990). The relative instructional efficiency of small group computer-based training. *Journal of Educational Computing, 6*, 329–341.

Su, P. C. (Ed.). (2003). *Xinxi wangluo shidai de Hanyu Pinyin (Hanyu Pinyin in the information and network age)*. Beijing: Yuwen Chubanshe.

Tao, L., & Boulware, B. (2002). E-mail: Instructional potentials and learning opportunities. *Reading & Writing Quarterly, 18*, 285–288.

Tao, L., & Reinking, D. (2000). E-mail and literacy education. *Reading & Writing Quarterly, 16*, 169–174.

Topping, K. J., & McKenna, M. C. (1999). Introduction to electronic literacy. *Reading & Writing Quarterly, 15*, 107–110.

Wang, J. (1995). *Dangdai zhongguo de wenzi gaige (Language reforms in modern China)*. Beijing: Dangdai Zhongguo Chubanshe.

Wang, L. J. (2003). *Hanyu Pinyin yundong yu Hanminzu biaozhunyu (The movement of the phonetic scripts of Chinese and standard language of Han nationality)*. Beijing: Yuwen Chubanshe.

Wang, X. D. (2001). *Zhongxiaoxue xinxi jiaoyu xianzhuang yu fazhan (Current situation and development of ICT education in primary and secondary schools)*. Retrieved January 15, 2005, from www.edu.cn/20011106/3008345.shtml

Wang, X. D. (1996). Guanyu zhongxiaoxue jisuanji shuru fangfa (On Chinese character input methods for primary and secondary students). *Zhongwen xinxi, 12*(1), 58–59.

Warschauer, M. (2001). Millennialism and media: Language, literacy, and technology in the 21st century. *AILA Review, 14*, 49–59.

Wenhui Daily (2004). *2003 Shanghai xinxihua pandian: jiating jisuanji pujilu chao 60% (An overview of Informatization in Shanghai, 2003: Household computer availability exceeds 60%)*. Retrieved January 15, 2004, from http://tech.sina.com.cn/it/2004–01–07/1324278746.shtml

World Bank (2003). *ICT at a glance: China*. Retrieved January 4, 2004, from http://www.worldbank.org/cgi-bin/sendoff.cgi?page=%2Fdata%2Fcountrydata%2Fict%2Fchn_ict.pdf

Xie, Y. R. (1998). Xiaoxue yuwen "sijiehe" jiaogai dui xuesheng xuexi xingqu yu xingwei de yingxiang fenxi (The effects of "sijiehe" experiment of primary school Chinese teaching on the students' learning interests and learning behavior). *Dianhua jiaoyu yanjiu, 19*(1), 90–95.

Xie, Y. R. (1997). Xiaoxue yuwen "sijiehe" jiaogai shiyan yanjiu jiaoxue xiaoguo (The effect of "sijiehe" experiment of primary school Chinese teaching). *Dianhua jiaoyu yanjiu, 18*(3), 72–80.

Xu, J. L. (1999). *Yuyanwenzixue ji qi yingyong yanjiu (Linguistics and applied linguistics)*. Guangzhou: Guangdong Jiaoyu Chubanshe.

Yan, Y. X. (2000). The politics of consumerism in Chinese society. In T. White (Ed.), *China briefing 2000: The continuing transformation* (pp. 159–193). New York: M. E. Sharpe.

Yu, S. Q., Wu, J., & Li, W. G. (2002). Yunyong xiandai jiaoyu jishu jinxing xueke jiaoxue gaige de xianfeng: "Sijiehe" jiaogai shiyan yanjiu xiangmu de huigui yu zhanwang (Pioneer in integrating modern education technology in school curriculum: A retrospect on "sijiehe" experiment). *Dianhua jiaoyu yanjiu, 23*(3), 36–46.

Zhang, P. (1992). *Hanyu xinxi chuli yanjiu (Studies of Chinese information processing)*. Beijing: Beijing Yuyan Xueyuan Chubanshe.

Zhang, Z. (1998). CALL for Chinese: issues and practice. *Journal of the Chinese Language Teachers Association, 33*(1), 51–82.

Zhou, Q. (1999). Duomeiti jishu yu xinxing shizi jiaoxue (Multimedia technology and new character teaching method). *Kecheng jiaocai jiaofa, 19*(11), 16–21.

Zhong, W. (2003). Jiaoyu xinxihua jianshe, zhuduo wenti yao jiejue (Many problems to be solved in educational informatization). *Zhongguo jiaoyu bao*, March 27, p. 3.

IV

TEACHER EDUCATION AND PROFESSIONAL DEVELOPMENT

14

Using Technology to (Re)Conceptualize Preservice Literacy Teacher Education: Considerations of Design, Pedagogy, and Research

Charles K. Kinzer
Teachers College, Columbia University

Dana W. Cammack
Montclair State University

Linda D. Labbo
University of Georgia

William H. Teale and Ruby Sanny
University of Illinois at Chicago

THE NEED TO (RE)CONCEPTUALIZE PRESERVICE TEACHER DEVELOPMENT AND THE ROLE OF TECHNOLOGY IN THAT DEVELOPMENT

Teacher education appears to have changed little in half a century or more. Although various instructional models, from traditional classroom instruction to apprenticeship/internship approaches, have gained and lost favor during this time,[1] preservice education programs continue, appropriately, to address three areas: knowledge of subject matter, knowledge of instructional processes and procedures, and implementation of appropriate processes and procedures in the classroom. Yet, for all of the innovations that have been and are being tried, it has generally been the case that teacher education programs are more successful at enhancing future teachers' knowledge of subject matter and instructional procedures than at developing their instructional decision-making abilities (e.g., see Munby, Russell, & Martin, 2001)—even though the making of moment-to-moment decisions about what to teach, when to teach it, and how to best do so is perhaps what characterizes the most effective classroom teachers.

---

[1]The handbooks of research on teacher education (Sikula, Buttery, & Guyton, 1996) and on teaching (Richardson, 2001) contain several discussions of these and other models.

It has been noted that future teachers appear to rely more on their own experiences as learners than on the knowledge provided to them by their teaching methods courses, and that field experiences may have more effect on future teachers' development than does coursework (e.g., Griffin, 1989). In light of such findings, Borko and Putnam (1996) and Feiman-Nemser and Remillard (1996) cite the need to change teachers' beliefs about teaching and learning, and advocate doing so through constructivist perspectives and situated cognition. Borko and Putnam note the following factors as contributing to successful teacher learning:

1. Addressing teachers' [existing] knowledge and beliefs about teaching, learners, learning, and subject matter;
2. Providing teachers with sustained opportunities to deepen and expand their knowledge of subject matter;
3. Treating teachers as learners in a manner consistent with the programs' vision of how teachers should treat students as learners;
4. Grounding teachers' learning and reflection in classroom practice; and
5. Offering ample time and support for reflection, collaboration, and continued learning. (Borko & Putnam, 1996, pp. 700–701).

These points have been applied to literacy teacher education in various ways. For example, Snow, Burns and Griffin (1998) propose that teacher education prepare future teachers for the complexities of classrooms by closely connecting preservice teacher education with what we know about effective instructional practices. Others agree that teacher preparation programs must move beyond simple presentations when preparing teachers for the complexities of classroom contexts (e.g., Alvermann, 1990; Bransford, Brown, & Cocking, 1999). Traditional lecture-based, preservice education experiences do not adequately prepare future teachers, largely because these approaches cannot adequately address the components presented herein. In addition, many current preservice courses do not integrate technology effectively, despite the fact that these preservice teachers will almost certainly be required to use technology in their own classrooms.

In fact, we believe that traditional methods used in teacher education are hard pressed to provide the experiences that address the items on Borko and Putnam's list. Furthermore, we suspect that without the inclusion of technological tools, these methods may be unable to provide the experiences. Even teacher education programs with substantial field-based components frequently come up short because they rely on unique and individualized experiences for each preservice teacher. For example, when preservice teachers come together in a student teaching seminar to share their classroom experiences and ask questions that might help them solve a problem, each preservice teacher approaches questions and reflections from his or her unique field experience classroom. Therefore, collaborative reflection is difficult to achieve. In effect, each individual's field experience is unique, and the potential benefits of collective experience are dissipated into what may be regarded as 20 or more teacher education programs (depending on the number of students in the class), rather than a single, powerful, connected program. Preservice peers, while empathetic to and supportive of each other, cannot closely relate to field experiences in which they are not grounded. As a result, reflection activities intended to mediate underlying beliefs and perceptions about teaching lose much of their power.

Consider, for example, the differences in the impact of reflective discussion in the following two scenarios. The first involves two individuals, one of whom has had field experiences in a second-grade classroom at Brewer Elementary School and another who was involved in a third-grade classroom at Cavasos Elementary (all names are pseudonyms). They come to their student teaching seminar class to discuss their respective experiences. Each individual briefly presents his or her field experience and asks for comments and suggestions. The student teacher at Brewer Elementary receives support and generic comments from her peers, but is left to reflect individually about what took place and how her beliefs and knowledge operate within Brewer's unique environment.

However, what if we could enable future teachers to participate in a shared experience that serves as a focal point for later discussion and grounds the teaching and learning of subject matter knowledge and instructional procedures while student teachers share their individual field experiences? In the second scenario, regarding the student teacher from Cavasos Elementary, individual presentations about unique field experiences are related to a shared context. The group then discusses similarities and differences between the shared context and the individual's unique preservice placement. As a result, group reflections and suggestions become more specific and beneficial in affecting individuals' underlying beliefs. In effect, the shared experience facilitates bringing peer reflections to bear on individuals' field placement discussions. (See Roskos, Vukelich, & Risko, 2002 for a discussion of research on reflection and reflective practice related to literacy.)

Multimedia technologies that present cases of classroom practice offer especially promising opportunities to provide students with situations like the second scenario just described. Through the delivery of visual and linguistic information on the Internet, students can share a common experience that grounds further learning in a rich socio-constructivist environment. The project, Case Technologies to Enhance Literacy Learning (CTELL) that we have developed (http://ctell .uconn.edu/home.htm), attempts to move toward the second example by merging two instructional perspectives—anchored instruction and case-based learning methods—through the use of video embedded in interactive multimedia cases delivered over the Internet or on CD-ROM.

Case-based methods, common in business, law and medicine, are becoming more accepted in educational settings, but there are important differences to consider in cases used in various content domains (Williams, 1992). For example, cases in law are based on precedent, but cases in classrooms cannot be viewed in this way. Educational practice, as a social and cultural endeavor, does not act on strict rules of precedence because classrooms are dynamic and changing environments. Lesson plans written by and for one teacher often fail when used by a different teacher, perhaps a substitute, because the context has changed and precedence does not apply. The importance of understanding the context within which teachers make their instructional decisions cannot be overemphasized. As discussed later, video provides possibilities for contextualizing instruction in ways not possible through print-based cases.

With the recognition of the importance of context as a facilitative factor in knowledge acquisition (Munby, Russell, & Martin, 2001), case-based instruction has become increasingly popular in teacher education (see discussions by Merseth, 1991, 1994; Schulman, 1995; Silverman & Welty, 1995; Lundeberg, 1999, Sykes & Bird, 1992). Case-based methods in education provide students with a contextual understanding of how complex teaching and learning can be (Bowers et al., 2000). Cases fit well into constructive, interactive pedagogies like anchored instruction (Kinzer & Risko, 1998) in that they allow for multiple entry points and perspectives to be explored. Many believe that such a complex field as teacher education is best taught by situating instruction in complex spaces like cases (Ferdig, Roehler, & Pearson, 2002). Teaching and learning are both situated in real-life spaces that are complicated, changeable, and difficult to assess. Case-based instruction provides a scaffolded sense of such complexity in ways that help preservice teachers begin to negotiate classroom situations (Hughes, Packard, & Pearson, 2000).

Case-based instruction has been presented as being quite different from transmission models, largely associated with lecture formats in traditional preservice teacher-education methods courses, that are prevalent in teacher education (e.g. see Risko, 1995). A comparison of many case-based methods, which presuppose exploration and problem-solving by a learner, and transmission models, which are analogous to filling empty vessels, might begin with the underlying assumptions of how case-based methods are used in the classroom. These include provision for analysis of data, thought of as the content of the case (in our instance, this includes video of classroom teaching, students' written work, interviews, and so on, as detailed later). Case content also is viewed as including the context(s) where instructional procedures are used and modified, as well as factors and variables that must be considered when choosing and implementing instructional decisions. Cases therefore allow preservice teachers to bridge from theory into the complexities of practice (Greenwood, 1996). As noted in the section that follows, computer technologies that include interactive, multimedia learning environments offer preservice teacher instructors unique avenues for effective case-based instruction. Indeed, computer tools and content offer distinctive affordances that are difficult to realize in print-based forms.

A Brief Discussion of the Promise of Technology Combined with Case-Based Methods

Casebooks for use in reading education are increasing in availability but, as Kinzer and Risko (1998) point out, there are important differences between print- and even videotape-based cases and those delivered through video on digital, random-access media. Although print-based cases can provide shared knowledge for discussion purposes, they are limited in utility when viewed from a perspective of access and analysis. Print-based cases are usually written after the fact and cannot truly capture a classroom's complexity. They present a single viewpoint and lay out events within a complex space in a linear format. Classrooms, however, are rarely that simple. Video images, combined with text, offer much richer possibilities for understanding classrooms (Baker, 2000; Hughes et al., 2000; Catalyst Web, 2004; Ferdig et al., 2000).

Videotape is capable of capturing a classroom's complexity but cannot be quickly rewound and re-viewed—a critical requirement in preservice classes. While videotape is able to play a scene from start to finish, it has significant shortcomings if a student asks for a particular part to be replayed so that a question or clarification can be addressed. Yet deeper analysis takes place when a segment of a classroom interaction is viewed more than once and analyzed from a variety of perspectives. At present, only random-access delivery systems (i.e., CD-ROM, DVD and digital video over the Internet) allow such functions. And these are important functions if we desire to address the calls for reforms as capsulated on Borko & Putnam's (1996) list, shown earlier.

Random-access video as part of case design allows one to revisit a scene to analyze what is occurring from multiple perspectives, and viewing a classroom from multiple perspectives is important in gaining knowledge about classroom complexity. Random access also allows a preservice instructor to break a class into groups with multiple assignments—perhaps various groups or individuals focusing on a particular student, on the teacher, on the instructional materials and procedures being used, and so on, and to revisit a single piece of video to look at each of these items as they arise in class discussions. By looking repeatedly at a video segment from different perspectives and for different purposes, one is left with a deeper understanding of the interaction of factors that are involved in the respective instructional situation.

In the case of the CTELL project, this means that the case content is taken from authentic classrooms with enough data provided in the case so that learners can analyze and compare classroom cases to enhance their understanding of instructional decisions and to foster the ability to suggest alternatives. In addition to video of classroom instruction, the data may include any or all of the following: children's test scores, their parents' thoughts, the teachers' experience as expressed in interviews, and so on. In case-based instruction, analysis and reflection are critical, and cases provide learners with opportunities to revisit the data and decisions in the case, along with the chance to consider alternative solutions. Revisiting case content provides a more sustained and recursive learning environment; reflection occurs in groups and individually as part of case analysis.

Traditional, transmission methods operate from a different set of assumptions, which make it difficult to meet the goals set out in Borko and Putnam's (1996) list. Most transmission methods present procedural steps and their appropriate uses to learners in a direct rather than a constructivist mode. Thus, students typically absorb facts about teaching methods and procedures. Even when instruction provides information about the use of instructional methods and procedures in classrooms in a general sense, this does not facilitate a deep understanding of the arena(s) where these methods might be implemented and under what conditions. This teaching model usually provides a "one-shot" exposure to the content within a course; revisiting content occurs largely when learners re-read their notes or assignments, usually in preparation for an examination. Further, reflection in transmission models is usually done outside the instructional situation and is linked to lecture content rather than to a decision-making process.

This is not to say that transmission models are inappropriate in all situations—after all, at times the most effective way to provide knowledge is to tell someone a fact. However, we argue that when instructional methods are intended to be used in a decision-making sense, and when knowledge is to be transferred into complex classroom contexts, then analysis, reflection, decision-making, and opportunities to learn recursively are critical. This is precisely what case-based methods require and is a reason why cases are popular in law, business, and medical education where linking facts and procedures to decision making are valued. Thus, CTELL uses case-based instruction with a significant video component, accessed through random-access technology, as one aspect in its effort to enhance preservice literacy education. The other aspect in which video plays a central role is as an instructional anchor, described in the next section.

Anchored Instruction as a Factor in CTELL Cases

Anchored instruction (CTGV, 1997) and situated cognition (Brown, Collins, & Duguid, 1989; Feiman-Nemser & Remillard, 1996) provide a context where all participants in the learning environment (teacher and students) experience a situation that becomes the springboard for future learning. Anchored instruction has been used successfully in elementary-grade mathematics and literacy classrooms (e.g. Cognition and Technology Group at Vanderbilt, 1997). In CTELL, the use of anchored instruction follows the outline provided by colleagues at Vanderbilt University:

> We emphasize the importance of anchored instruction because, in many educational settings . . . students often have not had the opportunity to experience the types of problems that are rendered solvable by the knowledge we teach them. They treat the knowledge as an end rather than as a means to important ends. . . . The common denominator in all these cases is that new information is treated as facts to be learned rather than as knowledge to be used.
>
> A major goal of anchored instruction is to help students experience the kinds of problems that experts in an area encounter and to understand how core concepts in a discipline help clarify these problems. We want them to transform knowledge from mere facts into useful tools. We also want to provide a common context that can be explored by students, teachers, parents, and others so that they have a common ground for communication. (CTGV, 1997, p. 25)

As discussed elsewhere (Kinzer & Risko, 1998), anchored instruction serves to mitigate three major issues confronted by all teachers, including instructors in preservice literacy classes: (1) teachers face students with a wide range of backgrounds; (2) there is often little shared knowledge among teacher and students, and (3) knowledge often remains inert; it is not accessed and used in appropriate situations.

The importance of mitigating these issues in preservice education is easily seen when one asks students to "think back to when you were taught to read." Some students report to us that they were taught in classrooms with desks in rows; others had flexible arrangements. Some were taught through a decoding emphasis, and others through more holistic programs. Some recall much drill and practice; others recall extensive use of children's literature. Differences in what each student brings to the task impacts shared knowledge among students in a class and between students and preservice instructor. Teachers and students must be able to link given knowledge to new knowledge, and course instructors must be able to refer to knowledge that students bring to the class and to draw examples from this knowledge. However, when there is a discrepancy across the prior knowledge within class members, this end is difficult to achieve. Anchored instruction addresses issues of background knowledge and shared knowledge by providing a contextualized task experienced by teacher and learners, which then becomes the background and shared knowledge from which instructional examples can be drawn and used as a common reference point during instruction. CTELL uses the notion of anchored instruction in its design of cases and in the recommended instructional procedures used in case-based instruction. Not only is a CTELL case in itself a shared experience, but each individual case includes in its design a "video anchor segment." This approximately 20-minute video anchor is intended to be viewed initially in its entirety by each learner, before other parts of the case can be accessed. Anchored instruction, as instantiated in an online learning environment, weaves together authentic classroom content with interactive navigational and communicative tools that amplify and enhance constructivist and socio-constructivist learning opportunities.

Using Technology Through the Design of the CTELL Cases

Designing instructional materials is a complex, multifaceted process, particularly in relation to the integration of technology. Design must consider questions such as, "What is curriculum and instruction?" "How should a learner progress through the material?" and "What support for reflection and communication can be provided?" In addition, instructional materials using technology must also consider what medium, or combination, to use to support material access and exploration. What media are aligned with the best way to achieve curricular goals? Certain media, including paper-based and electronic cases, afford different things. Paper-based cases are often more linear and do not offer as many opportunities for multiple perspectives (Baker, 2000). Other questions to consider are the following: How should students (and teachers) access and use the materials? What interface issues must be considered in the development of multimedia, Internet-based cases? Different modes of access and interface layout afford different things; how information is presented affects how the case is defined and viewed (Baker, 2000).

All of these areas were considered by our project team before shooting video to incorporate into the cases and then constructing our case interface and overall structure. Overlaid on the previously-noted questions were questions such as, "What video should we shoot?" and "How should we edit the video to make it consistent with case-based and anchored instructional pedagogy?" as well as "How should the interface present the components of a case?" "What information is most important to present right away?" and "What can be embedded further into the cases?"

In deciding on what video to shoot, an important preliminary decision was to capture footage that would allow us to design instructional cases that incorporate principles of effective reading instruction. Thus, we examined previous reviews of the literature, including national reports (e.g., Snow, Burns & Griffin, 1998; NRP, 2000), other subsequent literature not addressed in these reports, and position statements from professional organizations with regard to effective reading/

literacy instruction (e.g., IRA/NAEYC Position Statement on Early Literacy). Our review of the literature yielded 12 principles that we believe are supported by the literature as underlying effective reading instruction. The 12 principles formed the basis of the overarching curriculum covered by the CTELL cases and were used as written guidelines for filming, collecting artifacts from classrooms, and editing the classroom video that was incorporated into the finished case (see also, Teale, 2002; Teale, Kinzer, Labbo, & Leu, 2002).

The expanded version of the principles that grounded the video and the overarching content for each case appear in Appendix A and are summarized here: (1) teacher knowledge, insight, and orchestration skills; (2) building on home backgrounds; (3) development of foundational literacy knowledge, skills, and interests; (4) phonemic awareness instruction; (5) decoding instruction; (6) comprehension instruction; (7) independent reading; (8) developing reading fluency; (9) integrating reading and writing; (10) integrating computer and Internet technology into early literacy instruction; (11) early assessment and instructional intervention; and (12) enthusiasm for and engagement in reading. Additionally, because the research base for effective computer and Internet technology integration was sparse at the onset of the study (Kamil, Kim, & Intrator, 2000), we surveyed and interviewed 150 K–3rd grade teachers who were nominated for participation because of their exemplary use of computers in the classroom. Content analysis resulted in the identification of 11 facets of effective computer and Internet technology integration (principle 10; Teale, 2002) that were instrumental in selecting classroom cases where teachers were integrating computer technologies in exemplary ways.

It is important to note that the 12 principles are not presented as separate items or headings within a case or anchor video, but are shown as operating together in a classroom where reading instruction occurs. One benefit of the CTELL cases is that they provide materials in which students see that these principles operate in a classroom over time—not all are present at any given lesson, activity, or teacher-student interaction, but rather are part of an effective instructional program. Our cases show instruction across the space of 4 days to 3 weeks, and students learn how the principles of effective practice are incorporated into effective literacy instruction over time. The ability to view instruction over time, even if edited, is a clear benefit of video over print-based case instruction.

Our next decision was to determine the boundaries of our cases. A case can be built around a single child, a single teacher, a single lesson, a single management issue, and so on. In order to teach the complexities of classroom reading instruction, we decided to focus our cases on classrooms. Thus, the cases consist of a variety of items that teachers need to consider in classroom reading instruction. They include, as much as possible, elements within a classroom (e.g., children, materials, etc.) as well as elements that impact classroom instruction but are not physically found in the classroom (e.g., parents' desires and beliefs about school and literacy, school philosophy and demographics, etc.). Some of these items are physical artifacts that have been digitized through scanning and then placed into the case (e.g., children's work, teachers' lesson plans, summaries of children's test scores, diagrams of classroom layout, and so on), while other components of the case are represented through video (e.g., interviews with parents, teachers, school administrators, experts in the field, and children, as well as video of several specific lessons). Thus, our cases incorporate video and non-video items, something that recent advances in the ability to present a wide variety of media through the Internet allows. Figure 14.1 depicts both the structure of our cases and details their specific content.

As seen in Figure 14.1, our cases are comprised of an interface and the case content. The interface includes tool functions that facilitate reflection, provide for constructivist exploration of the case environment, and allow for socio-constructivist communication with others. The interface also includes administrative functions so that a course instructor can leave messages and

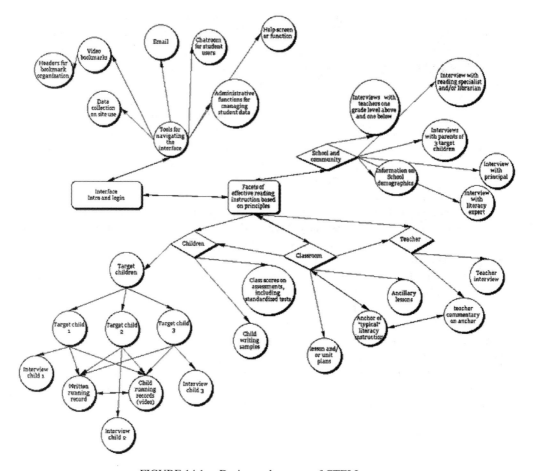

FIGURE 14.1.   Design and content of CTELL cases.

assignments for students, define areas that students should look at, and so on. The tools include e-mail and chat room capabilities, help functions, and bookmark functions used to define segments of the video within a case that can be easily revisited and sent to others via e-mail. The interface allows users to segment the video, revisit scenes within larger video segments, e-mail portions of video to peers for class discussion purposes, and create video portfolios for refection and assessment purposes. These interactive capabilities are what make the multimedia case powerful. Without an interface that organizes the case components and allows for repeated interactive access, video could only be viewed in linear form.

The content aspects of CTELL cases relate to facets of classroom instruction and decision making, and include school/community information (school demographics, interviews with teachers in the target school, parents, the school administrator, and literacy experts in the field), classroom-instructional aspects (the anchor segment, lesson plans, ancillary teaching segments, and teacher commentary), and student aspects of the case (three target children who are highlighted in each case, running records on these children, standardized test scores for all children in the class, and children's interviews and writing samples). In all, cases contain approximately 55 minutes of video and much additional material—from test scores to students' work, to teacher commentary. Exploring the rich content of the cases through an anchored instruction procedure and using support tools like the bookmarking and portfolio functions provided through the interface allow students to understand the context in which instructional decisions are made and in which instructional procedures are implemented.

It is important to note that case-based instruction does not use the components of cases as examples (Kinzer & Risko, 1998). Cases that incorporate video are immediate and powerful, and there is a danger that preservice teachers will adopt a "do what is shown" mindset. To mitigate this and to facilitate problem solving and decision making, we decided to provide multiple cases in each of the grades—K, 1, 2, and 3. Preservice teachers are required to explore more than one case at a given grade level. This makes clear that underlying principles of effective practice can be realized in multiple ways, that teachers modify instructional procedures and practices differently, and that no two teachers use instructional procedures in exactly the same way. Thus, preservice teachers come to realize that memorizing or mimicking what is shown on a video is not the goal. Rather, they must determine how and why instructional practices are working across classroom cases to embody effective principles of reading instruction in various settings. This leads them away from using video and cases as examples to using them in a constructivist, knowledge-acquisition, and decision-making process. Examples imply that one should do what is seen; case-based instruction implies that one must come to an understanding, through the data available in the case, about teacher decisions and the reasons for and outcomes of those decisions.

We feel that current technology that permits the use of video within case-based, anchored instruction allows preservice course instructors to meet Borko's and Putnam's (1996) criteria in ways not before possible. The unique combination of new streaming video possibilities via the Internet, more readily accessible broadband connections that are replacing modem and dial-up access, higher-speed computers and CD-ROM/DVD players, and affordable, high-capacity data storage have converged to the point where the limitations of print-based, videotape-based, and even CD-ROM-based media no longer apply. Thus, as seen in Figure 14.1, the CTELL cases are able to build in tools that facilitate reflection and communication. Using the Internet as a delivery system, CTELL cases allow an instructor to house, on a university's computer server, all of the case materials pictured in Figure 14.1 for the 11 K–3 cases. Students can, from their dorm room, computer lab or other broadband-available area, connect to these cases and, after logging in with their password, manipulate the video in the cases, move through the cases, and capture segments of video for user-defined playback. They can participate in predefined or user-defined reflections, make reflective notes, go back to modify or print them, bookmark segments of video, and send that bookmark to another learner (or to the instructor or other expert) for comment and discussion. Participants can then comment on and discuss the video segment and/or other items, such as students' work or the teacher's lesson plan, and reflect on what they are seeing and learning.

Figure 14.2 shows the main screen from the CTELL interface, which implements the design schematic just discussed. A sample anchor video and description of CTELL classroom implementation by an instructor can be seen at http://ctell.uconn.edu/.

CTELL Case Design as a Teaching Function. As part of our fidelity to an anchored instruction model, all cases begin with an anchor video segment that is central to the case. This 18–21- minute-long segment must be viewed before any other aspect of the case can be used. This anchor segment provides the common experience, and thus the shared knowledge, across the learners (and their course instructor) in a preservice class. Instruction of procedures, class discussion, and examples can be easily related to this common experience by the course instructor or the individual students in the course. Thus, when sharing a unique field experience or sharing their own primary-school reading experiences, preservice teachers can inform peers much

Control tabs for navigation to various video areas,
class information, expert and other interviews, etc.

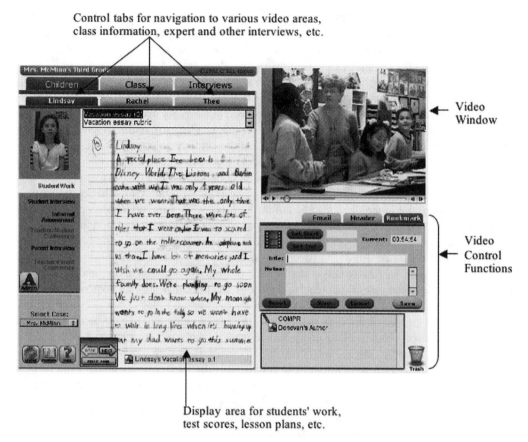

Video
Window

Video
Control
Functions

Display area for students' work,
test scores, lesson plans, etc.

FIGURE 14.2.   Sample screen from a CTELL multimedia case.

more easily, facilitating grounded discussion. Consider, as mentioned previously, the difference between trying to explain how one learned to read to someone who was not in a similar setting as a child. Without a shared experience, one is left to assume that inferences will be made that will be close to what is intended. Conversely, when shared knowledge is available through seeing an anchor, discussion can proceed along the lines of, "Remember when the case teacher had the small group discussion about the story they were reading? Well, in my situation things were the same up to the point where she . . . but then my second-grade classroom was different because . . . " Much richer, grounded, and more meaningful discussion with less miscommunication occurs when shared knowledge is provided through an anchor (Risko, 1995). Thus, CTELL cases require that the video anchor segment be the first contact with a case, so that all participants can reflect on, communicate about, and ultimately springboard beyond the cases in meaningful ways.

Of course, being able to do so implies that *all* participants in a class have seen the case's anchor segment. We therefore advocate that the first class session be devoted to viewing the video anchor segment as a group, with discussion following. Although the anchor can be viewed individually as homework, we have found that the group experience and subsequent discussion are better at building a classroom learning community around the cases and typically lead to more productive follow-up discussions.

The second phase of anchored instruction is that learners become expert enough in the anchor to discuss it, draw examples from it, and use it as a common reference in subsequent discussions throughout the course (or even the remainder of the preservice program). To reach this point requires multiple viewing and activities that involve students in thinking deeply about the structure and content related to literacy curriculum and classroom instruction represented in the anchor. One way to accomplish this deep reflection is what McLarty, Goodman, Risko, Kinzer, Vye, Rowe, and Carson (1990) have called "segmenting the case." The video anchor, by group consensus, is broken into logical sections, and labels for each segment are agreed upon. These labels become reference points to the anchor, allowing discussion to move in the "shorthand" that typically occurs within communicative groups. Segmenting allows learners to say things such as, "Remember the albatross vocabulary scene? Isn't that a counter-example to what we read about in our assigned article for today?" These common reference points, arising from shared knowledge, cannot come from only one viewing; they require focused work to gain expertise with the video anchor's content.

Once these two steps (group viewing of the anchor and analytic reflection activities such as segmenting) occur, the case is primed for exploration and can move in directions determined by the individual learner, by group consensus, or by the course instructor. If the instructor wishes to provide open-ended questions, such as "Come to class prepared to discuss the make-up and needs of the three focal children in the case," then students can explore children's test scores, their writing samples, video interviews, and so on. Or, the instructor can ask a more focused question, such as "Why would the teacher have chosen to work with *that* particular group of three students?" and the preservice teacher could explore the case to explain and critique the teacher's grouping decisions. Another possibility is that in response to the question, "What are the procedural steps that Ms. Kosiba uses in the book discussion scene?" learners could relate what they see her doing in the video with the steps for book discussion outlined in their textbook or other course readings. Students might also, as a class or a small group, be asked to agree on where to start the overall case exploration once the video anchor has been viewed—do they want to begin with some information about parental support and expectations? With children's standardized test scores? With video interviews that provide information from the teacher or children in the class? With demographic information about the school? With other information that teachers use to make instructional decisions? Using projection capabilities, the preservice course instructor can use group consensus procedures to show the agreed-upon beginning point, and discussion and teaching can move on from there. Recall that random access allows movement to any part of the case, so starting points and links across case content can easily occur as students question or bring up additional issues during any discussion. Recall also that the case, delivered over the Internet, allows students to explore it as a homework assignment from their dorm rooms or using any computer with a high-speed Internet connection. Thus, due to the flexible nature of case content, navigational tool use, and communicative functions, an instructor's implementation of the cases may vary widely. A central part of the CTELL project is figuring out how instructors utilize the cases for preservice teacher education.

Lessons Learned from Initial Implementation

Four of the 11 multimedia-based cases that comprise CTELL were implemented by 20 instructors teaching preservice literacy education courses at universities in the states of Connecticut, Georgia, Tennessee, Illinois, Kentucky, and Texas, from July 15, 2002 through December 15, 2002. Instructors initially attended a two-day workshop that presented the cases, provided instructions for using the interface, shared theoretical bases for case-based instructional approaches, and recommended instructional methods for using the cases in an anchored-instruction learning environment. Following the workshop and throughout the time that they used the cases, instructors voluntarily participated in listserv conversations where they posted and shared implementation issues and problems, asked questions, and shared strategies. This additional use of the technological capability of the listserv allowed instructors from varied geographical locations to communicate ideas, ask questions, and support one another. Although initially unforeseen, the positive qualities of the listserv were invaluable in learning to implement these multimedia cases.

During this implementation period, 230 unique messages were posted to this listserv. These messages were captured and inserted into the NUD*IST qualitative data analysis program, where each message was read and coded into categories related to the use of the multimedia cases. Standard qualitative analysis techniques were followed by coding each line according to emerging categories upon initial reading that were then refined on a subsequent pass. Analysis of the coded categories resulted in patterns of messages that are informative with regard to CTELL implementation in these classrooms, and serve to provide information that we believe other users of Internet-based multimedia cases will find valuable, as well as other users of technology more generally. Each of these patterns is discussed below in terms of lessons that we learned as a result of the listserv message analysis.

Lesson 1: The cases, especially the video within the cases, provided "value added" to the courses in which they were used. It was clear that instructors felt that the cases provided their students with beneficial, contextualized experiences that were unavailable to them in the past. Instructors frequently mentioned how students related the video in the cases to field experiences, and how this sharpened and made resulting class discussions more meaningful. Instructors also noted that random access capabilities for exploring multiple cases provided unique occasions for preservice teachers to make connections between theory and practice. The following quotations, taken from the listserv dataset, are indicative of this pattern in the data:

- "I felt the video gave me [and my students] true insight of how a class is actually conducted. . . . I liked how the video showed us how Mrs. Gordon conducted her classroom routine, and how others can make an example from her teaching. . . . I felt that I was observing the classroom directly. With a click of the button we can meet parents and students and listen to their conversation. These videos are going to be a great way to observe different classrooms and get insight on some efficient ways on helping students learn." (LD, 9/16/02)

- "I have been delighted with the way the CTELL cases have worked with my classes. . . . The second time we used the cases was after lots of reading theory work. I had just done a simulation on voice-to-print matching. . . . We actually deconstructed the video and it was fabulous. . . . it deepened their understanding of exactly what the teacher does to reinforce the speech-to-print match concretely in the classroom. . . . All of this was related to theory. My students really got it! . . . Students concretely understood what went on and why it went on. Theory and practice understanding is leading their development. . . . CTELL cases allow my students to understand the theory to practice relationships in such concrete ways. I think because of this understanding, they will readily enact these literacy events in their own classrooms with a better understanding of not only how to do it but more importantly why they are designing a literacy learning event in such a way." (CA, 10/10/02)

- "The students in my reading classes typically create a literacy continuum to examine the development of readers preK–Grade 5. . . . This past week they worked in groups and examined the cases for examples and evidence to add to their continuum—I was really encouraged by the number of instructional strategies and student behaviors they identified and used on their continuums. This is proving to be a very interesting way to connect our course content to the cases. I am finding that the more they revisit the cases from different angles, the more they are seeing—I anticipated this happening, but it is still exciting to see as a teacher." (WM, 11/3/02)

All instructors had positive things to say about the value of the cases for their students' learning. This is most important to keep in mind while considering the lessons learned about points of frustration when dealing with cases delivered over the Internet, as described below.

Lesson 2: When learning to use new technologies, frustrations can result—but frustrations can be dealt with successfully and the integration of new technology can proceed, if certain conditions exist. The listserv dataset indicated that instructors experienced frustration stemming from issues relating to technical support and/or factors related to using the technology or interface. The largest pattern of responses dealing with instructor frustration spoke to the need for technical support and university infrastructure that facilitates faculty if they wish to work with the new technologies required for the integration of web-based delivery of video. Most video that is delivered over the Internet requires the use of a broadband connection for each computer. Modems are simply too slow to allow adequately-sized video to be sent and received over the Internet. Computers also must have enough memory to buffer the video stream that is being downloaded, as well as the appropriate web browsers and application software that are required to play the video (for CTELL cases, this means that QuickTime and Shockwave, available at no cost, must be loaded on users' computers).

To address anticipated computer configuration and software requirements, before classes began instructors contacted their respective computer lab managers and technical support staff with specifications of their needs. Instructors provided lead time to lab managers and other technical support personnel to ensure, for example, that computers would have the appropriate web browsers and that QuickTime and Shockwave would be loaded on classroom presentation and laboratory computers. Several instructors also requested items such as headphones for each computer in a laboratory setting (e.g., "We are getting headphones for our lab since when students play the CTELL cases there a cacophony of sound erupts." (LD, 8/30/02)). Without headphones, a class of students who watch different parts of a case have difficulty hearing the audio accompanying the scene that they are watching. However, instructors who request that computers be appropriately configured or that resources such as headphones be ready for use when they enter a classroom to teach become quickly frustrated when this is not the case, as shown in the representative comments below:

- "... [there are] problems with our lab that we are working on. Finally got ten computers in the lab working ... WHAT A HEADACHE!" (RJ, 9/26/02)
- "... We have had a problem with not having enough computers and not having splitters on the headphones. Our tech. staff tells me that they can't or won't put splitters on them. Is it that difficult?" (CB, 10/9/02)

Technical support is required periodically as instructors encounter difficulties with computers or server issues in their classrooms, as well as issues related to the ability to project the video and audio from an instructors' station. A clear pattern of messages in our dataset indicated instructors' frustration with what they viewed as non-responsiveness on the part of technical support staff. Although the level of responsiveness may well be an issue of misunderstanding or miscommunication, the frustration exhibited is real. It may stem from levels of user sophistication (that is, technical staff who are well versed in computers might think a problem is trivial, while an instructor may think a problem is overwhelming), but when instructors think that their students are being disadvantaged because equipment does not work or problems are not addressed, they become vocal about these issues very quickly. The message that follows is indicative of a substantial number of messages in our database that showed frustration with what was viewed as non-responsiveness by support staff:

- "I have typically had to deal with [technical and lab issues] by myself since the technology is dropped off & there's no one around to troubleshoot immediately when the need arises. This has been the case for the past six weeks or more. I have tried accessing the videos from a computer lab that was (theoretically) configured with Shockwave and QuickTime and I have tried accessing the videos from my classroom. Both efforts proved to be fruitless and draining of my energy since I have tried to troubleshoot the technical problems personally. The typical response from tech support is that it's working from their work station . . . implying that the problem is with me or the computer I am using. I think tech support works on the principle that if the faculty member goes away, so does the problem! When asked about the problems with the server, the ready response is that it's fixed as of 'this morning.' Temporary bandages fall off and the problem still exists. I have stopped nagging but the problem is still there. . . . The class as a whole has not used them [the video cases] since we can't access them. I can show you every class agenda where the videos were part of the structure of the class and document each time that I was unable to access the videos! I have tried to use the same set of clips for THREE weeks without success. I have attached the class agendas to show the dates that we planned to use the videos but were unable to do so because of the technical problems. . . . The [university] technical staff are being sent this message & I'd ask that they be contacted directly since I am spent!" (RC, 11/3/02)

In addition to technical support, instructors also discussed university policies that they felt hindered their implementation of the multimedia cases into their teaching. For example, use of web-delivered video requires that instructors preview the video and bookmark segments for later class use or to choose appropriate readings and other experiences to parallel what is shown. Often, this preparation requires reviewing the cases at home prior to class. Some instructors felt that universities should provide some support for this professional activity, as shown in the following representative message, which discusses the need for support of off-campus activities as well as on-campus technical support:

- ". . . I was not able to convince my college to provide me with a portable computer that would allow me to work at home, so I finally had to bite the bullet and buy a new one myself. . . . [when classes started] I had no computer to use at home, the projector that I had in our 'smart room' didn't work, and I was so frustrated that I could hardly deal with it anymore. . . ." (GJ, 9/29/02)

Finally, unanticipated needs for ongoing support surfaced, even when computers were working properly and the case materials were being appropriately used. One instructor noted unforeseen problems that resulted because, throughout any given day, multiple users populated a computer laboratory. As seen in the following quotation, this multiple-user environment resulted in unexpected changes to computer configurations. The message also points out that unexpected delays in ordering needed supplies or equipment cause difficulties:

- "... problems have occurred in the changes students from other classes have made to computers [in the lab] before my students come in to work!!! For example, computers that were checked and readied earlier in the day, have had the audio cables pulled out or muted, confusing my students and taking time for the techie guys to figure out.... The computer lab does not yet have headphones or junction boxes for all the students, so it is noisy and distracting as they all work at the same time. (Some students like noise as they work.... others do not.....). The headphones have been ordered, as have the junction boxes, but they have not arrived yet ... maybe soon!!!!!! In short, it's all working, but it isn't always calm or exactly smooth...." (FF, 10/6/02)

The need for computers in instructors' classrooms to be properly configured is something that technical support staff and university administrators must confront directly and with sensitivity. Instructors who are making a shift from modes of teaching that have felt comfortable and successful for years are likely to give up on moving to video and technology integration if this process becomes unwieldy or too difficult. Yet, even when technical support is helpful and when all equipment issues are moot, frustration can result due to users' unfamiliarity with required computer software or the technology used to implement web-delivered multimedia. For example, instructors at times planned activities and then were unable to complete tasks (such as assigning student passwords) because of unfamiliarity with the software interface, an application program or how to project the multimedia for students' viewing. These "user errors" were also a clear pattern in our dataset, as reflected in comments such as,

- "I feel incredibly stupid; I just realized I had left out one of the underscores [when trying to assign passwords] ... yes, I had spent an entire week making the same error over and over again! I'm sorry!! I just managed to get online!!" (GJ, 9/29/02)

Additional comments in this category showed that instructors made errors in accessing the software or in requesting technical support with enough lead time for classroom implementation to occur.

Although this category of messages could be designated as representing user errors, such difficulties are real and might cause less motivated instructors to give up as they transition to integrating web-based multimedia in their courses. None of the CTELL instructors did so, but we feel that has much to do with support structures that were provided through the CTELL listserv and by CTELL project staff, in addition to support that was available to instructors through instructors' respective universities.

Lesson 3: The multimedia cases provided a motivational aspect for instructors, even when frustrations surfaced.   There seemed to be a motivational aspect to using the multimedia cases, resulting in instructors' persevering in the face of the frustrations noted above. There were frequent messages on the listserv indicating that, once technical problems were solved, things righted themselves quickly. For example, GJ's message of frustration with having to purchase a new laptop for home use and being "so frustrated I could hardly deal with it" in terms of not having a working projector in her classroom continued with the following comment:

- "... now that I have a working computer at home, I think things will be better. Two weeks ago they finally replaced the projector in the smart room so that we can now at least see the image on the screen when I use the cases. Until this time, the video would flip like an old filmstrip; it was like watching under strobe lights. Well, anyway, today I spent the morning setting my first bookmarks (hurray!) and I'm very excited again. . . ." (GJ, 10/20/02)

In looking at this category of responses, it seems that student feedback and the enhanced results seen in class discussions and contextualized teaching can quickly dissipate frustration, once problems are solved. Thus, it is important that technical support personnel continue to problem solve, continue to keep in close contact with instructors as solutions are determined and implemented, and continue to respond to issues as quickly as possible throughout a semester. Instructors who feel that problems are being addressed rather than ignored seem to persevere in using these new technologies in their courses. And, once problems are solved, instructors quickly go on to teaching and to implementing effective instruction.

Lesson 4: A listserv or other method of sharing problems, solutions, and ideas fosters a sense of community, decreases isolation, and mitigates "giving up" on integrating multimedia cases into existing courses. Critically important to the implementation of the multimedia cases was the provision of a listserv for instructors. This listserv became an area where participants could share their ideas, their victories, their frustrations and their solutions to problems. As we analyzed the listserv postings, it became clear that a sense of community developed among the instructors. They used the listserv to post problems and ask for solutions, but they also posted messages about co-authoring papers or presenting their use of the multimedia cases at professional conferences. The listserv decreased the sense of isolation for instructors, who realized that difficulties they might be experiencing with this new mode of instruction were common within the community, and that solutions and benefits were available to them. For example, after one instructor posted that her technical support staff had solved a problem with the laboratory computers, the following message appeared:

- "Is there any way you or one of the techs can tell us . . . how it was solved? It will add to our collective experience and may help others. Glad it worked for you" (HM, 9/29/02).

Similar exchanges occurred for specific requests for information, as in the following quotations:

- "I was able to access all the parts of cases 3, 5, and 7, but I still cannot get to the administrative portion of case 1 . . . Obviously, my computer has the capabilities to handle the cases because the others work. What do you recommend that I do?" (FF, 9/3/02)
- "My students and I are having trouble viewing bookmarks. We are clicking on the bookmark we want to view and then clicking on 'view.' Am I forgetting something?" (CB, 9/12/02)
- [Response to CB's question, above:] ". . . you can either check with your technical person or see the section in the 'CTELL Case Interface Manual' under 'Information on upgrading your browser's plugins.' If you need more information, you can call me or e-mail me." (CC, 9/21/02)
- "This is very helpful information, V. I am guessing, since the cases stopped playing after a few seconds, that your connection speeds at home are too slow for the online cases. Do you have broadband (high-speed Internet)? If so, what is the rate of your connection? . . . One strategy you could try is to use an identical machine at your university (with the appropriate shockwave and Quicktime plugins) to see if the Internet connection speed is the problem. . . ." (LD, 9/25/02)

- "I am having the exact same problem as V. I am trying to access the cases from a high-speed Internet connection using Explorer 5 with Macs. All of our machines have the newest Shockwave. I am caught in this same loop. I download the newest Shockwave and it puts me in the same loop and I get the exact same message as V. I have the same problem with all of the cases. [would like suggestions] Thanks." (CA, 9/27/02)

The requests for problem solutions and the willingness of participants to share strategies resulted in a sense of community and seemed to keep instructors going, mitigating a desire to "give up" when things did not go well. The sharing of information, however, went beyond the sharing of problems to professional discussions of teaching strategies. Thus, the professional conversation through the listserv supported instructors in integrating computer technologies into reading methods courses in ways that were supportive of existing instructional strategies, transactive with established instructional strategies, or entirely transformative.

Borko & Putnam (1996) explain that when curricular techniques are new, instructors initially use the innovation in ways that support their existing knowledge, beliefs, and practices. Transactions with established instructional practices occur as instructors begin to envision new purposes for the technology. In other words, subtle changes to established instructional strategies occur as instructors go through the process of interacting with the new technologies. Thus, as some instructors began to interact with the CTELL interface, their use of various case content, navigational tools, and support from the professional listserv began to subtly shift the nature of classroom discussion and student assignments. Transformation occurs when technology is a positive stimulus for organizational and pedagogical changes in conventional instruction (Labbo & Reinking, 1999). The sharing of ideas, the sense of camaraderie, and the sense of community that developed over the listserv is clearly seen in the following representative quotations:

- "Could you tell me more how you set up the class? Did you give them discussion prompts before you had them work with the various parts of the cases or did you simply say view these segments and talk about them in terms of comprehension? Did you talk about what to look for in terms of comprehension before splitting them up into teams? I am interested in doing something like this. The three short lesson segments you referred to—are these segments from the anchor [or] someone else? I would appreciate any input you can give me on how to set up the class for this activity. Thank you." (CB, 11/5/02)
- [Response to CB's question, above:] "CB, I will e-mail my instruction sheet from my computer at home. We had been talking about comprehension and who sets the curriculum for the last two weeks. They had already read the textbook chapter on comprehension. I think that much more can be absorbed from the anchors and other parts AFTER there has been discussion and reading. If nothing else, they are able to name behaviors that they see. . . ." (BB, 11/7/02)
- "My plan for Friday is just to allow exploration with the McCollum case individually. They have just gone out to begin their field experience with Writers' Workshop. I am anxious to see if they will begin to view the cases in a different light. Let you know." (CB, 11/19/02)
- "I just had to share what many of the students are doing with the videos. They meet after class and use the projection device and instructor's computer to watch the CTELL videos. It looks like they are watching a movie—lunch, snacks, sodas, 'happy faces'. . . . I observed a lot of interaction; e.g., instructional conversations, evaluations of strategies viewed, comparisons of case studies (textbook, CTELL, and the teacher candidate authentic case study), and much more. It's a good CTELL day!" (MS, 10/29/02)

The sense of community and the sharing of ideas through the provision of the listserv cannot be overemphasized in its importance in keeping instructors involved in case use. The listserv allowed instructors to deal with the frustrations that occurred because of technical support issues, because of instructors' lack of computer knowledge, or because of difficulties with the interface. Without the listserv, we feel that frustrations could well have caused instructors to give up on case/video implementation. However, being able to see that others had similar issues and were able to deal with them, and having the ability to ask a question or ask for help and quickly receive one or more responses appeared to make problems seem manageable, facilitating instructors' willingness to continue integrating the multimedia cases into their courses even when difficulties arose. In addition, the level of professional discussion about multimedia use in classes also contributed to a sense of working in an important professional area. Instructors grew and learned from each other as they implemented the video and other case material into their classes using an anchored-instruction, case-based approach.

The ideas for teaching that came out of using the multimedia cases, together with access to the listserv, resulted in ever-expanding notions of how the cases might be effectively used. The following exchange is indicative of communication within the group that showed a pattern of an idea being shared, then taken up and extended by another participant who shared the extension possibility with the community on the listserv:

- ". . . when students do have access to the videos, the results are quite exciting. You're invited to visit one student's electronic portfolio at [address removed for confidentiality purposes] to examine how she addresses the videos in her reflections." (RC, 11/4/02)
- [Response to RC:] "I LOVE your student's electronic portfolio. It is a wonderful archive of their thinking! I am excited about trying a similar format perhaps in place of a discussion board. They could add revisions of their thinking across our course sequence." (KC, 11/4/02)

SUMMARY AND CONCLUSION

The goal of this chapter was to provide those who are interested in designing and using technology in preservice literacy education with information on creating the kind of preservice education that Borko and Putnam (1996) and others advocate. This was done from the perspective of the CTELL project, a large-scale effort that has created 11 multimedia cases, delivered over the Internet, and is examining the implementation of those cases in 20 universities across six states, as well as using other supplemental technologies such as listservs as support.

To summarize, designing any technology for instructional purposes requires a clearly articulated theoretical framework with regard to pedagogy and content, as well as the technological knowledge and capabilities. As implemented in the multimedia cases described previously, specifying a framework guides filming and editing decisions as well as decisions around the development of an interface, making it more likely that the finished product will encompass desired content and facilitate desired pedagogy. Without a clearly articulated framework and "shooting list" of instructional content and principles for later instructional use, video becomes simply a serendipitously-filmed event. Without that same framework, the interface is nothing more than a holding tank where all the information of a case can be found. This theoretical frame shaped every decision related to the development and implementation of these cases in preservice literacy classrooms.

With regard to implementation, we noted that issues related to technical support and university infrastructure are necessary factors in helping instructors use multimedia technologies, delivered over the Internet, in their courses. In addition, providing a sense of community through a listserv mitigates feelings of isolation, helps solve problems, and provides instructors with a way to share ideas and implementation strategies.

Finally, the teaching implementation ideas and comments posted by the instructors using CTELL multimedia cases show that using random-access video together with additional artifacts within a case-based approach can help meet many of the criteria noted by Borko and Putnam (1996), and discussed in the introduction to this chapter. Using the cases as a foundation, instructors were able to address preservice teachers' existing knowledge as related to a video anchor that was available to all class participants. The cases, through the random access ability provided as a function of the web-based delivery system, allowed revisiting elements within the cases and thus enabled sustained opportunities for learning. Using an anchored-instruction, case-based approach facilitated instructors' ability to provide opportunities for thinking, critical analysis, reflection, and comparison of one's views to more expert "others." The multimedia cases of classroom practice allowed instructors to refer to instruction in a contextualized, grounded manner and the availability of a portfolio function and presentation capability allowed students to share their knowledge with their peers.

Of course, other valuable efforts also are underway to merge new technologies with case-based instruction and to use multimedia in preservice education. For example, Reading Classroom Explorer (Hughes, Packard, & Pearson, 2000; http://www.eliteracy.org/rce/; accessed 2/3/03) provides students the opportunity to explore classroom environments, reflect on the teaching of others, and provides "real world portraits of literacy teaching and learning." Baker (2000) has created multimedia cases and portfolios for preservice teachers, and an increasing amount of instructional video for preservice and in-service teachers is becoming available on the Internet (see, for example, the California Learning Interchange, http://www.gse.uci.edu/cli/vcliteracyprekunit01.html, which includes video of parents, teachers, and small-group instruction along with commentary; accessed 2/3/03). These and other projects show the interest and direction that many are taking to meet the goals of preservice education through the use of multimedia—goals that have been historically difficult to accomplish in traditional instructional formats.

We believe that technologies such as multimedia representations of cases, Internet-based communication forms such as listservs, discussion boards, Wikis, and others hold great potential for restructuring preservice literacy education in ways that are more consistent with learning theory and educational beliefs about effective ways to teach and learn. To return once more to the points outlined by Borko and Putnam (1996), these kinds of technologies create opportunities for students to interact around shared experiences such as multimedia cases through random-access video and classroom artifacts. These interactions can be facilitated through face-to-face classes or through other means of communication such as classroom discussion boards, e-mail lists, or instant chat capabilities that provide students with additional, supported opportunities to analyze classroom practices and deepen their own understanding while addressing their existing knowledge and beliefs. Many of these technologies, like the CTELL case interface, can be used to teach preservice teachers in a manner that is consistent with the ways these teachers will teach their students; rather than presenting preservice literacy educators with a scripted curriculum, technological resources can be implemented in a constructivist manner similar to the methods taught within the course. This symbiosis between content and pedagogy then can extend beyond the classroom through these communication technologies available online. Through the implementation and use of technologies in preservice literacy classrooms, preservice education is moving ever closer to the ideal—a better way of educating literacy teachers and, by extension, their future students.

REFERENCES

Alvermann, D. E. (1990). Reading teacher education. In W. R. Houston, M. Haberman, & J. Sikula (Eds.), *Handbook of research on teacher education* (pp. 687–704). New York: Macmillan.

Baker, E. A. (2000). Case-based learning theory: Implications for software design. *Journal of Technology and Teacher Education, 8*(2), 85–95.

Borko, H., & Putnam, R. (1996). Learning to teach. In D. C. Berliner & R. C. Calfee (Eds.), *Handbook of educational psychology* (pp. 673–708). New York: Macmillan.

Bowers, J., G. Kenehan, et al. (2000). Designing Multimedia Case Studies for Preservice Teachers: Pedagogical Questions and Technological Design Solutions: 6.

Bransford, J. D., Brown, A. L., & Cocking, R. R. (1999). *How people learn: Brain, mind, experience, and school: Expanded edition.* Washington, DC: National Academy Press.

Brown, J. S., Collins, A., & Duguid, P. (1989). Situated cognition and the culture of learning. *Educational Researcher, 18*, 32–41.

Catalyst Web (2004). Virtual Case. Accessed March 7, 2004 from *http://catalyst.washington.edu/catalyst/tools/vcase.html* Seattle, EA: University of Washington.

CTGV (The Cognition and Technology Group at Vanderbilt). (1997). *The Jasper project: lessons in curriculum, instruction, assessment, and professional development.* Mahwah, NJ: Lawrence Erlbaum Associates.

CTGV (Cognition and Technology Group at Vanderbilt). (1990). Anchored instruction and its relationship to situated cognition. *Educational Researcher, 19*, 2–10.

Feiman-Nemser, S., & Remillard, J. (1996). Perspectives on learning to teach. In F. B. Murray (Ed.), *The teacher educators' handbook: Building a knowledge base for the preparation of teachers* (pp. 63–91). San Francisco: Jossey-Bass.

Ferdig, R. E., Roehler, L. R., & Pearson, P. D. (2002). *Building electronic discussion forums to scaffold preservice teacher learning: Online conversations in the Reading Classroom Explorer.* Ann Arbor, MI: Center for the Improvement of Early Reading Achievement, Technical Report No. 3-021.

Greenwood, G. E. (1996). Using the case method to translate theory into practice. *The Case for Education: Contemporary Approaches for Using Case Methods.* J. A. Colbert, K. Trumble, and P. Desberg (Eds.). Boston, MA: Allyn and Bacon: 57–78.

Griffin, G. A. (1989). A descriptive study of student teaching. *Elementary School Journal, 89*, 343–364.

Hughes, J. E., Packard, B. W., & Pearson, P. D. (2000). Preservice teachers' perceptions of using hypermedia and video to examine the nature of literacy instruction. *Journal of Literacy Research, 32*(4), 599–629.

Hughes, J. E., B. W. L. Packard, et al. (2000). The Role of Hypermedia Cases on Preservice Teachers' Views of Reading Instruction. *Action in Teacher Education, 22*(2a): 24–38

International Reading Association (2001). Preparing Students for Their Literacy Future: A Position Statement on Literacy and Technology. Newark, DE: IRA.

Kamil, M. L., Kim, H., & Intrator, S. (2000). Effects of other technologies on literacy and literacy learning. In M. L. Kamil, P. B. Mosenthal, P. D. Pearson, R. Barr (Eds.), *Handbook of reading research* (Vol. 3, pp. 773–791). Mahwah, NJ: Lawrence Erlbaum Associates.

Kinzer, C. K., & Leander, K. (2003). Technology and the language arts: Implications of an expanded definition of literacy. In J. Flood, D. Lapp, J. R. Squire, & J. M. Jensen (Eds.), *Handbook of research and teaching the English language arts* (pp. 546–566). Mahwah, NJ: Lawrence Erlbaum Associates.

Kinzer, C. K., & Risko, V. J. (1998). Multimedia and Enhanced Learning: Transforming Preservice Education. In D. Reinking, M. McKenna, L. Labbo, & R. Kieffer (Eds.), *Handbook of technology and literacy: Transformations in a post-typographic world* (pp. 185–202). Hillsdale, NJ: Lawrence Erlbaum Associates.

Leu, D. (2000). Literacy and technology: Deictic consequences for literacy education in an information age. In M. Kamil, P. Mosenthal, & P. D. Pearson (Eds.), *Handbook of reading research III* (pp. 743–770. Mahwah, NJ: Lawrence Erlbaum Associates.

Lundenberg, M. A. (1999). Discovering teaching and learning through cases. In M. A. Lundeberg, B. B. Levin, & H. L. Harrington (Eds.), *Who learns what from cases and how?* (pp. 3–23). Mahwah, NJ: Lawrence Erlbaum Associates.

Merseth, K. (1991). *The case for cases in teacher education.* Washington, DC: American Association of Colleges of Teacher Education and American Association of Higher Education.

Merseth, K. K. (1994). Cases, case methods, and the professional development of educators. ERIC Digest, ERIC Clearinghouse on Teaching and Teacher Education, Washington, DC: 4.

McLarty, K., Goodman, J., Risko, V. J., Kinzer, C. K., Vye, N., Rowe, D. W., & Carson, J. (1990). Implementing anchored instruction: Guiding principles for curriculum development. In J. Zutell & S. McCormick (Eds.), *Literacy theory and research: Analysis from multiple perspectives* (39th NRC Yearbook, pp. 109–120). Chicago: National Reading Conference.

Munby, H., Russell, T., & Martin, A. K. (2001). Teachers' knowledge and how it develops. In V. Richardson (Ed.), *Handbook of research on teaching* (4th ed.). Washington, DC: American Education Research Association.

NRP Report www.nichd.nih.gov/publications/nrp/report.htm

Sikula, J. P. (Ed.), Buttery, T. J., & Guyton, E. (1996). *Handbook of research on teacher education.* New York: Macmillan.

Snow, C. E., Burns, M. S., & Griffin, P. (Eds.). (1998). *Preventing reading difficulties in young children.* Washington, DC: National Academy Press.

Richardson, V. (Ed.). (2001). *Handbook of research on teaching* (4th ed.). Washington, DC: American Educational Research Association.

Richardson, V., & Placier, P. (2001). Teachers change. In V. Richardson (Ed.), *Handbook of research on teaching* (4th ed., pp. 905–947). Washington, DC: American Educational Research Association.

Risko, V. J. (1995). Using videodisc-based cases to promote preservice teachers' problem solving and mental model building. In W. M. Linek & E. G. Sturtevant (Eds.), *Generations of literacy* (pp. 173–187). Pittsburgh, KS: College Reading Association.

Roskos, K., Vukelich, C., & Risko,. V. J. (2002). Reflection and learning to teach reading: A critical review of literacy and general teacher education studies. *Journal of Literacy Research, 33*(4), 595–636.

Schulman, L. S. (1992). Toward a pedagogy of cases. In J. H. Shulman (Ed.), *Case methods in teacher education* (pp. 1–30). New York: Teachers College Press.

Silverman, R., & Welty, W. M. (1995). Teaching without a net: Using cases in teacher education. In J. A. Colbert, P. Dresberg, & K. Trimble (Eds.), *The case of education* (pp. 159–171). Boston: Allyn & Bacon.

Sykes, G. and T. Bird (1992). Teacher education and the case idea. *Review of Research in Education.* G. Grant. Washington, DC, American Educational Research Association. 18.

Teale, W. H., Leu, D. J., Labbo, L. D., & Kinzer, C. (2002). The CTELL project: New ways technology can help educate tomorrow's reading teachers. *The Reading Teacher, 55*(7), 654–659.

Teale, W. H. (August, 2002). *A synthesis of principles and practices of effective early literacy instruction: The results of research reviews, a national survey, and interviews with teachers who use technology for literacy instruction in outstanding ways.* World Congress of the International Reading Association. Edinburgh, Scotland.

Williams, S. M. (1992). Putting case-based instruction into context: Examples from legal and medical education. *The Journal of the Learning Sciences, 2,* 387–407.

APPENDIX A
Foundational Principles of Effective Reading Instruction Embedded
in CTELL Cases (Teale, et al., 2002).

1. Teacher knowledge, insight, and orchestration of instruction
   The teacher's knowledge, ability to make principled, insightful, instructional decisions for individual children, and the ability to orchestrate effective instruction for the group of children being taught are more influential factors in student literacy achievement than knowing particular procedures for instruction or following scripted lesson plans.

2. Language, culture, home background, and literacy instruction
   Providing school reading instruction that builds on young children's language, culture, and home background enhances their chances for success in learning to read and write.

3. Emergent literacy foundations
   Basic early literacy concepts, skills, and positive attitudes that form the foundation for subsequent reading and writing achievement are developed by immersing young children in literacy-rich classrooms.

4. Phonemic awareness instruction
   Instructional activities that develop children's phonemic awareness increase reading achievement, when individual children have not acquired this important knowledge.

5. Decoding Instruction
   Instruction in the sound-symbol correspondences of language (often called phonics instruction) is positively related to student achievement in reading.

6. Comprehension instruction
   Instructional activities that develop children's abilities and strategies for comprehending written language enhance reading achievement.

7. Independent reading
   The more young children read a variety of texts that interest them, the more likely they are to achieve well in reading.

8. Fluency instruction
   Fostering the development of reading fluency through appropriate instructional activities and extensive opportunities to read fluently is associated with higher reading achievement.

9. Integrating writing and reading
   Providing writing instruction linked to reading instruction enhances achievement in reading as well as in writing.

10. Technology and early literacy development
    Integrating computer and Internet technologies into literacy instruction in the early grades of school provides the foundation for continued learning of both conventional and digital literacies as children proceed through school.

11. Early assessment and instructional intervention
    Monitoring children's early literacy development through ongoing classroom assessment and providing instruction based on the diagnostic information obtained, including appropriate instructional intervention to children who fall significantly behind, enhances the chances that children will achieve satisfactorily in reading and writing.

12. Enthusiasm for reading and writing

   Teaching in ways that foster young children's enthusiasm for and engagement with reading and writing enhances the likelihood that they will learn to read and write successfully and become lifelong readers and writers.

ACKNOWLEDGEMENTS

1. Readers are referred to Kinzer and Risko (1998), which the authors wish to acknowledge as a precursor to the current work.
2. This material is based on work supported by the National Science Foundation under Grant No. 0089221. Any opinions, findings, and conclusions or recommendations expressed are those of the authors and do not necessarily reflect the views of the National Science Foundation.

Video- and Database-Driven Web Environments for Preservice Literacy Teaching and Learning

Richard E. Ferdig
University of Florida

Laura R. Roehler
Michigan State University

P. David Pearson
University of California–Berkeley

In this chapter, we will summarize and highlight our work with the Reading Classroom Explorer (RCE). RCE is a video- and database-driven Web environment used to help preservice teachers explore exemplary literacy instruction. Over the course of the past five years, we have developed and implemented RCE in multiple states with literally hundreds of teacher candidates. We will highlight five years of research, with the hope of providing readers critical insight into the development, implementation, and research of an electronic learning environment for literacy teacher education. We hope readers will gain a complete understanding of Reading Classroom Explorer's theoretical rationale, operational principles, and empirical effectiveness from this chapter.

A major difficulty facing preservice literacy instructors is the ability to provide teacher candidates with field experiences in classrooms aligned with the pedagogical and theoretical foci of university preparation programs (Ferdig, Roehler, & Pearson, 2002). Some teacher candidates quickly sense this and report frustration with the tension they see between field experiences and the reform-oriented instructional techniques from their methodology classes (Hughes, Packard, & Pearson, 1998a). They also express concern about the conventional pedagogy of their methods classes that is "limited to articles, books and lectures about methods of teaching reading and writing" (Ferdig, Hughes, Packard, & Pearson, 1998, p. 30).

Even when the field experiences are strong, teacher candidates do not necessarily possess the tools to transform observations and practice into instances of deep reflection and ways of acting (see Dunkin, Precians, & Nettle, 1993; Feiman-Nemser & Buchman, 1986; Goodman & Fish, 1997). Moreover, granting access to strong apprenticeships does not guarantee meaningful experiences (Kinzer & Risko, 1998), access to diverse approaches to language and literacy instruction, or an introduction to diverse student perspectives (intellectually, ethnically, or culturally). Some teacher candidates face the danger of being in a field experience that will not prepare them for the pedagogical or student diversity they will experience in their teaching positions; others face the danger of not being prepared to take advantage of being in a model apprenticeship.

These concerns led us to develop a video- and database-driven, Web learning environment, the Reading Classroom Explorer (RCE).[1] RCE was designed to provide multiple opportunities for teacher candidates to develop rich understandings about teaching and learning in classrooms where diversity of pedagogical approaches and diversity of student populations are evident. In this chapter, we describe RCE and its theoretical underpinnings. We highlight findings from five years of data collection on the implementation, use, and evaluation of teacher candidates using RCE. We then conclude with lessons learned regarding the development and implementation of a video- and database-driven, Web-based learning environment.

THE THEORETICAL UNDERPINNINGS BEHIND RCE

RCE is based upon four important theoretical underpinnings: the nature of learning in ill-structured domains, the importance of cases in complex learning, collaboration in apparently individual learning contexts, and component architecture.

First, teaching, and thus helping teacher candidates learn to teach, is a complex and ill-structured domain (Spiro, Coulson, Feltovich, & Anderson, 1988). Research has suggested that hypermedia can be an effective tool in providing access, exploration, and ease of navigation in these complex domains (Hughes, Packard, & Pearson, 1998b). The notion of navigating these complex domains is described in greater detail in a chapter by Spiro in this same volume.

Second, learning in complex domains such as teacher education is often best achieved with case-based instruction (Shulman, 1992; Doyle, 1990; Ferdig et al., 2002). Hypermedia environments provide one way of responding to this call for vivid, explicit cases of exemplary practice (Bransford, Kinzer, Risko, Rowe, & Vye, 1989; Kinzer & Risko, 1998). It is possible to deliver cases that portray exemplary literacy instruction without using multimedia. However, research indicates that students who work in multimedia environments generate higher-level questions than students in classes without multimedia (Risko, Yount, & McAllister, 1992). Research also suggests that "students in these [multimedia] classes refer to the cases to guide their teaching in practicum settings" (Kinzer & Risko, 1998, p. 199; also see Risko, 1995; Risko, Peter, & McAllister, 1996). Thus, providing a case-based multimedia environment allows teacher candidates to view and review cases at different times, with different questions, and in different contexts (educationally and professionally). That, in turn, scaffolds their learning while providing tools to support their teaching in internship years.

A third important underpinning of RCE is a recent push to utilize collaboration and social interaction (Kinzer & Risko, 1998). This rise in interest is due, in part, to a pedagogical and theoretical interest in social-cultural views of learning. From this position, talk in interaction (Schegloff, 1991) or dialogue is a tool mediating the advancement of thinking for individuals as well as the development of community through the establishment of accepted discourse, history of experience, and shared purpose (Vygotsky, 1978; Rogoff, 1995; Wertsch, 1991). Vygotsky (1978) theorized that word meaning—or more broadly, the dynamics of meaning making—develops through the social process of language use over time.

Given this perspective, teacher candidates can benefit to a large degree from being able to view and review mental images of teaching. However, they may not be guaranteed access to the

---

[1]RCE is available online at: http://www.eliteracy.org/rce

language, vocabulary, and conversation needed to internalize those models into their own conceptions of teaching and learning. Social interaction online (asynchronous discussion forums or synchronous chat rooms) might be able to provide access to that discourse-based mediation.

A final underpinning relates to notion of *component architecture* (Ferdig, Mishra, & Zhao, 2004). Component architecture means that the system is not created as an entire entity, but rather the sum of many parts. Rather than having a simple system that aims at accomplishing one or two major goals, the engine behind the tool has many features. From a developer's perspective, it means that if one part fails, pedagogically or technically, the overall system can still operate by employing compensatory sub-systems. From an educator's viewpoint, it provides an opportunity to address diversity in learning, taking into account learning styles, prior experience, and individual needs (Jonassen & Grabowski, 1993; Gardner, 1983). Instructors guiding students can choose appropriate activities; self-guided students can tailor their instruction to meet their particular learning interests and needs—or at least their perceptions of their needs, whether accurate or not. Thus, a student who believes herself to be a visual learner can exploit visual features of the learning environment while a student who claims to be a verbal learner can do likewise. At the very least, then, the system offers students the illusion, if not the reality, of meeting their needs. Although the overarching goal of RCE is to improve teacher candidate learning through video-based exemplars, the system (again both technically and functionally) is comprised of smaller scaffolding activities that allow multiple, often verbal, treks through the complex domain (e.g., discussion forums and notepads).

THE READING CLASSROOM EXPLORER

Drawing on this conceptual framework, RCE was developed with many features designed to facilitate student learning. Upon entering the Web site, users have a chance to learn more about the RCE system (including the research behind its use). They can also log in to RCE (see Figure 15.1).

The log-in page is a very important feature of the RCE system. First, it provided us with the opportunity to have multiple and diverse users. Instead of only having the user who watches videos, we also have space for instructors to log in and monitor the progress of their teacher candidates. More importantly, creating a log-in system means that users have access to their personal history within RCE. They can return to the system from any location with Internet access and find their collection of favorite movies. They can find notes that they have taken, or perhaps even publicly shared, on particular clips. They can also find their contributions to discussion forums and papers they have composed online.

In design, at least, the main user of the RCE system is the preservice teacher. RCE was conceptualized as a complement to the texts, lectures, and field experiences that are typically associated with a reading or language arts methods class. In addition to some common navigational features (Frequently Asked Questions—FAQ, getting help, changing preferences), a teacher candidate encounters four major activities: *Select Movie Clips*, *Notes*, *Paper*, and *Discussion Forum*. The core of the RCE system is the video collection of exemplary literacy instruction. There are 10 different schools in the RCE collection, six of which are the original videos from the Center for the Study of Reading at the University of Illinois, Urbana-Champaign. From those 10 schools, there are over 250 smaller video clips that focus on specific teaching methods (See Table 15.1). The "Select Movie Clips" function is a way for students to peruse that database (see Figure 15.2).

There are five main ways for RCE users to search for movie clips. Teacher candidates will search for clips by *school* (i.e, San Antonio, East Lansing, Harlem, etc.) if they want to follow the curriculum of a particular teacher or the diversity of a particular classroom. Candidates can watch

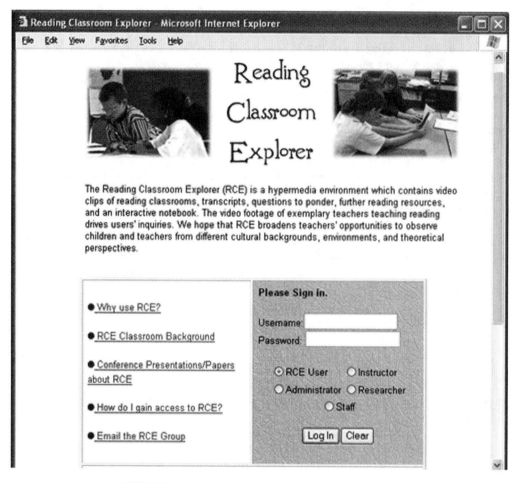

FIGURE 15.1.   Reading classroom explorer log-in page.

the entire video for that school, or they can watch particular clips. Instructors often show the entire video when using RCE in a large group setting. A RCE user can also search by *theme*. We consider themes to be the table of contents at the beginning of a book. There are 27 themes, and they are categorized under Schwab's (1978) notions of *teachers*, *students*, *curriculum*, and *context*. Examples of themes include "Linguistically Diverse Readers and Writers" and "Oral Language Development" (See Table 15.2).

If the themes act as the table of contents in the beginning of the book, the keywords act as the index in the back of the book. Searching by keywords returns fewer hits, but there are over 200 keywords; examples include *word recognition*, *decoding*, and *independent reading*. Each movie clip contains a transcript; students can search by this transcript to find particular terms in the dialogue. The final search method is for RCE users to view clips they have not viewed.

Regardless of the search method, upon selecting a clip, teacher candidates are sent to a page containing that particular clip as well as additional clip-related information to scaffold their learning. From a technological perspective, the RCE engine was built using a database and dynamic Web pages. Thus, although there are over 240 clips, there is actually only one clip view-

TABLE 15.1
Classrooms and movie titles in the Reading Classroom Explorer

**Allen Street School—
33 (Lansing, MI)**

- Assessing Questions
- Colleagues
- Community Resources
- Community Support
- Concept Map & Reading
- Content Area Literacy
- District-wide Books
- Forming Groups
- Group Organization
- Information Sources
- Informational Books
- Journal Share
- Journal Writing
- Knowledge Sources
- Learning Strategies
- Literacy Corner
- Newspaper Field Trip
- Organizing Ideas
- Organizing Information
- Publishing
- Read & Summarize
- Reading Books
- Reading Strategy—KWL
- Report Writing
- School Description and
  Introduction
- Share Journals
- Student Interviews
- Study Topics
- Topic Folders
- Want to Know
- What did I learn
- What do I know

**Bench Mark School—
27 (Media, Pennsylvania)**

- Book Conferences
- Compare & Contrast
- Context Strategy
- Draft Writing
- Integrated Program
- Invented Spelling
- Language Experience
- Making Predictions
- Model Decoding
- Parental Support

- Peer Tutoring
- Personal Reactions
- Positive Attitudes
- Reading Flexibly
- Reading Program Principles
- Reading Skills
- Reading With Parents
- Research to Practice
- School Library
- Small Group Lesson
- Sounds Activity
- Spelling Activity
- The Benchmark Program
- Vowel Variability
- Weekly Words
- Word Games
- Word Wall

**East Park Elem. School—
15 School (Danville, IL)**

- Author Identification
- Background information
- Great Books Club
- Group Reading
- Guided reading
- Independent reading
- Intro to Writing
- Introduction: Creating a
  literate culture
- News Activity
- Reading and Writing in Social
  Studies
- Reading Rules
- School support for literacy
- Semantic Web
- Writing
- Writing Help

**Elliot Elem. School—
28 (Holt, MI)**

- Activating Prior Knowledge
- Assigning the Writing task
- Book club: Overview
- Case Overview
- Compare & Contrast:
  An Overview
- Discussing their questions
- Introducing Assignment

- Introducing book club
- Introduction to unit
- Launching the unit: An
  Overview
- Literature Discussion
- Mini Plays: An Overview
- Picture Book Share
- Posting the questions
- Practicing speeches
- Preassessment activity
- Preparing to practice
- Scaffolding student writing
- Setting the purpose
- Small group discussion
- Small Group Performance
- Small Group Practice
- Small group pre-reading
- Small group reading
- Speech Presentations
- Teacher Modeling
- Writing before discussion
- Writing Their Paragraphs

**Kamehameha Elem. School—
27 (Honolulu, HI)**

- Assessment
- Choosing Stories
- Clarifying Content
- Confirm Predictions
- Connection with Story
- Hawaiian Classroom
- Overlapping Speech
- Picture Prediction
- Prior Knowledge
- Purpose for Reading
- Purpose for Reading II
- Rereading
- Responsive Questions
- Seatwork Assignment
- Seatwork Assignment 2
- Story Choice
- Story Discussion
- Story Interpretation
- Story Prediction
- Story Themes
- Student Connections
- Student Experience
- Teaching Strategy

(*continued*)

TABLE 15.1 (*Continued*)

- Theme Development
- Tie to Experiences
- Use of Charts
- Verifying Content

Mahalia Jackson Elem. School—26 (Harlem, NY)

- Books on Tape
- Choral Reading
- Classroom Organization
- Explaining Spelling
- Good Talk
- Independent Reading
- Large Group Mini Lesson
- Literature for children, Diversity
- Morning Message
- Ms. Martine's Philosophy
- Multi-level teaching, teacher interview
- Parent Involvement I
- Parent Involvement II
- Peer Sharing
- Process Reading and Writing
- Reading Materials, Harlem
- Reading Together
- Story Grammar, Overview
- Story Grammar, Teacher reflection
- Story Grammar, Whole class writing
- Suggesting Literature
- Teacher Sharing
- Teaching Skills
- Thoughts on Planning
- Writing Conference, Damian
- Writing Conference, Monica

National School— 18 (A variety of Locations)

- Assessing (ment?) of Comprehension (Jacob)
- Assessment of Comprehension (Carey)
- Assessment of Phonics (Beatriz)
- Assessment of Phonics (Christopher)

- Assessment of Phonics (Juan)
- Discussing Themes (Schneewind)
- Discussion (Hannah and Matthew)
- Integrated Curriculum (Karson)
- Intertextual Discussion (Allegria)
- Intertextual Discussion (Dillon)
- Personal Experience (Ashanti)
- Prediction (Alyssa)
- Prediction (Fulbrecht)
- Reading Strategies (Rachel)
- Rhyming and Assessment (Kimberly)
- Self-Correction (Daniella)
- Self-Correction (Jasmin)
- Self-Monitoring (Chelsea)

Neal Elem. School— 24 (San Antonio, TX)

- Admin Support—Interview
- Choral Reading Practice
- Class Description
- Creating Morning Message
- Culminating activity
- Description of Writing Development
- Emergent Literacy
- Field Trip
- Free Reading
- Home and School Connection—Int.
- Independent Activities
- Integrating the Language Arts—Int.
- Letter Sounds
- Letters & Words
- Modeling
- Morning Message
- Progression of Reading Skills—Int.
- Reading Friendly Letters
- Story reading
- Story Sharing
- Teacher Reading
- Words

- Writing Lesson
- Writing Mail

Post Oak Elem. School— 29 (Lansing, MI)

- Class Discussion—All Clips
- Class Discussion—Beginning of Lesson
- Class Discussion—Conclusion
- Class Discussion—Considering Equality
- Class Discussion—Discussing Liberty
- Class Discussion—Emotional Freedom
- Class Discussion—Exploring the topic
- Class Discussion—Listening to each other
- Class Discussion—Reading from dictionary
- Class Discussion—Returning to the Text
- Class Discussion—Scaffolding strategies I
- Class Discussion—Scaffolding strategies II
- Class Discussion—Student inquiry
- Overview for Whole Case
- Planning—Cultivating wonder
- Planning—Making connections
- Planning—Students asking questions
- Planning—Students taking ownership
- Planning—Taking risks
- Planning—Teacher and student roles
- Planning—Teacher goal
- Planning—Textual connections
- Planning sessions—All Clips
- Post lesson Conversation— A Dilemma
- Post lesson Conversation— All Clips
- Post lesson Conversation— Conclusion

(*continued*)

TABLE 15.1 (*Continued*)

- Post lesson Conversation—
  Initial thoughts
- Post lesson Conversation—
  Returning to text
- Post lesson Conversation—
  Scaffolding

**Red Cedar Elem. School—
27 (East Lansing, MI)**

- Emergent Writer—Abby
- Emergent Writer—Ilya
- Emergent Writer—Kathy
- Intermediate Writer—Max
- Intermediate Writer—Paige
- Introduction: Emergent
  Writer—Abby
- Overview—1st Grade Writing
  Conferences

- Teacher Interview—
  1st Grade Writing Conferences
- Writing Conference
  (Arthur Books)
- Writing conference
  (Arthur Stories #2 & #3)
- Writing conference
  (Arthur Story #1)
- Writing conference
  (Bluebirds #1 continued)
- Writing conference
  (Bluebirds #1)
- Writing conference (Cat Story)
- Writing conference (Cedar
  Point)
- Writing conference (Daisies,
  Recycling)
- Writing conference
  (Disneyland)

- Writing conference (Easter)
- Writing conference (Green
  Sun, Pot of Gold)
- Writing conference (Kite in
  the House)
- Writing conference
  (Leprechaun)
- Writing conference
  (Leprechaun, Green Sun)
- Writing conference
  (Leprechaun, Green, Spring)
- Writing conference
  (Leprechaun, Writing at Home)
- Writing conference (Play,
  Chicken Pox, Beach)
- Writing conference (Vacation,
  Tulips, Favorite Place)
- Writing conference (Wake up,
  Sun)

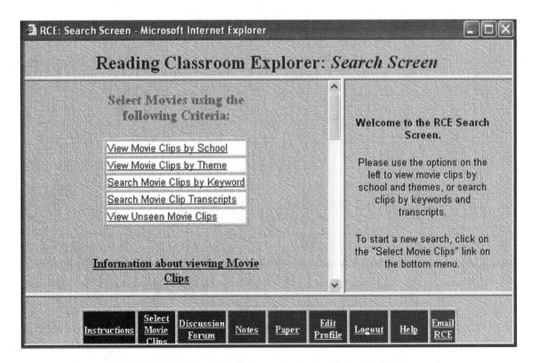

FIGURE 15.2. Reading classroom explorer movie selection page.

TABLE 15.2
Themes of Movies in the Reading Classroom Explorer

Teachers (93)	Students (81)
• Goals and objectives (31) • Management strategies (14) • Organizing instruction (37) • Planning (9) • Professional Development (2)	• Accomplished readers and writers (17) • Assessment (13) • Beginning/emergent readers and writers (32) • Linguistically diverse readers and writers (2) • Roles during Literature Discussions (9) • Special needs readers and writers (8)
Curriculum (229)	**Context (43)**
• Developing attitudes towards reading and writing (10) • Developing strategies and skills for reading and writing (35) • Gaining knowledge through reading and writing (8) • Literature-based instruction (38) • Oral language development (6) • Phonics or skill-based instruction (15) • Play in the classroom (2) • Reading instruction (26) • Reading materials (13) • Reading/writing connection (9) • Valuing real world experience (16) • Writing Conference (4) • Writing instruction (47)	• Administrative and Collegial support (5) • Creating a literate environment (25) • Home/school connection (13)

ing page; that page gets dynamically populated with a different clip each time a user makes a new choice about what clip to view. When the clip changes, so does all of the scaffolding material. The clips and the scaffolding material all reside in a data base. When a given clip is selected, so are all of the bits of scaffolding that go with it. Figure 15.3 is an example of a RCE user who has decided to view a clip on writing conferences.

One of the components built into the RCE engine is a Real Video Streaming Server. When RCE users select a video clip, they only have to wait a few seconds before the clip starts playing, regardless of the length of the clip or movie. Each clip is accompanied by a transcript as it is often difficult to hear voices in movies, particularly when videotaping children. Video segments often consist of teachers and students talking about artifacts (i.e., journals) that they have created. Any artifacts for the movies are included so teacher candidates get a complete picture of the teaching session.

After viewing the clip, RCE users may have thoughts about what they have seen. The Notepad allows them to record reactions to the movie. If they are unsure of what to look for in the movie, questions are provided; these questions are related to the themes that categorize the movie. If a teacher candidate would like more information, they have the opportunity to "View Other's Responses." This button triggers a dynamic search of the database that returns ALL of the responses to this clip that ALL other users have chosen to share publicly. Most, not all, clips are linked to articles in popular journals. Some of the articles are accessible directly through live

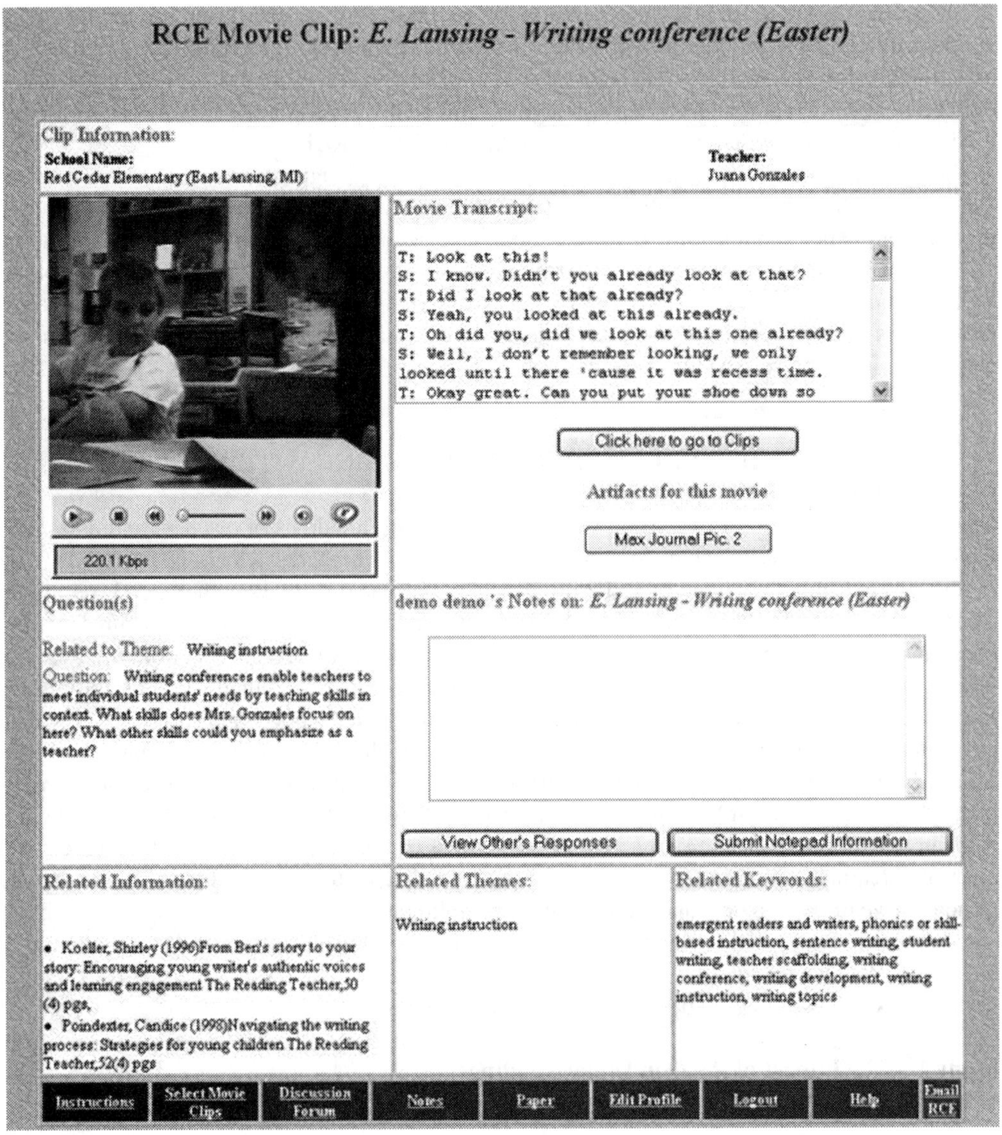

FIGURE 15.3   Reading classroom explorer sample clip page.

links; others require a trip to the library. Finally, if they would like to view more clips related to the theme or keyword associated with a previously viewed movie, they can click on the appropriate word.

At any point in time, teacher candidates can access their notes listed in chronological order according to viewed movies. Teacher candidates also have the opportunity to submit a paper to their instructor. They can use their notes to write their papers; they can also embed links to video clips as evidence to support their claims. Anyone reading that paper can click on a hyperlink to view the video associated with their text.

The final feature of RCE is the discussion forum. There are two discussion forums for every teacher candidate. The first discussion forum is a general forum that is accessible by everyone that uses RCE. This provides for cross-classroom communication and evaluation of videos. The second forum is particular to a given class in a given university. As a side benefit, the forum can be used by an instructor for conversations beyond the purview of RCE.

A second main user of RCE is the preservice reading or language arts methods instructor. Creating an online environment allowed us to create an instructor log-in, where the instructor can read student paper submissions. Instructors can also access the student discussion forums as well as a discussion forum strictly for instructors. They are given access to a database of other RCE instructors in order to facilitate cross-classroom dialogue and assignments. Finally, they have access to an instructor lesson plan database that contains ideas on how other teachers are using RCE in the preservice literacy classroom.

STUDIES ON TEACHING AND LEARNING WITH RCE

Over the course of the past five years, we have worked with hundreds of teacher candidates and their respective preservice instructors in five states (Ferdig, Hughes, Packard, & Pearson, 1998; Ferdig, Love, Boling, & Fang, 2002; Ferdig, Roehler, & Pearson, 2002; Boling, 2003; Ferdig & Roehler, 2003; Ferdig, Roehler, Boling, Knezek, Pearson, & Yadav, 2004). Our main research questions across the entire project have centered around four main areas. First, does the use of a video- and database-driven learning environment impact teacher candidates' understandings of literacy instruction? Second, what are the roles of the tools that support and surround the video environment? In other words, do the supporting tools (i.e., discussion forum, notepad, etc.) significantly impact the ability to teach or learn with RCE? Third, what are the roles of the non-technology factors in implementing a preservice literacy tool? For example, how significant is the instructor or the class environment in the success or failure of such a tool? Finally, can an electronic learning environment such as RCE help preservice teacher candidates better understand the role of pedagogical and student diversity in literacy instruction?

In the remainder of this chapter, we report on three studies that attempted to answer these questions. We also discuss the importance of the findings and the lessons learned for literacy teacher education with video-based e-learning technologies.

Study 1—The Impact of RCE on Understandings of Literacy Instruction

In our first study, we set out to examine preservice teachers' understanding of literacy instruction after using RCE in their methodology classes (Ferdig, Roehler, & Pearson, 2002). The study was conducted with 32 teacher candidates in the fall semester of a year-long elementary methodology class at a large Midwestern university. Like many teacher education programs, 90% of the teacher candidates were white and female.

The teacher candidates were divided into eight teams of four students. After a brief tutorial on how to use RCE, they were asked to individually explore the system and find five video clips that demonstrated optimum learning opportunities for elementary school children. After finding five videos, they were asked to post their list to the discussion forum, justifying why each video was an example of an optimum learning opportunity.

Once all four group members had posted their clips, they were to winnow their 20 clips down to 10, using the discussion forum as a medium to defend their choices for inclusion in the final list. The final assignment was to write a group paper highlighting these 10 clips and justifying why their group felt these were exemplary video clips of optimum learning opportunities. At the end of the study, there were over 230 postings to the forum.

The learning conversations from the forum were analyzed using both qualitative (constant comparison analysis, Glaser & Strauss, 1967) and quantitative (correlation analysis) tools. Interrater reliability between two of the researchers was established at 97%. For the qualitative methodology, the forum interaction transcripts were read and reread to capture the flow of conversations. Patterns that signaled surface and deep-level understandings of optimum learning opportunities were noted and compiled.

Two patterns emerged from the data: *intertextuality* and *engagement*. Intertextuality (Hartman, 1995) is the degree to which responses mentioned multiple texts, experiences, and examples that moved beyond the texts of the video cases. These comments and reflections included past, present, or future personal experiences; references to the collaborating teachers and their teaching materials in their field placements; ideas learned in the course and other courses; or responses to the work of other colleagues in the course. For an entry to be considered intertextual, at least one of these features had to be present.

The second dimension reflected the amount of engagement with the ideas in the clip, specifically in relation to teaching and learning. At the lower end, responses simply reiterated what happened in the movie clip, with no rationale for selecting it. Furthermore, responses included no explanation of why the clip illustrated something important about teaching and learning. Conversely, at the high end, responses demonstrated a deeper understanding by considering and explicating the relationship between what they had seen and teaching and/or learning.

Discussion forum postings were sorted into one of four categories. The postings were rated as either high or low on both the engagement and the intertextuality scales, as summarized and exemplified in Table 15.3.

Table 15.2 showcases the types of responses and the percentage attributed to each group. A striking finding is that the quantity of responses does not predict the quality. Note that Group 7 posted the second highest number of postings, but contributed the most number of NENI responses. Group 2, conversely, contributed the second lowest number of postings, but one of the higher EI response percentages. In short, more is not necessarily better when it comes to the impact of electronic postings on understanding the issues in a pedagogical space.

Second, when both elements (Engagement and Intertextuality) were present in the discussions, the subsequently submitted student papers (justifying their choices) exhibited the highest quality. This suggested that groups who used the RCE discussion forum to demonstrate uptake and intertextuality illustrated evidence of understandings and connections in the development of thinking about literacy teaching and learning. The most plausible explanation is that when the students used the discussion forum in ways that went beyond reiteration or summaries of the video texts, this created opportunities to internalize thoughts on what it meant to be a teacher. It gave students the opportunity to talk, think, and thus internalize information leading to expertise in literacy teaching and learning.

From this early foray into RCE, we were able to address the first two of our research questions. First, teacher candidates who used RCE successfully displayed deeper understandings of teaching and learning. Thus, we found evidence that RCE did improve preservice teachers' understanding of literacy instruction. Second, data suggested that groups who used the discussion forum with high levels of engagement and intertextuality were scaffolded in the development of richer thinking skills. The most plausible explanation of this effect is that the discussion forum created an opportunity to reflect on what it meant to be a teacher and to envision the type of teacher each was becoming.

TABLE 15.3
Examples of Postings that Exemplify High and Low Levels of Intertextuality and Engagement

		Intertextuality	
		High	*Low*
Engagement	High	I liked the approach used by the teacher. She used the prediction approach. This approach gave the students a chance to use their prior knowledge of the subject. This approach gave the students a chance to think about the future. It also gave the students a chance to use their imaginations. Each student was given a chance to say their prediction. Predicting seemed to be a helpful way for the students to understand the story of caterpillars. I have seen this approach used in my internship school. I hope to use this approach in reading when I have my own classroom.	Teaching story grammar can allow the students to write their own story with a plot and a point of view which will help make sense to the reader. Teaching grammar may also help develop a story that is more enjoyable and comprehendible.
	Low	Do you think that story reading could work with older students? I'm wondering if reading aloud a chapter book after lunch or at the end of the day and then talking about it a bit would be beneficial to students as I have seen done in many classrooms."	[We] feel that the teacher had a very good idea to have the children bring in items or pictures of items that began with the letter of the week.

It was not just the video environment, but also the electronic discussion forum in conjunction with the video clips that represented a unique opportunity for teaching and learning. The RCE forums retained many of the benefits of discourse and dialogue (the opportunity to socially interact) while offering the metalinguistic and meta-analytic advantages of print (Olson, 1994). Learners were presented with a tool to share thoughts and ideas informally. However, because ideas were recorded, learners could go back and review their own thoughts or peruse and respond to the thoughts of others. In doing so, teacher candidates developed patterns (habits) of careful thinking that could carry over into their teaching experiences, where they are more involved in ongoing assessment and monitoring of student learning.

Study 2—The Impact of the Instructor and Environment on RCE

In the first study, we found evidence to suggest teacher candidates who used RCE successfully deepened their understanding of literacy instruction. More importantly, the discussion forum provided a necessary complement to the video exemplars. However, we were left wondering what "successful use" meant. In other words, why did some students succeed when others did not? Is it necessary to suggest that video- and database-driven e-learning environments only help some teacher candidates and not others?

TABLE 15.4
Variation in the Engagement and Intertextuality of Responses across Groups

Group #	Overall Score	% of NENI	% of ENI	% of NEI	% of EI	Total Postings
1	3.61	4	41	1	53	68
2	2.64	8	42	17	33	12
3	2.10	14	52	0	34	29
4	2.16	38	8	23	31	13
5	1.85	9	48	9	33	33
6	1.50	0	71	14	14	7
7	1.44	80	15	5	0	40
8	0.69	78	22	0	0	18

In a second study, we set out to replicate our early findings (Ferdig & Roehler, 2003). In addition, we decided to examine the various teachers and classrooms that would be using the RCE. Three hundred thirty-one teacher candidates participated in five separate American universities. Although the syllabi and use of RCE differed, major course objectives, content and assignments were similar.

The methodology, as well as the data collection and analyses, were similar to the first study, with three exceptions. The first difference was the size of the data set. Quantitative analysis was completed on this larger set of data to examine whether learning had occurred. We discovered that teacher candidates in this study showed a significantly increased understanding of literacy teaching and learning and high amounts of intertextuality (Ferdig et al., 2004). As with the first study, students who positively used the discussion forum as evidenced by engagement and intertextuality demonstrated more growth of knowledge, skills, and dispositions (see Suh et al., 2002; Oliver et al., 2002). Thus, we were able to replicate our results from the first study.

The second difference was that RCE was used more extensively throughout the term than in the first study. Thus it had, at the very least, a greater opportunity to influence learning and attitudes among the preservice candidates. The third difference was methodological. We collected qualitative data and formed cases of classrooms, teacher candidates, and instructors. This qualitative data included classroom observations, classroom assignments, surveys, and interviews. Such data allowed us to understand why some students and/or some classrooms had difficulty, and then to determine potential solutions based on what made other students' gains and learning possible. The data were examined using constant comparison analysis (Glaser & Strauss, 1967) to explore patterns of preservice and teacher educator use. What follows are patterns with specific examples across the case studies in terms of the instructor and the environment in which RCE was implemented (also see Boling, 2003; Ferdig, Love, Boling, & Fang, 2002; Ferdig et al., 2004; Oliver et al., 2002).

RCE was successful in constructivist, discourse-based classrooms. In our first study, only one classroom was used for data collection; thus, we were not able to examine classroom or teacher differences. The second study contained 331 students from 12 classrooms and five universities. We found a positive relationship between certain teacher educators and the number of students in their classrooms who used the discussion forums to demonstrate uptake and intertextuality (Suh et al., 2002). In reviewing the case studies of the classrooms, teacher educators had differing levels of success in using RCE (Boling, 2003).

We did not examine or categorize the instructional approach of the teacher educators prior to this study. We had made the assumption that because they were all using a similar syllabus, as well as RCE in similar ways, the teacher educator variable would be held somewhat constant. However, in reviewing the cases, we found that some classrooms were more"discourse friendly" than others. A "discourse-friendly environment" was defined in our study as a learning community where dispositions such as sensitivity, responsibility, risk taking, trustworthiness, and allowing others the freedom to differ were presented, modeled, discussed, and applied with ongoing reflection occurring in many ways. As one might expect, this type of environment was evident in the classrooms where teacher educators revealed that they believed in and tried to teach from a constructivist approach (Boling, 2003). Teachers in our study who did not use discourse as a means to knowledge construction found it difficult to successfully integrate RCE and the complementing discussion forum in the classroom. Conversely, students in discourse-friendly environments found legitimate opportunities to participate in an environment the instructor believed was useful (Boling, 2003).

RCE was successful when instructors aimed content at the high end of the students' Zone of Proximal Development.   A main tenet of Vygotsky's theory is the importance of aiming instruction at the upper boundaries of a student's "Zone of Proximal Development" or "ZPD" (Brown & Ferrara, 1985). The goal is to use content that is at the high end of students' ZPD, where learning takes place with adult guidance or collaboration with more knowledgeable or more capable others and gradually move toward independence.

Two of our instructors, Elizabeth and Amy,[2] were experienced teacher educators who were attempting to integrate the Reading Classroom Explorer into their teaching for the first time. Many of the students were having a great deal of success (both self- and instructor-described), and their discussion forum postings were very interactive. However, both instructors were having a difficult time getting some of their students involved in using RCE. Elizabeth and Amy met to determine what could be done. Their meetings were unproductive, until they decided to invite some of the students to the meetings. They found that some of these students felt unprepared to join in the conversations. Elizabeth and Amy realized that they were not providing enough scaffolding for some students to participate. They were asking students to discuss things that they were not able to do—regardless of whether the conversations were electronic or not. The discussions seemed to be outside of their ZPD. Elizabeth and Amy provided additional support and instruction, through e-mail, RCE movie clips, and additional readings, and these non-participating students quickly became active in the discussions.

RCE assignments were successful when seminally related to class objectives.   Sarah was a teacher educator with the same level of experience as Amy and Elizabeth, but was located at a different institution. She was in her second year of using RCE, and found success using RCE movie clips to introduce topics for class discussion. Unfortunately, she reported that there were numerous practical and theoretical questions that were not answered due to time constraints. She introduced the discussion forum as an opportunity for students to ask additional questions. She found three results from her work (Ferdig, Love, Fang, & Boling, 2002). First, students began to have longer discussions about topics in class because they knew that other questions could be asked later on the forum. Rather than trying to "get their question in," they were content to discuss others' questions. Second, Sarah discovered that more questions were being asked in the dis-

---

[2]Pseudonyms have been used throughout the paper to protect the identity of those involved in the research.

cussion forum than were normally asked in class. We attribute this to the aforementioned benefit of discussion forums giving each student an equal voice. Finally, Sarah found that other students were willing to contribute answers to questions that their colleagues had asked. This provided another opportunity for growth and sharing.

Successful RCE instructors were those who modeled interactions with RCE. A fourth teacher educator involved in the study was Sally. Sally had been teaching preservice literacy courses for over 20 years and she was the most experienced user of RCE (she had been using it for 3 years). The value of modeling appropriate thinking was very evident in Sally's use of the discussion forum. She had the students view RCE movie clips in class and then respond to the clips in the forum by answering questions that she had posed for them. She explained that they were to put their responses on the forum and then respond to others' entries. The students' responses were simply descriptions of the teaching they viewed. Based on our initial analysis (Ferdig & Roehler, 2003), many of these postings were simply reiterations, without engagement or intertextuality.

After several instances of only explaining the task, Sally modeled how to respond to the entries of other users by using supportive comments and challenging questions. Interestingly enough, she did not do this intentionally. A student asked her a question on the forum, and Sally responded. In her response, she posted her thoughts, but also included a question for further thought. Within a day or so, the same student responded to Sally's question. Sally immediately responded to the student' response and the entries led to a substantive conversation. Once the students understood how to do the task, they took ownership and the discussion forum became a site for promoting understandings about literacy teaching and learning.

RCE instructors was successful between classes when instructors recognized the importance of the cohort effect. One common feature of excellent teacher education programs is the use of cohorts (Fullan, 2001; also see Teitel, 1997; Huey, 1996). Many universities and colleges of education use a cohort model in educating preservice teachers, and thus it becomes imperative for teacher educators to examine cohorts in relation to technology integration (Seifert & Mandzuk, 2004; Laffey, 2004; Thompson, Schmidt, & Davis, 2003). In other words, the success or failure of technologies like RCE can be attributed (in part) to the social structure of the cohort.

In our study (Ferdig & Roehler, 2003), our final teacher educator was Barbara. Barbara was the most experienced of the teacher educators, but was a self-described techno-phobe. Barbara's class completely failed to use RCE for any meaningful pedagogical purpose (Haltiwanger & Ferdig, 2003; Ferdig, Love, Fang, & Boling, 2002). Data suggested at least two main reasons this occurred. First, although no one spoke out, we discovered later that no one in the class understood how to use the system. As students in cohorts draw mainly on their network of resources within the group (Fullen, 2001), not only was the instructor unaware of the problem, there were also no *inside* experts that could have provided guidance. Having the instructor spend additional time with a few of the students could have alleviated this crisis. "People as resources" is not an original idea; however, a cohort's apprehension to seek out the help of an outsider or an unfamiliar person should not be underestimated.

Second, and perhaps most obvious, was the notion of time. The students in Barbara's class—as well as most cohort classes (Fullen, 2001)—spent five days a week, and almost six hours a day in classes together. When they were not in classes, many of them lived together (an intended or unintended outcome of the cohort grouping), and they also partnered for their practicum activities. When the teacher gave the assignment for them to go home and converse online about RCE, the students did not see the need or the value to do so, particularly because they spent so much time together. This was in stark contrast to other classes who chose to participate across universities, thus making the interaction more authentic and necessary (Ferdig & Roehler, 2003). The cohort effect is certainly not the only cause of students not valuing the online writing experience. In addition, problems with cohorts are just beginning to be examined (Bullough, Clark, Wentworth, & Hansen, 2001; Teitel, 1997). However, it is one of the causes that can be prevented with careful planning that provides teacher educators with opportunities to interact with those outside of their immediate cohort.

Study 3—The Impact of RCE on Students' Views of Diversity

Data from Study 2 suggested that the teacher and class environment play a large role in the success or failure of e-learning environments. Accounting for these variables, data also provided evidence that RCE could help preservice teachers come to deeper and more intertextual understandings about literacy instruction. We still did not have evidence, however, that RCE could help students learn about pedagogical and student diversity—one of the main goals of the project.

With that in mind, we developed a survey to examine three main areas: 1) teacher candidates' comfort with technology; 2) teacher candidates' understanding of important literacy teaching and learning strategies (pedagogical diversity); and 3) teacher candidates' understanding of student diversity (Suh et al., 2002). One hundred eighty-five teacher candidates from four universities were selected to participate in this study. The preservice teachers came from seven different classrooms within those four institutions, with four classrooms being chosen as experimental classes (106 teacher candidates) and three as control classes (76 teacher candidates).

Teacher candidates at each of the institutions were enrolled in a preservice literacy methodology course. The researchers in this study provided introductory RCE lessons and support to the individual instructors, but each individual instructor was allowed to use RCE in whatever way fit into their existing curriculum. Students were given the survey as a pre-test in the beginning of the semesterand then again as a post-test at the end of the semester.

Data analyses revealed that 11 of the items on the survey exhibited significant differences between the control and experimental groups in the final post-test. Three of those items related to teacher candidates' comfort with technology. The survey results showed that teacher candidates who had used RCE in their classroom reported significantly higher comfort in surfing the Web (2A, $p < .05$), conducting research on the Web (2C, $p < .05$), and watching video on the Web (2G, $p < .01$) (See Table 15.5).

These results are not surprising given the fact that many preservice classrooms do not yet heavily rely on technology for instruction. Thus, teacher candidates in the experimental group would all get experience with surfing, research, and watching video on the Web as these are the main components of RCE. These results also replicate RCE work from the aforementioned Study 1 (Ferdig, Roehler, & Pearson, 2002).

Four of the post-test items revealing significant experimental/control effects related to teacher candidates' understanding of teaching and learning strategies and skills related to literacy instruction. Teacher candidates who used RCE said they felt more prepared to assess student work in an effort to modify their literacy teaching strategies (7H, $p < .1$). They reported a significantly higher understanding of how to use children's literature (i.e., narrative and/or information texts) in teaching and learning (8G, $p < .01$). Teacher candidates using RCE placed a significantly higher importance on diversifying their instructional strategies for learning how to write (5B, $p < .05$) and for learning reading skills and strategies (5A, $p < .01$).

The final four items on the post-test exhibiting significant between control and experimental groups related to teacher candidates' understanding of student diversity. Preservice teachers in

TABLE 15.5
Means, Standard Deviations, and Levels of Significance

Experimental Group		N	Mean	Std. Deviation	Std. Error Mean
			Group Statistics		
A2	experimental	106	.99	9.71E−02	9.43E−03
	control	79	.92	.27	3.00E−02
C2	experimental	106	.93	.25	2.42E−02
	control	79	.82	.38	4.32E−02
G2	experimental	106	.85	.36	3.49E−02
	control	79	.30	.46	5.21E−02
F4	experimental	106	3.80	.42	4.11E−02
	control	79	3.65	.60	6.75E−02
A5	experimental	106	3.21	.81	7.90E−02
	control	79	2.81	.93	.11
B5	experimental	106	3.17	.83	8.10E−02
	control	79	2.89	.88	9.87E−02
A6	experimental	106	3.11	.85	8.30E−02
	control	79	2.80	1.03	.12
B7	experimental	106	3.18	.83	8.02E−02
	control	78	2.87	.76	8.63E−02
H7	experimental	106	3.31	.70	6.75E−02
	control	78	3.10	.77	8.67E−02
G8	experimental	106	3.41	.67	6.54E−02
	control	78	3.10	.83	9.41E−02
A10	experimental	106	3.83	.38	3.66E−02
	control	78	3.67	.53	5.96E−02

experimental classrooms understood more clearly that students' attitudes about reading and writing can vary across grade levels (10A, $p < .05$). They also felt more prepared to develop a curriculum that would include the perspectives, experiences, and contributions of groups from different backgrounds and cultures (7B, $p < .05$). Teacher candidates using RCE placed more importance on the home language, new languages (ESL), and/or dialects (6A, $p < .05$). Finally, they placed value in schools needing to develop motivated, independent readers who could enjoy literature (4F, $p < .05$).

IMPLICATIONS AND LESSONS LEARNED

The Reading Classroom Explorer was created to help preservice teachers learn about literacy instruction, as well as to prepare them for pedagogical and student diversity in teaching and learning. In our studies, we have provided evidence that students using video- and database-driven e-learning environments can develop deeper understandings of teaching and learning. They are apt to intertextualize what they learn. Our most recent work suggests that they will accomplish these goals while cultivating an appreciation for pedagogical and student diversity.

These goals and accomplishments can be realized provided developers and implementers of such systems are aware of the environmental factors that surround their implementation, use,

TABLE 15.5
Means, Standard Deviations, and Levels of Significance
from Independent Samples Test (*Continued*)

		Levene's Test for Equality of Variances		t-test for Equality of Means					95% Confidence Interval of the Difference	
		F	Sig.	t	df	Sig. (2-tailed)	Mean Difference	Std. Error Difference	Lower	Upper
A2	Equal variances not assumed	24.817	.000	2.115	93.514	.037	6.65E−02	3.14E−02	4.08E−03	.13
C2	Equal variances not assumed	24.115	.000	2.243	125.514	.027	.11	4.96E−02	1.31E−02	.21
G2	Equal variances not assumed	25.035	.000	8.695	142.566	.000	.55	6.27E−02	.42	.67
F4	Equal variances not assumed	13.420	.000	1.977	133.076	.050	.16	7.91E−02	−4.10E−05	.31
A5	Equal variances assumed	.067	.795	3.084	183	.002	.40	.13	.14	.65
B5	Equal variances assumed	.291	.590	2.240	183	.026	.28	.13	3.38E−02	.53
A6	Equal variances assumed	2.262	.134	2.276	183	.024	.32	.14	4.20E−02	.59
B7	Equal variances assumed	.473	.492	2.578	182	.011	.31	.12	7.21E−02	.54
H7	Equal variances assumed	.267	.606	1.928	182	.055	.21	.11	−4.91E−03	.42
G8	Equal variances assumed	.217	.642	2.731	182	.007	.30	.11	8.41E−02	.52
A10	Equal variances not assumed	23.477	.000	2.337	132.345	.021	.16	7.00E−02	2.51E−02	.30

and evaluation. In our research, there were specific factors related to the teacher and the ways in which the teacher managed the classroom that enabled or constrained the possibilities of the technology. Those factors included the appropriate use of discussion forums, an understanding of the cohort model, a need for modeling, the production and use of content at the high end of the student's ZPD, the use of environments with assignments that are seminally related to the course objectives, and the implementation of the environment into a constructivist classroom that contains discursive practices. These factors must be accounted for in implementing hypermedia systems for complex domains.

There are numerous lessons to be learned from our research, and not all of them are transparently inferable from the research findings. For instance, one of the decisions that future developers will have to make is to choose depth or breadth. RCE provides a tremendous number of clips across many schools. Other video-based e-learning environments (e.g. CTELL; see Teale, Leu, Labbo, & Kinzer, 2002; and Kinzer, Labbo, Leu, & Teale, 2003) tend to focus on one child or one school, but develop a much larger case study. Another important question relates to the engine behind the learning tool. RCE currently contains videos, a notepad, a paper-writing mechanism, discussion forums, and additional features for the videos (i.e., articles, artifacts, and transcripts). However, it was created to be used by a preservice instructor. Stand-alone users, such as in-service teachers, might need more scaffolding. The engine behind the tools is just as important to allow for future developments such as a "choose your own experience" scaffolding option. A final example relates to video. Our research team has spent countless hours trying to determine exactly what makes a good "case." RCE currently only contains clips that have been judged by experts to illustrate "best practices." Should video-based e-learning systems contain examples of not so exemplary practice so students learn to discriminate between practices that either promote or retard student engagement and learning?

These are questions we have struggled with in the development and implementation of RCE over the past 5 years. These dilemmas notwithstanding, our research has provided important evidence that Web-based learning environments such as RCE can make a difference in literacy instruction. There are two important areas that future research needs to follow. First, our future research needs to ask the right questions. Although we found statistical significance in our work, there have been some cases where there was no statistical significance in our findings (see Suh et al., 2002 and Oliver et al., 2002). In one case, the instructor in the experimental group was new to teaching. RCE was an important scaffold for her in helping deliver reform-oriented content. The control instructor, however, was an experienced, extraordinary instructor. It was not surprising, in this case, that we did not find significant differences. However, we realized after the study was over, that perhaps we were asking the wrong questions. Perhaps our survey was asking questions that had a ceiling effect. We were asking if students had learned in their classes, and both classes had learned. It is possible that there was other learning taking place that was not being measured. Our feeling is that it relates more to time than content. If Web-based learning environments provide innovative ways to traverse complex domains, then unexpected outcomes may not be evident until much later (i.e., when a teacher candidate becomes a classroom teacher). Future research needs to study the impact of hypermedia on preservice teachers in longitudinal studies.

A second issue that lies ahead of us turns on the issue of who has the authority to judge the appropriateness or exemplary character of a video or a clip. In RCE and other "best practice" videos, the developers hold that authority. We did not include practices that we deemed problematic. But one can imagine a video environment in which an instructor provides students with criteria or rubrics that they use to identify, select, and judge clips along a scale of *exemplariness*. And one can even imagine requiring students to develop the criteria or rubrics for themselves. In fact, an ideal environment would allow instructors to control this sort of scaffolding for themselves. One step beyond might be the video streaming done right from the field experience. Students would be able to see, capture, and explore streaming video from literacy classrooms to challenge notions of reform-oriented techniques in school environments. Future research needs to examine and anticipate these possibilities in order to maximize our effectiveness.

ACKNOWLEDGMENTS

The authors would like to thank the editors of this handbook for their guidance and leadership with this chapter. The authors would also like to thank the Reading Classroom Explorer development and research team at Michigan State University and the University of Florida for their support with this work.

REFERENCES

Boling, E. C. (2003). The transformation of instruction through technology: Promoting inclusive learning communities in teacher education courses. *Action in Teacher Education, 24*(4), 64–73.

Bransford, J., Kinzer, C., Risko, V., Rowe, D., & Vye, N. (1989). Designing invitations to thinking: Some initial thoughts. In S. McCormick & J. Zuttell (Eds.), *Cognitive and social perspectives for literacy research and instruction: Thirty-eighth yearbook of the National Reading Conference* (pp. 35–54). Chicago: National Reading Conference.

Brown, A. L., & Ferrara, R. A. (1985). Diagnosing zones of proximal development. In J. V. Wertsch (Ed.), *Culture communication, and cognition: Vygotskian perspectives* (pp. x, 379). New York: Cambridge University Press.

Bullough, R. V., Jr., Clark, C., Wentworth, N., & Hansen, M. (2001). Student cohorts,school rhythms, and teacher education. *Teacher Education Quarterly.* Spring, 97–110.

Doyle, W. (1990). Case methods in the education of teachers. *Teacher Education Quarterly, 17*(1), 7–15.

Dunkin, M. J., Precians, R. P., & Nettle, E. B. (1993). Effects of formal teacher education upon student teachers' cognitions regarding teaching. *Teaching and Teacher Education, 10*(4), 395–408.

Feiman-Nemser, S., & Buchmann, M. (1985). Pitfalls of experience in teacher preparation. *Teachers College Record, 87*(1), 53–65.

Ferdig, R. E., Hughes, J. E., Packard, B. W., & Pearson, P. D. (1998). Expanding resources in teacher education: The Reading Classroom Explorer. *Journal of Reading Education, 23*(4), 30–31.

Ferdig, R. E., Love, J., Boling, E., & Fang, Z. (December, 2002). Technology and preservice literacy methodology courses: Understanding the role of the teacher as implementer. In D. Mike (Chair), Exploring the Use of Video and Web-Based Tools in Literacy Preservice Instruction: The Design, Implementation, and Evaluation of Two Federally Funded Literacy Projects. Symposium conducted at the *National Reading Conference*, Miami, FL.

Ferdig, R. E., Mishra, P., & Zhao, Y. (2004). Component architectures and web based learning environments. *Journal of Interactive Learning Research, 15*(1), 75–90.

Ferdig, R. E., & Roehler, L. R. (2003). Student engagement in electronic discussions: Examining online discourse in literacy preservice classrooms. *Journal of Research on Technology in Education, 36*(2), 119–136.

Ferdig, R. E., Roehler, L. R., Boling, E. C., Knezek, S., Pearson, P. D., & Yadav, A. (2004). Teaching with video cases on the web: Lessons learned from the Reading Classroom Explorer. In A. Brown & N. Davis (eds.), *The world yearbook of education 2004: Digital technology, communities and education*, pp. 164–175, RoutledgeFalmer, London.

Ferdig, R. E., Roehler, L., Pearson, & P. D. (2002). Scaffolding preservice teacher learning through web-based discussion forums: An examination of online conversations in the Reading Classroom Explorer. *Journal of Computing in Teacher Education, 18*(3), 87–94.

Fullan M. G. (2001). Teacher educator as advocate. Paper presented at the *Annual Meeting of the Association of Teacher Educators*, New Orleans.

Gardner, H. (1983). *Frames of mind: the theory of multiple intelligences.* New York: Basic Books.

Glaser, B. G., & Strauss, A. L. (1967). *The discovery of grounded theory.* Chicago: Aldine.

Goodman, J., & Fish, D. R. (1997). Against-the-grain teacher education: A study of coursework, field experience, and perspectives. *Journal of Teacher Education, 48*(2), 96–107.

Haltiwanger, G., & Ferdig, R. E. (March, 2003). Cohorts, e-learning, and technology integration: Technology diffusion in three preservice literacy classrooms. Paper presented at the *Society for Information Technology and Teacher Education* (SITE) national conference, Albuquerque, New Mexico.

Hartman, D. K. (1995). Eight readers reading: The intertextual links of proficient readers reading multiple passages. *Reading Research Quarterly, 30*(3), 520–561.

Huey, G. L. (1996). *The impact of cohort group membership on preservice teachers.* Unpublished master's thesis, Iowa State University, Ames.

Hughes, J. E., Packard, B. W., & Pearson, P. D. (1998a, December). Expanding notions: The effect of hypermedia and video on preservice teachers' conceptions of becoming a teacher. Paper presented at the *American Educational Research Association*, San Diego, CA.

Hughes, J. E., Packard, B. W., & Pearson, P. D. (1998b). Reading Classroom Explorer: Navigating and conceptualizing a hypermedia learning environment. *Reading Online* [Online serial]. Available: www.readingonline.org/research/explorer/

Jonassen, D. H., & Grabowski, B. L. (1993). *Handbook of individual differences, learning, and instruction*. Hillsdale, NJ: Lawrence Erlbaum Associates.

Kinzer, C, Labbo, L. D., Leu, D. J., & Teale, W. H. (2003, May). CTELL: Case Technologies in Literacy Learning. Reading Research 2003. Presentation at the one-day research conference preceding the 48th Annual meeting of International Reading Association Annual Conference, Orlando, FL.

Kinzer, C. K., & Risko, V. J. (1998). Multimedia and enhanced learning: Transforming preservice education. In D. Reinking (Ed.), *Handbook of literacy and technology: Transformations in a post-typographic world* (pp. 185–202). Mahwah, NJ: Lawrence Erlbaum Associates.

Laffey, J. (2004). Appropriation, mastery and resistance to technology in early childhood preservice teacher education. *Journal of Research on Technology in Education, 36*(4), 361–82.

Oliver, S., Pearson, P. D., Suh, Y., Park, H., Ferdig, R. E, & Yadav, A. (2002). Examining the development of teacher knowledge in a hypermedia learning environment. In S. Oliver (Chair), Assessing the Impact of the Reading Classroom Explorer (RCE) on Literacy Learning. Symposium conducted at the *American Educational Research Association* (AERA) Annual Meeting, New Orleans, LA.

Olson, D. R. (1994). *The world on paper*. New York: Cambridge University Press.

Risko, V. J. (1995). Using videodisc-based cases to promote preservice teachers' problem solving and mental model building. In W. M. Linek & E. G. Sturtevant (Eds.), *Generations of literacy* (pp. 173–187). Pittsburg, KS: College Reading Association.

Risko, V. J., Peter, J., & McAllister, D. (1996). Conceptual changes: Preservice teachers' pathways to providing literacy transaction. In E. Sturtevant & W. Linek (Eds.), *Literacy grows* (pp. 103–119). Pittsburg, KS: College Reading Association.

Risko, V. J., Yount, D., & McAllister, D. (1992). Preparing preservice teachers for remedial instruction: Teaching problem solving and use of content and pedagogical knowledge. In N. Padak, T. V. Rasinski, & J. Logan (Eds.), *Inquiries in literacy learning and instruction* (pp. 179–189). Pittsburg, KS: College Reading Association.

Rogoff, B. (1995). Sociocultural activity on three planes. In J. V. Wertsch, P. del Rio, & A. Alvarez (Eds.), Sociocultural studies of mind (pp. 139–164). New York: Cambridge University Press.

Schegloff, E. A. (1991). Conversation analysis and socially shared cognition. In L. B. Resnick, J. M. Levine, & S. D. Teasley (Eds.), Perspectives on socially shared cognition (pp. 150–171). Washington, DC: American Psychological Association.

Schwab J. J. (1978). The practical: Translation into curriculum. In: I. Westbury, & N. J. Wilkof (Eds.) Science, curriculum and liberal education: Selected essays (pp. 365–383). Chicago, IL: The University of Chicago Press.

Seifert, K., & Mandzuk, D. (2004). How helpful are cohorts in teacher education? Paper presented at the *25th Forum for Ethnography in Education*, Philadelphia, Pennsylvania, USA, February 27–28, 2004.

Shulman, L. (1992). Toward a pedagogy of cases. In J. Shulman (Ed). Case methods in teacher education (pp. 1–30). New York: Teachers College Press.

Spiro, R. J., Coulson, R. L., Feltovich, P. J., & Anderson, D. K. (1988). Cognitive Flexibility Theory: Advanced knowledge acquisition in ill-structured domains. In V. Patel (Ed.), *Tenth annual conference of the Cognitive Science Society* (pp. 375–383). Hillsdale, NJ: Lawrence Erlbaum Associates.

Suh, Y., Pearson, P. D., Oliver, S., & Park, H. (2002). Examining changes in preservice teachers' practices and dispositions toward reading. In S. Oliver (Chair), Assessing the Impact of the Reading Classroom Explorer (RCE) on Literacy Learning. Symposium conducted at the *American Educational Research Association* (AERA) Annual Meeting, New Orleans, LA.

Teale, W. H., Leu, D. J., Labbo, L. D., & Kinzer, C. (2002). The CTELL project: New ways technology can help educate tomorrow's reading teachers. *The Reading Teacher, 55*(7), 654–659. Available online at: http://www.readingonline.org/electronic/RT/4–02_Column/index.html

Teitel, L. (1997). Understanding and harnessing the power of the cohort model in preparing educational leaders. *Peabody Journal of Education, 72*(2), 66–85.

Thompson, A. D., Schmidt, D. A., & Davis, N. E. (2003). Technology collaboratives for simultaneous renewal in teacher education. *Educational Technology Research and Development, 51*(1), 71–87.

Vygotsky, L. S. (1978). *Mind in society.* Cambridge, MA: Harvard University Press. Theme: Technology and Field

Wertsch, J. V. (1991). *Voices of the mind.* Cambridge, MA: Harvard University Press.

"P, not-P and possibly Q": Literacy Teachers Learning from Digital Representations of the Classroom

Colin Harrison, Daniel Pead, and Mary Sheard
University of Nottingham

REPRESENTATION, TEACHER LEARNING, AND VIDEO

"Almost all forms of learning involve information that is represented in different forms," argued van Someren and his co-workers in their introduction to a ground-breaking book on learning and multiple representations (van Someren et al., 1998, p. 1). The authors of this chapter aim to interpret this assertion in relation to teacher development, and attempt to address the complex issue of how teachers learn from multiple representations that are presented using electronic media.

The central topic of this chapter is research into teachers' learning, and the particular form of representation on which we focus is learning from video, especially digital video. We argue that there is a good deal of work to be done in this relatively new field, and that defining the research agenda is an important part of that work. We give as much attention to the preservice uses of representations of teaching as to in-service teaching, since, as the chapters by Ferdig et al. and Kinzer et al. in this volume suggest, video representations of teaching are as prevalent in teacher preparation as in the professional development of teachers. In exploring the issue of how we learn from video, and moving towards a research agenda, in later sections of the chapter we look in some detail at the design and delivery of two of the most important U.S. approaches to presenting digital video: Reading Classroom Explorer (RCE; for a fuller treatment of RCE see the Ferdig et al. chapter in this volume) and Case Technologies to Enhance Literacy Learning (CTELL; for a fuller account of the CTELL project see the Kinzer et al. chapter in this volume) and then at a UK entrant to the field, Interactive Classroom Explorer (ICE). We also offer some conclusions about the potential of Web-based video for preservice and in-service teacher development.

ENHANCING TEACHER EFFECTIVENESS: MODELS OF DELIVERY AND MODES OF REPRESENTATION

A good deal is known about the characteristics of excellent literacy teachers (National Reading Panel, 2000; Taylor et al., 2000; Pressley et al., 2001), but much less about precisely how literacy teachers learn and what part witnessing the practice of other teachers (in real-life classrooms, through videotaped lessons or more recently, from digitized video of classrooms) contributes to that learning. The comprehensive Center on English Learning and Achievement (CELA) reviews of research into teacher professional development (CELA, undated; Langer, 2001) take as their starting point a conceptual framework based on the notion of the reflective practitioner, a teacher who has developed an internalized conception of "what is working and not working" (Schon, 1983, 1987), and in our view these studies provide a valuable starting point for considering the issue of representation in teacher learning. The CELA paper cites the views of Hillocks (1999, p. 128) on how the process of internalization operates: "We might say the teacher has a subject matter goal or image that serves as a template against which he or she may judge the impact of each move in light of the context in which the former move was made." This perspective is in harmony with Schon's model, but it also clearly highlights the issue of representation, and raises the question of how a teacher develops, reviews and updates the internalized images that serve as a template for his or her planning and classroom activity.

The point here is not to suggest that all teacher learning is based on representations stored in visual memory, but rather to emphasize that teachers' professional development, even when it involves video material, has tended to be delivered through what Spillane (2000) called a "quasi-behaviorist" approach, with programs consisting primarily of explanations and demonstrations of preferred teacher behaviors. In a study that involved interviewing 40 administrators, lead teachers, and curriculum specialists who were involved on a regular basis in promoting instructional change in their district, Spillane reported that 85% espoused an essentially Skinnerian approach, with new knowledge "treated in separate chunks—content knowledge, knowledge about teaching strategies, knowledge about materials and technology" (Spillane, 2000, p. 10), and with very poor integration of this knowledge into the teachers' earlier, current or future models of how to teach. The formats used in this type of professional development included workshops, in-class demonstration lessons, videotapes, and curricular materials, and teachers were motivated to participate through a variety of external motivators such as rewards and sanctions. The problem with this approach was not that district leaders entirely ignored the issue of coherence of their curriculum for teacher learning, but rather that coherence was mostly understood at a very broad and not at a personal level. Spillane clearly favored a situated learning approach (Lave & Wenger, 1991) that was essentially Vygotskian, especially if (as occurred in only a single instance) the district leader sought to ally this with a "quasi-cognitive" perspective, with teacher development clearly linked to curriculum development. When this occurred, and the content of the curriculum for teacher learning was determined by teachers' needs as they attempted to implement the new curriculum, then significant teacher learning and change could occur.

Some of the teachers in the nine districts studies by Spillane (2000) learned from video of classrooms, but many did not, or not in ways that influenced their practice. Clearly the contexts for learning were crucial here, but we also want to suggest that, although it may have been overlooked because of its complexity and inaccessibility, it is important for researchers to consider the issue of how teachers learn from representations. We want to suggest in this chapter that, particularly in the light of the increasing importance of digital representations of classrooms as sites for intended teacher learning, it is worthwhile to try to shift the balance of discussion into the area of learning from visual representation, even if we have to acknowledge from the outset that the field is relatively new, that our analytical tools for exploring representations are underdeveloped, and that our conclusions will necessarily be tentative.

How do teachers acquire the internalized representations of "what works" and "what might work" on the basis of which they construct templates for their own planning and delivery of content, and which guide their notions of what it is to construct an environment that is conducive to learning? Clearly, a major goal of any preservice program is to help to construct in the mind of a beginning teacher a conceptual framework within which such pedagogical templates might be built. However, we also need to acknowledge that the 15,000 hours or so of teaching that teachers themselves witnessed as school students (Rutter et al., 1979) are likely to have had a significant impact on the construction of a beginning teacher's array of available representations, an impact so enduring that many of those representational templates may be impervious to revision and updating, at least in the short term. It is also important to note that much of the teaching witnessed by school students who become teachers may have been variable in quality or even uniformly poor, and its impact might have been negative as well as positive, in that the dominant representations stored were memorable as events but ineffectual in terms of pedagogy.

Although our main focus is on teacher learning through video, it is important to give some attention to the broader research into literacy teachers' professional development, and to seek to discern areas that can be related to our theme of teachers' learning from multiple representations. In the section of its report that produced an overview of research into teacher education and reading instruction, the National Reading Panel (NRP, 2000) offered the following conclusions:

- provided they are well-funded and well-supported in terms of providing time for teachers to learn, interventions in teacher education and professional development are successful in improving literacy;
- improvement in classroom teaching leads directly to higher achievement on the part of learners;
- teacher attitudes change as a result of successful interventions, and without such changes in attitudes, it is extremely difficult to effect changes in practice;
- no single method of teaching that was investigated showed unquestioned superiority, but rather an eclectic mix of methods was successful (NRP, 2000, pp. 5–13, 5–14).

The mechanisms of teachers' learning related to representation are not highlighted in these conclusions, but the two issues of time for reflection and teacher motivation certainly are, and deserve comment. In a far-sighted definition written 25 years ago, Lunzer and Gardner (1979, p. 5) characterized comprehension as "the willingness and ability to reflect on what is read." In the context of this chapter, motivation (or "willingness . . . to reflect") on the one hand, and the "ability to reflect" on the other, are most certainly factors that are not only central to the development of comprehension in general, but also highly relevant to the concept of the reflective practitioner to which we wish to link our discussion of representation.

Under what conditions do attempts to change teacher behavior succeed or fail? Fullan (2000) has attempted to answer this question in some detail, and his analysis has relevance for the present discussion, not least because the UK government has distributed significant amounts of video material to every school in England as part of the National Literacy Strategy, and Fullan and his team at the Ontario Institute for Studies in Education (OISE) have led the evaluation of the effectiveness of this initiative (see Department for Education and Skills, 2001, for a description of the Strategy; see Barber, 2001, for an early evaluation of the National Literacy Strategy; see Department for Education and Skills 1999, 2000, and 2003 for sources of videotaped or CD-ROM material aimed at supporting teachers' implementation of the Strategy). According to Fullan, there was a "massive failure" of reform initiatives in the 1960s and 1970s, because innovations were based on disseminating materials that were adopted (or not adopted) by individuals, without systemic change at classroom, school, district, and regional levels. Systemic change, argued Fullan (2000, p. 23), had to involve teachers, but it also had to be about putting in place integrated and coherent reform initiatives, supported by strong and complex partnership networks.

If we accept Fullan's (2000) analysis, effective change at the macro level needs to motivate teachers, to encourage reflection, and to be connected to coherent and integrated system-level reforms. What does research tell us, however, about the nature of change at the level of the individual? Perhaps not surprisingly, given the NRP's strict criteria for experimental or quasi-experimental designs, with data linked to student outcomes, only a few studies were reported that linked specific teacher development interventions to positive effects on learners, and these had relatively little overlap in terms of shared variables. However, for the purposes of this chapter, even if the studies analyzed by the Panel did not provide a meta-analysis of trends, there were some very useful indications of the place that video could play in contributing to the development of teachers' understanding.

The study of Copeland and Decker (1996), for example, on group discussion of video by preservice teachers of fourth-grade students, provided strong evidence of teacher change, in that the teachers' ability to interpret and understand the video data improved after the group discussion activities. Three weeks after they had discussed the videos, the student teachers were able to adopt, transform, or create new topics related to what they had discussed on the video. In a similar vein, a study by Klesius, Searls, and Zielonka (1990) compared two approaches to introducing material to preservice teachers: lecture plus discussion and video plus simulation. There were no short-term differences between the two groups, but interestingly, there was a relationship between the use of video and teachers' subsequent recall: the preservice teachers instructed with videotape and simulation retained and used the information better, and for a longer, period of time.

Interpreting the implications of studies involving video can be problematic. Baker (1977) for example, in one of the earliest reported studies using video for teacher development, showed tapes to experienced teachers and encouraged the use of a variety of reading strategy models. The results of the intervention were promising: both teachers and their students improved, but it is not clear whether video was a determining factor in that improvement. The same problem applies to a number of other studies that included video and that were reported by the NRP as being associated with teacher or student improvement, or both.

There is a similar problem in attempting to assess the distinctive part played by the use of video representations in one of the most fully researched teacher development initiatives in recent years, Reading Recovery (Clay, 1995; Hobsbaum, & Leon, 1999). The training of Reading Recovery teachers is a year-long procedure, involving a great deal of on-the-job training, one-to-one teaching of individual students and large- and small-group discussion of the teaching strategies of each novice Reading Recovery teacher, whose work is observed by the group through one-way glass, and also videotaped to facilitate fuller reflection, discussion, and review. Here the ability to review and reflect is central, but any specific part played by video is difficult to separate from other effects.

There are some important points to note from these studies, even if they are no more than indicative of where a fuller research effort might be targeted. First, many of these studies adopted a case-based approach: the implicit (or explicit) pedagogical stance is that models of teaching presented as cases would provide a useful basis for discussion and learning; Second, all the studies used group discussion, and again, the implicit contrast would be with models of teacher development that disseminated video material that was intended to provide models for emulation, but without opportunities for collaborative or collegial reflection on those models. We should also note the importance of attempting to monitor teacher change over time and recall the important classical study of Morrison and his co-workers (1969), which showed that after 3 years, teachers who were working without sustained support eventually reverted to the methods of teaching that they had been using initially and jettisoned the materials and approaches which had been advocated in the innovation.

DIGITAL VIDEO FOR TEACHERS: THE CASE OF CTELL

Producing video of classrooms is costly in terms of participants' time, and it is also costly in terms of production and distribution, but there is no shortage of evidence, on both sides of the Atlantic, that universities, publishers and national agencies are pinning their faith in the potential of digital video to exemplify and spread models of good practice. The preamble to the video archive of the Teachers Network.org (Teachers Network, 2004) is instructive as an example of this confidence. Under a banner reading *Streaming Video Showcasing the Work of Exemplary Teachers*, the introduction for teachers reads:

> With a shortage of teachers nationwide, but particularly in the New York City area, more and more educators are entering school this fall with little or no hands-on classroom experience. Overcrowded classes, pressure to "teach to tests," and a more diversified student population will also put added stress on this new crop of teachers. Guidance in the form of professional development, via the Internet, is now available, providing access to an archive of wisdom and best practices from some of the greatest teachers on the front lines. Teachers Network, with a grant from the AT&T Foundation, has developed a series of interactive streaming videos, which offers practical instruction for the novice teacher, and serves as a form of "digital mentoring."
>
> (Teachers Network Web, 2004)

A digital archive, on this analysis, can not only remedy the problem of a lack of positive models of good practice in the new teacher's own experience of schooling, it can even make good a lack of classroom experience of the sort provided by a traditional teacher preparation program. But the apprenticeship model implied by this quotation from the Teachers Network philosophy appears nearer to Spillane's (2000) "quasi-behaviorist" approach than a situated or quasi-cognitive model, and it is with a critique of such approaches that the CTELL team begin an explanation of their approach (Schrader et al., 2003).

The CTELL group owes much of its genesis to the work on teachers' learning from video and CD carried out at Vanderbilt University for a number of years (Risko, 1995; Kinzer & Risko, 1998). Kinzer and Risko made the point that many preservice teachers are not offered examples of practice that are encountered in context-rich or complex situations. Instead, the materials tend to offer imagined scenarios or show lessons taped under ideal conditions. As a result, candidate teachers are often denied opportunities to engage in analysis, reflection, or decision-making in ways that enable them to begin thinking like an expert or considering how to modify the learned procedures in ways that meet differing instructional needs of real children in real classrooms. The CTELL group quotes with approval the work of Spiro on cognitive flexibility theory (Spiro et al., 1991), which discusses how experts differ from novices in their learning, and the ways in which advanced knowledge acquisition in ill-structured domains is likely to occur. In our view, the approach advocated by Spiro et al. deserves close attention, and it is worth reviewing in more detail exactly what was called for. A cognitive flexibility approach to learning would:

- Seek to avoid oversimplification
- Value multiple representations
- Value case studies
- Define meaning as use
- Prefer flexible schemata

- Seek interconnectedness
- Value human support systems to develop complexity management. (Spiro et al., 1991, p. 611–3)

The CTELL team aimed to meet all these criteria in their case-based Internet-delivered approach to providing digital video of exemplary classrooms (Schrader et al., 2003). In harmony with the general approach advocated by Spillane (2000) that combines a situated learning perspective with a quasi-cognitive perspective, the CTELL group aims to provide case-based anchored instruction, in which the video case provides not a disassociated exemplar of good practice, but rather a macro-context for learning through gaining multiple perspectives in what is essentially a problem-solving model of learning (Shyu, 1997).

In the CTELL project, digital video cases provide a context within which candidate teachers can engage with a task environment that has the goal of addressing some critically important instructional issues, including attention to different student backgrounds, the sharing and development of knowledge between instructor and students, and the challenge of making knowledge "accessible rather than inert" (Schrader et al., 2003, pp. 320–321). Candidate teachers can work in small groups and be given different tasks on the jigsaw principle, with subsequent reporting back from "expert" groups to the home group, with the instant-access search facility of digital video significantly enhancing the group's ability to navigate swiftly across the whole lesson to any point, but also enabling the users to view and discuss repeatedly key segments of the video that invite close scrutiny.

The research goals of CTELL are bold: the project aims to develop case-based instructional methods that can (1) enhance preservice teacher candidates' knowledge of best practices for teaching reading, (2) result in the implementation of these practices in the candidates' classrooms when they become teachers, and (3) foster teachers who teach in ways that positively and significantly affect children's reading achievement. This is a tall order, not least because as one of us has observed, there are a number of assumptions that need to be met before CTELL's goals of enhancing student achievement in reading can be judged to have been met (Harrison, 2002). Harrison argued that CTELL is attempting to meet these additional goals:

- Identify best practice
- Digitize and distribute that practice to candidate teachers
- Change candidate teacher behaviors
- Transfer that practice to the teacher's first school
- Improve the reading of the students in that school
- Enhance test results of the students in that school. (Harrison, 2002)

The difficulty for the CTELL team is that each of these areas is problematic, not least since each goal is causally related to the next.

First, on the issue of how challenging it is to locate examples of exemplary practice, we shall cite a tape-recorded event from a conference presentation on a related project that also makes use of "exemplary" video clips that took place in 1999 (Brenner et al., 1999). In a symposium session, the CIERA team was demonstrating an early version of RCE at the National Reading Conference, and groups of reading researchers who had viewed early examples of "exemplary classroom teaching" had their discussions on a video extract taped as data by the CIERA team (Hughes, Packard, & Pearson, 2001). The result was predictable: hardly a single delegate was ready to concede that the "exemplary" teaching was exemplary. Instead, many colleagues in the discussion judged what the teacher was doing to be less than optimal, or at the very least agreed that the concept of exemplary was problematic.

Next, on the issue of providing Internet access to dozens of video clips, we need a realistic appraisal of the issue of access. Unless every candidate teacher has broadband wireless or Ethernet access, it is likely that there will be problems in accessing and viewing the video, particularly when a candidate teacher is out on practicum experience.

Other potential challenges that the CTELL project has to meet concern the possible changes in the belief system of candidate teachers. Here again there are problems: (a) concept maps (used as indices of changes in candidate teacher knowledge, reported in Schrader et al., 2003) may or may not reflect such changes; (b) any changes may be transitory, and may evaporate when a beginning teacher embarks on their first post; and (c) a new teacher may be relatively successful or unsuccessful, but to have that success represented in the students' test scores, and to be confident that any success is attributable to the CTELL case-based activities rather than to all the other influences that impinge on a beginning teacher, is another matter (Harrison, 2002). Our point here is not to question whether the CTELL project might have a positive influence on the representations that candidate teachers construct that will guide their later behavior in the classroom, but rather to draw attention to how difficult it is to pinpoint causality in teacher learning, and to link that learning confidently to student outcomes many months (or even years) later.

The CTELL team is to be congratulated on having put together one of the boldest, most methodologically complex and most technically challenging research projects in the field of literacy research, and when we come to suggest a research agenda for the future, their efforts will have made a very important contribution to our points of departure. CTELL appears to have great potential: its theoretical underpinnings are sound, its arguments supporting case-based learning are strong, its mode of delivery appears to be robust, and its evaluation model is ambitious. The project is a longitudinal study, and it will be important therefore to track its impact using both local and global perspectives, over a sustained period.

DIGITAL VIDEO FOR TEACHERS: THE CASE OF READING CLASSROOM EXPLORER

Reading Classroom Explorer (RCE) was conceived with the highly creative and ambitious goal of providing an online repository of segments of exemplary practice in reading instruction that could be accessed by students and faculty in any cooperating institution in the US. Clearly the project was predicated on the assumption of good Internet access, but provided this was in place, users would be able to access over 240 video clips of good practice, illustrating many aspects of teaching that any one institution would find difficult to offer its candidate teachers. The clips not only featured many important aspects of literacy teaching, including work with children for whom English was an additional language and with those who had special educational needs, they also illustrated small group and large group teaching, discussion groups and partner reading, with students in the age range pre-school to fifth grade.

Like CTELL, RCE offered not only on-demand video, but also additional resources, including text transcripts, audio clips, and supplemental reading material such as research articles related to the topic illustrated on the video. The RCE team gave a good deal of thought as to how the video would be used, in particular encouraging the juxtaposition of linked resources for comparison purposes, and the use of five search-support tools: (1) the opportunity to search by case (a particular school); (2) by theme (in effect a type of contents list); (3) by keyword (in effect an index); (4) by lexical item in the text transcript; or (5), from a list of "not previously viewed" clips. RCE also provided users with an online notepad, and the capability to view the notes of others, or, potentially, to view the RCE-related coursework of other candidate teachers. Users could post commentaries or notes to an asynchronous online forum. As research data on the use of RCE became available, evidence emerged that candidate teachers' initial assumptions about teaching were indeed challenged (Boling and Roehler, 2002; Ferdig, Roehler, & Pearson, 2002) and that instructional ideas were integrated into new lesson plans (Boling, 2003).

The potential of RCE to influence and move forward good practice in the field of Internet-delivered video may be limited, since CIERA was not funded as a permanent organization, but its contribution is, in our view, likely to be enduring, not least because of the ambitious scale of its digital repository of representations of literacy practices and the fact that these have been made available so widely. As we move towards suggesting a research agenda in this area, RCE's contribution to the field will deserve particular consideration.

DIGITAL VIDEO: DEFINING THE RESEARCH AGENDA

In the "New Directions in Research" piece on *Media and online literacy studies* in *Reading Research Quarterly* (Volume 38, 3, 2003), Leander (2003) makes the point that since 1998 the field of research into literacy and technology has changed significantly in three ways. First, our focus on electronic text has been widened to a focus on electronic media; second, our research has begun to move beyond the traditional settings of classroom, school, and lecture hall into the home and into mobile learning; third, there is an increasing acceptance of the need for researchers to focus on the issue of identity—to acknowledge the identity of the participants, and to be aware of the sociocultural contexts within which we are studying online literacies. These emphases are not new; Spiro et al. (1991) were arguing over a decade ago that newer technologies implied the need not only for cognitive flexibility on the part of learners, but also that researchers should adopt approaches that took account of complex, hybrid representational environments for learning. Equally, Lave and Wenger's (1991) account of situated learning emphasized the need for us to attempt to understand that learning occurs in a sociocultural context and that an account of learning that fails to account for this may be seriously deficient. How do these issues impact our emerging research agenda? Our suggestion is that they overlap with the issues already highlighted in earlier sections—namely the need to study representations, the need to look at mobile learning (and the related issues of access to mobile learning), and the need to study the sociocultural contexts of learning.

Clearly we could generate a potentially infinite list of researchable questions, but in our view, there are three areas of research that are implied from the analyses earlier in this chapter that urgently need particular attention. These questions are as follows:

- How do we define, and how do we use (or indeed, should we use) the concept of "exemplary" in digital representations of teaching from which we want others to learn?
- How might we research and how should we report issues of access and technical expertise in relation to the use of digital video?
- If we are serious in wanting to take a situated learning perspective in researching how teachers make use of digital representations of teaching, how might this be accomplished?

We shall comment briefly on each of these agenda items, and then (with some trepidation) shall describe a video interface that, we hope, has some potential in addressing at least some aspects of the agenda.

We want to suggest that the concept of the exemplary lesson is problematic. As we mentioned earlier, when a group of academics was asked to discuss an RCE clip, the immediate reaction was to question the validity of the term *exemplary* in relation to the extract that everyone had viewed. This was not an isolated or surprising reaction, in our view. Two of the authors of this chapter have worked with a number of groups of teachers in England in recent years, and have found that, even if teachers found a video useful as the basis for discussion, and agreed that the teacher on the video was a skilled practitioner, it was generally not the case that they agreed that the teaching was exemplary. What teachers often wanted to do was to replace the implied authority structure of the video, which was vertical (with the teacher positioned at a low point in an authority hierarchy, and as the recipient of knowledge on how to teach) with something different. Figure 16.1 shows this vertical authority structure, with the viewing teachers squeezed between the input from content developers and the output of improved teaching and higher standards.

Figure 16.2, by contrast, presents a horizontal authority structure, with the teachers viewing the video recognized as professional equals and invited to position themselves as co-operative participants seeking to understand how teaching and learning are taking place. As well as viewing video material that is provided, users also have access to comments posted in a discussion forum and to new content generated by fellow users.

The second agenda item takes a technical perspective on the situated learning theme; if learning takes place in an individual's life, in a unique sociocultural context, then the learner's knowl-

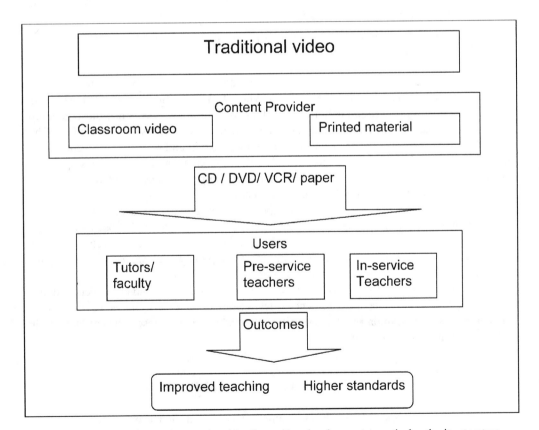

FIGURE 16.1.   Traditional exemplar video for teacher development—vertical authority structure.

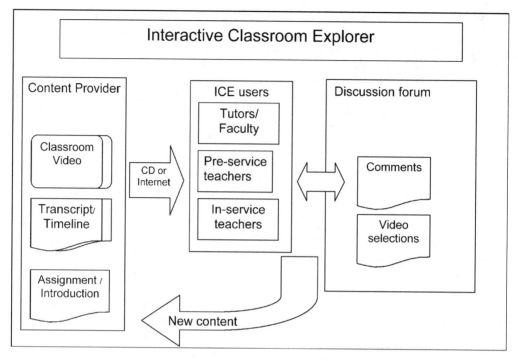

FIGURE 16.2.   Interactive Classroom Explorer—horizontal authority structure.

edge and understanding of the affordances of the computer, the local network, and the Internet are likely to influence that learning and should not be ignored. What we are saying is that researchers tend not to report issues around technical problems or Internet access, since these generally seem to be irrelevant to our main concern, namely how literacy teachers acquire models of better practice. But, we would argue, such issues as authentication and password protocols, access times, Internet cache lag, and bandwidth can significantly impact a potential user's opportunities for learning. These issues need to be both researched more fully and reported more frankly, since they are an important part of the learning process.

The third agenda item is for us the most important. If we agree that teachers' learning is not simply a matter of assimilation, and that learning is generally something that occurs in a highly complex social context, then we need to give careful thought to how we research and how we report that learning, and if it is difficult to capture that complexity, then we need to develop new tools that are valid, non-invasive and reliable in order to do the job.

In our view, both CTELL and RCE have enormous potential to extend our understanding of how teachers (both candidate and experienced) learn from digital video. But we have developed Interactive Classroom Explorer with the specific aim of addressing the research agenda items that we have identified as particularly important.

INTERACTIVE CLASSROOM EXPLORER

Interactive Classroom Explorer (ICE) is a computer-mediated interface for viewing and critiquing digital video. It has been funded in the UK by grants from the Teacher Effectiveness

Enhancement Programme (TEEP) and Science Enhancement Programme (SEP) projects, supported by the Gatsby Foundation. The aim of ICE is to present digital video for exploration and discussion (face-to-face, online or offline) in a way that offers much more flexibility than is available with traditional video (whether stored on tape, on CD, or on DVD), and with certain contextual resources than are not offered by some of the more recently developed Internet-based interfaces.

Traditional taped video essentially offers four tools for exploration: playback, pause, fast forward, and fast rewind. ICE aims to offer a suite of tools, enabling the user to perform the following functions:

- to play back a video while scrolling through a "timeline" containing a transcript, lesson plan, and/or other annotations;
- to create "video quotations" (i.e., video clips from one frame to five minutes in length) that can be pasted into e-mails or a discussion area;
- to display as "pop-ups" resources associated with the video (e.g., still images of whiteboards, student work, copies of worksheets etc.), selected either from a menu or from hyperlinks in the time-line;
- to work (as in the right-hand half of the screen in Figure 16.3) with a collection of tasks, videos, timelines, texts, and other resources that form a "module" containing an interactive professional development activity.

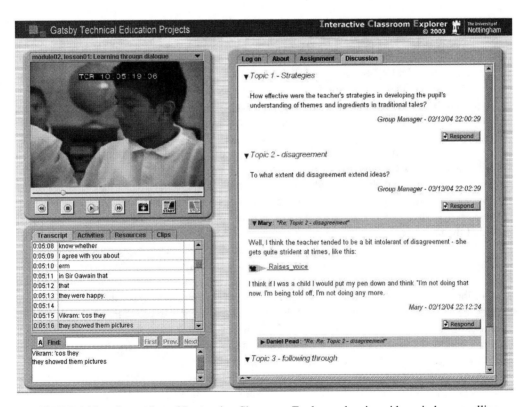

FIGURE 16.3. Screenshot of Interactive Classroom Explorer, showing video window, scrolling transcript and resources window, and online bulletin board/discussion area.

Traditional video is generally distributed in educational contexts by providers such as governments or publishers with a view to disseminating good or exemplary practice. What viewers of such videos sometimes want to do, however, is to problematize and question the exemplars shown on a video, and to discuss whether the examples of teaching that are being shown do indeed demonstrate successfully the good practice that is claimed. Those who distribute such videos are often aware that this will happen (and indeed might wish to encourage such discussion), but with a traditional video playback system this is not easy (Schrader et al., 2003).

ICE aims to facilitate such professional conversations by offering an environment that can permit much closer attention to the content, discourse, and pedagogy of a lesson or other teaching and learning event. With ICE, the user can perform the following tasks:

- begin their viewing having read a context-setting introduction
- use the scrolling second-by-second timeline, a text search tool that scans the discourse transcript or event record (usually a lesson plan) to navigate directly to any point in the video that merits closer attention.
- draw upon the video, the transcript, the lesson plan, and the pop-up resources (student work, screenshots of teacher or students' computers, worksheets, etc.) to provide a much richer evidence base upon which to review and make judgments about teaching and learning.
- select their own "video quotations" (from one frame to 5 minutes in length) that can be stored in a personal file area, or pasted with commentary into e-mails or discussion board messages.

Our own work in the University of Nottingham Classroom Language Action Research Group (UNCLAG) in the School of Education has shown that many teachers not only choose to critique videos of suggested exemplary practice, but would prefer to be able to upload their own video material in order to contribute to a debate about how to teach a particular skill or topic (Harrison et al., 2004). The development of ICE has therefore been phased, with the final phase aiming to permit the uploading of video material supplied by users (subject to appropriate screening and editing procedures) that can be used to extend professional analysis and debate. Such material might, for example, have been recorded in the user's own school, and might (given appropriate permissions and data protection clearance) greatly extend the availability of material related to a key area of pedagogical debate.

In our view, ICE has the potential to meet the goals of the research agenda described in the sections earlier in this chapter. What we wish to argue is that the "video quotation" tool (which has been programmed such that video quotations take up negligible space in an e-mail message, provided the user at each end of the communication has the source video file) offers a significant advance in maximizing the potential of video, in two ways. First, it enables teachers to learn more from video, by offering a range of tools and resources to facilitate close attention to those sections that are deemed important, and second, it offers opportunities for collaborative exploration of video, that can deepen the level of analysis significantly. For the user, the opportunities for learning through ICE are manifold: teachers will be able to use ICE working in a small group, or on their own, online or offline. But ICE also has, in our view, significant potential as a research tool; we believe that it can provide information about how teachers learn from the representations of teaching that have hitherto been unavailable.

Traditional video essentially offers a legitimated and monovalent view of learning (Kinzer & Risko, 1998), a single model of how to teach. By contrast, we favor a view of teacher learning that is closer to that of Spiro and his associates, in their representation of learning in complex domains (Spiro et al., 1991). We would characterize many traditional approaches as offering what in formal logic could be described as a proposition, P, whose message is an assertion: "this is how good teaching should proceed." But what we have found is that teachers, being teachers, want to challenge proposition P, to adopt the "not-P" position, and to say, "Hold on—I'm not sure I want to agree that this is exemplary teaching." Many of the teachers we have worked with have wanted to say, "That classroom does not look like a classroom that I recognize as existing in the real world—the children are too well-scrubbed and polite!" Other teachers have said, "I don't accept that this teacher really understands the concept or the teaching technique she is supposed to be demonstrating here."

What we have also found is that many teachers wish to go further, and to be able to say, "If you really want to see this skill taught, you need look no further than lessons in my school." This we might call the "Possibly Q" position, in that it is introducing a new proposition into the equation, an alternative representation of reality, one based in a classroom they know well—their own or that of a close colleague.

What we hope to explore, using ICE, is how teachers use representations of teaching to enhance their own learning, and what we are suggesting is that their use of the "video quotation" tool may well provide a window into this process. Our initial work has begun by collecting focus group and transcript data on how teachers view, comment on, and learn from regular video. We are using knowledge elicitation procedures and domain discourse analyses to develop a taxonomy of teachers' learning moves as they reflect on video.

The pilot tasks on which we have been working involve relative brief segments of video (6–10 minutes in length), on which teachers are invited to comment. For example, in one UK-government funded video that we are using, children in a Year 6 class (fifth grade in US schools) are working on suspense writing. In the video, the children start by analyzing a suspense paragraph that the teacher has prepared, and within the ICE environment we ask teachers to consider how effective they consider the teacher's strategies to have been in developing pupils' understanding of how a writer may introduce and build suspense.

To guide their thinking, the teachers are asked:

- Do you consider you have learned from this material? [Offering an opportunity to accept the "P" position]
- If so, could you elaborate?
- If you consider that you have not learned from this material, could you give your reasons? [Offering space for a "not-P" response]
- How would you present this lesson? [Offering space for a "Possibly Q" response].

The teachers are then invited to identify a video quotation of between 10 seconds and 1 minute in length that they feel raises important issues for developing practice in teaching this aspect of writing, and to share the clip and their thoughts about the significance of the issues they have identified within the ICE discussion environment. They are also asked to revisit the ICE online site and to take the discussion forward interactively, by responding to at least one other respondent in one or more additional postings.

As in all computer-based applications, the user interface is a central determinant of response, and our hope is that the ICE environment will offer new opportunities for teachers to critique and comment and to engage with the critiques and comments of other professionals. As may be seen from the screenshot in Figure 16.3, there are a number of clickable tabs under the video image, and these make it a "one-click" operation to identify the start or stop point of a video quotation. It is also a one-click operation to paste a video clip into the discussion area on the right of the screen, or to view a video clip posted by another teacher, and that clip will transfer together with its associated transcript, activities, and resources. This will be valuable for teachers, since it will offer them opportunities for sharing their professional insight and wisdom in new and transparent and rich ways. But what it will give us as researchers will be priceless: a window on what teachers see as significant in representations of classroom practice and direct evidence of what they are learning, on their own and from each other.

What we aim to be able to present are accounts of how teachers learn from the more flexible and extensive digital resources of ICE. In particular, we aim to explore the extent to which the video quotations generated by ICE become the propositions (P, Q and R, if you will), and the surrounding discourse the logical operators on those propositions (as in "P," "not-P," "Possibly Q," or "Definitely R"), at the point where representational templates for classroom action are critiqued and edited, then saved or rejected as elements in a teacher's future professional repertoire. Our initial research efforts using ICE will be focussed on in-service teacher development, but we do believe that ICE has the potential to be used with preservice teachers, particularly where there is a significant distance-learning element in their school-based experience, and we hope to be able to report on this area too in the near future.

CONCLUSION

It is all too easy to dismiss, or to appear to dismiss, the work of other researchers in the field, and to present one's own team's work, albeit inadvertently, as likely to be the key to all mythologies. It is also easy to describe in glowing terms a pilot-phase research tool (which naturally has no flaws that have been discovered thus far). One of the pleasing aspects of our close study of CTELL and RCE has been the degree of congruence between the work of these teams and that of the group that has been developing ICE, in terms of theoretical underpinning. It will be interesting to see over the coming years how the different user interfaces, client groups, and research orientations yield different types of data to enhance our understanding of how teachers learn from representations of teaching.

ACKNOWLEDGMENTS

The authors wish to acknowledge the invaluable support of the TEEP and SEP projects in funding ICE, and to thank the Teacher Training Agency for its encouragement of the initial project, the Qualifications and Curriculum Authority for permitting us to use its video material, and the teachers who have contributed their time and expertise to ICE.

REFERENCES

Baker, J. E. (1977). Application of the in-service training/classroom consultation model to reading instruction. *Ontario Psychologist, 9*(4), 57–62.

Barber, M. (2001). The National Literacy Strategy—recognition of success. *Literacy Today, 26.* Web version at http://www.literacytrust.org.uk/Pubs/barber.html. Accessed 19 January 2005.

Boling, E. C. (2003). The transformation of instruction through technology: promoting inclusive learning communities in teacher education courses. *Action in Teacher Education, 24*(4), 64–73.

Boling, E. C., & Roehler, L. (2002). *Preparing educators for diverse classrooms: teacher candidates investigate written and hypermedia cases.* Paper presented at the symposium "Preparing Educators for

Diverse Classrooms" at the Annual Meeting of the American Association of Colleges of Teacher Educators (AACTE), New York.

Brenner, D. G., Hughes, J. E., Ferdig, R., McVee, M. B., Norman, P., Packard, B., Roehler, L., & Pearson, P. D. (1999, December). *Exploring a literacy hypermedia environment: Learning from your own journeys through the Reading Classroom Explorer.* Paper presented at the National Reading Conference, Orlando, FL.

Center on English Learning and Achievement. (undated). *Features of Successful Professional Development: The Knowledge Base for Teacher Learning.* http://cela.albany.edu/research/partnerC1.htm Accessed 11 February 2004.

Clay, M. M. (1995). (Revised edition). *Reading recovery: A guidebook for teachers in training*, Auckland, NZ: Heinemann.

Copeland, W. D., & Decker, D. L. (1996). Video cases and the development of meaning making in preservice teachers. *Teaching and Teacher Education, 12*, 467–481.

Department for Education and Skills (1999). *National Literacy Strategy Training Pack.* Publication reference NLS54. London: DfES.

Department for Education and Skills. (2000). *Progression in phonics for whole class teaching CD ROM.* Publication reference DfES 0604/2001. London: DfES.

Department for Education and Skills. (2001). *The National Literacy Strategy Framework for Teaching.* Publication reference DfES 0500/2001. London: DfES.

Department for Education and Skills. (2003). *Guided reading: Supporting transition from KS1 to KS2.* Publication reference DfES 0064/2003. London: DfES.

Ferdig, R. E., Roehler, L., & Pearson, P. D. (2002). Scaffolding preservice teacher learning through Web-based discussion forums: an examination of online conversations in the Reading Classroom Explorer, *Journal of Computing in Teacher Education, 18*(3), 87–94.

Fullan, M. (2000). The return of large scale reform. *Journal of Educational Change, 1*, 15–27.

Harrison, C. (2002). *C-TELL: intentionality, causality and attribution.* Paper presented at the IRA World Congress on Reading, Edinburgh, 2002.

Harrison, C., Pead, D., & Sheard, M. (2004, December). *"P, not-P and possibly Q"—How the Interactive Classroom Explorer (ICE) interface can support teacher professional development.* Paper presented at the National Reading Conference, San Antonio TX.

Hillocks, G. W., Jr. (1999). *Ways of thinking, ways of teaching.* New York: Teachers College Press.

Hobsbaum, A., & Leon, A. (1999). *Catalyst for change: The impact of Reading Recovery in the United Kingdom.* Viewpoint 10, University of London Institute of Education.

Hughes, J. E., Packard, B. W.-L., & Pearson, P. D. (2001). *Preservice teachers' experiences using hypermedia and video to learn about literacy instruction.* CIERA Technical Report 00–06. Available: http://www.ciera.org/library/archive/index.html Accessed 25 February, 2004.

Kinzer, C., & Risko, V. (1998). Multimedia and enhanced learning: Transforming preservice education. In D. Reinking, M. McKenna, L. Labbo, & R. Kieffer (Eds.), *Handbook of technology and literacy: Transformations in a post-typographic world* (pp. 185–202). Hillsdale, NJ: Lawrence Erlbaum Associates.

Klesius, J. F., Searls, E. F., & Zielonka, P. (1990). A comparison of two methods of direct instruction of preservice teachers. *Journal of Teacher Education, 41*(4), 34–43.

Langer, J. A. (2001). *Excellence in English in middle and high school: How teachers' professional lives support student achievement.* Albany, NY: National Research Center on English Learning & Achievement. [http://cela.albany.edu/eie1/main.html] Report downloaded 17 August 2001.

Lave, J., & Wenger, E. (1991). *Situated learning: Legitimate peripheral participation.* Cambridge, England: Cambridge University Press.

Leander, K. (2003). Writing travelers' tales on new literacyscapes. *Reading Research Quarterly, 38*, 392–397.

Lunzer, E. A., & Gardner, W. K. (1979). *The effective use of reading.* London: Heinemann Educational.

Medwell, J., Wray, D., Poulson, L., & Fox, R. (1998). *Effective teachers of literacy.* Exeter: University of Exeter School of Education.

Morrison, C., Harris, A. J., & Auerbach, I. T. (1969). Staff after-effects of participation in a reading research project: A follow-up study of the craft project. *Reading Research Quarterly, 4*, 366–395.

National Reading Panel. (2000). *Teaching children to read: An evidence-based assessment of the scientific research literature on reading and its implications for reading instruction.* Washington, DC: National Institute for Child Health and Human Development.

Pressley, M., Wharton-McDonald, R., Allington, R., Block, C. C., Morrow, L., Tracey, D., Baker, K., Brooks, G., Cronin, J., Nelson, E., & Woo, D. (2001). A study of effective grade–1 literacy instruction. *Scientific Studies of Reading, 5*, 35–58.

Risko, V. (1995). Using videodisc-based cases to promote preservice teachers' problem solving and mental model building. In W. M. Linek & E. G. Sturtevant (Eds.), *Growing literacy* (pp. 173–187). Pittsburgh, PA: College Reading Association.

Rutter, M., Maughan, B., Mortimore, P., & Ouston, J., with Smith, A. (1979). *Fifteen thousand hours: Secondary schools and their effect on children.* Cambridge: Harvard University Press.

Schon, D. A. (1983). *The reflective practitioner.* New York: Basic Books.

Schon, D. A. (1987). *Educating the reflective practitioner.* San Francisco: Jossey-Bass.

Schrader P. G., Leu, Jr., D. J., Kinzer, C. K., Ataya R., Teale W. H., Labbo L. D., & Cammack, D. (2003). Using Internet delivered video cases to support preservice teachers' understanding of effective early literacy instruction: An exploratory study. *Instructional Science, 31*(4–5), 317–340.

Shyu, H. (1997). Anchored instruction for Chinese students: Enhancing attitudes toward mathematics. *International Journal of Instructional Media, 24*(1), 55–63.

Spillane, J. P. (2000). *District leaders' perceptions of teacher learning* (CPRE Occasional Paper Series OP 05). Philadelphia, PA: Consortium for Policy Research in Education. Accessed 25 February 2004. Available online: http://www.cpre.org/Publications/op-05.pdf

Spiro, R. J., Feltovich, P. J., Jacobson, M. J., & Coulson, R. L. (1991). Cognitive flexibility, constructivism, and hypertext: Random access instruction for advanced knowledge acquisition in ill-structured domains. *Educational Technology, 31*(5), 24–33.

Taylor, B. M., Pearson, P. D., Clark, K., & Walpole, S. (2000). Effective schools and accomplished teachers: Lessons about primary-grade reading instruction in low-income schools. *Elementary School Journal, 101*, 121–165.

Teachers Network. (2004). *Videos for teachers: Successful teaching strategies in elementary and middle school classrooms.* http://www.teachersnetwork.org/media/Accessed 10 February 2004.

van Someren, M., Boshuizen, H. P. A., de Jong, T., & Reimann, P. (1998). Introduction. In M. van Someren, HPA Boshuizen, T. de Jong, & P. Reimann (Eds.), *Learning with multiple representations.* Oxford: Pergamon.

Wragg, E. C., Wragg, C. M., Haynes, G. S., & Chamberlin, R. P. (1998). *Improving literacy in the primary school.* London: Routledge.

17

The Role of Technology in
the Professional Development
of Literacy Educators

Michael C. McKenna
University of Virginia

Kenneth M. Proctor
Georgia Department of Education

How can technology help to achieve the primary goal of professional development in literacy, that of enhancing the proficiency of educators in order to optimize student learning? This question is the chief focus of the present chapter, but answering it requires that we first establish a conceptual foundation of professional development. We examine how technology is building on that foundation in a variety of current initiatives. Finally, we attempt to distill common principles from these initiatives that might guide future endeavors.

THE ENDS AND MEANS OF PROFESSIONAL DEVELOPMENT

Sparks and Loucks-Horsley (1990) proposed five models of professional development, which we find useful in categorizing present-day technology applications. In the individually guided model, teachers pursue expertise in areas reflecting perceived need or personal interest. In the observation-and-feedback model, teachers grow by analyzing their own practice in collaboration with a colleague. The curriculum development/improvement model begins with a specific problem (such as low reading achievement) and entails collaborative activities designed to address it through curriculum design and implementation. The inquiry model engages teachers in the pursuit of a topic of mutual interest, providing them with a system of support and guidance. Finally, the training model targets specific learning objectives, always highly focused and, as a result, often narrow in scope. Walpole and McKenna (2004) have suggested that none of these models is likely to be effective in meeting the professional development needs of a struggling school, and that a far-reaching hybrid model should be crafted. "A comprehensive system will include mechanisms for individual support, informed by observation and feedback, all designed to develop curriculum and to train teachers to implement it, in a context of inquiry about the effects of the total program on teachers and children" (Walpole & McKenna, 2004, p. 187).

Duffy (2004) in effect placed the training model in a category of its own, by distinguishing between the "training" and the "educative" models of professional development. So labeled, the training model obviously has little to recommend it, and Duffy expressly associated it with scripted instruction. We argue, however, that the educative model, which accords teachers the professional status they deserve, can be represented as a narrow-to-broad spectrum and that the narrow end may include the kind of "training" Duffy sought to avoid. Thus, where Duffy saw a dichotomy, we see a continuum.

Toward the narrow end, a scientifically-based conceptualization of best practice grounds professional development activities that lead teachers to implement such practice. Teachers who are unaware of this conceptualization are deemed, from this perspective, to be "underprepared" (Sweet, 2004, p. 39). Toward the narrow end, professional development may concern itself with learning a new program or with mastering one or more instructional strategies, perhaps those endorsed by the National Reading Panel (NICHHD, 2000) or the International Reading Association through its *Standards for Reading Professionals* (IRA, 2003a) and its position paper on teacher education (IRA, 2003b).

Toward the broad end of the continuum, teachers become flexible decision makers, employing research-based methods, but adapting instruction to classroom contexts and unanticipated eventualities. They are still responsible for applying evidence-based methods, but they must also manage, coach, encourage, and support if they are to be highly effective. Toward the broad end, professional development may include not only these targets but less well-structured ones. For example, Block, Oakar, and Hurt (2002) concluded that the type of expertise needed by reading teachers varies by grade level, and they labeled desired roles as those of "guide," "guardian," "encourager," "supporter," "demonstrator," "manager," "coach," and "adaptor." The sort of staff development germane to learning how to implement a new core program or how to operate a laptop does not seem very conducive to the assumption of such roles.

At its narrowest, then, professional development may amount to little more than rote training in techniques or procedures; at its broadest, it may address reflective and adaptive implementations based on broad cognizance of student needs and the instructional context. We feel it is fair to say that professional development may initially target the narrow end of this continuum if teachers are to acquire proficiency in validated instructional strategies, but that it is unwise to target the broader end until these strategies are understood.

A comprehensive program of professional development in reading is one in which research-based instructional techniques are fostered together with the reflective practice necessary to employ them effectively. The National Reading Panel took such a stance in presenting evidence for specific instructional methods, while at the same time endorsing professional development resulting in thoughtfully responsive teachers (NICHHD, 2000).

What sort of professional development is likely to achieve this comprehensive outcome? Its characteristics are relatively well established and align closely, we will argue, with several present-day technology initiatives. Vacca (1994) distilled four general principles from research into effective professional development. It should, she contended, be "hands-on, relating directly to teaching and learning; individual, evoking a personal, reflective response; collaborative, joining professionals in working partnerships; [and] gradual and long-term, taking time and commitment" (p. 672). It is notable that Vacca's stance is constructivist. She acknowledges that the result will be "differing beliefs" (p. 672), so that divergent outcomes are acceptable. This stance may be a consequence of focusing on the broad end of the instructional continuum at the expense of the narrower proficiencies associated with evidence-based pedagogy. Indeed, these same four principles can easily ground a more comprehensive notion of professional development, one grounded in scientific evidence. The Learning First Alliance (LFA) (2000) has published guidelines that include individual teacher reflection, peer support, collaborative teams, and an extended time frame. These recommendations are similar to Vacca's but were explicitly intended to guide professional development in "scientifically validated practices" (p. 1). Teacher practice is therefore expected to converge in the implementation of these practices, but to diverge in accordance with student data and classroom contexts (see Lyons & Pinnell, 2001).

We offer two examples of comprehensive professional-development systems grounded in scientifically-based reading instruction (SBRI). In the first, Mesmer and Karchmer (2003) reported how professional development that embraced the LFA guidelines was successfully implemented in two schools with reading projects funded by the Reading Excellence Act, a federal program that embraced SBRI. They began their project with clear instructional goals, but they came to realize that teacher expertise varied considerably. It became necessary to adapt their initial plan in order to address the assessed professional-development needs of the teachers. In the second example, Moats (2004) reported two projects in which collaborative activities resulted in convergent thinking about best practice. She observed that teachers had limited tolerance for lecture and that successful sessions included more engaging activities, such as "when teachers prepared demonstrations for one another, read aloud with one another, worked as groups to answer questions, toured each other's classrooms, viewed videotapes of peers at work, or put themselves in the shoes of the children" (p. 283). While clear and consistent as to the content that reading teachers must acquire, she recommended "an approach that engages their affect and imagination, is respectful of their concerns, and that shows them the connection between what is being learned and the job they have to do" (p. 284). In our view, Moats' conclusions about effective professional development parallel to a remarkable degree the established principles of student learning—namely, that active engagement is indispensable, that students must realize the relevance of their learning, and that peer and family contexts may either impede or enhance achievement.

When the experiences of Vacca, Mesmer and Karchner, and Moats are considered collectively, it is clear that similar approaches to professional development can lead to remarkably different outcomes. When teacher learning is not grounded in research-based methods, we can anticipate a diversity of practice based on philosophy and instinct. When professional learning is anchored by validated methods, similarity of practice can be expected, together with variations based on context and data-driven planning. That is to say, remarkably different ends can be obtained by employing the same means, such as Vacca's four general principles of effective professional development. This is possible because, at its best, professional development occasions high levels of engagement, true depth of processing, and a focus on practical application.

USING TECHNOLOGY TO PROVIDE
PROFESSIONAL DEVELOPMENT

Business-driven advances in technology have steadily infused professional development. Even in conventional "stand-and-deliver" sessions, transparencies have given way to PowerPoints, and note-taking may now involve laptops and personal digital assistants. Newer forms of technology-facilitated professional development, representing a clear break with the past, are of two types. One is teacher directed and entails the use of Internet resources to address problems that a teacher has identified or areas of professional interest a teacher wishes to pursue. The second is more formal and less ad hoc in nature. In this section, we will describe each of these two forms in turn, citing specific exemplars in the process.

Ad hoc Applications

Online resources.   The Internet already affords teachers a host of resources related to literacy instruction. Together these resources provide the basis of self-directed professional development, mostly ad hoc in nature but valuable nonetheless. In designing the professional-development Web site for Georgia's Reading First, we compiled nearly 200 literacy sites and organized them into 21 categories. These include informative Web sites (e.g., author sites, literacy organizations, online reference tools, search engines, interactive sites for young readers, children's literature, and so forth) and sites offering downloads (e.g., cyberguides, online texts, PowerPoints, research reviews, etc.). We found categorizing difficult because of the multiple functions and extensive cross-linking of many sites, but the primary focus of a given site is still useful for access. (See "Literacy Links" at http://www.georgiasouthern.edu/~mmckenna/garf.html)

The popularity of these Web sites appears to be considerable, judging both from anecdotal evidence and commercial longevity. Research into how teachers utilize these sites is scant, however, and important questions have yet to be answered. Which types of sites are most useful? For which, if any, can a causal link with teacher practice or student achievement be substantiated? Can characteristics of site design be distilled in order to guide development of future sites? As new sites appear and old ones sometimes vanish without warning, a Darwinian analogy is compelling. Such a comparison is further apropos in that the dynamics of Web-site evolution are not yet well understood.

Discussion groups.   Systems permitting teachers to share expertise, offer commentary, and pose questions take synchronous form in chat rooms and instant messaging and asynchronous form in listservs and discussion boards. Chat rooms and discussion forums are often components in larger projects, and they can have rather specific focuses. The RTeacher listserv, developed by Donald Leu while at Syracuse University and now administered by the International Reading Association, allows teachers from the English-speaking world to share thoughts, pose questions, and voice opinions on a wide range of current issues (http://www.reading.org/resources/community/discussions.html). More focused discussion occurs at the site of the International Dyslexia Association, where discussion forums are established on a variety of topics (http://www.interdys.org/forum). Such forums provide supportive environments in which teachers are free to pursue self-selected paths toward their own professional development. In their revised standards, the National Staff Development Council (2001) advocates the establishment of professional learning communities, and these electronic meeting places are clearly a means to that end, in effect extending the community far beyond conventional limits by bringing together teachers unlikely to cross paths in "real life."

Systematic Applications

The proliferation of teacher utility sites and open-ended forums offers an exciting but peripheral approach to systematic, meaningful teacher education. In designing coherent programs, the question is how technology can embody the principles of effective professional development. Pang and Kamil (2004) reviewed the still rather limited research base underlying technology use in the professional development of literacy educators. Their conclusions are useful in framing both what we know and how we might design future applications. They found evidence that video of teaching episodes can be useful in modeling effective practice for teachers. When, in more recent years, video has come to be digitized for Internet, CD, or DVD access, it affords the additional advantage of allowing teachers to navigate through it in hypermedia environments, in combination with other information, in order to pursue specific learning objectives. Finally, they concluded that e-mail, Web logs, discussion boards, and similar vehicles permit teachers to interact in a supportive learning environment while examining instructional issues.

We now examine several current initiatives that incorporate these conclusions in unique ways. Each seeks to provide or facilitate professional development by encouraging exploration and self-reflection. Each is grounded in real-world applications that convert theory into practice. Each reflects the broadly based principles suggested by by Vacca (1994), the Learning First Alliance (2000), and the National Staff Development Council (2001). We believe that each application yields clues about the design of future technology-based professional development projects for literacy educators.

Case Technologies to Enhance Literacy Learning (CTELL). In this ambitious initiative (see Kinzer, Cammack, Labbo, Teale, & Sanny, this volume), 11 extensive K–3 classroom cases are presented to preservice teachers. These cases give teacher educators and their preservice students random access to information such as classroom and school demographics, commercial programs in use, test score summaries, samples of children's work, lesson plans, room layout, video of lessons, and recorded interviews with students, teachers, principals, and parents. Preservice teachers can share comments via e-mail and chat rooms, as well as in college class settings. Each CTELL case unfolds across time (from 4 days to 3 weeks). Each case begins with a video clip of the classroom, from 18 to 21 minutes long. This clip is viewed at the outset so that it grounds, or "anchors," all subsequent study and discussion. Preservice teachers are required to explore and contrast multiple cases at a given grade level. This requirement is designed to avoid conveying the impression that there is a single best way to deliver instruction, to make clear instead that the "underlying principles of effective practice can be realized in multiple ways" (Kinzer et al., this volume, p. 285). Three children in each CTELL classroom case are the focus of extensive data gathering, so that students can examine them in depth.

Reading Classroom Explorer (RCE). This project (Hughes, Packard, & Pearson, 2000; see also Ferdig, Roehler, & Pearson, this volume) takes a different approach to preservice teacher education, providing over 240 video clips of exemplary instruction (with transcripts) organized around 27 themes. Unlike CTELL, these clips lack rich contextualizing data, but the principal focus here is on instructional methods. Like CTELL, the hypermedia environment permits students to navigate in order to realize individual purposes, but the route is largely across episodes rather than through a dataset concerning a single case. One of the goals of RCE is to provide vicarious experience with diverse students, which is often not provided through student teaching placements. Students can post notes about the clips, accessible by other students and their instructor. The variety of clips invites useful comparisons and contrasts across teachers, and clips can be accessed by school or theme. A central question is whether studying exemplary videos translates into enhanced practice, especially in the case of undergraduates, who have yet to enter an instructional context of their own (Harrison, Pead, & Sheard, this volume).

Interactive Classroom Explorer (ICE). Like CTELL and RCE, this UK initiative presents digital video of instructional episodes to practicing teachers (see Harrison, Pead, & Sheard, this volume). ICE's approach differs, however, in that there is no *a priori* assumption that the videos necessarily capture "exemplary" instruction. Its developers argue that teachers and teacher educators alike tend to disagree as to what constitutes exemplary instruction. In the context of ICE, teachers are therefore urged from the outset to view each clip critically, using assigned readings to ground subsequent instruction. A multimedia e-mail system permits teachers to "quote" from the videos by embedding brief excerpts within e-mail messages in order to reinforce their points; search tools are provided to help them locate key instances within a transcript or clip. Teachers may also upload video clips of their own teaching when they wish to offer an alternative to how a given method is best implemented.

Teacher self-study.   Analysis of video, with the assistance of an administrator, a peer, or a literacy coach, is a widely recommended practice (Joyce & Showers, 2002; Walpole & McKenna, 2004). Using a computer and a digital camcorder makes it possible for the observer first to edit the video and then share selected segments with the teacher in a conference setting. Where all parties are willing, a group of teachers may benefit from examining and analyzing the same taped episodes. A fruitful path may be to contrast a video episode from an external source, such as RCE or ICE (regardless of whether it is considered exemplary), with video of a teacher's own attempt to employ a given technique.

Extended Cases in Reading Acquisition (ECRA).   This project, sponsored by Georgia's Reading First program, provides an extensive database of children's progress in Grades K–3 (McKenna & Walpole, 2004; McKenna, Walpole, & Proctor, 2005). Data are collected three times per year, and as children pass from one grade to the next, their case studies are extended to include the new data. For a complete case (first available in the summer of 2008), it is possible to track a child's reading development from the beginning of kindergarten to the end of third grade across 12 data collection points. (Less extensive cases, due to attrition or to a child's initial availability later than the beginning of kindergarten, are also included.) Each case is multimedia in nature, including test results; written descriptions of the child; the commercial core, supplemental, and intervention programs in use; background pertaining to the school context; interviews with parents, teachers, and children; audio clips of oral reading; and a scanned spelling sample (PALS) (see Invernizzi & Meier, 2000; Invernizzi, Meier, Swank, & Juel, 1997). The cases also offer commentary concerning important inferences from the data and the multiyear trajectories portrayed. Because the cases are publicly available, they can be linked to university courses and to formal professional development programs. Suggestions for examining the cases, including study guides, are provided. Figure 17.1 presents the home page for a particular child. While numerical and categorical data are available in an Excel file for use by researchers, it is the cases themselves that make professional development possible. Teachers can use a search engine to identify children similar to one or more of the challenging students they themselves may serve. They can contrast children on different growth trajectories and infer the causes. They can test hypotheses about the impact of approaches and programs. In their revised 2001 standards, the National Staff Development Council encourages the use of disaggregated student data to help

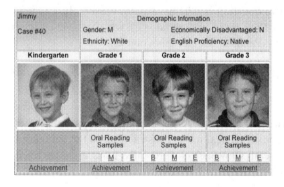

FIGURE 17.1   One child's home page in the ECRA system.

set learning priorities for individual teachers and evaluation of impact using multiple data sources. The Extended Case Studies provide models of how these priorities can be instantiated in teachers' instructional settings.

Cybermentoring. This project was initiated by Gerald Maring and his colleagues at Washington State University (Maring, Levy, & Schmid, 2002). Preservice teachers use Internet technologies (e.g., teleconferencing, e-mail, web-page development) to directly support the learning of K–12 children in remote classrooms. While the mentoring is provided by third- and fourth-year undergraduates to students, professional development occurs both for the preservice teachers involved and for the practicing teachers, who self-reflect as they provide guidance. The preservice teachers begin by learning about effective literacy strategies. Next, they apply the strategies in content-focused contexts, such as helping first graders develop a classroom newspaper or assisting seventh graders in preparing science projects. Figure 17.2 shows an undergraduate videoconferencing with a student. Given that the International Reading Association's position statement on preservice teacher preparation calls for mentoring during the first five years of teaching (IRA, 2003b), cybermentoring proactively embraces this standard by incorporating mentoring prior to employment. Although the primary mentoring is for children, the teacher mentoring received by undergraduates is notable.

Virtual clinic. The use of technology to simultaneously enhance teacher expertise and provide services to K–12 students can occur at many levels of teacher development. While cybermentoring engages undergraduates in student learning, McKenna, Reinking, and Labbo (1999)

FIGURE 17.2   A preservice teacher provides cybermentoring to a secondary science student.

have suggested a more specialized application that they call the virtual clinic. Here, data pertaining to a struggling child are relayed to a university-based clinic for analysis by reading specialists in training and their instructors. Envisioned as a means of providing expert analysis to remote geographic areas, the virtual clinic has the potential to contribute to the professional development of children's classroom teachers and field-based reading specialists as well as the specialists in training. While improvements in technology make the idea of a virtual clinic increasingly feasible, we know of no functioning example. "What is needed," they concluded, "is the emergence of a model project suitable for adaptation elsewhere" (McKenna, Reinking, & Labbo, 1999, p. 362). Such a project might entail submission of case information that includes agreed-upon measures and formats so that judgments can be readily reached and suggestions offered in a timely manner.

Multimedia units.   In a more conventional way, state departments of education, universities, and private companies have begun to use technology in order to provide professional development. The New York State Reading Academies are one example of a modular approach, in which eight 10-hour modules are available online (http://www.nyreading.com/academies/NY/overview/index.jsp). Teacher learning is only partially independent, however, in that teachers participate in 20-person cohorts engaging in online discussions led by an Academy "coach." The USDOE-sponsored Light Bridge project (http://www.sonoma.edu/lightbridge) offers online lessons on specific topics (including, but not limited to, reading) supported by video clips. Teachscape (http://www.teachscape.com) is a private company that, like Light Bridge and the New York Academies, also provides study modules, but tailors its offerings to district needs and combines online work with in-person sessions. Like Light Bridge, Teachscape is not limited to literacy. We view these as among the first of many staff development agencies that will rely on the Internet for a portion of its delivery.

CHARACTERISTICS OF SUCCESSFUL
TECHNOLOGY APPLICATIONS

We offer these projects as exemplars of how technology can be used to address both the narrow and broad ends of the professional-development continuum. In Table 17.1 we organize the exemplars according to the six major approaches we have discussed. Each has the capacity to focus on specific teacher competencies without losing sight of the contextual factors and the need to flexibly differentiate instruction. They nest the consideration of instructional techniques within the context of real examples. This is true even of the loosely structured discussion forums, as anyone familiar with them can attest.

There may be a lesson in these projects for the design of new ones. Based on their common traits and on how those traits reflect the research on effective professional development, we can distill characteristics of technology applications that have a high probability of success.

1. *The technology should use multimedia to contextualize specific instructional methods.* Technology may be uniquely situated to address the broad and narrow ends of the professional-development spectrum simultaneously. One of the early (Goodman, 1989) and enduring (Allington, 2002) objections to the use of scientifically-based reading research is that such research typically disregards the contexts in which instructional methods must ultimately be applied. For example, when teachers learn about graphic organizers (certainly an indisputable example of SBRI), they may begin at the narrow end of the spectrum (learning what graphic organizers are, how they can be used instructionally, etc.) and then move to the broad end by observing teach-

TABLE 17.1
Approaches to the Use of Technology for Professional Development in Literacy

Basic Approach	Subtypes	Examples
Online Resources	Informative Web Sites	IRA, Author Sites, Reference Tools
	Downloadable Resources	SEDL, FCRR, CIERA
Discussion Groups	Synchronous	Chat Rooms (RCE, CTELL)
	Asynchronous	Listservs (RTeacher)
		Discussion Forums (RCE, ICE)
Case Studies	Student based	ECRA
	Classroom based	CTELL
Video Episodes	Exemplary Instruction	RCE
	Unrated Instruction	ICE
	Teacher Self-Study	Peer and Literacy Coaching
Multimedia Units	Topical Units	NY Reading Academies
		Light Bridge
	Online Courses	University Graduate Programs
Clinical Experiences	Preservice Teachers	Cybermentoring
	Specialists	Virtual Clinic

ers introduce them in classroom contexts, by watching students construct them, by examining student work containing organizers, or by hearing how individual children react to them. Technology places the full range within the professional developer's grasp, from narrow to broad, from general to contextualized.

2. *The technology should provide a rich depiction of actual children.* The promise of multimedia is to portray children multidimensionally. While their true complexity can never be captured, teachers can gain a reasonable idea of their backgrounds, needs, and growth trajectories from data housed in hypermedia environments. We suspect that hearing children read and respond to interview probes, listening to their parents and teachers, and watching video clips of children in classroom settings will help humanize cases for teachers who are learning about reading development and how to foster it. Such information richly contextualizes assessment results and can lead to nuanced interpretation and insights.

3. *The technology should permit instructive contrasts among examples.* Projects like RCE, CTELL, ICE, and ECRA offer educators the chance to note similarities and differences among instructional episodes, classrooms, and children, respectively. Multiple examples make it possible to infer overarching principles, which is key to the subsequent application of such principles in classroom practice.

4. *The technology should facilitate collaboration and engagement.* In their revised standards, the National Staff Development Council (2001) advocates the establishment of professional learning communities, and the involvement and guidance of school and district leaders. Each of the systematic uses of technology described in this chapter has a collaborative component. While independent use is possible, their developers foresaw interaction among educators as the most effective approach, with the technology merely providing a focus and facilitating that interaction.

5. *The technology must eventually become "invisible" to be most effective.* If technology is to facilitate how teachers process the information and ideas presented through professional development, then it must function transparently, without calling attention to itself at the expense of

content learning (Bruce & Hogan, 1998). We suspect that this reality has occasioned the observable trend among staff developers away from glitzy PowerPoints and toward more workmanlike presentations in which form follows function. The goal, then, is to "use technology as a tool, not as a focus" (Maring, Levy, & Schmid, 2002, n.p.), but this goal can only be achieved when the technology used has become second nature to teachers (the recipients of professional development). Anyone familiar with technology innovations can attest to the early distraction of their novelty and to their subsequent effectiveness as the newness waned. This trend may be inevitable with any new application, including audio and video clips, discussion forums, and other uses associated with the initiatives described in this chapter.

In the early stages of a new application, professional development may require that technology be a focus as well as a medium (Pang & Kamil, 2004). Teachers must learn how it works and how it can help them. This focus is necessary not only to facilitate teacher learning of professional-development content but to equip teachers with the know-how to incorporate new technology applications into their own instruction (Strickland, 2004). The technology specialist may play a central role in familiarizing teachers with the applications they may be required to use as part of the professional-development process (Proctor & Livingston, 2001). This goal cannot be realized through the specialist's independent efforts, however. Proctor (1998) summarized the importance of a team approach to effective technology implementation on any scale. He discussed the necessity for administrators, technology personnel, and teachers to be involved in short- and long-range comprehensive technology planning.

USING TECHNOLOGY TO EVALUATE
PROFESSIONAL DEVELOPMENT

Despite near-universal acknowledgement of the need for professional development, its impact on student achievement is difficult to substantiate (Guskey, 2002; Guskey & Sparks, 1996), even though some studies have documented such a link (see Anders, Hoffman, & Duffy, 2000). Sometimes increased student achievement is not clearly recognized as the ultimate goal (Killion, 2002). Even when it is, gauging the impact of professional development on student growth is challenging.

Joyce and Showers (2002) asserted that four conditions are required if professional development is to affect achievement to a meaningful degree:

- A community of professionals comes together who study together, put into practice what they are learning, and share the results.

- The content of staff development develops around curricular and instructional strategies selected because they have a high probability of affecting student learning—and, importantly, student ability to learn.

- The magnitude of change generated is sufficient that the students' gain in knowledge and skill is palpable. What is taught, how it is taught, and the social climate of the school have to change to the degree that the increase in student ability to learn is manifest.

- The processes of staff development enable educators to develop the skill to implement what they are learning. (p. 4)

These conditions suggest that the link between professional development and student achievement is both indirect and subject to intervening influences. Guskey (2000) suggested that the impact of professional development is typically assessed simply by asking teachers to comment on the session they attend. However, the ultimate goal of most professional development is enhanced student achievement, and teachers' impressions can hardly be a proximate indicator of an achievement impact. While teacher impressions can constitute useful feedback for improving future sessions (Learning Point Associates, 2004), it is also important to assess what teachers actually learn through professional development activities. And yet, for two reasons, teachers' learning of the session content may or may not lead to their attempting to implement the instructional strategies to which they have been exposed. To begin with, school and district factors may help or hinder implementation. Moats (2004) observed that school and district contexts can militate against effective teacher learning when existing policies are at odds with such learning. Simple logistics can also stand in the way. For example, if teachers learn about a new reading strategy that cannot be implemented because of the time demanded by an adopted core program, then implementation cannot be expected to occur. The second reason is that teachers may simply choose not to implement newly introduced strategies, despite adequate knowledge of how to do so and despite the fact that nothing in the classroom or school context is likely to prevent them.

Guskey accordingly recommends that effective evaluation of professional development be multifaceted. Teacher impressions as well as the extent of their learning should be gauged. Classroom and school factors likely to assist or impede implementation must be evaluated. The degree of actual implementation must also be determined. Then, if and only if implementation has occurred to an adequate extent, student outcomes must be surveyed. Although the National Reading Panel has concluded that effective implementation of validated instructional strategies can be expected to result in improved student achievement (NICHHD, 2000), this expectation is by no means certain and does not absolve us from the responsibility of evaluating the causal link. Nor can student achievement alone be used as the index of professional development's effectiveness.

To summarize, Guskey has suggested that the causal steps leading from professional development to enhanced student achievement are these:

1.   professional development occurs;
2.   positive teacher impressions about the professional development result;
3.   teachers adequately learn the content of the professional development;
4.   the inhibiting effects of school-level factors are negligible;
5.   teachers ultimately implement the content of the professional development; and finally
6.   student achievement improves as a result of the implementation.

If we leapfrog the intervening steps (namely, the extent of teacher learning, the possible effects of intervening school factors, and the extent of teacher implementation) and attempt to gauge the impact of professional development in terms of student achievement alone, then nuanced appreciation of what actually occurred is impossible.

Guskey's perspective is that the evaluation of professional development must be articulated from start to finish if credible conclusions are to be reached. Technology applications are possible at each stage of this process. Teacher reaction and learning can be gauged by discussion postings, listservs, or online exams. Electronic portfolios have also shown promise in stimulating reflection and self-appraisal (Kieffer, Hale, & Templeton, 1998). In fact, excellent online resources are available for this purpose through the Online Evaluation Resources Library (OERL) (www.oerl.sri.com). Contextual factors might be gauged in the same manner, especially if administrators take part and discussions are unrestricted and possibly anonymous. When follow-up classroom visits by the professional development provider are not feasible, implementation can be judged through video tapes, using rubrics to organize and evaluate instructional episodes. Our work with

Reading First in Georgia has entailed the rubric-based analysis of both audio and videotapes of content redelivery, and the resulting feedback has been well received by those observed. This application is similar to the use of video to mentor first-year teachers in the Pathwise system (Lane, 2004). Finally, student outcome data may present itself through technology more rapidly than it has in the past. Using computerized classroom assessments such as DIBELS (http:// dibels.uoregon.edu) and PALS (http://pals.virginia.edu), teachers (and professional development evaluators) can gauge changes in student achievement in specific areas. Such data can then be reasonably tied to the implementation of new strategies. Statistical packages and spreadsheets represent yet another technology application ideal for this purpose (Killion, 2002). For older students, class grades recorded either through digital grade books or software systems, such as Parent Connect, designed to keep parents apprised of student progress, can also be used as an indicator of professional development impact.

CONCLUSIONS

Professional development in literacy presently reflects an expanding range of technology applications. Like many educational innovations, some of these applications are well ahead of research into their effectiveness. However, many are fashioned on the basis of sound principles of teacher learning, and evidence of impact is beginning to accrue.

These applications now provide effective patterns for creating new ones. One potentially fruitful path may be to employ established ideas in tandem. From the six basic types of applications we have described, productive combinations suggest themselves. Consider well-delineated, longitudinal child cases nested within a series of classroom cases as a cohort of children advances from grade to grade. Imagine a virtual community in which practicing teachers conduct cybermentoring by offering insights to preservice teachers concerning a CTELL-like classroom case. Envision a system in which preservice and in-service teachers share responses to exemplary video clips. Contemplate a virtual learning community in which data for challenging readers are discussed during videoconferences and contrasted with archived case studies by teachers and university-based specialists while undergraduates "eavesdrop." As new applications emerge, they may comprise such hybrids, or they may constitute newly conceived basic types, themselves subject to subsequent mergers with existing types. The potential for creative uses of technology to facilitate teacher learning about literacy seems limitless.

REFERENCES

Allington, R. L. (2002). *Big Brother and the national reading curriculum: How ideology trumped evidence*. Portsmouth, NH: Heinemann.

Anders, P. L., Hoffman, J. V., & Duffy, G. G. (2000). Teaching teachers to teach reading: Paradigm shifts, persistent problems, and challenges. In M. L. Kamil, P. B. Mosenthal, P. D. Pearson, & R. Barr (Eds.). *Handbook of reading research* (Vol. 3, pp. 719–742). Mahwah, NJ: Lawrence Erlbaum Associates.

Birman, B. F., Desimone, L., Porter, A. C., & Grant, M. S. (2002). Designing professional development that works. *Educational Leadership, 59*(8), 28–33.

Block, C. C., Oakar, M., & Hurt, N. (2002). The expertise of literacy teachers: A continuum from preschool to grade 5. *Reading Research Quarterly, 37*, 178–206.

Bruce, B. C., & Hogan, M. P. (1998). The disappearance of technology: Toward an ecological model of literacy. In D. Reinking, M. C. McKenna, L. D. Labbo, & R. D. Kieffer (Eds.). *Handbook of literacy* and technology: Transformations in a post-typographic world (pp. 269–282). Mahwah, NJ: Lawrence Erlbaum Associates.

Dole, J. A., & Osborn, J. (2004). Professional development for K–3 teachers: Content and processes. In D. S. Strickland & M. L. Kamil (Eds.). *Improving reading achievement through professional development* (pp. 65–74). Norwood, MA: Christopher-Gordon.

Duffy, G. G. (2004). Teachers who improve reading achievement: What research says about what they do and how to develop them. In D. S. Strickland & M. L. Kamil (Eds.). *Improving reading achievement through professional development* (pp. 3–22). Norwood, MA: Christopher-Gordon.

Ferdig, R. E., Roehler, L. R., & Pearson, P. D. (2006). Video and database-driven web environments for pre-service literacy teaching and learning. In M. C. McKenna, L. D. Labbo, R. D. Kieffer, & D. Reinking (Eds.). *International handbook of literacy and technology* (vol. 2, pp. xxx–xxx) (??). Mahwah, NJ: Lawrence Erlbaum Associates.

Goodman, K. S. (1989). Whole-language research: Foundations and development. *The Elementary School Journal, 90*, 207–221.

Guskey, T. R. (2000). *Evaluating professional development.* Thousand Oaks, CA: Corwin Press.

Guskey, T. R. (2002). Does it make a difference? Evaluating professional development. *Educational Leadership, 59*(6), 45–51.

Guskey, T. R., & Sparks, D. (1996). Exploring the relationship between staff development and improvements in student learning. *Journal of Staff Development, 17*(4), 34–038.

Harrison, C., Pead, D., & Sheard, M. (2006). "P, not-P and possibly Q": Literacy teachers learning from digital representations of the classroom. In M. C. McKenna, L. D. Labbo, R. D. Kieffer, & D. Reinking (Eds.). *International handbook of literacy and technology* (vol. 2, pp. xxx–xxx) (??). Mahwah, NJ: Lawrence Erlbaum Associates.

Hughes, J. E., Pakard, B. W., & Pearson, P. D. (2000). Preservice teachers' perceptions of using hypermedia and video to examine the nature of literacy instruction. *Journal of Literacy Instruction, 32*, 599–629.

International Reading Association. (2003a). Standards for reading professionals (2003 Revision). Newark, DE: Author. Available: http://www.reading.org/resources/issues/reports/professional_standards.html

International Reading Association. (2003b). *Investment in teacher education in the United States: A position statement of the International Reading Association.* Newark, DE: Author. Available: http://www.reading.org/resources/issues/positions_preparation.html

International Reading Association (2001). *Preparing students for their literacy future: A position statement on literacy and technology.* Newark, DE: Author. Available: http://www.reading.org/positions/investment.html

Invernizzi, M., & Meier, J. (2000). *Phonological awareness literacy screening: Grades 1 to 3.* Charlottesville, VA: University of Virginia.

Invernizzi, M., Meier, J., Swank, L., & Juel, C. (1997). *Phonological awareness literacy screening: Kindergarten.* Charlottesville, VA: University of Virginia.

Joyce, B., & Showers, B. (2002). *Student achievement through staff development* (3rd ed.). Alexandria, VA: Association for Curriculum and Supervision Development.

Kieffer, R. D., Hale, M. E., & Templeton, A. (1998). Electronic literacy portfolios: Technology transformations in a first-grade classroom. In D. Reinking, M. C. McKenna, L. D. Labbo, & R. D. Kieffer (Eds.). *Handbook of literacy and technology: Transformations in a post-typographic world* (pp. 145–164). Mahwah, NJ: Lawrence Erlbaum Associates.

Killion, J. (2002). *Assessing impact: Evaluating staff development.* Oxford, OH: National Staff Development Council.

Kinzer, C. K., Cammack, D. W., Labbo, L. D., Teale, W. H., & Sanny, R. (2006). Using technology to (re)conceptualize pre-service literacy teacher education: Considerations of design, pedagogy and research. In M. C. McKenna, L. D. Labbo, R. D. Kieffer, & D. Reinking (Eds.). *International handbook of literacy and technology* (vol. 2, pp. xxx–xxx) (??). Mahwah, NJ: Lawrence Erlbaum Associates.

Lane, D. M. (2004). The use of videotape in a classroom setting. In D. S. Strickland & M. L. Kamil (Eds.). *Improving reading achievement through professional development* (p. 246). Norwood, MA: Christopher-Gordon.

Learning First Alliance. (2000). *Every child reading: A professional development guide.* Washington, DC: Author.

Learning Point Associates. (2004). Keeping professional learning on track with evaluation. *Notes and Reflections*, Issue 6, Spring 2004, pp. 1–15. Available: http://www.ncrel.org/info/notes/

Lyons, C. A., & Pinnell, G. S. (2001). *Systems for change in literacy education: A guide to professional development.* Portsmouth, NH: Heinemann.

Maring, G. H., Levy, E. W., & Schmid, J. A. (2002). Variations on a cybermentoring theme: Six literacy projects involving preservice teachers and students across grade levels. *Reading Online, 6*(4). Available: http://www.readingonline.org/articles/art_index.asp?HREF=maring2/index.html

McKenna, M. C., Reinking D., & Labbo, L. D. (1999). The role of technology in the reading clinic: Its past and potential. In D. H. Evensen & P. Mosenthal (Eds.). *Reconsidering the role of the reading clinic in a new age of literacy*, pp. 347–364. JAI Press. [Volume 6 of *Advances in Reading/Language Arts*]

McKenna, M. C., & Walpole, S. (2004, June). *An Internet database of longitudinal case studies in reading.* Paper presented at the meeting of the Society for the Scientific Study of Reading, Amsterdam, The Netherlands.

McKenna, M. C., Walpole, S., & Proctor, K. M. (2005). *Using online cases studies to enhance teacher expertise in reading assessment and instruction.* Paper presented at the meeting of the International Reading Association, San Antonio.

Mesmer, H. A., & Karchmer, R. A. (2003). REAlity: How the Reading Excellence Act took form in two schools. *The Reading Teacher, 56*, 636–645.

Moats, L. C. (2004). Science, language, and imagination in the professional development of reading teachers. In P. McCardle & V. Chhabra (Eds.). *The voice of evidence in reading research* (pp. 269–287). Baltimore: Brookes.

National Institute of Child Health and Human Development (NICHHD). (2000). *Report of the National Reading Panel. Teaching children to read: An evidence-based assessment of the scientific research literature on reading and its implications for reading instruction.* (NIH Publication No. 00-4769). Washington, DC: U. S. Government Printing Office. Available: http://www.nationalreadingpanel.org

National Staff Development Council. (2001). *Standards for staff development* (Revised). Oxford, OH: Author. Available: http://www.nsdc.org/standards

Pang, E. S., & Kamil, M. L. (2004). Professional development in the uses of technology. In D. S. Strickland & M. L. Kamil (Eds.). *Improving reading achievement through professional development* (pp. 149–168). Norwood, MA: Christopher-Gordon.

Proctor, K. M. (1998). *Increasing the use of technology by classroom teachers: The role of the system technology specialist.* Unpublished doctoral dissertation. Valdosta State University, Valdosta, Georgia.

Proctor, K. M., & Livingston, M. J. (1999). The role of technology specialist: Case studies of change agents. *Research in the Schools, 6*(2), 25–32.

Sparks, D., & Loucks-Horsley, S. (1990). Models of staff development. In R. Houston (Ed.). *Handbook of research on teacher education* (3rd ed., pp. 234–250). New York: Macmillan.

Strickland, D. S. (2004). Introduction. In D. S. Strickland & M. L. Kamil (Eds.). *Improving reading achievement through professional development* (pp. 43–48). Norwood, MA: Christopher-Gordon.

Sweet, R. W. (2004). The big picture: Where we are nationally on the reading front and how we got here. In P. McCardle & V. Chhabra (Eds.). *The voice of evidence in reading research* (pp. 13–44). Baltimore: Brookes.

Vacca, J. L. (1994). What works for teachers in professional growth and development. *The Reading Teacher, 47*, 672–673.

Walpole, S., & McKenna, M. C. (2004). *The literacy coach's handbook.* New York: Guilford.

V

▼▼▼▼▼▼▼

THE POTENTIAL OF TECHNOLOGY IN KEY DIMENSIONS OF LITERACY

Technology and the Engaged Literacy Learner

Linda B. Gambrell
Clemson University

It is clear that technology is becoming more important as a teaching and learning tool both at home and in our schools. Classrooms today look and feel very differently from the classrooms of 30 years ago, primarily because of the increased use of technology. Our students are more proficient than ever before in using technology to search for information, to answer questions of interest, and to find out about other people's ideas and opinions about various topics. It is no surprise that many students find technologically mediated reading and writing to be highly motivating and engaging.

In classrooms today it is common to see students using e-mail and informational sites on the Internet. In a recent visit to a middle-grades classroom, students were logged on to Booktalks (http://nancyKeane.con/booktalks). The booktalks are more like movie trailers than book reviews. They are intended to hook the reader. In an elementary classroom, children were logged on to Between the Lions (http://pbskids.org/lions), a Web site based on the popular PBS program that offers stories, games, and songs designed to promote reading as a fun pastime. Other students in this same classroom were logged on to National Geographic Kids Magazine (http://www.nationalgeographic.con/ngkids/) and Scholastic News Zone (http://teacher.scholastic.com/scholasticnews/).

WE ARE NOW A CYBERNATION

As I think about how technology relates to classroom environments I am reminded of themes that emerged in a survey conducted by the National School Boards Foundation (NSBF) in 2000. The survey revealed interesting trends in the use of technology and yielded implications for P–16 education. The NSBF study surveyed 1,735 randomly sampled American households with children ages 2 to 17 on the use of technology. One conclusion of the study was that we are now a cybernation, and that this is especially true for today's children. In over half the households surveyed, at least one child used the Internet and three out of four teenagers were online.

We are seeing much more use of the Internet in classrooms, particularly as a resource for locating and researching topics of study. The NSBF reported that 52% of school-age children who used the Internet reported using it for schoolwork at least once a week. This finding illustrates the connection between school and home Internet use. In addition, approximately 30% of children in the NSBF reported using the Internet at least once a week for general learning activities not connected with school.

In the NBSF study, 53% of the students who reported using the Internet said they watched less TV as a result. In the past, educators have often viewed television as taking away time from reading. It appears that use of the Internet may diminish the amount of time that children view television. Of particular note was the survey finding that 73% of the students who reported using the Internet said they spend more time reading books as a result of Internet use. These findings appear promising and suggest that technology may even increase interest and growth in reading.

TECHNOLOGY AND SUSTAINED ENGAGEMENT WITH TEXT

How does technology promote engagement, particularly as it relates to learning from text? Much of what we know about literacy engagement provides insights about the importance and relevance of the role of technology in learning from text. In Flippo's (2001) study of reading experts, there was compelling agreement on the importance of literacy motivation, or engagement with text. Many of the points of agreement among the reading experts were grounded in the belief that motivation is an important outcome of literacy instruction. Flippo's study revealed congruence across theoretical perspectives, research findings, and reading experts that the following class-room characteristics foster reading engagement: access to reading materials, opportunities for self-selection, and social interactions about text. Technology in the classroom can enhance these three classroom characteristics in important ways.

Access to reading materials.   There is no doubt that the Internet enriches access to text, particularly informational text. Over the past two decades, reading research has highlighted the importance of increasing young children's exposure to informational text. Prior to the 1990s, our elementary schools favored the use of narrative with young children. In 1993, Pappas published a landmark study that raised significant questions about whether narrative text should be the primary or dominant text used with young children. In her study of kindergarten children, she found that children were just as successful in reenacting informational text as they were with stories. Pappas challenged the "narrative as primary" notion, stating that an exclusive emphasis on reading "story" in the early grades limits children's experiences with other forms of text and may result in creating a barrier to full access to literacy. Adding to the research base on young children's exposure to informational text, Duke (2000) explored the degree to which informational texts were actually included in first-grade classrooms, and in what ways. Duke's study revealed that young children lack the exposure to informational text needed to build the familiarity, comfort, and confidence required to become proficient readers of informational text in the later grades.

At about the same time that reading researchers such as Pappas (1993) and Duke (2000) were emphasizing the need for young children to have increased exposure to informational text, another phenomenon was occurring; the computer was becoming an integral thread in the fabric of our classrooms and our culture. The computer and the Internet have put information literally at the fingertips of both teachers and students. Students can pursue their interests in a range of topics and locate information from a wide range of sources. It may not be an exaggeration to say that gone are the days when teachers refer students to traditional hardback encyclopedias or other resource books to locate information. While these resources still serve an important role in our classrooms, it is increasingly likely that our students are "logging on" and "Googling" a topic on the Internet. Clearly, technology has dramatically increased our access to text and the opportunity for students to explore their reading interests in a variety of ways.

Opportunities for self-selection.   One of the most important features of technology in the classroom is the opportunity for self-selection. Self-selection of topics, texts, and types of resources has dramatically increased as a result of access to the Internet.

Research continues to document that reading engagement is high in classrooms that provide access to text and opportunities for students to choose topics of interest (Allington & McGill-Franzen, 1993; Elley, 1992; Gambrell, 1995; Flippo, 2001). One of the most robust findings in the psychological literature is that choice is related to motivation. Consequently, it is no surprise that self-selection of reading material is strongly linked to increased engagement with text (Gambrell & Morrow, 1996; Palmer, Codling, & Gambrell, 1994). Schiefele's (1991) research documented that students who were allowed and encouraged to choose their own reading materials expended more effort in learning and understanding the material they read.

Increases in motivation and sustained engagement with text have been reported for a range of students who self-selected reading materials, including remedial readers (Mayes, 1982) and adolescent students with discipline problems (Coley, 1981). These studies suggest that motivation to read is linked to increased engagement with text, thereby helping students gain much needed practice and experience.

Social interactions about text.   Theories of motivation and engagement with text emphasize that learning is facilitated by social interactions with others. A number of reading studies have documented that social interaction promotes literacy achievement, higher-level cognition, and intrinsic desire to read (Almasi, 1995; Guthrie, Schafer, Wang, & Afflerbach, 1995). In addition, studies have also shown that a classroom environment that fosters social interaction is more likely to foster intrinsic motivation to read as compared to more individualized solitary learning environments (Ames, 1984; Deci, Valerand, Pelletier, & Ryan, 1991; Guthrie, Schafer, Wang, & Afflerbach, 1995). Guthrie et al. (1996) found that students who talked with others about text were more intrinsically motivated to read, and they read more widely and more frequently than students who were not as socially interactive.

Sharing and exchanging ideas with others about books, stories, and informational text is an important factor in developing engaged and motivated readers. In Flippo's (2001) study of reading experts, there was agreement among the experts about the importance of the role of social interaction in reading. Specifically, there was agreement that students should be encouraged to talk about and share different kinds of reading in a variety of ways with many others.

Classrooms today are supporting and nurturing social interactions about text through the use of online book clubs, discussion groups, and journal writing. Technology has also introduced new and interesting ways for students to socially interact with others about text. Early on, teachers provided opportunities for students to engage in e-mail exchanges with students in other towns, states, and even countries about books they were reading. The newest form of technology that promotes social interaction is the "blog" (Web logs, or online journals).

I recently had a personal experience that revealed the power of the blog, particularly with respect to revealing multiple interpretations of a text. I ran across a report of a survey conducted by the National Endowment for the Arts, entitled "Reading At Risk" (2004). The key finding was that the reading of "literary" books by American adults was declining rapidly, especially among younger adults. I was intrigued. I wanted to know more about this study, so I went on the Internet to find the actual report so that I could read it in detail. After I read the report, I found newspaper articles on the Internet from across the country about the survey and its findings. The newspaper articles revealed additional insights about the survey, particularly the fact that only the reading of traditional books was considered in this study, and the key findings related only to the reading of novels, short stories, poetry, or plays during leisure time reading. When I clicked on to several blogs, I found people talking about the increasing role of informational reading, and the use of technologically mediated reading. I found questions being raised about definitions of "reading" and "literary reading." As I reflected on this experience, I realized how my understanding of the survey had been broadened by reading other sources and how my interpretation had expanded as a result of reading what others thought about the survey and its findings.

According to Parker (2004), the "blogosphere" is a potential boon to problem solving of a higher order. Clearly, technology supports social interaction in a variety of ways, including e-mail exchanges and blog sites, so that students can share and read the ideas of others.

Technology, particularly the use of the Internet, has the potential to enhance literacy engagement and motivation to read. The ability to access information via the Internet increases daily, giving students the ability to self-select reading materials and resources, as well as the ability to explore what others think about text ideas. Literacy researchers are becoming increasingly aware of the powerful role of technology in literacy development and its potential to enhance literacy achievement.

FROM SKEPTICAL TO ENTHUSIASTIC: EMERGING VIEWS OF TECHNOLOGY

In working with parents, preservice, and in-service teachers, I have found that views of technology have moved from skeptical to enthusiastic. In the NSBF (2,000) survey, parents were even more positive about computers than their children. They reported overwhelmingly that the Internet is a powerful tool for learning. While 36% of the families reported that they purchased the home computer for their children's education, over 45% of the families reported that their children are actually using it for that purpose now. My experiences suggest that parents and teachers are increasingly viewing technology as an important literacy and learning tool.

This message was brought home recently when I heard one of our teacher education majors speak to members of the Clemson University Health, Education, and Human Development Advisory Board. Morgan Bowie, a senior at Clemson University majoring in Elementary Education, was completing her student teaching in a fourth-grade classroom. Her comments reflect the trends and issues in technology better than anything I could say:

> During my four years in the teacher education program I had the opportunity to take many courses that enabled me to grow as a student and a professional. Of all the courses I have taken, none has prepared me more for my student teaching experience than my technology class. I learned everything from how to make PowerPoint [presentations] to how to create and edit I-movies. When I first took the class, I didn't think most classrooms used this type of technology. However, when I stepped into my fourth-grade classroom and saw the abundance of technological tools that I could use to implement lessons, I was amazed. My classroom had 10 computers, 5 PC's and 5 I-Macs, 20 Pal Pilots, an LCD projector, 4 digital still cameras, and 2 digital video cameras. After seeing fourth-grade students use this technology, I realized that education technology is a powerful tool that can be used to improve student motivation and achievement.
>
> Technology gives students a tremendous range of instructional and learning opportunities. For example, students in my social studies class researched statesmen of the U.S. They then recorded their presentations using digital recording devices. This was loaded into the I-Mac computer and then the students added sound, sound effects, and transitions to create a multimedia presentation. Instead of pretending to record a newscast interviewing statesmen, the students actually created their own news program that was viewed by other students. The students became experts who assumed the responsibility for their own learning, and the learning of their peers.

I have seen that children, as writers, seek to be heard by "real audiences." They also want to see the relationship between what they are asked to do in their classrooms and what is going on in the rest of the world. Providing students with opportunities to share their ideas using technology enables them to find real purposes for their learning. They begin to see themselves as able to contribute to their own learning and the learning of their peers. I have learned so much in my student teaching experience, but the most rewarding part has been seeing every student want to learn and help others learn by using technology.

Not every classroom will have the wealth of technology found in the one where Morgan did her fourth-grade student teaching. Nonetheless, the trend is clear that classrooms are increasing in the acquisition and use of technology, and preservice and in-service teachers are becoming increasingly skilled at providing a range of learning opportunities for students that are only possible through technology.

With respect to motivation and literacy learning, there are a number of questions that need to be explored through research. Research is needed that will explore the increased use of technology in the classroom and the shift from time spent watching television to time spent on the Internet and the effects on literacy and learning. In addition, we need to know more about text engagement and motivational factors that are associated with the use of technology, particularly as they relate to literacy development and achievement.

SUMMARY

As intuitively appealing as technology may appear, it will be little more than a sophisticated novelty unless teachers are equipped with the skills needed to use it effectively in support of literacy instruction. Technology has the potential to significantly increase access to text, opportunities for self-selection, and social interactions about text. With technology on the increase, it is important that teachers become more aware of the positive impact technology can have on students' literacy engagement, motivation, and achievement.

REFERENCES

Allington, R. L., & McGill-Franzen, A. (1993, October 13). What are they to read? Not all children, Mr. Riley, have easy access to books. *Education Week*, 26.

Almasi, J. F. (1995). The nature of fourth graders' sociocognitive conflicts in peer-led and teacher-led discussions of literature. *Reading Research Quarterly, 30*, 314–351.

Ames, C. (1984). Achievement attributions and self-instructions under competitive and individualistic goal structures. *Journal of Educational Psychology, 76*, 478–487.

Coley, J. D. (1981). Non-stop reading for teenagers: What we have learned and where we go from here. Paper presented at the annual meeting of the College Reading Association, Louisville, KY. (ERIC Document Reproduction Service No. ED 211951.)

Deci, E. L., Valerand, R. M., Pelletier, L., & Ryan, R. (1991). Motivation and education: The self-determination perspective. *Educational Psychologist, 26*, 325–347.

Duke, N. (2000). 3.6 minutes per day: The scarcity of informational texts in first grade. *Reading Research Quarterly, 35*, 202–224.

Elley, W. B. (1994). *The IEA study of reading literacy: Achievement and instruction in thirty-two school systems*. Exter: BPCC Wheatons.

Flippo, R. F. (2001). *Reading researchers in search of common ground*. Newark, DE: International Reading Association.

Gambrell, L. B. (1995). Motivation matters. In W. M. Linek & E. G. Sturtevant (Eds.), *Generations of literacy: Seventeenth yearbook of the College Reading Association* (pp. 2–24). Harrisonburg, VA: College Reading Association.

Gambrell, L. B., & Morrow, L. M. (1996). Creating motivating contexts for literacy learning. In L. Baker, P. Afflerbach, & D. Reinking (Eds.). *Developing engaged readers in school and home communities* (pp. 115–136). Hillsdale, NJ: Lawrence Erlbaum Associates.

Guthrie, J. T., Schafer, W., Wang, Y., & Afflerbach, P. (1995). Relationships of instruction to amount of reading: An exploration of a social, cognitive, and instructional connection. *Reading Research Quarterly, 30*, 8–25.

Mayes, F. J. (1982). U.S.S.R. for poor readers. *Orbit, 13*, 3–4.

National School Boards Foundation Technology Survey (2000).

Palmer, B. M., Codling, R. M., & Gambrell, L. B. (1994). In their own words: What elementary children have to say about motivation to read. *The Reading Teacher, 48*, 176–179.

Pappas, C. C. (1993). Is narrative "primary"? Some insights from kindergartners' pretend readings of stories and information books. *Journal of Reading Behavior, 25*, 97–129.

Parker, K. (September 15, 2004). Bloggers bring new layer of truth to the information age. *The Greenville News. Greenville, SC.*

Reading At Risk: A survey of Literacy Reading in America (2004). National Endowment for the Arts, Research Division Report #46.

Schiefele, U. (1991). Interest, learning, and motivation. *Educational Psychologist, 26*, 299–323.

19
▼▼▼▼▼▼▼

More than Skill and Drill: Exploring the Potential of Computers in Decoding and Fluency Instruction

Melanie R. Kuhn
Rutgers Graduate School of Education

Steven A. Stahl
University of Illinois at Urbana–Champaign

Given the number of concepts students in the primary classroom need to develop, it may seem excessive to argue that computers should be part of the literacy curriculum. And when looking at many of the computer programs that are available for home use, it may even seem as if technology is fine for games, but that it is not an effective use of children's time in terms of literacy learning. However, computers have significant potential to assist students with both their word recognition and their fluency development in ways that can complement traditional print based materials (e.g., Labbo & Kuhn, 2000; Merrow, 2001; Reinking, 1998). Indeed, computers have the capacity to become an important part of reading instruction in the primary grades. It is the goal of this chapter to discuss this potential by identifying unique and effective ways in which computers can be used within the classroom in order to become an integral part of the literacy curriculum.

DECODING INSTRUCTION

Decoding is a key component in learning to read (e.g., National Reading Panel, 2000)—one that allows learners to identify words independently and provides a means of access to the meaning of print (Stahl, 1998). Since the vast majority of words that students encounter in beginning texts are words that already exist in their spoken vocabulary, once the readers determine what the words are, they can begin to make sense of what is written. Students must develop a base of sight words along with a range of strategies for recognizing words in text if they are to become skilled at decoding. Further, once students are able to apply this knowledge to text, it is equally important that students learn to recognize words automatically in order to ensure that they become fluent readers (Chall, 1996; Schwanenflugel, Hamilton, Kuhn, Wisenbaker, & Stahl, 2004; Stanovich, 1980).

Unfortunately, for many people, the concept of decoding instruction brings to mind the teaching of words in isolation or the use of synthetic phonics to create nonsense words. However, there is a significant disconnect between instruction designed to develop word recognition though skill and drill and the kind of decoding instruction that is designed to ensure learners can independently read connected text. Regrettably, for the most part, early versions of phonics software emphasized skill and drill. While such instruction allows students to become extremely competent at recognizing words in isolation, there is no guarantee that this ability will transfer when the learners attempt to read connected text (Fleisher, Jenkins, & Pany, 1979–1980; Levy, Abello, & Lysynchuk, 1997; Spring, Blunden, & Gatheral, 1981).

While we do not consider it necessary to embed the instruction itself, it is crucial that learners are provided with extensive opportunities to practice what they have learned as part of their decoding instruction through the reading of enjoyable books, magazines, poetry, or their own writing (e.g., Cunningham, Hall, & Defee, 1998; Kuhn & Stahl, 2003, Rasinski, 2003). It is this combination of word recognition work and its application through wide reading that appears to be key in ensuring that learners solidify their understanding of English orthography (Adams, 1990; Ehri, 1995, 1998).

In order to ensure that time spent on the computer assists students with their word recognition, McKenna (2002) has outlined seven principles that can be used to identify programs that are effective at promoting phonics instruction. To begin with, the instruction should be systematic and direct. Second, it should facilitate the teacher's ability to monitor the student's literacy development. Third, the programs should help students progress from alphabetic decoding, where individual letters are the focus, to orthographic decoding, in which knowledge of spelling patterns and rimes are used. Next, onset-and-rimes should be emphasized. Fifth, it should allow students to make and break words using virtual manipulatives. Sixth, it should progress from monosyllabic to multisyllabic words. And, finally, it should maximize time on task.

One unique way in which computers could integrate these principles and support effective decoding instruction is by creating "bundled" programs that would allow for both decoding activities and practice of targeted principles to occur. For instance, Trachtenburg (1990) suggested a whole-part-whole approach to phonics. Under this design, students are introduced to a given phonics element through the reading of a story by the teacher. In her example, a class was introduced to the short "a" sound using *Angus and the Cat* (Flack, 1931). The students then spent time working with a word slotter to practice the short "a" sound by making a series of cvc, or consonant-vowel-consonant, words with the targeted vowel. The lesson was completed with the teacher's reading aloud of another classic piece of children's literature that stresses the short "a" sound, such as *The Cat in the Hat* (Seuss, 1957) or *Who Took the Farmer's Hat?* (Nodset, 1963). Further, a range of texts that emphasizes the concept can be incorporated into the classroom library for the students to peruse on their own.

An adaptation of this whole-part-whole approach to phonics instruction for computers would not only incorporate these seven principles, it would also adapt easily to the needs of the individual learner. Further, it could be designed for either independent instruction or reinforcement across a range of concepts. To begin with, a variety of stories could be presented in a CD-ROM format. Each of these stories could be narrated in a number of ways. The entire story could be automated, with the print being highlighted as it is read, either in a word-by-word manner or in appropriate phrases, so that the student is able to simply enjoy the text while being exposed to the print-speech match. Alternatively, the student could be in control of the way the story unfolds by using the mouse or touchpad to decide when to turn the page, when to have the text read, or even when individual words or phrases should be repeated. This would allow students to reinforce concepts of print in addition to developing letter-sound relationships (Labbo & Kuhn, 1997).

The second component of the lesson could incorporate several phonics activities related to the concept that is being focused on. For example, students could be asked to work with a word slotter as was suggested in the original article. However, the students would be able to complete this activity by manipulating virtual versions with the assistance of the mouse or touchpad. As each word is generated, the computer could record it on a virtual notepad. The students could then sort the words into three categories: real, pretend, and a group they are uncertain about (e.g., tam). The computer could then provide immediate feedback for students. For example, if the student touched the word with a stylus, the computer could pronounce it. This could assist students who are working on blending individual letters or onsets and rimes by ensuring they had access to the correct pronunciation. The computer could also highlight the words that are real and provide verbal definitions for them. The student could then resort them into two categories, real and pretend. In this way, it would be possible to ensure that any misidentified word was correctly sorted.

Another activity could involve the student rereading the text, with or without computer narration, and listing all the words that contain the short "a" sound. Again, students who were able to work independently could find and list the words themselves, whereas, the computer could highlight and pronounce examples for those students who need greater support. In this way, the program could be designed to scaffold the individual learner by varying the difficulty level. After the student identified these words, the computer could create a list of them. Students would then have the opportunity to sort them in a variety of ways, for example, by rime, initial letter, or part of speech. Alternatively, the students could write out the words both as they find them and as they sort them in order to provide a record for the teacher to monitor. Similarly, if the computer incorporated a word processing program as part of the software "bundle," the students could type out the words in order to create a record. After completing the decoding work, the students would have the opportunity to select another text in order to further reinforce the targeted concept. The second text could be used in any of the ways outlined for the introductory text. A further option could involve creating extension activities for the unit using a program like Kidpix®, in which a variety of activities are available. For example, it would be possible to create character stamps and a background based upon the story that would allow the students to expand upon the story (Labbo & Kuhn, 1997). Since these programs integrate both drawing and writing, students could use both media to express themselves. Importantly, by providing them the opportunity to write, the students will be making important letter-sound associations for themselves and further internalizing their ability to decode and encode text.

Another study that integrated the principles (McKenna, 2002) outlined above was that conducted by Beck and Roth (1987). This study involved the use of two games designed to promote students' orthographic knowledge, Construct-A-Word and Hint and Hunt. Construct-A-Word involved the construction of real words from "word beginnings" and "word endings" or onsets and rimes. When a student formed a real word by correctly matching an onset and rime, the word was transferred into a word box on the side of the screen. When the stack was full, the round ended, and feedback was provided as to time and the number of words made. The goal for each subsequent round was to create a greater number of words in a shorter period of time. Any pseudowords that were created were identified as such for the learner, and if the student needed help identifying real words, they would be identified first aurally and then visually.

Hint and Hunt, on the other hand, was designed to help students develop speed and accuracy with vowels and vowel diagraphs. In this game, a word was presented aurally and the students would either find or create a word that matched the one they heard. The computer provided the learner with an introduction to the vowel combinations at each level and points were given based on the number of correctly identified words and the amount of time it took to find them. This technology provided unique and effective approaches to reading development through the computer's ability to speed up the presentation of the word elements, its ability to provide timings for the learner, and its ability to provide feedback or guidance as the learner needed it. Both of these programs were successful with struggling fourth-grade readers, assisting them in developing their word recognition skills as well as their comprehension at the word and proposition/sentence level, but not at the passage level. Since developing word recognition is an important component of the total reading process, these programs could assist learners by developing their decoding in a game-like atmosphere. Further, if this was integrated into a whole-part-whole approach, it would not only give students the opportunity for enjoyable practice with key aspects of their word recognition development, it could also be followed with practice reading a range of texts, in the manner outlined above, that could reinforce this learner. By combining this kind of word-recognition practice with the reading of connected text, it may be that learners will be assisted in the development of their passage comprehension, as well as their decoding.

FLUENT READING

As students' word-recognition ability continues to develop, larger numbers of words are incorporated into their sight-word lexicon (Ehri, 1995) and the focus of their learning shifts from developing basic decoding skills to fluent reading (Chall, 1996). While it is important to emphasize fluency throughout a child's literacy development, decoding needs to be stressed early on in order to ensure that students are able to identify words they encounter in text independently. As students begin to internalize the sound-symbol relationships, however, a greater emphasis needs to be placed on developing automatic word recognition. Similarly, expressive reading and appropriate phrasing need to be a focus of literacy instruction at this point if students are to become fluent readers.

Fluent and disfluent readers differ in a number of ways (Kuhn & Stahl, 2003; National Reading Panel, 2000). Disfluent readers read either in a word-by-word manner or by grouping words in ways that do not parallel spoken language (Dowhower, 1991; Reutzel, 1996; Schreiber, 1991). Further, their word recognition is often arduous, and their reading is monotonous. Fluent readers, on the other hand, are not only accurate and automatic in their decoding, they make appropriate use of phrasing, pitch, and emphasis in their reading (Chall, 1996; Dowhower, 1991; Schreiber, 1991). In so doing, they manage to make their oral reading sound like spoken language (Stahl & Kuhn, 2002).

However, fluency is not only important in terms of the way reading sounds; it also plays a role in readers' ability to construct meaning from text. This occurs in two ways. First, when word recognition is laborious, readers spend a disproportionate amount of their attention trying to identify individual words (LaBerge & Samuels, 1974). As a result, it takes a significant amount of time to read a text, or a portion of a text. It is, therefore, unlikely that they have enough attention left for comprehending what is read. In order to ensure that learners have enough attention available to access meaning, decoding needs to become automatic. According to many researchers (e.g. Adams, 1990; Stanovich, 1980), the development of automatic word recognition best occurs through practice. This practice involves repeated exposure to English orthography. Further, such practice appears to be most effective when there is repeated exposure to connected text (Chomsky, 1978; Dahl, 1979; Dowhower, 1989).

Next, the use of expression, or prosody, and appropriate phrasing in reading also appear to contribute to comprehension. Prosody is comprised of a series of features including intonation, emphasis, rate, and the regularly reoccurring patterns of language (Hanks, 1990; Harris & Hodges, 1981, 1995). As with students who find decoding arduous, disfluent readers experience difficulty with both their phrasing and their use of appropriate expression (Dowhower, 1991; Reutzel, 1996; Schreiber, 1991). However, studies indicate that disfluent readers at all age levels demonstrate improved comprehension when text is presented in appropriate phrase units for the reader (e.g., Cromer, 1970; O'Shea & Sindelar, 1983; Weiss, 1983). As such, it seems that fluent readers are not only automatic and expressive readers, but readers who can construct meaning from text as well.

As with McKenna's (2002) guidelines for effective computer-based phonics instruction, Rasinski (2003) has identified four principles that should be incorporated into effective fluency instruction. The first is to provide modeling of fluent reading for the students through the expressive rendering of text. Second, it is important to provide learners with support or assistance, such as is given through echo or choral reading. This allows them access to material that would otherwise be inaccessible. The third is to provide students with plenty of opportunities to practice, such as through repetition or supported reading. As with any complex task, practice allows a procedure to become fluid. The final suggestion is that students spend time practicing appropriate phrasing in order to move beyond the word-by-word or inappropriate phrasing that often characterizes disfluent reading and that interferes with readers' comprehension.

There are a number of approaches designed specifically to develop fluent reading, including repeated readings (Samuels, 1979), *Fluency-Oriented Reading Instruction* (Stahl & Heubach, in press), and the use of audio-taped books to scaffold students' reading (Carbo, 1978; Chomsky, 1978). One unique way that computer-aided instruction can expand upon these strategies is by providing scaffolding that allows students to work independently. For example, the creation of a series of talking books, similar to CD-ROMs that present an animated version of text, could be used as an aid to the development of fluent reading. While the basic format of talking books already exists, they could be easily adapted as part of an assisted reading design in a manner similar to that of audio-taped books that are the basis of the reading-while-listening strategy. Reading-while-listening involves students repeatedly listening to the books at the upper end of their instructional level while reading along with the text until they are able to render the material fluently (Chomsky, 1978). This approach could be modified for talking books, providing a format that is different from audiotapes in two ways. The most obvious difference is that animation can accompany the text in the computer-aided version. However, a second difference with particular implications for the development of fluent reading involves the way in which the text itself is presented. Talking books allow a learner to see the text as it is being read. That is, the text can be highlighted in meaningful phrases as it is being expressively read, thereby ensuring that the reader focuses on phrase units that maintain the meaning of the story, a key aspect of fluent reading.

Next, as speech recognition continues to improve, computers have the potential to "listen" to students as they read a text. The computers can then provide feedback in terms of not only individual words, but also in terms of appropriate phrasing and the use of prosodic elements that contribute to students' understanding of text. It may also be possible to create a record of a student's reading, including information on rate and accuracy. This would allow a student to more easily complete a series of repeated readings, a process that requires students to read a "short, meaningful passage several times until a satisfactory level of fluency is reached" (Samuels, 1979, p. 404). By recording and automatically analyzing texts, the computer could provide students with a highly motivating record of their reading growth over a short period of time. Such implementation of computer-aided literacy development can be seen through the work done at both Soliloquy Learning (Adams, 2004) and Project LISTEN (Mostow & Beck, in press) where voice recognition and computer rendering of text provide students with scaffolding that aids their reading development. Each of these approaches would, or does, make use of technology to assist students in developing accurate and automatic word recognition along with the prosodic elements of fluent reading in a way that expands traditional classroom literacy practice.

CONCLUSIONS

Given the potential computers have to help students with their decoding and reading fluency, rather than seeing computers as an unnecessary distraction from literacy learning, or at best a complex reward system, we believe that they can become an integral part of primary grade classrooms and their use can become central to the literacy learning of children. As such, we hope effective applications will continue to be developed and integrated into the classroom curriculum.

REFERENCES

Adams, M. J. (1990). *Beginning to read: Thinking and learning about print.* Cambridge, MA: M.I.T. Press.

Adams, M. J. (2004). *A research-based approach ensures reading success.* Needham Heights, MA. Soliloquy Learning: [Online] Available: http://soliloquylearning.com/research_paper.html

Beck, I. L., & Roth, S. F. (1987). Theoretical and instructional implications of the assessment of two microcomputer word recognition programs. *Reading Research Quarterly, 22,* 197–218.

Carbo, M. (1978). Teaching reading with talking books. *The Reading Teacher, 32,* 267–273.

Chall, J. S. (1996). *Stages of reading development.* (2nd ed.). Fort Worth, TX: Harcourt-Brace.

Chomsky, C. (1978). When you still can't read in third grade? After decoding, what? In S. J. Samuels (Ed.), *What research has to say about reading instruction* (pp. 13–30). Newark, DE: International Reading Association.

Cromer, W. (1970). The difference model: A new explanation for some reading difficulties. *Journal of Educational Psychology, 61,* 471–483.

Cunningham, P. M., Hall, D. P., & Defee, M. (1998). Non-ability-grouped, multilevel instruction: Eight years later. *The Reading Teacher, 51,* 652–664.

Dahl, P. R. (1979). An experimental program for teaching high speed word recognition and comprehension skills. In J. E. Button, T. Lovitt, & T. Rowland (Eds.), *Communications research in learning disabilities and mental retardation* (pp. 33–65). Baltimore: University Park Press.

Dowhower, S. L. (1989). Repeated reading: Theory into practice. *The Reading Teacher, 42,* 502–507.

Dowhower, S. L. (1991). Speaking of prosody: Fluency's unattended bedfellow. *Theory in Practice, 30*(3), 158–164.

Ehri, L. C. (1995). Phases of development in learning to read words by sight. *Journal of Research in Reading, 18,* 116–125.

Ehri, L. C. (1998). Grapheme–phoneme knowledge is essential for learning to read words in English. In J. L. Metsala & L. C. Ehri (Eds.), *Word recognition in beginning literacy* (pp. 3–40). Mahwah, NJ: Lawrence Erlbaum Associates.

Flack, M. (1931). *Angus and the cat.* New York: Doubleday.

Fleisher, L. S., Jenkins, J. R., & Pany, D. (1979–1980). Effects on poor readers' comprehension of training in rapid decoding. *Reading Research Quarterly, 15,* 30–48.

Hanks, P. (Ed.). 1990. *The Collins English dictionary.* Glasgow, GB: William Collins & Co. Ltd.

Harris,T. L., & Hodges, R. E. (Eds.). 1981. *A dictionary of reading and related terms.* Newark, DE: International Reading Association.

Harris, T. L., & Hodges, R. E. (Eds.). 1995. *The literacy dictionary: The vocabulary of reading and writing.* Newark, DE: International Reading Association.

Kuhn, M. R., & Stahl, S. (2003). Fluency: A review of developmental and remedial strategies. *The Journal of Educational Psychology, 95,* 1–19.

Labbo, L. D., & Kuhn, M. R. (1997, November). *Computers and emergent literacy: Expanding upon reading.* Paper presented at the College Reading Association, Boston, MA.

Labbo, L. D., & Kuhn, M. R. (2000). Weaving chains of affect and cognition: A young child's understanding of considerate and inconsiderate CD storybooks. *Journal of Literacy Research, 32,* 187–210.

LaBerge, D., & Samuels, S. J. (1974). Toward a theory of automatic information processing in reading. *Cognitive Psychology, 6*, 293–323.

Levy, B. A., Abello, B., & Lysynchuk, L. (1997). Transfer from word training to reading in context: Gains in fluency and comprehension. *Learning Disability Quarterly, 20*, 173–188.

McKenna, M. C. (2002). Issues in technology: Phonics software for the new millennium. *Reading & Writing Quarterly, 18*, 93–96.

Merrow, J. (2001). Double click: Threat or promise? *The magazine of the Harvard Graduate School of Education, 45*(1), 22–25.

Mostow, J., & Beck, J. (in press). When the Rubber Meets the Road: Lessons from the In-School Adventures of an Automated Reading Tutor that Listens. In B. Schneider (Ed.), *Conceptualizing Scale-Up: Multidisciplinary Perspectives.*

National Reading Panel. (2000). *Teaching children to read: An evidence-based assessment of the scientific research literature on reading and its implications for reading instruction. Reports of the subgroups.* Bethesda, MD: National Institutes of Health. [Online] Available: http://www.nichd.nih.gov/publications/nrp/

Nodset, J. L. (1963). *Who took the farmer's hat?* New York: Harper & Row.

O'Shea, L. J., & Sindelar, P. T. (1983). The effects of segmenting written discourse on the reading comprehension of low- and high-performance readers. *Reading Research Quarterly, 18*, 458–465.

Rasinski, T. V. (2003). *The fluent reader: oral reading strategies for building word recognition, fluency and comprehension.* New York: Scholastic.

Reinking, D. (1998). Introduction: Synthesizing technological transformations of literacy in a post-typographic world. In D. Reinking, M. C. McKenna, L. D. Labbo, & R. D. Kieffer (Eds.). *Handbook of literacy and Technology: Transformations in a post-typographic world* (pp. xi–xxx). Mahwah, NJ: Lawrence Erlbaum Associates.

Reutzel, D. R. (1996). Developing at-risk readers' oral reading fluency. In L. R. Putnam (Ed.), *How to become a better reading teacher* (pp. 241–254). Englewood Cliffs, NJ: Merrill.

Samuels, S. J. (1979). The method of repeated readings. *The Reading Teacher, 32*, 403–408.

Schreiber, P. A. (1991). Understanding prosody's role in reading acquisition. *Theory into Practice, 30*(3), 158–164.

Schwanenflugel, P. J., Hamilton, A. M., Kuhn, M. R., Wisenbaker, J., & Stahl, S. A. (2004). Becoming a fluent reader: Reading skill and prosodic features in the oral reading of young readers. *The Journal of Educational Psychology.*

Seuss, Dr. (1957). *The cat in the hat.* New York: Random House.

Spring, C., Blunden, D., & Gatheral, M. (1981). Effect on reading comprehension of training to automaticity in word-reading. *Perceptual and Motor Skills, 53*, 779–786.

Stahl, S. A. (1998). Understanding shifts in reading and its instruction. *Peabody Journa lof Education, 73*, 31–67.

Stahl, S. A., & Heubach, K. (in press). Fluency-oriented reading instruction. *Journal of Literacy Research.*

Stahl, S. A. & Kuhn, M. R. (2002). Making it sound like language: Developing fluency, Center for the Improvement of Early Reading Achievement Commentary. *The Reading Teacher, 55*, 2–4.

Stanovich, K. E. (1980). Toward an interactive-compensatory model of individual differences in the development of reading fluency. *Reading Research Quarterly, 16*, 32–71.

Trachtenburg, P. (1990). Using children's literature to enhance phonics instruction. *The Reading Teacher, 43*, 648–654.

Weiss, D. S. (1983). The effects of text segmentation on children's reading comprehension. *Discourse Processes, 6*(1), 77–89.

Family Literacy and Technology: Challenges and Promising Constructive Designs

Patricia A. Edwards, Ph.D.
Michigan State University

The practice of family literacy has occurred for generations, but the two words were not unified as a concept until 1983, when Denny Taylor published her dissertation, *Family literacy: Young children learning to read and write.* The purpose of her 1977 study was to "develop systematic ways of looking at reading and writing as activities that have consequences in and are affected by family life" (1983, p. xiii). Her groundbreaking ethnographic study carefully described the ways that families support the literacy development of their children and is considered to be the beginning of current research, practice, and interest in the area of family literacy.

Taylor (1997) revealed that "no single narrow definition of 'family literacy' can do justice to the richness and complexity of families, and the multiple literacies, including often unrecognized local literacies that are part of their everyday lives" (p. 4). Nevertheless, DeBruin-Parecki and Krol-Sinclair (2003) reported that "once the term *family literacy* was coined, its meaning became subject to broad interpretation to suit the context in which it was mentioned and implemented" (p. 1). Purcell-Gates (2000) suggests that this occurred when family literacy gained the attention of scholars across a wide range of scholarly traditions; researchers in psychology, emergent literacy, beginning reading, anthropology, and sociology began investigating family literacy practices from a variety of different philosophical stances (Anderson, 1995; Burgess, 1997; Edwards, 2003; Edwards, 1993; Heath, 1983; Morrow, 1983; Purcell-Gates & Dahl, 1991; Teale, 1984).

The lack of a universally accepted definition of family literacy has not curtailed family programs from emerging all over the world. Though such programs were not new in the late 1980s, their growth and national prominence were enhanced by the development of the privately endowed National Center for Family Literacy and the federally funded Even Start Act (1988). Some 20 years later, there are thousands of family literacy programs serving thousands and thousands of families in a variety of ways. Paratore (2001) reported that elementary and secondary school teachers and administrators looking for solutions to assist low-achieving students have found family literacy programs to be a lifeline they can grab. Gadsden (1994) summarized the disagreement and dissension that characterize the work in family literacy as emerging from two seriously conflicting premises: one that perceives the family's lack of school-like literacy as a barrier to learning, and the other that sees the home literacy practices that are already present—however different they may be from school-based literacy—as a bridge to new learning. Rather than choosing sides in the debate, however, Gadsden argues that both premises may be useful. She suggests that educators might adopt a reciprocal approach predicated on an understanding that teachers need to instruct parents in school-based literacy and also seek to learn about and integrate parents' existing knowledge and resources into school curricula.

I agree with Gadsden that we should incorporate new learnings (learning?) from families; so do researchers like Wiley (1996) who warns, however, that "[i]n order for incorporation to occur, teachers need knowledge of the language, communication styles, and literacy practices of their students" (p. 149). I have suggested elsewhere (Edwards, 2003), however, that the reality is that "it is extremely difficult for teachers to gain this much-needed knowledge in a nine-month period of time" (p. 97).

As a scholar in family literacy, what I find so intriguing is that there is an intense controversy within the research community concerning family literacy programs that show families how to participate in school-like activities. For example, researchers have warned that "educating" parents for a specific kind of literacy interaction—namely, family literacy programs that "train" parents how to read to their children—is in effect "blaming the victim" in a deficit-model of learning development, and they point out that literacy is already an integral part of the home life (Anderson & Stokes, 1984; Erickson, 1989; Hearron, 1992; Taylor & Dorsey-Gaines, 1988). It has also been suggested that family literacy educational programs imply that homes of poor, minority, and immigrant children are "lacking in literacy" (Anderson & Stokes, 1984; Auerbach, 1989; Chall & Snow, 1982; Delgado-Gaitan, 1987; Erickson, 1989; Goldenberg, 1984) or that these programs do not recognize that "literacy is not something which can be pasted onto family life; it is deeply embedded within it" (Macleod, 1996, p. 130). Another criticism is that these programs "have perpetuated the 'we know, you don't know' dichotomy" (Shockley, 1994, p. 500).

Surprisingly, there appears to be little or no controversy within the research community when it comes to showing families how to integrate technology as part of their family life. Interaction between humans and computers has greatly increased as we embark into the 21st century. The ability to access computers and the Internet has become increasingly important to completely participate in the economic, political, and social aspects of not just America, but the world. However, not everyone has access to this technology. The idea of the "digital divide" refers to the growing gap between the underprivileged members of society—especially the poor, rural, elderly, and handicapped portions of the population who do not have access to computers or the Internet—and the wealthy, the middle class, and the young Americans living in urban and suburban areas who have ready access. Consequently, it comes as no surprise that most researchers, politicians, policymakers, and civic groups agree that there is a significant "digital divide" separating American information "haves" and "have nots."

In 2001, the United States General Accounting Office stated, "Because the Internet is still in a relatively early stage of commercial deployment, these socioeconomic and geographic differences in Internet usage are not surprising and may not be long lasting" (p. 7). Clark and Gorski (2002) believe, however, that this statement expresses a flawed interpretation of the data on three levels. They reported that GAO's conclusions:

- Assume that the privileged should have quicker access to new technologies than others who are socioeconomically disadvantaged.
- Do not consider it problematic that people in rural areas cannot access new technologies due to inadequate technological infrastructure.
- Assume that these gaps will close naturally in due course—as if this will somehow magically disappear so that there is no need to be concerned with the facts as they exist now.

Clark and Gorski (2001) also believe that recent reports by both the United States Department of Commerce and the United States General Accounting Office show clear evidence that the digital divide is unfortunately as large as ever and favors the privileged over the disadvantaged in our society. The digitally exiled are still being kept from the electronic tools that are crucial in this age of digital literacies.

As a result, over the last 5 years the metaphor of the digital divide has continued to be part of the national discourse in the United States, an abstract symbol that condenses public concerns about social inequality and evokes hopes for solutions related to the use of information technology. The digital divide is a potent resource whose symbolic properties and communicative power have activated a wide array of participants in the policy debates about how to create a more just society.

Statistical data issued by the National Technical and Information Administration (1998, 1999, 2000) were deployed as evidence to justify this assertion and were regularly invoked to demonstrate the need for a concerted programmatic response and to stimulate a community of interest (Stone, 1997). The statistics classified the population according to geography, race, income, employment, age, gender, and education.

Although great advances have been made in rural connectivity in recent years, with the gap between rural and urban households owning a computer decreasing from 2.7% in 1994 to 1.6% in 2001 (Economic and Statistics Administration, 2001). The gap between rural households and urban households with Internet access actually increased between 1998 and 2001. More rural households may have computers, but may not be using them to effectively access the worldwide information system. Figures 20.1 and 20.2 also suggest that White and Asian Americans are more likely to have home computers and Internet access regardless of whether they are living in urban, rural, and suburban areas. Blacks and Hispanics are less likely to have this technology regardless of where they are living.

Looking at U.S. households separated into racial categories, Figure 20.3 presents the stark reality of disparity across racial groups as it relates to access of computers; access to this digital tool

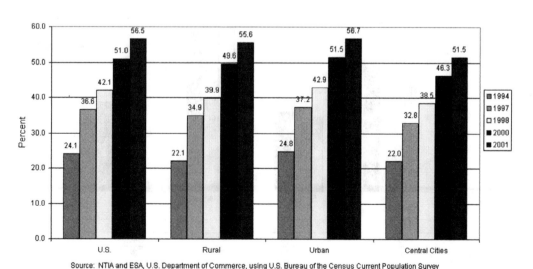

Percent of U.S. Households with a Computer By U.S., Rural, Urban, and Central Cities, 1994, 1997, 1998, 2000, 2001

Source: NTIA and ESA, U.S. Department of Commerce, using U.S. Bureau of the Census Current Population Survey supplements

FIGURE 20.1. Percent of U.S. households with a computer.

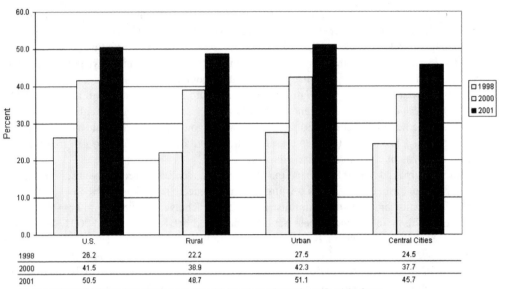

Percent of U.S. Households with Internet Access, By U.S., Rural, Urban, and Central Cities, 1998, 2000, 2001

	U.S.	Rural	Urban	Central Cities
1998	26.2	22.2	27.5	24.5
2000	41.5	38.9	42.3	37.7
2001	50.5	48.7	51.1	45.7

Source: NTIA and ESA, U.S. Department of Commerce, using U.S. Bureau of the Census Current Population Survey supplements.

FIGURE 20.2.   Percent of U.S. households with internet access.

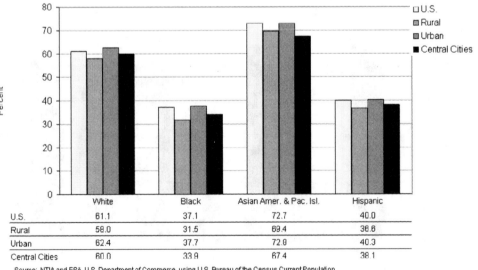

Percent of U.S. Households with a Computer By Race/Hispanic Origin, By U.S., Rural, Urban, and Central Cities, 2001

	White	Black	Asian Amer. & Pac. Isl.	Hispanic
U.S.	61.1	37.1	72.7	40.0
Rural	58.0	31.5	69.4	36.6
Urban	62.4	37.7	72.8	40.3
Central Cities	60.0	33.9	67.4	38.1

Source: NTIA and ESA, U.S. Department of Commerce, using U.S. Bureau of the Census Current Population Survey supplements.

FIGURE 20.3   Percent of U.S. households with computer by race/hispanic origin.

in the home is most definitively divided along racial lines. The U.S. culture seems to systematically exile persons racially from the tools that are generally agreed upon to be indispensable in the
digital age we live in. Rural Black households show the smallest number of computers in homes
(31.5%) when compared to any other racial and demographic category. However, this number is
almost equal to the percentage of urban Blacks who use home computers (37.7%).

In Figure 20.4, the digital divide becomes even more evident. We again see the outcomes
of racial grouping of persons who do not have access to the Internet in their households. Again
the two racial groups (Blacks and Hispanics) are exiled from the tools needed to compete and sur-
vive in this new economy.

Figures 20.5 and 20.6 provide additional evidence that socioeconomic factors greatly influence one's access to the information system, ultimately determining the size of the gap.

The statistical evidence supports the case that there is a digital divide between the "haves"
and the "have nots." Levesque (2000) correctly noted that "[f]amily literacy practitioners [as well
as researchers] understand that the education of children and their parents is interconnected. Connecting literacy learning with technology is a powerful means of breaking the intergenerational
cycle of low educational levels and poverty. Family literacy programs have the programmatic
structure to integrate educational technologies with play activities shared by parents and their
preschool children" (p. 5). Other researchers (Bowie, 2000; Ginsburg, Sabatini, & Wagner, 2000)
agree that as we enter the 21st century, technology serves as a symbol of equity or a solution to
equity problems—whether gender-, race-, or economically-related. For example, members of
the Black Family Network are running a series of workshops and seminars to educate and
empower these families through technology in 21 states, including the District of Columbia, and
one site in Toronto, Canada.

**Percent of U.S. Households with Internet Access, By Race/Hispanic Origin, By U.S.,
Rural, Urban, and Central Cities, 2001**

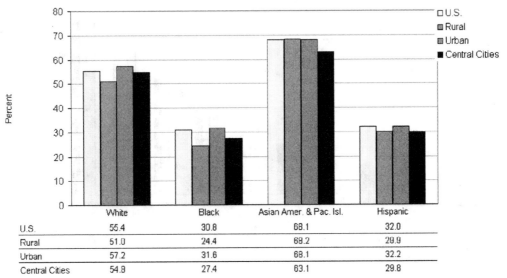

	White	Black	Asian Amer. & Pac. Isl.	Hispanic
U.S.	55.4	30.8	68.1	32.0
Rural	51.0	24.4	68.2	29.9
Urban	57.2	31.6	68.1	32.2
Central Cities	54.8	27.4	63.1	29.8

Source: NTIA and ESA, U.S. Department of Commerce, using U.S. Bureau of the Census Current
Population Survey supplements.

FIGURE 20.4.   Percent of U.S. households with internet access by race.

Percent of U.S. Households with a Computer By Income, By U.S., Rural, Urban, and Central Cities, 2001

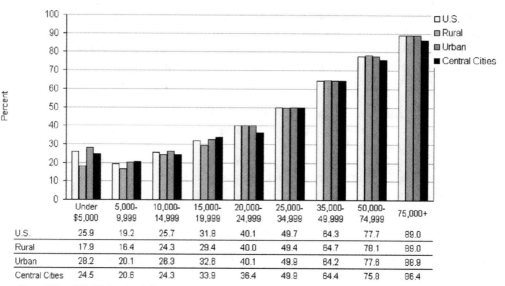

	Under $5,000	5,000-9,999	10,000-14,999	15,000-19,999	20,000-24,999	25,000-34,999	35,000-49,999	50,000-74,999	75,000+
U.S.	25.9	19.2	25.7	31.8	40.1	49.7	64.3	77.7	89.0
Rural	17.9	16.4	24.3	29.4	40.0	49.4	64.7	78.1	89.0
Urban	28.2	20.1	26.3	32.8	40.1	49.9	64.2	77.6	88.9
Central Cities	24.5	20.6	24.3	33.9	36.4	49.9	64.4	75.8	86.4

Source: NTIA and ESA, U.S. Department of Commerce, using U.S. Bureau of the Census Current Population Survey supplements.

FIGURE 20.5   Percent of U.S. households with a computer by income.

Percent of U.S. Households with Internet Access, By Income, By U.S., Rural, Urban, and Central Cities, 2001

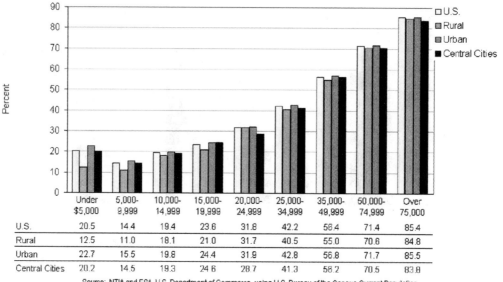

	Under $5,000	5,000-9,999	10,000-14,999	15,000-19,999	20,000-24,999	25,000-34,999	35,000-49,999	50,000-74,999	Over 75,000
U.S.	20.5	14.4	19.4	23.6	31.8	42.2	56.4	71.4	85.4
Rural	12.5	11.0	18.1	21.0	31.7	40.5	55.0	70.6	84.8
Urban	22.7	15.5	19.8	24.4	31.9	42.8	56.8	71.7	85.5
Central Cities	20.2	14.5	19.3	24.6	28.7	41.3	56.2	70.5	83.8

Source: NTIA and ESA, U.S. Department of Commerce, using U.S. Bureau of the Census Current Population Survey supplements.

FIGURE 20.6.   Percent of U.S. households with internet access by income.

In a 1995 article, "In school or out: Technology, equity, and the future of our kids," Rockman highlighted four examples of school districts in the early 1980s reaching out to at-risk families and children. His first example highlighted the Houston, Texas, independent school district. The district pursued an aggressive program to provide equity of computer access to disadvantaged, at-risk students. To create greater equity with more affluent students, the district reached out to inner-city students and developed a range of activities including: a software library for parents, computer camps for disadvantaged students, parent training and loaner computers, business-school partnerships, technology magnet schools, and mobile computer classrooms.

Rockman's next two examples focused on the Oakland, California, school district. In inner city Oakland, children were connected by computer and modem to suburban schools to share ideas and resources, and they worked together on common projects. Extending the school-room into the larger world was a motivating and enriching experience for inner-city children. In another disadvantaged Oakland school, donated computers were sent home for the semester so children could do homework, play educational games, and get their parents involved with the school.

Rockman's final example was one in which the school-home connection was carried much further. In the Buddy project in Indianapolis, Indiana, fourth graders received a computer, printer, and modem to take home and use until they moved into middle school. For most of the families, this was the first computer in the house, and it was almost always the only one available to all members of the family. Students received instruction in school about how to use computers and were taught how to help their parents and siblings learn. Parents, too, could attend after-school sessions to learn more. And through telecommunications, parents and teachers could communicate, everyone knew what the homework assignments were, and kids could work together after school on projects.

More recently, Ginsburg, Sabatini and Wagner (2000) described two promising programs aimed at helping traditionally under-served families to gain home-based access to Information Communication Technology (ICT) and opportunities to learn. One program, LINCT (Coalition, Learning and Information Networking for Community—via Telecomputing), seeks to help communities achieve digital equity through a locally managed learn-and-earn process. The communities cooperate with corporations to generate a sustainable supply of donated, recyclable technology, and to provide ICT trainers. In South Phoenix, Arizona, low-income families can "buy" their own home computer, following 100 hours of service on the program as a tutor, a tutee, or a tutor supervisor.

A second program is Neighborhood Networks, which offers access to advanced technology, with training and support, to help residents increase their earning power and move off welfare and other public subsidies. Seed capital is provided to establish computer centers in privately owned apartment buildings. The centers are sustained financially by contributions from local partners in each community and by income generated from the centers' own business initiatives. They offer welfare-to-work initiatives, classes in General Education Development (GED) high-school equivalent qualifications, basic computer literacy training, and resume writing—with use of computers in a home-based environment that is convenient for families. Parents can acquire skills that increase their employment marketability, while children can use the technology for school projects. These examples are but a few of the programs currently underway that use technology as part of larger efforts assisting underprivileged families and children.

The above examples clearly indicate the importance of creating opportunities for low-income families and children to have access to technology. Also, these examples demonstrate that helping these families and children in crossing the digital divide is essential for what Lesvesque (2000) calls "age-appropriate educational success and economic self-sufficiency" (p. 5).

In the remainder of this paper, I focus on the ways that the research community has developed family literacy programs (though there is only one such program) that integrate educational technologies and prepare families for success in a society increasingly dependent upon, even driven by, technology. I address some of the challenges researchers have faced in their efforts to integrate technology into these family literacy programs and suggest ways the research community should respond to these challenges. I highlight some proposals that have appeared recently arguing that the design of educational systems should incorporate a constructivist approach rather than an instructional approach. I provide a rationale for why I think family literacy programs should incorporate these constructivist approaches. Lastly, I present a call for additional research to be conducted on integrating technology in family literacy programs.

INTEGRATING TECHNOLOGY IN FAMILY LITERACY
PROGRAMS: SOME CHALLENGES

In my review of the literature, I found only one study that addressed the question of how family literacy programs integrate educational technologies and prepare families for success. Levesque (2000) explored this question as a statewide evaluation consultant for a Midwestern state's Even Start family literacy programs. Over a one-year period, at nine program sites, she observed and interviewed literacy staff and led several distance-learning workshops for practitioners.

Consistent with a recent federal report (NTIA, 1999), Levesque (2000) concluded that adults with less education, especially low-income parents in family literacy programs, who could perhaps benefit most from the Internet's educational value, are being left behind. For example, Levesque (2000) never once observed an adult learner using the Internet. In addition, the adults spent the majority of their time practicing keyboard skills such as typing, making personal greeting cards using Print Shop, or practicing basic study skills. A gap persists between those who have access to new technologies and those who do not.

Levesque (2000) found that several possible explanations account for the difficulties of integrating technology into family literacy programs. In the rural programs, for example, Levesque (2000) observed the existence of recycled technology, in the form of numerous outdated computers in need of serious repair. In addition, administrative problems plagued a rural site. For example, one adult basic educator refused to use computer-aided instruction software or to allow her students to use a word processor to prepare for the GED. In another instance, computers were removed from the infant/toddler rooms, which was inconsistent with the goals of promoting rich parent-child interactions in center-based family literacy programs.

More positively, Levesque (2000) observed digital learning that connected families with meaningful information. She also documented the motivation to learn how to become skilled readers. These spanning-the-gap experiences included learning experiences that were matched to each adult's personal goals, such as desktop publishing projects involving family stories and personal greeting cards, or practicing for a standardized achievement test. Ultimately, family literacy programs should match learners' goals and interests with appropriate educational technology (Levesque, 2000).

Earlier in this paper, I highlighted the intense controversy within the research community concerning "educating" parents for a specific kind of literacy interaction—namely, family literacy programs that "train" parents how to read to their children. Also, I provided evidence that researchers, politicians, policymakers, and civic groups agree that there is a significant digital divide separating American information "haves" and "have nots." Despite the controversy around family literacy programs that show families how to participate in school-like activities, and despite the overall acceptance of the need to incorporate technology into family programs, I argue that both perspectives should be accepted and supported. Constructing programs that (1) provide skills to families and (2) study the contexts of family life to inform school-based educational programs are consistent with contructivist learning principles. By paying attention to these principles, we will be better able to study, as well as support, families in providing them with access to the technological tools needed to reduce "divides" and create equitable access for all.

PROMISING CONSTRUCTIVIST DESIGNS FOR FAMILY LITERACY PROGRAMS

Constructivist designs provide the opportunity for learners to make linkages between new knowledge and the context of existing knowledge (Poplin & Stone, 1992). A key characteristic of this view, then, is that learners "construct" their own knowledge (Peterson, Fennema, & Carpenter, 1988–89). A major goal of constructivist learning is learning to learn, or metacognition, which prepares the learner for life-long learning.

From the constructivist perspective, technology should be used to deliver computer-based applications emerging from authentic tasks with multiple representation in order to engage students in exploratory learning (Collins, Brown, & Newman, 1990; Roblyer, Edwards, & Haviluk, 1997). Constructive learning benefits from support provided by computer applications because the complexity of world situations can be presented in a flexible and versatile format to accommodate the diverse individualized processes of constructing knowledge.

Levesque's third observation—spanning the gap—is the most critical for integrating technology in family literacy programs. I agree with Levesque's (2000) observation that family literacy programs "can help adults to use technology to achieve personal learning goals, develop communication skills, accommodate individual learning styles and disabilities, enhance self-esteem, and increase employability skills" (p. 5). In order to successfully do this, I believe these family literacy programs should consider the six principles of constructivist design proposed by a group of researchers at the Institute for Learning Technologies at Teachers College, Columbia University (Black, Thalheimer, Wihder, de Soto, & Picard, 1994). The six principles of constructivist design that they proposed and their sources are:

1. Set the stage but have the **students generate the knowledge** for themselves as much as possible (Jacoby, 1978; Black, Carroll, & McGuigan, 1987).
2. Anchor the knowledge in **authentic situations** and activities (Cognition and Technology Group at Vanderbilt, 1990).
3. Use the **cognitive apprenticeship** methods of modeling, scaffolding, fading, and coaching to convey how to construct knowledge in authentic situations and activities (Collins, Brown, & Newman, 1990).
4. Situate knowledge in **multiple contexts** to prepare for appropriate transfer to new contexts (Gick & Holyoak, 1983).
5. Create **cognitive flexibility** by ensuring that all knowledge is seen from multiple perspectives (Spiro, Feltovich, Jacobson, & Coulson, 1991).
6. Have the students **collaborate** in knowledge and construction (Johnson & Johnson, 1975).

The six principles of constructivist design allow family literacy programs to do what Lesvesque suggests "to address the learners' learning goals and interests" (p. 5). Practitioners and researchers agree that learners come to family literacy programs with a wide range of goals and interests, and technology should be utilized in a way that authentically addresses the learners' identified goals and interests.

In addition, the six principles could serve as a way of finding a common definition of how to use technology with learners across family literacy programs as well as a way of providing the equity that researchers and practitioners are looking for. In particular, the six principles have the potential of achieving Lesvesque's belief that "[c]onnecting literacy learning with technology is a powerful means of breaking the intergenerational cycle of low educational levels and poverty" (p. 5). I agree. However, I believe that in order for technology to have an indelible impact on these families, those coordinating family literacy programs must begin to think carefully about how technology is integrated into, as well as presented to, the families they serve. The six principles of constructivist design are a framework that can be used to meaningfully integrate technology into family literacy programs.

Since I only found one study focused on integrating technology into family literacy programs, there is a dire need to conduct more research in this area. For example, using interpretative methodologies, researchers can focus on the perspectives of various participants in family literacy programs. (How do parents, for example, make sense out of the information they receive in a family literacy program? How do instructors perceive their roles in the programs?) Similarly, survey research can illuminate the relationships between characteristics of family literacy programs and outcomes (e.g., continued use of technology, literacy skills). I suggest that the research community develop studies to address the six principles of constructivist design.

Finally, I suggest that researchers examining family literacy/technology issues must attend to the dual aspects of family literacy research that involve efforts to (1) effectively provide parents with tools that enable success in school or workplace learning contexts and (2) develop rich models of the needs, interests, resources, and knowledge of families to inform the design of educational programs. For example, **principle one** would involve attention to the ways in which technology learning is structured so that learners themselves can become active and independent learners, pursuing personal goals, and learning how to learn. Adequate support would be provided initially to frame the task, but the aim of such a program would be to provide learners with the knowledge needed to set personal goals and to use technology at times and in ways that are individually meaningful. This has implications for how educational programs are constructed in terms of what tasks are presented (who decides what to learn), how assistance is provided (it should scaffold greater autonomy, not lead to reliance on a "teacher"), as well as when and where families work on this. **Principle two** would attend to the personal utility of such knowledge. As mentioned earlier, many educational contexts in which technology is provided do not use it in ways that lead to greater equality of economic opportunity or educational access. Using a computer to practice basic remediation skills operates as little more than a worksheet. For technology to be truly transformative, it must provide skills and resources that enable families to better achieve goals that are meaningful to them. **Principle three** would attend to using technology as a means for modeling and scaffolding to help families construct knowledge in authentic situations. Learners can continuously practice with adequate support around interests and goals that they view and believe are authentic situations for them. This has implications for preventing drop-outs from family literacy programs and enhancing learner commitment. **Principle four** would attend to using technology across multiple contexts to assist families in thinking about how information learned in family literacy programs might transfer to new contexts. Simulation-based technology practice sessions could help the family literacy program coordinator and learner locate potential problems across multiple contexts, as well as how to correct these problems. **Principle five** would attend to using technology as a means for helping families view knowledge from multiple perspectives. This has implications for broadening and strengthening learners' capacity to critically examine their own learning. Again, this means greater "buy in" for the learner, the potential for improving their decision-making ability, and increasing their higher-order thinking skills. **Principle six** would attend to allowing learners to collaborate with the family literacy coordinator in designing and constructing a program of study for themselves. This provides the equality and balance many families have wanted from their participation in family literacy programs. These six principles, in my opinion, provide the opportunity for the research community to conduct new lines of research around family literacy and technology that attend to both the need to provide skills to the family and at the same time learn from them and create educational contexts that more effectively provide access to the kinds of literacies valued in this new millennium.

REFERENCES

Anderson, J. (1995). Listening to parents' voices: Cross cultural perspectives on learning to read and to write. *Reading Horizons, 35*, 394–413.

Anderson, A. B., & Stokes, S. J. (1984). Social and institutional influences on the development and practice of literacy. In H. Goelman, A. Oberg, & F. Smith (Eds.), *Awakening to literacy* (pp. 24–37). Exeter, NH: Heinemann.

Auerbach, E. R. (1989). Toward a social-contextual approach to family literacy. *Harvard Educational Review, 59*(2), 165–181.

Black, J. B., Thalheimer, W., Wilder, H., de Soto, D., & Picard, P. (1994). Constructivist design of graphic computer simulations. http://www.ilt.columbia.edu/publications/cdgcs.html

Black, J. B., Carroll, J. M., & McGuigan, S. M. (1987). What kind of minimal instruction manual is most effective? In P. Tanner & J. M. Carroll (Eds.), *Human factors in computing systems and graphic interface.* Amsterdam.

Black Family Network. http://www.blackfamilynet.net/soon/nationwide_2002%20participant.html

Bowie, N. A. (2000). The digital divide: Making knowledge available in a global context. In *Schooling for tomorrow: Learning to bridge the digital divide* (pp. 37–50). Centre for Educational Research and Innovation, National Center on Adult Literacy (NCAL), Paris, France: Organisation for Economic Co-operation and Development (OECD).

Burgess, S. (1997). The role of shared reading in the development of phonological awareness: A longitudinal study of middle- to upper-class children. *Early Childhood Development and Care, 127/128*, 191–199.

Chall, J. S., & Snow, C. (1982). *Families and literacy: The contributions of out of school experiences to children's acquisition of literacy.* A final report to the National Institute of Education. Cambridge, MA: Harvard Graduate School of Education.

Clark, C., & Gorski, G. (2001). Multicultural education and the digital divide: Focus on socioeconomic class background. *Multicultural Perspectives, 4*(3), 25–36.

Cognition and Technology Group at Vanderbilt (1990). Anchored instruction and its relationship to situation cognition. *Educational Researcher, 20*, 2–10.

Collins, A., Brown, J. S., & Newman, S. E. (1990). Cognitive apprenticeship. In L. B. Resnick (Ed.), *Knowing, learning and instruction: Essay in honor of Robert Glaser.* Hillsdale, NJ: Lawrence Erlbaum Associates.

DeBruin-Parecki, A., & Knol-Sinclair, B. (2003). Introduction. In A. DeBruin-Parecki & B. Knol-Sinclair (Eds.), *Family literacy: From theory to practice* (pp. 1–6). Newark, DE: International Reading Association.

Delgado-Gaitan, C. (1987). Mexican adult literacy: New directions for immigrants. In S. R. Goldman and K. Trueba (Eds.), *Becoming literate as second language learners* (pp. 9–32). Norwood, NJ: Ablex.

Edwards, P. A. (2003). The impact of family on literacy development: Convergence, controversy, and instructional implications. NRC Annual Review of Research Address. In J. V. Hoffman, D. L. Shallert,

C. M. Fairbanks, J. Worthy, & B. Maloch (Eds.), *52nd Yearbook of the National Reading Conference* (pp. 92–103). Milwaukee, WI: National Reading Conference.

Edwards, P. A. (1993). *Parents as partners in reading: A family literacy training program* (2nd ed.). Chicago: Children's Press.

Erickson, F. (1989). Forward. Literacy risks for students, parents, and teachers. In J. Allen and J. Mason (Eds.), *Risk makers, risk takers, risk breakers: Reducing the risks for your literacy learners (pp. xiii–xvi).* Portsmouth: NH: Heinemann.

Gadsden, V. L. (1994). *Understanding family literacy: Conceptual issues facing the field.* Philadelphia: University of Pennsylvania National Center for Adult Literacy.

Gick, M. L., & Holyoak, K. J. (1983). Schema induction and analogical transfer. *Cognitive Psychology, 12*, 306–355.

Ginsburg, L., Sabatini, J., & Wagner, D. A. (2000). Basic skills in adult education (Ed:and ?) the digital divide. In *Schooling for tomorrow: Learning to bridge the digital divide* (pp. 77–89). Centre for Educational Research and Innovation, National Center on Adult Literacy (NCAL), Paris, France: Organisation for Economic Co-operation and Development (OECD).

Goldenberg, C. C. (1984, October). *Low-income parents' contributions to the reading achievement of their first-grade children.* Paper presented at the meeting of the Evaluation Network/Evaluation Research Society, San Francisco.

Heath, S. B. (1983). *Ways with words. Language, life and work in communities and classrooms.* New York: Cambridge University Press.

Hearron, P. F. (1992). *Kindergarten homework in nonmainstream families: The school-family interace in the ecology of emergent literacy.* Unpublished doctoral dissertation, Michigan State University, East Lansing, MI.

Jacoby, L. L. (1978). On interpreting the effects of repetition: Solving a problem versus remembering a solution. *Journal of Verbal Learning and Verbal Behavior, 17*, 649–667.

Johnson, D., & Johnson, R. (1975). *Learning together and alone.* Englewood Cliffs, NJ: Prentice-Hall.

Levesque, J. (2000). Across the great divide: Can family literacy programs prepare families for a technology-driven society? The potential is there. *Focus on Basics*, Vol. 4, Issue C., 1–5.

Macleod, F. (1996). Integrating home and school resources to raise literacy levels of parents and children. *Early Child Development and Care, 117*, 123–132.

Morrow, L. M. (1983). Home and school correlates of early interest in literature. *Journal of Educational Research, 76*, 221–230.

National Technical Information Administration (1998). *Falling through the Net II: New data on the digital divide.* Washington, DC: U. S. Department of Commerce, National Telecommunications and Information Administration.

National Technical Information Administration (1999). *Falling through the Net: Defining the digital divide.* Washington, DC: U. S. Department of Commerce, National Telecommunications and Information Administration.

National Technical Information Administration (2000). *Closing the digital divide.* Washington, DC: U. S. Department of Commerce, National Telecommunications and Information Administration.

National Telecommunications and Information Administration. *Falling through the net: Defining the digital divide. A report on the telecommunications and information technology gap in America. July 1999.* Washington, DC: National Telecommunications and Information Administration, U. S. Department of Commerce. http://www.ntia.doc.gov/reports.html

Paratore, J. R. (2001). *Opening doors, opening opportunities: Family literacy in an urban community.* Boston: Allyn and Bacon.

Peterson, P., Fennema, E., & Carpenter, T. (1988–1989). Using knowledge of how students think about math. *Educational Leadership, 46*(4), 42–46.

Poplin, M. S., & Stone, S. (1992). Paradigm shifts in instructional strategies: From reductionism to holistic/constructivism. In W. Stainback & S. Stainback (Eds.), *Controversial issues confronting special education: Divergent perspectives.* Boston: Allyn and Bacon.

Purcell-Gates, V. (2000). Family literacy. In M. L., Kamil, P. B. Mosenthal, P. D. Pearson, & R. Barr (Eds.), *Handbook of reading research* (Vol. 3, pp. 853–870). Mahwah, NJ: Lawrence Erlbaum Associates.

Purcell-Gates, V., & Dahl, K. (1991). Low-SES children's success and failure at early literacy learning in skills-based classroom. *Journal of Reading Behavior, 23*, 1–34.

Rockman, S. (June, 1995). *In school or out: Technology, equity, and the future of our kids.* Communications of the ACM. New York, NY.

Roblyer. M. D., Edwards, J., & Havriluk, M. A. (1997). *Integrating educational technology into teaching.* Columbus, OH: Prentice Hall.

Shockley, B. (1994). Extending the literate community: Home-to-school and school-to-home. *The Reading Teacher, 47*, 500–502.

Spiro, R. J., Feitovich, P. J., Jacobson, M. J., & Coulson, R. L. (1991). Cognitive flexibility, constructivism, and hypertext. *Educational Technology, 39*, 24–33.

Stone, D. (1997). *Policy paradox: The art of political decision making.* New York: W.W. Norton & Company.

Taylor, D. (1997). *Many families, many literacies: An international declaration of principles.* Portsmouth, NH: Heinemann.

Taylor, D. (1983). *Family literacy: Young children learn to read and write.* Portsmouth, NH: Heinemann.

Taylor, D., & Dorsey-Gaines, C. (1988). *Growing up literate: Learning from inner-city families.* Portsmouth, NH: Heinemann.

Teale, W. H. (1984). Reading to young children: Its significance for literacy development. In H. Goelman, A. Oberg, & F. Smith (Eds.), *Awakening to literacy* (pp. 110–121). Portsmouth, NH: Heinemann.

United States General Accounting Office [GAO], (2001). *Telecommunications: Characteristics and choices of Internet users.* Washington, DC.

Wiley, T. G. (1996). *Literacy and language diversity in sociocultural contexts, Literacy and language diversity in the United States.* Center for Applied Linguistics and Delta Systems Co., Inc.

Comprehension and Technology

Nell K. Duke
Michigan State University

Elizabeth Schmar-Dobler
Emporia State University

Shenglan Zhang
Michigan State University

By now it is trite to say that literacy has been changed fundamentally by the advent of computer-based and Internet technologies. Indeed we now write not of literacy, but of literacies, in part due to the influence of these technologies (New London Group, 1996). Terms like hyperlink, icon, and URL join phoneme, grapheme, and punctuation in our talk about text. The role of educators includes teaching children to contend with a whole new set of texts and contexts for reading. Indeed, so much has changed, and so much continues to change, that "no single theoretical perspective exists to explain the full range of changes to literacy" (Leu, Kinzer, Coiro, & Cammack, in press).

"Comprehension" is also developing new meanings and new emphases. Consider the familiar heuristic for comprehension of the text, activity, and reader in sociocultural context (e.g., Rand Reading Study Group, 2002). Many texts in electronic environments have unique characteristics (e.g., hyperlinks, embedded videoclips), many activities carried out in electronic environments are distinct (e.g., searching the Internet for information, editing a document in track changes mode), and each *reader* brings to the comprehension process particular knowledge and experience with technology and reading. The sociocultural contexts in which all this is occurring often reflect widespread influence of technology. Inevitably, then, there are differences in comprehension in electronic contexts. These differences raise a host of new questions about comprehension teaching and learning, identified throughout this chapter.

This is not to say that everything in comprehension is different in an electronic age. As will also be evident later in this chapter, there are a great many similarities between comprehension processes in electronic environments and comprehension processes with printed texts. In fact, even something viewed as a hallmark of reading in electronic environments—nonlinear reading—is actually also observed in comprehension in print contexts. For example, using a printed encyclopedia, you might look up information about Kashmir, read an entry on that, and then decide that you also need to know about India, read an entry on that, and then decide you should read about Pakistan, and read an entry on that. You have begun in the middle of the book, turned to an entry toward the front, and then back to a passage toward the back. That is nonlinear reading. Many other print reading activities—perusing a magazine, using an index, consulting a dictionary or field guide, flipping back to find a favorite passage, flipping ahead to find out whodunit—are also fundamentally nonlinear. Hypertext is not the only format that enables non-linear reading (cf. Boyle, 1997; Childers & Hentzi, 1995).

So there is both similarity and difference in comprehension processes, and comprehension teaching and learning, in print and electronic contexts (Figure 21.1). In the next section, we support this conclusion with respect to research on comprehension processes in electronic environments. We focus on hypertext, as this is a central form of text in these environments and one that has been the subject of some research. Following that, we discuss what is known about teaching comprehension in and of electronic environments, again noting both similarities and differences with teaching in printed texts. Throughout this chapter, we identify areas in comprehension and technology in need of further research.

COMPREHENSION PROCESSES IN HYPERTEXT

A fundamental question to ask about comprehension in electronic contexts regards what comprehension processes look like (Kamil & Lane, 1998). Researchers have begun to address this question, mostly focusing on strategies of skilled adult hypertext readers. Thus far, research suggests that skilled hypertext readers utilize a number of comprehension strategies (Altun, 2000; Baker and Brown, 1984; Coiro & Dobler, 2003; Foltz, 1996; Hillinger & Leu, 1994; Kim & Kamil, 1999; Lachman, 1989; Lawless & Kulikowich, 1994; Schmar, 2002; Sutherland-Smith, 2002; Verhij, Stoutnesdijk, & Beishuizen, 1996; Yang, 1997). These include:

Setting Reading Purpose; Planning. Skilled hypertext readers have a reading goal in mind and make a mental plan which typically follows a cycle of goal setting, searching, evaluating, and setting a new goal.

Activating Prior Knowledge. The prior knowledge used by skilled readers of hypertext requires not only knowledge of the topic, but also knowledge of the navigational features

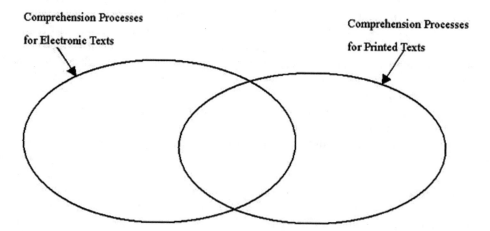

FIGURE 21.1. *Relationships Between Comprehension Processes for Electronic Texts and Comprehension Processes for Printed Texts.* This figure represents the position that there are some comprehension processes in common among electronic and printed texts, some processes unique to electronic texts, and perhaps a few processes unique to comprehension of printed texts.

of hypertext, and these two kinds of prior knowledge influence each other. Readers use this knowledge to understand, to locate and identify necessary information, and to prevent getting "lost" in navigation.

Previewing. Skilled hypertext readers preview the text before reading, for example scanning a page or pages before making reading decisions, and as a way of gleaning an overview of the text.

Predicting. An important part of hypertext comprehension is making predictions in order to determine what links to click to obtain useful information. Skilled hypertext readers are familiar with all kinds of context cues, both semantic and electronic, that can aid them in making good predictions.

Attending to Text Structure and Main Idea. Skilled hypertext readers identify the main idea and the text structure within the focal text and among linked texts.

Evaluating the Text and Text Information. Skilled hypertext readers also evaluate the quality and the value of the information in each link and distinguish relevant from irrelevant information.

Monitoring. Hypertext readers monitor their comprehension as a way of determining their path or their construction of meaning, perhaps even more so than the reader of linear text. Indeed, skilled hypertext readers continually monitor their reading, particularly in relation to their reading goal.

It is important to note that some of the research cited herein has been conducted with hypertext not on the Internet but in a closed context, sometimes with the hypertext actually created for use in the study. Findings may be altered or expanded when more research is conducted with naturally-occurring and Internet-based hypertexts. Moreover, the account is based on a limited number of studies. The field has not yet met Spires and Estes' (2002) call for a "rich theoretical description of the comprehension processes" (p. 123) in hypertext reading environments, but it does have a start.

Striking about the list of comprehension strategies is its similarity to lists of strategies generated by research on skilled readers with printed texts. Setting reading purpose and planning, previewing and predicting, attending to text structure, identifying main idea, evaluating the text, and monitoring have all been identified in research as things good readers do when they read printed texts (Duke & Pearson, 2002; Pressley & Afflerbach, 1995; Pressley, 2000). Indeed, in his review of previous studies, Altun (2000) concluded that skilled readers tend to "transfer their printed-text reading strategies to the computer environment" (p. 38). That said, it seems that these strategies play out in different ways or have different emphases in hypertext reading. Consider predicting, for example. In reading printed fictional narrative text, predicting involves thinking about what might happen next in the story. One might make a reading decision on the basis of that prediction—for example, deciding that what you predict will happen next is so unpleasant or contrary to your preferences that you will discontinue reading—but most of the time the prediction does not prompt a reading decision of that magnitude, but rather in a sense lends inertia to the reading. In contrast, in hypertext reading, some predictions in fact prompt a fundamental decision about the reading—whether to click on a link or access that text at all. This happens in reading printed informational text as well—for example, when someone decides not to read the next section of a text because they predict it will contain information irrelevant to their needs. However, reading printed informational text also can include a more linear approach, in which the person simply reads every page, one after the other, without active decision-making about what and where to read next. The structure of most hypertexts does not afford this simple linear approach. In hypertext, predicting *entails* a heightened emphasis on decision-making.

The point that hypertext comprehension demands the reader take an active role in text construction, by forcing decisions about what to click, what not to click, and so on, cannot be overstated. A reader encounters a myriad of choices, which can possibly cause cognitive overload and impair comprehension. Indeed, some studies have found hypertext more difficult to read than linear text (Gordon, Gustavel, Moore, & Hankey, 1988; Rouet, Levonen, Dillon, & Spiro, 1996), where too many choices can divert the attention of otherwise strong readers. The importance of bearing in mind one's reading purpose, interests, prior knowledge, and so on may be heightened in hypertext comprehension. The active role the reader must take may require more "cognitive energy" (van Oostendorp & de Mul, 1996) or an extended set of thought processes (Coiro, 2003) to make meaning from hypertext.

Another strategy listed above that takes on heightened emphasis in hypertext contexts, particularly on the Internet, is the need to evaluate information (e.g., Coiro & Schmar-Dobler, 2003; Leu, Kinzer, Coiro, Cammack, in press) and further, to "draw connections between resources of diverse and multiple perspectives" (Coiro, 2003, p. 461). This is not unique to Internet reading, with such demands also part of conducting research with printed texts for a report or term paper, for example. However, the task is different and perhaps more complex in Internet reading, which involves adeptly using a search engine, selecting appropriate and useful Web sites, locating, understanding and evaluating the information, and comparing and contrasting this information with a reader's prior knowledge and new information found at other Web sites. Such a complex process requires an effective and efficient use of comprehension strategies along with the additional skills of navigating and critical reading. The role of the Internet reader as an evaluator of the truthfulness of text is a new one for many readers, who typically give little thought to evaluating printed text. We need to further delve into this evaluative role and the most effective ways to teach readers to think critically about information found on the Internet. Unfortunately, research specifically on Internet comprehension is in its infancy. In a meta-analysis, Coiro, Leu, Kinzer, Labbo, and Teale (2003) found 80 studies on comprehension and technology, but only three of these studies focused on comprehension and the Internet. Several researchers have recognized the need for clarification of the comprehension processes used by Internet readers (e.g., Spires & Estes, 2002; Duke & Pearson, 2002; Coiro, 2003; Leu, Kinzer, Coiro, & Cammack, in press; RAND Reading Study Group, 2002).

Another emphasis in skilled hypertext reading seems to be minimizing reader disorientation. In reading hypertext, the reader must play an active role in making sense of a sequence of text nodes (van Oostendorp & de Mul, 1996), recognizing or understanding "where they are" in the hypertext. When readers are disoriented, they do not know where they are, where they want to go in hypertext, and how to get there (Kim & Hirtle, 1995). Disorientation can be caused by readers' lack of prior knowledge (Calisir & Gurel, 2003; Lawless, Brown, Mills, & Mayall, 2003; McDonald & Stevenson, 1996; McDonald & Stevenson, 1998; Potelle & Rouet 2003), and confusing text structure in a hypertext (Dee-Lucas & Larkin, 1992; Calisir & Gurel, 2003; Mohageg, 1992; Waniek, et al., 2003). It appears that different skilled readers take different approaches to avoiding disorientation. Altun (2000) noted that they "have a tendency toward their own way of navigation instead of what they have been given" (p. 50). Experienced readers also adopt some time management skills. For example, Altun also found that they open multiple windows and read one while waiting for another to download. This reading strategy reflects the concept that in hypertext, "reading is a multilayered cognitive activity" (Rouet et al., 1996, p. 5).

Clearly, there is a general need for more research on comprehension processes with hypertext, particularly with naturally-occurring and Internet-based hypertexts. One specific area in need of further investigation is how strategies differ and do not differ for different genres of text. Comprehension processes for fictional narrative hypertext and informational hypertext, for example, are very likely to be different, as they are in print contexts (Duke, 2003). And reading informational hypertext might be different from reading persuasive hypertext, and so on. Another set of questions regards the impact of purposes on hypertext comprehension processes. Different purposes of hypertext reading also have different effects on text comprehension and require different reading strategies. For instance, processes used when the purpose is to find information may differ a great deal from those used when the purpose is to browse or pass time. Greater understanding of features of particular genres of hypertext, and how those compare to features of those genres outside in print contexts, will also be important (e.g., Schmar-Dobler, 2003).

There is a critical need for better understanding of how hypertext comprehension develops. Much of the research thus far has been conducted with adult readers. We are just beginning to learn about children's comprehension of hypertext, how this develops over time, and how individual differences are manifest in younger readers' hypertext comprehension. Thus far, there is evidence that hypertext poses significant challenges for comprehension for developing readers. For example, in a study of third graders, researchers found that several children did not click on any hyperlinks within a text, some did not know that hyperlinks could be clicked or what they did, and one clicked on each and every hyperlink in a text (Pang & Kamil, 2003). On the other hand, research also suggests some competency with hypertext. Skilled fifth-grade readers were found to use a variety of comprehension strategies when reading on the Internet, including identifying important ideas, making inferences, predicting, and monitoring their comprehension (Schmar, 2002). We need to understand much more about children's comprehension processes with hypertext at different points in development and given different instructional backgrounds.

TEACHING COMPREHENSION WITH AND OF HYPERTEXT

What roles can hypertext play in teaching comprehension? It seems that there are at least two potential contributions. First, hypertext can be useful as a tool for teaching comprehension broadly speaking. Software programs and Web sites have been developed for teaching comprehension not only of hypertext but of many other types of text. Second, hypertext is one specific, and important, type of text for children to learn to comprehend. In both comprehension settings, hypertext serves as an extension of printed text with opportunities for the use of traditional comprehension strategies along with new cognitive challenges.

Using Hypertext to Teach Comprehension

How can hypertext help teach comprehension? Although there is much more research needed in this area, thus far it appears that the unique features of hypertext can provide opportunities for the development of scaffolded support systems within a text to aid in comprehension. The multilinear nature of hypertext provides for the use of text resources or "reading aids that act directly upon a particular text" (Gillingham, 1996, p. 79). Some of these text resources in essence make text more comprehensible, for example by providing hyperlinked definitions for low frequency vocabulary (Lachman, 1989; Feldman & Fish, 1991) and alternative presentation of ideas through sound and images (Reinking & ChanLin, 1994). Others actually teach or reinforce specific comprehension strategies, such as when reminders to access prior knowledge are provided (Gillingham et al., 1989).

The use of hypertext, with an emphasis on the unique ways it can be adapted for learning, has been found to engage struggling readers in ways that "may help compensate for inadequate reading ability" (McKenna, Reinking, Labbo, & Kieffer, 1999, p. 113). For example, the Thinking Reader (Center for Applied Special Technology, 2004) is a software program providing various levels of comprehension assistance within a computer-supported reading environment. Digital versions of children's literature are enhanced with speech-to-text capabilities and an online glossary to make the text more understandable. Particular reading strategies, such as predicting, summarizing, and questioning, are prompted with links to sounds and images. Metacognition is encouraged by asking readers to reflect on their reading progress. All this can be tailored to the reader's individual needs, for example with the amount of text read aloud and hints for strategy use varied by reader. Another example of a hypertext resource for teaching comprehension is available at the Web site CNN Learning Resources (http://www.literacynet.org/cnnsf/). Learning Resources provides access to current and past CNN news stories along with interactive comprehension activities focusing on determining word meaning, sequencing details, or drawing conclusions.

Based on the literature currently available, Coiro, Leu, Kinzer, Labbo, and Teale (2003) concluded that a variety of computer technologies appear to have the potential to assist readers with comprehension, including ILS systems, multiple mediated texts, speech supported text, and Internet technologies. However, of course, teachers must make appropriate decisions about the use of technology to teach reading comprehension for the teaching and learning potential of technology to be realized. The authors argued that teachers should focus on collaboration, individual differences of learners, and the ways comprehension outcomes are defined and assessed.

Teaching Comprehension of Hypertext

If hypertext poses substantial and in some respects unique challenges for comprehenders, another essential question is how to teach readers to comprehend this special form of text—to "learn to orchestrate sophisticated strategies to become literate in this complex environment" (Eagleton, Guinee, and Langlais, 2003). Unfortunately, there is very little research in this area, and there is a substantial need for this research. Recall the examples presented earlier of developing readers' comprehension processes with hypertext. It seems likely that these children would benefit from instruction in hypertext comprehension. Thus far, studies in the reading of hypertext have found that readers need explicit instruction in the use of hypertext resources (Shapiro, 1988; Gillingham, Garner, Guthrie, & Sawyer, 1989), such as links, to be able to take full advantage of the opportunities provided by the uniqueness of hypertext. Such instruction will likely need to be accompanied by instruction in comprehension strategies that apply more broadly (Duke & Pearson, 2002). Figure 21.2 represents our guess as to the relationship between instruction inside and outside of hypertext contexts. Some comprehension instruction may be specific to hypertext environments—for example regarding interpreting URLs to make decisions about where to read next in a text. Some may be specific to print environments—for example that that assumes an entirely linear reading. Other instruction may occur in hypertext environments but apply to both hypertext and printed texts, or occur in printed texts but apply as well to hypertext. For example, the strategy of monitoring comprehension can be taught in and apply to either context, though the extent to which instruction can transfer from one context to another is a question in need of research.

Critical questions include not only *how* to teach comprehension of hypertext, but also *who* should teach comprehension of hypertext. Does this responsibility lie with the classroom teacher, the reading specialist, the instructional technology facilitator, or all of them? Researchers have called not only for an understanding of how to teach the skills needed to comprehend on the Inter-

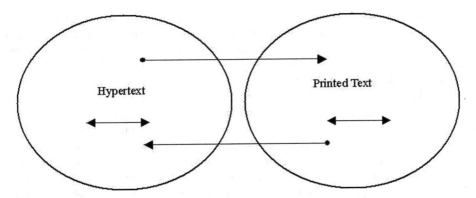

FIGURE 21.2. *Relationships Between Comprehension Instruction for Hypertext and Printed Text.* The arrows represent instruction. Instruction can occur specifically for printed texts, specifically for electronic texts, or can occur within one text but apply to the other as well.

net, but also for an understanding of how to assess those skills (Coiro, 2003; Rand Reading Study Group, 2002). Early work in this area highlights the need for assessment tools that assess the ability to locate, understand, and evaluate Internet text.

DIRECTIONS FOR FUTURE RESEARCH ON COMPREHENSION

The similarities and differences of comprehension processes, teaching, and learning between printed and electronic texts emphasized throughout the chapter have exciting consequences for research in comprehension. On the one hand, there are many new research questions to explore— we have much to learn about comprehension processes in electronic environments. These questions include:

- What are comprehension processes in use with hypertext?
  How do processes compare with comprehension of printed texts?
  How do processes compare for different genres of hypertext?
  How do processes compare for different purposes for reading?
- What does hypertext comprehension look like at different points in development and given different instructional backgrounds?
- What individual differences in hypertext comprehension development are evidenced?
- How can hypertext help teach comprehension?
- How can we teach comprehension of hypertext?
- To what extent does comprehension instruction in hypertext transfer to printed texts and vice-versa?
- Who will teach comprehension of hypertext?
- How will we assess readers' ability to read this critical form of text?

At the same time, there is potential for research in electronic contexts to reinvigorate comprehension research more broadly. For example, a focus on the navigational aspects of hypertext reading may help spur additional research on navigation of printed texts (a relatively neglected area in past research; Symons, MacLatchy-Gaudet, Stone, & Reynolds, 2001) and greater attention in general to navigational aspects of comprehension. Research on comprehension in electronic environments may even inspire us to rethink fundamental theories of comprehension. For example, the simple view of reading (Gough & Tunmer, 1986), which remains highly influential, holds that reading comprehension is comprised of decoding and listening comprehension. However, many comprehension processes in electronic environments (and outside them as well, though to a lesser degree) are not captured in decoding or listening comprehension. Integrating the reading of icons, para-linguistic markers, photos, charts, graphs, videoclips, and other multimedia with reading written text is part of comprehension in electronic contexts and does not have a direct correlate in decoding or listening comprehension. For this and other reasons, the simple view of reading comprehension is not serving us well (Duke et al., 2005); research on comprehension in electronic environments may help bring about this realization. Electronic environments have the potential to be one of the best things to happen to the field of reading comprehension in this field's history. With comprehension researchers working together inside and outside of electronic contexts, we can develop a more powerful, comprehensive, and dynamic understanding of comprehension than ever before. Off we go!

REFERENCES

Altun, A. (2000). Patterns in cognitive processes and strategies in hypertext reading: A case study of two experienced computer users. *Journal of Educational Multimedia and Hypermedia, 9,* 35–55.

Baker, L., & Brown, A. L. (1984). Cognitive monitoring in reading. In J. Flood (Ed.). *Understanding reading comprehension: Cognition, language, and the structure of prose* (pp. 21–44). Newark, DE: International Reading Association.

Boyle, T. (1997). *Design for multimedia learning.* London: Prentice Hall.

Calisir, F., & Gurel, Z. (2003). Influence of text structure and prior knowledge of the learner on reading comprehension, browsing and perceived control. *Computer in Human Behavior, 19,* 135–145

CAST eReader [Computer Software]. Wakefield, MA: CAST, Inc. Retrieved September, 2005 from http://www.cast.org/products/ereader/index.html

Childers, J., & Hentzi, G. (Eds.) (1995). *Columbia dictionary of modern literary and cultural criticism.* New York: Columbia University Press.

Coiro, J. (2003). Reading comprehension on the Internet: Expanding our understanding of reading comprehension to encompass new literacies. *The Reading Teacher, 56,* 458–464.

Coiro, J., Leu, D. J., Kinzer, C. K., Labbo, L., & Teale, W. (2003). *A review of research on literacy and technology: Replicating and extending the NRP subcommittee report on computer technology and reading instruction.* Paper presented at the annual meeting of the National Reading Conference, Scottsdale, AZ.

Coiro, J., & Schmar-Dobler, E., (2003). *Exploring how skilled readers use reading strategies while locating information on the Internet.* Paper presented at Annual Meeting of the National Reading Conference, Scottsdale, AZ.

Dee-Lucas, D., & Larkin, J. H. (1995). Learning from electronic texts: Effects of interactive overviews for information access. *Cognition & Instruction, 13,* 431–468.

Duke, N. K. (2005). Comprehension of what for what: Comprehension as a non-unitary construct. In S. Paris & S. Stahl (Eds.), *Current issues in reading comprehension and assessment* (pp. 93–104). Mahwah, NJ: Erlbaum.

Duke, N., & Pearson, P. D., (2002). Effective practices for developing reading comprehension. In A. E. Farstrup & S. J. Samuels (Eds.). *What research has to say about reading instruction* (pp. 205–242). Newark, DE: International Reading Association.

Duke, N. K., Pressley, M., Hilden, K., Golos, D. Halladay, J., Zhang, S., Fingeret, L., Park, Y., & Reynolds, J. M. (2005). *The simple view of reading is probably too simple.* Paper presented at the National Reading Conference, Miami, FL.

Eagleton, M. B., Guinee, K., & Langlais, K. (2003). Teaching Internet literacy strategies: The hero inquiry project. *Voices From the Middle, 10*(3), 28–35.

Feldman, S. C., & Fish, M. C. (1991). Use of computer-mediated reading supports to enhance reading comprehension of high school students. *Journal of Educational Computing Research, 7*(1), 25–36.

Foltz, P. W. (1996). Comprehension, coherence, and strategies in hypertext and linear text. In J.-F. Rouet, J. J. Levonen, A. Dillon, & R. J. Spiro (Eds.). *Hypertext and Cognition* (pp. 109–136). Mahwah, NJ: Lawrence Erlbaum Associates.

Gillingham, M. G. (1996). Comprehending electronic text. In H. V. Oostendorp, & S. de Mul (Eds.). *Cognitive aspects of electronic text processing* (pp. 77–98). Norwood, NJ: Ablex.

Gillingham, M. G., & Garner, R. (1992). Readers' comprehension of mazes embedded in expository texts. *Journal of Educational Research, 85*, 234–241.

Gillingham, M. G., Garner, R., Guthrie, J. T., & Sawyer, R. (1989). Children's control of computer-based reading assistance in answering synthesis questions. *Computers in Human Behavior, 5*, 61–75.

Gordon, S., Gustavel, J., Moore, J., & Hankey, J. (1988). The effects of hypertext on reader knowledge representation. In *Proceedings of the 32nd Annual Meeting of the Human Factors Society, 32*, 296–300. Santa Monica, CA: The Human Factors Society.

Gough, P. B., & Tunmer, W. E. (1986). Decoding, reading, and reading disability. *Remedial and Special Education, 7*, 6–10.

Hillinger, M. L. & Leu, D. J. (1994). Guiding instruction in hypermedia. *Proceedings of the Human Factors and Ergonomics Society's 38th Annual Meeting*, 266–270.

International Reading Association. (2001). *Integrating literacy and technology in the curriculum: A position statement.* Retrieved January 13, 2003, from http://www.reading.org/positions/technology.html

Kamil, M., & Lane, D. (1998). Researching the relationship between technology and literacy: An agenda for the 21st century. In D. R. Reinking, L. D. Labbor, M. McKenna, & R. Kieffer (Eds.). *Literacy for the 21st century: Technological transformations in a post-typographic world* (pp. 323–342). Mahwah, NJ: Lawrence Erlbaum Associates.

Kim, H., & Hirtle, S. C. (1995). Spatial metaphors and disorientation in hypertext browsing. *Behaviour and Information Technology, 14*, 239–250.

Kim, H. S., & Kamil, M. L. (1999, December). *Exploring hypertext reading and strategy use for structured vs. unstructured texts.* Paper presented at the National Reading Conference, Orlando, FL.

Kristeva, J. (1984). *Revolution in poetic language.* New York: Columbia University Press.

Lachman, R. (1989). Comprehension aids for on-line reading of expository text. *Human Factors, 31*, 1–15.

Lawless, K. A., & Kulikowich, J. M. (1994). *Reading comprehension, navigation and hypertext.* Paper presented at the annual meeting of the Southwestern Educational Research Association, San Antonio, TX.

Leu, D. J., Kinzer, C. K., Coiro, J., & Cammack, D. (2004). Towards a theory of literacies emerging from the Internet and other ICT. In R. B. Ruddell & N. Unrau (Eds.). *Theoretical Models of Processing Reading, 5th Edition* (pp. 1568–1611). Newark, DE: International Reading Association.

Lawless, K. A., Brown, S. W., Mills, R., & Mayall, H. J. (2003). Knowledge, interest, recall and navigation: A look at hypertext processing. *Journal of Literacy Research, 35*, 911–934.

New London Group, The. (1996). A pedagogy of multiliteracies: Designing social futures. *Harvard Educational Review, 66*, 60–92.

Pang, E. S., & Kamil, M. L. (2001). Reading hypertext: Comprehension and strategies of third grade students. In D. L. Schallert, C. M. Fairbanks, J. Worthy, B. Maloch, & J. V. Hoffman (Eds.). 51st Yearbook of the National Reading Conference Yearbook (pp. 333–343). Oak Creek, WI: National Reading Conference.

Potelle, H., & Rouet, J. (2003). Effects of content representation and readers' prior knowledge on the comprehension of hypertext. *International Journal of Human-Computer Studies, 58*, 327–345.

McDonald, S., & Stevenson, R. (1996). Disorientation in hypertext: The effects of three text structures on navigation performance. *Applied Ergonomics, 27*(1), 61–68.

McDonald, S., & Stevenson, R. (1998). Effects of text structure and prior knowledge of the learner on navigation in hypertext. *Human Factors, 40*(1), 18–27.

McKenna, M. C., Reinking, D., Labbo, L. D., & Kieffer, R. D. (1999). The electronic transformation of literacy and its implications for the struggling reader. *Reading & Writing Quarterly, 15*, 111–126.

Mohageg, M. F. (1992). The influence of hypertext linking structures on the efficiency of information retrieval. *Human Factors, 34,* 351–367.

RAND Reading Study Group. (2002). *Reading for understanding: Towards an R&D program in reading comprehension.* Santa Monica, CA: Rand Education.

Reinking, D. (1988). Computer-mediated text and comprehension differences: The role of reading time, reader preference, and estimation of learning. *Reading Research Quarterly, 23,* 484–498.

Reinking, D., & ChanLin, L. (1994). Graphic aids in electronic texts. *Reading Research and Instruction, 33,* 207–232.

Reinking, D., & Rickman, S. S. (1990). The effects of computer-mediated texts on the vocabulary learning and comprehension of intermediate-grade readers. *Journal of Reading Behavior, 22,* 395–411.

Reinking, D., & Schreiner, R. (1985). The effects of computer-mediated text on measures of reading comprehension and reading behavior. *Reading Research Quarterly, 20,* 536–552.

Rosenblatt, L. (1978). *The reader, the text, the poem.* Carbondale, IL: Southern Illinois University Press.

Rouet, J., Levonen, J., Dillon, A., & Spiro, R. (Eds.). (1996). *Hypertext and cognition.* Mahwah, NJ: Lawrence Erlbaum Associates.

Reinking, D., & Mason, G. E. (Eds.). (1987). *Reading and computers: Issues for theory and practice.* NY: Teachers College Press.

Schmar, E. S. (2002). A collective case study of reading strategies used by skilled fifth graders reading on the Internet. (Doctoral Dissertation, Kansas State University). *Dissertation Abstracts International, 63,* 4227.

Schmar-Dobler, E. (2003). Reading on the Internet: The link between literacy and technology. *Journal of Adolescent and Adult Literacy, 47,* 80–85.

Shapiro, A. (1998). Promoting active learning: The role of system structure in learning from hypertext. *Human-Computer Interaction, 31,* 1–36.

Smolin, L. I., & Lawless, K. A. (2003). Becoming literate in the technological age: New responsibilities and tools for teachers. *The Reading Teacher, 56,* 570–577.

Spires, H. A. & Estes, T. H. (2002). Reading in Web-based learning environments. In C. C. Block & M. Pressley (Eds.). *Comprehension instruction: Research-based best practices* (pp. 115–125). New York: The Guilford Press.

Spruijt, S., & Jansen, C. (1999). The influence of task and format on reading results with an online text. *IEEE Transactions on Professional Communication, 42*(2), 92–100.

Sutherland-Smith, W. (2002). Weaving the literacy Web: Changes in reading from page to screen. *The Reading Teacher, 55,* 662–668.

Symons, S., MacLatchy-Gaudet, H., Stone, T. D., & Reynolds, P. L. (2001). Strategy instruction for elementary students searching informational text. *Scientific Studies of Reading, 5*(1), 1–33.

Tapscott, D. (1998). *Growing up digital: The rise of the net generation.* New York: McGraw-Hill.

van Oostendrop, H. (1996). Studying and annotating electronic text. In J. Rouet, J. Levonen, A. Dillon, & R. J. Spiro (Eds.). *Hypertext and cognition* (pp. 137–148). Mahwah, NJ: Lawrence Erlbaum Associates.

van Oostendorp, H., & de Mul, S. (Eds.) (1996). *Cognitive aspects of electronic text processing.* Norwood, NJ: Ablex Publishing.

Verheij, J., Stoutjesdijk, E., & Beishuizen, J. (1996). Search and study strategies in hypertext. *Computers in Human Behavior, 12,* 1–15.

Waniek, J., Brunstein, A., Naumann, A., & Krems, J. F. (2003). Interaction between text structure representation and situation model in hypertext reading. *Swiss Journal of Psychology, 62*(2), 103–111.

Wixson, K., & Peters, C. (1984). Reading redefined: A Michigan Reading Association position paper. *The Michigan Reading Journal, 17,* 4–7.

Yang, S. C. (1997). Information seeking as problem-solving using a qualitative approach to uncover the novice learners' information-seeking processes in a Perseus hypertext. *Library & Information Science Research, 19*(1), 71–92.

22

▼▼▼▼▼▼▼

Technology Use and Needed Research in Youth Literacies

Donna E. Alvermann
University of Georgia

The potential of the Internet and other forms of information and communication technologies (ICTs) to redefine the field of youth literacies has garnered considerable attention of late, especially among professional organizations committed to supporting youth's interests in ICT-related literacies. For example, the International Reading Association (2002) and the National Reading Conference (Alvermann, 2002) commissioned separate position papers that called for integrating new literacies and technology in middle and high school curricula. The College Reading Association dedicated a themed issue of *Reading Research and Instruction* to exploring new literacies (Bean & Readence, 2002), and the International Reading Association's *Reading Research Quarterly* featured five essays on media and online studies (Hagood, Leander, Luke, Mackey, & Nixon, 2003) as part of its New Directions in Research initiative. Not to be left out, organizations within the private sector also made their intentions known. For instance, the Alliance for Excellent Education (Kamil, 2003) and the Carnegie Corporation of New York (2004) issued policy briefs that underscored, among other things, the importance of integrating literacy and technology in secondary classrooms.

Given this interest in the potential of ICTs to redefine youth literacies as a field, it seems reasonable, first, to identify current trends in the ICT literature, and then, to examine those trends for what they might tell us about needed research on technology applications at the middle and high school level. By technology applications, I mean the use of the Internet and other digital technologies in both academic and nonacademic settings. To limit the scope of this chapter, I focused on information published after 1998, the year in which the first edition of the *Handbook of Literacy and Technology: Transformations in a Post-typographic World* (Reinking, McKenna, Labbo, and Kieffer, 1998) appeared. Although the intervening period of time is relatively short, I believe it is sufficient for marking trends in rapidly changing ICT-related literacies.

CURRENT TRENDS IN ICT-RELATED LITERACIES

This section begins by taking into account the findings from three large-scale surveys of youth's online literacy practices. These findings are meant to provide a context for the more detailed analysis of the current trends in ICT-related literacies in school and home/community settings that follow.

Surveys of Youth's Online Literacy Practices

Two reports from the Pew Internet and American Life Project and a separate report by the USC Annenberg School Center for the Digital Future were the data sources for the following synthesis of online youth literacy practices. In the first Pew Internet report (Lenhart, Simon, & Graziano, 2001), project personnel surveyed 754 online youth ages 12–17 and their parents. Both groups agreed that the Internet is essential for completing homework, with a majority saying that the Internet has virtually replaced the library as a source of information.

The second Pew Internet report (Levin, Arafeh, Lenhart, & Rainie, 2002), based on information gathered from 14 racially diverse and gender-balanced focus groups ($N = 136$ middle and high school students representing 36 different schools), describes numerous uses that Internet-savvy youth attribute to the Net. Referring to it as "virtual textbook and reference library, as virtual tutor and study shortcut, as virtual study group, as virtual guidance counselor" (n.p.), the youth in this study report that there is a substantial disconnect between how they use the Internet in school under their teachers' direction and how they use it after school on their own. For the most part, students' use of the Internet occurs outside of school where they say they are free from "heavy-handed filtering" and the "uninspiring quality of Internet-based assignments" (n.p.). Project staff concluded that "Internet-savvy students are coming to school with different expectations, different skills, and access to different resources" (n.p.).

In a report entitled *Surveying the Digital Future: Year Four*, researchers from the USC Annenberg School Center for the Digital Future (2004) compared responses from 2,000 users and non-users representing all age ranges, from 12 to >65. Perhaps not surprisingly, Internet use is highest for those age 24 and under, with use among those age 18 and under approaching 100%. The 10 trends the USC Annenberg School researchers identified were the following:

1. In America, the digital divide is closing, as new divides emerge (e.g., home vs. public access; broadband vs. modem access).
2. The media habits of the nation have changed, and continue to change (e.g., less TV viewing; little negative effect on personal and social activities).
3. The credibility of information on the Internet is dropping.
4. A variety of issues affecting online purchasing are just beginning to surface.
5. The "geek-nerd" perception of Internet users is dead.
6. Privacy and security concerns remain.
7. The Internet has become the primary source of information for users.
8. Parents and children perceive the benefits and drawbacks of Internet use differently.
9. E-mailing is both a great convenience and a source of irritation.
10. Broadband is changing everything (e.g., the tasks people undertake online vary according to the mode of access).

School Contexts

Much of what was originally written about using technology to mediate students' understanding of text and motivation for learning in the first edition of the *Handbook of Literacy and Technology: Transformations in a Post-typographic World* (Reinking, McKenna, Labbo, & Kieffer, 1998) remains a trend today. Examples of current contributions to this trend can be found in edited collections (Jetton & Dole, 2004; Verhoeven & Snow, 2001), in syntheses and reviews of the literature (Edyburn, 2001; Kamil, Intrator, & Kim, 2000; Lou, Abrami, & d'Apollonia, 2001), as well as in peer-refereed journal articles (Hobbs & Frost, 2003; Windschitl & Stahl, 2002). This body of literature on school contexts for ICT studies is classroom centered and relies largely on pragmatism as defined by Dillon, O'Brien, and Heilman (2000) as its lens for interpreting the impact of digital technologies on young people's literacy learning. It is a rich literature comprised of studies on language/text and mind/cognition that are situated in real-world contexts and that typically require instructional interventions for addressing attitudes and beliefs as much as cognitive changes in learners.

A second trend within school contexts for ICT-related literacy studies is a call for negotiating the multiple realities of technology in literacy research and instruction (Labbo & Reinking, 1999). The construct *multiple realities* builds on Leu's (1997) notion of *deixis*, a linguistic concept that marks quick shifts in the meanings of words (e.g., *old* and *new*) when the frame of reference changes. Applied to ICT-related literacies, deixis refers to continual changes (or multiple realities) wrought by rapid advances in technology use that often undermine long-standing assumptions about reading and writing. Labbo and Reinking (1999) have argued that technology should be studied not as a monolithic topic within literacy instruction but rather "as a set of possibilities in relation to multiple realities" (p. 479). They suggest that this multiple realities view of technology use in school contexts can provide guidance to teachers, especially when there are competing goals for ICT-related literacy instruction. Such might be the case when the goals within a single school range from "seeing new technologies as extensions of the status quo to seeing new technologies as a potential catalyst for transforming instruction" (p. 488).

The three studies presented next illustrate quite dramatically the variation found in technology use when a multiple realities perspective is employed. Karchmer (2001) used this perspective to frame her exploratory study of 13 classroom teachers' perceptions of how the Internet influenced literacy and literacy instruction in their classrooms. She identified several distinctions between elementary and secondary school teachers' perceptions of the Internet's influence on their instruction, one of which was the finding that five of the six secondary teachers in her study did not believe that providing opportunities to publish on the Internet increased their students' motivations to produce quality written work. Interestingly, this finding stood in stark contrast to what seven of the eight elementary teachers believed. Karchmer interpreted it (and other findings) in light of the multiple realties perspective. In a qualitative study that uncovered serious flaws in the assumptions guiding two Silicon Valley high schools' policies on ICT use, Cuban, Kirkpatrick, and Peck (2001) reported that "access to equipment and software seldom led to widespread teacher and student use" (p. 813). The researchers offered two interrelated explanations for these and several other anomalies observed, all of which suggested the usefulness of Labbo and Reinking's (1999) multiple realities framework for interpreting classroom practices. Finally, although not identified specifically as a multiple realities study, Williams and Williams' (2000) attempt to use ICTs to teach EFL learners who had previously not been able to understand their teacher or the course requirements would seem to fit the perspective's emphasis on the importance of flexibility in meeting classroom realities.

Home and Community Settings

A third trend, though one that is not yet well represented in the literature, is a form of inquiry that focuses on youth's digital literacy practices in home and community settings. With a few notable exceptions (e.g., Chandler-Olcott & Mahar, 2003; Lankshear & Knobel, 2003; Leander & McKim, 2003; Lewis & Finders, 2002), literacy researchers have opted to focus on academic contexts, with only an occasional foray into exploring how digital literacies acquired in school connect to those used in home and community (Beach & Bruce, 2002; King & O'Brien, 2002; Lankshear & Snyder, 2000). Despite its relative newcomer status, there is evidence to suggest that the trend in studying youth's home and community digital practices is likely to grow, especially among researchers inquiring into how ICTs mediate youth's social spaces to produce new insights related to identity formation and what it means to be literate in a digital age.

Scholars who locate their work in spatial theories of youth's digital practices, such as Leander and his colleagues (Leander, 2002, 2003; Leander & McKim, 2003; Leander & Sheehy, 2004), make use of current thinking in social and cultural geography to generate insights for interpreting ICT-related literacies. They also represent an important shift in the study of online literacies. For example, Leander et al.'s work reflects what can be learned by moving away from a fixation on technology as a tool and toward mapping what Lemke (2003) refers to as ecosocial systems—digital spaces in which youth produce and enact new literate identities, not unlike those described in Neilsen's (1998) study of a rural high school's introduction to the Internet in the first edition of the *Handbook of Literacy and Technology: Transformations in a Post-typographic World.*

Other researchers interested in ICT-related literacies in home/community settings have used a variety of theoretical perspectives, including critical, sociocultural, and poststructural, to inquire into how young women enact their identities through digital literacies (Lewis & Finders, 2002), how constructions of gender influence (and are influenced by) ICT-mediated literacy practices outside of formal academic settings (Chandler-Olcott & Mahar, 2003); how juxtaposition of traditional and intermedial literacies can redefine the competence of youth who struggle to read (O'Brien, 2003); and how Internet communities of practice support L2 (a second language, as opposed to a first, or native/mother tongue language) learning and positive change in self-perceptions of what it means to be literate (Lam, 2001).

NEEDED RESEARCH ON TECHNOLOGY
USE IN YOUTH LITERACIES

Although it is too early to lay out a broad agenda for ICT-related literacy research, a few interim questions to guide researchers in their work that are specific to the trends just identified seem in order. These questions are in line with the 10 central principles that Leu, Kinzer, Coiro, and Cammack (2004) identified as having emerged from their review of the literature on the Internet and other ICTs in preparation for developing a more comprehensive theoretical framework for online literacies.

Question: Given that youth report that Internet access is essential for completing homework and yet find most Internet-based assignments "uninspiring," how might teachers alter their approach to making assignments?

Researchers interested in addressing this question may find Hinchman and Lalik's (2002) interpretation of the scenariating strategy described in Lankshear and Knobel (2003) particularly helpful. *Scenariating*, which means considering a number of possibilities, is a process for raising important "what-if" questions that a group can then take into account when seeking to change how things have traditionally been done.

Question: Given the transactional nature of ICTs and youth literacies (i.e., ICTs produce changes in youth literacies just as youth literacies produce changes in ICTs), what is needed to transform existing tools and forms of strategic knowledge into "new" resources for locating, evaluating, and effectively using ICT-related information?

Studies that might be designed to answer this question are clearly in need of a collaborative framework, for the onus is not on researchers alone but rather on the shared knowledge and expertise that youth and their teachers can bring to the project. Examples of how all three parties who share a stake in answering this question can be encouraged to participate in the project are available in Hull and Schultz's (2002) edited book on bridging out-of-school literacies with classroom practice. This resource, while not exclusively focused on ICT-related literacies, provides practical ideas for tapping into the expertise of individuals whose work in informal learning centers, such as home and community organizations, makes them particularly valuable.

Question: Given that significant strides are being made to enlarge the scope of inquiry related to ICTs and youth literacies (e.g., studies that draw on perspectives outside the conventional literacy paradigms), what theoretical and methodological issues need to be addressed, and why?

Here, the focus is on the type of research to be conducted rather than on the design of specific studies. A concern, perhaps more implied than directly stated, is the possibility that in our haste to open up the field of ICT-related youth literacies, we might unintentionally stifle trends that are yet "unborn." For example, if the field were to privilege research traditions that focus on the relationship between language/text and mind/cognition over those that view ICT texts as socially, culturally, and historically constructed (or if the privileging were in reverse), what views might be lost that represent other perspectives, such as "new realism" (Hruby, 2001)?

Of paramount concern is that studies of ICT-related youth literacies take into account the global/local tensions underlying the autonomous view of literacy. Collins and Blot (2003) argue along with others (e.g., Brandt & Clinton, 2002) that socioculturalists and ethnographers, in trying to correct for an earlier conception of literacy as a deterministic force in social evolution (Goody, 1986), have relied too heavily on localized, or contextualized, accounts of literacy practices. They point out that although revisionist historical research and situated ethnographic studies of people's multiple literacies have largely discredited the autonomous view of literacy—a view that assumes a deterministic force in social evolution—the fact remains that literacy studies generally, and ICT-related literacy studies in particular, have yet to take into account the tenacity of this key aspect of the model.

In sum, although the three questions just posited are far from fulfilling the need for a comprehensive research agenda on ICT-related youth literacies, they may prove useful in starting the conversation. As with all relatively new areas of research, ICT youth literacies stand to gain from the sustained intellectual and material engagement of all who are interested in the potential of this research to inform a broader audience.

REFERENCES

Alvermann, D. E. (2002). Effective literacy instruction for adolescents. *Journal of Literacy Research, 34*, 189–208. (Also available at http://www.nrconline.org)

Andrews, R. (2004). Conclusion. In R. Andrews (Ed.). *The impact of ICT on literacy education* (pp. 202–214). London: RoutledgeFalmer.

Beach, R., & Bruce, B. C. (2002). Using digital tools to foster critical inquiry. In D. E. Alvermann (Ed.). *Adolescents and literacies in a digital world* (pp. 147–163). New York: Peter Lang.

Brandt, D., & Clinton, K. (2002). Limits of the local: Expanding perspectives on literacy as a social practice. *Journal of Literacy Research, 34*, 337–356.

Carnegie Corporation of New York. (2004). *Reading next: A vision for action and research in middle and high school literacy.* New York: Author.

Chandler-Olcott, K., & Mahar, D. (2003). "Tech-savviness" meets multiliteracies: Exploring adolescent girls' technology-mediated literacy practices. *Reading Research Quarterly, 38,* 356–385.

Collins, J., & Blot, R. K. (2003). *Literacy and literacies: Texts, power, and identity.* Cambridge, UK: Cambridge University Press.

Cuban, L., Kirkpatrick, H., & Peck, C. (2001). High access and low use of technologies in high school classrooms: Explaining an apparent paradox. *American Educational Research Journal, 38,* 813–834.

Dillon, D. R., O'Brien, D. G., & Heilman, E. E. (2000). Literacy research in the next millennium: From paradigms to pragmatism and practicality. *Reading Research Quarterly, 35,* 10–26.

Edyburn, D. L. (2001). 2000 in review: A synthesis of the special education technology literature. *JSET 16*(2). Retrieved January 4, 2004 from http://jset.unlv.edu/16.2/Edyburn/first.html

Goody, J. (1986). *The logic of writing and the organization of society.* Cambridge, UK: Cambridge University Press.

Hagood, M. C., Leander, K. M., Luke, C., Mackey, M., & Nixon, H. (2003). New directions in research: Media and online literacy studies. *Reading Research Quarterly, 38,* 386–413.

Hinchman, K. A., & Lalik, R. (2002). Imagining literacy teacher education in changing times: Considering the views of adult and adolescent collaborators. In D. E. Alvermann (Ed.). *Adolescents and literacies in a digital world* (pp. 84–100). New York: Peter Lang.

Hobbs, R., & Frost, R. (2003). Measuring the acquisition of media-literacy skills. *Reading Research Quarterly, 38,* 330–355.

Hruby, G. G. (2001). Sociological, postmodern, and "new realism" perspectives in social constructionism: Implications for reading research. *Reading Research Quarterly, 36,* 48–62.

Hull, G., & Schultz, K. (Eds.). (2002). *School's out! Bridging out-of-school literacies with classroom practice.* New York: Teachers College Press.

International Reading Association (2002). *Integrating literacy and technology in the curriculum: A position statement of the International Reading Association.* Newark, DE: Author.

Jetton, T. L., & Dole, J. A. (Eds.). (2004). *Adolescent literacy research and practice.* New York: Guilford.

Kamil, M. (2003). *Adolescents and literacy: Reading for the 21st century.* Washington, DC: Alliance for Excellent Education.

Kamil, M. L., Intrator, S. M., & Kim, H. S. (2000). The effects of other technologies on literacy and literacy learning. In M. L. Kamil, P. B. Mosenthal, P. D. Pearson, & R. Barr (Eds.). *Handbook of reading research* (Vol. 3, pp. 771–788). Mahwah, NJ: Lawrence Erlbaum Associates.

Karchmer, R. A. (2001). The journey ahead: Thirteen teachers report how the Internet influences literacy and literacy instruction in their K–12 classrooms. *Reading Research Quarterly, 36,* 442–466.

King, J. R., & O'Brien, D. G. (2002). Adolescents' multiliteracies and their teachers' needs to know: Toward a digital détente. In D. E. Alvermann (Ed.). *Adolescents and literacies in a digital world* (pp. 40–50). New York: Peter Lang.

Labbo, L. D., & Reinking, D. (1999). Negotiating the multiple realities of technology in literacy research and instruction. *Reading Research Quarterly, 34,* 478–492.

Lam, W. S. E. (2000). L2 literacy and the design of the self: A case study of a teenager writing on the Internet. *TESOL Quarterly, 34,* 457–482.

Lankshear, C., & Knobel, M. (2003). *New literacies: Changing knowledge and classroom learning.* Buckingham, UK: Open University Press.

Lankshear, C., & Snyder, I. (2000). *Teachers and techno-literacy: Managing literacy, technology and learning in schools.* St. Leonards NSW, Australia: Allen & Unwin.

Leander, K. M. (2002, December). *Situated literacies, digital practices, and the constitution of space-time.* Paper presented at the annual meeting of the National Reading Conference, Miami, FL.

Leander, K. M. (2003). Writing travelers' tales on new literacyscapes. (RRQ Online Supplement). Retrieved October 7, 2004 from http://www.reading.org/Library/Retrieve.cfm?D=10.1598/RRQ.38.3.4&F=RRQ–38–3–Hagood-supp_3.html

Leander, K. M., & McKim, K. K (2003). Tracing the everyday "sitings" of adolescents on the Internet: A strategic adaptation of ethnography across online and offline spaces. *Education, Communication & Information, 3,* 211–240.

Leander, K. M., & Sheehy, M. (Eds.). (2004). *Spatializing literacy research and practice*. New York: Peter Lang.

Lemke, J. L. (2000). Across the scale of time: Artifacts, activities, and meanings in ecosocial systems. *Mind, Culture, and Activity, 7*, 273–292.

Lenhart, A., Simon, M., & Graziano, M. (2001). *The Internet and education: Findings of the Pew Internet & American Life Project. Washington, DC: Pew Internet and American Life Project*. Retrieved May 30, 2003 from http://www.pewinternet.org/reports/toc.asp?Report=39

Leu, D. J. (1997). Cathy's question: Literacy as deixis on the Internet. *The Reading Teacher, 41*, 62–67.

Leu, D. J., Jr., Kinzer, C. K., Coiro, J. L., & Cammack, D. W. (2004). Toward a theory of new literacies emerging from the Internet and other information and communication technologies. In R. B. Ruddell, & N. Unrau (Eds.). *Theoretical models and processes of reading* (5th ed., pp. 1570–1613). Newark, DE: International Reading Association.

Levin, D., Arafeh, S., Lenhart, A., & Rainie, L. (2002). *The digital disconnect: The widening gap between Internet-savvy students and their schools*. Washington, DC: Pew Internet and American Life Project. Retrieved July 4, 2004 from http://www.pewinternet.org/report_display.asp?r=67

Lewis, C., & Finders, M. (2002). Implied adolescents and implied teachers: A generation gap for new times. In D. E. Alvermann (Ed.). *Adolescents and literacies in a digital world* (pp. 100–113). New York: Peter Lang.

Lou, Y., Abrami, P. C., & d'Apollonia, S. (2001). Small group and individual learning with technology: A meta-analysis. *Review of Educational Research, 71*, 449–521.

Neilsen, L. (1998). Coding the light: Rethinking generational authority in a rural high school telecommunications project. In D. Reinking, M. McKenna, L. Labbo, & R. Kieffer (Eds.). *Handbook of literacy and technology: Transformations in a post-typographic world* (pp. 129–143). Mahwah, NJ: Lawrence Erlbaum Associates.

O'Brien, D. (2003, March). Juxtaposing traditional and intermedial literacies to redefine the competence of struggling adolescents. *Reading Online6*, (7). Retrieved January 20, 2004 from http://www.readingonline.org/newliteracies/lit_index.asp?HREF=obrien2/

Reinking, D., McKenna, M., Labbo, L., & Kieffer, R. (Eds.). (1998). *Handbook of literacy and technology: Transformations in a post-typographic world*. Mahwah, NJ: Lawrence Erlbaum Associates.

USC Annenberg School Center for the Digital Future. (2004). *The digital future report: Surveying the digital future, year four*. Retrieved September 30, 2004 from http://www.digitalcenter.org

Verhoeven, L., & Snow, C. E. (Eds.). (2001). *Literacy and motivation: Reading engagement in individuals and groups*. Mahwah, NJ: Lawrence Erlbaum Associates.

Williams, H. S., & Williams, P. N. (2000). Integrating reading and computers: An approach to improve EFL students' reading skills. *Reading Improvement, 37*, 98–100.

Windschitl, M. & Stahl, K. (2002). Tracing teachers' use of technology in a laptop computer school: The interplay of teacher beliefs, social dynamics, and institutional culture. *American Educational Research Journal, 39*, 165–205.

23

Dispelling Spelling Assumptions: Technology and Spelling, Present and Future

Shane Templeton
University of Nevada, Reno

DISPELLING SPELLING ASSUMPTIONS: TECHNOLOGY AND SPELLING, PRESENT AND FUTURE

A broad perspective on literacy and language in the 21st century suggests increasingly sophisticated spell checkers, grammar checkers, voice recognition software, and the reality of multiple literacies that cross all manner of contexts and formats. One might wonder if we are at last on the cusp of a new age in which those who are literate in English or who aspire to literacy might finally be released from the need to master what many believe is an illogical, inconsistent, and irrational spelling system. The first assertion is most certainly true; the second, almost certainly, is not. In order to effectively ground an investigation of spelling and technology, two common assumptions about spelling need to be dispelled: First, because the spelling system is illogical, it can only be mastered through drill and rote memorization; second, spelling is primarily a skill for writing (Templeton, 2003).

During the last quarter of the 20th century, linguistic analyses of the English spelling system converged with developmental and experimental research to reveal that 1) although it is not strictly an alphabetically-based system, the spelling system of English is much more consistent and logical than commonly assumed—at the level of sound, and significantly, at the level of meaning or morphology; and 2) learning to spell is a conceptual, developmental process. Ironically, much of spelling instruction, past and present, has proceeded in stark contrast with these insights—the phonocentric perspective (Templeton & Morris, 2000), the expectation that the spelling system should represent phonemes on a one-to-one basis—has held powerful sway. English spelling or *orthography* does represent the sounds of the language more consistently when variables such as the effects of *position* within a word are considered (Hanna, Hanna, Hodges, & Rudorf, 1966; Venezky, 1999): for example, the /j/ sound is never spelled *dg* at the beginning of a word, only within a word; "long a" is never spelled *ai* at the end of a word, only within a word. When spelling does not appear to represent sound as consistently, it is because there is a tradeoff with the visual representation of meaning; units of meaning or *morphemes*—prefixes, suffixes, base words, and word roots—tend to be spelled similarly, thus visually preserving the meaning relationships that they share. The silent *n* in *solemn* is pronounced in the related word *solemnity*; although the vowels represented in the letter sequence *telepath* are pronounced differently in the words *telepathy* and *telepathic*, their spelling remains consistent, indicating the semantic relationship that the words share.

In their acquisition of English orthographic knowledge, cognitive and linguistic factors predispose learners to focus on sound-spelling relationships earlier in development and on morphology-spelling relationships in the intermediate years and beyond (Allal, 1997; Templeton & Bear, 1992). One might argue that most individuals learn how to spell in spite of how they are taught, but Hughes and Searle (1997) captured the legacy of such instructional histories in education when they observed that teachers' "own knowledge of the spelling system is largely implicit or relatively poorly understood. For example, they may teach spelling as a solely sound-based system long after that is useful . . . If we teachers do not believe that spelling has logical, negotiable patterns, how can we hope to help children develop that insight?" (p. 133). That insight applies to reading words as well: Investigations primarily in the areas of cognitive psychology and connectionist theory reveal that spelling or orthographic knowledge plays a critical role in the word recognition process during reading (e.g., Perfetti, 1993, 1997).

How best can teachers facilitate students' negotiation and learning of the logical patterns in English spelling? First, they should assess students' orthographic knowledge with a qualitative spelling inventory (Masterson, Apel, & Wasowicz, 2002; Bear, Templeton, & Warner, 1991; Ganske, 1999; Morris, Blanton, Blanton, Nowacek, & Perney, J., 1995, Schlagal, 1992); this reveals where students fall along a continuum of spelling development. This developmental determination in turn provides information about the particular spelling patterns and features that students may most productively explore. Masterson, Apel, and Wasowicz (2002) developed a software program for speech and language teachers that addresses the link between assessment and instruction; such programs hold promise for classroom teachers as well. The process of learning orthographic patterns appears to occur best through comparing and contrasting different spelling patterns (Invernizzi & Hayes, 2004; Templeton & Morris, 2000). For example, transitional readers and writers at the early "within-word pattern" spelling developmental stage would compare and contrast words such as *trap* and *skim* with *cape* and *time* to determine how the long vowel sound is represented; more advanced readers and writers would compare and contrast words such as *predictable, acceptable, profitable* and *edible, feasible, plausible* to determine when the suffix *–able* or *–ible* is used.

What are the implications for technology and spelling of the more significant role that orthographic knowledge plays in the enterprise of literacy? The balance of this review addresses this question in terms of, first, instructional assessment and delivery, and second, implications for the future of spelling and technology.

There is no extensive research literature addressing the effectiveness of computer-assisted instruction in spelling versus conventional instruction, although studies involving regular education, special education, and learning-disabled subjects have been conducted (e.g., Berninger, Abbot, Rogan, Reed, Abbot, Brooks, Vaughan, & Graham, 1998; Cunningham & Stanovich, 1990; Gates & Goodling, 1997; Watson, 1988; Weber & Henderson, 1989). A number of studies employing randomized control trials have reported no significant effects favoring one type of instructional delivery over another, although a meta-analysis by Torgerson and Elbourne (2002) of these studies opined that the studies were conducted within the contexts and assumptions of "old" conceptions of literacy and technology. In addition, the content of the instruction in computer-assisted formats was traditional skill-and-drill; the results of a study by Weber and Henderson (1989), however, in which words were compared, contrasted, and sorted according to different vowel patterns, were promising. Importantly, the effects of new, more engaging and interactive formats need to be explored, though the type or nature of instructional content will need to be addressed as well. Students' word consciousness, or degree of metalinguistic awareness necessary for developing a rich and interconnected vocabulary, may be facilitated by designing interactive engagements with words in which the processes of word formation are visually and aurally modeled and instructed, from the alphabetic level on through the morphological. In this latter regard, there is significant potential for interfacing spelling and vocabulary development in the intermediate grades and beyond (Templeton, 2004). As an example, an engaging and interactive format would support students' growth from becoming aware of and understanding the spelling-meaning relationships among known words such as *oppose/opposition*, *resign/resignation* to the introduction of an unfamiliar word to explain the troublesome spelling of a known word. For example, a student who knows the meaning of the word *neutral* but misspells it *neutrile* would be presented the unfamiliar word *neutrality*, in which the vowel in the second syllable becomes accented and its spelling is straightforward, thereby providing an explanation for the spelling of the unaccented second syllable in *neutral*. Similarly, the misspelling of *harmony* as *harminy* would be corrected by presenting the word *harmonious*. In the process of learning correct spelling for known words, students' vocabulary knowledge is extended through the introduction of unknown words that are related in spelling and meaning, or morphologically.

Spell check is the most notable spelling-based technological aid, though students who confidently respond to their teachers with the all-too-familiar "I don't have to learn how to spell because the computer will do it for me" often acknowledge, albeit grudgingly, that one has to know a bit about how words are spelled in order to use spell check—the best spell check is the one inside their head; and second, most of a student's writing, at least in school, is still of the pen-and-paper variety. A number of small standalone devices are available into which students may type a "sound spelling," for example, and the device generates the probable conventional spelling; for example, *majikle* yields *magical*. These may be helpful for particularly troublesome words, but they are often suggested as support for students who are truly struggling as readers and writers. Though supportive, such devices should not be used exclusive of a focused, more systematic word study program.

What is the potential for voice recognition software to ameliorate spelling difficulties— indeed, for eliminating the need for attention to the written structure of words at all in the composing process? Here, the discussion, based on an understanding of how knowledge about words develops and the role of this knowledge in both reading and writing, takes a more speculative turn. When considering the implications of technology for spelling, we unavoidably consider those implications for the broader composing process in writing as well. First of all, because orthographic knowledge underlies writing and reading, ignoring instruction in word structure affects reading ability as well as writing ability; the screen, in other words, must still be read. Extending the argument further, however: Students won't need to read the screen because the computer will read back what has been dictated, and others can listen to the composition as well without the need to read it. At most, orthographic knowledge will be logographic rather than alphabetic because internationally-recognized icons will guide the encoding and decoding processes. The circle is completed; we return to our oral/aural roots and written representation of language withdraws into the stuff of oral history, and eventually, of legend. As Lanham observed, "The long reign of black-and-white textual truth has ended" (1993, p. x). (Missing number? Or, actually p. x?)

From the intermediate grades on, engaging students in this speculative vision as it spins out from an initial focus on spelling often leads to exciting if not animated discussion. Students may be closer than their teachers to some scholars' reflections on the implications of language in cyberspace: The "space" in which writing occurs may quite significantly influence how writing is conceptualized and used (Bolter, 1991; Bolter & Grusin, 2000; Lanham, 1993). Over time, as students compose more frequently in word processing and other presentation formats, the fluidity of the screen as opposed to the static nature of the page may come to influence their conception of the process and the product of writing. Here we are moving beyond the parochial realm of orthography, of course, but it will be very interesting to research the manner in which ortho-graphic knowledge will evolve within this more fluid compositional context.

This latter aspect is beginning to be explored at the present time. How will the orthographic etiquette of online composing develop, and how will it affect the acquisition of conventional orthographic knowledge? Instant messaging and e-mail accept, if not encourage, a more flexible orthographic license, including a rapidly-expanding corpus of emoticons. On the other hand, maintaining a log on the Web—a *blog*—may require more attention to formal conventions because the audience is potentially much larger. Posting other types of compositions on the Web would also require attention to standard orthographic conventions. Another area of enquiry is the pace at which the technology, most importantly the Internet, is affecting the coining and dis-semination of terms. Certainly, our subjective experience suggests that the pace is quite rapid. As students negotiate this burgeoning lexicon, it will be interesting to study the degree to which their attention to words may be increased. Will they in fact attend more to the structure or orthog-raphy of words and their nuances of meaning? Will the processes of word formation, for exam-ple, become more engaging and transparent?

In summary, the short-term instructional implications of technology for spelling are a more engaging facilitation of learning the spelling of specific words as well as, more importantly, the development of students' conscious awareness of the logic that guides spelling at the level of sound and the level of meaning. In the longer term, although technological support for the entire composing process will continue to evolve in unforeseeable, albeit compelling, ways, so too will the role that orthographic knowledge will play in support of encoding and decoding the content of this process.

REFERENCES

Allal, L. (1997). Learning to spell in the classroom. In Perfetti, C. A. & L. Reiben (Eds.). *Learning to spell: Research, theory, and practice across languages* (pp. 129–150). Mahwah, NJ: Lawrence Erlbaum Associates.

Bear, D. R., Templeton, S., & Warner, M. (1991). The development of a qualitative inventory of higher levels of orthographic knowledge. In J. Zutell & S. McCormick (Eds.). *Learner factors/teacher factors: Issues in literacy research and instruction* (Fortieth yearbook of the National Reading Conference; pp. 105–110). Chicago, IL: National Reading Conference.

Berninger, V., Abbot, R., Rogan, L., Reed, E., Abbot, S., Brooks, A., Vaughan, K., & Graham, S. (1998). Teaching spelling to children with specific learning disabilities: the mind's ear and eye beat the com-puter or pencil. *Learning Disability Quarterly, 21*, 106–122.

Bolter, J. D. (1991). *Writing Space: The computer, hypertext and the history of writing*. Hillsdale, NJ: Lawrence Erlbaum Associates.

Bolter, J. D., & Grusin, R. (2000). *Remediation: Understanding new media*. Cambridge, MA: MIT Press.

Cunningham, A. E., & Stanovich, K. E. (1990). Early spelling acquisition: Writing beats the computer. *Jour-nal of Educational Psychology, 82*, 159–162. (159–162?)

Ganske, K. (1999). The Developmental Spelling Analysis: A measure of orthographic knowledge. *Educa-tional Assessment, 6*, 41–70.

Gates, W. M., & Goodling, S. C. (1997). The relative effectiveness of learning options in multimedia com-puter-based fifth-grade spelling instruction. *Educational Technology Research and Development, 45*, 27–46.

Hanna, P. R., Hanna, J. S., Hodges, R. E., & Rudorf, H. (1966). Phoneme-grapheme correspondences as cues to spelling improvement. Washington, DC: United States Office of Education Cooperative Research.

Hughes, M., & Searle, D. (1997). *The violent "e" and other tricky sounds: Learning to spell from Kindergarten through Grade 6.* Portsmouth, NH: Stenhouse.

Invernizzi, M., & Hayes, L. (2004). Developmental-spelling research: A systematic imperative. *Reading Research Quarterly, 39*, 216–228.

Lanham, R. A. (1993). *The electronic word: Democracy, technology, and the arts.* Chicago: The University of Chicago Press.

Masterson, J. J., Apel, K., & Wasowicz, J. (2002). SPELL: Spelling performance evaluation for language and literacy. Evanston, IL: Learning by Design, Inc.

Morris, D. Blanton, L., Blanton, W. E., Nowacek, J., & Perney, J. (1995). Teaching low-achieving spellers at their "instructional level." *Elementary School Journal, 96,* 163–178.

Perfetti, C. A. (1993). The representation problem in reading acquisition. In P. B. Gough, L. C. Ehri, & R. Treiman (Eds.). *Reading acquisition* (pp. 145–174). Hillsdale, NJ: Lawrence Erlbaum Associates.

Perfetti, C. A. (1997). The psycholinguistics of spelling and reading. In C. A. Perfetti, L. Rieben, & M. Fayol (Eds.). *Learning to spell: Research, theory, and practice across languages* (pp. 21–38). Mawah, NJ: Lawrence Erlbaum Associates.

Schlagal, R. (1992). Patterns of orthographic development into the intermediate grades. In S. Templeton & D. R. Bear (Eds.). *Development of orthographic knowledge and the foundations of literacy: A memorial Festschrift for Edmund H. Henderson* (pp. 31–52). Hillsdale, NJ: Lawrence Erlbaum Associates.

Templeton, S. (2003). Spelling. In Flood, J., Lapp, D., Squire, J. R., & Jensen, J. M. (Eds.). *Handbook of research on teaching the English language arts* (2nd ed., pp. 738–751). Mahwah, NY: Lawrence Erlbaum Associates.

Templeton, S. (2004). The vocabulary-spelling connection: Orthographic development and morphological knowledge at the intermediate grades and beyond. In J. F. Baumann & E. J. Kame'enui (Eds.). *Vocabulary instruction: Research to practice* (pp. 118–138). New York: Guilford Press.

Templeton, S., & Bear, D. R. (Eds.) (1992). *Development of orthographic knowledge and the foundations of literacy: A memorial Festschrift for Edmund H. Henderson.* Hillsdale, NJ: Lawrence Erlbaum Associates.

Templeton, S., & Morris, D. (2000). Spelling. In M. Kamil, P. Mosenthal, P.D. Pearson, & R. Barr (Eds.). *Handbook of reading research: Vol. 3* (pp. 525–543). Mahwah, NJ: Lawrence Erlbaum Associates.

Torgerson, C. J., & Elbourne, D. (2002). A systematic review and meta-analysis of the effectiveness of information and communication technology (ICT) on the teaching of spelling. *Journal of Research in Reading, 25*, 129–143

Venezky, R. L. (1999). *The American way of spelling: The structure and origins of American English orthography.* New York: Guilford Press.

Watson, A. J. (1988). Developmental spelling: A word categorizing instructional experiment. *Journal of Educational Research, 82*, 82–88.

Weber, W. R., & Henderson E. H. (1989). A computer-based program of word study: Effects on reading and spelling. *Reading Psychology, 10*, 157–171.

Vocabulary Development and Technology: Teaching and Transformation

Camille L. Z. Blachowicz
National-Louis University

Janet Beyersdorfer
C.C.S.D. 21, Wheeling, IL

Peter Fisher
National-Louis University

VOCABULARY DEVELOPMENT AND TECHNOLOGY: TEACHING AND TRANSFORMATION

Children enter school with significant "meaningful differences" in levels of vocabulary knowledge (Hart & Risley, 1995). Some begin school with thousands of hours of exposure to books and experiences that develop rich and deep vocabularies; others come with limited experiences with words and concepts. Unfortunately, these differences widen as time goes on and may contribute to the difficulties many children experience in becoming readers (Becker, 1977; Cunningham & Stanovich, 1998; National Reading Panel, 2000.)

In 2001, about 75% of 5-year-olds in the United States were computer users with 25% of them Internet users; over 50% of 9-year-olds and at least 75% of 15- to 17-year olds used the Internet (De Bell & Chapman, 2003. p. iv), although the "digital divide" splits computer and Internet access and use along socioeconomic and demographic lines. For many students, then, technology has become one avenue to learning that would seem a "natural" fit for vocabulary learning. Research on good vocabulary learning suggests that to develop vocabulary knowledge it takes:

- a word rich environment
- active, motivated engagement on the part of the learner
- multiple exposures to and ways to access words and both contextual and definitional information about words, and
- the development of independent word learning strategies.

With the increase in the time learners spend with technology and increased access to technology (NCES, 2003), educational researchers see natural links between the points just enumerated and what technology can provide and facilitate. Technology can provide an interactive, motivating, textual environment where strategy use is required and multiple exposures to vocabulary and vocabulary meanings are provided.

Several comprehensive reviews of technology and literacy learning, as well as the excellent prior volume of this handbook, have provided a sketch of what we know about the general landscape of technology and literacy (Kamil, Intrator, & Kim, 2000; Leu, 2000). In this landscape, research on vocabulary learning with technology is in its infancy and has been somewhat equivocal in its outcomes (Gildea, Miller, & Wurtenberg, 1990; Koren, 1999). Like any new area of study, it has raised more questions than it has answered. The focus of this chapter, therefore, is on looking at the possibilities technology provides for the development of meaning vocabulary (as opposed to word recognition of words already known) and to suggest some issues for continuing and deepening the research in this area. Because we bring to this review two differing perspectives, that of literacy educators interested in technology (Blachowicz & Fisher) and of a technology educator trained in literacy (Beyersdorfer), we look at vocabulary and technology from two perspectives which we think are provocative for educators—how electronic texts can be used for teaching and learning vocabulary and how technology is transforming vocabulary.

VOCABULARY AND ELECTRONIC TEXTS

In his excellent review of the potential of electronic texts for transforming early reading instruction, McKenna (1998) notes that the use of electronic texts for literacy learning makes great intuitive sense as well as having a research foundation. One area of literacy research in particular informs our understanding of how electronic text may influence word knowledge. A primary way in which young readers are exposed to new vocabulary is within the context of supported storybook reading. The language of even very simple storybooks is more advanced than the language use in talk (Cunningham & Stanovich, 1998). When an adult or more expert reader shares a storybook, they make the concepts and vocabulary of the text accessible through interactive discussion (Snow, 1991), through asking questions, adding or clarifying information and by urging the listener to respond in active meaningful ways (Whitehurst et al., 1994; Whitehurst et al., 1999). Increased active engagement in storybook reading has been found to be linked to increased vocabulary learning (Senechal, Thomas, & Monker, 1995; Hargrave & Senechal, 2000.) Storybooks made available through computers and videodiscs in schools, with built-in mediation and support, have generated some research in relation to vocabulary development.

While the studies cited by McKenna in his review (1998) were primarily focused on the development of word recognition, there are several studies that have focused on electronic texts and meaning vocabulary. Many electronic books for school use have animation cues which provide a rich context for word learning. Though the research has been somewhat equivocal on the use of electronic texts without mediation (Matthew, 1997; Moore & Smith, 1996), Higgins and Hess (1999) found that this technology is more effective for learning when adult facilitation was provided. So a natural question about vocabulary learning from technology is, "What types of mediation are most effective in facilitating vocabulary learning from electronic texts?" A concurrent question is, "Can this type of mediation be provided within the text itself?"

One study which addressed these questions used videodisc technology with which elementary students could access mediation in the form of definitions and illustrative sentences. The study suggested that learners knew when to ask for help, but were not able to judge whether or not definitions or illustrative sentences would be most helpful in expanding their word knowledge (Gildea, Miller, & Wurtenberg, 1990). Students tended to ask for definitions which helped them less than illustrative sentences or information-rich pictures, both of which were more facilitative of learning than definitions. The researchers suggest, since these were older students, that looking for directions was a result of prior instruction. This is a conclusion which suggests that in-text facilitation does not exist in a vacuum and provides another question for research: the connection between learning from technology and extra-technological instructional influences.

Three other studies look at the issue of facilitation from another angle. Koren (1999), working with second language learners, found that facilitation which called for active inferencing on the part of the learner was one key to word learning from electronic text. Students learned more from tasks which required inferencing from context than they did from glossed texts, where students have the ability to call up definitions, graphics, or video explanations. Pawling's (1999) case studies of high school students found that metacognitive reflection was an important part of learning and that the students welcomed working on and responding to electronic text where "no one was there to make fun of your answers." Lastly, an excellent study by Xin and Reith, (2001) with learning disabled students used video to anchor text by presenting a prior knowledge video followed by interactive text that highlighted new vocabulary words. These anchor presentations were then mediated by instructional sentence comprehension and cloze tasks which resulted in greater learning than the anchored text alone, an effect that was strongest for students with learning disabilities.

In all, looking back at what we know about word learning generally, electronic texts can be both motivating and effective for word learning when they provide or couple their presentations with facilitation which calls on the students to actively engage with the words. The current studies raise questions about the type and placement of the mediating instruction. Further, they are all of short and limited duration so that longer term, richer studies will inform us further on the promise of electronic texts for developing meaning vocabularies.

VOCABULARY AND THE INTERNET GENERATION

Looking at the research on electronic texts can give us clues to develop new ways we teach and develop vocabulary. Coming at the issue of vocabulary and technology from the other direction, we might also ask, "In what ways are emerging electronic technologies transforming the vocabulary we teach?" We see four possible connections:

1. *Technology provides interactive environments to gain, refine, and practice word knowledge.*

In the first section of this paper we have discussed the ways in which technology, particularly electronic texts, provides interactive environments to gain, refine, and practice word knowledge. Other familiar opportunities include vocabulary builders/tutorials (A_Word_A.Day www.wordsmith.org/awad), drill and practice activities (Word Confusion http://www.funbrain .com/words.html), quizzes to boost GRE, SAT, TOEFL/TOEIC scores (SuperVocab.com http://supervoca.net), or games (Vocabulary University http://www.vocabulary.com/.) These are some of the most obvious ways in which technological innovations exemplify best practice in word learning.

Technology associated with word learning has a significant role to play in the writing process. Vocabulary is central to the students' use of concept mapping programs to plan their writing (Kidspiration and Inspiration). Students write offline using word processing software with an electronic spell checker, style checker, dictionary, and thesaurus to support word choice, or online with Web logs (a form similar to journaling), bulletin boards, or e-mail messages. WebQuests, scavenger hunts, and telecommunication projects provide electronic contexts for collaboration and word learning that blend reading, writing, and speaking. "Technology brings to your classroom the capability to connect dynamic, interactive vocabulary with reading, writing, spelling and content area learning" (Fox & Mitchell, 2000, p. 66).

2. *Technology modifies definitions and generates vocabulary in response to innovation.*

In the digital age, familiar words have acquired new meanings. The formerly straightforward request, "What's your address?" may now be met with the response, "Do you want my e-mail address, Web address or street address?" Other words share a similar fate. Bulletin boards have moved from the classroom to cyberspace and windows open, close, minimize, and maximize on computer screens. The Internet, cellular phones (cell phones, cells) e-commerce, and e-mail are new terms. In addition, acronyms have been added to our lexicon including CD, DVD, and PDA (not "public displays of affection" as was the meaning of this term to earlier generations).

An even more intriguing view of word meanings in electronic texts can be proposed. First, consider that the electronic context of a word is expanded if the word is a hyperlink to speech, a graphic, a movie, and/or another document. Multiple contexts are possible, each adding to the reader's understanding of the word's meaning. Second, graphics do replace words. Emoticons or smileys, a graphical shorthand using punctuation marks that connote feelings, are used in e-mail messages to replace words. In *Radical Change: Books for Youth in a Digital Age*, Dresang (1999) suggested, "Books in the digital world use visual information in place of words and vice versa" (p. 81). She uses the concept "synergy" to describe "when words become pictures and pictures become words" (p. 88). Dresang further suggests that, "Graphics merge with words to create meaning" (p. 88), describing four relationships between words and pictures in the digital world: "words that tell the story, by their size, color and position; words that are superimposed or incorporated into the illustration; colors that are used symbolically and often performing the function of words; and text that cannot be distinguished from illustration, and vice-versa" (p. 91).

3. *Technology demands the development of technical vocabulary to participate in and discuss experiences with electronic environments.*

The terms may refer to the computer (desktop, hard drive, mouse), the actions of computing (delete, highlight, scroll), or computer operations (formatting, opening, saving). Going online introduces a lexical set of technical concepts: firewall, provider, router, server, modem, and cable. There are terms associated with computer maintenance: virus, plug-ins, download, upgrades, and patch. These concept words go beyond naming technology components; the user must understand the relationships among the words in order to effectively complete the tasks undertaken.

4. *Technology exemplifies the synergy between domain knowledge and vocabulary knowledge.*

Lastly, and perhaps most significantly, vocabulary knowledge merges with content area knowledge when students make use of technology for gaining information. The connection of vocabulary and search strategies is a synergistic one. Technology users rely upon domain knowledge and its conceptual vocabulary to effectively and efficiently locate pertinent information online.

Unfortunately, the search navigation profiles of users do not reflect a high degree of success. Although elementary students learn about the organization of a library (fiction, nonfiction, reference) and the system used to arrange books on the shelves, even mature students may lack a conceptual understanding of a search engine database and how to use it. To compile a directory, human editors index pages and organize them in a series of hierarchical, conceptual menus. A search engine employs software programs called spiders or bots to collect key words from web page metatags, titles, and pages to create a keyword index to the database. When users submit a query with a specific syntax, they attempt to match their query terms with those in the database index to return pertinent search results.

The key to those searches is individual words and terms, in other words, vocabulary knowledge and the strategies to use this knowledge. In terms of vocabulary knowledge, access to information is constrained by knowledge of conceptual vocabulary regarding the search topic, word choice for the query, and knowledge of a search engine's syntax and conventions. Although search engine tutorials are found throughout the Web, search strategy among student users is poorly developed (Fidel, 1999; Schacter, Chung, & Dorr, 1998), and their experience is marked by inefficient navigation and failed learning outcomes.

Research has examined some of the problems that students have in developing a successful search strategy. The first challenge may come from the navigation map. McDonald and Stevenson (1999) found that a conceptual navigation map was important for learning whereas a spatial map increases efficiency but not effectiveness. Second, students must often rely on prior knowledge of the topic to successfully navigate to the needed information (Boechler & Dawson, 2002) and the type of navigational strategy is related to the level of knowledge one has within the domain of study, its concepts, and terminology (Lawless & Kulikowich, 1998; Lawless and Mills, (2002). Third, the student's perception of their own Internet work strategy seems to influence their learning success regardless of the search strategy they used (Priemer and Schon, 2002). Fourth, the user's search query may not produce optimal results. Bilal (2002) reported retrieval rates for seventh graders ranging from 50 to 73%. In another study, 54 graduate students were asked to locate three items on the Web: a picture of the Mona Lisa, the complete text of Robinson Crusoe or David Copperfield, and a recipe of an apple pie with a photograph. Of the 162 tasks examined, only 88 tasks (54.5%) were successful (Nachmias & Gilad, 2002).

Based on their data, Nachmias and Gilad (2002, 478–481) described six search engine strategies. These rest upon conceptual and vocabulary knowledge of the topic and the conventions of Web searching. The strategies were: a) keyword search—typing the query subject, Mona Lisa; b) wide search definition—using a broad query term such as art and painting; c) complex search—using more than one keyword, "Mona Lisa" "Louvre"; d) using general knowledge—searching for the Mona Lisa using Leonardo da Vinci; e) computer convention—including a file suffix, i.e., gif or jpeg; and f) Boolean search terms, Louvre and Mona Lisa. It is interesting to note that to employ these strategies, vocabulary knowledge is indispensable.

Furthermore, crafting the search query only brings students to a results list. The significance of word knowledge again emerges as students search a Web site for information. Here we turn to the experts on document design and Web site usability. Schriver (1997) states, "The first decision that people make when confronted with a document is whether or not to read. . . . we choose not only whether to read but also how to read" (p. 164). Neilson (2000) pointed out that 79% of readers scan a page for keywords (often used as links), meaningful subheadings, and bulleted lists. He recommended Web pages with half the word count of print, reinforcing word choice as critical to Web designer's writing style. (pp. 101–104). Clearly, keywords—often used as traditional text structure markers—act as guideposts to the data students seek.

In summary, technology influences students' vocabulary acquisition and information gathering strategies by a) providing interactive environments to gain, refine, and practice word knowledge, b) modifying existing definitions and generating new vocabulary in response to innovation, c) demanding development of technical vocabulary to participate in and discuss experiences with electronic environments, and d) demanding that the user rely on domain knowledge and its related conceptual vocabulary to effectively and efficiently locate pertinent online information. Continuing investigation into the role of vocabulary in the search strategy of students is a most critical research area. As people view the Internet as an important source of accurate information, effective and efficient search strategies will become more critical to the decision-making processes of its users.

CONCLUDING REMARKS

Technology is clearly changing both the nature of our interaction with text and the vocabularies we use to do so. Research in other areas of literacy education suggests some conclusions and questions that still need to be answered.

First, we know that children learn vocabulary from wide reading of books, magazines, and other forms of text. We also know that students are motivated to use technology in their daily lives. What we need to know is if technology is being used by the same students who read widely in other forms of text, or is it appealing to a new population of readers? If it is, they will be reading electronic text that is almost always not a traditional fiction format. Does this fact impact on incidental word learning?

Second, we know that vocabulary is learned through multiple exposures to words in a variety of ways. Electronic text and other forms of technology provide opportunities for greater interaction with new concepts and vocabulary. Are the nature of the exposures in electronic text different, perhaps more efficient, than in traditional text in terms of word learning?

Third, we know that many students do not use dictionaries, glossaries, and other resources to aid word learning with traditional textual forms. Given the easy access to resources for word learning through technology, are certain types of students (for example, poorer readers, or those with different learning styles) differentially impacted by such resources? In relation to such mediated learning, we also need to know more about effective ways to facilitate word learning for all students with technology in our classrooms.

Answers to these questions and others will increase our understanding of vocabulary learning and teaching even as technology is changing and shaping our lives in different ways.

REFERENCES

A Nation Online: How Americans are expanding their use of the Internet. U.S. Department of Commerce, February 2002. [Electronic Version] found January 4, 2004 at http://www.ntia.doc.gov/reports/anol

Becker, W. C. (1977). Teaching reading and language to the disadvantaged—what we have learned from field research. *Harvard Educational Review, 47*, 518–543.

Bilal, D. (2002). Perspectives on children's navigation of the World Wide Web: Does the type of search task make a difference? [Electronic Version] at http://www.emeraldinsight.com/Insight/ViewContent Servlet?Filename=Published/EmeraldFullTextArticle/Articles/2640260205.html. *Online Information Review, 26*, 108–116.

Boechler, P. M., & Dawson, M. R. W. (2002). Effects of navigation tool information on hypertext navigation behavior: A configural analysis of page-transition data. *Journal of Educational Multimedia and Hypermedia, 11*(2), 95–115.

Cunningham, A. E., & Stanovich, K. E. (1998). What reading does for the mind. *American Educator*, Spring/Summer, 8–17.

DeBell, M., & Chapman, C. (2003). Computer and Internet use by children and adolescents in 2001: Statistical analysis report. National Center for Education Statistics [Electronic Version] found January 4, 2004 at http://nces.ed.gov/pubs2004/2004014.pdf

Dresang, E. T. (1999). *Radical Change: Books for Youth in a Digital Age.* H. W. Wilson. Co.

Fidel, R. (1999). A visit to the information mall: Web searching behavior for high school students. *Journal of the American Society for Information Science, 50*(1), 24–37.

Fox, B. J. & Mitchell, M. J. (2000). Using technology to support word recognition, spelling, and vocabulary acquisition. In S. B. Wepner, W. J. Valmont & R. Thurlow. (Eds.). *Linking Literacy and Technology*, Newark: International Reading Association, 42–75.

Gildea, P. M., Miller, G. A., & Wurtenberg, C. L. (1990). Contextual enrichment by videodisk. In D. B. Nix & R. Spiro (Eds.). *Multimedia: Exploring ideas in high technology.* Hillsdale, NJ: Lawrence Erlbaum Associates.

Hargrave, A. C., & Senechal, M. (2000). A book reading intervention with pre-school children who have limited vocabularies: The benefits of regular reading and dialogic reading. *Early Childhood Research Quarterly, 15,* 75–95.

Hart, B., & Risley, T. R. (1995). *Meaningful differences in the everyday experience of young American children.* Baltimore: P.H. Brookes.

Higgins, N., & Hess, L. (1999). Using electronic books to promote vocabulary development. *Journal of Research in Computing Education, 31*(4), 425–430.

Kamil, M. L., Intrator, S. M., & Kim, H. S. (2000). The effect of other technologies on literacy and literacy learning. In Kamil, M. L., P. B. Mosenthal, P. D. Pearson & R. Barr. (Eds.). *Handbook of reading research: Volume III* (pp. 771–790.). New York: Longman.

Koren S. (1999). Vocabulary instruction through hypertext: Are there advantages over conventional methods of teaching? *Teaching English as a Second or Foreign Language, 4*(1), 1–13.

Lawless, K. A., & Kulikowich. J. (1998). Domain knowledge, interest, and hypertext navigation: A study of individual differences. *Journal of Educational Multimedia and Hypermedia, 7*(1), 51–70.

Lawless, K. A., Mills, R., & Brown, S. (2002). Children's hypertext navigation strategies. [Electronic Version] at http://www.iste.org/Content/NavigationMenu/Publications/JRTE/Issues/Volume_341/Number_3_Spring_20021/Childrens_Hypertext_Navigation_Strategies.htm. *Journal of Research on Technology in Education, 34*(3), 274–284.

Leu, D. J. (2000). Literacy and technology: Deictic consequences for literacy education in an information age. In Kamil, M. L., P. B. Mosenthal, P. D. Pearson & R. Barr. (Eds.). *Handbook of reading research: Volume III* (pp. 743–770). New York: Longman.

Matthew, K. (A comparison of the influence of interactive CD-ROM storybooks and traditional print storybooks on reading comprehension. *Journal of Research on Computing in Education, 29*(3), 263–275.

McDonald, S., & Stevenson, R. (1999). Navigation in hyperspace: An evaluation of the effects of navigational tools and subject matter expertise on browsing and information retrieval in hypertext. *Journal of Educational Hypermedia and Multimedia, 8*(1), 43–64.

McKenna, M. C. (1998). Electronic texts and the transformation of beginning reading. In Reinking, D., McKenna, M. C., Labbo, L. D., & Kieffer, R. D. (Eds.). *Handbook of literacy and technology: Transformations in a post-typographic world.* Mahwah, NJ: Lawrence Erlbaum Associates.

Moore, M., & Smith, L. (1996). Interactive computer software: The effects on young children's reading achievement. *Reading Psychology, 17*(1) 43–64.

Nachmias, R., & Gilad, A. (2002). Needle in a hyperstack: Searching for information on the World Wide Web. *Journal of Research on Technology in Education. 34*(4), 475–486.

National Reading Panel (2000). *Report of the National Reading Panel: Teaching children to read.* Washington, D.C.: National Academy Press.

Neilson, J. (2000). *Designing Web useability.* Indianapolis, IN.: New Riders Publishing.

Pawling, E. (1999). Modern languages and CD-ROM based learning. *British Journal of Educational Technology, 30,* 163–176.

Priemer, B., & Schon, L. H. (2002). *Hypertext navigation strategies and learning outcomes.* [Electronic Version] December 22, 2003. http://www.didaktik.physik.hu-berlin.de/...reimer_online_educa_2002.pdf

Senechal, M., Thomas, E., & Monker, J. (1995). Individual differences in 5 year olds' acquisition of vocabulary during storybook reading. *Journal of Educational Psychology, 87,* 218–229.

Schacter, J., Chung, G. K. W. K., & Dorr, A. (1998). Children's Internet searching on complex problems: Performance and process analysis. *Journal for Information Science, 49,* 840–850.

Schriver, K. A. (1997). *Dynamics of Document Design.* NY: John Wiley and Sons.

Snow, C. (1991). The theoretical basis of the Home-School Study of language and literacy development. *Journal of Research in Childhood Education, 6,* 5–10.

Whitehurst, G. J., Epstein, J. N., Angell, A. L., Payne, A. C., Crone, D. A., & Fischel, J. E. (1994). Outcomes of an emergent literacy intervention in Head Start. *Journal of Educational Psychology, 86,* 542–555.

Whitehurst, G. J., Zevenberg, A. A., Crone, D. A., Schultz, M. D., Velting, O. N., & Fischel, J. E. (1999). Outcomes of an emergent literacy intervention from head Start through second grade. *Journal of Educational Psychology, 91,* 261–272.

Xin, J. F., & Rieth, H. (2001). Video-assisted vocabulary instruction for elementary school students with learning disabilities. *Information Technology in Childhood Education Annual,* 87–104. Norfolk, VA: AACE.

WEBSITES

A. Word_A.Day www.wordsmith.org/awad
SearchEngineWatch.com. http://searchenginewatch.com/
SuperVoca.com: Your Vocabulary Builder Site. http://suspervaco.com
Word Confusion http://www.funbrain.com/words.html
Vocabulary University. http://www.vocabulary.com

SOFTWARE

Kidspiration and Inspiration from Inspiration Software Company.
http://www.inspiration.com

25

▼▼▼▼▼▼▼

Technology and Writing

Karen Bromley
Binghamton University

Rapid changes in information and communication technology (ICT) require regular redefinitions of literacy. Many of us can no longer consider ourselves "literate;" rather we must accept the continuing need to "become literate" (Gee, 2003; Leu, 1997; Leu & Kinzer, 2003). New technology related to writing requires constant change in our literacy to adjust to word processing software upgrades, new computer programs, and new composing concepts (e.g., e-zine, html, e-book, WEB editors, filters, ALT text, synchronous and asynchronous communication). For many of us, becoming literate is a social endeavor, and how we acquire literacy has changed. Often, we interact with others to learn how to use a new word processor, create a web page or html, use e-mail, or participate in a discussion board. We are only recently beginning to recognize the possibilities ICT has for enhancing communication and exploring language and literacy (Reinking, McKenna, Labbo, & Kieffer, 1999).

Today, perhaps more than ever before, technology is transforming writing. Instead of replacing one kind of writing with another however, we are adding to our repertoire of process and product tools (Bruce, 1998). Past notions of writing that included paper, pencil, standard conventions, and the isolated writer are changing in dramatic ways for students, parents, educators, researchers, administrators, and policy makers. This chapter provides a brief overview of the technology-writing relationship, trends in writing related to technology, and questions for future research.

THE TECHNOLOGY-WRITING RELATIONSHIP

Technology has enhanced the basics of effective teaching and learning about writing and it has made the writing process easier. Technology has changed our ways of writing, thinking, and communicating, and it has affected both what is written and how it is written (Daiute, 1985: Farnan & Dahl, 2003). Because much computer-based writing never becomes words on a printed page, but rather is read directly from a video screen, the computer has become "a new communications medium" that facilitates traditional paper-based writing and allows other forms of writing as well (Bruce & Levin, 2003). Writing with technology allows for combining the use of paper and pencil with use of the computer and wireless technologies. For example, a writer may refer to handwritten notes or an outline and several Web sites to compose a draft using a word processor on a wireless laptop. A colleague's suggestions for revision may be done on paper or may appear as comments in the margins of an e-mailed file. As well, writers can now send text accompanied by images, graphics, sound, and video with fonts in different languages and text displayed in different orientations. Technology has extended the concept of audience and users routinely write to each other using not only paper, pencil, and pen, but also via instant messaging (IM), e-mail, discussion boards, chat rooms, and listservs.

Technology also affects who is writing. Many more technology users are writers because of word processors, presentation software, WEBpage programs, desktop publishing, and Internet publishing. In a recent study of schools, 75% reported a majority of teachers use computers daily, 77% reported a majority of teachers have school-based e-mail addresses, and two-thirds said a majority of teachers use the Internet for instruction (Cramer & Smith, 2002, p. 10). Student writing with word processors has become a "commonplace fixture in language arts classrooms" (Bruce & Levin, 2003). Since 87% of classrooms have at least one Internet computer and 85% of schools have Internet access (National Center for Education Statistics, 2002), there are also many more opportunities for students to write online for their peers and sharpen their writing skills as they do so (Kehus, 2003; Smolin & Lawless, 2003). The writing of students with disabilities is motivated and facilitated with enhanced word-processing programs that include multimedia, speech synthesis, word prediction, and online dictionaries (Kamil, Intrator, & Kim, 2000).

Research suggests computers have a positive impact on student writing. Students using computers tend to write longer compositions, add more to their writing, and revise more (Daiute, 1985; Farnan & Dahl, 2003). Because technology makes it easier to compose and revise, identify problems with text, and share texts, students learn to be better writers and readers (Bruce & Levin, 2003). In addition, student collaboration seems to occur more frequently when compositions are accessible for reading on computer screens (Baker & Kinzer, 1998), and variety and complexity of language use increases during creative writing projects on the computer (Kamil, Intrator, & Kim, 2000). Online writing centers provide access to writing resources, offline centers, e-mail links, and handouts, and students can submit papers for online tutoring (Leander, 2003). There are hundreds of word-processing programs, myriad software tools for planning and organizing for writing, and text editors make revising easier. Spell checkers and grammar checkers give feedback more quickly than a teacher can, thus freeing the teacher to support the writer's idea development, clarity, and style. Of course, the ability to cut and paste from multiple sources may enhance both creative thinking and plagiarism, but online sources make it easier to identify a writer's use of others' ideas without giving credit (Kehus, 2003).

However, there are some caveats related to technology-enhanced writing. Schools in many urban and rural high-poverty areas do not have computers or workable computers. Many families living in poverty do not have computers. Many schools do not provide technology support to help teachers use technology to enhance writing. Technology may foster a product-oriented approach toward writing as students focus on presenting work attractively using clip art and animation, rather than focusing on content, and frustration with software may inhibit planning and revising (Baker & Kinzer, 2003). The cost of technology that permits writing with the full complement of hypermedia and ICT may not be reflected in benefits to student learning and achievement. And, because technology changes so rapidly, it is expensive for schools with meager resources available for instructional resources to remain up-to-date (Bruce & Levin, 2003). Reading and editing from a video screen may not be as comfortable for the eye and may be less efficient than from paper (Kamil, Intrator, & Kim, 2000). Of course, factors such as keyboarding skill, complexity of word processors, motivation, attitudes, audience, the process used for writing with technology, and teachers' instructional goals affect how and what writers compose.

NEW DIRECTIONS

Technology-enhanced writing will be visible in more K–12 classrooms in the future. The IRA's position statement, *Integrating Literacy and Technology in the Curriculum* (2001), recommends that instruction and assessment in reading and writing include the new literacies of ICT. It exhorts teachers to integrate Internet and other ICT into the literacy curriculum because "Proficiency at using the new literacies of networked information technologies has become critical to our students' success in the workplace and their daily lives" (p. 2). Reading and writing assessments need to include ICT literacies because research shows that many students prefer to use word processors to complete writing assignments, and research suggests that 20% more students will pass state writing assessments if they can use them (Russell & Plati, 2000).

As literacy instruction and ICT converge, the central role teachers play in guiding student learning will increase, not decrease (Leu, Kinzer, Coiro, & Cammack, 2003). "Teachers will be challenged to thoughtfully guide students' learning within information environments that are richer and more complex than traditional print media, presenting richer and more complex learning opportunities for both themselves and their students" (p. 58). Thus, work that examines authentic cases and practical classroom applications (Karchmer, 2001; Richards & McKenna, 2003; Teale, Leu, Labbo, & Kinzer, 2002) will be needed to help teachers conceptualize and structure integrated lessons using technology-enhanced writing. And, more teachers will begin to connect out of school literacies with classroom writing (Alvermann, Moon, & Hagood, 1999; Grisham in Pailliotet, 2003).

Other new directions in writing are emerging as a result of technology's influence. Changes in notions of authorship and text will continue as new ways of collaborating and writing across distance and time emerge. More online publishing will undoubtedly occur, providing the benefit of quicker access to information as well as the need for critical literacy. Online texts such as *Education for an Information age: Teaching in the Computerized Classroom* (Poole & Jackson, 2003) available at http://www.pitt.edu/~edindex/InfoAge4index.html and electronic journals will augment paper texts like *Linking Literacy and Technology: A Guide for K–8 Classrooms* (Wepner, Valmont, & Thurlow, 2000) and paper journals like *The Journal of Computer Assisted Learning*.

Other changes in the form of writing will continue to occur. One example is IM, a quick way to communicate online using acronyms that require fewer keystrokes than conventional English. The message, ***wu with w and ict 2day*** *(What's up with writing and information and communication technology today?)* illustrates how technology and audience have affected writers' spelling, punctuation, and form. IM users have created a new language (accessible in online acronym dictionaries) for use with computers, cell phones, or personal digital assistants (PDAs). As this type of informal writing finds its way into student journals, assignments, and tests, it will require teachers to rethink standards for writing and the form of classroom writing in relationship to ICT.

Another result of technology-enhanced writing is global access and an ever-shrinking world. The Web offers teachers access to the work of other teachers around the world and opportunities to share their own creative work. Connections established among students within our country and around the world through electronic networks will continue to bring students closer together. The creation of personal web pages by students and teachers throughout the world that include photos, stories, music, and graphics makes users more public and accessible (Bruce, 1998). These connections can help erase cultural, ethnic, linguistic, and economic barriers as users come to know each other through technology-enhanced writing.

DIRECTIONS FOR FUTURE RESEARCH

Research is needed to better understand the complex nature of technology-related writing. Questions posed by researchers include the following. What will it mean to compose in the 21st century (Yancey, 2004)? How will traditional literacy contribute to the new literacies of the

Internet (Leu & Kinzer, 2002)? What are the consequences for reading and writing instruction as the boundaries between author and reader disappear (Bruce & Levin, 2003)? How do text preparation and presentation, including graphics, hypermedia, and layout, affect meaning making (Kamil, Intrator, & Kim, 2000)? How do current copyright laws need to change to address new forms of disseminating information electronically? (Reinking, 1996). What is the role of facilitative devices on students' writing processes and writing quality (Farnan & Dahl, 2003)? How do age, cognitive development, and writing style impact technology-related writing (Daiute, 1985)? Other questions arise as well, e.g., How does technology-related writing affect student learning? How do student-student interactions and student-teacher interactions in writing conferences change as a result of writing with ICT? How can technology-enhanced writing better serve students from diverse backgrounds? In what ways should curriculum, instruction, and assessment change to incorporate technology-related writing? What factors cause shifts in teacher thinking about writing with ICT? How can teachers' instructional goals be met using technology-enhanced writing? How can teacher education programs prepare preservice teachers to integrate technology with writing? How will the English language continue to change as technology and writing co-mingle? These are but a few of the questions educators will undoubtedly need to seek answers to in the future in order to better understand the complex nature of technology's impact on writing.

REFERENCES

Alvermann, D. E., Moon, J. S., & Hagood, M. C. (1999). *Popular culture in the classroom: Teaching and researching critical media literacy.* Newark, DE: International Reading Association.

Baker, E., & Kinzer, C. K. (1998). Effects of technology on process writing: Are they all good? In T. Shanahan & E. V. Rodriquez-Brown (Eds.). *Forty-seventh yearbook of the national reading conference* (pp. 428–440). Chicago, IL: National Reading Conference.

Bruce, B. C. (1998). Learning through expression. *Journal of Adolescent and Adult Literacy, 42*(4), 306–310.

Bruce, B., & Levin, J. (2003). Roles for new technologies in language arts: Inquiry, communication, construction, and expression. In J. Flood, D. Lapp, J. R. Squire, & J. M. Jensen (Eds.). *Handbook of research on teaching the English language arts, 2nd ed.* (pp. 649–657). Mahwah, NJ: Lawrence Erlbaum Associates.

Cramer, S., & Smith, A. (2002). Technology's impact on student writing at the middle school level. *Journal of Instructional Psychology, 29*(1), 3–14.

Daiute, C. (1985). *Writing and computers.* Reading, MA: Addison Wesley.

Farnan, N., & Dahl, K. (2003). Children's writing: Research and practice. In J. Flood, D. Lapp, J. R. Squire, & J. M. Jensen (Eds.). *Handbook of research on teaching the English language arts, 2nd ed.* (pp. 993–1007). Mahwah, NJ: Lawrence Erlbaum Associates.

Gee, J. P. (2003). *What video games have to teach us about learning and literacy.* New York: Palgrave Macmillan.

Integrating literacy and technology in the curriculum: A position statement of the International Reading Association (2001). Retrieved on January 6, 2004 from http://www.reading.org/resources/issues/positions_technlogy.html

Kamil, M. L., Intrator, S. M., & Kim, H. S. (2000). The effects of other technologies on literacy and learning. In M. L. Kamil, P. B. Mosenthal, P. D. Pearson, & R. Barr (Eds.). *Handbook of reading research, vol. III* (pp. 771–788). Mahwah, NJ: Lawrence Erlbaum Associates.

Karchmer, R. A. (2001). The journey ahead: Thirteen teachers report how the Internet influences literacy and literacy instruction in their K–12 classrooms. *Reading Research Quarterly, 36*, 442–466.

Kehus, M. J. (2003). Opportunities for teenagers to share their writing online. In B.C. Bruce (Ed.). *Literacy in the information age: Inquiries into meaning making with new technologies* (pp.148–158). Newark: DE: International Reading Association.

Leander, K. (2003). Laboratories for writing. In B.C. Bruce (Ed.). *Literacy in the information age: Inquiries into meaning making with new technologies* (222–232). Newark, DE: International Reading Association.

Leu, D. J., & Kinzer, C. K. (2003). Toward a theoretical framework of new literacies on the Internet: Central principles. In R. C. Richards & M. C. McKenna (Eds.). *Integrating multiple literacies in k–8 classrooms: Case commentaries and practical applications* (pp. 18–38). Mahwah, NJ: Lawrence Erlbaum Associates.

Leu, D. J., Kinzer, C. K., Coiro, J., & Cammack, D. (Forthcoming). Toward a theory of new literacies emerging from the Internet and other ICT. In R. Ruddell and N. Unrau (Eds.). *Theoretical models and processes of reading, 5th ed.* Newark, DE: International Reading Association.

Leu, D. J. (1997). Caity's question: Literacy as deixis on the Internet. *The Reading Teacher, 5,* 62–67.

National Center for Education Statistics (2002). *Internet access in public schools and classrooms: 1994–2000.* Retrieved on January 6, 2004 from http://nces.ed.gov/pubsearch/pubsinfo.asp?pubid=2002018

Pailliotet, A. W. (2003). Integrating media and popular-culture literacy with content reading. In R. C. Richards & M. C. McKenna (Eds.). *Integrating multiple literacies in k–8 classrooms: Case commentaries and practical applications* (pp. 172–189; Grisham pp. 180–181). Mahwah, NJ: Lawrence Erlbaum Associates.

Poole, B. J., & Jackson, L. (2003). *Education for an information age: Teaching in the computerized classroom, 4th ed.* Retrieved January 6, 2004 from http://www.pitt.edu/~edindex/InfoAge4index.html *Reading online.* Retrieved January 6, 2004 from http://www.readingonline.org/

Reinking, D., McKenna, M. C., Labbo, L., & Kieffer, R. (Eds.) (1999). *Literacy for the 21st century: Technological transformations in a post-typographic world.* Mahwah, NJ: Lawrence Erlbaum Associates.

Reinking, D. (1996). Reclaiming a scholarly ethic: Deconstructing "intellectual property" in a post-typographic world. In D. J. Leu, C. K. Kinzer, & K. A. Hinchman (Eds.). *Literacies for the 21st Century: Research and practice* (pp. 461–470). Forty-fifth Yearbook of the National Reading Conference. Chicago, IL: National Reading Conference.

Richards, J. C., & McKenna, M. C. (Eds.) (2003). *Integrating multiple literacies in k–8 classrooms: Case commentaries and practical applications.* Mahwah, NJ: Lawrence Erlbaum Associates.

Russell, M., & Plati, T. (2000). *Mode of administration effects on MCAS composition performance for grades four, eight, and ten.* Chestnut Hill, MA: National Board on Educational Testing and Public Policy.

Smolin, L. I., & Lawless, K. A. (2003). Becoming literate in the technological age: New responsibilities and tools for teachers. *The Reading Teacher, 56,* 570–577.

Teale, W. H., Leu, D. J., Labbo, L. D., & Kinzer, C. (2002). The CTELL project: New ways technology can help educate tomorrow's reading teachers. *The Reading Teacher, 55,* 654–659.

Wepner, S. B., Valmont, W. J., & Thurlow, R. (Eds.) (2000). *Linking literacy and technology: A guide for K–8 classrooms.* Newark, DE: International Reading Association.

Yancey, K. B. (2004). Made not only in words: Composition in a new key. Keynote address. Conference on College Composition and Communication. San Antonio, TX. Retrieved January 16, 2004 from http://www.ncte.org/profdev/conv/cccc04/featured/114905.htm

Real and Imagined Roles for Technology in Acquiring Second-Language Literacy

Elizabeth B. Bernhardt
Stanford University

Whenever the adjectival phrase "second-language" is added to any noun phrase, an immediate and critical need to dissect the two phrases separately and then to examine their conflation arises. "Second-language literacy and technology" is most assuredly no exception to axiom. Certainly, "second-language literacy" carries with it a set of challenges often referred to as double and triple jeopardy. These challenges include learning a new oral language; learning about literacy processes in general; learning a written language that does not match the oral dimension of the first language; trying to comprehend words and sentences in the second language; and attempting to integrate all of these components simultaneously into a coherent and culturally consistent meaning. The potential for overload and for misunderstanding is vast. A short circuit in any of these multiple processes can push a comprehender into chaos.

Technology in many of its guises complexifies any literacy activity by adding a layer of knowledge that a reader must acquire. When the literacy activity is as multifaceted as second-language literacy, the space for discussion and challenge grows exponentially. A reader within a unilingual environment indeed must learn how the technology operates; a reader within a second-language environment must not only acquire literacy processes specific to the technology at hand, but must also bring to the processes the complexities of a different language and risks a much higher potential for misunderstanding.

A review of what research says is the most effective use of technology for enhancing second-language literacy would be short indeed. Few, if any, studies have been conducted that focus specifically on comprehension outcomes. The next years will and must surely produce important work in this regard. Some studies do examine how second-language readers interact with technology based on specific instructional designs particularly in the arena of using conventional as well as electronic dictionaries, and these studies provide some helpful grounding for the present. Hence, the present provides the opportunity to speculate on what the components of an effective technology-based or technology-enhanced second-language literacy experience should include. The first step lies in understanding what is known about the acquisition of second-language literacy and how dimensions of that data base might be reflected in effective uses of technology.

A THUMBNAIL SKETCH OF SECOND-LANGUAGE READING DEVELOPMENT

To overstate and oversimplify the case for second-language literacy is to put it in the following equation: Second-language "grammatical" knowledge, plus first language "literacy" knowledge, plus unknown elements explain "second-language literacy." There is no question that the more a second-language reader knows of a particular language's grammar and vocabulary, the better the second-language reader will be able to read. While this statement would appear to be far too obvious, the just-learn-the-grammar-of-the-language argument falls far short of explaining or enabling a second-language reader to comprehend. Research indicates that a second element, native language literacy knowledge, must inevitably come into play (Bernhardt & Kamil, 1995; Bosser, 1991; Carrell, 1991; Royer & Carlo, 1991; among others). These studies and others document that the better the second-language reader is able to read in his/her first language, the higher the probability of success in a second (Greene, 1997). While this statement would appear to be fairly intuitive—understanding literacy processes is universal across languages—it, too, similar to the argument regarding grammatical knowledge, falls short of enabling a second-language reader to comprehend. In fact, the two elements combined (second-language grammatical knowledge and first-language literacy) seem to account for only around half of the second-language comprehension process. The other 50% of the process is unknown. Certainly, speculating on what elements could constitute that unknown dimension is not difficult. Variables such as interest in a given topic, knowledge about it, urgency to understand, and so forth must be involved in second-language comprehension. In spite of what would appear to be reasonable, studies have yet to provide any additional concrete data on what constitutes the "unknown."

Work derived from the above has examined the nature of the second-language "language knowledge" that successful second-language comprehenders possess. While consistency across studies has not yet been reached and only adult populations have been examined in any depth, a key factor in second-language knowledge is vocabulary knowledge. In fact, estimates hold it as constituting the overwhelming portion of necessary language knowledge (Brisbois, 1996). Again, this appears to be a logical and intuitive finding. Given the clear role that vocabulary knowledge plays in successful first-language reading, it is hardly surprising that it plays a crucial role in second-language comprehension. There is further little surprise in the fact that vocabulary and technology are interesting variables for investigation.

VOCABULARY KNOWLEDGE AS A KEY VARIABLE

Studies about how second-language learners learn new words or compensate for unknown words fall into three categories. The first category includes studies that investigate the role of traditional vocabulary lists and dictionaries. Davis (1989) found that vocabulary lists provided to learners prior to reading enhanced comprehension. No follow-up to how many of the words were actually acquired was conducted, although Hulstijn, Hollander, and Greidanus (1996) provide some evidence in this regard. They found that Dutch learners of French who were most able to acquire incidental vocabulary through reading had access to marginal glosses. In like manner, Luppescu and Day (1993), examining Japanese learners of English, found positive effects on vocabulary learning from the use of dictionaries. Jana, Amritavalli, and Amritavalli (2003), studying Hindi-speaking learners of English, as well as Laufer and Hadar (1997), report some skepticism, however, about the direct instruction of words with the use of dictionaries.

A second arena of investigation examines the polar opposite: the acquisition of words with no external support. Most of the studies in this area argue that the contexts surrounding words play critical roles in the acquisition of word meaning. They therefore cast doubt on the genuine utility of dictionaries that tend to provide a one word meaning or translation. Leung (2002), for example, found that extensive reading did indeed foster vocabulary acquisition, while Laufer (2003) expressed skepticism that significant numbers of L2 (second language) words could be acquired through extensive reading. Pulido (2003) and Jiang (2002) each noted in their studies that examining either dictionaries or extensive reading *per se* are not fruitful lines of inquiry without also considering the role of second-language proficiency as well as the nature of the first language and culture in understanding the meanings of new L2 words.

A third area of investigation is comprised of studies that consider the contexts in which learners will use word learning aids and how they go about intentionally learning new words. Lawson and Hogben (1996) investigating English-speaking learners of Italian underlined the importance of repetition in new L2 word learning as did Sanaoui (1995) who investigated the learning strategies of 50 English language learners in Canada. Hulstijn (1993), whose subjects were 82 Dutch learners of English, examined the conditions under which learners employ word learning strategies. Hulstijn found effects for both general literacy knowledge and for task. In others words, the greater the literacy level, the lower the chances of looking up words. Further, the comprehension task also determined the extent to which learners confronted individual words. When the task was a general summary, learners tended to look up fewer words than when they knew in advance that they would have to answer an explicit question.

Anecdote and observation indicate that second-language readers turn to dictionaries as primary aids for comprehension. This brief review of vocabulary research leaves the question open about the overall effectiveness of marginal glosses and, when in use, the best version of a marginal gloss. Technology clearly enables much more elaborate glossing, containing considerably more information regarding words, their collocations, morphological forms, as well as connotations and denotations. Technology aside, little, if any, research clearly addresses the impact and influence of word assistance on second-language comprehension.

TECHNOLOGY TO ENHANCE SECOND-LANGUAGE COMPREHENSION

Some studies have examined computer-assisted second-language comprehension. These studies share many commonalities with the studies on the use of dictionaries. This commonality is, of course, hardly surprising given that the bulk of "assistance" in the second-language comprehension process inevitably involves word meaning and, consequently, must rely on dictionaries in one form or another. The computer assisted language learning (CALL) literature regarding second language comprehension can also be grouped into three categories. The first area presents findings regarding the effective design of computer assistance; the second, how learners interact with computer assisted materials; the third, echoes previous findings regarding individual differences in the use of computer assistance.

Pictorial representations accompanied by text seem to have the greatest productive value in assisting second-language learners with word meaning. Chun and Plass (1996a; b) found that German learners had higher comprehension scores when reading second-language material if they were given pictures and text to help them understand. In an extension of this work, Jones and Plass (2002) found that French learners remembered words better if the words were annotated with pictures. This finding is consistent with that of Secules, Herron, and Tomasello (1992) who found that adding video materials to second-language texts enhanced the comprehension of foreign language texts because students were forced into a global comprehension strategy rather than focusing on micro elements of language. In two separate studies of learners of French, Grace (1998; 2000) investigated the nature of text presented in CALL software. She found that translations were critical for any second-language text used in such software. She argues that "sentence-level translations increase the likelihood of making correct associations" (p. 533) and found that learners had higher second-language word retention rates if they had translations available. Another method to help students acquire word meanings was demonstrated by Nikolova (2002). She had subjects create multimedia annotations for texts and found a significant positive effect on vocabulary acquisition.

How second-language learners choose to interact with computer-assisted materials is another important domain. Aust, Kelley, and Warren (1993) compared Spanish learners' conventional dictionary use with online dictionary use. They found that learners used the online format more often, but also indicated that this increased dictionary usage did not bring about higher comprehension rates. They conclude in their study that efficiency is enhanced, but not comprehension. Liu (1995), investigating non-native speakers of English reading in English, similarly found no relationship between learners' comprehension and the number of times they accessed technology-based vocabulary assistance. With further study, Liu and Reed (1995) indicated that English-as-a-second-language learners could enhance their vocabulary knowledge through the use of hyper-mediated vocabulary assistance. These findings appear to be consistent with many findings in the general literacy literature: readers may know a word out of context, but fail to bring that knowledge to bear during the comprehension process.

The third area in CALL regarding second-language comprehension focuses on individual differences. Black (1991), similar to Hulstijn (1993), found that the task learners are asked to perform regulates the effectiveness of different kinds of computer presentation. She found, for example, if learners are asked to do a construction task (such as recall) that they needed definitions, but if they were given recognition tasks, examples were preferable. Yoshii and Flaitz (2002), also similar to Hulstijn (1993), found that proficiency level interacted with word annotation type over time. When presented with texts and pictures, all learners performed well in an immediate test of words. Differences emerged over time, however, on the number of vocabulary words retained. One of the few CALL studies that examined both vocabulary and grammatical knowledge is Heift (2000). She found that when German learners were in an environment which gave them corrective feedback in both grammar and vocabulary, the overwhelming majority of the learners responded to and acted on the feedback given. No comprehension measures were taken, however. A final consistent finding regarding word learning is Harrington (1994) and the Palm Education Pioneers Program (SRI, 2002). Learners trying to acquire vocabulary must have systematic review capabilities. These capabilities are easy to develop and customize in computer-based environments.

The main focus in this discussion has been on vocabulary and dictionary use principally because the research on second-language comprehension emphasizes the criticality of word knowledge for success in understanding. Returning, however, to the research base in second-language reading forces into discussion the unknown 50% of the process which research has been unsuccessful at explaining. Some important work in technology and second-language reading regarding user attitudes has emerged and is promising in bringing insights into the second-language reading process (Davis & Lyman-Hager, 1997; Brantmeier, 2003). Issues such as interest and background knowledge, content beliefs and expertise have not yet been explored in a digital environment. The impact of trying to provide second-language readers with important cultural background (in a language they understand) without confounding misunderstanding with misunderstanding is critical research for the future. An excellent review of many of these features is found in Chun and Plass (1997).

REALISTIC AND IMAGINED USES OF TECHNOLOGY IN SECOND-LANGUAGE SETTINGS

This essay is focused fundamentally on cultures that have technology of all kinds available in abundance. In some sense, this is a "real" world. Yet, any contemporary discussion of technology must address the issue of resources as a central concern. Within second-language contexts across the globe the resource issue is even more crucial. While the internet and computers and cellular technologies may have reached all the corners of the globe, concerns over access remain. Indeed, in North America most schools and public libraries are on the Net; and admittedly, most cities around the globe are connected. This does not mean, however, that those connections are convenient. Given the poverty and crises that children and adults face from Redbud, Louisiana to Port au Prince, Haiti, to Bangalore, India, to Rio de Janeiro, Brazil, where even getting to a school is a challenge and where having a school with electric power is not a given; where books are luxuries (Elley, 1991); and school, let alone classroom libraries, are the stuff of dreams, gives a very different perspective on the notion of "technology." Beyond the challenges presented in this brief sketch of the relationship of technology to the enhancement of vocabulary development, and by default then comprehension, lies the much greater challenge for literacy educators of working with children and adults who must read to learn in a language they do not speak natively. While Western researchers ponder the worthy questions of how best to design hypermediated learning tools for second-language populations, an equally important set of questions is how to physically connect millions of persons across the globe to high-quality and accurate written materials of any kind.

Perhaps the Internet is the answer. It can provide the cheap and worldwide distribution of materials, no printing or shipping costs, no out-of-date materials. One could imagine a world in which books are an old and outmoded technology. This view works in a world of unlimited electric power and biennial hardware changes. It is, however, hard to imagine that such a world will ever exist even in the next generations. Perhaps translation software is the answer—software that could reflect culture, discourse style, and beauty with a 100% accuracy in basic content. But such software would bring about a nightmarish homogeneity in literacy use.

There are times when literacy in a second language appears to be an annoyance in the literacy curriculum and that perhaps technology can cure it. This is a wrong-headed notion. Reading in multiple languages and the complexities and frustrations introduced by multilinguality into the literacy learning and use process should be embraced and welcomed. Developing technologies that value and accept difference and ambiguity, enabling communication in multiple languages rather than relying on one language, should be the objective of all literacy educators.

REFERENCES

Aust, R., Kelley, M. J., & Warren, R. (1993). The use of hyper-reference and conventional dictionaries. *Educational Technology Research & Development, 41*(4), 63–73

Bernhardt, E. B., & Kamil, M. L. (1995). Interpreting relationships between L1 and L2 reading: Consolidating the linguistic threshold and the linguistic interdependence hypotheses. *Applied Linguistics, 16*(2), 16–34.

Black, A. (1991). On-line consultation of definitions and examples: Implications for the design of interactive dictionaries. *Applied Cognitive Psychology, 5*(2), 149–166

Bossers, B. (1991). On thresholds, ceiling, and short circuits: The relation between L1 reading, L2 reading, and L1 knowledge. *AILA Review, 8*, 45–60.

Brantmeier, C. (2003). Technology and second language reading at the university level: Informed instructor's perceptions. *The Reading Matrix, 3*(3), 50–74.

Brisbois, J. (1995). Connections between first- and second-language reading. *Journal of Reading Behavior, 24*(4), 565–584.

Carrell, P. (1991). Second language reading: Reading ability or language proficiency? *Applied Linguistics, 12*, 159–179.

Chun, D., & Plass, J. (1996). Facilitating reading comprehension with multimedia. *System, 24*(4), 503–519.

Chun, D. M., & Plass, J. L. (1996). Effects of multimedia annotations on vocabulary acquisition. *Modern Language Journal, 80*(2), 183–198.

Chun, D. M., & Plass, J. L. (1997). Research on text comprehension in multimedia environments. *Language Learning and Technology, 1*(1), 60–81.

Davis, J. (1989). Facilitating effects of marginal glosses on foreign language reading. *Foreign Language Annals, 21*, 547–550.

Davis, J. N., & Lyman-Hager, M. (1997). Computers and L2 reading: Student performance, student attitudes. *Foreign Language Annals, 30*(1), 58–72.

Elley, W. (1991). Acquiring literacy in a second language: The effects of book-based programs. *Language Learning, 41*(3), 375–411.

Grace, C. A. (2000). Gender differences: Vocabulary retention and access to translations for beginning language learners in CALL. *Modern Language Journal, 84*(2), 214–224.

Grace, C. A. (1998). Retention of word meanings inferred from context and sentence-level translations: Implications for the design of beginning-level CALL software. *Modern Language Journal, 82*(4), 533–544

Greene, J. (1997). A meta-analysis of the Rossell and Baker review of bilingual education research. *Bilingual Research Journal, 21*, 103–122.

Harrington, M. (1994). CompLex: A tool for the development of L2 vocabulary knowledge. *Journal of Artificial Intelligence in Education Special Issue: Language learning, 5*(4), 481–499.

Heift, T. (2000). Error-specific and individualised feedback in a Web-based language tutoring system: Do they read it? *ReCALL: Journal of Eurocall Special Issue: Selected papers from EUROCALL 2000, 13*(1), 99–109.

Hulstijn, J. H. (1993). When do foreign-language readers look up the meaning of unfamiliar words? The influence of task and learner variables. *Modern Language Journal, 77*(2), 139–147.

Hulstijn, J. H., Hollander, M., & Greidanus, T. (1996). Incidental vocabulary learning by advanced foreign language students: The influence of marginal glosses, dictionary use, and reoccurrence of unknown words. *Modern Language Journal, 80*(3), 327–339.

Jana, A., Amritavalli, V., & Amritavalli, R. (2003). Students' understanding of dictionary entries: A study with respect to four learners' dictionaries. *Indian Journal of Applied Linguistics, 29*, 5–20.

Jiang, N. (2002). Form-meaning mapping in vocabulary acquisition in a second language. *Studies in Second Language Acquisition, 24*, 617–37.

Jones, L. C., & Plass, J. L. (2002). Supporting listening comprehension and vocabulary acquisition in French with multimedia annotations. *Modern Language Journal, 86*, 546–561.

Knight, S. (1994). Dictionary: The tool of last resort in foreign language reading? A new perspective. *Modern Language Journal, 78*(3), 285–299.

Laufer, B. (2003). Vocabulary acquisition in a second language: Do learners really acquire most vocabulary by reading? Some empirical evidence. *Canadian Modern Language Review, 59*, 567–87

Laufer, B., & Hadar, L. (1997). Assessing the effectiveness of monolingual, bilingual, and "bilingualized" dictionaries in the comprehension and production of new words. *Modern Language Journal, 70*, 350–354.

Lawson, M. J., & Hogben, D. (1996). The vocabulary-learning strategies of foreign-language students. *Language Learning 46*(1), 101–135.

Leffa, V. (1992). Making foreign language texts comprehensible for beginners: An experiment with an electronic glossary. *System, 20*(1), 63–73.

Leung, C. Y. (2002). Extensive reading and language learning: A diary study of a beginning learner of Japanese. *Reading in a Foreign Language, 14*, Apr 2002.

Liu, M. (1995). Contextual enrichment through hypermedia technology: Implications for second-language learning. *Computers in Human Behavior Special Issue: Hypermedia: Theory, Research, and Application, 11*(3–4), 439–450.

Liu, M., Reed, W. M. (1995). The effect of hypermedia assisted instruction on second language learning. *Journal of Educational Computing Research 12*(2), 159–175.

Luppescu, S., & Day, R. (1993). Reading, dictionaries, and vocabulary learning. *Language Learning, 42*(2), 263–287.

Nikolova, O. (2002). Effects of students' participation in authoring of multimedia materials on student acquisition of vocabulary. *Language Learning and Technology, 6*(1), 100–122.

Plass, J. L., Chun, D. M., Mayer, R. E., & Leutner, D. (2003). Cognitive load in reading a foreign language text with multimedia aids and the influence of verbal and spatial abilities. *Computers in Human Behavior, 19*(2), 221–243.

Pulido, D. (2003). Modeling the role of second language proficiency and topic familiarity in second language incidental vocabulary acquisition through reading. *Language Learning, 53*, 233–84

Royer, J., & Carlo, M. (1991). Transfer of comprehension skills from native to second language. *Journal of Reading, 34*(6), 450–455.

Sanaoui, R. (1995). Adult learners' approaches to learning vocabulary in second languages. *Modern Language Journal, 79*, 115–28.

Secules, T., Herron, C., & Tomasello, M. (1992). The effects of video context on foreign language learning. *Modern Language Journal, 76*(4), 480–490.

SRI International. *Palm Education Pioneers Program: Final evaluation report.* SRI: Menlo Park, CA.

Yoshii, M., & Flaitz, J. (2002). Second language incidental vocabulary retention: The effect of picture and annotation types. *CALICO Journal, 20*, 33–58.

27

Diversity, Technology, and the Literacy Achievement Gap

Kathryn H. Au
University of Hawai'i

The purpose of this brief commentary is to look at issues of diversity, specifically, relationships between technology and the literacy achievement of students of diverse backgrounds. By students of diverse backgrounds, I mean students who differ from their mainstream peers along three lines: ethnicity, social class, and primary language. In the United States, students of diverse backgrounds are African American, Asian American, Latino/a, and Native American in ethnicity, and they come from poor and working class families. These students speak a home language other than standard American English, such as Spanish or African-American vernacular English.

My commentary centers on two major points. First, I argue that technology is likely to contribute to a widening of the literacy achievement gap between students of diverse backgrounds and mainstream students. This prediction grows not from concerns with technology per se but with the bias in the instruction typically provided to students of diverse backgrounds. Second, I suggest that technology can definitely be used to close the literacy achievement gap, but that successful projects require educators to move outside of familiar patterns.

POSSIBLE WIDENING OF THE
LITERACY ACHIEVEMENT GAP

Students of diverse backgrounds, as a group, achieve scores on large-scale tests of literacy achievement far lower than those of mainstream students. For example, in the United States results of the National Assessment of Educational Progress show that African-American and Hispanic students in Grade 12, on average, are reading at a level typical of White and Asian/Pacific-Islander students in Grade 8 (Grigg, Daane, Jin, & Campbell, 2003). These differences in achievement have been evident since the advent of large-scale testing. Recent evidence suggests that the gap is not widening and may, in some instances, be narrowing slightly. Nevertheless, differences in achievement remain substantial and troubling.

Technology may contribute to a widening of the literacy achievement gap through the introduction of new forms of literacy that require students to engage in complex, higher-level thinking. For example, Reinking (1995) looks at how computers and electronic texts have contributed to changes in reading and writing in the post-typographic era. Electronic texts lend themselves to interaction because they are so malleable that they blur the distinction between reader and writer. The greater interactivity and malleability of electronic texts invite readers to participate as writers, and this active construction of meaning can impose new cognitive demands. Another difference is what Reinking calls the "ascendancy of non-verbal elements" such as photos, icons, drawings, movies, narration, and music (Reinking, 1995, p. 23). The creators of a multimedia presentation must consider how the different elements, such as visual images and printed text, can best be coordinated to convey a message, a cognitively complex process.

I view most of the shifts brought about by electronic text and other media in a highly positive light, because of their potential for empowering students of diverse backgrounds to gain information not previously accessible, to express their ideas in dynamic new ways, and to reach audiences around the world. Leu (2002) notes that new literacies open additional avenues for cultural understanding. In particular, I can see how students of diverse backgrounds could engage in exchanges with those from cultural contexts similar to or different from their own, and through these exchanges gain insights into other cultures while becoming reflective about their own cultural identities. Many have noted how the Internet can contribute to a healthy disruption of existing power relations, because individuals and small groups can effectively establish a presence and communicate with a large audience, privileges previously limited to those with extensive resources.

My concerns do not stem from the changes to literacy being spurred by technology, because I regard these changes as potentially of great positive value to students of diverse backgrounds. Instead, my concern is with the well-documented tendency for schools to provide students of diverse backgrounds with literacy instruction that centers on lower-level skills rather than higher-level thinking. My fear is that this tendency will prevent students of diverse backgrounds from gaining experiences with the generative potential of technology and from developing the cognitive strategies required to engage successfully in new forms of literacy. Bruce and Levin (2003), along with other researchers, highlight the uses of new media for communication, expression, inquiry, and construction and the benefits to learners from engagement with these new media. The constructivist teaching required if students are to realize these benefits is directly opposed to the transmission models of instruction typically seen in schools enrolling large numbers of students of diverse backgrounds.

Many studies verify the dominance of transmission models of instruction in classrooms with students of diverse backgrounds. Fitzgerald (1995) concluded in her review that English-language learners tended to receive instruction heavily oriented toward lower level skills, such as phonics and pronunciation. Studies of elementary schools indicate that students of diverse backgrounds are frequently placed in the lowest reading group within the classroom or sent to remedial reading classes (Bartoli, 1995). The instruction they receive in these situations focuses on lower-level skills of decoding with little of the attention to comprehension and higher-level thinking observed in reading lessons given to other students (Allington, 1983). Research in secondary schools reveals the same pattern. Oakes and Guiton (1995) found in their study of a large urban high school that a disproportionate number of Latino students were placed in the vocational track, where teachers did not have high expectations for their academic performance and did not provide them with challenging content.

In short, the bias toward instruction in basic skills and away from constructivist teaching and higher-level thinking has been well documented in studies of schools serving students of diverse backgrounds. This relative neglect of instruction in higher-level thinking with text, including strategies of comprehension and composition, may easily contribute to a limiting of students' classroom experiences with technology, even when their schools offer computers and Internet access. When schools adopt literacy programs based on transmission models and a heavy emphasis on lower-level skills, computers are more likely to be treated as electronic workbooks for further reinforcement of skills. Although many software programs are available, those for drill-and-practice are by far the most common in classrooms (Zhao, Tan, & Mishra, 2000). Students of diverse backgrounds may have few opportunities to use computers for the purposes of composing new texts, integrating information from multiple sources, creating hypermedia projects, and communicating with e-mail when strategies of comprehension and composition are not emphasized in the school's program.

USING TECHNOLOGY TO CLOSE
THE LITERACY ACHIEVEMENT GAP

The quality of students' experiences with technology in institutional settings becomes a critical question in efforts to close the literacy achievement gap. The families of students of diverse backgrounds often lack the resources to make technology available at home. Unlike their mainstream peers, whose homes often have computers and Internet access, students of diverse backgrounds usually rely on schools and other institutions for opportunities to engage in generative uses of technology.

Reports about successful efforts to close the literacy achievement gap through the use of technology provide ideas about the form successful institutional efforts might take. I briefly discuss three promising projects.

Vasquez (2002) describes La Clase Mágica, one of the longest running and best documented efforts to use technology to promote the academic achievement and self-esteem of students of diverse backgrounds. La Clase Mágica grew from the Fifth Dimension, an after-school project to encourage literacy and higher-level thinking for meaningful purposes in a motivating context (Mayer, Quilici, & Lavezzo, 1997). The heart of the Fifth Dimension is a computer game in which students attempt to complete a maze using reading, writing, and strategic thinking to solve problems introduced in each new room. To get help in solving problems, students communicate online with the Wizard who created and maintains the Fifth Dimension.

The original project failed to attract Mexican-American students, despite its location in the community where these students lived. Vasquez accepted the challenge of adjusting the Fifth Dimension to meet the goal of involving Mexican-American students in technology in an enriching way. She made a number of changes that proved effective in turning the situation around. These included relocating the project to a church attended by Mexican-American families, changing the language used in the computer program from English to Spanish, and infusing elements of Mexican culture. In addition, Vasquez involved community members in making decisions about the project, and community members gradually took on the major responsibility for running the project.

The Dreamweaver project conducted with Aboriginal students in Australia had its intellectual roots in the Fifth Dimension and La Clase Mágica (Kaptizke et al., 2000). The goal of the Dreamweaver after-school program was to teach students to design and construct their own web pages. (Although the program bears the same name as a popular program for designing Web sites, the two are not connected.) Through participation in the program, students and their families became acquainted with a university environment, and the hope was that this contact might lead students to pursue higher education. The Dreamweaver, who played a role parallel to that of the Wizard in the Fifth Dimension, assisted students by collaborating with them in the production of their web pages. Students conversed with the Dreamweaver online, and older students were slated eventually to take on the role of the Dreamweaver. The researchers analyzed the students' web pages and conducted interviews with administrators, teachers, students, parents, and members of the community. Gains were noted in students' literacy performance, as well as in their social interactional skills and motivation to learn. Students' confidence increased in particular from the opportunity to tutor others. This project represented a step forward from La Clase Mágica, in that students' cultural backgrounds were taken into consideration from the outset and students were involved in generative uses of the computer shaped by their own interests.

Searider Productions is a project based at Wai'anae High School, located in a low-income, rural community in Hawai'i (Essoyan, 2002). About two-thirds of the students are Native Hawaiians. The project is directed by Candy Suiso, a teacher who was raised in the community and is herself a graduate of the school. Suiso's intentions for the project are not only to give students proficiency in new media, but also to raise pride in the community, which tends to be stereotyped as a dangerous and undesirable area. In their media classes, students learn the procedures necessary to run the school newspaper, create Web sites, and produce videos. Students' work is of such high quality that Searider Productions wins contracts to prepare videos for large companies in Hawai'i, in addition to Web sites for both businesses and non-profit organizations. Students have won numerous local, national, and international awards for productions ranging from documentaries to music videos.

While students are initially attracted by the high-tech equipment, they soon find that they must learn to write well. They write news stories for the school paper, then rewrite the stories for television and radio broadcasts. For video productions, students draft scripts, prepare storyboards, and maintain audiovisual log sheets. Many students who previously lacked the motivation to do well in school gain the incentive to excel academically through their involvement with Searider Productions. They spend long hours hard at work, frequently into the evenings. Some students become sufficiently proficient in media productions to gain admission to colleges with well-regarded media programs.

CONCLUSION

What do these successful projects suggest about how technology can be used to close the literacy achievement gap between students of diverse backgrounds and their mainstream peers? First, technology projects must be rooted in the cultures and communities of the students being served. I find it interesting that, as often as not, successful technology projects occur in after-school settings, rather than during the school day. Unless an insider to the school and community, such as Suiso, is involved, innovative technology projects may have a difficult time taking hold, given the curricular and social complexities and constraints typical of many schools. Second, technology projects seem to work best when they present students of diverse backgrounds with challenging, generative tasks that require them to read, write, and think in new and demanding ways. The time, energy, and thought students devote to participate effectively in these projects suggests that they are readily able to take advantage of constructivist forms of instruction that give them the knowledge and strategies needed to engage with new forms of literacy and electronic media. Third, while much more research is needed to document both the academic and social effects of successful technology projects, preliminary results point to substantial benefits in both the cognitive and affective dimensions.

These conclusions point to guidelines for researchers interested in exploring the potential of technology to close the literacy achievement gap. The field needs many more studies of well-designed programs that utilize technology to help students of diverse backgrounds grow as readers, writers, and thinkers. Clearly, researchers and educators must continue to study the conditions under which such programs can become part of the culture of the school, as well as of the community, so that students can experience benefits over the long term. Success with a school-based program will likely depend on the researcher's ability to involve respected insiders at the school.

Programs exploring the potential of technology can be coordinated with, or even embedded in, thematic units and project-based learning in both elementary and secondary schools where the emphasis is on generative thinking and the integration of concepts across content areas. In these rich instructional contexts, researchers should seek careful, thorough documentation of student learning, including test results plus classroom-based evidence, such as that contained in electronic or traditional portfolios. Research must establish a clear connection between innovative programs and improved academic achievement by students of diverse backgrounds, in order to make a strong case for the potential of technology to close the literacy achievement gap.

REFERENCES

Allington, R. L. (1983). The reading instruction provided readers of differing abilities. *Elementary School Journal, 83*(5), 548–559.

Bartoli, J. S. (1995). *Unequal opportunity: Learning to read in the U. S. A.* New York: Teachers College Press.

Bruce, B., & Levin, J. (2003). Roles for new technologies in language arts: Inquiry, communication, construction, and expression. In J. Flood & D. Lapp & J. R. Squire & J. M. Jensen (Eds.). *Handbook of research on teaching the English language arts* (Second ed., pp. 649–657). Mahwah, NJ: Lawrence Erlbaum Associates.

Leu, D. J. (2002). The new literacies: Research on reading instruction with the Internet. In A. E. Farstrup & S. J. Samuels (Eds.). *What research has to say about reading instruction* (Third ed., pp. 310–336): International Reading Association.

Essoyan, S. (2002). *Waianae video program helps students stand out* [Web article]. Honolulu Star-Bulletin. Retrieved December 23, 2002, from the World Wide Web: http://starbulletin.com/2002/12/23/news/story3.html

Fitzgerald, J. (1995). English-as-a-second-language reading instruction in the United States: A research review. *Journal of Reading Behavior, 27,* 115–152.

Grigg, W. S., Daane, M. C., Jin, Y., & Campbell, J. R. (2003). *The nation's report card: Reading 2002* (NCES 2003–521). Washington, DC: U.S. Department of Education, Institute for Education Sciences.

Kaptizke, C., Bogitini, S., Chen, M., MacNeill, G., Mayer, D., Muirhead, B., & Renshaw, P. (2000). Weaving words with the Dreamweaver: Literacy, indigeneity, and technology. *Journal of Adolescent and Adult Literacy, 44*(4), 336–345.

Mayer, R. E., Quilici, J., & Lavezzo, A. (1997). Cognitive consequences of participation in a "fifth dimension" after-school computer club. *Journal of Educational Computing Research, 16*(4), 353–370.

Oakes, J., & Guiton, G. (1995). Matchmaking: The dynamics of high school tracking decisions. *American Educational Research Journal, 32*(1), 3–33.

Reinking, D. (1995). Reading and writing with computers: Literacy research in a post-typographic world. In K. A. Hinchman & D. J. Leu & C. K. Kinzer (Eds.). *Perspectives on literacy research and practice, Forty-fourth yearbook of the National Reading Conference* (pp. 17–33). Chicago: National Reading Conference.

Vasquez, O. A. (2002). *La Clase Mágica: Imagining optimal possibilities in a bilingual community of learners.* Mahwah, NJ: Lawrence Erlbaum Associates.

Zhao, Y., Tan, S. H., & Mishra, P. (2000). Teaching and learning: Whose computer is it? *Journal of Adolescent and Adult Literacy, 44*(4), 348–354.

Can Technology Support Emergent Reading and Writing? Directions for the Future

Lea M. McGee
University of Alabama

Donald J. Richgels
Northern Illinois University

CAN TECHNOLOGY SUPPORT EMERGENT READING AND WRITING? DIRECTIONS FOR THE FUTURE

The purpose of this chapter is to explore the role that technology might play in supporting the literacy development of preschool children. We deliberately choose to focus this chapter only on children in preschool rather than children in the broader age ranges usually associated with emergent reading and writing. That is, many children beyond preschool age—in kindergarten and even in early first grade—are not yet reading or writing conventionally; they are children considered emergent readers and writers. However, we will argue that the literacy accomplishments and instructional needs of preschoolers, while overlapping with emergent readers and writers in kindergarten and even in first grade, are not precisely the same as those of children beyond preschool. In this chapter, we explore the unique contributions that technology might make for children in the very early stages of literacy development before they reach kindergarten and experience today's press toward convention, and before they develop the foundational early literacy accomplishments that are often requirements for other uses of technology (for example, see McKenna, Labbo, and Reinking's 2003 description of nonreaders' ability to read electronic text or LEP children's use of speech-synthesizer software to read invented spellings). We wish to make clear that we will not review current research on computer usage with preschool children, mostly because there is so little research in this area. Nor will we critique current software programs aimed at preschool literacy, although we will make some comments about some pieces of software where appropriate. Rather, we will speculate on technology that would be useful in supporting and extending preschoolers' emergent reading and writing that we hope will be available in the future.

PRESCHOOL EMERGENT READERS AND WRITERS: THEIR UNIQUE LITERACY ACCOMPLISHMENTS AND NEEDS

Literacy development begins early in a child's life—for many children their progress toward being readers and writers is well underway by their first birthday. By the time they reach three, and certainly by 4 years of age, these children are active participants in reading and writing events in their homes and preschools (Clay, 1975; McGee & Richgels, 2004). They pretend to write birthday cards, find environmental print meaningful, and pretend to read favorite storybooks, often with nearly perfect memory for the text. Children engage in these and other literacy activities because they observe family members engaging in them and want to participate as well. Numerous research studies, especially case studies, have documented the variety of emergent literacy concepts that young children develop as a consequence of growing up in homes and preschools in which they are immersed in literacy-embedded events (e.g., Baghban, 1984; Ballenger, 1999; Bissex, 1980; Cochran-Smith, 1984; Rowe, 1998). So it is not surprising that preschoolers similarly explore the computer using its tools in unconventional ways to create meaningful activities and symbols (Labbo, 1996). It is important to keep in mind that at these early ages, children's pretend reading and writing—whether with books, paper and pencils, or computers—is unconventional, but nonetheless just as critical for their future literacy development as more conventional learning (McGee & Richgels 2003).

Because children's unconventional literacy processes and products are an important hallmark of preschool children's reading and reading, the International Reading Association and National Association for the Education of Young Children's (IRA/NAEYC,1998) description of the phases of development of early literacy begins with the phase of Awareness and Exploration. In this phase, children know few or no alphabet letters, are not aware of the directionality of print, and have not acquired phonological and phonemic awareness abilities called for in recognizing rhyme or alliteration. They do however, demonstrate a conscious awareness of the existence of print in their environment and a rudimentary awareness of how members of their family use that print in their daily lives. They are aware that printed symbols "stand for" or symbolize particular meanings. Only later, and rooted in children's awareness of the functionality of print and its symbolic potential to communicate messages, do children gain the more conventional emergent literacy concepts demanded in kindergarten (McGee & Purcell-Gates, 1997; Purcell-Gates, 1986; 1995). Exemplary preschool classrooms afford children many experiences in which print is used to communicate messages for a variety of pretend and real purposes. Children explore the ways that print is powerful in shaping lives within and beyond classrooms. Teachers carefully plan activities to expand children's awareness of print and its many and varied uses within children's communities and across the world.

These activities may be overlooked in today's kindergartens with pressure to have children master foundational skills. For example, in Alabama children in mid-year of kindergarten are expected to be able to select words based on a target phoneme and isolate up to 24 phonemes within 2 minutes. By the end of the kindergarten year, they are expected to segment 35 phonemic units from spoken words, also within 2 minutes. While children in preschool *do* begin to develop these conventional concepts amid increasing calls for preschools to be accountable for delivering instruction in these foundational skills (see the Early Reading First part of the Leave No Child Left Behind legislation), the development of these skills is intertwined with children's unconventional explorations of literacy's purposes. Preschool children learn to recognize the conventional alphabet letter names at the same time that they operate with very unconventional ideas about the purpose and role of alphabet letters in communicating messages intended to serve a variety of different purposes. Most preschool teachers are accepting of children's unconventional concepts while at the same time providing some instruction aimed at helping children reach some conventional level of literacy development.

How then to use technology in preschool to maintain its playful approach in which unconventional use of literacy is celebrated at the same time that children are given opportunities to learn more conventional knowledge? We offer some suggestions for how to integrate computers into the daily activities offered in typical preschools and then make suggestions for software development that would be useful in helping 3- and 4-year-olds learn some of the basic conventions of print. We discuss three ways that computer technology can be used in preschool: integrated into activities, centers, and theme studies to support discovery and exploration of the communicative and functional purposes of print; as an "adult scribe" in which the computer assumes the role of helping children write messages from dictation; and as a game center in which children can learn more conventional literacy skills.

TECHNOLOGY AND ITS ROLE IN COMMUNICATING FOR A VARIETY OF PURPOSES

In this portion of the chapter we speculate on possible ways technology could be infused into the preschool classroom, much as literacy experts recommend that more traditional reading and writing tools such as paper and pencil be integrated into the classroom (Roskos & Neuman, 2001). Traditional tools for reading and writing are carefully selected and infused into classroom centers so as to suggest the "authentic" purposes served by those objects in real life. For example, clipboards with pretend lumber order forms are placed in the block area to prompt children to plan buildings, order materials, and pretend to be construction bosses and architects. Coupons, household bills, and checkbooks are placed in the home living center to prompt children to pretend to pay bills and sort coupons before going grocery shopping. Recording forms are placed in science centers for children to draw objects that sink and float or to make a tally of how many children like chocolate, vanilla, or strawberry ice cream.

Teachers demonstrate how to use the print props that are integrated into various centers during whole group discussions. Or, teachers may join in children's play to demonstrate new uses of the tools and provide children with the names of literacy activities and props (Neuman & Roskos, 1993). In these language- and literacy-rich environments, children explore the print props as they pretend to use them in ways that are based on their own experiences. They gain new understandings of print uses as they play with other children and their teacher, who demonstrate different understandings about the functions and purposes of particular print props.

In the same way, computers can be integrated into centers in ways that would reflect the authentic and functional uses of computers in real life situations. For example, the art center could become a computer graphics art center over several weeks (we do not recommend mixing computers with the messy media usually found in a preschool art center!). Today children can scan in photographs and other art work and use graphics programs (such as Kid Pix2) to stamp or draw on the photographs (see Labbo, Eakle, & Montero, May 2002). In the future we envision even more child-friendly versions of these programs and tools. Children would have access to easy-to-operate printers, scanners, digital cameras, and computers with an updated preschool-friendly graphics program. With these tools and with the support of their teacher or assistant, children could enjoy digital painting and photo editing. We envision that future graphics programs would be able to follow simple voice commands that would expand children's art-related vocabulary. That is, children might point the mouse at a photo they have downloaded from the digital camera and speak several commands such as "color red," "size smaller," and "repeat picture," and the computer would be able to execute these and other standard commands. For example, preschoolers could scan in leaves gathered from the school playground, resize the leaves, create a montage of several copies of the same leaf, color each leaf a different color, and print out their computerized art work complete with a digitized artist's signature.

The computer could have many pretend uses in the dramatic play centers. McKenna, Labbo, and Reinking (2003) describe a travel center in which children print tickets, timetables, maps, and passports. These authors imply that children would create these props on the computer in pretend play as they would an actual computer in a travel agency. However, simple programs that would allow children to access these forms and pretend to type on them are not currently available. Yet, the *idea* of creating these print props for children to use in dramatic play is used in many classrooms. Teachers simply use graphics or even word processing programs to create and print their own props. In the busy lives of preschool classrooms, teachers would greatly benefit from software programs that would allow them to click and print these print items without having to create them. For example, teachers could select *restaurant* and then print copies of menus, blank food orders, credit cards, checks, and placemats. Or, they might select *doctor's office* and print blank copies of patient charts, prescription pads, appointment books and cards, and x-ray charts. These print props could easily be placed in a variety of preschool centers to increase the amount of interactions children have with print-in-use.

In the future, we envision that new programs for pretend play using the computer could be created. For example, children might pretend to pay bills in a special pretend virtual banking program. They could receive bills via pretend e-mail, get paid via a pretend electronic deposit, and be able to pay the electric and telephone bill. Preschool children are not readers, so all of these printed messages would be accompanied by icons and other simple picture clues and by automatic voice messages. Children's responses to e-mails would likely be strings of letters randomly typed into the computer. The computer could "read" these messages by responding with 25 to 30 randomly selected messages that could make sense. These programs would prompt children to write other e-mail messages, make bank deposits, or pay bills electronically. After children complete their banking, the program would automatically provide a printout of pretend checking account balances or deposit slips.

Similar programs for pretend grocery shopping would allow children to select familiar foods and drag icons into a shopping cart. The program would highlight the written words on the food products and speak those words when children click on the words. Children could write grocery lists by speaking words and seeing those words appear in print. Or, children could select a grocery list, click on the words so they are spoken aloud by the computer program, and then shop for those items. The computer would provide helpful hints such as saying, "You are looking for toothpaste, are you in the section where you would find toothpaste? Toothpaste begins with the letter *T*. Do you see a letter *T* on any of the grocery items here? No, you selected toothbrush, see the picture of the toothbrush on the box? Try again and look for a box with a *T* that does not have a brush." (Today's computer programs such as Riverdeep's Reading Destination are not very useful to preschoolers when they remove activities from their functional context and only provide yes or no feedback rather than help on strategies for getting the right answer.)

A similar pretend program could be developed for children to use in a restaurant dramatic play center. The restaurant pretend program would be like those currently used in restaurants for selecting food to be ordered and sent to computers in the kitchen to direct cooking. Children could order food by touching icons and words of food, and another computer could print out or display the food order to pretend cooks. Finally, waiters and waitresses could print out copies of bills.

TECHNOLOGY AND ITS ROLE AS AN ADULT SCRIBE

In our speculation above about a future program to support children's pretend grocery shopping play, we mentioned children creating a grocery list by speaking and seeing their words appear as print. This would represent one of the most significant future developments in computer-assisted literacy learning. Currently, computers have text-to-speech recognition capability (e.g., Write Out Loud, by Don Johnson, Inc., which allows the computer to read aloud conventionally spelled print). We look forward to the generation of literacy software that would turn the computer into a scribe, responding to children's spoken words with print. That print then would have all the capabilities of electronic text. It could be read back by the computer, and it could be manipulated (cut and pasted into a variety of documents; reformatted, including in a variety of colors and fonts; displayed on screens; and printed).

The computer-as-scribe could be used in a special drama activity. Paley (1990) described a preschool storytelling and playacting activity that encourages children's creative composing at the same time that it illustrates for them many of the functions of print. She writes children's stories as they dictate them and talks with them about their stories throughout the day, encouraging them to incorporate the stories into their dramatic play. At the end of the day, she reads a dictated story while the storyteller and selected classmates act it out. Classmates' commentaries on the dramatized story can result in revision of the story and the dramatization.

The computer-as-scribe can be available to more children and at more times of the day than when the teacher is the only scribe. Located in the dramatic play center, a computer-as-scribe, especially when it has read-back and text-manipulation capabilities (the latter accomplished with the sort of voice-recognition commands we discussed earlier), can support continuous storytelling, story-influenced play, and dramatization with revisions. These processes are directly analogous to the drafting and revising essential to the process writing approach that children will experience in the primary grades, when they have more conventional reading and writing abilities.

Teachers will have the ability to track multiple computer-taken dictations. They may drop in on children's story telling and dramatizing, read the dictated texts, ask questions that confirm or clarify meanings, suggest next steps, and assist in manipulations of the electronic texts, such as by making conventionally formatted scripts for use in practicing the dramatization of a favorite story (one that will be used beyond a single day's pretend play) or by creating play bills and posters for stories that children wish to perform for audiences beyond their classroom. Children will not be able to read the scripts, but the scripts can be augmented with icons and other simple pictures (e.g., a fireman's hat to mark a fireman-character's lines), and with its read-back capability, the computer can act as prompter. The script can be displayed on a large screen, and one child, the director, can point to the line of dialogue or teacher-inserted stage direction that he or she wants the computer to voice. With a scrolling option, the computer will display only one line of script at a time, with the next line appearing only when the director calls for it.

In the future, music will be another source of electronic text, supported by the computer-as-scribe. Dyson (2003) has documented children's use of popular music in their creation of literary texts. We envision that future dictation programs will generate an electronic text from a music CD or from children's singing into a microphone. Read-back, formatting, and display of musical texts is especially supportive of children's learning to track print, that is, their pointing to the correct printed word for each spoken (or sung) word (this is sometimes called finger-point reading). Teachers can manipulate the electronic texts—with line arrangement, highlighting, and insertion of icons and simple picture cues—to facilitate students' attending to salient words, words that are most likely to be meaningful to them because of their familiarity with the lyrics of the favorite song from which the text originated. Children's karaoke-like performances of such songs can be supported by electronic text in the same ways as are their story dramatizations. For example, a displayed text of a song can be used for rehearsal, and parts of the text can be imported into a concert bill or poster.

The computer-as-scribe will turn children's spoken and sung texts into written texts. We also look forward to computer programs that will turn children's writing and drawing on paper into electronic texts. Already, document cameras can display what is on paper, and scanners can turn texts and pictures into electronic files. We envision future generations of these technologies that can take an image from a document camera and instantly give it the features of an electronic text. A child's story with letter-like forms, invented spellings, and drawings will be placed under a document camera, which displays it on a screen. Any part of the image on the screen can then be highlighted by moving and clicking with a mouse. That part can then be imported into other texts, reformatted, and read by the computer. For example, a child highlights a string of mock letters, reads into a microphone what those letters mean, and the computer turns them into conventional spellings, which the computer reads back. The child can then use those spellings in a new document and can move a picture from his own original image into that document.

TECHNOLOGY AND ITS ROLE AS "TEACHER" OF CONVENTION

Technology is currently most familiar in preschool classrooms used in a center where children play literacy-related games. There are hundreds of software programs aimed at young children, and most of them teach alphabet recognition, phonics, and word building. Some are elaborate systems aimed at the school market and billed as entire reading programs (e.g., Riverdeep's Reading Destination), while others are aimed at the home market and teach only a few skills (e.g., LeapFrog's *Leap Phonics Library, Phonics Writing Desk*, and *Fridge Phonics Magnetic Letter Set*). Most programs have voice directions and the capacity to speak the name of the letters aloud when children point at the letters. What is missing—and we would envision would be added in the future—would be the capacity of the computer to understand children's speech as they identify letters and articulate phonemes, as well as to provide more elaborate strategic feedback to children's incorrect answers.

Today's alphabet learning games assume children can distinguish among letters and are merely learning to recognize each of the unique letters by name. In the future, alphabet games would be designed to help children learn to distinguish among letters that are usually not unique to young children (Gibson, Gibson, Pick, & Osser, 1962). For example, a game might display a variety of *M's* and *W's* printed in different fonts and invite children to separate them into two groups. Speech would be included in other games so that the computer says a letter the child is to search for, and the child must click on that letter given an array of several easily confused letters. For example, the child could be asked to search for an *N* with the computer screen displaying *M, W, Z,* and *N.* When children select a wrong letter, that letter could be superimposed on the correct letter *N* and the child told why the letter is incorrect. For example, the computer could say, "letter *M* has four lines"—as the four lines in the letter are highlighted—"and the letter *N* has only three lines"—as these three lines are highlighted. Or, if the child incorrectly selected the letter *Z* for *N,* the computer would say, "*Z* has three lines but the lines go across, down, and across"—as these lines are highlighted—"but the letter *N* has three lines that go down, down across, and down"—as these lines are highlighted.

Similarly, children could command that the computer write letters. The child would speak a letter name and that letter would be slowly written for the child one line at a time, followed by an interesting sound effect with its phoneme or an animal or object beginning with that letter appearing. Children could click on the letter to get its name and its sound or other pictures that begin with the letter. Similarly, children could demand that the computer "write" or "spell." For example, a child could say, "write *dog*," and the computer would slowly produce the written word, saying each letter as it was written. Or, the child could say, "spell *dog*," and the computer would say the letters and each letter on the keyboard would light up so that the children could hit that letter and then spell the word. Other games would involve the child being asked to name letters quickly as they are shown on the screen. The computer could count the number of letters children correctly name in a one-minute interval.

Most current software focuses on helping children learn letter-sound associations rather than develop phonemic awareness. In most activities, even when labeled phonemic awareness, children are shown letters or written words and are asked to listen for the sound or select words with a target sound (e.g., *Reading Destination*). We envision that in the future, software would be aimed more directly at phonemic awareness. For example, a program might be developed to introduce children to 35–40 phonemes in isolation. Moving graphics could show, for example, a heart beating as the /d/ is repeatedly pronounced, followed by a motor boat with /m/ phoneme pronounced. Children could say each phoneme and the moving graphic could appear. Or, the computer could speak a target phoneme or word and the child be shown a screen with four boxes. When clicked, each of the boxes would show a short video of a child pronouncing a word. The child must identify the box in which the child on the video is saying a word with the target phoneme or that begins with the same phoneme as the target word. Or, children could listen to all four boxes and then find the two that have children pronouncing rhyming words.

HARDWARE NEEDS

Currently, most early childhood classrooms have only one computer that is frequently 10 or more years old. These large computers with "worksheet" like games and activities do not serve young children well. Many middle-class children have more sophisticated computer toys at home (e.g., LeafFrog's Disney Princess Laptop). The future of technology in preschool is more likely going to require a different approach to hardware more like that used currently in the toy industry. Smaller, reasonably priced, portable computers that are designed for a few specific purposes would better allow computers to be integrated within preschool centers. For example, like the Disney Princess Laptop, small toy computers could be designed to support pretend play. Such computers could be programmed for many pretend activities such as going to the "doctor's office," "restaurant," "grocery store," or "lumber yard" as described earlier in this chapter.

Real computers with Internet access will still be needed in preschool (see http://www.geoc ities.com/Athens/Acropolis/4616/projects/projects.html or http://gsh.lightspan.com/pr/_cfm/Get Detail.cfm?pID=155 for a description of an Internet project involving preschoolers all over the world gathering, categorizing, and identifying leaves or http://www.globalschoolhouse.org/pr/ _cfm/index.cfm to search for other projects). However, wireless laptop computers need to replace the large desktop models with screens that take up far too much space in the cramped spaces of most early childhood classrooms. Laptops could be arranged on a table for center time and put away, like other table top games, when not needed. Printers would also need to become specialized. Color printers would be essential for art centers; extra large printers could be used to print poster-sized charts for shared reading. Larger-sized scanners with some three-dimensional capacity would also be needed to in order to scan preschool-age children's paintings, collages, and other art constructions.

IN CONCLUSION

In this chapter, we have suggested ways that future technologies might support children's literacy learning, especially in the early stages of that learning when they are exploring the meanings and functions of print and do not often recognize nor easily produce conventional forms. We have suggested technology use in contexts that allow for children's play and other forms of social interaction appropriate to early childhood education. Our examples illustrate ways computers might support preschoolers' gaining awareness of the functionality of print and its symbolic potential to communicate. Such awareness is essential to children's later acquisition of such literacy conventions as phoneme-letter correspondence knowledge and word identification ability. We look forward to technologies that provide preschoolers with engaging, meaningful, and purposeful experiences with the power of the written word, experiences that are formed from the preschoolers' own input and shaped by their own manipulations (and those of their teachers) to suit unique classroom interests and needs. Learning to read and write is critical, but it is not at the top of a list of developmental interests and needs in a preschool classroom. However, with the technological presence envisioned in this chapter, learning the ways of reading and writing can be a constant but unobtrusive companion to more important developments of preschoolers, their social and emotional growth in a company of learners.

REFERENCES

Baghban, M. (1984). *Our daughter learns to read and write: A case study from birth to three.* Newark, DE: International Reading Association.

Ballenger, C. (1999). *Teaching other people's children: Literacy and learning in a bilingual classroom.* New York: Teachers College Press.

Bissex, G. (1980). GYNS AT WRK: A child learns to write and read. Cambridge, MA: Harvard University Press.

Clay, M. M. (1975). *What did I write?* Auckland, New Zealand: Heinemann.

Cochran-Smith, M. (1984). *The making of a reader.* Norwood, NJ: Ablex.

Dyson, A. H. (2003). *The brothers and sisters learn to write: Popular literacies in childhood and school cultures.* New York: Teachers College Press.

Gibson, E., Gibson, J., Pick, A., & Osser, H. (1962). A developmental study of discrimination of letter-like forms. *Journal of Comparative Physiological Psychology, 55*, 897–906.

International Reading Association and National Association for the Education of Young Children (IRA/NAEYC 1998). Learning to read and write: Developmentally appropriate practices for young children. *Reading Teacher, 52*, 193–216.

Labbo, L. (1996). A semiotic analysis of young children's symbol making in a classroom computer center. *Reading Research Quarterly, 31*, 356–385.

Labbo, L., Eakley, A., & Montero, M. (2002, May). Digital language experience approach: Using digital photographs and software as a Language Experience Approach innovation. *Reading Online 5*, Available: http://www.readingonline.org/electronic/elec_index.asp?HREF=labbo2/index.html

McGee, L., & Purcell-Gates, V. (1997). Conversations: So what's going on in research in emergent literacy? *Reading Research Quarterly, 32*, 310–318.

McGee, L., & Richgels, D. (2003) *Designing early literacy programs: Strategies for at-risk preschool and kindergarten children.* New York: Guilford Press.

McGee, L., & Richgels, D. (2004). *Literacy's beginnings: Supporting young readers and writers* (4th ed.). Boston, MA: Allyn and Bacon.

McKenna, M., Labbo, L., & Reinking, D. (2003). Effective use of technology in literacy instruction. In L. Morrow, L. Gambrell, & M. Pressley (Eds.). *Best practices in literacy instruction* (2nd ed.) (pp. 307–331). New York: Guilford Press.

Neuman, S., & Roskos, K. (1993). Access to print for children of poverty: Differential effects of adult mediation and literacy-enriched play settings on environmental and functional print tasks. *American Educational Research Journal, 30*, 95–122.

Paley, V. G. (1990). *The boy who would be a helicopter: The uses of storytelling in the classroom.* Cambridge, MA: Harvard University Press.

Purcell-Gates, V. (1986). Three levels of understanding about written language acquired by young children prior to formal instruction. In J. Niles & R. Lalik (Eds.). *Solving problems in literacy: Learners, teachers & researchers.* Thirty-fifth Yearbook of the National Reading Conference (pp. 259–265). Rochester, NY: National Reading Conference.

Purcell-Gates, V. (1995). *Other people's words: The cycle of low literacy.* Cambridge, MA: Harvard University Press.

Roskos, K., & Neuman, S. (2001). Environment and its influences for early literacy teaching and learning. In S. Neuman & D. Dickinson (Eds.). *Handbook of early literacy research* (pp. 281–292). New York: Guilford Press.

Rowe, D. (1998). The literate potentials of book-related dramatic play. *Reading Research Quarterly, 33*, 10–35.

29

▼▼▼▼▼▼▼

Information Technology and the Literacy Needs of Special Populations: Ode to FedEx and Dairy Farmers

Edward J. Kame'enui and Joshua U. Wallin
University of Oregon

INFORMATION TECHNOLOGY AND THE LITERACY NEEDS OF SPECIAL POPULATIONS: ODE TO FEDEX AND DAIRY FARMERS

As we prepare this chapter for the *Handbook of Literacy and Technology*, the future in the form of 2004 looms imminently and transparently on the horizon, waiting for the arrow of time to issue its inevitable invitation. Handbooks are charged with at least two taxing and unenviable burdens: (a) to offer a succinct but trenchant narrative of the past and (b) to extract viable trends from the current research literature and offer reasonable predictions of what the future portends. When the topics of literacy and technology are invoked and special populations—children identified with disabilities—are added to the mix of topics, the challenge of capturing the past and predicting the future appears whimsical, if not reckless. Nevertheless, the challenge is a worthy one, and we are pleased to offer our brief assessment of how technology might best be considered and employed to benefit children identified with unique literacy needs. We initiate this challenge by first offering two examples that have nothing to do with literacy (which is why they were selected), but are illustrative of the compelling, yet ubiquitous nature of information technology in a global economy. We use these examples to underscore the potential applications of information technology to literacy, in general, and to special populations, in particular, that have distinctive literacy and reading needs.

What FedEx and Dairy Farmers Can Teach Us About Information Technology

In an article published in *Business Week* (March 23, 1998) entitled, "Why the Global Economy is Here to Stay," Jeffrey E. Garten, former Dean of the Yale School of Management, asserted that "globalization seemed to be the wave of the future" and is being driven by "truly global companies" such as FedEx (p. 21). Garten observed:

> Delivering some 2.8 million packages in 210 countries each day, FedEx is pushing globalization faster and deeper, not just because it is adding more planes and routes but because it is using

information technology to reengineer its clients' worldwide supply and distribution systems. In the process, global sourcing and sales are becoming an ever more integral part of these companies' ways of operating. Indeed, FedEx has become the global logistical backbone for many of its corporate customers. It manages their worldwide inventory, warehousing, distribution, and customs clearance, using state-of-the-art technology . . . FedEx can perform these functions because it can electronically track where any shipment is at any given moment, and it can guarantee on-time delivery. (p. 21)

In another article entitled, "Cream of the Crop" (*Horizon Air Magazine*, April 1998), author Allison Peacock celebrates the pride Northwest dairy farmers take in their products and work. In describing this industry, Peacock unwittingly offers another application of information technology:

At noon, the cows wait for one of their daily turns in the milking stall . . . Soon, milk fills each clear vestibule attached to the milking apparatus. From there, it flows to a huge collection tank in the building's entryway. A computerized system keeps track of how much milk each cow gives each time. Obrist (owner of Fairview Acres Dairy Inc.) can look up any cow on his computer and track her milking yields for weeks at a time, noting at a glance when she is at peak production or if her health is ailing. (p. 13)

The examples of FedEx and Obrist, the dairy farmer, reveal provocative and important features of information technology that may hold promise for applications in literacy and reading, including, for example: (a) creation of an information technology infrastructure (e.g., a logistical backbone and nervous system) that shapes the needs of clients from how their resources, inventory, and warehouses are fashioned and managed, to how their supply and distribution systems are engineered; (b) real-time electronic tracking of specific outcomes and products on both a local and global scale; and (c) utilization and application of information in a longitudinal time frame that includes linking current performance to past performance trajectories.

The FedEx and dairy farmer examples provoke an interesting and important set of questions and laments specific to applications of literacy and reading:

1. If FedEx can (as of December 2003) employ information technology to track approximately 5.4 million packages in over 215 countries each day, what promise does this information technology hold for tracking and promoting the literacy and reading needs of *all* children each day, including special populations, as they progress from Kindergarten to Grade 3, when all children are expected to be "readers" (*No Child Left Behind*, 2002)?

2. If Obrist, the dairy farmer, can employ information technology to gauge the current health and productivity of his milking cows, what can school administrators and classroom teachers reasonably expect from this information technology in gauging the reading health and productivity of *all* children, including special populations who require "specially designed" literacy and reading instruction that requires administrative challenges for teachers?

3. If FedEx can employ information technology to reengineer its clients' worldwide supply and distribution system, how can we take this information technology to scale in complex host environments known as schools, to reengineer the distribution of student performance information at the classroom, school, and district levels?

4. If a dairy farmer can track the milking yields of cows for weeks to determine their productivity, can we apply and sustain this information technology longitudinally, systemically and systematically in complex organizations like schools when the information involves the performance of children reading in an alphabetic writing system?

5. If information technology can be readily applied to the delivery of packages and the productivity of milk, can this same technology honor the developmental nature of reading in an elaborate symbolic system that is nested in a complex organization where the stakes are nothing less than children's future?

In the remainder of this chapter, we briefly characterize the literacy and reading needs of students identified with disabilities, as well as the research on beginning reading in general, along with its application to special populations. In addition, we describe a set of reading assessment measures and a Web-based database system that permits schools and districts to enter student performance reading data online and immediately generate automated reports. Finally, we offer a few comments about future applications of the Web-based assessment system as an extension of information technology's power to change systems.

Research on Literacy and Reading Needs of Special Populations

A defining characteristic of the performance of children identified with special needs is they are typically behind in reading development and performance when compared with their same-age peers (Bradley, Danielson, & Hallahan, 2002; National Research Council, 1998; Kame'enui, 1993; Vaughn & Briggs, 2003). The scientific evidence on the causes and correlates of reading failure and success is substantial and persuasive (Adams, 1990; Lyon, 1995; National Research Council, 1998; National Reading Panel, 2000). One of the most consistent and compelling findings of this empirical research is that the trajectory of reading success or failure begins early in a child's formal schooling, long before Grade 3. Furthermore, in the absence of intensive, systematic, and strategic intervention, children's reading growth and development are conspicuously resistant to change (Good, Simmons, & Smith, 1998; Juel, 1988; Torgesen, 2001). Moreover, the scientific evidence appears to support Bloom's (1964) pronouncement more than 40 years ago that "growth and development are not in equal units per unit of time" (p. 204). For beginning reading, this suggests that some reading skills and experiences are more important at certain points in a child's reading growth and development than others, particularly those involving phonological awareness, alphabetic understanding (or phonics), vocabulary development, fluent reading of connected text, and reading comprehension (Adams, 1990; Lyon, 1995; National Research Council, 1998; National Reading Panel, 2000).

The question of either preventing delayed reading development or accelerating reading growth is central to the design and implementation of reading instruction for special populations. The research designed to answer this question is formative, complex, and significant (Bradley, Danielson, & Hallahan, 2002; Foorman, 2003; Simmons, Kame'enui, Stoolmiller, Coyne, & Harn, 2003; Swanson, Harris, & Graham, 2003; Torgesen, Rashotte, Alexander, Alexander, & MacPhee, 2003), because it must necessarily unpack experimentally multiple sets of messy and complex individual (e.g., a special needs child), group (e.g., an intervention reading group comprised of children with special literacy needs vs. whole class reading group), and system (e.g., clear reading goals and standards; professional development support for teachers; coaching support for inexperienced teachers; adoption of a core, comprehensive reading program) interactions that involve a range of nested factors at the school (e.g., urban vs. rural), classroom (e.g., large vs. small), teacher (e.g., experience and evidence of success with children who have special reading and literacy needs), and instructional program levels (e.g., core reading program vs. supplemental reading program vs. intervention reading program) in a developmental framework (e.g., Kindergarten to Grade 3) in which select reading skills and experiences (e.g., teaching phonemic segmentation in the middle of Kindergarten vs. building text reading fluency at the end of Grade 2) are invoked at appropriate and necessary stages of reading development and instruction.

These complexities aside, paramount to a child's reading growth and development is "a reading assessment system within an information technology framework" that permits teachers and administrators to discern formatively and summatively if a child is making adequate growth and progress on critical reading skills and experiences, not only at particular points in time (Adams, 1990; Kame'enui, 1998; Kame'enui, Good, & Harn, in press), but in "real time" to ensure that each and every child is "learning enough" (Carnine, 2000). In a real sense, what is needed is not unlike the information technology applications revealed and employed by FedEx and dairy farmer Obrist. What is needed is an information technology system of sufficient scale, efficiency, and structure, coupled with a set of reading assessment measures that will permit the timely, valid, reliable, and useable renderings of children's reading performance for teachers and administrators to use in real-time instructional situations for timely and effective instructional decision-making. On its face, such an information technology system seems utterly fanciful, but it is *not*. In the remainder of this chapter, we describe a set of beginning reading measures, the Dynamic Indicators of Basic Early Literacy Skills (DIBELS), and an example of an information technology system, the DIBELS Data System, that exploits some of the prominent features revealed earlier in the examples of FedEx and the dairy farmer.

DIBELS: A Measurement System of Indicators to Determine Reading Growth and Development

There are literally hundreds of beginning reading assessment instruments available to assess the complex construct of reading in an alphabetic writing system. These assessments are ostensibly designed to accomplish one or more of the following purposes: (a) screening, (b) diagnosis, (c) progress monitoring, and (d) outcome. Not surprisingly, the technical adequacy of reading assessment instruments varies mightily, including the target domain or dimensions of reading, the scoring structure, the reliability, validity, and decision-making utility of the measures, the time and frequency of administration, the characteristics of the normative sample, the assessment format, the grade-level performance index, and so on (see Kame'enui, 2002).

Clearly, different reading assessment instruments are designed to provide different kinds of information for different purposes and contexts. The Dynamic Indicators of Basic Early Literacy Skills (DIBELS) (Good & Kaminski, 2002), like many traditional reading assessment instruments, is designed to assess reading performance in the areas of phonological awareness, phonics, fluency, and reading comprehension. However, unlike most traditional reading assessment measures, DIBELS is unique in its decision-making utility, time and frequency of administration, assessment format, and indexing of reading performance. Specifically, DIBELS is a set of seven standardized, individually administered measures of prereading and early reading and literacy development, designed to be very brief (i.e., administration time of each measure is 1 minute) fluency measures used for screening, diagnosis, progress monitoring, and outcome evaluation. The DIBELS measures assess early literacy domains deemed "essential" in both comprehensive reports from the National Reading Panel (2000) and National Research Council (1998), including phonological awareness, alphabetic understanding, automaticity and fluency with the code, and reading comprehension.

Important to the decision-making utility of DIBELS and to its theoretical, conceptual, and psychometric "fit" within an assessment framework of beginning reading writ large is that the measures are considered to be indicators of reading growth and development. As a system of indicators, DIBELS is designed primarily to index a child's reading growth and development, similar to indexing a person's body temperature using a thermometer, or body weight using a scale, or blood pressure using a sphygmomanometer. Because this indexing takes only a minute per measure, it can be repeated frequently, reliably, and at significantly less cost in time than traditional beginning reading screening, progress monitoring, and outcome measures. In addition, DIBELS is anchored to "cut scores" or performance benchmarks that, if met, are predictive of later reading proficiency. Thus, the measures can be used in the early identification of students who are not making adequate progress (i.e., not meeting the appropriate benchmarks on specific measures at specific points in time) in their reading growth and development (Good, Simmons, & Kame'enui, 2001; Kame'enui, Good, & Harn, in press). These decision-making utility features of DIBELS make it conceptually and psychometrically distinctive from other traditional reading measures, and enormously powerful for use in an information technology system.

The DIBELS Web site is located at http://dibels.uoregon.edu/. The Web site includes descriptions and tutorials on each of the measures, technical reports on the technical adequacy of DIBELS, logistical information on implementing DIBELS in a school, and contact information for trainers. The measures themselves are *free* to download for use from the Web site (*http:// dibels.uoregon.edu/measures/materials.php*).

The DIBELS Data System as an Example of Applied Information Technology

The decision-making utility features of DIBELS (e.g., 1-minute, fluency-based indicators of essential reading skills, numerous alternate forms for repeated administrations, used within a predictive validity framework) make it ideal in an information technology system. We have created such a system specific to DIBELS called the DIBELS Data System (http://dibels.uoregon.edu/data/). This system is a Web-based database that permits schools and districts to enter student DIBELS data online and generate automated reports. The benefits to using the DIBELS Data System are numerous, including (a) receiving results of student performance at the district, school, class, and individual student level immediately after data entry; (b) receiving a wide range of different reports (e.g., histograms, district norms, box plots, scatter plots, individual student performance by class, and many others); and (c) identifying students at risk of reading difficulties. In addition, the Data System permits the creation of a national, longitudinal database that can be harvested and analyzed to address a range of statistical and measurement issues. At the time of this writing, the DIBELS Data System consists of 10,880 schools for the 2005–2006 academic year, across 3,275 districts in the U.S. and Canada, totaling over 2.4 million students in Grades K–3.

In determining the platform for the DIBELS Data System, three primary criteria were employed: ease of use, scalability, and cost-effectiveness. Because the system had to be easy for schools to use, a Web-based interface was set up so that schools were not required to install separate client software. The only requirements for the Data System are Internet access and a Web browser. The interface was designed to be simple and have few graphics, to improve compatibility for users with older Web browsers or slow Internet access.

In addition to easy to use, the system had to be scalable to accommodate a large user base. The original DIBELS reports were written as Visual Basic scripts in Excel, which required excessive management. The reports became difficult to manage even with less than 100 participating schools. Schools received a template spreadsheet to enter student names and scores and send back. DIBELS personnel ran the data through Excel scripts and sent the results back to schools.

Clearly, another approach was required that permitted schools to administer, enter data, and print reports without negotiating this cumbersome and archaic process, and without direct involvement from DIBELS personnel in each step.

Finally, the costs to build and manage the system had to be constrained to keep fees low. At the same time, performance had to be high enough to accommodate hundreds or thousands of schools. The cost to use the current DIBELS Data System is one dollar per child per year.

The selected software was chosen for its performance, ease of use, and reliability. Most of the software for this project is based on the Open Source model (http://www.opensource.org/docs/definition.php). A community of programmers and users develop Open Source software and provide updates to the community. Because of this, an Open Source project which has gained a critical mass of users often has better performance and reliability than comparable commercially-available alternatives. It also means most Open Source software packages are available free of charge or at lower than traditional commercial rate.

The basic data entry and administrative tools for the Data System were available and went live in September, 2000. Due to the Web-based nature of the interface, new administrative functions or new reports could be written and made immediately available to all users. By spring 2001, all the original DIBELS reports had been duplicated in the Data System. New tools have been added, including additional features and reports.

CONCLUSION

In his book, *Powershift*, Alvin Toffler (1991), noted author of *Future Shock*, observed, "For from now on the world will be split between the fast and slow. To be fast or slow is not simply a matter of metaphor. Whole economies are either fast or slow. Primitive organisms have slow neural systems. The more evolved human nervous system processes signals faster. The same is true of primitive and advanced economies. Historically, power has shifted from the slow to the fast—whether we speak of species *or* nations" (p. 397, original emphasis).

One could argue that Toffler's assertions are also true of primitive and advanced disciplines of inquiry. Unless educational researchers, practitioners, and administrators committed to literacy and beginning reading can advance an information technology research, infrastructure and capacity-building agenda that takes full advantage of the kinds of applications rendered in the examples of FedEx, Obrist the Oregon dairy farmer, and the DIBELS Data System, we will be saddled with a slow information technology system. Such a state does not augur well for students who require human and pedagogical nervous systems to process symbolic signals faster and more imaginatively than the status quo. The time is ripe for a power shift in literacy and beginning reading from slow to fast information technology systems. If we can do it for packages and dairy cows, we ought to be able to do it for all children, especially children with special needs who need the best instruction and information systems currently available.

REFERENCES

Adams, M. J. (1990). *Beginning to read: Thinking and learning about print*. Cambridge, MA: MIT Press.
Bloom, B. S. (1964). *Stability and change in human characteristics*. New York: Wiley.
Bradley, R., Danielson, L., & Hallahan, D. P. (Eds.). (2002). *Identification of learning disabilities: Research to practice*. Mahwah, NJ: Lawrence Erlbaum Associates.

Caplan, G., & Grunebaum, H. (1967). Perspectives on primary prevention. *Archives of General Psychiatry, 17,* 331–346.

Carnine, D. W. (2000). *A consortium for Evidence in Education (CEE).* Unpublished manuscript.

Foorman, B. (Ed.). (2003). *Preventing and remediating reading difficulties: Bringing science to scale.* Timonium, MD: York Press.

Garten, J. E. (March 23, 1998). Why the global economy is here to stay. *Business Week.*

Good, R. H., & Kaminski, R. A. (Eds). (2002). *DynamiciIndicators of basic early literacy skills* (6th ed.). Eugene, OR: Institute for the Development of Educational Achievement. Available: http://dibels.uoregon.edu

Good, R. H., Simmons, D. C., & Kame'enui, E. J. (2001). The importance and decision-making utility of a continuum of fluency-based indicators of foundational reading skills for third-grade high-stakes outcomes. *Scientific Studies of Reading, 5*(3), 257–288.

Good, R., III, Simmons, D. C., & Smith, S. (1998). Effective academic interventions in the United States: Evaluating and enhancing the acquisition of early reading skills. *School Psychology Review, 27*(1), 45–56.

Juel, C. (1988). Learning to read and write: A longitudinal study of 54 children from first through fourth grades. *Journal of Educational Psychology, 80,* 437–447.

Kame'enui, E. J. (2002). *An analysis of reading assessment instruments for K–3.* Eugene, OR: Institute for the Development of Educational Achievement, University of Oregon.

Kame'enui, E. J., Good III, R., & Harn, B. A. (In press). Beginning reading failure and the quantification of risk: Reading behavior as the supreme index. In W. L. Heward, T. E. Heron, N. A. Neef, S. M. Peterson, D. M. Sainato, G. Cartledge, I. Gardner, R., L. D. Peterson, S. B. Hersh, & J. C. Dardig (Eds.). *Focus on behavior analysis in education: Achievements, challenges, and opportunities* Upper Saddle River, NJ: Prentice Hall/Merril.

Kame'enui, E. J. (1993). Diverse learners and the tyranny of time: Don't fix blame; fix the leaky roof. *The Reading Teacher, 46,* 376–383.

Kame'enui, E. J. (1998). The rhetoric of all, the reality of some, and the unmistakable smell of mortality. In J. Osborn & F. Lehr (Eds.). *Literacy for all: Issues in teaching and learning* (pp. 319–338). New York: Guilford.

Lyon, G. R. (1995). Research initiatives in learning disabilities: Contributions from scientists supported by the National Institute of Child Health and Human Development. *Journal of Child Neurology, 10,* 120–126.

National Reading Panel (2000). *Teaching children to read: An evidence-based assessment of the scientific research literature on reading and its implications for reading instruction: Reports of the subgroups.* Bethesda, MD: National Institute of Child Health and Human Development.

No Child Left Behind, 2002, Title I, Part B, Student Reading Skills Improvement Grants, Subpart 1, Reading First.

National Research Council (1998). *Preventing reading difficulties in young children.* Washington, DC: National Academy Press.

Peacock, A. (April 1998). Cream of the crop. *Horizon Air Magazine.*

Simeonsson, R. J. (1994). Promoting children's health, education, and well-being. In R. J. Simeonsson (Eds.). *Risk, resilience, & prevention* (pp. 3–11). Baltimore: P. H. Brookes.

Simmons, D. C., Kameenui, E. J., Stoolmiller, M., Coyne, M. D., & Harn, B. (2003). Accelerating growth and maintaining proficiency: A two-year intervention study of kindergarten and first-grade children at risk for reading difficulties. In B. Foorman (Eds.). *Preventing and remediating reading difficulties: Bringing science to scale* (pp. 197–228). Timonium, MD: York Press.

Swanson, H. L., Harris, K. R., & Graham, S. (Ed.). (2003). *Handbook of learning disabilities.* New York: The Guilford Press.

Toffler, A. (1991). *Powershift: Knowledge, wealth and violence at the edge of the 21st century.* New York: Bantam.

Togesen, J., Rashotte, C., Alexander, A., Alexander, J., & MacPhee, K. (2003). Progress toward understanding the instructional conditions necessary for remediating reading difficulties in older children.

In B. Foorman (Eds.). *Preventing and remediating reading difficulties: Bringing science to scale* (pp. 275–297). Baltimore: York Press.

Torgesen, J. K., Alexander, A. W., Wagner, R. K., Rashotte, C. A., Voeller, K. K. S., & Conway, T. (2001). Intensive remedial instruction for children with severe reading disabilities: Immediate and long-term outcomes from two instructional approaches. *Journal of Learning Disabilities, 34*(1), 33–58, 78.

Vaughn, S., & Briggs, K. L. (Eds.). (2003). *Reading in the classroom: Systems for the observation of teaching & learning.* Baltimore, MD: Paul H. Brookes.

30

▼▼▼▼▼▼▼

Integrating Reading Assessment and Technology

Barbara J. Walker and Sandra K. Goetze
Oklahoma State University

While current policies call for more high-stakes assessments in the form of standardized and criterion-based tests, research on effective schools demonstrates that teachers use alternative assessments such as observations and listening to children read to monitor student growth (Taylor, Pearson, Clark & Walpole, 2002). However, we are increasingly reliant on tests, rather than our daily observations and interactions with students, to evaluate growth. This chapter proposes that technology can enhance and promote literacy assessments, specifically, alternative assessments. In other words, teachers will more frequently use alternative assessments because technology will make it easy and data will be more accessible for instructional decision-making. First, we discuss some views on assessment including traditional assessments and alternative assessments. Then, we propose ways technology can enhance alternative assessment. Finally, we take a peek at the future and offer some final comments.

Standardized tests are being used to make high-stakes decisions about teachers and their students. These standardized tests represent only a snapshot of reading performance on a single day, in unfamiliar circumstances, and on unfamiliar tasks (short, densely written passages) that require a single right answer to questions posed in a multiple-choice format. These high-stakes tests are not in line with current views about the constructive nature of the reading process (Pearson & Hamm, 2005). For instance, the importance of prior knowledge for both word recognition and comprehension are not measured by current standardized tests. The constructive nature of reading is complex— focusing on meaning that is constructed with the text, the reader, and within the context of the literacy situation. These recent views of literacy acquisition also encompass the sociocultural theory which posits that problem-solving in literacy is a multifaceted, dynamic activity depending to a great extent on the context in which it is situated. Situated learning occurs through interactions that provide individuals with an opportunity to interact with more knowledgeable peers (including teachers and parents), thus deepening their understanding (Vygotsky, 1978).

Along with these views, Feuerstein, Rank, and Hoffman (1979) introduced the notion of dynamic assessment, where students are assessed while they are completing a task such as reading a passage. An informed teacher measures learning by noting growth, changes in the task, and how much effort the teacher and the student expend. Thus, assessment and instruction occur simultaneously during the instructional event (Walker, 2004), creating ongoing assessments in the midst of student learning. These shifts in our views of literacy and assessments call for assessments that use authentic tasks and texts, ask for more complex responses which include the influence of background knowledge, and instruction that reflects a group interaction. The high-stake assessments that currently predominate in our schools are not congruent with more recent views of literacy development and assessment.

According to Duffy and Cunningham (2001), authentic assessments which are "sympathetic to constructivist's principles will require new conceptions of such traditional concepts as reliability and validity" (p. 186). Not only do authentic assessments call into question these traditional concepts of assessment, but also technology is challenging these traditional notions. Using hand-held devices like cell phones and personal digital assistants (PDAs), data is easily shared by the beaming capability; therefore, teachers must rethink how students are assessed. Even now, teachers have no knowledge of the silent beaming of data from student to student and, consequently, traditional assessments do not function effectively in the new technological environment. For example, using cell phones which allow instant messages, students can share data beaming information to each other or wirelessly on the Internet. This creates questions for educators about the effectiveness of traditional assessments when these new technologies are used to communicate information when taking exams. This ability to share data so easily causes one to question traditional assessments and look for alternatives.

Thus, as our views of literacy change to a constructivist and socio-cultural perspective and technology challenges traditional assessment forms, alternative assessments may be the response for both summative assessment to evaluate schools and formative to make instructional decision. We are attempting "to change the form and purpose of classroom assessment to make it more fundamentally a part of the learning process" (Shepard, 2000, p. 6). According to Shepard, movement toward formative assessment is more in line with a learning culture as opposed to current culture which limits access to language and ways of knowing which are not evaluated through standardized instruments.

Rather than a snapshot, these new assessments provide an ongoing video of students' behaviors. These alternative assessments include activities from authentic text and context that demonstrate student growth as they interact in a learning community. For example, some performance assessments involve reading a long passage from a piece of authentic literature. After reading, students discuss the passage in a group setting and finally write a response and/or a summary. Rubrics are used to assess student performance (Pearson, Spalding, & Myers, 1998; Pearson & Hamm, 2005). Thus, these assessments focus on the students' responses to authentic stories rather than the recognition of correct answers from a contrived text. They also focus on authentic tasks and projects that reveal a depth of understanding rather than evaluation of surface understanding as in standardized tests. Instead of scores, these assessments rely on informed judgments by teachers and other professionals. Using rubrics where descriptions of various qualities (e.g. poor, acceptable, and superior) on key factors are used to assess a response allows teachers to read and decide on the merit of the response. Many ready-made rubric models can be accessed on the Web. Other alternative assessments often engage students in the assessment process asking them to evaluate and reflect on their progress toward literacy learning. In other words, students engage in self-assessment (Tierney, Crumpler, Bertlesen, & Bond, 2003). Other alternative assessments include parental reflection on learning involving assessment conversations among students, parents, and teachers (Johnston, 2003). One form of this type of assessment is student-led conferences where students describe their literacy behaviors while explaining their work to their parents (Tierney, et. al., 2003, Walker, 2004). Portfolios are often used as a vehicle to demonstrate the new literacy behaviors learned. Adding to this conversation of literacy assessment is the recent inclusion of technology to produce electronic portfolios and display student data (Kieffer, Hale, & Templeton, 1998).

Technology Can Enhance Alternative Assessments

Technology has potential for enhancing the use of assessments that have become associated with more recent views of literacy. As we explain the ways technology can strengthen assessments, particularly alternative assessments, we suggest possibilities for the future. Although there are certainly others, we focus on five features of integrating technology and assessment. They are using assessments that are a remix, gathering data efficiently to inform instruction, saving teacher time so they have more time to interact with children, displaying assessments in multimedia environments, and communicating assessments within a larger community.

Technology Creates New Assessments Through a Remix

One concept that provides opportunities to move toward more formative assessments is the concept of "remix." Remix strives to provide diverse learners with multiple ways to demonstrate their understanding. For example, an electronic portfolio which includes some standard measures may also include robust reflection from both teacher and student. This type of reflection is referred to as "remix" (Lessig, 2004) since students literally create a new and significantly different product when they add reflection. Using an electronic portfolio, students are easily able to connect reflections from two or more artifacts and explain their learning using multiple artifacts. New movements such as Creative Commons, suggest technology assists students to describe or elaborate richness of detail from the learner's perspective in multimedia environments such as the Internet.

According to Barrett (2000), the use of electronic portfolios can bring together two different technology processes: multimedia project development and portfolio development. Literacy processes are embedded in both as learners read, write, and reflect using this two-pronged development process. The resulting artifacts and reflections provide means for teachers to assess student growth. Further, it is suggested by Reinking (1998) that since development of electronic portfolios is complex in nature, students may actually gain both linear and non-linear literacy processes. This phenomenon was observed in the research completed by Myers, Hammett, and McKillop (1998) where students created hypermedia artifacts and were able to gain greater understanding of literacy processes through the ways they could digitally manipulate their artifacts. Currently, we use rubrics to assess these portfolios and projects; however, in the future, we will rethink how we assess these literacy artifacts as more tools become available through technology.

Technology Facilitates Gathering Data

The process of gathering student data with technology is not a new phenomenon since schools have gathered data on students for years; however, the gathering of data for authentic literacy assessment purposes via computer desktop and PDA computers is a relatively new phenomenon. Several proprietary software packages and some shareware development projects through universities have created literacy assessments. They are now readily available to the classroom teacher and reading specialist through programs that work with hand-held computers, such as PDAs. The use of hand-held applications for literacy assessment includes informal reading inventories, graded word lists, and the ability to take running records. When using PDAs to take running records, the teacher evaluates learning within the literacy event and can make judgments about a student's reading immediately. The teacher is given choices in pop-up menus for miscue types, along with space to make written notations. Currently, text passages are limited to those available on the Web at specific sites where there are passages for assessment; however, in some instances you have to pay for access. From the PDA, these data are regularly uploaded to the desktop computer from a docking cradle, and a variety of reports can subsequently be generated. Outcomes from this PDA assessment movement have created Web-based databases so that teachers can download an informal reading inventory or leveled text passage to a hand-held computer and make notations as the child reads. The school reading specialist or literacy coach taking several records is able to go from classroom to classroom with a PDA and hard copy of text for the child to read, while collecting data quickly and efficiently. Even standardized evaluations include inclusion of technology, such as PDAs to take data and immediately analyze it along with input from the assessment specialist. The Dynamic Indicators of Basic Early Literacy Skills (DIBELS) is an example of a standardized reading assessment and the ability to enter data with a PDA. The DIBELS software is utilized to support test administration and analysis as a way to decrease cognitive load on the literacy coach or teacher. Both standardized individual assessments and authentic assessments increase the ability to input student data into the PDA, which frees the teacher to listen more closely to the child while recording the data. This new use of the PDA to gather data may allow the teacher to focus more attention on the child and the accurate recording of test data.

This process of gathering data with technological tools is useful and expeditious; however, human decision-making, with regard to reading performance, is still decided by the teacher. In the future, we believe teachers will be able to type passages on a Web site, transfer them to the hand-held computer, and use them to assess the students on whatever type of text they are reading in class.

More traditional teacher assessments are also transferable to hand-held devices through an Internet freeware program called Handy Sheets (Goknow, 2003). This freeware software for hand-held computers allows teachers to create Web-based documents which students can use for assessment either on the Internet or downloaded to their hand-held devices. This technology is available to help teachers create checklists, classroom assessments that call for multiple right answers, and open-ended responses as suggested in the research on alternative assessments (Pearson & Hamm, 2005; Tierney, et al., 2003).

Data can also be gathered by using tools like Go and Observe which have been developed for assessing teachers at the University of Michigan (Merit Network, 2003). The hand-held program GO and Observe contains assessment tools to observe teachers and could be modified for observing children. A similar tool is the program Observation Log for Teachers, 1.0 by ADL-software (2003) which enables teachers to take multiple observations and characterize them in multiple ways. In these programs, teachers are able to record anecdotal records of students' literacy behaviors as they are teaching. This continuous description of literacy learning helps inform instructional decision-making.

Technology Saves Time So Teachers Can Focus on Their Students

According to Hargreaves, Earl, and Schmidt (2002), "Time is one of the most frequently cited problems in regard to implementing alternative assessments" (p. 75). Consequently, time-saving production seems to be a common thread for the integration of technology and alternative assessment. If technology has the ability to make a mundane task easier, teachers are more likely to embrace it. This is just the case with rubrics and the creation of them. Creating rubrics can be a time-consuming process; however, when teachers are able to view a database of completed rubrics, which are adaptable to their classroom needs, they become more attractive. Rubistar (High Plains Region Technology Education Consortium, 2003) is such a database. By providing models for teachers who are just beginning to use rubrics in their teaching and assessment, the

Rubistar database creates a virtual zone of proximal development (Vygotsky, 1978). With a multitude of topics and the ability to create their own blank rubric, teachers at all levels, including higher education, are harnessing this power. Rubistar becomes the user's electronic filing cabinet of rubric assessments, which can be used again and modified each time. Each rubric is unique and generates its own URL, which makes it easily printable and linked to web pages.

Using PDAs to calculate data related to an oral reading or a think-aloud assessment saves time in the mathematical calculations. The teacher can access calculated data from the Web site. The effort for calculating miscues is done by the computer along with translating the miscue notations to a student database file. Data of this nature then becomes "beamable" to a reading specialist, another classroom teacher, or a parent, allowing teachers more time to focus on individual children. As teachers interact with individual children, the PDA codes data related to reading and thinking with input from the teacher using pop-up menus and written notations. The input from the teacher increases sensitivity to the processes of reading, rather than accuracy, thus increasing their understanding of how children read.

Technology Can Expand Assessment by Displaying Artifacts

Gathering data and saving time are only two ways to utilize the power of technology for literacy assessment. Technology also provides a place to display student artifacts that may include multimedia reflections or responses. Barrett (2000) describes seven generic types of software for creating electronic portfolios: databases, hypermedia software, multimedia authoring software, Internet pages (HTML), Adobe Acrobat (PDF files), multimedia slideshows, and video. These technological tools assist students by converting the artifacts to digital formats and allowing students to add a reflection to multiple artifacts. The ability to add reflections through multimedia enhancement eliminates the need to write reflections by hand, allowing those who find writing difficult to reflect in depth by recording their reflections. Electronic portfolios provide a space for students to juxtapose pieces of their writing with their reflections, drawings, video, and audio within a public space such as a web page on the Internet. Electronic portfolios enhance alternative assessment because you have more choices of types of artifacts to include within the portfolio for literacy evaluation. For example, more students are able to use drawing, visual displays of information, and multimedia projects, as well as written work, in their portfolio by scanning or transferring them to a personal Web site.

Recently, portals have emerged to house electronic portfolios and the use of portals provides secure access for both the author and viewer of the documents. Portals are a secure entrance into a Web site, which allows assessment to be shared among stakeholders. These new portals for electronic portfolios harness the power of drop-and-drag add-ins for reflection along with the ability to include feedback forms for the authors that do not require programming knowledge. Essentially, all the architecture for the portal site is completed and learners focus on reflection and artifact selection over architecture development. Portals provide the structure for the content residing in the electronic portfolio so the student can focus on content while not being burdened by cognitive default because of needing to know programming language (Rouewt, Levonen, Dilon, & Spiro, 1996). This allows for more contextualized remix as parents, grandparents, and teachers provide responses to the artifacts that the learner has provided. These Web-based portfolios will allow for multiple stakeholders to evaluate and talk about the artifacts, thus, creating interactive assessments (Tierney, et. al, 2003). In the future, sharing assessment information through Web-based means will provide for multiple opportunities for parents, students, teachers, and administrators to interact about student growth.

Technology Provides a System for Communicating Information

Broadening the lens of alternative assessment has the potential to expand our conceptualization of literacy. Technology is advancing our thinking about definitions of literacy. According to Flood and Lapp (1995), definitions of being literate have changed greatly over the last 150 years. Years ago, it only took one's signature to identify the literate person, while today we often describe a literate individual in multiple ways. A salient example is Reinking's (1989) view of the way digital forms of text are replacing printed forms: "This shift has consequences for the way we communicate and disseminate information, how we approach the task of reading and writing, and how we help people become literate" (p. XV). This is of particular interest for literacy assessment as the processes of collecting data and sharing data are user-friendlier; hence, more time can be spent on the human element of decision-making. At least two examples of Web-based literacy assessments that provide information that school personnel and stake holders can easily understand are the Phonological Awareness Literacy Screening assessment (Partridge, Invernizzi, Meier, & Sullivan, 2003) and Let's Go Learn (McCallum, 2003) .

Phonological Awareness Literacy Screening assessment (PALS) is one example of a project that took a standard assessment format and established a Web-based version for the state of Virginia (Partridge et al., 2003). The notion that PALS has utilized a shareable format for collecting and disseminating data across the state of Virginia adds to the ease of the process of assessment for teachers in this state. The advantages of this system are that it supports transient students, provides reports across groups of schools, and facilitates easy access for teachers across all districts. The biggest advantage of an assessment system such as PALS is its basic design and user-friendly interface. PALS is intuitive to users because is contains an Internet-based spreadsheet system, which utilizes teacher input data and then provides teachers with feedback and reports. The ability to disaggregate the data and utilize one's data in multiple ways makes it a powerful tool to better understand student instructional needs. This can all be done on the PALS Web site without extensive knowledge of spreadsheets or databases. School personnel and stake-holders can easily understand generated reports, and users of the system can easily enter data. How the PALS Web-based assessment system links assessment and instruction is clearly an advantage of PALS since there is much evidence to support the reciprocal relationship between assessment and instruction. If the future is to link literacy assessment with instructional decisions and provide e-support so that teachers have instructional choices based on best practice, then we have arrived—and technology has become more relevant to teacher's needs. Consequently, users now demand excellent instructional design with shareable formats, which are user-friendly. The future may change these literacy assessments into self-assessments with the support of technology along with shareable learning objects like a model for a self-assessment chart or a model conversation about assessment that may be available via the Internet. The use of learning objects is already creating standards for high levels of shareability.

THE FUTURE

Imagine a "Napster-like" database for literacy assessments and an instructional strategy that utilizes a "TIVO-like" process, which is a digital recording device for television, and unlike the VCR, it learns your viewing preferences and makes personal files based on these preferences. The file-sharing component would select those assessments and preferences—for example, those appropriate for a third-grade classroom—and deliver them to the user's mailbox. The more it is utilized, the more the system learns the preferences of the user. Sound far-fetched? Powerful file-sharing databases, like Napster, which support multiple disciplines, are already popping up. Literacy assessments could be one possible file-sharing system. It takes time to find learning objects, like a video case study or a running record, within the assessment database because often the formats are not similar (Gibbon, Nelson, & Richards, 2000). New advances with meta-data will allow us to embed a code within a file so that anyone can manipulate it or use at any time, thus, searching will be more powerful. This will be very useful to schools, as many learning object assessments will not have to be recreated each time they are used. An example of this is a rubric for a multimedia assignment. Imagine searching the file-sharing network, much like putting in a request for a journal article, and then have the documents show up in your mailbox. The system will learn the user's needs and preferences and make instructional or assessment suggestions.

Probably closer to reality is the notion that sophisticated voice-activated programs will allow students to read into a computer or handheld device which can then record and print their oral reading and response. Thus, both the teacher and the student can use information not only about accuracy, but also about miscues and the thinking behind them. Students would be able to review their miscues and discuss the thinking behind their reading in individual teacher-student conferences (Goodman & Merrick, 1996). The voice-activated technology also would enable students to complete a retelling orally by talking into a computer that can subsequently be programmed to describe and assess the response. Even more authentic is that students would be able to think aloud into a computer. The think-aloud protocol would allow students to dictate their thoughts into the computer as they read. After that, the computer would print out their thinking so that both the teacher and student could describe the thinking process that occurred. In these processes, students are "active, engaged, and challenged contributors to their own learning" (Hargreaves et al., 2002). Further, the future may bring the ability to scan student writing and then be able to evaluate it. For example, in a performance assessment that calls for a written response from a student, it might be possible to scan the response and have the computer holistically evaluate it using an already developed rubric. Is the computer that intelligent? Only time will tell.

Final Caveats and Comments

Even though technology is changing the way we conduct assessments, we must be cautious that it does not erode teacher judgment. Over reliance on technology to assess students can decrease the amount of personal and professional knowledge that teachers have about the students in their classrooms. For example, voice-activated technology may supplant teachers actually listening to students read, thus teachers would not know their students as readers. Using multiple rubrics downloaded from the Web may take away thoughtful decision-making on the part of teachers. They may become reliant on ready-made rubrics rather than using the Web-based rubrics as a model for creating their own. Teachers, parents, and students may talk past each other because they use different assessment criteria for what constitutes success, and the online communication might not allow negotiating the meaning of assessment tasks. On the other hand, suggested assessment criteria may be posted on the Web so that teachers, parents, and students can negotiate their understanding about what constitutes growth in literacy. Technology may help the transition to more effective alternative assessment techniques so that more teachers will use these techniques with confidence. Finally, the promise of technology is that it can give teachers, students, and parents the power and ability to describe literacy learning, rather than give it a numerical value.

In conclusion, technology can become an integrated tool in alternative assessment that encourages students to assume responsibility for their own learning, make assessment a continuous ingredient in the learning process, and root it in authentic experiences that ask students to construct and apply a range of understandings (Hargraves et al., 2002). We have proposed that technology can enhance alternative assessments by remixing assessments, gathering data, saving time, displaying artifacts, and providing a system for communicating information. Even though the integration of reading assessment and technology enhances the use of alternative assessments, we must not be seduced into abandoning teachers' judgment and their ". . . professional prerogative" (Pearson & Valencia, 1987 p. 3) when making decisions about student assessment and instruction.

REFERENCES

ADLsoftware (2003). Observation log for teachers 1.0 [computer software]. Retrieved from http://adlsoftware.homestead.com

Barrett, H. (2000). Creating your own electronic portfolio: Using off-the-shelf software (to?) showcase your own or student work. *International Society for Technology in Education:* Retrieved: January 9, 2004 from the World Wide Web: http://www.iste.org

Creative commons (2004). [Web site]. Retrieved from http://www.creativecommons.org

Duffy, T. M., & Cunningham, D. J. (2001). Constructivism: Implications for the design and delivery of instruction. In D. H. Jonassen (Ed.). *Handbook of research for educational communications and technology* (pp. 170–198). Association for educational communications and technology. Mahwah, NJ: Lawrence Earlbaum Associates.

Feuerstein, R. R., Rand, Y., & Hoffman, M. B. (1979). *The dynamic assessment of retarded performance.* Baltimore, MD: University Park Press.

Flood, J., & Lapp, D. (1995). Broadening the lens: Toward an expanded conceptualization of literacy. In K. Hinchman, D. J. Leu, & C. K. Kinzer (Eds.). *Perspectives on literacy research and practice.* Forty-fourth yearbook of the The National Reading Conference (pp. 1–16). Chicago, IL: National Reading Conference.

Gibbons, A. S., Nelson, J., & Richards, R. (2000). The nature and origin of Instructional objects. In D. A. Wiley (Ed.). *The instructional use of learning objects.* Bloomington, IN: Association for Educational Communications and Technology.

GoKnow, Inc., (2003). Handy sheets (Computer software). http://www.goknow.com

Goodman, Y. M., & Marek, A. M. (1996). Retrospective miscue analysis. In Y. M. Goodman & A. M. Marek (Eds.). *Retrospective miscue analysis: Revaluing readers and reading* (pp.39–49). Katonah, NY: Richard C. Owen Publishers.

Haregreaves, A., Earl, L., & Schmidt, M. (2002). Alternative assessment reform. *American Educational Research Journal, 39,* 69–95.

Hodgins, Wayne. (2000). *Into the future* [Online]. Available: http://www.learnativity.com/download/MP7.PDF

Johnston, P. (2003). Assessment conversations. *The Reading Teacher, 57,* 90–92.

Jonassen, D. H. (2000). *Computers as mindtools for schools.* Upper Saddle River, NJ: Merrill.

Kieffer, R. D., Hale, M. E., & Templeton, A. (1998). Electronic literacy portfolios: Technology transformations in a first-grade classroom. In D. Reinking, M. C. McKenna, L. D. Labbo, & R. D. Kieffer (Eds.). *Handbook of literacy and technology: Transformations in a post-typographic world* (pp. 145–163). Mahwah, NJ: Lawrence Erlbaum Associates.

Lessig, L (2004). *Free culture.* New York: Penguin Press.

McCallum, R. (2003). *Let's go learn.* [Online]. Available: http://www.letsgolearn.com

Meritt Network (2003). Go and Observe [computer software]. Retrieved from http://observe.merit.edu

Myers, J., Hammett, R., & McKillop, A. (1998). Opportunities for critical literacy and pedagogy in student-authored hypermedia. In D. Reinking, M. C. McKenna, L. D. Labbo, & R. D. Kieffer (Eds.). *Handbook of literacy and technology: Transformations in a post-typographic world* (pp. 63–91). Mahwah, NJ: Lawrence Erlbaum Associates.

Partridge, H., Invernizzi, M, Meier, J. & Sullivan, A. (2003). Linking assessment and instruction via Web-based technology: A case study of a statewide early literacy initiative. *Reading Online*, Retrieved Decem-ber 22, 2003 from the World Wide Web: http://www.readingline.org

Pearson, P. D., & Hamm, D. (2005). The history of reading comprehension assessment. In S. G. Paris & S. A. Stahl (Eds). *Children's Reading Comprehension and Assessment*. Mahwah, NJ: Lawrence Erlbaum Associates.

Pearson, P. D., Spalding, E., & Meyers, M. (1998). Literacy assessment in the New Standards Project. In M. Coles & R. Jenkins (Eds.). *Assessing Reading to Changing Practice in Classrooms* (pp. 54–97). London: Routledge.

Pearson, P. D., & Valencia, S. (1987). Assessment, accountability, and professional prerogative. In J. E. Readance & S. Baldwin (Eds.). *Research in literacy: Merging perspectives* (pp. 3–16). Rochester, NY: National Reading Conference.

Reinking, D. (1998). Introductions: Synthesizing technological transformations of literacy in a post-typographic world. In D. Reinking, M. C. McKenna, L. D. Labbo, & R. D. Kieffer (Eds.). *Handbook of literacy and technology: Transformations in a post-typographic world* (pp. xi–xxx). Mahwah, NJ: Lawrence Erlbaum Associates.

Rouet, J., Levonen, J., Dillon, A., & Spiro, R. (1996). *Hypertext and cognition.* Mahywah, NJ: Lawrence Earlbaum Associates.

Rubitstar (2003). High Plains Region Technology Consortium. Retrieved from http://rubistar.4teachers.org

Shepard, L. A. (2000). The role of assessment in a learning culture. *Educational Researcher, 29,* 4–14.

Taylor, B. M., Pearson, P. D., Clark, K. F., & Walpole, S. (2000). Effective schools and accomplished teach-ers: Lessons about primary-grade reading instruction in low-income schools. *Elementary School Jour-nal, 101,* 121–165.

Tierney, R. J., Crumpler, T. P., Bertelsen, C. D., & Bond, E. L. (2003). *Interactive assessment: Teachers, parents and students as partners.* Norwood, Massachusetts: Christopher-Gordon Publishers. 197 pp.

Vygotsky, L. (1978). *Mind in society: The development of higher psychological processes.* Cambridge: Harvard University Press.

Walker, B. J. (2004). *Techniques for reading assessment and instruction.* New York: Prentice Hall.

Author Index

Numbers in *italics* indicate pages with multiauthored sources.

Index